ADMINISTRATIVE
LAW
AND PROC

FOURTH EDITION

By

RICHARD J. PIERCE, JR.
Lyle T. Alverson Professor of Law
George Washington University Law School

SIDNEY A. SHAPIRO
University Distinguished Chair in Law
Wake Forest University School of Law

PAUL R. VERKUIL
Professor of Law
Cardozo Law School, Yeshiva University

FOUNDATION PRESS
New York, New York
2004

Foundation Press, a Thomson business, has created this publication to provide you with accurate and authoritative information concerning the subject matter covered. However, this publication was not necessarily prepared by persons licensed to practice law in a particular jurisdiction. Foundation Press is not engaged in rendering legal or other professional advice, and this publication is not a substitute for the advice of an attorney. If you require legal or other expert advice, you should seek the services of a competent attorney or other professional.

© 1985, 1992, 1999 FOUNDATION PRESS
© 2004 By FOUNDATION PRESS
                    395 Hudson Street
                    New York, NY 10014
                    Phone Toll Free 1–877–888–1330
                    Fax (212) 367–6799
                    fdpress.com
Printed in the United States of America

ISBN 1–58778–529–3   (hard cover)

ISBN 1–58778–530–7   (soft cover)

 *TEXT IS PRINTED ON 10% POST CONSUMER RECYCLED PAPER*

In memory of
Kenneth Culp Davis
who defined the field
for over 50 years

*

PREFACE TO THE FOURTH EDITION

In the preface to the Third edition, we acknowledged our inability to predict the future in this field, which has by now become our mantra. Since the last edition, who could have imagined that there would be an impeachment of a President that would have been topped by a Supreme Court ordered outcome of a presidential election? Our polity will be hard pressed to top those events, even in as contentious an election year as we are experiencing in 2004.

The political dimension of Administrative Law has understandably captured the headlines. In the preface to the last edition, we noted the "switch" in divided government from a Republican to Democratic President and from a Democratic to Republican Congress. Are we now at the end of the era of divided government? After all, the Republicans are in charge of both political branches and, through (often highly contested) judicial appointments, increasingly in control of the third. But we see the pendulum swinging back to the divided branch scenario precisely because that state reflects our political equilibrium.

For us, politics is one means of handicapping the prospects for the administrative state. Traditionally, the Republican hegemony could be predicted to produce "less" government and therefore activities of the bureaucracy would be curtailed if not terminated. But the horrible events of September 11, 2001 made even that prediction hazardous. The Homeland Security Act[1] puts administration in the foreground in many areas, notably immigration policy, administrative due process and, in a broad sense, information policy. In that regard, The Critical Infrastructure Information Act of 2002 and its impact upon FOIA is highlighted in a new Section 8.4.

The Bush administration has otherwise been predictable in such matters as OMB's more stringent review of agency regulations, at least in terms of the number of agency rules returned for further analysis compared to the Clinton years. One little noticed regulatory review statute, The Information Quality Act,[2] which deals with "correcting" government and privately collected information, also bears close scrutiny as a regulatory tool. We have discussed it in Section 8.7 of this edition.

---

1. Pub. L. No. 107-296 (2002), 116 Stat. 2135 (2002).

2. Pub. L. No. 106, §515 (2001).

PREFACE TO THE FOURTH EDITION

The Courts have thankfully not been as active in the last five years as the two political branches have been. We do not have any major doctrinal shifts to record, but the relationship of <u>Chevron</u> deference to <u>Skidmore</u> "deference" continues to occupy the Supreme Court and the courts of appeal. The Third branch may well become more assertive as various applications of the Homeland Security Act work their way through the system.

Finally, we noted in the prior preface that a major assessment of the field was underway with the ABA Administrative Law Project. That project has now been completed and a Blackletter Statement has been published[3]; this synopsis may be of interest to students seeking a quick overview of the field that we parse much more carefully in this treatise.

The authors want to thank James Chang and Robert Mead for their help on the preparation of this Fourth edition.

RICHARD PIERCE
SIDNEY SHAPIRO
PAUL VERKUIL

Washington, D.C.
Winston Salem, NC
New York, NY

July 2004

---

3. Verkuil, Duffy and Herz, A Blackletter Statement of Administrative Law, 54 Ad. L. Rev. 1 (2002).

PREFACE TO THE THIRD EDITION

In the Preface to our second edition we fortunately "disavowed any ability to predict the future path of administrative law." We renew that disavowal in this edition, but in so doing highlight some of the major, albeit unpredictable, events in the seven years that have expired since our last edition.

Surely the biggest events affecting our subject have been political in nature. The blockbuster is of course President Clinton's impeachment. From our perspective, which focuses on the political relationships between and among the branches, the antagonism between Congress and the White House over impeachment may well condition future interbranch relationships. Moreover, the concept of "perpetual divided government" which we noted in our second edition did an unexpected flip—few would have believed before the November 1992 elections that the Democrats would control the executive branch and the Republicans the legislative, this fact, plus the impact of Reagan and Bush appointees on the federal judiciary, can easily undermine fixed assumptions about regulatory policies.[1] But then again, the Democratic White House has not behaved in predictable ways either. The Reinventing Government initiative, under Vice President Gore's direction,[2] in fact brought Republicans and Democrats closer together on issues of government management. Moreover, President Clinton's statement, early in his second term, that we are living in the "post-big government" era[3] was also meant to close the political gap. The long term effect of impeachment on these political relationships will undoubtedly produce more confusion than innovation in the field of government management and by extension in the subject of our study, administrative law.

In the reinventing era, all agency budgets for ambitious regulatory initiatives have been constrained, but few agencies have been terminated. In fact, only two agencies have been eliminated: the Interstate Commerce Commission (ICC) and the Administrative Conference of the United

---

1. Consider the outcome in the census sampling case, Dept. of Commerce v. United States House of Representatives, 119 S.Ct. 765 (1999) (5 to 4) where the democratic Executive Branch wanted to use sampling techniques for determining appropriations to states, and where the Republican Congress wanted to withhold funds for that purpose. The flip in branch division also changes the assumptions underlying the appropriations process.

2. *See* A. Gore, Report of the National Performance Review: Creating a Government that Works Better & Costs Less (Sept. 7, 1993).

3. President Clinton, Radio Address to the Nation, June 27, 1996.

States (ACUS). As the ICC was the oldest independent agency, created in 1887, its long overdue passing is more to be noted as a historical fact than as evidence of regulatory reform. As to the ACUS, demise has come much quicker and is much to be regretted. The ACUS was the only place in government where private sector academics and practitioners, regulatory and executive branch officials, and members of the judiciary could gather to discuss and promote proposals for administrative reform.[4] From the perspective of your three authors, who served over the years as consultants and/or members of the Conference, its intellectual influence will be sorely missed. We wish Vice President Gore would put ACUS back on his "reinvention" list.

The hegemony of the *Chevron* case over the field of judicial review of administrative action, while noted in our last edition, is now complete. It is the most extensively cited case in the Courts of Appeals and persistently if inconsistently relied upon by the Supreme Court. All indications are that judicial deference is alive and well, which we applaud. But given the shifts in the field, we cannot help but anticipate the moment when the pendulum begins to swing back. Judicial review in the era of reinvention and deregulation has the potential to become a contentious issue. As established expectations are thwarted, new alliances and antagonisms will emerge. For example, the interaction between the Takings Clause and deregulation will likely increase pressures on the judiciary to review agency actions.[5]

A milestone to note is that the Administrative Procedure Act (APA) celebrated its 50th birthday in 1996. While this anniversary was not front page stuff, it was a significant event within the administrative law community.[6] The administrative state was in a sense legitimated by the procedures that the APA established at the end of the New Deal. The APA and its related statutes continue to provide an organizing vehicle for government intervention into private sector activities. And its anniversary has occasioned not just praise but also proposals for reform and renewal. An attempt to "describe" the field of administrative law is underway,[7] which we will watch and record for the next edition. While at least one of us has doubts about the wisdom of such a project, it comes at a propitious time considering the developments already noted above. Of

4. *See* Symposium on ACUS, 30 Ariz.L. Rev. 1 (1998).

5. *See* J. Sidak & D. Spulber, Deregulatory Takings and the Regulatory Contract: The Competitive Transformation of Network Industries in the United States (1997).

6. *See* Symposium, The Future of the American Administrative Process, 49 Ad.L. Rev. 149 (1997).

7. In October 1998, the Section of Administrative Law and Regulatory Practice of the American Bar Association embarked on an ambitious project under the direction of one of the authors as Chief Reporter, to state the field of administrative law.

one thing we can be sure—these and other activities will provide us with plenty of material for the next edition.

RICHARD PIERCE
SIDNEY SHAPIRO
PAUL VERKUIL

Washington, D.C.
Lawrence, Kansas
New York, New York

June, 1999

*

SUMMARY OF CONTENTS

CHAPTER ONE

THE POLITICAL NATURE OF THE ADMINISTRATIVE PROCESS

CHAPTER TWO

THE LEGAL NATURE OF THE ADMINISTRATIVE PROCESS

CHAPTER THREE

LEGISLATIVE CONTROL OF ADMINISTRATIVE DISCRETION

CHAPTER FOUR

EXECUTIVE CONTROL OF ADMINISTRATIVE
DISCRETION

CHAPTER FIVE

JUDICIAL CONTROL OF AGENCY DISCRETION—
THRESHOLD ISSUES

CHAPTER SIX

JUDICIAL CONTROL OF ADMINISTRATIVE
DISCRETION—PROCEDURAL ISSUES

CHAPTER SEVEN

JUDICIAL CONTROL OF ADMINISTRATIVE
DISCRETION— SUBSTANTIVE ISSUES

CHAPTER EIGHT

ACCESS TO PRIVATE AND PUBLIC INFORMATION

CHAPTER NINE

FAIRNESS AND POLITICAL ACCOUNTABILITY

*

TABLE OF CONTENTS

CHAPTER THREE

LEGISLATIVE CONTROL OF ADMINISTRATIVE DISCRETION

CHAPTER FOUR

EXECUTIVE CONTROL OF ADMINISTRATIVE DISCRETION

CHAPTER FIVE

**JUDICIAL CONTROL OF AGENCY DISCRETION—
THRESHOLD ISSUES**

CHAPTER SIX

JUDICIAL CONTROL OF ADMINISTRATIVE DISCRETION—PROCEDURAL ISSUES

TABLE OF CONTENTS

CHAPTER SEVEN

JUDICIAL CONTROL OF ADMINISTRATIVE DISCRETION— SUBSTANTIVE ISSUES

CHAPTER EIGHT

ACCESS TO PRIVATE AND PUBLIC INFORMATION

CHAPTER NINE

FAIRNESS AND POLITICAL ACCOUNTABILITY

TABLE OF CONTENTS

ADMINISTRATIVE
LAW
AND PROCESS

*

Chapter One

THE POLITICAL NATURE OF THE ADMINISTRATIVE PROCESS

§ 1.1 Private and Public Law Contrasted

Two essentially different models exist in this country for the resolution of social problems and disputes, depending on whether they involve private or public law. *Private law* typically involves a lawsuit brought by a private party usually against another private party in a state or federal court. According to this model, the judge will determine impartially which claims have greater merit. In making that decision, the judge typically will be bound to follow an existing set of precedents or statutory provisions that limit the scope of the decision that can be made.

Public law typically involves an attempt by a governmental administrator to regulate the conduct usually of many persons under legislative standards designed to promote the public interest. While an agency may have to give a hearing to parties affected by a proposed action, the procedures used often will be less formal than those used in a private law trial and no judge will be involved. In reaching a decision, the administrator will typically have considerable discretion since the applicable laws will have delegated the responsibility to make the necessary policy decisions to the administrator's agency. Finally, the administrator, like the trial judge, is responsible to reviewing courts, but agency decisions are also subject to review by the executive and legislative branches, and, for some forms of proceedings, this review can be concurrent with the regulatory proceeding itself.

The distinctions between public and private law are not precise. Normally, for example, the responsibility for implementing broad legislative standards is assigned to administrative agencies. Courts, however, are sometimes also assigned that responsibility. The federal judiciary enforces the Sherman Act, for example, which broadly prohibits "monopolization" and "restraints of trade" under 15 U.S.C. Section 1. Moreover, even when the primary responsibility for enforcing broad legislative standards is assigned to agencies, the courts normally review agency decisions. Thus, the judiciary is not limited to the enforcement of private rights, but it is also a partici-

1

pant in the enforcement of public law as well. Further, in order to remedy unconstitutional agency action, judges have overseen remedial actions on the part of schools, prisons, mental health facilities, the police and public housing.[1] Finally, even traditional public law functions, such as the management of prisons, can be turned over to private entrepreneurs. In this situation, the courts must decide whether public or private law rules apply.[2]

Despite the fact that the private and public law models overlap, there are distinctions between the two types of law that are worth pursuing. The public law model is one that is used widely in Europe, and it is one that can be adopted in the United States with some benefit.

§ 1.2   Background to the Public Law and Private Law Distinction

Since the time of Justinian, most civil law jurisdictions have drawn distinctions between public and private law.[3] Three of the most important of these concern the organization of the judiciary, the nature of legal philosophy, and the manner of legal education.

In most civil law countries, two different judicial systems exist for the enforcement of private and public law. Private law, which consists primarily of civil and commercial law, is adjudicated in "ordinary" courts. Public law, which consists primarily of administrative and constitutional law, is adjudicated in "administrative" courts. The administrative courts have the power to annul virtually any administrative act for errors of fact, as well as law, and for cases of unlawfulness, as well as abuse of discretion. Most administrative court judges have expertise in an administrative law subject and some administrative courts are divided into subject matter sections such as tax courts, social security courts, and others.

1. *See* Sabel & Simon, *Destabilizing Rights: How Public Law Litigation Succeeds,* 117 Harv.L.Rev. 1015 (2004); Chayes, *The Role of the Judge in Public Law Litigation,* 89 Harv.L.Rev. 1281 (1976).

2. Consider Richardson v. McKnight, 521 U.S. 399 (1997), where the Court divided five to four over the issue whether private prison officials are entitled to the governmental function immunity under 42 U.S.C. § 1983. *See generally* Freeman, *Extending Public Law Norms*

Through Privatization, 116 Harv. L. Rev. 1285, 1302 (2003) (discussing whether privatization erodes the public law norms that constitutional and statutory limits are designed to protect).

3. J. Merryman, The Civil Law Tradition 98–108 (1969); Szladits, *The Civil Law System,* in II International Encyclopedia of Comparative Law 2–26 to 2–40 (1974); Merryman, *The Public Law–Private Law Distinction in European and American Law,* 17 J.Pub.L. 3 (1968).

Continental legal scholarship has stressed the distinction between public and private law in order to create a general conception of law. The codified private law exists to protect private property and freedom of contract from government intrusion. The sole function of the state is the recognition and enforcement of individual property and contract rights. The state performs this function by serving as a neutral referee when there is a dispute between private parties. By comparison, the public law, which generally is uncodified, exists to promote the "public interest". As a result, the state is considered to be a party, and not a referee. Further, the state, as the representative of the public interest, is thought to have interests "superior" to that of any private party involved in the dispute. In this manner, the state can be the "driving consideration" to "effectuate the public interest".[4]

Continental legal scholarship has also used the distinction between private and public law to support a strict separation of powers doctrine. This doctrine holds in part that the legislative, executive, and judicial branches cannot perform each other's functions.[5] The separate court system for private and public law matters serves this distinction.[6] Public law judges are not called upon to adjudicate private law matters. They therefore can be considered to be members of the executive branch. Conversely, private law judges are not called upon to adjudicate public law matters. The separate court systems thereby allow a stricter separation of powers than is possible in systems, like the one in this country, where the same court system adjudicates both types of law. Of course, as with our system, it is not always clear even in Continental countries what legal actions are premised on public law and what are within the realm of private adjudication.[7]

Despite the considerable influence that the public and private law distinction has had in civil law countries, it has very little impact in common law jurisdictions. One reason is that the distinction made less sense in feudal England during the early development of the

4. J. Merryman, *supra* note 3, at 100–101.

5. *See infra* § 2.1.2.

6. Continental legal education has also been influenced by the distinction. Public lawyers are trained to be bureaucrats, not advocates, and a public law education encompasses instruction in political science and economics, as well as constitutional and administrative law.

See Carbonneau, *The French Legal Studies Curriculum: Its History and Relevance as a Model of Reform*, 25 McGill L.J. 445 (1980).

7. In France, for example, the Tribunals des Conflicts must adjudicate jurisdictional disputes between the administrative and ordinary courts. *See* L. Brown & J. Bell, French Administrative Law 144–45 (4th ed. 1993).

common law. Because both "public" and "private" rights were defined by property interests, no distinction was made between property ownership and public office of the type made in civil law. Another reason is that one set of courts became the source of review for legislative and executive actions, as well as for private disputes, and therefore there was no strict separation of powers of the European type. Finally, early American legal scholars tended to ignore the distinction as unnecessary to the synthesis of judicial decisions by subject matter, such as torts or contracts. This differed from the European tradition of seeking an overriding conceptual framework for public and private law. Most early administrative law scholars also adopted narrow definitions of administrative law that inhibited the development of a general conception of public law of the continental type. Professor Wyman in a 1903 book made a distinction between "internal" administrative law, which concerned the relationships of administrative decisionmakers, and "external" administrative law, which concerned the constitutional and statutory authority of agencies to impinge on the rights of private citizens.[8] For a time, the distinction was used to separate the field of public administration, which studied the creation and application of administrative policy, and the field of administrative law, which studied the judicial review of final agency actions.

Wyman's distinction was ultimately abandoned because scholars recognized that some problems of administrative law concerned internal procedures, organization and personnel administration.[9] A good example is the separation of the prosecutorial and judicial functions within an agency. Nevertheless, scholars still considered administrative law and public administration to be largely unrelated. Professor Carrow, for example, noted that "those subjects of administration not closely related to the exercise of administrative powers ... are of lesser interest in the study of administrative law. Thus such questions as the ones raised by the desirability of a single-head as against a broad type of administration, centralization as against decentralization of administrative agencies, civil service generally, or grants in aid to other governmental levels, are matters more clearly within the providence of public administration studies".[10]

---

8. B. Wyman, The Principles of Administrative Law Governing the Relations of Public Officers 1–23 (1903).

9. *See generally* W. Chase, The American Law School and the Rise of Administrative Government 61–69 (1982) (failure of scholarship to address "internal" law resulted in excessive agency discretion).

10. M. Carrow, Background of Administrative Law 17–18 (1948).

Scholars made another distinction which further served to narrow the focus of administrative law. This distinction was between "general" administrative law, which pertained to those procedural questions common to most agencies, and "special" administrative law, which pertained to the substantive law made by an agency and any unique procedures used. For law students, this distinction was made on the "practical" ground that it was "truly impossible to present both the general and all the specialized law in one book, nor could it be taught in one law school course".[11] As a result, "specialized" questions were left for specific subject matter courses such as federal trade regulation, taxation, or immigration and naturalization law.

The movement to de-emphasize the broader aspects of administrative law was not universal, however. Early scholars, such as Professors Goodnow and Freund attempted to establish links between public law, as practiced on the continent, and administrative law, as it developed in the United States.[12] Later authors contended that administrative law could not be understood apart from its broader contexts. In the introduction to his 1950 textbook, for example, Professor Hart reminded the reader that the central problem studied in both administrative law and political science was the "adjustment of authority and liberty".[13] Hart warned that the student who ignored this connection would "see important issues of administrative law as merely technical, and hence dull and meaningless questions" and would "be unable to make intelligent administrative law judgments". By comparison, Hart thought that the student "who reduces every question to the over-all problem will find administrative law of great significance precisely because it involves specific application of political theory."

Although the private-public law distinction has not become a staple of American administrative law scholarship, scholars have used the distinction to analyze legal developments in administrative and constitutional law. For example, Professor Mashaw has considered the different dimensions of the "right" to seek judicial review under "individualistic" (private law) and "statist" (public law) con-

11. R. Parker, Administrative Law 5 (1952).

12. *See* E. Freund, Administrative Powers Over Persons and Property: A Comparative Survey (1928); F. Goodnow, Comparative Administrative Law (1970) (reprint of 1893 edition).

13. J. Hart, An Introduction to Administrative Law With Selected Cases 23 (2d ed. 1950); *accord* Freund, *Historical Survey,* in the Growth of American Administrative Law 40 (1923).

ceptions.[14] The public and private law distinction has also been used to highlight the fact that when judges engage in constitutional adjudication, their decisions, especially concerning remedial action, inherently raise a problem of democratic responsiveness. As the *Chevron* case teaches us, judges are not elected and are not members of the "political" branches of government.[15]

Moreover, despite the failure generally to identify American administrative law as public law, administrative law scholarship is deeply committed to the view that administrative law must be understood in terms of its broader relationships. Scholars have examined other social science disciplines, political science, public administration, and economics, to evaluate how the administrative law and process can be better understood and improved.[16] Further, administrative law casebooks usually ask students to consider questions associated with the public administration, political science, or economic aspects of administrative law and process. Certainly, the authors of this treatise approach the subject of administrative law from this broader, interdisciplinary framework.

§ 1.3   The Relevance of the Public Law Model to Administrative Law

In civil law jurisdictions, public law is synonymous with administrative law. While there has been a reluctance overtly to make that connection in the United States, the authors believe that many current administrative law doctrines are nonetheless indirectly influenced by the concept of public law. We will propose a public law model that helps explain the relationship between administrative law and the process by which administrative decisions are reached.

The remainder of this chapter will describe the administrative process. Chapter Two will describe the relationship of that process to

---

14. Mashaw, *"Rights" in the Federal Administrative State,* 92 Yale L.J. 1129 (1984); *see also* B. Ackerman, Reconstructing American Law 23–37 (1984); Stewart & Sunstein, *Public Programs and Private Rights*, 95 Harv.L.Rev. 1193 (1982).

15. Chevron U.S.A., Inc. v. Natural Resources Defense Council, Inc., 467 U.S. 837 (1984); discussed *infra* at § 7.4.

16. *See, e.g.,* R. Baldwin & M. Cave, Understanding Regulation: Theory, Strategy & Practice ch. 3 (1999); C. Sun-

stein, Free Markets & Social Justice (1997); G. Robinson, American Bureaucracy: Public Choice & Public Law (1991); Kagan, *Presidential Administration*, 114 Harv. L. Rev. 2245 (2001); Croley, *Theories of Regulation: Incorporating the Administrative Process*, 98 Colum. L. Rev. 1 (1998); Farina, *Statutory Interpretation and the Balance of Power in the Administrative State*, 89 Col.L.Rev. 452 (1989); Pierce, *The Role of Constitutional and Political Theory in Administrative Law*, 64 Tex.L.Rev. 469 (1985).

administrative law. The nature of that process, and the interconnections between it and administrative law, form the public law model.

§ 1.4   The Nature of the Administrative Process

Four governmental institutions create public law. The legislature establishes an agency by passing enabling legislation that defines its role and its limitations. The legislature controls the agency subsequently through a combination of statutory controls, such as laws that overrule agency decisions, and non-statutory controls, such as oversight hearings. The President or a governor appoints the person or persons who will lead an agency, usually with the approval of at least one house of the legislature. The executive's staff monitors the agency's compliance with the administration's general regulatory philosophy or specific wishes in a given case. The agency is composed of its politically appointed leadership and usually a staff hired through a civil service system. Finally, the judiciary, who are usually political appointees, will determine whether an agency has acted within the limitations of its enabling act and the constitution.

Private parties are active in public law by participation in agency proceedings and by lobbying agency administrators, the executive, legislators, or the staff of those persons. Private participants include the firm or industry being regulated and other firms financially affected, both of which may participate through the use of trade associations, such as the American Chemistry Council, which represents chemical manufacturers, or the United States Chamber of Commerce. Public interest groups, such as the Environmental Defense Fund, Natural Resources Defense Council, OMB Watch, Public Citizen, and the Sierra Club, will also participate in some matters.

§ 1.4.1   The airbag controversy as a case study

Automobile manufacturers today routinely attempt to convince buyers to purchase their automobiles because they have installed more than the minimum mandatory airbags required by law. As the following story indicates, however, this was not always the situation. The series of events that led to today's use of airbags in cars nicely illustrates the interaction of the various institutions, private parties, and public interest groups that interact in public law.

In 1966, Congress passed the National Traffic and Motor Vehicle Safety Act which directed the Department of Transportation to "reduce traffic accidents and deaths and injuries to persons resulting from traffic accidents" by promulgating regulations that "shall be practical, shall meet the need for motor vehicle safety, and shall be stated in objective terms". The Department's general authority to promulgate such safety standards was delegated to the National Highway Traffic Safety Administration (NHTSA).[17]

One of the Department's and NHTSA's first efforts was a 1967 regulation that required all new automobiles to have seatbelts.[18] By 1972, however, the Department found that the level of seatbelt usage was too low to reduce traffic injuries significantly. A new regulation therefore was issued to require that all automobiles built after 1975 have either automatic seatbelts, which would deploy without any effort by the passenger to buckle them, or airbags, which would automatically inflate around passengers if an automobile was in an accident. The Department also required that all automobiles built between 1973 and 1975 be equipped either with passive restraints or with an "ignition interlock" that would not allow them to be started unless the car's seatbelts were buckled.[19]

In *Chrysler Corporation v. Department of Transportation*,[20] the Sixth Circuit affirmed the regulations, but their political life turned out to be short-lived. The automobile manufacturers had chosen to comply with the 1973 to 1975 regulations by installing ignition interlocks. The interlocks were so unpopular with the public that Congress received numerous complaints. The lawmakers reacted by passing the Motor Vehicle and School Bus Safety Act Amendments of 1974. The law prohibited the Department from requiring the interlocks. It also provided that any future passive restraint regulations promulgated by the agency had to be submitted to Congress for its review and that Congress could veto them by a concurrent resolution of both houses.[21]

Passive restraints then became a political ping-pong ball. William Coleman, President Ford's Secretary of Transportation, withdrew the existing regulations and proposed that a demonstration project involving as many as 500,000 cars be mounted to smooth the way for public acceptance of passive restraints. When President Carter appointed Brock Adams as Secretary a few months later, the Department changed its mind and reissued a regulation requiring passive restraints starting in 1982.[22] The regulation survived scrutiny by

---

17. 15 U.S.C. §§ 1381, 1392(a); 49 C.F.R. § 1.50(a) (delegation of Secretary's authority to NHTSA). *See generally* J. Mashaw & D. Harfst, The Struggle for Auto Safety (1990).

18. 32 Fed.Reg. 2408, 2415 (1967).

19. 37 Fed.Reg. 3911, 3912 (1972).

20. 472 F.2d 659, 675 (6th Cir.1972).

21. 15 U.S.C. § 1410b. The Supreme Court later declared the legislative veto to be unconstitutional. See *infra* § 3.5

22. 42 Fed.Reg. 34,289, 34,297 (1977).

Congress, which did not use its legislative veto authority, and it was affirmed in *Pacific Legal Foundation v. Department of Transportation* by the District of Columbia Circuit.[23] In February 1981, however, Drew Lewis, appointed Secretary by President Reagan, withdrew the regulation on the ground that automobile manufacturers planned to meet the regulation by use of automatic seatbelts that could easily be detached.[24]

In *Motor Vehicle Manufacturers Association v. State Farm Mutual Automobile Insurance Company,* the Supreme Court heard a challenge to the Department's decision by several insurance companies, which believed that passive restraints would lower insurance costs, and by several public interest groups.[25] The decision was defended by the Department and by the Motor Vehicle Manufacturers Association, which believed that passive restraints would increase automobile costs without any corresponding benefit. The Court remanded the regulation back to the Department on the ground that the agency could not withdraw it without a more logical explanation of its actions. The Court found that while NHTSA offered reasons why it did not make sense to require automatic seatbelts, it offered no rationale for why it did not require the installation of airbags.

In 1984, Secretary of Transportation Elizabeth Dole promulgated a new passive restraint rule which required the automobile manufacturers to install either automatic seatbelts or airbags in all automobiles after 1989.[26] The regulation provided, however, that it would not go into effect if two-thirds of the nation's population were covered by state laws requiring the use of manual seatbelts before April 1, 1989, and if those laws met the minimum criteria set out in the regulation. Although lobbyists from the automobile manufacturers swooped down on state legislatures in a $15 million campaign for the adoption of laws requiring the use of seatbelts, the campaign failed. Most states did enact seatbelt laws, but most of these did not meet the minimum criteria specified in the regulation and the regulation requiring the use of passive restraints went into effect.

By the late 1990s, airbags were practically a standard technology. In 1997, of the 100 million cars and trucks on the roads, about 55 million had driver-side airbags, and some 28 million also had passenger side airbags. Nevertheless, the government's mandate continued

---

23. 593 F.2d 1338, 1349 (D.C.Cir. 1979), cert. denied 444 U.S. 830 (1979).

24. 46 Fed.Reg. 21,205–208 (1981).

25. 463 U.S. 29 (1983).

26. Federal Motor Vehicle Safety Standard: Occupant Crash Protection, 49 Fed.Reg. 28,962 (1984).

to be controversial.[27] NHTSA discovered that in addition to the 1,700 lives saved by airbags since the mid–1980s, airbags were responsible for causing the deaths of 55 persons, including 35 children. The problem was that airbags explode with such great force that they are a threat to small adults and children. The agency had originally assumed that airbags of this force were necessary to protect drivers and passengers because they might not be wearing seatbelts. The agency issued warnings to the public not to place small children in the front seat of cars with passenger side airbags and it amended its regulation to permit car owners who were endangered to install a switch to shut off airbags.

§ 1.4.2 Lessons for public law

The automakers' resistance to the legal imposition of airbag technology involved many of the common elements of a public law matter. The Department of Transportation was given broad discretion to decide how to reduce traffic injuries which it chose to exercise initially in the form of requiring passive restraints. The issue throughout the following years of contention was whether such a requirement served the public interest of protecting people and reducing the cost of automobile accidents. Resolution of the issue involved a statutory amendment and other oversight by Congress, successive changes implemented by each of four new Presidential appointees, and three different lawsuits. Participants in most of those events included industry groups which supported and opposed the proposals and public interest groups which supported them.

The seatbelt example indicates that the administrative law process is bound up with the practice of politics. This chapter will address the nature of the relationship between that process and politics. To consider this issue, it is important to recognize that there are two contending explanations for why regulation exists. One is that it serves some public or general social purpose. The other is that it serves the economic interest of some private group or groups.

§ 1.5 The Public Interest Explanation for Regulation

Regulation can serve the public interest in two ways.[28] First, it can address "market failure" or the absence of one or more of the

---

27. *See* S. Shapiro & J. Tomain, Regulatory Law & Policy: Cases & Materials 32 (3d ed. 2003).

28. For an analysis of the public interest explanation of regulation, see C. Sunstein, After the Rights Revolution: Reconceiving the Regulatory State 47–73 (1990); Verkuil, *Understanding the "Public Interest" Justification for Government*

factors necessary for an efficient market. A private market is "efficient" when it produces only those goods and services most desired by consumers. Second, regulation is justified on the ground that the outcome of markets, although efficient, is inconsistent with important collective social values.

§ 1.5.1   Regulation to improve information

Without accurate and adequate product information, consumers can purchase goods and services that will fail to perform adequately, or that will harm them or their property. Markets will be inefficient in these circumstances because consumers with accurate and adequate information about those consequences would have purchased other products.

Inadequate information occurs because of market flaws of various types.[29] For example, some sellers, like itinerant roofers, do not depend significantly on repeat sales. They are free to mislead consumers because future sales do not require maintaining consumer good will. In other markets, information about the performance of products is too expensive for consumers to obtain. For example, information about the efficacy and safety of pharmaceutical drugs or pesticides can be developed only after time-consuming and costly scientific testing. Because consumers are unlikely to undertake the testing on their own, some sellers may exploit the consumer's lack of knowledge to sell a drug or pesticide that performs poorly or is dangerous.

Two forms of regulation have been created to address the problem of inaccurate and inadequate consumer information. Some agencies, like the Federal Trade Commission (FTC), are authorized to prohibit sellers from "false or deceptive acts or practices" in the sale of their products or services.[30] Other agencies prohibit the sale of goods or services unless a license is first obtained from the agency. The agency conditions the availability of a license on the seller's meeting certain requirements that are intended to set a minimum level of quality for the goods and services. States license occupations

---

Actions, 39 Acta Juridica Hungarica 141 (1998).

29. *See* Lyndon, *Information Economics and Chemical Toxicity: Defining Laws to Produce and Use Data,* 87 Mich. L.Rev. 1795 (1989); Reich, *Toward a New Consumer Protection,* 128 U.Pa.L.Rev. 1, 19–31 (1979); *compare* Pitofsky, *Beyond Nader: Consumer Protection and the Reg-*

ulation of Advertising, 90 Harv.L.Rev. 661, 663–67 (1977) (markets generally will not produce adequate consumer information) *with* Posner, *The Federal Trade Commission,* 37 U.Chi.L.Rev. 47, 61–65 (1973) (markets generally will produce adequate consumer information).

30. 15 U.S.C. §§ 45, 52.

for this purpose. Federal agencies, such as the Food and Drug Administration (FDA) and the Environmental Protection Agency (EPA), license the sale of products also for this purpose.[31]

§ 1.5.2 Regulation of competitive conditions

An efficient market also requires numerous sellers and buyers. Under these conditions, a market price will prevail at which sellers will produce exactly the supply of goods and services demanded by buyers at that price. This result is efficient because both shortages and oversupply are avoided.

The type of competitive conditions that produce appropriate buyers and sellers will not always be present. Several types of regulation have been adopted to remedy those situations. The antitrust laws, for example, prohibit a firm from anti-competitively exploiting a monopoly market position or two or more firms from engaging in an agreement or conspiracy to restrain trade unreasonably.[32] The states regulate firms, such as local natural gas companies, that have a monopoly, to prevent them from exploiting their lack of competition by charging a price higher than that which would occur in a competitive market.[33]

§ 1.5.3 Regulation for externalities and free-riders

An efficient market also requires that consumers pay a market price that reflects the value of the resources used in the production of the product. If a manufacturing process, for example, produced toxic vapors that made persons ill, the manufacturer should pay for the medical expenses of those persons and include them as part of the price for which the product is sold. If the manufacturer does not pay those costs, the product will be overproduced. There will be more demand for the product than if it were sold at a higher price that reflected the damages its production caused.

Under some market circumstances, a manufacturer will adjust the price of a product because persons who are adversely affected by its production will bargain for that result.[34] In most markets, however, so many persons are affected that the costs of negotiating the necessary bargain are prohibitive. The tort system compensates for

31. *See* 21 U.S.C. §§ 351–360ee (drug and device regulation); 7 U.S.C. §§ 136–136y (pesticide regulation).

32. 15 U.S.C. §§ 1–2.

33. *See* A. Kahn, The Economics of Regulation: Principles & Institutions ch. 1 (1988); J. Harrison, T. Morgan, & P. Verkuil, Regulation & Deregulation: Cases & Materials ch. 3 (2d ed. 2004).

34. *See* Coase, *The Problem of Social Cost,* 3 J.Law & Econ. 1 (1960).

that problem by forcing manufacturers to pay for the harmful consequences of many of their actions. Further, Congress has reached the judgment that agency regulation is necessary to avoid additional injuries. Agencies such as the Environmental Protection Agency (EPA) and the Occupational Health and Safety Administration (OSHA) have the authority to order manufacturers to lessen pollution and other dangerous conditions.[35]

Some products, like national defense or police services, will not be produced in private markets because of what is called the "free-rider" problem. These products, called "public goods," have the unique character that consumption of them by one consumer does not diminish the possibility of consumption by another consumer. As a result, public goods must be purchased by the government if they are to be purchased at all. Otherwise, every consumer will attempt to become a free rider by waiting for someone else to purchase the product so that it can be used for free. Government regulation concerning the method and collection of taxes ensures that each citizen pays a share of the cost of governmental purchases of public goods.

§ 1.5.4 Regulation for Social Goals

Even if a market system is efficient, it may produce outcomes that citizens find inappropriate. Citizens also rely on regulation to address these non-economic goals. As Cass Sunstein explains:

> First, citizens may seek to fulfill individual and collective aspirations in political behavior, not in consumption. As citizens, people may seek the aid of the law to bring about a social state in some sense higher than what emerges from a market ordering. Second, people may, in their capacity as political actors, attempt to satisfy altruistic or other-regarding desires, which diverge from the self-interested preferences characteristic of other markets. Third, political decisions might vindicate what might be called meta-preferences or second-order preferences. A law protecting environmental diversity and opposing consuming behavior is an example.[36]

Besides the endangered species act, scholars have sought to justify other types of health and safety and environmental law on the basis

---

35. *See* Pierce, *Encouraging Safety: The Limits of Tort Law and Government Regulation,* 33 Vand.L.Rev. 1281, 1289 (1980). While health and safety and environmental regulation can be justified on the basis of market failure, there is a debate over whether the failure is an economic problem or a social problem. See *infra* §§ 1.5.4.

36. C. Sunstein, supra note 16, at 57–58.

of collective social values.[37]

Other regulatory responses concern the distribution of wealth. Efficient markets may produce a distribution of wealth that a majority of citizens find unsatisfactory because some people are too poor to live a humane existence.[38] Wealth is redistributed to needy persons, both directly through methods such as food stamps, and indirectly through subsidies to areas like housing and community development. The function of administrative agencies in redistributive activities is to determine the eligibility of persons and institutions to receive payments.

§ 1.6 Regulatory Reform

Whatever the justification, regulation in the United States is ubiquitous. It is difficult to think of many activities in which businesses and individuals engage that is not affected, at least indirectly, by regulation. The scope and extent of regulation has caused scholars to raise questions about its utility. In particular, critics have contended that the benefits of many forms of regulation are less than the costs of the regulation.[39] Regulation is economically efficient when benefits exceed costs because the total value of society's resources will have been increased. By comparison, when benefits are less than costs, society is spending more money to produce a social benefit than it is worth and thereby wasting scarce resources. Supporters of regulation counter that benefits do exceed costs for health and safety and environmental regulation, that a cost-benefit standard is an inappropriate measure of whether there should be regulation because it is extremely uncertain and biased, and that many forms of regulation have equitable goals which cannot be measured by an economic measurement.[40]

The debate concerning the costs and benefits of regulation will continue for the foreseeable future.[41] The liveliness of the debate,

---

37. *See, e.g.*, L. Heinzerling & F. Ackerman, Priceless: On Knowing the Price of Everything and the Value of Nothing (2004); S. Shapiro & R. Glicksman, Risk Regulation At Risk: Restoring a Pragmatic Approach (2003).

38. A. Okun, Equality and Efficiency: The Big Trade-off 6–22 (1975).

39. *See, e.g.*, C. Sunstein, supra note 16; Risks, Costs, and Lives Saved: Getting Better Results From Regulation (R.

Hahn ed. 1996); S. Breyer, Breaking The Vicious Circle: Toward Effective Risk Regulation (1993); W. Viscusi, Fatal Tradeoffs: Public and Private Responsibilities for Risk (1992); S. Breyer, Regulation and Its Reform 147–53 (1982).

40. *See, e.g., supra* note 37.

41. *See infra* § 9.5 (discussing regulatory analysis and political accountability).

however, should not obscure the fact that the critics of government regulation have already made a significant contribution to public policy. Several types of regulatory programs have been ended or modified because their costs were greater than their benefits. For example, Congress has abolished the Civil Aeronautics Administration (CAB) and ended price and entry regulation of the airline industry. Similarly, Congress has ended regulation by the Federal Energy Regulatory Commission (FERC) of petroleum prices. Partial deregulation has occurred for other forms of transportation and for broadcasting.

Besides deregulation, critics argue that the form of regulation can be changed to decrease its costs. They contend that agencies should adopt regulatory techniques, wherever feasible, that do not remove decisions about the sale and purchase of products from consumers.[42] For example, states or municipalities could replace occupational licensing with techniques that would increase the amount of information that consumers would have about the quality of the service being offered. The advantage of these techniques is that consumers are allowed to determine for themselves what minimum level of quality they will accept. Because consumers make that decision, a possibly erroneous prejudgment by an agency about what consumers prefer is avoided.[43]

§ 1.7   The Public Choice Explanation for Regulation

The public interest explanation for regulation identifies the economic or social purpose for which the regulation was established. The purpose is either to improve the efficiency of a market or to address market outcomes that are inconsistent with social values. Regulation can also be explained as the product of political forces.

Politics has been defined as "who gets what, when, and how" and in this sense all regulation is political.[44] Because regulatory decisions produce groups of persons who will benefit and groups of persons who will lose, each side competes concerning the outcome of proposed policies. Competition over regulatory outcomes is normally conducted by interest groups who represent citizens affected by the proposed decisions. Trade and producer organizations, labor unions,

---

42. S. Breyer, Regulation & Its Reform, *supra* note 39, at 191–96.

43. Moore, *The Purpose of Licensing*, 4 J.Law & Econ. 93, 104–06 (1961); Rose, *Occupational Licensing: A Framework for Analysis*, 1979 Ariz.State.L.J. 189, 191.

44. H. Lasswell, Politics: Who Gets What, When, How (1936); *see also* R. Leone, Who Profits: Winners, Losers, and Government Regulation (1986).

environment associations, and similar groups bargain with members of Congress, presidential aides, and administrators concerning the outcome of regulatory issues.[45] This competition has been interpreted as a market process similar to private market decisionmaking. Interest groups demand more or less regulation according to the self-interest of their members and public officials supply more or less regulation according to what would benefit their self-interest.[46]

The idea that the regulatory process is best understood as a market-like process is part of the "public choice" explanation of politics. The public choice approach has been defined as "the economic study of nonmarket decisionmaking, or simply the application of economics to political science."[47] The basic premise of this method is that individuals are egoistic, rational utility maximizers, who pursue their own self-interest whether they are acting in private markets, purchasing consumer goods, or in public markets, voting or serving as public officials. Other scholars have challenged this view of human nature, and this challenge is explained in the next section. First, however, this section describes how the regulatory process can be explained as the product of demand and supply and discusses some of the implications of such a perspective.

§ 1.7.1   The demand for and supply of regulation

Interest groups are of two types. "Public" and "private" interest groups are distinguished by the type of regulation they demand. Public interest groups seek regulation that has a widely dispersed economic or social effect. Environmental groups, for example, have supported air quality regulations that benefit the thousands of persons who live in polluted areas. By comparison, private interest groups support results that have a narrowly dispersed economic effect. The Motor Vehicle Manufacturers Association is a good example. As related earlier, the Association actively opposed efforts by the Department of Transportation to promulgate a regulation requiring

---

45. *See* J. Chubb, Interest Groups and the Bureaucracy: The Politics of Energy 18–41 (1983); R. Noll, The Political Economy of Deregulation: Interest Groups and the Political Process 26–52 (1983).

46. Stigler, *The Theory of Economic Regulation*, 2 Bell J. Econ. & Management Sci. 3, 11–13 (1981); Peltzman, *Toward a General Theory of Regulation*, 19 J.Law & Econ. 211, 212–13 (1976); Pos-

ner, *Theories of Economic Regulation*, 5 Bell J.Econ. & Management Sci. 335, 343 (1974); *see generally*, S. Reiter & J. Hughes, *A Preface on Modeling the Regulated United States Economy*, 9 Hofstra L.Rev. 1381 (1981).

47. D. Mueller, Public Choice II 1 (1989); *see generally, Symposium on the Theory of Public Choice*, 74 Va.L.Rev. 167 (1988).

the installation of passive restraints in automobiles. The Association's efforts were intended to benefit the automobile manufacturers by allowing them to avoid the increased costs that would have reduced the demand for new cars.

Private groups do not always oppose regulation, but sometimes seek it because it would be economically beneficial. The profession to be licensed, for example, has usually supported occupational licensing. One reason is that it often eliminates competitors that cannot meet the licensing standards and therefore it raises prices to consumers.[48] Private groups can also benefit from regulation in other ways. Scholars argue, for example, that the railroads supported the creation of the Interstate Commerce Commission, to substitute more lenient federal supervision for stricter state regulation.[49] Similarly, chemical manufacturers have sought federal regulation of the identification of chemical hazards to avoid inconsistent and sometimes stronger state laws.[50]

When interest groups clash over whether new regulations should be adopted, the outcome will depend on which group or groups can offer the greatest rewards to the legislators or administrators responsible for the decision. The medium of exchange is the repayment of past favors or the creation of a stock of credits useful for obtaining future favors.[51] In the case of elected officials, the favors concern activities that will affect the person's chances for reelection. In the case of unelected administrators, the favors concern activities that will affect the person's career objectives. The activities could improve the person's professional advancement (a better job outside of the agency), bureaucratic advancement (a bigger budget and more prestige for the agency), or political advancement (increased opportunity for elected office).[52]

---

48. *Cf.* Rose, *supra* note 43, at 193–94 (regulations create barriers to entry).

49. G. Kolko, Railroads and Regulation 34–39 (1965); M. Josephson, The Politicos 526 (1938); *but see* Purcell, *Ideas and Interests: Business and the Interstate Commerce Act,* 54 J.Am.History 561 (1967) (commission was also supported as being in the public interest).

50. *See* Schroeder & Shapiro, *Responses to Occupational Disease: The Role of Markets, Regulation, and Information,* 72 Geo.L.J. 1231, 1288–89 (1984).

51. Weingast, *Regulation, Reregulation, and Deregulation: The Political Foundations of Agency–Clientele Relationships,* 44 Law & Contemp. Probs. 147, 150–65 (Winter 1981).

52. *See* P. Quirk, Industry Influence in Federal Regulatory Agencies (1981); W. Niskanen, Bureaucracy and Representative Government (1971); G. Tullock, The Politics of Bureaucracy (1965); J. Buchanen & G. Tullock, The Calculus of Consent (1962); A. Downs, An Economic Theory of Democracy (paper text ed. 1965).

§ 1.7.2 Theories of capture

Decisionmakers can be expected to favor those groups that can benefit them the most in the ways just mentioned. Many times, however, many of the people who will be affected by a regulatory decision will not be represented by any group. In those circumstances, a phenomenon called "agency capture" could occur. An agency is captured when it favors the concerns of the industry it regulates, which is well-represented by its trade groups and lawyers, over the interests of the general public, which is often unrepresented.[53]

Private groups participate more than public groups in the formulation of policy because most regulatory decisions have a much greater impact on manufacturers and producers than they do on consumers. For example, some regulations confer a small economic benefit on each member of the public at a large cost borne by the few members of an industry. The benefits of cleaner air are spread over the entire population of an area, but the costs will be borne by electrical utilities and other manufacturers who pollute. Other regulations will impose small costs on each member of the public for the significant benefit of a few. The cost of milk price supports is spread over the population of everyone who buys milk, but the benefits accrue to a fairly small number of milk producers. In each of these instances, most members of the public will be only marginally affected by policy changes. As a result, only industry members find it economically worthwhile to pay the substantial costs of forming an organization to influence policy decisions.[54]

Although private interests have a better incentive to organize, public groups have had considerable success in influencing Congress and the agencies. For example, Professor Weidenbaum has identified forty-two federal laws passed between 1962 and 1978 that constitute "major" expansions of government regulation of business.[55] There are two reasons for this success. First, public interest groups are able to lower their organizational costs and increase their effectiveness when they can capitalize on the altruism of their donors, the efficiency of direct-mail fund raising, the support of foundations, the advantage of friendly media coverage, and the sympathy of friendly mem-

53. *See* Peltzman, *supra* note 46, at 212; Posner, *supra* note 46, at 341–43; *see also* M. Bernstein, Regulating Business by Independent Commission 90–95 (1955) (capture occurs when consumer coalition that caused agency to be formed dies out).

54. Wilson, *The Politics of Regulation,* in The Politics of Regulation 266–72 (J.Q. Wilson, ed. 1980).

55. M. Weidenbaum, Business, Government and the Public 7–10 (2d ed. 1981).

bers of Congress and the bureaucracy. Second, public interest groups are successful when they can create a political climate to offset the organizational advantages of private groups. Public interest advocates, like Joan Claybrook of Public Citizen, seek to mobilize "latent public sentiment (by revealing a scandal or capitalizing on a crisis), put the opponent on the defensive (by accusing them of deforming babies or killing motorists), and associating themselves with widely shared values (clean air, pure water, health and safety)".[56]

§ 1.8 The Relationship of the Public Interest and Public Choice Explanations

The public choice perspective has been challenged by scholars who believe that it offers useful insights into public behavior, but it fails as an all encompassing explanation for such behavior.[57] One problem with public choice theory is that many political acts are better explained as the result of altruism or ideology than as the product of self-interested behavior. As two thoughtful critics of public choice conclude, "no theory of government can ignore the powerful forces of individual self-interest. It is one-sided, however, to lose sight of the role of civic virtue."[58] According to this counter-interpretation of public life, social decisions provide an opportunity for citizens to give certain things a higher valuation than individuals choose, for one reason or another, in their private activities.[59]

Another aspect of public behavior that public choice theory does not take into account is that societies create institutional arrangements that channel public behavior towards public purposes.[60] For example, public behavior can be influenced by the existence of *organizational norms*. Organizations are structured so that decision-makers will consider whether actions they wish to take will serve the purposes of the organization. When the organization is an agency or

56. Wilson, *supra* note 54, at 266–72, 370; *see* M. Pertschuk, Revolt Against Regulation: The Rise and Fall of the Consumer Movement 12–23 (1982); Weaver, *Regulation, Social Policy, and Class Conflict,* 50 Public Interest 45, 52 (1978).

57. *See* Farina & Rachlinski, *Forward: Post–Public Choice?*, 87 Corn. L. Rev. 267 (2002).

58. D. Farber & P. Frickey, Law and Public Choice: A Critical Introduction 11 (1991); *see also* Rubin, *Beyond Public Choice: Comprehensive Rationality in the Writing and Reading of Statutes,* 66 N.Y.U.L.Rev. 1 (1991); Hovenkamp, *Legislation, Well–Being and Public Choice,* 57 U.Chi.L.Rev. 63 (1990).

59. Beyond Self–Interest (J. Mansbridge ed. 1990); The Power of Public Ideas (R. Reich ed. 1988); *see also* Rubin, *Public Choice Phenomenology, and the Meaning of the Modern State: Keep the Bathwater, But Throw Out the Baby,* 87 Corn. L. Rev. 309 (2002).

60. *See* Nonet, *The Legitimation of Purposive Decision,* 68 Cal.L.Rev. 263 (1980); *see also* Frug, *The Ideology of Bureaucracy in American Law,* 97 Harv. L.Rev. 1277 (1984).

the Congress, decisionmakers will defend their actions in terms of the public interest because that is the purpose of those organizations. In addition, public behavior can be influenced by *legal norms*. In agencies, the decisionmaking process is structured by legal procedures that require an administrator to take actions only when they serve the public purpose for which the agency was created. The nature and effect of these two constraints is explained further in the next two sections.

§ 1.9   Organizational Norms

Sociologists argue that because organizations exist for a purpose, members will establish "norms" or mutual expectations of what constitutes acceptable behavior. These can be quite indefinite and general, in the form of unwritten purposes and values, or quite specific, in the form of written guidelines. Members are expected to justify their actions in terms of these norms. As a result, the acceptability of various actions to other members will be based on the strength of the logical connection between the reasons given for the actions and the principles, values, or guidelines, to which they relate.[61]

Decisionmakers in agencies will find it in their self-interest to justify their actions in terms of the purposes for which their agency exists to obtain the support and approval of other members of the organization. Decisions will be justified in terms of the organization's purpose also as a matter of professional socialization. Decisionmakers are often trained as lawyers, scientists, engineers, public administrators, or economists, where the emphasis is to solve problems by the use of rational analysis rather than by political negotiation and accommodation.[62]

Choices concerning the structure of government agencies have been made to create stronger organizational norms. The civil service system, for example, was created in the belief that persons hired, trained, and retained on the basis of expertise and job performance

61.   Nonet, *supra* note 60, at 268–73. For an excellent account of the role of organizational and professional influences in administrative decisionmaking, *see* J. Mashaw, Bureaucratic Justice (1983).

62.   *See* F. Mosher, Democracy and Public Service 101, 109 (2d ed. 1982)

(because professionalism rests on specialized knowledge, science, and rationality, there "are *correct* ways of solving problems"); Wilson, *The Study of Administration,* 2 Political Sci.Q. 197, 209 (1887) ("The field of administration is a field of business . . . removed from the hurry and strife of politics. . . . ").

will be more acceptable as decisionmakers than those persons whose sole qualifications are their political contacts.[63]

There are clear limits to the influence of organizational norms, however. If the expectations produced by organizational and professional pressures are sufficiently general and abstract, administrators will feel free to respond to their self-interest to a considerable degree. For example, the scientific evidence used by agencies like EPA, OSHA and FDA to determine whether a chemical is carcinogenic is often indefinite and subject to conflicting interpretations by various experts. In this circumstance, an administrator can choose any one of several answers concerning the level of exposure at which a chemical becomes dangerous. The administrator therefore is free to make a policy judgment which can be influenced by the dynamics of public choice theory.[64]

§ 1.10   Legal Norms

Under the public choice model of politics, the decisionmaker will make that decision which satisfies the largest number of groups possible and minimizes the displeasure of the others. The nature of decisionmaking is "interactive" because it is a bargaining process where the decisionmaker attempts to reconcile competing claims with the agreement of those who advocate them. Under a legal system of decisionmaking, the emphasis is on the advocacy of conflicting viewpoints and their logical resolution by the decisionmaker. The process is a "rational" one in the sense that the decision that is reached must be justified in terms of the applicable legal rules and precedent.[65]

There are two such sources of administrative law and precedent. The Constitution places limitations on Congress and on administrative agencies concerning the types of powers they can possess and the methods by which those powers can be executed. Congress further sets the limits of acceptable agency action when it establishes the laws under which an agency will operate. For the administrator, any

---

63. Kaufman, *Emerging Conflicts in the Doctrines of Public Administration,* in The Politics of the Federal Bureaucracy 75 (A. Altshuler ed. 1968) ("The slogan of the neutral competence school became, 'Take administration out of politics.' "); *cf.* H. Heclo, A Government of Strangers: Executive Politics in Washington 240–64 (1977) (Well-organized, higher career civil service is the key to better control by politically appointed administrators.).

64. *See* Schroeder & Shapiro, *supra* note 50, at 601–07; McGarity, *Substantive and Procedural Discretion in Administrative Resolution of Science Policy Questions: Regulating Carcinogens in EPA and OSHA,* 67 Geo.L.J. 729, 731–32 (1979); Bazelon, *Coping With Technology Through the Legal Process,* 62 Cornell L.Rev. 817, 824 (1977).

65. *See* C. Lindblom & D. Cohen, Usable Knowledge (1979).

accommodation of interest groups must be justifiable under the applicable constitutional and legislative limitations. Particularly, the administrator must be able to defend the decision as being one that serves the economic and social purposes for which the agency was created.

The influence of legal norms, like organizational norms, will be limited if the applicable constitutional and legislative rules under which an agency operates are too general and abstract. In these circumstances, the administrator will have more discretion to interact with interest groups because the results of any bargain can be more easily defended as being consistent with vague and broad limitations, than with specific and narrow constraints.[66]

66. *See* Scalia, *Rulemaking as Politics*, 34 Ad.L.Rev. v, v (1982) (Chairman's message, Summer 1982).

Chapter Two

THE LEGAL NATURE OF THE ADMINISTRATIVE PROCESS

§ 2.1 Administrative Law and Democratic Legitimation

Governmental actions in a democracy must be justified according to democratic principles or they will be open to political challenge. Administrative law is an attempt to justify regulatory decisions by placing them within the context of the "classical" or "liberal" definition of democracy. But important questions concerning the legitimacy of the administrative process itself have arisen because agency government has developed in a manner that appears to violate the classical definition.[1] This chapter will examine the nature of the regulatory process and its democratic legitimacy.

§ 2.1.1 The "classical" or "liberal" definition of democracy

The principles of American democracy are built on the "liberal" philosophical and political movements that came to dominate England and Europe in the three centuries before this country was founded. Liberalism grew out of the Renaissance's assertion that individuals should use reason to question "received beliefs" such as those of church dogma. It developed into the Enlightenment's faith that reason could explain the nature of life and society. Liberalism attacked the economic and social restrictions that had grown out of feudalism on the ground that if people were given liberty to learn, to think, and to act, they would form a better society. Liberalism therefore promoted the values of liberty, natural rights, and government by consent.[2]

---

1. J. Freedman, Crisis and Legitimacy: The Administrative Process and American Government 10 (1978) ("[T]he criticism of the administrative agencies has been animated by a strong and persisting challenge to the basic legitimacy of the administrative process itself"); *see* J. Mashaw, Greed, Chaos, and Governance: Using Public Choice to Improve Public Law (1997) (offering theories of administrative legitimacy).

2. *See* J. Pennock, Liberal Democracy: Its Merits and Prospects 9–16 (1950); *see generally* L. Hartz, The Liberal Tradition in America 3–27 (1955). Related is the classical liberal movement of economics which supports a laissez-faire market

Liberal political values influenced the type of government structure that was chosen in America. The notion of government by consent was implemented by providing for an electoral system, but one which would operate to protect citizens from the actions of their own government. The Jeffersonian Republicans insisted that majority rule had to be qualified by the vigorous protection of those freedoms that make political and social interaction between citizens possible. As a result, specific liberties, or natural rights, were proclaimed in, and protected against governmental interference by, a Bill of Rights. For those rights that were not absolutely protected, governmental interference could proceed only after the operation of a legal process. The Constitution, for example, guaranteed the right to trial by jury in criminal cases, preserved it in civil cases, and provided due process for invasions of life, liberty, and property in all cases.[3]

§ 2.1.2   The role and meaning of separation of powers in democratic theory

The Madisonians, or Federalists, believed that liberal political values required even greater restraints on majoritarian decisions.[4] These statesmen believed that merely providing for free and open discussion and due process did not necessarily promote reasonable decisions by the majority. As a result, they favored a separation of powers in which governmental authority was divided into three types (legislative, executive, and judicial). Separation of powers was understood to guard against the abuse of power by committing each type of government power to a separate, equal, and independent group of persons.

Separation of powers is a concept more readily accepted than understood. It is frequently mentioned in the Federalist papers as the basis for justifying the tripartite system of government that emerged from the constitutional convention.[5] The Supreme Court has endorsed its application to modern government in emphatic terms.[6] But

system. *See* M. Friedman, Capitalism & Freedom (1962); F. Hayek, Law, Legislation, and Liberty (1973) (three volumes). Modern "liberalism" which advocates regulation to promote distributive justice and equality, should not be confused. *See* J. Galbraith, Economics and the Public Purpose (1973); J. Rawls, A Theory of Justice (1971).

   3. U.S. Const., Amends. 5, 6 and 7.

   4. *See* L. Lipson, The Democratic Civilization (1964); L. Caldwell, The Admin-

istrative Theories of Hamilton & Jefferson (1964).

   5. Alexander Hamilton referred to the "celebrated maxim requiring a separation of the departments of power" in Federalist No. 81 at 507 (A. Hamilton) (B. Wright ed. 1961). *See also* Federalist Nos. 47, 48, and 51 (J. Madison).

   6. INS v. Chadha, 462 U.S. 919 (1983).

its historical roots are not easily discerned and it is not obvious how the concept of separated powers ensures democratic legitimacy.[7] It is not even a self-evident proposition in England whence the roots of American democracy can be traced.[8]

The best explanation of its historical relevance is that uncovered by Professor William Gwyn,[9] who has linked the separation of powers doctrine to the basic proposition of natural justice that no man can be a judge in his own cause.[10] This proposition was early understood in England when, after the "Glorious Revolution" of William and Mary, the monarchy was deprived of the opportunity to adjudicate cases against the Crown even though it was under royal authority that all judges were appointed. Thus, separation of powers creates the conditions necessary to avoid conflicts of interest between law makers, enforcers, and deciders that would arise if each could invade the other's functions.[11] In this manner, the doctrine serves as a fundamental underpinning of limited government.

Under the classical definition, administrative agencies would comply with democratic principles as long as their operation was consistent with the concepts of government by consent, by rule of law, and by separation of powers. Agencies thus would have to be accountable to popularly elected officials, operate according to legal procedures that provided for due process, and not involve the combination of legislative, executive, and judicial functions. Each of these requirements will be elaborated upon in subsequent chapters.

---

7. *See* Fallon, *"The Rule of Law" as a Concept in Constitutional Discourse*, 97 Colum. L. Rev. 1 (1997); Verkuil, *Separation of Powers, The Rule of Law and the Ideal of Independence*, 30 W & M L. Rev. 301, 307–311 (1989) (emphasizing the rule of law aspect of separation of powers).

8. In England, the executive branch, as a reflection of the party in power, dominates the legislative branch. Moreover, the members of the judiciary have traditionally been appointed through the Lord Chancellor, who presides over the House of Lords. But due to recent changes imposed by membership in the European Community, the office of the Lord Chancellor is being abolished and the appointment of judges will be by an independent commission. Stevens, *Reform in Haste & Repent in Leisure: Lolanthe, The Lord High Executioner and*

Brave New World, 24 J. Legal Studies 1 (2004).

9. *See* W. Gwyn, The Meaning of the Separation of Powers 127–28 (1965).

10. *Id.* at 6–7. Professor Gwyn refers to the rule of law basis for the separation of powers as the "purest version" of the doctrine. *Id.* at 128 n. 1. *See also* A.V. Dicey, Introduction to the Study of the Law of the Constitution, 183–205 (10th ed. 1959).

11. Lord Coke first emphasized the importance of separating judicial and prosecutorial roles in Bonham's Case, 8 Coke Rep. 113b, 118a, 77 Eng. Rep. 646, 652 (1610). *See also* Arnett v. Kennedy, 416 U.S. 134, 197 (1974) (White, J. concurring and dissenting) (quoting *Bonham's Case*, for the proposition that no man shall be a judge in his own cause).

§ 2.1.3 "Liberal" and "pluralistic" democracy contrasted

The Jeffersonian and Federalist conceptions of democracy are regarded by modern democratic theorists as inadequate to explain how politics presently works. Their "classical" conception assumed that the legislature and the chief executive would be responsible to citizens through the electoral process. In fact, many people do not vote; those who do frequently fail to study a candidate's voting record in any detail, and those who know the record must make an undifferentiated judgment anyway concerning the hundreds of different decisions made by the incumbent.[12] As a result, many of an incumbent's decisions will not affect his chances for reelection, except through the interest group process. As detailed in the last chapter, some people now receive representation through interest groups, which carefully monitor decisions of importance to them.[13]

A "pluralistic" concept of democracy attempts to account for the lack of popular participation and the role of interest groups in the governmental process. According to this account, governmental decisions are democratic, despite the lack of popular participation, because the public is represented by various political activists, like interest groups. As long as the interests of a representative section of citizens are expressed in this fashion, a pluralistic bargaining process is supposed to produce a reasonably just and stable division of the benefits and burdens of the country's social and economic life.[14] Thus, the fact that voters are ill-informed, or even irrational, will not prevent the formation of a democratic process.[15]

In the pluralistic concept, an agency must be structured in a manner that facilitates the participation of groups in the decision-making process in order to ensure the agency's power is checked by the power of the participating groups. Further, government must be open, rather than secretive, so that groups find out what actions are

12. *See* J. Choper, Judicial Review and the National Political Process 13–15 (1980); M. Margolis, Viable Democracy 79 (1979); T. Mann, Unsafe at Any Margin: Interpreting Congressional Elections 46 (1978).

13. *See supra* §§ 1.7–1.7.1.

14. *See* R. Dahl, Pluralistic Democracy in the United States (1967); R. Dahl & C. Lindblom, Politics, Economics & Welfare (1953); R. Dahl, Preface to Democratic Theory (1956); *see generally* D. Truman, The Governmental Process (1955); J. Schumpter, Capitalism, Socialism & Democracy (1950).

15. *See* E. Purcell, The Crisis of Democratic Theory: Scientific Naturalism & the Problem of Value (1973) (pluralism is a response to doubts about natural law and human rationality in philosophy, social science, and law after 1910); *see also* D. Price, America's Unwritten Constitution: Science, Religion and Political Responsibility (1983).

contemplated and seek to support or oppose those actions as warranted.[16]

Critics challenge the pluralists' attempt to legitimize existing political arrangements on the ground that in effect it justifies the delegation of governmental decisionmaking to private parties. Since decisions are reached by a bargaining process, the role of public officials is to arrange the necessary negotiations. Thus, in this system, there is no necessity for public officials to make an independent judgment of whether the public interest has been served. As a result, a "discontinuity between politics and government" is created whereby policy is made free from the restraints imposed by the classical definition of democracy, which assumed that public policy would be made by elected officials. The net result, the critics conclude, is that government has developed policies that better serve private interests than the public interest.[17]

The conflict over how to legitimize democratic government is important for administrative law. If the classical conception is considered essential to promote the public interest, then the role of administrative law, as an essential element of the classical model, should be increased and strengthened. If the pluralistic conception is considered sufficient for regulation to be considered legitimate, then the role of politics can be increased. There is, however, another concept of democracy that suggests a third way of legitimizing agency government.

§ 2.1.4　The "republican" definition of democracy

Pluralists presume that government is legitimized through pluralistic bargaining and compromise. Those who adhere to a "civic republican" conception of democracy challenge this assumption.[18] They attribute many of the important structural features of the federal government to the influence of classic republicanism on the founders, particularly on James Madison.[19] Influenced by Aristotle, republicanism calls on citizens to subordinate their private interests

16. D. Yates, Bureaucratic Democracy: The Search for Democracy and Efficiency in American Government 13 (1982).

17. T. Lowi, The End of Liberalism: The Second Republic of the United States 36–41 (2d ed. 1979); see also R. Wolff, The Poverty of Liberalism (1968); G. McConnell, Private Power and American Democracy (1966); H. Kariel, The Decline of American Pluralism (1961); C. Mills, The Power Elite (1956); see generally supra §§ 1.7–1.7.2.

18. Readers should not confuse "civic republicans" with those who are members of the "Republican" party.

19. See C. Sunstein, After the Rights Revolution: Reconceiving the Regulatory State 14–18 (1990); see generally G. Wood, The Creation of the American Republic 1776–1887 (1969).

to the public good through political participation in an ongoing process of collective self-determination,[20] which leads to personal betterment, or "civic virtue," through active citizenship.

Framers influenced by republican ideas differed about how best to promote a "republican" government. Some, like Thomas Jefferson, sought to develop a virtuous citizenry by restricting the size of the national government and by depending on direct self-rule at the local level. According to Professor Sunstein,

> Madison turned this idea on its head. In his view it was a large republic, with comparatively well-insulated representatives, that would be uniquely able to produce a well-functioning deliberative democracy. While a small republic would be torn by factional warfare, the representatives of a large one would be able to escape the pressures of powerful groups and engage in the deliberative tasks of politics. Within a large republic the various factions would be so numerous as to cancel each other out, making it more likely that representatives would serve the common good.... Madison abandoned the classic republican belief in direct self-rule by the citizenry without rejecting the fundamental faith in deliberative democracy.[21]

Sunstein and others attribute important structural elements in the Constitution, particularly checks and balances, to an effort to promote deliberation and stem factionalism.

The civic republican ideal rejects the "pluralistic assertion that government can, at best, implement deals that divide political spoils according to the pre-political preferences of interest groups."[22] Instead, a republican conception argues that governmental decisions are valid only if they relate to some public value, and public values are discovered through deliberation. For this reason, "democratic practices provide a setting in which citizens or their representatives can seek the common principles that underlie their disagreements."[23] In other words, "government's primary responsibility is to enable the citizenry to deliberate about altering preferences and to reach consensus on the common good."[24]

20. *See* Sunstein, *Beyond the Republican Revival*, 98 Yale L.J. 1539, 1547–48 (1988).

21. C. Sunstein, *supra* note 19, at 15.

22. Seidenfeld, *A Civil Republican Justification for the Bureaucratic State*, 105 Harv. L. Rev. 1512, 1514 (1992).

23. S. Shapiro & J. Tomain, Regulatory Law & Policy 74 (3d ed. 2003).

24. Seidenfeld, *supra* note 22, at 1514.

Modern reformers who adhere to civic republicanism may favor different administrative law reforms than persons who seek to implement a liberal or pluralistic conception of democracy.[25] The issue for civic republicans is what institutional arrangements are most likely to promote deliberative decisionmaking and the justification of decisions according to public values.

§ 2.2 Beginnings of the Administrative Law Process

Each of the previous conceptions of democracy seeks to reform government in a manner to make it more legitimate. The legitimacy of agency government, however, did not become an issue until the last part of the nineteenth century.[26] The federal government had engaged in few regulatory functions before that period and almost all of those encouraged economic growth by subsidizing business or the purchase of public goods. For those functions, administrators were delegated narrow powers with reasonably specific limitations.[27] The laissez-faire atmosphere, however, permitted economic abuses and governmental corruption which resulted in a demand for significant regulatory initiatives.

In the Progressive era of the last half of the nineteenth century, the demand for regulation was led by the agrarian interests, who believed that they were economically exploited by the railroads and other monopolies, and by Progressive religious and social leaders who objected to business trusts, unscrupulous industries, and corrupt politicians.[28] The states responded with regulation of railroads, grain elevators, and other monopolies, but the Supreme Court essentially halted that activity when it ruled the states could not constitutionally regulate interstate commerce.[29] With state regulation blocked, Congress was influenced to create the Interstate Commerce Commission (ICC) in 1887 to supervise competition in the railroad industry.[30] Other regulatory initiatives were the 1906 Pure Food and Drug Act,

25. *See infra* § 2.6 (discussing impact of theories of democracy on future of administrative process).

26. For an insightful history of federal regulation, see Rabin, *Federal Regulation in Historical Perspective,* 38 Stan. L.Rev. 29 (1985).

27. S. Breyer, R. Stewart, C. Sunstein & S. Spitzer, Administrative Law and Regulatory Policy 17–18 (5th ed. 2002); T. Lowi, *supra* note 17, at 94.

28. M. McGerr, A Fierce Discontent: The Rise and Fall of the Progressive

Movement 1870–1920 (2003); R. Crunden, Ministers of Reform: The Progressive's Achievement in American Civilization (1889–1920) 163–66 (1982); R. Cushman, The Independent Regulatory Commissions 37–40 (1941).

29. Wabash, St. L. & P. Ry. Co. v. Illinois, 118 U.S. 557 (1886) (holding that states could not regulate interstate railroad traffic within their borders).

30. Interstate Commerce Act of 1887, 24 Stat. 379 (codified as amended at 49 U.S.C. §§ 10101–11917).

which created the forerunner of today's Food and Drug Administration (FDA),[31] the 1907 Meat Inspection Act,[32] and the 1914 Federal Trade Commission Act, which authorized the FTC to prevent unfair competition.[33]

The ICC was structured in a fashion that did not neatly fit within the separation of powers paradigm.[34] First, Congress delegated to the agency the full ambit of government authority. Although the ICC was given some fairly specific responsibilities to execute, it was also given policy-making flexibility to regulate in the "public interest, convenience, and necessity." This meant the ICC shared the legislative power created in the Congress by Article I of the Constitution.[35] Moreover, the ICC was to determine railroad price rates by use of an adversary hearing in which agency administrators were to be the judges, an intrusion upon the power of the judicial branch in Article III.[36] Finally, ICC commissioners were presidential appointees, but they could not be removed except "for inefficiency, neglect of duty or malfeasance in office."[37] This restriction created what is now known as the "independent agency" because of its partial independence from both the President and Congress. The ICC could make "laws" without Congressional legislation, determine railroad rates without appearing before a judge, and its administrators could not be fired by the President for doing so except for the statutorily prescribed reasons.

Although the other agencies created in the Progressive era shared many of these variations from the separation of powers paradigm, they and the ICC were successfully absorbed into the governmental framework. One reason was that judicial review significantly constrained the actions of the agencies.[38] Another reason was

---

31. 34 Stat. 768 (codified as amended at 21 U.S.C. §§ 301–392).

32. 34 Stat. 1260 (codified as amended at 21 U.S.C. § 601).

33. 38 Stat. 717 (codified as amended at 15 U.S.C. §§ 41–58).

34. J. Landis, The Administrative Process 10–15 (1938).

35. "All legislative Powers herein granted shall be vested in a Congress of the United States, which shall consist of a Senate and House of Representatives." U.S. Const. Art. I, § 1.

36. "The judicial power of the United States shall be vested in one Supreme Court, and in such inferior Courts as Congress may from time to time ordain and establish.... " U.S. Const. Art. III, § 1.

37. Interstate Commerce Act of 1887, *supra* note 30, at § 11.

38. *See, e.g.,* FTC v. Raladam Co., 283 U.S. 643 (1931) (both competitors and consumers must be injured by deceptive act before FTC can act); FTC v. Klesner, 280 U.S. 19 (1929) (statutory requirement of public harm must be specific and substantial); FTC v. Gratz, 253 U.S. 421 (1920) (FTC act applied only to unfair methods of competition condemned at common law in 1914).

that, although the agencies had been given decisionmaking flexibility, decisions were made by an adversary hearing system similar to that used to settle civil disputes. Use of this system legitimized the agency's policy-making flexibility by placing its actions well within the rule of law framework.[39]

§ 2.3   The Administrative Process and the New Deal

The number of federal agencies and their involvement in private markets grew dramatically during President Roosevelt's first term, as the government sought to spur the economy out of the depression and to address the urgent needs of the unemployed and displaced.[40] The banking system came under federal control,[41] the 1933 and 1934 Securities Acts regulated stock exchanges and the sale of securities,[42] the National Industrial Recovery Act established a minimum wage and set maximum hours for workers[43] and the National Labor Relations Board (NLRB) regulated the relations between labor unions and management.[44] Compared with their Progressive predecessors, the New Deal agencies were significantly more involved in the regulation of private markets under mandates that were often more indefinite and vague.[45] Further, some of the agencies were not required to use adjudicatory procedures before taking action.[46]

Critics, especially from the business community, complained that power-mad bureaucrats constituted an unconstrained "fourth branch of government."[47] The term, which is still commonly used,[48] was

---

39. S. Kelman, Regulating America, Regulating Sweden: A Comparative Study of Occupational Safety and Health Policy (1981) ("The history of administrative procedure in the United States is one of imposition of adversary proceedings on government agencies ... to deal with objections to the very legitimacy of administrative decisionmaking.").

40. *See* A. Schlesinger, The Coming of the New Deal (1959).

41. Banking Act of 1933, 48 Stat. 162 (codified as amended at 12 U.S.C. §§ 221–522); *see also* Banking Act of 1935, 49 Stat. 684 (codified as amended at 12 U.S.C. §§ 221–522).

42. Securities Act of 1933, 48 Stat. 74 (codified as amended at 15 U.S.C. §§ 77–bbbb); Securities Act of 1934, 48 Stat. 881 (codified as amended at 15 U.S.C. §§ 78a–kk).

43. National Industrial Recovery Act, 48 Stat. 195 (1933).

44. National Labor Relations Act of 1935, 49 Stat. 449 (codified as amended 29 U.S.C. §§ 141–187).

45. H. Friendly, The Federal Administrative Agencies: The Need for Better Definition of Standards 13–14 (1962).

46. *See, e.g.,* A.L.A. Schechter Poultry Corp. v. United States, 295 U.S. 495, 533 (1935) (National Industry Recovery Act "dispenses with any administrative procedure ... ").

47. Report of the Committee with Studies of Administrative Management in the Federal Government 39–43 (1937).

48. *See* Process Gas Consumers Group v. Consumer Energy Council, 463 U.S. 1216, 1219 (1983) (White, J. dissenting).

intended to delegitimize the administrative process by distinguishing between agencies and the liberal precepts of the classical theory. These complaints made some headway in the Supreme Court,[49] but they made no impression politically because of the popular support for the economic goals of the Roosevelt administration.[50] Once the crisis of the Depression had abated after World War II, however, serious consideration was given to dormant notions of liberal democratic theory.[51] Then the passage of the Administrative Procedure Act (APA) ushered in the modern era of administrative law.[52]

§ 2.4   The Administrative Process and the Modern State

The years between 1960 and 1980 witnessed a significant increase in regulatory activity.[53] Initiatives included the formation of new departments such as Energy (DOE)[54] and Education,[55] and of new agencies, such as the Environmental Protection Agency (EPA),[56] the Occupational Health and Safety Administration (OSHA),[57] and the Consumer Product Safety Commission (CPSC).[58] Further, the

49. *See, e.g.,* Humphrey's Executor (Rathbun) v. United States, 295 U.S. 602 (1935) (President could not remove FTC commissioner for policy disagreements); Schechter Poultry Corp. v. United States, 295 U.S. at 542 (NIRA constituted a violation of the constitutional prohibition against delegation of legislative powers); United States v. Butler, 297 U.S. 1 (1936) (Agriculture Adjustment Act unconstitutional as regulation of intrastate commerce and as invalid exercise of general welfare clause); *compare* NLRB v. Jones & Laughlin Steel Corp., 301 U.S. 1 (1937) (National Labor Relations Act valid because intrastate activities affect interstate commerce).

50. J. Auerbach, Unequal Justice: Lawyers and Social Change in Modern America 194–95 (1976); A. Schlesinger, *supra* note 40, at 489–507.

51. *See* Verkuil, *The Emerging Concept of Administrative Procedure,* 78 Colum.L.Rev. 258, 264–76 (1978) (history of the development of the APA); *see generally,* Stewart and Sunstein, *Public Programs and Private Rights,* 95 Harv. L.Rev. 1195, 1246–49 (1982) (APA was a "compromise" in which broad delegations of discretion were tolerated as long as they were checked by extensive procedures).

52. Administrative Procedure Act of 1946, 60 Stat. 237 (codified as amended at 5 U.S.C. §§ 551–59).

53. *See* M. Weidenbaum, Business, Government, and the Public 7–10 (2d ed. 1981) (forty-two federal laws passed between 1962 and 1978 to regulate business); M. Pertschuk, Revolt Against Regulation: The Rise and Fall of the Consumer Movement 5 (1982) (twenty-five consumer, environmental or social regulatory laws passed between 1967 and 1973).

54. Department of Energy Act of 1977, Pub.L. 95–91, 91 Stat. 565 (codified as amended at 42 U.S.C. §§ 7101–7375).

55. Department of Education Act of 1979, Pub.L. No. 96–88, 93 Stat. 696 (codified as amended at 20 U.S.C. §§ 3401–3510).

56. Reorganization Plan No. 3 of 1970, 35 Fed.Reg. 15623 (1970).

57. Occupational Health and Safety Act of 1970, Pub.L. No. 91–596, 84 Stat. 1592 (codified as amended at 29 U.S.C. §§ 651–678).

58. Consumer Product Safety Act of 1972, Pub.L. No. 92–573, 86 Stat. 1207 (codified as amended at 15 U.S.C. §§ 2051–83).

regulatory authority of existing agencies was increased. For example, the Federal Trade Commission was authorized to regulate consumer credit reporting agencies, debt collection practices, and product warranties,[59] the Department of Housing and Urban Development was authorized to regulate interstate land sales,[60] and the Food and Drug Administration was authorized to regulate the marketing of new pharmaceutical drugs that are not effective.[61] Other changes involved increased funding of agencies like the Department of Housing and Urban Development (HUD) and the then Department of Health, Education, and Welfare as part of President Johnson's Great Society effort to eradicate poverty, hunger and inadequate education.[62]

Some of the new initiatives significantly differed from earlier efforts. Since many of the social problems that were being addressed cut across industry lines, like pollution, discrimination, or work and product safety, agencies were given jurisdiction to regulate the entire economy. Many earlier agencies, like the Interstate Commerce Commission (ICC) or the Federal Communications Commission (FCC), were limited to a single industry or a group of related industries like transportation or radio communications.[63] Moreover, many of these agencies were given considerable discretion with which to carry out their regulatory mission. Congress establishes an agency's authority in its enabling act by defining its powers and the factual circumstances in which those powers can be used. Even the earliest of these delegations ceded some discretion to agencies, but modern statutes are often particularly broad and vague, and therefore open-ended, concerning the limitations on an agency.[64]

A third change was that decisionmaking was by "rulemaking" instead of "adjudication". Rulemaking under the APA constitutes a legislative-type of hearing where the participation of parties is limited to submitting comments, almost always only in a written form. Adjudication consists of a trial-type hearing with most of the procedures commonly associated with that type of proceeding, including

---

59. Consumer Credit Protection Act of 1968, Pub.L. No. 90–321, 82 Stat. 146 (codified as amended at 15 U.S.C. §§ 1681–81t, 1692a–o (1982)); Magnuson–Moss Warranty–Federal Trade Commission Improvement Act, Pub.L. No. 93–637, 88 Stat. 2183 (codified as amended at 15 U.S.C. §§ 2301–12).

60. Interstate Land Sales Full Disclosure Act, Pub.L. No. 90–448, 82 Stat. 590 (codified as amended at 15 U.S.C. §§ 1701–20).

61. Federal Food, Drug, and Cosmetic Act of 1962, Pub.L. No. 87–781, 76 Stat. 780 (codified as amended at 21 U.S.C. §§ 321–60).

62. *See* S. Levitan, The Great Society's Poor Law 3–13 (1969).

63. *See* M. Weidenbaum, *supra* note 53, at 18–20.

64. *See infra* § 3.1.

the right to present oral evidence and cross-examine witnesses.[65] The change-over is attributable to the removal of any constitutional requirement that adjudication is necessary for purposes of due process,[66] to the relative efficiency of rulemaking because it involves fewer procedures, and to the tactical desire of agencies to eliminate substantive and procedural issues that can embroil the agency in additional litigation.[67]

§ 2.5   The Administrative Process and Democratic Theory

The role of administrative law in the development of regulatory policy was originally thought to be to ensure that the process was consistent with the "liberal" values of the classical model of democracy. Robert Rabin has noted that a "strong tradition of constitutionalism, embodied in a commitment to the separation of powers, due process, and judicial review, buttressed by a lingering attachment to laissez-faire ideology, provided the under-pinning for administrative norms that came to define the traditional approach to administrative law".[68] Richard Stewart has summarized four such norms.[69] First, the imposition of administratively determined actions is authorized by the legislature through rules that control agency action. Second, the decisional procedures used by the agency must ensure agency compliance with the authorizing legislative directives. Third, judicial review must be available to ensure that an agency will utilize impartial and accurate decisionmaking procedures and will comply with legislative directives. Fourth, agency decisional processes must facilitate the exercise of such judicial review.

These norms promote the liberal values of government by consent, separation of powers, and due process. Policy decisions are made by the legislature which is democratically elected and politically accountable. Administrative agencies are limited to the execution of congressional policy decisions, although this function inevitably involves some discretion because the relationship between specific

---

65. *Compare* 5 U.S.C. § 553 (procedures for informal rulemaking) *with* 5 U.S.C. §§ 554–557 (procedures for adjudication); *see infra* § 2.6.

66. *See* Bi–Metallic Investment Co. v. State Bd. of Equalization, 239 U.S. 441 (1915); *see generally infra* § 6.3.

67. *See* Hamilton, *Rulemaking on a Record by the Food and Drug Administration,* 50 Tex.L.Rev. 1132, 1153–55 (1972); Robinson, *The Making of Admin-*

istrative Policy: Another Look at Rulemaking and Adjudication and Administrative Procedure Reform, 118 U.Pa. L.Rev. 485, 507–35 (1970).

68. Rabin, *Administrative Law In Transition: A Discipline in Search of An Organizing Principle,* 72 N.W.L.Rev. 120, 125 (1977).

69. Stewart, *The Reformation of American Administrative Law,* 88 Harv. L.Rev. 1669, 1671–75 (1975).

actions and congressional goals and standards will not always be apparent. This discretion, however, cannot be used until the procedural requirements of the APA are met. Finally, the judicial branch will police the other two branches by measuring whether the legislative decisions violate any constitutional prohibitions, whether an administrative agency has used the decisional standards required of it by Congress, and whether the procedural obligations of the APA have been met.

Professor Stewart has emphasized the congruence between his four norms and classical democracy by summarizing the connection as the "transmission-belt thesis".[70] If all four norms are met, then administrative agencies are a transmission belt for congressional policy decisions. The reality, however, is different because the development of administrative law has been somewhat inconsistent with each of the four norms.

§ 2.5.1 The delegation problem

The rather typical broad and vague delegations of legislative authority are inconsistent with the first and third norms—legislative authorization of administrative action and judicial review to ensure compliance with legislative directives. When delegations are open-ended, the imposition of administratively determined sanctions will not be confined, except in a broad sense, by the rules that control agency action. The agency, not Congress, will make the policy decisions significant to a regulatory program.[71] Moreover, these broad and vague delegations make it difficult for the judiciary to determine whether an agency has acted within the boundaries of its legislative mandate. When those limitations are stated in an open-ended fashion, they are usually capable of several interpretations and the judiciary is often left with the difficult job of determining which interpretation was meant by Congress.[72]

A Supreme Court case involving OSHA illustrates both of those inconsistencies. In *American Textile Manufacturers Institute, Inc. v. Donovan,* the Court interpreted OSHA's authority to set exposure limitations for toxic chemicals that would "most adequately assure *to the extent feasible* . . . that no employee would suffer material impairment" of his or her health.[73] Industry groups contended that the phrase "to the extent feasible" meant that OSHA had to establish that the benefits of a regulation exceeded its costs in order to act,

---

70. *Id.* at 1675.

71. *See infra* § 3.1.

72. *See infra* Chapter 7.

73. 452 U.S. 490 (1981).

while OSHA and several labor unions contended that no such limitation was intended. An important policy issue was involved. OSHA required industry to limit employee exposure to hazards through the use of expensive manufacturing controls instead of more inexpensive personal protective devices. For example, to abate dangerous noise, OSHA ordered expensive noise dampers to be installed around machinery instead of requiring employees to wear ear plugs that muffled the sound. Critics doubted OSHA could factually establish that the more expensive way of protecting employees produced benefits that exceeded costs,[74] but the Supreme Court concluded that was unnecessary. The Court found that the legislative history, which "concededly" was "not crystal clear", supported OSHA's interpretation that a cost-benefit analysis was unnecessary.[75]

§ 2.5.2   The rulemaking problem

The common use of rulemaking is inconsistent with the second and fourth norms. The second norm was that an agency should use decisional procedures that ensured agency compliance with its legislative directive and the fourth norm was that those procedures should facilitate judicial review. Adjudication under the APA serves those objectives nicely. A trial-like proceeding is held in which participants present documentary evidence and witnesses, and have the right to cross-examine other witnesses.[76] The documents and testimony form a record from which the agency must justify its decision in written form.[77] The reviewing court thereby has a full and complete record of all adversarial efforts to determine the substantive propriety of the agency's action.

Rulemaking procedures satisfy the two norms of adequate procedures less well. The APA requires that an agency engaged in rulemaking must allow the parties to submit written comments and must produce a "concise general statement of its basis and purpose" for any rule that is promulgated.[78] Although agencies must now comply with additional procedures that have been imposed by the courts,[79] statutes,[80] and by presidential Executive Orders,[81] a reviewing court

---

74. *See, e.g.,* Nichols & Zeckhauser, *Government Comes to the Workplace: An Assessment of OSHA,* 49 The Public Interest 39 (1977); *see generally* Schroeder & Shapiro, *Responses to Occupational Disease: The Role of Markets, Regulation, and Information,* 72 Geo.L.J. 1231, 1256–64 (1984).

75.   452 U.S. at 514.

76.   5 U.S.C. §§ 554, 556–557.

77.   *Id.* at §§ 554(a), 556(e); *see infra* § 7.5.

78.   *Id.* at § 553(c).

79.   *See* Citizens to Preserve Overton Park, Inc. v. Volpe, 401 U.S. 402 (1971); *see generally infra* §§ 7.5–7.7.

80.   *See infra* § 9.5.3.

81.   *See infra* § 9.5.2

will not have a record in which the participants present documentary evidence, witnesses, and cross-examination.[82]

Concern has been expressed that a court may be hampered by the lack of adversarial procedures in rulemaking, especially for technologically complex matters. For example, *Ethyl Corporation v. EPA* involved a regulation that required gasoline manufacturers to eliminate lead as an additive.[83] The rule, which forced automobile manufacturers to redesign their engines to use unleaded gasoline, was based on rather vague scientific evidence concerning the health dangers posed by car emissions. To approve the propriety of the EPA's action, the court reviewed the persuasiveness of that evidence. In a concurring opinion, Judge Bazelon worried that this review invited "judges of opposing views to make plausible-sounding, but simplistic judgments of the relative weight to be afforded various pieces of technical data". He noted that this problem might be avoided if rulemaking contained additional procedural safeguards "which by their nature serve to illuminate the underlying facts", and to "prevent erroneous decisions on the merits from occurring."[84]

Vague and ambiguous legislative delegations and agency reliance on rulemaking are inconsistent with the four norms of administrative law identified by Professor Stewart, which means these attributes of the administrative process are also inconsistent with the classical definition of democracy. These aspects of the administrative process give administrators additional discretion and thereby free them to participate in, and respond to, the pluralistic interest group process. If these changes are to be considered as consistent with a democratic regulatory process, then they must also be defended within the context of pluralistic or republican democracy.

§ 2.6 The Future of Administrative Law and Process

The future of administrative law will depend in part on whether the classic, pluralist or republican conception of democracy will prevail. Under the classical theory, the role of administrative law would be increased in an attempt to constrain administrative discretion. Under the pluralistic theory, additional attempts to constrain administrative behavior would be political in nature and involve greater oversight by the executive and legislative branches. Under a

---

82. *See* Vermont Yankee Nuclear Power Corp. v. Natural Resources Defense Council, Inc., 435 U.S. 519 (1978); *see generally infra* § 6.4.9.

83. 541 F.2d 1 (D.C.Cir.1976) (*en banc*), cert. denied 426 U.S. 941 (1976).

84. 541 F.2d at 66 (Bazelon, J. concurring).

republican theory, reform is directed towards making the administrative process more deliberative. Civic republicans therefore favor judicial review and other forms of oversight which they believe have the potential to enforce deliberative norms in agency decisionmaking.

These different conceptions of the administrative process can produce disagreement concerning what is the appropriate future of the administrative process. For example, as noted earlier,[85] the liberal conception of democracy is threatened when Congress delegates authority to agencies in a broad and vague manner. A "liberal" reformer therefore would favor requiring Congress to delegate authority to agencies in a specific and narrow fashion, rather than in a broad and vague one. The legal system has a means of accomplishing that result. As will be explained in Chapter Three, the Supreme Court is in a position to decide whether Congress can legislate in its usual broad and vague manner. Some justices and several important scholars have urged the Court to use its authority to force Congress to change its ways and use its legislative powers to confine the discretion of agencies.[86] By comparison, Professor Seidenfeld defends broad delegations to agencies on the ground that "having administrative agencies set government policy provides the best hope of implementing civic republican's call for decisionmaking informed by the values of the entire polity."[87] According to this view, the policy experience and expertise of administrators makes it more likely that administrative process will focus on policy arguments and public values as compared to legislative deliberations.

Professor Rubin seeks another method of ensuring the legitimacy of agency action.[88] He argues that it is time to rewrite the APA according to the modern realities of how agencies actually function. He proposes the new act should be "based on the prevailing conception of administrative governance as an instrumentally rational process carried out by institutions with defined jurisdiction, a hierarchical structure, expert staff, and continuous operation." He would therefore replace the principle of "private participation," now used to organize the APA, with the principle of instrumental rationality, and

---

85. *See supra* § 2.5.1 (the delegation problem).

86. American Textile Manufacturers Inst. v. Donovan, 452 U.S. 490, 543 (1981) (Rehnquist, J. dissenting, joined by Burger, C.J.); J. Ely, Democracy and Distrust 132–34 (1981); T. Lowi, *supra* note 17, at 93; *see generally infra* § 3.4.

87. Seidenfeld, *supra* note 22, at 1515.

88. Rubin, *It's Time to Make the Administrative Procedure Act Administrative*, 89 Corn. L. Rev. 101 (2002).

hold agencies accountable according to the rationality of their actions.

Some civic republican reformers favor giving judges an important role in overseeing the administrative process.[89] Judges can meet this objective by vigorously enforcing the requirement that agencies fully and completely explain the nature of their reasoning process. Some courts have required agencies to give a "hard look", or a high degree of scrutiny, to whether a proposed action will serve the public interest.[90] Others object on pluralist-related grounds that activist review delays agencies from meeting their statutory duties and involves unelected federal judges in resolving political issues.[91]

Jody Freeman, however, argues for more and better deliberation between regulators and interested parties.[92] She favors an administrative process that is "a problem-solving exercise in which parties share responsibility for all stages of the rule-making process, in which solutions are provisional, and in which the state plays an active, if varied, role." This "collaborative governance" assumes that multi-stakeholder processes are more likely than the traditional rule-making processes "to be sites at which regulatory problems are redefined, innovative solutions [are] devised, and institutional relationships [are] rethought." This claim rests on the republican principle that "unanticipated or novel solutions are likely to emerge from face-to-face deliberative engagement among knowledgeable parties who would never otherwise share information or devise solutions together."

Other recent or proposed changes would attempt to constrain administrative discretion by subjecting the agencies to additional political oversight. Elena Kagan endorses "presidential administration" consisting of enhanced and proactive supervision of the agencies by the White House.[93] In her view, "presidential administration . . . advances political accountability by subjecting the bureaucracy to the control mechanism most open to public examination and most

---

89. *See, e.g.,* Sunstein, *Interest Groups in American Public Law,* 38 Stan. L. Rev. 29, 61 (1985).

90. *See* Diver, *Policymaking Paradigms in Administrative Law,* 95 Harv. L.Rev. 393, 409–413 (1981); *see generally infra* § 7.5.2.

91. *See, e.g.,* McGarity, *The Courts and the Ossification of Rulemaking: A Response to Professor Seidenfeld,* 75 Tex. L. Rev. 525 (1997) (criticizing activist

review); *see, also,* Seidenfeld, *Hard Look in a World of Techno–Bureaucratic Rationality: A Reply to Professor McGarity,* 75 Tex. L. Rev. 559 (1997) (supporting activist review).

92. Freeman, *Collaborative Governance in the Administrative State,* 34 UCLA L. Rev. 1 (1997).

93. Kagan, *Presidential Administration,* 114 Harv. L. Rev. 2245 (2001).

responsive to public opinion." A more radical proposal is that certain types of rules would not take effect until passed as laws by the legislature.[94] Administrators could also be chosen by direct election as they are in some states.[95] Civic republicans, however, are less enthusiastic about these electoral reforms. Despite their preference for citizen involvement, they are suspicious of day-to-day politics because of the influence of self-interest and the lack of deliberation.

An extended discussion of democratic theory and administrative reform is beyond the scope of this section or this book. This discussion, however, does indicate that the design and structure of the administrative process is related in important ways to the nature of the government and of the democratic process. It also reveals the difficulty of determining how best to constitute our democracy. Our preference is that reforms address the actual nature and problems of the regulatory process, rather than an abstract conception of the ideal nature of democracy.[96]

Finally, there may be a limit to the extent to which bureaucratic discretion can be controlled by the "external" forces of politics and law. Professor Jerry Mashaw argues that "an internal law of administration that guides the conduct of administrators" is necessary because of the inadequacies of the external forces.[97] Mashaw believes that managerial rationality, which is based on the rules of behavior that evolve in organizations and professions, can create "images of 'good administration' that guide bureaucratic behavior ... and permit evaluation and hierarchical control" that are "at least as coherent as external conceptions of justice and the rule of law".[98]

94. *See infra* § 3.5.

95. *See* Stewart, *supra* note 69, at 1791–93.

96. *See* Pierce, *The APA and Regulatory Reform*, 10 Ad.L.J. Rev. 81 (1996); Shapiro, *A Delegation Theory of the APA*, 10 Ad. L.J. 89 (1996).

97. J. Mashaw, Bureaucratic Justice: Managing Social Security Disability Claims 16, 227 (1983).

98. *Id.*

Chapter Three

LEGISLATIVE CONTROL OF ADMINISTRATIVE DISCRETION

§ 3.1 Methods of Legislative Control

Congress has a wide variety of means, both statutory and non-statutory, by which it can seek to control agency discretion. The enabling legislation under which an agency will operate can specify its degree of authority. Specific agency decisions can be overruled by passing legislation or they can be rendered moot by the simple expedient of changing the agency's jurisdiction. Appropriations can be wielded to punish or reward agencies and restrictions can be placed on the use of appropriated funds. Besides these traditional methods of control, Congress adopted a process for legislative review of new regulations in 1996. This process requires agencies to submit all new rules for legislative review, stays the implementation date of major rules to give Congress the opportunity to review them before they are effective, and establishes special procedures to adopt legislation that would bar an agency from adopting a regulation.[1]

Congress can also shape administrative decisions indirectly by applying political pressure through the use of committee reports, through budgetary, oversight, or investigatory hearings and hearings on the nominations of administrators, and through direct communications with administrators. The effectiveness of this last group of controls can be increased by requiring that agencies report to Congress before they act, by utilizing the General Accounting Office to investigate agency conduct, and by employing the Congressional Budget Office to consider the economic effects of government programs.[2]

1. A more detailed description of congressional review of rules can be found *infra* at § 9.5.4.

2. Senate Comm. on Gov'n Affairs, Vol. II Congressional Oversight of Regulatory Agencies, S.Doc. No. 95–26, 95th Cong., 1st Sess. (1977) [hereinafter cited as Senate Study]; A. Maass, Congress and the Common Good 172–253 (1983); L. Dodd & R. Schott, Congress and the Administrative State 155–275 (1979); M. Kirst, Government Without Passing Laws (1979); Kaiser, *Congressional Action to Overturn Agency Rules: Alternatives to the "Legislative Veto"*, 32 Ad. L.Rev. 667, 710–11 (1980); Krasnow &

Congress has occasionally explicitly specified the circumstances in which an agency can act in its enabling legislation. Under the National Gas Policy Act of 1978, for example, the Federal Energy Regulatory Commission (FERC) applies pricing formulas set by Congress to determine the maximum price that can be charged for natural gas.[3] In other cases, Congress has eschewed detailed instructions of that sort, but it has still provided a relatively meaningful standard. For example, the Federal Trade Commission (FTC) is authorized to prohibit "unfair practices", by which Congress meant those acts that violated the letter or the spirit of the antitrust laws or acts that otherwise unreasonably injure consumers.[4] In most cases, however, Congress has given agencies considerably more discretion by passing enabling acts that are effectively standardless.

There are three types of such standardless delegations. Congress sometimes has failed to provide any standards to indicate when or how an agency is to act. In the Economic Price Stabilization Act, the President was authorized to "stabilize" wages and prices to prevent inflation without any further indication of his allowable scope of action.[5] In other cases, Congress provides a standard so broad that it is capable of an elastic interpretation. The Federal Communications Commission (FCC), which is authorized to regulate the transmission of radio signals for the "public interest, convenience, and necessity",[6] has been able to regulate television stations, television networks and cable television operators, even though those last two businesses usually do not directly involve any radio transmissions.[7] A final class of statutes provides so many inconsistent standards that any action can be defended as consistent with one or more of them. The

Shooshan, *Congressional Oversight: The Ninety–Second Congress and the Federal Communications Commission,* 10 Harv.J. on Legis. 297, 317–20 (1973).

3. 15 U.S.C. §§ 3312–19.

4. 15 U.S.C. § 45; *see* FTC v. Sperry & Hutchinson Co., 405 U.S. 233, 244 (1972).

5. Economic Price Stabilization Act of 1970, Pub.L. No. 91–379, 84 Stat. 799. *See infra* § 3.4.3 (discussing constitutionality of act).

6. 47 U.S.C. §§ 303, 307.

7. *See* United States v. Midwest Video Corp., 406 U.S. 649 (1972) (regulation of cable television); United States v. Southwestern Cable Co., 392 U.S. 157 (1968) (regulation of cable television); Mt. Mansfield Television, Inc. v. FCC, 442 F.2d 470 (2d Cir.1971) (regulation of television networks); *see also* In re Permian Basin Area Rate Cases, 390 U.S. 747, 779–80 (1968) (authority to set rates that were "just and reasonable" authorized Federal Power Commission (FPC) to engage in nontraditional methods of regulation such as area rates and price ceilings); American Trucking Ass'ns v. Atchison, T. & S.F. Ry. Co., 387 U.S. 397, 415–16 (1967) (Interstate Commerce Commission authorized to regulate shipping for trailers on railroad flatcars despite an agency interpretation for twenty-five years it did not); *but see* NAACP v. FPC, 425 U.S. 662, 670 (1976) (Commission's broad authority did not include civil rights enforcement).

Emergency Petroleum Allocation Act, for example, required the President to promulgate a regulation for the mandatory allocation of petroleum products that protected the public health, maintained public services and agricultural operations, preserved a sound and competitive petroleum industry, allocated crude oil to refiners to permit them to operate at full capacity, resulted in an equitable distribution of supplies to all parts of the country, promoted economic efficiency, and minimized economic distortion.[8]

The reasons for these broad and vague delegations are often political.[9] First, the pressures of interest group competition lead Congress to foster a compromise acceptable to the greatest number of groups. The adoption of broad and vague language is a strategy to accomplish that result. Second, while interest groups may be only generally affected by a decision to regulate, the means chosen to implement that decision can have a far greater impact on them. As a result, even when an agreement is reached about the need to regulate, no corresponding agreement can be reached concerning the regulatory details. Under those circumstances, the broad and vague delegation of authority to an agency is a way to prevent a consensus from being frustrated by continuing disagreement over particular issues. Third, members of Congress prefer a solution for which they receive initial credit for establishing a program and for which they can later offer themselves as intermediaries to bargain on behalf of constituents when an agency decides the specific issues left unresolved by Congress.

Even if Congress found it politically desirable to delegate authority more precisely, there are institutional limitations that would usually prevent it from doing so.[10] Many members of Congress lack the expertise necessary to understand the policy choices involved in complex regulations. Moreover, a regulatory agency often decides questions that could not have been anticipated at the time the statutory delegation was enacted. Congress could conceivably legislate on each question as it arose, but it almost certainly does not have the time, or the will, to do so. Finally, public choice analysis demon-

8.   15 U.S.C. § 753(b)(1).

9.   *See* M. Fiorina, Congress, Keystone of the Washington Establishment 41–49 (1977); Aranson, Gellhorn & Robinson, *A Theory of Legislative Delegation,* 68 Cornell L.Rev. 1, 38–39, 43–45 (1982); Stone, *The Twentieth Century Administrative Explosion and After*, 52 Calif.L.Rev. 513, 525 (1964).

10.   *See* Aranson, Gellhorn & Robinson, *supra* note 9, at 21–24; Davis, *A New Approach to Delegation,* 36 U.Chi. L.Rev. 713, 720 (1969); Redford, *Regulation Revisited,* 28 Ad.L.Rev. 543, 563–64 (1976).

strates the difficulty of aggregating diverse individual policy preferences into a coherent collective decision.[11] In his analysis of voting,
Kenneth Arrow demonstrated that majority rule can lead to indeterminate and shifting outcomes as legislators try to determine which of
three or more policy alternatives to choose,[12] and that coherence is
possible only if certain restrictions are posed on how majority preferences are aggregated.[13] In light of the difficulty of aggregating preferences into a stable result, Congress will find it easier to reach general
agreement on the need for regulation than on the precise regulatory
standards to be applied.

The same confluence of factors leads Congress to favor those of
its other methods of control that pose the fewest political and
institutional problems. Thus, while Congress holds hundreds of regulatory hearings and makes thousands of individual contacts with
agencies, there are many fewer attempts to overturn agency decisions
by passing a statute or by changing an agency's jurisdiction.[14] Until it
was declared to be unconstitutional, the legislative veto was popular
because it did not require any substantive changes in an agency's
enabling legislation or require Congress to propose alternatives to
agency regulations that were rejected. Although exercise of a veto did
represent a policy choice by Congress, it failed to indicate to an
agency what alternative decision, if any, should be implemented.
Congress could avoid that decision because of the manner in which
most vetoes operated. When an agency was subject to a veto, it had to
delay implementation of its actions for a specified period of time.
During that period, Congress had authorized that either House, or
both Houses, could "veto" the agency's decision by passing a resolution to that effect. Congress had included 295 veto provisions in 196
different statutes.[15]

When Congress does use statutory controls, it also favors those
that avoid difficult policy decisions and therefore are easier to pass.
Congress has sought to preempt agency action more frequently by
changing an agency's jurisdiction, or by prohibiting the use of agency

---

11. *See* D. Farber & P. Frickey, Law & Public Choice 38–52 (1991).

12. K. Arrow, Social Choice & Individual Values (1951).

13. *See* K. Shepsle & M. Bonchek, Analyzing Politics: Rationality, Behavior, and Institutions 68 (1997).

14. *See* Kaiser, *supra* note 2, at 669–87 (frequency of use of statutory controls 1973–78).

15. Abourezk, *The Congressional Veto: A Contemporary Response to Executive Encroachment on Legislative Prerogatives*, 52 Ind.L.Rev. 323, 324 (1977); *see generally* Bruff & Gellhorn, *Congressional Control of Administrative Regulation: A Study of Legislative Vetoes*, 90 Harv. L.Rev. 1369 (1977) (five case studies of Congressional veto attempts).

funds to enforce a previous decision, than by legislating a substantive solution.[16] Of the available methods of control, financial constraints are often preferred because appropriations riders can be added on the floor of either House and need not undergo the lengthy committee process. Like the veto, jurisdictional and appropriations actions usually fail to add any specificity to an agency's mandate.

Although Congress tends to take actions which create or preserve an agency's discretion, this is not always the case. In the 1980s, for example, Congress reacted to what it perceived as the mismanagement of the Environmental Protection Agency (EPA) by adopting detailed substantive criteria to limit how EPA implemented its regulatory responsibilities, and by imposing strict deadlines or schedules to govern EPA rulemaking. These events suggest that Congress is capable of narrowing an agency's regulatory discretion, but will do so only when it has lost faith in the agency's commitment to its regulatory mission, its own staff has substantial expertise in the area, and there is broad support for the specific regulatory solution that Congress has chosen.[17]

§ 3.2   The FTC as an Illustration

A period in the history of the Federal Trade Commission (FTC) illustrates these trends in legislative oversight. In 1969, the American Bar Association and Ralph Nader agreed that the FTC was moribund and required immediate reforms.[18] Congress, by the use of oversight hearings and informal contacts, pressured the Commission to respond.[19] By 1975, the FTC had reacted in a sufficiently favorable fashion that Congress awarded the agency considerable new powers

---

16. *See, e.g.,* Soft Drink Interbrand Competition Act, 15 U.S.C. §§ 3501–3503 (removing some soft drink trademark licensing agreements from reach of antitrust laws); Saccharin Study and Labeling Act § 3, 21 U.S.C. § 348 note (18-month moratorium on FDA ban of saccharin or saccharin products); Consumer Product Safety Commission Improvements Act of 1976, § 3(e), 15 U.S.C. § 2080 note (removing CPSC jurisdiction of firearms); *see generally* Kaiser, *supra* note 2, at 710.

17. Shapiro & Glicksman, *Congress, The Supreme Court, and the Quiet Revolution in Administrative Law,* 1988 Duke L.Rev. 819.

18. Report of the ABA Committee to Study the Federal Trade Commission (1969); E. Cox, R. Fellmeth & J. Schultz, "The Nader Report" on the Federal Trade Commission (1969).

19. *See* R. Katzmann, Regulatory Bureaucracy: The Federal Trade Commission and Antitrust Policy 147, 156–57 (1980); Kovacic, *The Federal Trade Commission and Congressional Oversight of Antitrust Enforcement,* 17 Tulsa L.J. 587, 590–91 (1982) (congressional forces pushed FTC to boundaries of antitrust enforcement in 1970's); Weingast & Moran, *The Myth of the Runaway Bureaucracy: The Case of the FTC,* Regulation, May/June 1982, at 34 (key legislative leaders supported FTC reform efforts).

to regulate.[20] The FTC used, or proposed to use, those powers to regulate a wide-ranging group of industries including funeral homes, used cars, television advertising, and the professions, law included. Predictably, these entities resisted administrative controls by demanding that Congress stifle the process. A cooperative Congress agreed.[21]

Many of the controls used by Congress to reign in the FTC were nonstatutory in nature. For example, although Congress did not pass a proposed exemption from FTC jurisdiction for professionals, the Commission altered its plans because of congressional consideration of the proposal.[22] A legislative attempt to exempt the used car industry from proposed FTC regulations concerning disclosures about mechanical reliability and warranties failed, but a group of Senators sent the Commission a letter informally expressing their opposition to those regulations. Cognizant of the Congressional opposition, the FTC significantly narrowed its original conception of the rule.[23] When the rule was promulgated, it was vetoed by Congress anyway.[24]

Statutory amendments sought to achieve oversight by narrowing the FTC's authority or jurisdiction to act. The so-called Federal Trade Commission Improvements Act of 1980 withdrew the Commission's authority to promulgate a trade rule concerning industry standards and certifications, prohibited any rule concerning commercial advertising through the fiscal year 1982, suspended the Commission's rulemaking proceeding for children's advertising until a proposed rule could be published, and limited the agency's rulemaking

---

20. Magnuson–Moss Warranty–Federal Trade Commission Improvement Act of 1975, Pub.L. No. 93–637, 88 Stat. 2183 (codified at 15 U.S.C. §§ 45–48, 2301–2311) (FTC granted limited rulemaking authority for warranty matters and broad powers to issue trade regulations).

21. *See* S. Tolchin & M. Tolchin, Dismantling America: The Rush to Deregulate 143–88 (1983); M. Pertschuk, Revolt Against Regulation: The Rise and Pause of the Consumer Movement 73–77 (1982); Gellhorn, *The Wages of Zealotry: The FTC Under Siege,* Regulation, Jan./Feb. 1980, at 33.

22. *See* S. 1991, 96th Cong., 2d Sess., 126 Cong.Rec. S2015–18 (daily ed. Feb. 6, 1980) (proposed by Sen. McClure); *FTC is Cautious about Health–Plan Rule on*

Eve of Senate Debate of Agency Power, Wall St.J., Feb. 6, 1980, at 15, col. 1.

23. H.R. 7584, Amend. No. 1659, 96th Cong., 2d Sess., 126 Cong.Rec. S27,-242 (daily ed. Sept. 25, 1980); Antitrust & Trade Reg.Rep. (BNA) No. 983, at A–2 (Oct. 2, 1980); Warner, *FTC is Softening Used–Car Dealer Rule As Fear of Congressional Veto Takes Toll,* Wall St.J., Apr. 14, 1981, at 4, col. 1.

24. 128 Cong.Rec. S5402 (daily ed. May 18, 1982) (Senate veto); 128 Cong. Rec. H2882 (daily ed. May 26, 1982) (House veto); *see generally* Consumers Union v. FTC, 691 F.2d 575 (D.C.Cir. 1982) (per curiam), *affirmed sub nom.* United States Senate v. FTC, 463 U.S. 1216 (1983) (veto declared unconstitutional).

authority to regulate the funeral home industry.[25] The Commission's jurisdiction to regulate some antitrust aspects of the soft-drink industry was also ended.[26]

During the Reagan administration, the FTC was a far less active regulatory force,[27] in part because of the appointment of administrators committed to a less intrusive role for the Commission in most economic affairs.[28] Few new regulations were issued and existing regulations were weakened. In addition, the Commission brought fewer enforcement actions in consumer protection and antitrust than under the Carter administration. Nevertheless, the Commission still managed to run afoul of Congress. A 1984 appropriations act prohibited the FTC from expending any funds on suits against municipalities in the absence of specific congressional authority.[29] The bill was a reaction to attempts by the FTC to establish that the cities of Minneapolis and New Orleans combined with existing taxicab owners in each location respectively to prevent the entry of new competitors.

The FTC example illustrates the potential effectiveness of congressional oversight. Congress was able to obtain in various situations either more or less regulation than the FTC favored.[30] The effectiveness of such oversight, however, depends in significant part on the diligence with which it is applied. Agencies can escape review because the oversight process overlooks them or subjects them to only superficial consideration. The reason is that oversight yields few political advantages to members of Congress, and it usually, therefore, occurs as an *ad hoc* response to a crisis or to intense political pressure of the type brought to bear by industries regulated by the FTC.[31]

The effectiveness of oversight also depends on an agency's ability to develop countervailing political pressure to resist congressional control. Interest groups and other agencies that support an agency's

25. Pub.L. No. 96–252, §§ 11, 18–20, 94 Stat. 374, 378, 391–93 (codified as 15 U.S.C. §§ 57a(i), 58).

26. *See* Soft Drink Interbrand Competition Act, *supra* note 16.

27. *See* Oversight of Federal Trade Commission Law Enforcement: Fiscal Years 1982 and 1983 Before the Commerce, Consumer, and Monetary Affairs Subcomm. of the House Comm. on Government Operations, 98th Cong., 1st Sess. 298 (1983) (statement of Michael Pertschuk, FTC Commissioner); Nader, *End Big Antitrust,* New York Times, March 4, 1983, at 29, col. 2.

28. *See generally infra* § 4.3.1. (executive control by appointments).

29. *See* 130 Cong.Rec. S10,192 (daily ed. Aug. 9, 1984).

30. *See generally* C. Foreman, Jr., Signals From the Hill: Congressional Oversight and the Challenge of Social Regulation (1988); H. Kaufman, The Administrative Behavior of Federal Bureau Chiefs 47–48, 164–65 (1981).

31. *See* Senate Study, *supra* note 2.

actions will lobby Congress to do likewise. Efforts, for example, to strip the FTC of its authority to order antitrust defendants to sell assets, unless their cases involved mergers, were defeated by the FTC with assistance from the National Small Business Administration.[32]

§ 3.3 Overview of Legal Limitations

Besides political and institutional influences, legislative decisions concerning how to structure and oversee agency government are constrained by legal limitations. Congress must respect constitutional requirements such as separation of powers and due process. In addition, it cannot force an agency to act in a manner inconsistent with the APA or its statutory mandate except by amending those statutes.

The constitutional requirement of separation of powers constrains how Congress can exercise its authority under Article I of the Constitution in three ways.[33] First, Congress is authorized to engage only in legislative and not executive or judicial functions. Some forms of oversight, such as restricting the President's authority to fire administrators except for certain specified reasons, have presented questions of whether Congress has engaged in other than legislative functions.[34] Second, Article I itself contains limitations which specify how Congress can use its legislative authority. Article I, for example, not only authorizes Congress to make laws for the subjects specified, but also prohibits Congress from delegating its law-making authority to another branch or other institution. Since administrative agencies in effect engage in law-making, the Supreme Court has had to define the limitations of that nondelegation prohibition.[35] The Supreme Court has also had to decide whether the legislative veto was consistent with the requirement in Article I that all legislation be passed by both Houses and presented to the President for a possible veto.[36] Finally, the Court has had to determine to what extent Congress can delegate to agencies the authority to exercise judicial powers consis-

---

32. *See* R. Arnold, Congress and the Bureaucracy: A Theory of Influence 35–71 (1979) (agencies make allocational decisions to please key members of Congress); Schorr, *FTC's Mike Pertschuk Tilts Against Congress to Keep Agency Power,* Wall St.J., Jan. 15, 1980, at 1, col. 1; *see generally* L. Dodd & R. Schott, *supra* note 2, at 221.

33. *See Symposium on Administrative Law: The Uneasy Constitutional Sta-* *tus of Administrative Agencies,* 36 Am. U.L.Rev. 277 (1987).

34. *See infra* § 4.4; *see generally* Fein, *Fighting Off Congress: A Bill of Rights for the Independent Agency,* 8 District Lawyer 37 (1983); Parnell, *Congressional Interference in Agency Enforcement: The IRS Experience,* 89 Yale L.J. 1360 (1980).

35. *See infra* § 3.4.

36. *See infra* § 3.5.

tent with Article III, which locates such powers in the judicial branch of government, and the Seventh Amendment, which guarantees a right to a jury trial in certain types of cases.[37]

Among the Bill of Rights protections, the due process clause is the most important for most types of administrative matters. The clause requires a minimum level of procedural process, a neutral decisionmaker, and certain limitations on the nature of contacts that a decisionmaker can have outside of the procedural process. The last two of those constraints can be implicated when members of Congress seek to pressure administrators to adopt a certain policy or outcome in a proceeding. Normally, an agency is free to accommodate the wishes of members of Congress as long as they are consistent with its statutory mandate. Certain types of political pressure, however, are a violation of due process or the APA regardless of the substantive outcome.[38]

§ 3.4   The Nondelegation Doctrine

The Constitution provides that "[a]ll legislative powers shall be vested in a Congress of the United States".[39] This provision is both a grant of power to the Congress and limitation upon its use. It prohibits Congress from delegating its legislative powers to any other institution. That prohibition, called the nondelegation doctrine, raises the issue whether broad and vague delegations constitute the unconstitutional delegation of legislative powers to administrative agencies.

§ 3.4.1   Cases prior to the New Deal

The Supreme Court first considered the nondelegation clause in *Brig Aurora,* which involved a statute that authorized the President to lift trade embargoes against France and England when they "ceased to violate the neutral commerce of the United States". The Court approved the legislation because the executive's authority was limited to taking the specific, prescribed action mandated by Congress when the "named contingency"—no more violations of neutral commerce—occurred.[40]

The "named contingency" test, however, was dropped in the first case where its use would not have permitted approval of the statute being challenged. In *Buttfield v. Stranahan,* the Court reviewed a statute that authorized the Secretary of the Treasury to establish

---

37. *See infra* § 3.7.

38. *See infra* § 3.6.

39. U.S. Const. Art. I, § 1; *see* Field v. Clark, 143 U.S. 649, 692 (1892) ("That

Congress cannot delegate legislative power ... is a principle universally recognized ... ").

40. 11 U.S. (7 Cranch) 382 (1813).

uniform standards of purity, fitness, and quality for imported tea.[41] Because the named contingency test would not sanction a cabinet officer's promulgation of rules and regulations, the Court substituted a "standards" test. The Court announced it would permit legislative delegations if Congress set sufficient standards to delimit clearly the scope of agency authority to regulate. As the Court explained in *United States v. Grimaud,* which involved the Department of Agriculture's authorization to make rules to conserve the national forests, agencies could be given the "power to fill up the details".[42]

The change of tests, however, was not sufficient in itself to approve some of the delegations the Court reviewed. In *Buttfield,* for example, the Supreme Court interpreted the legislative history to mean that the lowest grades of tea were to be excluded so that the Secretary's authority to set rules was limited sufficiently.[43] In *Mahler v. Eby,* the President's vague authority to deport undesirable aliens was upheld because ambiguous words used as standards had a "common understanding" when their historical context was considered.[44]

The switch of tests by the Court meant that a strict interpretation of the nondelegation prohibition would not be pursued. Instead the Court opted for a more pragmatic response that required Congress to establish a sufficiently "intelligible principle" to which the agency must conform in order that the judiciary would be able to determine whether an agency was meeting the intentions of Congress. Further, the Court accommodated vague delegations by finding a more definitive meaning for words used in legislative or administrative history.

§ 3.4.2   The New Deal cases

The favorable reception given to broad and vague delegations ended in the New Deal. In *Panama Refining Co. v. Ryan,* the Court declared unconstitutional a provision of the National Industrial Recovery Act (NIRA) that authorized the President "to prohibit ... the transportation in interstate ... commerce of petroleum ... produced or withdrawn from storage in excess of the amount permitted ... by state law.... "[45] The provision was intended to prevent the sale of "hot oil" that occurred when oil companies avoided state restrictions on how much petroleum they could sell by shipping more than the

---

41. 192 U.S. 470 (1904).

42. 220 U.S. 506, 517 (1911).

43. 192 U.S. at 496–97.

44. 264 U.S. 32, 40 (1924).

45. 293 U.S. 388 (1935); *see generally* P. Irons, The New Deal Lawyers 58–74 (1982) (background and history of the litigation).

allowable amount in interstate commerce. The Court concluded that the provision did not pass the standards test because it "[did] not state whether, or in what circumstances or under what conditions, the President is to prohibit the transportation of . . . petroleum . . . in excess of the state's permission". Since there was no such standard, the Court believed the President had been given "an unlimited authority to determine the policy and to lay down the prohibition, or not to lay it down, as he may see fit".

The sole dissenting opinion, by Justice Cardozo, argued that the statute did provide standards that limited the President's discretion in the first section of the NIRA. In that section, Congress had indicated that the purpose of the NIRA was to accomplish several goals, such as the elimination of unfair competition and the conservation of natural resources. Cardozo thought these goals offered the type of standards required by the previous case law, because any action to limit "hot oil" would have to be consistent with those goals. The majority opinion dismissed that section of the NIRA on the ground it was "simply an introduction of the Act. . . . "

In *A.L.A. Schechter Poultry Corp. v. United States,* a unanimous Court declared another and more important part of the NIRA to be unconstitutional.[46] The NIRA allowed firms in an industry to agree to codes of "fair competition" in order to eliminate forms of competition that kept prices low and prevented employers from paying higher wages to their workers. The President was authorized to enforce the codes as long as the trade group that proposed a code was representative of the firms in an industry, as long as the code would not promote monopolies, and as long as the code would serve the purposes of the NIRA stated in its first section. The government sought to punish Schechter Poultry for its wholesale violation of a poultry industry code and the company argued that the delegation to the President to approve codes lacked the necessary standards to be constitutional.

The government had contended that the standards used in the NIRA "codes of fair competition" contained the same type of vague phrase that had been used to authorize the Federal Trade Commission (FTC) to prevent "unfair methods of competition" or the Interstate Commerce Commission (ICC) to allow railroads to operate as the "public convenience and necessity may require".[47] The Court

---

46. 295 U.S. 495 (1935); *see generally* P. Irons, *supra* note 45, at 86–107.

47. 15 U.S.C. § 45 (FTC delegation); 49 U.S.C. § 1(20), *repealed by* Pub.L. No. 95–473, §§ 4(b)–(c), 92 Stat. 1466, 1470 (1978) (ICC delegation).

distinguished the other legislation, which it had previously approved as being consistent with the nondelegation clause, on two grounds. First, the Court said that the phrase "fair methods of competition" covered more industrial activities than the FTC mandate because it concerned both activities that were undesirable and had to be prohibited, and activities that were desirable and should be promoted. The FTC mandate concerned only the first area. Second, the Court focused on the FTC's and ICC's implementation of their statutory mandates through the use of adversary procedures, including a hearing and judicial review, whereas no such procedures were used under the NIRA.

The Court refused to accept the statement of congressional purposes in the first section of the NIRA as sufficient to constitute the necessary standards. This time Justice Cardozo agreed. In a concurring opinion, he indicated that the goals were not sufficient as standards because of the jurisdictional reach of the power given to the President. The Justice complained that "anything that Congress may do within the limits of the commerce clause for the betterment of business may be done by the President.... This is delegation running riot".[48]

Because the Supreme Court returned to approving broad and vague delegations after the New Deal cases,[49] they are often dismissed as being atypical and the consequences of the justices' considerable ideological opposition to the Roosevelt administration. The Court's analysis, however, is important to later case law.[50] Rather than overruling the previous cases, the Court distinguished them by declaring that the degree of specificity of the standards must be considered in relationship to the degree of power conferred on an agency and the procedural protections given to the persons subject to

48. A.L.A. Schechter Poultry Corp. v. United States, 295 U.S. 495, 553 (1935) (Cardozo, J. concurring). *See* A. Kaufman, Cardozo 512–13 (1998) (describing how Cardozo wrote numerous drafts of his famous concurring opinion).

49. One other federal statute was invalidated on the ground it constituted the delegation of legislative power to private parties. Carter v. Carter Coal Co., 298 U.S. 238 (1936); *but see* United States v. Rock Royal Co-op., Inc., 307 U.S. 533, 577–78 (1939) (requirement of producer approval for regulations to take effect not an invalid delegation); *cf.* Allen v. California Bd. of Barber Examiners, 25 Cal.App.3d 1014, 102 Cal.Rptr. 368 (1972) (delegations to boards consisting of private parties require narrow and specific standards); *see generally* Jaffe, *Law Making by Private Groups,* 51 Harv. L.Rev. 201 (1937).

50. Justice Brandeis is reported to have told a Roosevelt aide, Tommy Corcoran, immediately after *Schechter* was announced, "This is the end of this business of centralization and I want you to go back and tell the President that we're not going to let this government centralize everything." A. Schlesinger, The Politics of Upheaval 280 (1960).

that power. The Court thus continued to accept the delegation of the power to make rules to agencies. Vague delegations that otherwise might be excessive would pass muster if the scope of power was narrower, or if those subject to the agency's regulatory efforts were afforded sufficient procedural protection.

§ 3.4.3 Post New Deal cases

Since the New Deal, the Court has approved all of the legislation it has reviewed under the nondelegation clause. In some cases, the Court has followed the approach of Justice Cardozo in *Panama Refining* to determine that the goals and purposes stated in the preamble of an act constituted the necessary standards.[51] In other cases, the Court has followed *Buttfield* and *Eby* by using the legislative history or prior administrative usage and experience to give words a sufficiently narrow meaning.[52] In this process, the Court sometimes has construed a statute to avoid a nondelegation problem by choosing the one of two or more meanings that gave an agency the least power.[53] This technique avoids the fatal flaw of the legislation considered in *Schechter*, where the breadth of power conferred was an important consideration.

The Court has also turned to other means to conclude that a statute was sufficiently definite. Congress has been given more leeway when its actions have involved the conduct of a war or foreign affairs on the ground that the executive requires greater flexibility in those areas.[54] The Court even has justified vague legislation in part on the ground that if an administrator acted in a manner inconsis-

51. *See, e.g.,* Yakus v. United States, 321 U.S. 414, 423 (1944) (boundaries of delegation to World War II Office of Price Administration contained in statement of purposes of Act).

52. *See, e.g.,* Zemel v. Rusk, 381 U.S. 1, 18 (1965) (delegation to Secretary of State authorized "only those passport refusals and restrictions 'which it could fairly be argued were adopted by Congress in light of prior administrative practice' "); Fahey v. Mallonee, 332 U.S. 245, 250 (1947) (delegation to Federal Home Loan Bank Board to take over and restructure regulated lending institutions intended to follow "well-defined" State administrative "practices").

53. *See, e.g.,* National Cable Television Ass'n, Inc. v. United States, 415 U.S. 336, 342–44 (1974) (delegation to Federal Communications Commission to prescribe fees or charges for agency services narrowly construed to mean services of value to the regulated industry, not the public); Kent v. Dulles, 357 U.S. 116, 129–30 (1958) (delegation to Secretary of State to issue passports interpreted to exclude power to deny on ground of political belief).

54. *See, e.g.,* Zemel v. Rusk, 381 U.S. 1, 17 (1965) (delegation to Secretary of State to issue passports approved because Congress in dealing with foreign affairs "must of necessity paint with a broader brush"); Yakus v. United States, 321 U.S. 414, 422–23 (1944) (delegation to Office of Price Administration to regulate prices was "a war emergency measure").

tent with Congressional intentions, Congress could order any necessary changes through oversight or legislation.[55]

By its willingness to engage in favorable statutory interpretation to meet the "standards" test and to augment that test with other considerations, the Supreme Court has created a body of case law that can be used to approve even exceedingly broad and vague delegations. Nevertheless, there are those who would like the Supreme Court to reinvigorate the doctrine, as discussed next.

§ 3.4.4 Reinvigoration of the Nondelegation Doctrine

While the Court has remained steadfast in rejecting nondelegation challenges concerning vague statutory language, some Justices have signaled their interest in a revitalized doctrine. In 1981, Chief Justice Burger and Justice Rehnquist held that OSHA's statutory mandate to protect workers from workplace health hazards was too vague to pass muster under the doctrine.[56] More recently, Justice Thomas proposed that the Court be less accepting of vague delegations when they are accompanied by substantial grants of power to an agency.[57] A group of scholars support a reinvigorated nondelegation doctrine, while other scholars are opposed. The authors are in the opposition camp for reasons that will be explained.

The issue of whether OSHA's statute violated the nondelegation doctrine came up in two related cases. The first case, *Industrial Union Department v. American Petroleum Institute,*[58] involved an Occupational Health and Safety Administration (OSHA) standard that limited the exposure of workers to benzene, a toxic chemical.[59] Congress instructed OSHA to set exposure limits for toxic materials, such as Benzene, that would "most adequately assure, *to the extent feasible* ... that no employee will suffer material impairment" of his or her health.[60] The American Petroleum Institute contended the phrase "to the extent feasible" required OSHA to establish that the benefits of the regulation exceeded its costs. OSHA insisted that the words "to the extent feasible" meant that it was technologically and

---

55. Arizona v. California, 373 U.S. 546, 594 (1963) (delegation to Secretary of Interior to apportion water of Colorado River in times of shortages upheld in part because if power was abused Congress could reduce Secretary's powers as necessary).

56. American Textile Manufacturers Institute, Inc. v. Donovan, 452 U.S. 490 (1981).

57. Whitman v. American Trucking Ass'n, 531 U.S. 457 (2001).

58. 448 U.S. 607 (1980).

59. The case is often referred to as the Benzene case.

60. Occupational Health and Safety Act, § 6(b)(5), 29 U.S.C. § 655(b)(5).

economically feasible for an industry to achieve the level of protection that OSHA ordered.

The nondelegation doctrine played two roles in the case. Four members of the Court held that the OSHA act required the agency to make a threshold determination that benzene posed a "significant health hazard" at the levels of exposure that were prohibited, and they used the nondelegation doctrine to justify this interpretation of OSHA's mandate. Since OSHA had not made a "significant risk" determination, the plurality returned the regulation to the agency for further findings.[61] A fifth member, then-Justice Rehnquist, found that the statutory provisions violated the nondelegation doctrine.[62]

The plurality's interpretation of OSHA's mandate was highly controversial because it was not well supported by the statutory language. The plurality, however, supported its interpretation on the ground that unless OSHA's authority was narrowed in this manner, there would be a violation of the nondelegation doctrine. Without its narrowing interpretation, the plurality pointed out that OSHA's authority to regulate was constrained only by the requirement of feasibility. If feasibility were the only limit, the plurality felt OSHA would have the authority to impose enormous clean-up costs on industry to reduce a minimal risk. This type of "sweeping delegation" would have been a violation of the nondelegation doctrine because Congress would have failed to indicate how such power was to be used.

The decision in *Industrial Union* did not reach the issue of whether the statutory reference to "feasibility" required OSHA to use a cost-benefit test to determine the extent to which workers were to be protected. In *American Textile Manufacturers Institute, Inc. v. Donovan,* a majority of the Court held that the statutory reference to "feasibility" did not require a cost-benefit analysis to impose an exposure regulation.[63] Justice Rehnquist, joined by Chief Justice Burger, dissented on the ground that the "feasibility" authorization violated the nondelegation prohibition because the word was not sufficiently defined by Congress and it was therefore only precatory.[64]

61. 448 U.S. 607 (1980) (plurality opinion). *See, also,* UAW v. OSHA, 938 F.2d 1310 (D.C. Cir. 1991) (remanding a safety regulation and requiring OSHA to demonstrate that a vague statutory mandate did not violate the nondelegation clause); UAW v. OSHA, 37 F.3d 665 (D.C. Cir. 1994) (accepting OSHA's construction of its statute as sufficiently definite to satisfy the nondelegation doctrine).

62. 448 U.S. 607, 675 (1980) (Rehnquist, J. concurring).

63. 452 U.S. 490 (1981).

64. 452 U.S. 490, 546–47 (1981) (Rehnquist, J. dissenting).

Echoing his concurring opinion in the *Benzene* case, Justice Rehnquist distinguished instances where Congress would be unable to delegate more specifically because of a lack of technical expertise, which he would permit, from cases like the OSHA statute which he characterized as demonstrating a lack of political will to decide hard policy issues. He believed that Congress had simply failed to decide whether or not a cost-benefit standard, or any other approach, was to be used, and the statute therefore did not have an "intelligible principle" to limit OSHA's actions. The majority opinion disagreed on the ground that the legislative history, which "concededly" was not "crystal clear", indicated that Congress intended feasibility to mean "capable of 'economic and technological accomplishment' ".

After these cases, the Court has continued to reject nondelegation challenges. In *Mistretta v. United States*,[65] for example, the Court rejected a challenge that Congress failed to specify in sufficient detail the authority of the United States Sentencing Commission, which had promulgated binding sentence guidelines for the federal courts. Congress' mandate was more specific than many other statutes that have survived a nondelegation challenge, and the Court routinely found that Congress had established an "intelligible principle." What is notable is Justice Blackmun's expression of tolerance for general delegations. He noted that the Court's implementation of the nondelegation doctrine "has been driven by a practical understanding that in our increasingly complex society, replete with ever-changing and more technical problems, Congress simply cannot do its job absent an ability to delegate power under broad general directives." Moreover, "[d]eveloping proportionate penalties for hundreds of different crimes by a virtually limitless array of offenders is precisely the sort of intricate, labor-intensive task for which delegation to an expert body is especially appropriate."

In *Whitman v. American Trucking*,[66] the Supreme Court both rejected a new interpretation of the nondelegation doctrine by the D.C. Circuit and upheld a key provision of the Clean Air Act using the traditional nondelegation approach. Congress required EPA in the Clean Air Act to promulgate National Ambient Air Quality Standards (NAAQS) and to review those standards periodically. After EPA changed the NAAQS for particulate matter and ozone, the plaintiff challenged its action on a number of grounds including a

---

65. 488 U.S. 361 (1989); *see, also,* Loving v. United States, 517 U.S. 748 (1996) (nondelegation doctrine not violated by statute authorizing the President to choose the "aggravating factors" that would authorize a court martial to impose a death penalty on a member of the armed services convicted of murder).

66. 531 U.S. 457 (2001).

nondelegation challenge. The Clean Air Act requires EPA to set standards "the attainment and maintenance of which . . . are requisite to protect the public health" with an "adequate margin of safety." The D.C. Circuit interpreted this provision to provide no intelligible principle because it lacked any determinate criteria for determining what constitutes a safe level of exposure. The circuit court, however, gave EPA an opportunity to avoid the unconstitutional delegation by adopting a restrictive construction of this section.

The Supreme Court first rejected the idea that EPA could "cure an unlawful delegation of legislative power by adopting in its discretion a limiting construction of the statute." The reason was simple: "The very choice of which portion of the power to exercise—that is to say, the prescription of the standard that Congress has omitted—would *itself* be an exercise of the forbidden legislative authority." It then rejected the nondelegation challenge because the "scope of discretion [the statute] allows is well within the outer limits of our nondelegation precedents." The Supreme Court backed up this conclusion by comparing the statutory standard to other standards that it had previously approved that were of comparable ambiguity. It endorsed the principle that "the degree of agency discretion that is acceptable varies according to the scope of the power congressionally conferred," but it noted that, it had "never demanded, as the Court of Appeals did, that statutes provide a 'determinate criterion' for saying 'how much [of the regulated] harm is too much' ", even in 'sweeping regulatory schemes'."

In his concurrence, Justice Thomas agreed with both aspects of the majority's decision, but he observed, "I am not convinced that the intelligible principle doctrine serves to prevent all cessions of legislative power."[67] He continued, "I believe that there are cases in which the principle is intelligible and yet the significance of the delegated decision is simply too great for the decision to be called anything other than 'legislative' ". Therefore, he was willing "on another day" to "address the question whether our delegation jurisprudence has strayed too far from our Founding Fathers' understanding of separation of powers."

Some scholars have agreed that the Supreme Court should consider revitalizing the nondelegation doctrine. They see this action as necessary to make agency government democratically legitimate.[68]

67. 531 U.S. at 920.

68. *See, e.g.,* D. Schoenbrod, Power Without Responsibility (1995); J. Ely, De-

These scholars argue that if Congress was forced to delegate in a more narrow and specific manner, two benefits would occur. First, many of the important policy decisions now made by agencies would instead be made by Congress. In this manner, regulatory decision-making would be located in a more democratically accountable body than the agencies, particularly since the agencies are often dominated by unrepresentative interest groups. Second, the courts will find it easier to determine whether agencies are acting within their mandates because those constraints will be more clearly specified.

Other scholars support the Supreme Court's refusal to reinvigorate the nondelegation doctrine,[69] and we are in this camp. As the *Mistretta* opinion recognizes, Congress' failure to adopt narrow and specific legislation is often attributable to the complexity of the technical questions that often accompany a decision to regulate and to the fact that, once a legislative decision is reached, it is more efficient to resolve details in administrative proceedings. Moreover, as discussed earlier,[70] these are only one of the institutional and political reasons why Congress has difficulty legislating specific details. Indeed, as noted earlier,[71] using majority rule to aggregate preferences about specific regulatory policies inherently works against reaching stable agreements on these issues. Thus, unless the Supreme Court permits Congress to pass general legislation, it will likely pass less regulatory legislation. In light of this reality, reinvigoration of the nondelegation prohibition would represent a political choice in favor of less regulation. This may be the desired outcome of those pushing for a revitalized nondelegation doctrine, but if it is, it suggests an approach that is reminiscent of the pre-New Deal substantive due process era.[72] For example, how will Justice Thomas know when Congress has delegated too much power and therefore a statute is unconstitutional?

mocracy & Distrust 132–34 (1980); J. Freedman, Crisis and Legitimacy: The Administrative Process and American Government 93–94 (1978); T. Lowi, The End of Liberalism: The Second Republic of the United States 93 (2d ed. 1979); Aranson, Gellhorn & Robinson, *supra* note 9, at 63–67; Wright, Book Review, 81 Yale L.J. 575, 582–83 (1972) (reviewing K. Davis, Discretionary Justice: A Preliminary Inquiry (1971)).

69. *See, e.g.,* Pierce, *Political Accountability and Delegated Power: A Re-*sponse to Professor Lowi, 36 Am.U.L.Rev. 391 (1987); Mashaw, *Prodelegation: Why Administrators Should Make Political Decisions*, 1 J.L., Econ. & Org. 1 (1985).

70. *See supra* § 3.1.

71. See *supra* notes 11–13 & accompanying text.

72. *See* Lochner v. New York, 198 U.S. 45 (1905); *see generally* McCloskey, *Economic Due Process and The Supreme Court: An Exhumation and Reburial*, 1962 Sup.Ct.Rev. 34.

Justice Rehnquist's position that the nondelegation prohibition should be used only when Congress fails to specify agency authority because of political, rather than pragmatic, reasons does not answer the previous objection. First, it requires predictions about inherently subjective factors—the reasons why Congress acted—and therefore involves the courts in the appearance, if not the actuality, of partisanship.[73] The inquiry is also inconsistent with the general reluctance of the Court to investigate legislative motives.[74] Second, it assumes that the lack of political will justifies use of the prohibition, but this assumption is questionable. Madison and his followers believed that the best government is one where power is organized competitively. They therefore created a congressional system intended to be *"politically* rational—not necessarily policy rational".[75] What makes Congress inherently democratic is that the accepted process for resolving conflict is accommodation of contending individuals, groups, parties, and ideologies. Thus, when Congress produces broad and vague legislative mandates, it is operating in the politically rational manner for which it was created. Holding Congress to a strict standard of specificity, or policy rationality, would be inappropriate for that reason.

Instead, Professor Stewart's recommendation that the Court use statutory interpretation to fill in the details of vague delegations, but construe the delegation in as narrow a manner as a reading of the legislative history will allow, seems the most appropriate stance.[76] This was essentially the position adopted by the plurality in the *Industrial Union Department* case.[77] This approach creates an incentive for Congress to act decisively, offers a predictable basis for the application of the prohibition, is consistent with the case law, and respects the political predicament of Congress.

§ 3.4.5 Nondelegation in the states

There has been more active use of the nondelegation doctrine in the states. Some states have used the nondelegation doctrine to rein in legislative discretion, although one state, Oregon, has dispensed

---

73. *See* Stewart, *The Reformation of American Administrative Law,* 88 Harv. L.Rev. 1669, 1696–97 (1975).

74. *See, e.g.,* Pacific Gas and Electric Co. v. State Energy Resources Conservation & Development Commission, 459 U.S. 817 (1982).

75. Davis, *Congress and the Emergence of Public Health Policy,* 10 Health Care Management 61, 69 (1985) (emphasis in original); *see generally supra* § 2.1.2.

76. Stewart, *supra* note 73, at 1697 n. 6.

77. *Supra* text accompanying note 61.

with the requirement altogether. Other states have employed the doctrine, but attempted to be more precise about what constitutes an "intelligible principle" for the purpose of enforcing the doctrine.

A Nebraska case, *Lincoln Dairy Company v. Finigan*,[78] illustrates the first result. The Nebraska Supreme Court struck down a delegation to the Director of the Department of Agriculture to "adopt, by regulation, minimum standards for the sanitary quality, production, processing, distribution, and sale of Grade A milk and Grade A milk products, and for the labeling of the same." The Court objected to the lack of legislative standards because a person might be subject to criminal penalties for violation of the regulations adopted by the Director. The justices explained, "It is axiomatic that the power to define crimes and criminal offenses is in the Legislature and it may not delegate such power to an administrative agency." Other states, however, disagree.[79]

Oregon, by comparison, rejects the requirement of the nondelegation doctrine. In *Warren v. Marion County*,[80] the Oregon Supreme Court held there "is no constitutional requirement that all delegation of legislative power must be accompanied by a statement of a standard circumscribing its exercise." Instead, "the important consideration is not whether the statute delegating the power expresses *standards*, but whether the procedure established for the exercise of the power furnishes adequate *safeguards* to those who are affected by administrative action." *Warren* upheld a statute that empowered county governments to establish building ordinances because the statute required an appeal procedure that "provided a sufficient safeguard to persons wishing to contest administrative action in the enforcement of the code." As for requiring standards, the justices thought this requirement to be meaningless: "It is now apparent that the requirement of expressed standards, has in most instances, been little more than a judicial fetish for legislative language, the recitation of which provides no additional safeguards to persons affected by exercise of the delegated authority."

78. 170 Neb. 777, 104 N.W.2d 227 (1960).

79. *See, e.g.*, Ohio v. Acme Scrap & Metal, 49 Ohio App.2d 371, 361 N.E.2d 250 (1974) (rejecting challenge to state air pollution regulations on ground that violations were a criminal offense). The United States Supreme Court has also rejected a challenge to agency regulations because an administrator defines what conduct is criminal. Touby v. United States, 500 U.S. 160 (1991) (nondelegation doctrine not violated by statute authorizing the Attorney General to designate drugs whose possession constituted a crime, despite the vague standards to be used in this decision).

80. 222 Or. 307, 353 P.2d 257 (1960).

A good example of the third tendency is *Thygesen v. Callahan,*[81] which involved an Illinois statute that authorized the Illinois Director of Financial Institutions to establish "schedules of maximum rates which can be charged for check cashing and writing of money orders by community currency exchanges and ambulatory currency exchanges." The Illinois Supreme Court followed a previous case which established a three-part test for the nondelegation doctrine: A law establishes an "intelligible principle" if it sufficiently identifies (1) the persons and activities potentially subject to regulation, (2) the harm sought to be prevented, and (3) the general means intended to be available to the administrator to prevent the identified harm. The court held that while the first prong was met, the legislature made no attempt to identify the harm to be prevented, or to set any "meaningful" standards to guide the agency in setting rates.

Various explanations have been offered for the greater popularity of the nondelegation doctrine in state courts. Justice Linde and Professor Bunn, for example, believe it is because states typically lack a sufficient legislative history for most statutes to allow statutory interpretation, because state court judges and practitioners are insufficiently familiar with federal administrative law cases, and because state court judges may be less deferential and more critical of the capacities of legislatures and agencies to act professionally, impartially, and reasonably.[82] Although some observers believe that states are moving in the direction of the federal approach,[83] because conditions are changing concerning the factors just mentioned, we believe that the long tradition in the states of invoking the nondelegation doctrine will not be excessively influenced by federal developments. For one thing, states have a continuing problem with delegation to private parties whereas that issue largely ended at the federal level during the New Deal.[84]

---

81. 74 Ill.2d 404, 24 Ill.Dec. 558, 385 N.E.2d 699 (1979); *see also* Fitanides v. Crowley, 467 A.2d 168 (Me.1983); Commissioner of Agriculture v. Plaquemines Parish Commission Council, 439 So.2d 348 (La.1983); Askew v. Cross Key Waterways, 372 So.2d 913 (Fla.1978); *see also* Texas Boll Weevil Eradication Foundation v. Lewellen, 952 S.W.2d 454 (Tex. 1997) (overturning a legislative delegation to private entity).

82. H. Linde & G. Bunn, Legislative and Administrative Processes 537 (1976); *see also* F. Cooper, 1 State Administrative Law 73–91 (1965); K. Davis, 1 Administrative Law Treatise § 3.14 (1978); B. Schwartz, Administrative Law § 2.13 (3d ed. 1991).

83. K. Davis, *supra* note 82, § 3.14.

84. *See* Texas Boll Weevil Foundation v. Lewellen, *supra* note 81.

§ 3.5 The Legislative Veto

Mindful of its habit of passing vague and broad delegations, Congress has sought methods to police the discretion it creates. One of the most widely used techniques was the legislative veto until it was declared to be unconstitutional. The Supreme Court sounded the death knell for the legislative veto in three cases. In *INS v. Chadha,* the Court declared unconstitutional a statutory provision that authorized either House of Congress to reverse decisions of the Attorney General concerning whether or not to deport aliens.[85] In *Chadha,* the Immigration and Naturalization Service (INS) had ordered Mr. Chadha to be deported after an adjudicatory hearing, the Attorney General had suspended that order, and the House of Representatives had reinstated it by vetoing the Attorney General's decision. Although *Chadha* involved an adjudicatory decision, the Supreme Court quickly indicated that its decision was to be given a broad reading by affirming two decisions by the Court of Appeals for the District of Columbia which had invalidated one and two-house vetoes of agency rules. The Court thereby eliminated the possibility that when agencies were engaged in rulemaking, a quasi-legislative activity, there would be a different result.

The Supreme Court's actions in two subsequent cases were per curiam and without opinion except to cite *Chadha.* In *Consumer Energy Council v. FERC,* the Court invalidated legislation that authorized either house to veto Federal Energy Regulatory Commission (FERC) regulations concerning the pricing of natural gas to industrial uses.[86] The Natural Gas Policy Act of 1978 was designed to shift a portion of the price increases resulting from deregulation of certain categories of natural gas from residential to industrial users in two phases covering first industrial boiler fuel facilities and then any industrial facility. After FERC had promulgated regulations intended to implement the second phase, the House passed a resolution vetoing the rule. In *Consumers Union v. FTC,* the Court invalidated legislation that authorized both houses of Congress to veto trade regulation rules issued by the Federal Trade Commission (FTC).[87] After the FTC had issued such a rule requiring warranty coverage and the disclosure of accurate information in connection

---

85. 462 U.S. 919 (1983).

86. 673 F.2d 425 (D.C.Cir.1982), affirmed sub nom. Process Gas Consumers Group v. Consumer Energy Council of America, 463 U.S. 1216 (1983) (per curiam).

87. 691 F.2d 575 (D.C.Cir.1982) (per curiam), affirmed sub nom. United States Senate v. FTC, 463 U.S. 1216 (1983) (per curiam).

with the sale of used cars, it was vetoed by a concurrent resolution passed by both houses.

The litigation of the three cases involved three objections to legislative vetoes. Opponents claimed that any veto provision that involved only one house of Congress violated the "bicameralism" requirement of Article I that no law can take effect without the concurrence of a majority of the members of both houses.[88] Opponents also argued that a one or two house veto violated another requirement of Article I that all laws have to be presented to the President for his approval or veto.[89] Finally, opponents argued that the veto provisions were unconstitutional infringements on the executive's power to execute the laws under Article II[90] and the judiciary's power to determine their legal effect under Article III.[91]

The Court in *Chadha* accepted the first and second objections that the bicameralism and presentment requirements were violated. The Court reasoned that the veto decision was "essentially legislative in purpose and effect" and the intention of the framers of the Constitution was that the legislative power of Congress could not be exercised except under those two constraints. The Court concluded that the action was "legislative" for two reasons. First, it altered Mr. Chadha's legal right to remain in the country because the decision could have been made absent the veto provision only by legislation to deport Mr. Chadha.[92] Second, it changed the scope of discretion of the Attorney General because it was a policy decision of the type that usually is considered to be legislative in character.

The majority's reasoning has an unsatisfying quality to it when the objections of Justices Powell and White are taken into account. Both Justices Powell and White disagreed with the Court's character-

---

88. Every Bill which shall have passed the House of Representatives and the Senate, shall, before it become a Law, be presented to the President of the United States; If he approve he shall sign it, but if not he shall return it, with his Objections, to that House in which it shall have originated.... If ... two thirds of that House shall agree to pass the Bill it shall be sent ... to the other House, ... and if approved by two thirds of that House, it shall become a Law.... U.S. Const. Art. I, § 7, cl. 2.

89. Every Order, Resolution, or Vote, to Which the Concurrence of the Senate and House of Representatives may be necessary (except on a question of Ad-

journment) shall be presented to the President of the United States; and before the Same shall take Effect, shall be approved by him, or being disapproved by him, shall be repassed by two thirds of the Senate and House of Representatives, according to the Rules and Limitations prescribed in the Case of a Bill. U.S. Const. Art. I, § 7, cl. 2–3.

90. U.S. Const. Art. II, § 1, cl. 1.

91. U.S. Const. Art. III, § 1.

92. The Court took no position on whether Congress constitutionally could enact legislation to deport an alien. 462 U.S. at 954 n. 17, 935 n. 8.

ization of the veto as a "legislative" act and the Court's reply to these objections is make-weight in character.[93] Justice Powell, who concurred in the judgment, argued that the veto was an improper invasion of the judicial sphere because it constituted a judgment that a certain statute applied to a certain set of facts.[94] The majority countered that since Mr. Chadha could not have appealed the Attorney General's decision to allow him to remain in the country, the House's action did not remove a case from the federal courts. Justice Powell objected that the Court's point was irrelevant because the House was engaged in an adjudicatory function that could be performed only by an impartial tribunal.

Justice White, in his dissent, argued that the Attorney General's decision was merely a recommendation and therefore the House's decision not to accept it was not a legislative act.[95] The majority replied that Justice White's interpretation would allow Congress to enact executive proposals without deliberation and debate merely by not vetoing them. The majority said the adoption of decisions by silence violated the purpose of Article I to guarantee deliberation and debate. Justice White's answer was that the Constitution does not and cannot guarantee that Congress will carefully debate all laws since laws that are passed without such deliberation are clearly still valid.

The majority made an argument that would have been a stronger answer to Justice White's objection. The Court reviewed the framers' intention that Article I was supposed to limit the ability of a majority in either House and in both Houses to act.[96] Article I first provides that "Every bill that shall have passed the House of Representatives and the Senate, shall, before it become a Law, be presented to the President . . . ". The article also requires that "Every Order, Resolution, or Vote to which the Concurrence of the Senate and House of Representatives may be necessary (except on a question of Adjourn-

93. *See generally* Strauss, *Was There a Baby in the Bathwater? A Comment on the Supreme Court's Legislative Veto Decision,* 1983 Duke L.J. 789, 794–801 (criticisms of Court's definition of a legislative act); Elliot, *INS v. Chadha: The Administrative Constitution, the Constitution, and the Legislative Veto,* 1983 Sup.Ct.Rev. 125.

94. INS v. Chadha, 462 U.S. 919, 959 (1983) (Powell, J. concurring).

95. INS v. Chadha, 462 U.S. 919, 967 (1983) (White, J. dissenting).

96. Presentment to the President and the Presidential veto were considered so imperative that the draftsman took special pains to assure that these requirements could not be circumvented. During the final debate on Art. I, § 7, cl. 2, James Madison expressed concern that it might easily be evaded by the simple expedient of calling a proposed law a "resolution" or "vote" rather than a "bill". 462 U.S. at 947.

ment) shall be presented to the President ... ".[97] The clear intent of adding the second stipulation was to prevent Congress from avoiding the presentment requirement applicable to a law by calling it something else. The second presentment requirement would invalidate a two-house veto authorization of the type in the *Consumers Union* case. Whether or not the veto could be characterized as "legislative," it appears to be within the ambit of the category "Order, Resolution or Vote" of Article I.

The one-house veto involved in *Chadha* and *Consumer Energy Council,* by comparison, would not fall within that requirement since action by only one house was necessary. The one-house veto, however, is a violation of the bicameralism requirement based on an extension of the previous argument. The bicameralism provision was motivated by the same premise as the presentment clause, but it operated as a check on the majority in each house of Congress, instead of a check on the majority of Congress as a whole. As the Court noted, the system of presentment and bicameralism represented the "Framers' decision that the legislative power of the Federal government be exercised in accord with a single, finely-wrought and exhaustively considered procedure". The framers therefore did not intend that Congress could avoid the presentment provision by enacting policy decisions by a vote of only one house. Considering the framers' intention, it would be anomalous to invalidate a two-house veto and approve a one-house one.[98]

The *Chadha* decision has been criticized by some scholars as being overly formalistic. For example, Professor Elliot argues that the "most that can be said ... is that the Constitutional Convention wanted the presentment requirement to apply to bills and to functional equivalents of bills". As a result, Elliot contends that the important issue is whether the use of the legislative veto "is an exercise of Article I power of the kind that requires presentment and bicameral action". Elliot concludes that the question cannot be answered by reference to the formal language of Article I alone because the framers did not anticipate the role of administrative agencies. Elliot instead would address the issue of separation of powers in light of the role of agencies in the administrative state. If this analysis were done, Elliot suggests that the Court could have reached a different result concerning the constitutionality of vetoes

97. U.S. Const. Art. I, § 7, cls. 2–3. Article I is more fully quoted *supra* at note 89.

98. *See* 462 U.S. at 948–51.

that had applied to agency rulemaking.[99]

The criticism that the Court decided *Chadha* too broadly is important if the Court thereby deprived Congress of a useful form of oversight for agency rulemaking. Justice White indicated that the *Chadha* decision struck down "in one fell swoop provisions in more laws enacted by Congress than the Court has cumulatively invalidated in its history". Nearly two-hundred statutes were affected. Justice White characterized the legislative veto in *Chadha* as an "indispensable political invention that allows the President and Congress to resolve major constitutional and policy differences, assures the accountability of independent regulatory agencies, and preserves Congress' control over [agency] lawmaking".[100] While the veto did have the advantage of being easier to adopt than statutory methods of oversight, its loss is not the serious blow that Justice White envisioned.

The oversight of the FTC, described earlier, illustrates how Congress can effectively rein in any agency by means other than a veto.[101] The problem with such oversight is that it is often unsystematic and shallow, but the experience with the veto indicated it was subject to the same problems. For example, in *Chadha,* Congress took up the issue of the veto one and one-half years after the Attorney General's decision and only seven days before the veto authority would have expired. The veto resolution was reported to the House by the Judiciary Committee only four days after it was introduced and before it had been printed and submitted to the rest of the House's members. The vote was based on a very short statement by Representative Eilberg that the Committee believed the action was required by the Immigration Act and it was passed without debate or recorded vote.[102]

The veto also increased some of the present problems of legislative oversight by accelerating the tendency of Congress to avoid difficult policy decisions whenever possible, and to allow committee and subcommittee chairpersons, or their staffs, to have a disproportionate role in the design of agency policies.[103] The legislative veto in the *Consumer Energy Council* case is a good example of the first

99. Elliot, *supra* note 93, at 133–34.

100. 462 U.S. at 972–73.

101. *See supra* § 3.2.

102. 462 U.S. at 926–27. The Supreme Court had some suspicion that neither the members of the House generally, nor Chairman Eilberg in particular, understood the consequences of passing the veto resolution. 462 U.S. at 927 n. 3.

103. *See* Bruff & Gellhorn, *supra* note 15, at 1417–19; Scalia, *The Legislative Veto: A False Remedy for System Overload,* Regulation, Nov./Dec. 1979, at 19.

tendency. The veto authorization substantially resulted from the fact that the energy legislation under consideration was highly controversial and difficult to pass despite its position as the centerpiece of President Carter's energy program. Although the rules passed by FERC were highly faithful to its legislative mandate, they were vetoed because when forced to decide, Congress decided it did not want to shift part of the burden of natural gas price increases to industrial users.[104]

As a veto replacement, Congress has adopted the process for legislative review of new regulations mentioned in the introduction to this chapter. The details and efficacy of this process are discussed in Chapter Nine.[105] This legislative mechanism resembles oversight models used by various states, which include staying the effective date of rules so that legislative oversight may occur, setting time limits on the duration of rules, and allowing legislative comments to become part of a rulemaking record for purposes of judicial review.[106] The Court already has indicated approval of "wait and see" provisions that postpone the effective date of rules until Congress has an opportunity to review them.[107]

Congress has additional options to attempt to gain additional control over agency rulemaking. It could impose the requirement that agencies justify their actions in terms of cost-benefit analysis, adopt a regulatory budget, or utilize sunset provisions. Chapter Nine considers the merits of the first proposal.[108] A regulatory budget would legislatively establish an upper limit on the cost of regulatory activities and apportion this sum among the individual regulatory agencies. Although the concept has received political and academic support, others oppose it as impractical, because of methodological problems and otherwise dubious merit.[109] One opponent observes, "Choosing a budget ceiling without consideration of regulatory bene-

---

104. *See* Strauss, *supra* note 93, at 810 n. 84.

105. *See infra* § 9.5.4.

106. Levinson, *Legislative and Executive Veto of Rules of Administrative Agencies: Models and Alternatives,* 24 Wm. & Mary L.Rev. 79, 98–104 (1982).

107. Sibbach v. Wilson, 312 U.S. 1 (1941), *cited with approval in* INS v. Chadha, 462 U.S. 919, 935 n. 9 (1983) (provision that Rules of Civil Procedure do not take effect until after reported to Congress was constitutional); *see* Tribe, *The Legislative Veto Process: A Law by*

Any Other Name, 21 Harv.J. on Legis. 1, 18–19 (1984).

108. *See infra* § 9.5

109. *See* Shapiro, *Political Oversight and the Deterioration of Regulatory Policy,* 46 Ad. L. Rev. 1, 34 (1994) (identifying supporters and opponents); *see generally* R. Litan & W. Nordhous, Reforming Federal Regulation 133–58 (1983); Wood, Laws & Breen, *Restraining the Regulators: Legal Perspectives on a Regulatory Budget for Federal Agencies,* 18 Harv.J. on Legis. 1 (1981).

fits is incoherent, and attempting to take benefits into account would significantly compound the methodological problems. Moreover, budget estimates, which are inherently imprecise, would invite partisan wrangling because opponents and supporters of regulation would advocate budget levels based on ulterior motives concerning the scope of federal regulation.''[110]

Finally, Congress can require sunset laws, as do some states, that force agencies to justify their existence periodically because their statutory authorizations have time limits.[111] The wisdom of this proposal is also doubtful. A method of oversight appropriate in some state governments may be unsuitable for the oversight of the more numerous and complex federal regulatory schemes. Moreover, this (or any other reform) will be useful only if it results in more systematic and thorough oversight.[112] Congress already has sufficient tools, however, to engage in such oversight if it wishes.

§ 3.6   Due Process as a Limitation

Congress attempts to influence administrators through political pressure in the ways previously described.[113] Two of the most common methods are hearings at which decisionmakers are questioned about their intentions regarding future actions and direct contacts. The latter are part of the pluralistic bargaining process by which decisions are reached where members of Congress offer their support for the agency in return for favorable consideration of their requests.

The Constitution requires that agency actions that adversely affect a person's life, liberty, or property be made by due process of law.[114] Due process has been interpreted to require a neutral or nonbiased decisionmaker[115] and the prohibition of certain types of ex parte contacts.[116] In applying these concepts, some courts have expressed an unwarranted suspicion concerning the role of politics in administrative decisionmaking. In our system of government, legislative oversight is an essential feature of the democratic accountability of agency government, and attempts to wring politics out of the

---

110. Shapiro, supra note 109, at 34.

111. *See Sunset Review—Effective Oversight Tool or New Political Football,* 32 Ad.L.Rev. 209–24 (1980) (panel discussion).

112. *See generally* Administrative Conference of the United States, Legislative Veto of Agency Rules after *INS v. Chadha* (1983) (transcript of panel discussion).

113. *See supra* § 3.1.

114. U.S. Const. Amend. 5; *see generally infra* § 6.3 (discussion of when Due Process clause requires a hearing and of what type).

115. *See infra* § 9.2 (discussion of rules concerning bias and prejudice).

116. *See infra* § 9.3 (discussion of rules for ex parte contacts).

process can reduce the potential of oversight. At the same time, however, constitutional limitations such as due process must be respected. These must be defined, however, with sensitivity concerning the actual nature of the administrative process, and not some idealized version of how it could work.[117]

§ 3.6.1   Congress and formal adjudication

One of the two prominent cases that define the present constraints imposed by the Due Process clause that affects legislative oversight of agency adjudication is *FTC v. Cement Institute*.[118] The Institute, a trade association, contended that the FTC commissioners who decided that the association's members had violated the antitrust laws were " 'prejudiced and biased against the Portland cement industry generally,' and that the industry . . . could not receive a fair hearing from the Commission". The charge was based on the fact that before the FTC had begun its proceedings, the commissioners had concluded the type of pricing system used by the cement industry was an antitrust violation. That opinion had been expressed in congressional hearings and in reports that the FTC was required to make to Congress.

The Supreme Court responded that the FTC was under no stronger constitutional compulsion than federal judges and that the judges were free to sit in cases where they had previously expressed an opinion concerning whether certain types of conduct were prohibited by law. The Court noted that merely because the Commission had expressed such an opinion, it did not mean that "the minds of its members were irrevocably closed on the subject of the [Institute's] practices". The Court said that the Institute had an opportunity during the FTC hearing to convince the commissioners that its practices were legally permissible.

Professor Davis has noted that the Court's requirement that the Institute prove the commissioners had "irrevocably closed minds" established a burden of proof that no litigant is likely to be able to meet.[119] He nevertheless supported the result because the Court's standard applies to "legislative" facts. "Legislative" facts are general

---

117. *See* Pierce, *Political Control Versus Impermissible Bias In Agency Decisionmaking: Lessons from Chevron and Mistretta,* 57 U.Chi.L.Rev. 481 (1990); *see also Agency Diplomacy: Relations With Congress and the White House, and Ethics in the Administrative Process,* 4 Admin.L.Rev. 3, 27–31 (1990) (Comments of David M. Klaus).

118. 333 U.S. 683 (1948); *cf.* Ash Grove Cement Co. v. FTC, 577 F.2d 1368, 1377 (9th Cir.1978) (FTC Report on legality of industry practices).

119. 3 K. Davis, Administrative Law Treatise § 19.2 (2d ed. 1980).

facts that help a decisionmaker decide questions of law and policy. They are to be distinguished from "adjudicative" facts which are facts that help the decisionmaker establish what happened at a particular time and place.[120] The facts in *Cement Institute* were legislative because they involved a determination of whether a certain type of pricing scheme violated an antitrust statute and not whether a particular company was in violation because it had engaged in this type of conduct.

Professor Davis argued that while decisionmakers should be neutral and unbiased concerning adjudicative facts, the situation is different for legislative facts.[121] He noted that if the country is to have experienced and thoughtful decisionmakers, they will have thought about issues of law and policy that they are likely to apply in specific cases. In fact, judges and administrators are chosen precisely because they have developed certain biases about law and policy which are favored by the politicians who choose them for their positions. The standard adopted by *Cement Institute* therefore is appropriate because it recognizes these realities.

In the second prominent case, *Pillsbury Co. v. FTC*, the Fifth Circuit held that a congressional oversight committee had improperly interfered with the FTC's decisional processes while a case was pending before it.[122] The FTC had brought an antitrust complaint against Pillsbury and, before a decision had been reached in that action, four of the five FTC commissioners had appeared at a committee hearing. During the hearing, first the chairman and then the other members were met with a hostile "barrage" of questions and statements criticizing the FTC's position concerning a legal issue relevant to the pending case. The court declared the oversight effort was "an improper intrusion into the adjudicatory processes" of the commission and therefore a violation of procedural due process.

In both cases, the court considered whether congressional oversight concerning issues of statutory interpretation involving legislative facts was constitutional. But in *Pillsbury* the hearing occurred at a time when resolution of the statutory interpretation issue directly affected the chances of Pillsbury to have the case dismissed.[123] The

120. *See* Davis, *An Approach to Problems of Evidence*, 55 Harv.L.Rev. 364, 402–16 (1942) (definition and comparison of legislative and adjudicative facts).

121. K. Davis, *supra* note 119, at § 19.3.

122. 354 F.2d 952 (5th Cir.1966).

123. The committee challenged the Commission's position that a mere showing of a substantial increase in the share of a market after a merger did not trigger a per se rule that would have obviated any need for the FTC to prove the

importance of this difference was noted by the court. Once a hearing is started, "Congress is no longer intervening in the agency's legislative function, but rather in its judicial function". On that basis, the court concluded that the danger of unfairness to the litigant as a result of such "powerful external influences" outweighed the insignificant disadvantage to Congress of forbidding such contacts. This difference between an ongoing proceeding and contacts outside of that context offers a reasonable basis by which to distinguish the two cases.

The *Pillsbury* court might have rested its decision on the grounds suggested by Professor Davis because the contested issues of fact were at least arguably adjudicative rather than legislative and the hearings at a minimum constituted intense external pressure to resolve the facts against Pillsbury. Instead, the Court announced a broader principle: "[W]hen [a congressional] investigation focusses directly and substantially on the mental decisional processes of a Commission in a case which is pending before it, Congress is . . . intervening [impermissibly] in the agency's . . . judicial function."

A more satisfactory method by which to police such contacts is found in the relatively new ex parte contact rule of the APA. The APA forbids the receipt by adjudicatory decisionmakers of any ex parte communication "relevant to the merits of the proceeding".[124] Application of the rule obviates any necessity of judging the consequences of the contact on an administrator and offers significant protection to litigants from possible unfairness.[125]

The APA rule is modeled after the prohibition of ex parte contacts in nonadministrative trials. The prohibition was based on the fact that under the type of advocacy system used in adjudication, such contacts can be unfair to one or more parties. In adjudication, the judge makes a decision based only on the evidence and arguments presented during the trial. As a result, each party has the same opportunity to attempt to rebut unfavorable presentations. That right is denied once the judge accepts ex parte communications relevant to the lawsuit.[126]

Even though Congress added a strict ex parte prohibition for agency adjudication, the law concerning limitations on congressional

merger was competitively harmful. 354 F.2d at 956.

124. 5 U.S.C. § 557(d)(1).

125. *See* Koniag, Inc., Village of Uyak v. Andrus, 580 F.2d 601 (D.C.Cir.1978),

cert. denied, 439 U.S. 1052 (1978) (concerning ex parte contacts by legislators that did, and did not, go to the merits of the case).

126. *See infra* § 9.3.1.

oversight is still unclear. Congress exempted itself from the application of this prohibition, at least as it relates to the practice of congressional inquiries concerning the status of pending proceedings.[127] Moreover, contacts with administrators outside of the context of a pending matter will not result in disqualification because the contact would have to result in that person's mind being irrevocably closed concerning the legislative facts and law being discussed.

§ 3.6.2   Congress and informal agency action

Agencies are subject to some requirements of neutrality[128] and ex parte prohibitions[129] when they engage in decisionmaking processes other than adjudication.[130] The nature of these requirements is discussed in Chapter Nine.[131] None of the prominent cases involved congressional contacts, but the rules developed by those cases could apply to members of Congress.

D.C. Federation of Civic Associations v. Volpe addressed the issue of limitations on congressional oversight of informal decisionmaking outside of the requirements of neutrality and ex parte contacts.[132] Two members of a three-judge panel held that the Secretary of Transportation, John Volpe, had failed to establish that a bridge proposed for federal funding met the statutory criteria that Congress had established for approval of such funding. Secretary Volpe's decision was adjudicatory because he had to determine whether there was evidence that this particular project met the various statutory criteria, but it was also informal because he did not need to hold a hearing to make that determination.

In addition to holding that the Secretary had failed to establish that the statutory requirements had been met, the panel majority also addressed the propriety of political pressure that had been placed on the Secretary to decide that the bridge qualified for the funding.

---

127. 5 U.S.C. § 557(b)(2); *see* K. Davis, *supra* note 119, § 18.7 (questioning whether "status inquiries" are intended to affect the merits of pending cases).

128. *See* Association of National Advertisers, Inc. v. FTC, 627 F.2d 1151 (D.C.Cir.1979), cert. denied 447 U.S. 921 (1980).

129. *See* Home Box Office, Inc. v. FCC, 567 F.2d 9 (D.C.Cir.1977), cert. denied 434 U.S. 829 (1977); Action for Children's Television v. FCC, 564 F.2d 458 (D.C.Cir.1977).

130. There are two such processes: informal rulemaking pursuant to 5 U.S.C. § 553 and informal adjudication. The latter function occurs whenever a decisionmaker is required to reach conclusions about adjudicative facts, but is not required by the agency's enabling act to hold a hearing to do so. *See* 5 U.S.C. § 554(a).

131. *See infra* § 9.2 (neutrality and bias); § 9.3 (ex parte contacts).

132. 459 F.2d 1231 (D.C.Cir.1971).

That pressure included a threat by the Chairman of the House Committee for the Affairs of District of Columbia, Representative Natcher, that funding for the district's new subway would be withheld until the bridge was approved. Judge Bazelon, one of the two-judge majority, interpreted the findings of the district court to mean that Secretary Volpe was influenced in his decision to approve the bridge by this political pressure.[133] Judge Bazelon concluded that the "impact of this pressure is sufficient, standing alone, to invalidate the Secretary's action" even if the Secretary had established the statutory criteria had been met. Judge Fahey, the other majority judge, decided that no holding was required concerning the legal effects of the political pressure because the Secretary had not established that the statutory criteria were met.

Both Judges Bazelon and Fahey, however, agreed concerning the applicable legal standards. They concluded that since Secretary Volpe's decision was one of informal adjudication, because no hearing was required by statute, the ex parte prohibitions established for formal adjudication by the law at that time were not applicable. The political pressure, however, was still relevant. The court held that upon remand, the Secretary had to "make new determinations based strictly on the merits and without regard to any considerations not made relevant by Congress in the applicable statutes". The court pointed out that considerations such as the possible loss of funding for the subway were not the type of factors included within those statutes.[134]

Sierra Club v. Costle,[135] which affirmed an EPA regulation establishing emissions standards for coal burning power plants, warns that *D.C. Federation* must be understood in light of the nature of legislative oversight. An environmental group had challenged the rulemaking on the basis of congressional pressure because EPA officials had met with Senator Byrd who " 'strongly' " expressed his views. Judge Wald drew a two-part test from *D.C. Federation.* First, was there

---

133. The district court found that "[t]he statement issued by the Secretary at the time he directed the [bridge to be restored for funding] indicates that the pressure on the rapid transit funds was a consideration at that time" and that "[t]here is no question that the pressure regarding the rapid transit appropriations was given some consideration at the time of the approval of the project...." 316 F.Supp. 754, 764–66 (D.D.C.1970).

134. 459 F.2d at 1248; *but see* 459 F.2d at 1261 (MacKinnon, J. concurring in part and dissenting in part) (trade-off between subway and bridge permissible under Act); *accord* Mashaw, *The Legal Structure of Frustration: Alternative Strategies For Public Choice Concerning Federally Aided Highway Construction,* 122 U.Pa.L.Rev. 1, 47–49 (1973).

135. 657 F.2d 298 (D.C. Cir.1981).

pressure to force EPA to decide upon factors not made relevant by Congress in the applicable statute? Second, was the agency's determination affected by those extraneous considerations?[136]

The Court concluded there was no persuasive evidence that either criterion was satisfied. Judge Wald explained:

> Americans rightly expect their elected representatives to voice their grievances and preferences concerning the administration of our laws. We believe it entirely proper for Congressional representatives vigorously to represent the interests of their constituents before administrative agencies engaged in informal, general policy rulemaking, so long as individual Congressmen do not frustrate the intent of Congress as a whole as expressed in statute, nor undermine applicable rules of procedure. Where Congressmen keep their comments focused on the substance of the proposed rule, and we have no substantial evidence to cause us to believe Senator Byrd did not do so here, administrative agencies are expected to balance Congressional pressure with the pressures emanating from all other sources. To hold otherwise would deprive the agencies of legitimate sources of information and call into question the validity of nearly every controversial rulemaking.

§ 3.7   Article III and the Seventh Amendment as a Limitation

Just as the Supreme Court has accommodated the delegation of legislative power to administrative agencies, it has also permitted Congress to authorize agencies to assert judicial powers. Nevertheless, the Court has established some boundaries beyond which Congress cannot go concerning Article III and the Seventh Amendment.

Article III provides that the "judicial Power of the United States shall be vested in one Supreme Court and such inferior Courts as the Congress may from time to time ordain and establish."[137] Since the Constitution gives Article III judges certain protections, such as lifetime tenure, the Supreme Court must be wary that adjudication by a non-Article III tribunal will deny litigants the protections associated with having Article III judges. In 1855, however, the Court made an important distinction between the adjudication of private rights, which may come under the protection of Article III, and public

---

136. An agency, however, cannot act on legislative pressure concerning factors relevant under a statute without first making an independent determination of the validity of the argument raised by legislators. SEC v. Wheeling–Pittsburgh Steel Corp., 648 F.2d 118 (3d Cir.1981).

137. U.S. Const. Art. III, § 1.

rights, which do not. In *Murray's Lessee v. Hoboken Land and Improvement Company,*[138] the Court upheld an act that authorized federal marshals to seize and sell property that belonged to a customs agent who failed to turn over to the government all of the money that he had collected for it. The Court rejected a claim that Article III precluded a determination by the Treasury Department whether the agent owed the government money (which would justify the seizure and sale of his land) because this determination involved "public rights," or rights arising under a federal statute, instead of "private rights," or rights arising under the common law or equity. The Court explained that Article III does not apply to public rights because of the doctrine of sovereign immunity. Since the federal government may not be sued without its consent, a litigant is entitled to sue in the federal court concerning rights created by an act of Congress only if that or another law consents to such a suit.

In *Crowell v. Benson,*[139] which overturned a lower court decision upholding an award of workers compensation benefits by the United States Employees' Compensation Commission, the Court added an important qualification to the previous case. Under the federal Longshoreman's and Harbor Workers' Compensation Act, the Commission was authorized to adjudicate whether an employer was required to pay compensation to an injured worker. In rejecting an argument that the Commission's adjudication violated Article III, the Court characterized the right at issue as being a "private right" because it concerned whether one private party owed another compensation. Nevertheless, the Court concluded that agencies can adjudicate private rights in the first instance so long as Article III courts retain sufficient review authority. Article III permits this arrangement because juries, masters, and commissioners had historically been assigned the function of fact-finders in lawsuits between private parties subject to appellate review by Article III judges.[140]

The framework established by these two cases—that non-Article III tribunals could adjudicate public rights without restriction and could adjudicate private rights if there were sufficient judicial review—stood undisturbed for nearly fifty years. In the 1980s, however, the Court revisited this area. In *Commodity Futures Trading*

---

138. 59 U.S. (18 How.) 272 (1855).

139. 285 U.S. 22 (1932).

140. The Court, however, said that there were two exceptions to its holding that an agency could adjudicate private rights. One exception provided that there would be *de novo* federal court review of "jurisdictional facts," but today this exception is moribund. The second exception, which was for "constitutional facts," is still valid today. *See infra* § 5.2.2.

Comm'n v. Schor,[141] a disgruntled customer sought damages from a professional commodities broker. The Commission was authorized to order the broker to pay such damages if a violation of CFTC regulations had occurred. The customer challenged on Article III grounds a CFTC rule that authorized the agency to adjudicate any common-law counterclaims the broker might have against the customer arising out of the same transactions about which the customer complained. Justice O'Conner applied a three-part test to determine the constitutionality of the Commission's jurisdiction over the common-law counterclaims. First, the Court inquired whether the essential attributes of judicial power had been vested in the agency. It examined the breadth of the agency's jurisdiction, the scope of judicial review, and whether the agency exercised incidental powers such as the subpoena power, contempt power, and the power to enforce its own orders. Justice O'Conner found the CFTC's jurisdiction concerned only a " 'particularized area of law,' " the merits of the Commission's decision were subject to judicial review, and the Commission's jurisdiction did not include excessive incidental powers. Second, the Court examined the nature and origin of the rights at issue. Although the rights arose from common-law, the Court decided that fact was not dispositive. Finally, the Court evaluated the concerns that drove Congress to vest jurisdiction in a non-Article III tribunal. The Court noted that Congress gave the CFTC the authority to resolve the counterclaims because it was more efficient than litigating them separately and because the Commission had expertise concerning the validity of the claims. Balancing these results, the Court held that the incursion on the judicial branch was "*di minimus.*"

Schor is a clear departure from *Crowell* since it rejects the public/private right distinction as an absolute basis for resolving Article III claims. For the same reason, it is a clear departure from *Northern Pipeline Construction Co. v. Marathon Pipe Line Co.*,[142] decided only four years earlier, which relied on the public/private right distinction to strike down the Bankruptcy Act of 1978. Instead, the Court relies on a "core function" test which asks whether agency adjudication supplants the essential or core functions of Article III adjudication. As compared to the approach in *Crowell*, the core function test is more lenient concerning the scope of agency adjudication of private rights since agency adjudication is not necessarily limited to initial fact-finding.

141.　478 U.S. 833 (1986).　　　　　**142.**　458 U.S. 50 (1982).

The impact that *Schor* has on agency adjudication of private rights was affected by *Granfinanciera, S.A. v. Nordberg*,[143] which involved a Seventh Amendment challenge. In *Granfinanciera,* a bankruptcy trustee alleged that a person had fraudulently acquired assets that previously had belonged to a bankrupt estate. The case was brought in bankruptcy court where the defendant was not entitled to a jury trial. The defendant argued that because private rights were involved, the Seventh Amendment applied. The Seventh Amendment provides that "In suits at common law, where the value in controversy shall exceed twenty dollars, the right of trial by jury shall be preserved."[144]

The Court first analyzed whether the defendant's claim concerned a public or private right. There is no right to a jury trial if the government is a party to a lawsuit because the Seventh Amendment refers to "suits at common law." Since a private right was involved, the Court next analyzed whether the proceeding was "equitable" or "legal" in nature. There is no right to a jury trial if a proceeding is "equitable" in nature because at the time the Seventh Amendment was adopted, proceedings in equity were tried before a chancellor in equity, who sat without a jury. The Court concluded this was a "legal" matter because historical evidence indicated this type of proceeding was treated as "legal" in the eighteenth century, and because an order to pay money is a legal, rather than an equitable, remedy.

Turning to defendant's Article III contention, the Court interpreted an earlier case, *Thomas v. Union Carbide Agricultural Protects Co.*,[145] as holding that the government did not have to be a party for a case to involve "public rights." Instead, the "crucial question in cases not involving the Federal Government is, whether 'Congress acting for a valid legislative purpose pursuant to its constitutional powers under Article I, [has] create[d] a seemingly "private" right that is so closely integrated into a public regulatory scheme as to be a matter appropriate for agency resolution with limited involvement by the Article III judiciary.' " Under this test, the Court determined that a bankruptcy trustee's right to recover a fraudulent conveyance was "more accurately characterized" as a private right because such suits

---

143.   492 U.S. 33 (1989).

144.   U.S. Const. Amend. 7.

145.   473 U.S. 568 (1985). *Thomas* upheld a law that permitted a pesticide manufacturer to obtain a license from the Environmental Protection Agency to sell a product based on scientific data submitted by another company. The statute provided for compulsory arbitration if the two parties could not agree on the amount of the compensation that the firm who used the information would pay to the firm who created it.

resemble state law contract claims. The bankruptcy court's adjudication of the matter was therefore unconstitutional.

Granfinanciera appears to limit the impact of *Schor*. In *Schor,* the Court held that an agency could adjudicate "private rights" as long as the adjudication did not invade a core function of the judiciary. Thus, in *Schor,* as in *Granfinanciera,* a non-Article III tribunal was asked to adjudicate a common law right of action. According to *Granfinanciera,* however, the Seventh Amendment prohibits delegating private rights to tribunals sitting without the aid of a jury. In a footnote, the majority appears to distinguish *Schor* on the ground that because the disgruntled consumer elected to pursue a remedy from the CFTC, rather than a district court, the person waived the right to have any counterclaims by the broker determined by an Article III judge. This suggests, however, that if a litigant does not make such a waiver, a jury trial would be required. If so, *Granfinanciera* would constitute an important limitation on the scope of *Schor*. If the Seventh Amendment requires a jury trial in any case where a public right is not involved, the *Schor* balancing test will not uphold any cases that a straight public/private law test will not also uphold. Thus, the Court appears in effect to have returned to the public/private rights distinction that it appeared to have abandoned in *Schor*.

Granfinanciera may be explained by the fact that the Court, when it decided *Schor,* did not anticipate the impact of the Seventh Amendment on Congress' authority to delegate to an agency the adjudication of a private right. Having considered the impact of the Seventh Amendment, the Court's apparent approach has merit. The Court should preserve a litigant's right to a jury trial unless it is waived. Moreover, even if it is waived, Congress may not delegate to an agency the adjudication of a private right based merely on such a waiver. As Justice O'Connor notes in *Schor,* a litigant cannot waive the structural interests that Article III protects. Thus, even in the presence of such a waiver, the Court must determine if agency adjudication of a private right invades a core function of the judiciary.

Chapter Four

EXECUTIVE CONTROL OF ADMINISTRATIVE DISCRETION

§ 4.1 The Need for Executive Control

Executive control over administrative agencies is indispensable if government is to be run efficiently and effectively. The President is in a unique position to manage the bureaucracy and to see the whole picture. In 1979, the ABA Commission on Law and the Economy concluded that the President had the constitutional power and duty to supervise executive branch policy-making and the Commission therefore urged Congress to increase and confirm presidential authority in this respect by statute.[1] James MacGregor Burns has described as "a crisis of the American Presidency" the failure of that office effectively to perform its leadership role.[2] As agencies grow in size, number, and complexity of mission, the necessity for executive branch coordination and implementation becomes a central tenet of bureaucratic management. Today, most would agree with the proposition that presidential administration can make agency government accountable.[3]

But it was not always this way. In 1937, for example, the President's Committee on Administrative Management, headed by Louis Brownlow, emphasized the need for presidential coordination of administrative agencies. The Committee saw agency decisionmaking as a "headless 'fourth branch' of the government containing a haphazard deposit of irresponsible agencies and uncoordinated powers".[4] References to the headless fourth branch highlight the problem of policy coordination and control.[5] Since 1937, there have been

1. ABA Comm. on Law and the Economy, Federal Regulation: Roads to Reform 78–80 (1979).

2. J.M. Burns, The Power to Lead—The Crisis of the American Presidency (1984).

3. *See* E. Kagan, Presidential Administration, 114 Harv. L. Rev. 2245, 2331 (2001).

4. Report of the Committee with Studies of Administrative Management in the Federal Government 39–43 (1937).

5. *See* Process Gas Consumers Group v. Consumer Energy Council, 463 U.S. 1216, 1219 (White, J. dissenting).

numerous proposals to increase executive control,[6] but the goal of efficient and effective management of agency government is still elusive.

One reason for lack of success of executive management is that, while many recognize the need for presidential control of government, they fear executive hegemony and the concomitant abrogation of the role of Congress. But even with the oversight powers discussed in Chapter Three, Congress is simply not in a position on a day-to-day basis to achieve the level of agency policy control that the President can. Only the executive branch is institutionally capable of employing, directing, and disciplining the officials whose responsibility it is to carry out the missions of agencies and departments.

Thus, today, executive control of the bureaucracy has become a bipartisan issue. Whether the motives of a given President are pro- or anti-regulation, there can be no progress without coordination and control. Nevertheless, presidential management presents its own accountability problems. First, the President must inevitably rely on staff members to perform this oversight function. As Glen Robinson has observed, "one should not suppose that, individually or collectively, these [staffers] are simply representatives of the president. In fact, these executive interveners are themselves part of the administrative bureaucracy and, as such, present the same type of monitoring and control problems . . . as the agencies they seek to influence."[7] Second, "elected officials who supervise administrative agents must themselves be accountable to the public. Unless this condition is met, one agency problem—voters' lack of control over elected officials—replaces another—the elected official's lack of control over bureaucrats."[8]

This Chapter explores the institutional and legal mechanisms that facilitate or inhibit the constitutional responsibility of the President to manage the bureaucracy and oversee the exercise of administrative discretion. Chapter Nine considers the procedural instruments used to promote the transparency of government to the voters, including the political accountability of White House policy oversight.

6. *See, e.g.,* E. Redford, The President and the Regulatory Commissions (1960).

7. G. Robinson, American Bureaucracy: Public Choice & Public Law 102 (1991).

8. Shapiro, *Political Oversight and the Deterioration of Regulatory Policy,* 46 Admin. L. Rev. 1, 20 (1994).

§ 4.2   The Constitutional Basis for Executive Control

In the scheme of separated and countervailing powers established in the Constitution, the Executive branch is given explicit powers in Article II to control and manage government. In the first place, Article II itself vests the Executive power in a President of the United States of America.[9] This power to execute the laws is, at its core, the power to carry out the congressional plan for the administrative state. By exclusively vesting this power in a single executive, the Constitution of necessity must have contemplated an individual with strong powers to exercise it.[10]

Beyond this over-arching grant of executive power, Article II makes reference to three specific implementing powers. The President is granted the power to appoint "Officers of the United States" with the advice and consent of the Senate.[11] The Appointments Clause of Article II requires "principal" officers to be appointed by the President with senatorial concurrence, but permits "inferior" officers to be appointed by the President or agency heads alone. Both categories of officers would be policy-makers in any administration.[12] This power provides the executive branch with the ability to place in subordinate roles those individuals designated to carry out policy and direct agency staff. In order to help ensure implementation, the President has the power to "require the Opinion, in writing, of the Principal Officer in each of the executive Departments".[13] Finally, and more broadly, the President is told that "he shall take care that the laws be faithfully executed".[14]

The importance of the "take care" clause can hardly be overstated. The President is told to oversee subordinates in the faithful execution of the laws. It imposes on the President a duty of supervision, but it also grants to the President by implication the power to delegate his authority to subordinates.[15] It is from this clause, and

---

9.   U.S. Const. Art. II, § 1, cl. 1. Professor Corwin has questioned whether the executive power mentioned at the outset of Article II was meant to be a grant of power as opposed to a designation of office. *See* E. Corwin, The President—Office and Powers 4–5 (4th ed. 1957). But the implications of that power, even narrowly read, would appear to contemplate control of the executive branch.

10.   The idea of a "plural executive," or a President acting with a council of state, was considered and rejected by the constitutional convention. *See* A. Schlesinger, The Imperial Presidency 382–86 (1973).

11.   U.S. Const. Art. II, § 2, cl. 2.

12.   *See infra* § 4.5 (discussion of distinction between "principal" and "inferior" officers).

13.   U.S. Const. Art. II, § 2, cl. 1.

14.   U.S. Const. Art. II, § 3.

15.   *See* Williams v. United States, 42 U.S. (1 How.) 290, 297 (1843) ("It is impossible for the President to Execute

the appointments clause, that the President's power to remove executive officials who fail in their duties derives its constitutional status.[16]

§ 4.3 Methods of Executive Control

The President's methods of control over administrative agencies are a function of the office and the one who holds it. There is no substitute for good political instincts and an ability to communicate. These qualities had much to do with the success of Franklin Roosevelt's and Ronald Reagan's administrations in controlling the bureaucracy and with the failure of their immediate predecessors to do so as effectively. While a President exercises control of agency discretion through apt political management, he does not do so alone. Effective management involves not just the President, but the Office of the President, where members of the White House staff are assigned the primary tasks of policy-making and control. The methods and techniques of agency oversight are a reflection of White House staff practices, attitudes, and experience. If the President has put together an effective management team, the chances to supervise agency decisionmaking in purposeful ways are greatly enhanced.

In the area of domestic policy, the staff must deal astutely with both Congress and the agencies. Matters of appointment, reorganization, budgeting, and policy-making are legislative, as well as administrative, concerns. The White House must understand and capitalize upon existing alliances and tensions between Congress and the agencies in order to make the bureaucracy respond to executive priorities. The following are some of the most obvious methods of control.

§ 4.3.1 The appointment process

William Howard Taft recognized long ago that "one of the functions which in a practical way gives the President more personal influence than any other is that of appointments."[17] The top policy-making members of administrative agencies must be appointed by the President, with the advice and consent of the Senate, or, with the approval of Congress, by the President or heads of Departments alone. This power to place in government those individuals who share

every duty, and every detail thereof, imposed upon him by Congress.") Congress recognized the practical necessity of this proposition in the Presidential Subdelegation Act of 1951, 3 U.S.C. § 301, which permitted the delegation of more than 400 duties then imposed directly upon President Truman. Since then it has been used by many presidents to delegate by executive order hundreds of more duties.

16. *See infra* § 4.4.2 (discussion of the scope and limits of the President's removal power in the context of independent agencies).

17. W.H. Taft, The President and His Powers 55 (1916).

the President's political views is at the heart of policy control in American government. The appointment power was given a strong endorsement in *Buckley v. Valeo*[18] when the Supreme Court rebuffed congressional attempts by statute to arrogate to itself the appointment of several members of the Federal Election Commission. The power to appoint, coupled with the power to remove, gives the President his most direct contact with the bureaucracy and links the White House to an agency's permanent staff.

The quality of agency appointments is obviously central to the effectiveness of administrative oversight, as Dean Landis advised President Kennedy in 1960.[19] Since then, there have been notable appointments like John Gardner to HEW by President Kennedy, Lee White to FPC by President Johnson, Miles Kirkpatrick to the FTC by President Nixon, Alfred Kahn to the CAB by President Carter, Mark Fowler to the FCC by President Reagan, William Reilly at the EPA by President George Bush, Robert Pitofsky to the FTC by President Clinton and Timothy Muris of the FTC by President George W. Bush. These officials have helped to implement their administrations' goals in exceptional fashion. That many of these appointments were to agencies denominated "independent" confirms that, despite an agency's alleged politically insulated character, a President's control over it is nonetheless substantial. The power to designate chairs of collegial independent agencies, even where members are serving fixed terms, is therefore a crucial aspect of the appointment process.[20]

In spite of the success that Presidents have had in controlling agencies through the appointment of good administrators, many have complained that most appointments to agencies have lacked distinction.[21] There are several explanations for this reaction. To some extent, the appointment process may negatively affect quality when selections are made on a basis other than merit and ability. But the problem may be more subtle than that. The evaluation of the quality of appointments is often done in terms of whether the administration

18.   424 U.S. 1 (1976).

19.   "The prime key to the improvement of the administrative process is the selection of qualified personnel." J. Landis, Report on the Regulatory Agencies to the President–Elect 66 (1960). *See* T. McGraw, Prophets of Regulation (1984).

20.   Chairs of independent agencies, except the Federal Reserve Board, can be designated from among its members by the President. The power of chairs to control the staff and policies of independent agencies is considerable and it has increased with the effect of the Sunshine Act on formal commissions meetings. *See* D. Welborn, Governance of Federal Regulatory Agencies 132–37 (1977). *See supra* § 9.4.

21.   Senate Comm. on Gov't. Affairs, Vol. I—The Regulatory Appointments Process, S.Doc. No. 95–25, 95th Cong., 1st Sess. 1 (1977) (appointments over the years have produced a "mixed record").

involved has furthered the goals of the agency as prescribed by Congress. A presidential appointment given low marks on this scale would not necessarily receive the same grade from the White House that appointed that person. A deregulatory administration may applaud an administrator, such as Alfred Kahn of the now defunct Civil Aeronautics Board (Carter appointee) or Michael Powell of the FCC (a Bush appointee), who may frustrate congressional committees by inhibiting an agency's ability to regulate. An activist administration may prefer an administrator who pushes his agency to its statutory limits (and beyond), even though its regulated constituency, and perhaps the courts, are at odds with the results. One thinks of Dr. David Kessler of President Clinton's Food and Drug Administration (FDA) in this regard.[22] Thus, the true worth of the administrators involved may be difficult to measure, since success is often in the eye of the beholder. But whatever the regulatory goals of an administration, good appointments remain the *sine qua non* of bureaucratic success or failure. Since all presidents want to be recognized as strong leaders, their appointment of administrators who are themselves capable of giving as well as receiving directives and orders helps assure this recognition.

§ 4.3.2   The reorganization process

The power to appoint policy-making members of administrative agencies is related to the power to reorganize the institutions of which they are a part. Bureaucratic structures are themselves shapers of attitudes and repositories of uncheckable discretion.[23] Reorganization puts new forces to work and signals the assertion of management control. A Senate study of federal regulation emphasized: "For an incoming administration, there are immediate and important benefits to be gained from reorganization: Changing structures and replacing key personnel is an opportunity for the President to assure the bureaucracy will be responsive to the needs and philosophies of his Administration."[24]

But the power to reorganize is not an inherently executive one; it is delegated to the President by Congress, often in a hedged fashion. History records only one instance in which the President received

---

22. Dr. Kessler convinced President Clinton to regulate tobacco, thereby setting in motion state settlements that changed the industry's accountability for injury to the public, even though the FDA's regulatory program was eventually set aside. *See* FDA v. Brown & Williamson, Tobacco Corp., 529 U.S. 120 (2000) (holding tobacco regulation exceeded FDA's jurisdiction).

23. *See* A. Downs, Inside Bureaucracy 158–67 (1967); *see also supra* § 1.9.

24. Senate Study, *supra* note 21, at 190.

reorganization authority without having to lobby hard for it; that occurred in March 1933 on the eve of Franklin Roosevelt's first term.[25] Thereafter, even FDR had to press Congress for renewal of reorganization authority, which was not always forthcoming.[26] For years, Congress has viewed the power as temporary and emergency in nature and has granted it reluctantly.

Congress did not establish a more comprehensive basis for reorganization until the Truman Presidency. The Reorganization Act of 1949[27] mandated that the President periodically examine agency structures and suggest changes in light of the following factors:

(1) promoting better execution of the laws and more effective management of the Executive branch;

(2) reducing expenditures and increasing efficiency and economy;

(3) consolidating and coordinating agencies and functions according to major purposes;

(4) reducing the number of agencies, and abolishing those which are unnecessary; and

(5) eliminating overlap and duplication between the agencies.

Authority under the Act expired in 1973. It was renewed in 1977 at the behest of President Carter and expired four years later.[28]

Since 1981 there has been no reorganization authority in place and Congress in the future may be unwilling to establish a statutory authority similar to past grants.[29] This is because Congress has always been reluctant to grant such authority without a legislative veto attached. In the aftermath of *INS v. Chadha*,[30] this may no longer be a feasible alternative.

---

25. The 1933 reorganization authority was to lapse in two years. Pub. L. 428, 47 Stat. 1489, 1517 (1933). *See* B. Karl, *Executive Reorganization and Presidential Power,* 1977 Sup. Ct. Rev. 1, 3.

26. President Roosevelt was denied the power to reorganize by Congress in 1937 after one of the great electoral landslides in history. It wasn't until 1939, with war on the horizon, that Congress granted him further reorganization authority. B. Karl, *supra* note 25, at 4–5. For a thorough historical analysis, see B. Karl, Executive Reorganization and Reform in the New Deal (1963).

27. Pub. L. 109, 81st Cong., 1st Sess., § 2(a) (1949).

28. 5 U.S.C. §§ 901, 905. The act was originally for 3 years, but was amended in 1980 to extend until 1981.

29. Even the recent creation of the Homeland Security Agency was done by extensive legislative action, not by a grant of reorganization authority to President Bush.

30. 462 U.S. 919 (1983).

This difficulty is one of the consequences of the *Chadha* decision that might not be apparent on first reading. *Chadha,* by broadly striking down all legislative vetoes, including those in reorganization acts, eliminated an executive accountability technique that posed few of the objections that led the Court to reject the legislative veto.[31] Justice White in his *Chadha* dissent, emphasized that "Reorganization Acts established the chief model for the legislative veto."[32] Since reorganization acts have long been sought by presidents who specifically attached the veto to their requests,[33] it produced a balanced political accommodation between the policy-making branches. The absence of a veto will make Congress less willing to grant the executive the desired power to reorganize. If it does not do so, the political controls upon agency operations will be reduced accordingly.

The President can still carry out internal reorganizations of agencies even without a reorganization act[34] and utilize the budget to affect organizational change. But the ability to shift major responsibilities from one agency to another will be hamstrung by the lack of a broader power to reorganize agencies themselves.

§ 4.3.3   The budgetary process

While Congress holds the purse strings, the President's responsibility to present the budget provides a substantial opportunity to engage in administrative agency oversight. All but a few administrative agencies must have their budgets approved by the President's policy-coordinating agent, the Office of Management and Budget (OMB).[35] The process of budget approval offers an excellent setting

---

31. *See* Strauss, *Was There a Baby in the Bathwater? A Comment in the Supreme Court's Legislative Veto Decision,* 1983 Duke L.J. 789, 806. Strauss suggests that reorganization acts are the product of legitimate "horse trading" between the President and Congress; he concludes that since they apply directly to the President, they "rarely appear in a form likely to attract or, more importantly, to justify judicial review". This last observation hints at the possibility that a renewed Reorganization Act, containing a legislative veto, might not even reach the courts to be challenged.

32. 462 U.S. at 968. *See also supra* § 3.5.

33. *Id.* Justice White notes that of the 115 reorganization plans submitted

to Congress over the years, 23 have been vetoed.

34. *See* Senate Study, *supra* note 21.

35. The Budget and Accounting Act of 1921, 31 U.S.C. § 1 granted the President the power to submit an annual budget for executive agencies to Congress; in 1939 the Act was amended to include independent commissions and boards within this authority. *Id.* at § 2. In 1970, the Bureau of the Budget, which had previously managed this assignment for the President, became the OMB. Reorganization Plan No. 2 of 1970, 84 Stat. 2085. Both the Consumer Product Safety Commission and the Commodities Futures Trading Commission, however, were granted the power to send their budget and legislative requests directly to Congress.

from the White House's perspective to review agency performance and establish program priorities. It is a time when, to understate the matter, OMB has the agencies' full attention. Since the enforcement of statutory responsibilities is tied to funding, the budget process gives the OMB a chance to emphasize priorities of the President that may or may not be instinctively shared by the agencies.

The budget process has an important impact on regulatory agencies since the Reagan Administration. The Reagan Administration utilized its control over the budget of regulatory agencies as part of an overall strategy to deregulate the economy and reduce the deficit. The Reagan OMB was successful in decreasing the rate of expenditures and reducing the number of regulatory personnel. The regulatory budget, however, turned upward once again during the Bush Presidency. During the Clinton Administration, regulatory agencies have been impacted by efforts to eliminate the federal budget deficit. The lack of budget increases (and in some cases budget decreases) have hampered the capacity of agencies to carry out their responsibilities in a timely manner.[36] The momentary occurrence of a federal budget surplus offered an opportunity to rectify this situation, but other pressing needs (particularly shoring up Social Security) and a general hostility toward government (and regulation) in many political quarters continues to constrict agency activities.

Another aspect of budgetary control is OMB's clearance function for agency proposals for legislation. Since legislative requests have budgetary implications, OMB can often reshape or kill legislative proposals by agencies that contradict presidential goals. Independent agencies may not be bound by this clearance process, but since almost all agencies are required to submit their budgets to OMB, the tendency is for them to submit their legislative requests as well, whether or not the President has final authority over their disposition.[37]

OMB plays additional (but nonbudgetary) roles concerning regulation which you will read about in Chapter Nine.[38] The Office of Regulatory Affairs (OIRA), a division of OMB, has been in charge of the efforts of every administration since President Reagan to oversee the agency rulemaking process. In addition, OIRA administers the

36. *See* Shapiro, *Substantive Reform, Judicial Review, and Agency Resources: OSHA As An Case Study*, 49 Ad. L. Rev. 645 (1997); Pierce, *Judicial Review in an Age of Diminished Resources*, 49 Ad. L. Rev. 61 (1996).

37. *See* L. Fisher, Presidential Spending Power 150–51 (1975).

38. *See infra* § 9.5 (discussing regulatory oversight).

Paperwork Reduction Act which is intended to reduce the paperwork burden on private industry. Agencies that seek to require private entities to provide information to the government or the public must first obtain OIRA's approval.

The powers of the President over the budgetary process provide numerous opportunities to exercise control by restraining the spending powers of agencies. Nevertheless, there have been several important efforts to enhance the President's role and authority. The President's power to impound funds appropriated by Congress, which provoked a lively political debate in the Nixon years, has since been controlled by legislation.[39] The huge budget deficit produced during the Reagan Administration (an increase to about $3.5 trillion (in 1992) from $1 trillion (in 1980)) produced two reactions involving the President's budget powers. First, Congress attempted to appoint the Comptroller General of the United States to monitor Congress' compliance with spending limitations it enacted and to eliminate spending that exceeded these limitations. In *Bowsher v. Synar*[40] the Supreme Court declared this effort to be unconstitutional because the Comptroller General could only be removed by Congress, yet he engaged in an executive function. This violated Article II, which vests in the President the power to execute the laws, because, the Court reasoned, Congress might utilize its power over the Comptroller General to influence how he implemented the budget act.

Second, the Congress passed legislation that empowered the President to exercise a "line-item" veto, but the Supreme Court also declared this initiative unconstitutional in *Clinton v. New York*.[41] Congress borrowed this idea from the states, many of whom provide their executive with line-item veto power, although there is no clear evidence that line-item vetoes by themselves actually reduce the level of state spending.[42] Under this authority, the President was authorized to cancel specific spending items or tax benefits passed by Congress. The idea was that the President, who has a national constituency, would be less susceptible than members of Congress to the impulse to create spending or tax benefits for specific constitu-

39. The Congressional Budget and Impoundment Control Act of 1974, 31 U.S.C. § 1301, requires congressional approval before the President can terminate programs or cut total spending.

40. 478 U.S. 714 (1986).

41. 524 U.S. 417 (1998).

42. Compare Devins, *Budget Reform and the Balance of Powers*, 31 W & M

L.Rev. 993 (1990) (finding little evidence that the states' line-item vetoes affect spending levels) with Crain & Miller, *Budget Process and Spending Growth*, 31 W & M L.Rev. 1021 (1990) (using regression analysis to uncover some connections between the item reduction veto and spending growth).

ents. After President Clinton exercised his power, by canceling one spending and one tax provision, the Court observed that his actions in "both legal and practical effect ... amended two Acts of Congress by repealing a portion of each" and that "[t]here is no provision in the Constitution that authorizes the President to enact, to amend, or to repeal statutes." Moreover, the President's actions were not authorized by his veto authority under the Constitution (i.e., Article I, § 7) because "the constitutional return occurs *after* the bill becomes law", and because the "constitutional return is of the entire bill" while the "statutory cancellation is of only a part."

The *Clinton v. New York* majority also rejected the government's argument that no legislative "amendment" occurred because the President was executing the line-item veto law. When Congress passed the line-item veto law, it provided that if the President made certain factual determinations, specified in the law, he was authorized to veto a spending or tax provision, and the money saved was to be used to reduce the deficit. This redirection, which was called the lock-box provision, meant that the President, acting on delegated authority, could prevent the budget and tax authorizations from having legal force or effect. However, because the money was redirected to deficit reduction according to the prior legislation, the President's actions had been authorized by law. The majority replied that since the impact of the President's veto, from the perspective of the persons who were to receive the spending and tax benefits, was to eliminate the benefits, the cancellation "was the functional equivalent of a partial repeal.... " The majority admitted the Court had many times approved delegations to the President to prevent some legislative provision from having legal effect, including the authority not to spend appropriated funds. The majority felt, however, that in none of these prior cases had Congress given the President "the unilateral power to change the text of a duly enacted statute."

As the logic of the dissenting opinions by Justices Breyer and Scalia in *Clinton v. New York* make clear, the Court's approach was exceedingly formalistic. Because the authorization for the President to redirect funds was in a different law than the spending and tax provision that the President vetoed, the majority insisted that he was rewriting the latter act. But this, as Justice Breyer explains, ignores the literal reality of what is going on:

> ... [I]t seems fair to say that, despite the Act's use of the word "cancel," the Act does not delegate to the President the power truly to *cancel* a line item expenditure (returning the legal status quo to one in which the item had never been enacted). Rather, it

delegates to the President the power to decide *how* to spend the money to which the line item refers—either for the specific purpose mentioned by the item, or for general deficit reduction via the "lockbox" feature.

These features of the law ... mean that it is not, and is not just like, the repeal or amendment of a law, or, for that matter, a true line item veto (despite the Act's title). Because one cannot say that the President's exercise of the power the Act grants is, literally speaking, a "repeal" or "amendment," the fact that the Act's procedures differ from the Constitution's exclusive procedures for enacting (or repealing) legislation is beside the point. The Act *itself* was enacted in accordance with these procedures, and its failure to require the President to satisfy those procedures does not make the Act unconstitutional.

For the dissenters, the relevant issue was whether Congress' empowerment of the President to exercise a line-item veto violated the nondelegation doctrine or other constitutional prohibitions, such as separation of powers, and they found that the legislation easily satisfied the Court's precedents in these areas.

The budget deficit also produced proposals to amend the Constitution to require the federal government to have a balanced budget, although this talk died out once the federal government achieved a budget surplus in the last years of the Clinton Administration. There is little talk of that kind of response to the Bush Administration's budget deficits today, perhaps because the task seems insurmountable. There is some evidence that such restrictions have worked to control spending (on a smaller scale) at the state level.[43] Ultimately, as the elimination of the budget deficit illustrates, control of spending requires the President and Congress to make the necessary hard choices to prevent deficit spending. In particular, it requires levying sufficient taxes to pay for the amount of government that is in place, or to reduce government to a size that current taxes will support. The failure of the President and Congress to do either during the Reagan Administration produced huge deficits and the resort to the extra-constitutional techniques described earlier.

---

43. Many states have constitutionally mandated balanced budget requirements. Recent research has demonstrated that the rate of budget growth is reduced in those states when combined with other legislative spending restraints such as the item reduction veto. *See* Crain & Miller, Budget Process and Spending Growth, *supra* note 42, at 1042–45 (documentating balanced budget amendments in 31 states).

§ 4.3.4   The policy-making process

No area of interaction with administrative agencies in recent years has been more lively than that of White House policy control. Since the early 1970s, the complexity of missions assigned individual agencies, and their sheer number, have required policy coordination by the executive. The White House recognized that although national goals such as a clean environment, low inflation, high employment and energy self-sufficiency were all placed in the hands of administrative agencies, they could not be achieved by agencies acting in isolation.

Executive Order 12,866 is the current version of a succession of executive branch efforts to require that agency rules undergo cost-benefit analysis supervised by OMB officials. The actual practice and implementation of the regulatory analysis process is reserved for later discussion.[44] What bears mention here is the idea that the White House can and should gain control of agency policy. For many years, it was thought that the agencies themselves should be responsible for the development of policy through rulemaking, and fears were expressed that White House intervention in that process would only reduce the incentives for agencies to act responsibly.[45] For example, a minority of the members of the ABA Commission on Law and the Economy thought that presidential policy controls were not a good idea even if Congress specifically approved them.[46]

The results of this assertion of policy control by the White House has been a demonstrable reduction in the numbers of regulations and, although this contention is controversial, an improvement in the quality of regulatory process. Knowing that they are subject to White House oversight, regulatory agencies have become more careful in their own assessments of the policy merits of proposed actions. Critics, however, contend that the White House itself is prone to making policy more to serve the President's partisan political preferences than to ensure appropriately balanced policy positions, and

---

44.   *See infra* § 9.5.

45.   *See* H. Friendly, The Federal Administrative Agencies; The Need for Better Definition of Standards 152–54 (1962).

46.   *See* ABA Commission on Law and the Economy, *supra* note 1, at 157 (remarks of William T. Coleman, Jr.). Judge Friendly, who had earlier doubted the advisability of executive control, modified his views as a member of the ABA Commission and concluded that "[s]omeone in Government, and in the short run that someone can only be the President, must have the power to make the agencies work together rather than push their own special concerns to the point that the country becomes ungovernable". *Id.* at 163.

that, despite more transparency, White House oversight is still insufficiently accountable to the public.[47]

The trend seems clearly in the direction of more White House control of agency policy, with or without congressional authorization.[48] Policy coordination and control could be increased by combining the budgetary and policy control functions of OMB. The idea of a "regulatory budget," designed to identify the total costs that agency regulations impose upon the public, is one method of merging the policy and budgetary functions of OMB. But the feasibility of such a plan has to be questioned. The complexity of the calculations involved would dwarf in magnitude (and in "softness") those calculations currently relied upon to establish justifications based upon cost-benefit analysis.[49] Thus, at the present time, regulatory policy control is a technique of executive management which has not fully exhausted its potential, but it may be on the verge of doing so.

§ 4.4   The Independent Agency Complication

The extent of the President's authority to appoint and to remove administrators has posed two issues for the Supreme Court. First, although the Constitution expressly mentions the President's power to appoint, it is silent on his authority to remove administrators. The power to appoint an administrator would seem to include a concomitant power to remove the same person, but the Supreme Court has made the matter more complicated. This "independent agency complication" is discussed below. Second, the Constitution requires that the President appoint "principal" officers of the United States, but it permits others to appoint "inferior" officials. As late as 1997, the Supreme Court was attempting to define how to distinguish a "principal" officer from an "inferior" one. This and other issues regarding the appointment of inferior officials is discussed in the following section.

Executive control of administrative discretion would be a far simpler proposition if the independent agency had not been launched with the establishment of the Interstate Commerce Commission in 1887. The notion of agency independence, born initially to insulate agency adjudication from improper influence, has over the years

47. For a discussion of White House oversight, regulatory analysis, and political accountability, *see infra* § 9.5.

48. Congress has had several bills before it which would have granted the White House policy control authority over both independent and executive agencies, but they have failed to pass. *See infra* § 9.5.5 (discussing proposed legislation).

49. *See* Shapiro, *Political Oversight and the Deterioration of Regulatory Policy*, 46 Ad. L. Rev. 1 (1994).

become a rallying cry for those, in Congress and out, who want to protect the agency from executive interference. The critical questions are: Independent for what purposes and from whom?

While the answers to these questions are complicated, one thing is clear. The Constitutional Convention had no awareness of (nor any interest in) the concept. Thus, references in Article II to presidential control of "executive Departments"[50] are not meant constitutionally to narrow control over other agencies subsequently labeled independent. In other words, the Constitution is neutral on the type of agency that should be subjected to executive control. In order to discern constitutional limits or differences concerning executive control over executive and independent agencies, one must therefore tease meanings out of the Constitution that are not apparent on the face of the document.

§ 4.4.1   Executive and independent agencies compared

Administrative agencies take a variety of organizational forms. There are the executive departments mentioned in the Constitution, which are attached to the cabinet officers who control them. These are by far the most important administrative organizations in terms of their policy role and budgetary responsibilities. The Departments of Defense, State, Justice, Agriculture and Health and Human Services (HHS) are prime examples. These departments have sub-agencies within them that, while still executive, are often organizationally distinct, such as the Food and Drug Administration (FDA) in HHS. There are also agencies that are separate from the executive departments, but are nonetheless "executive". The Environmental Protection Agency (EPA) and the Office of Management and Budget (OMB) are prominent examples. Finally, there are agencies designated "independent" by Congress. These agencies, frequently referred to as "regulatory," include familiar acronyms like the FTC (Federal Trade Commission), FCC (Federal Communications Commission), NLRB (National Labor Relations Board), and the SEC (Securities and Exchange Commission). Most of these agencies were established during the New Deal, but they also include older agencies like the Federal Reserve System,(and the FTC) and some new ones like the Consumer Product Safety Commission (CPSC), Commodity Futures Trading Commission (CFTC), the Federal Election Commission (FEC) and Nuclear Regulatory Commission (NRC). A few of the newer agencies, like the Federal Energy Regulatory Commission (FERC) and the Occupational Safety and Health Review Commission

50. *See* note 13 *supra* and accompanying text.

(OSHRC), are independent agencies located within executive departments, but most are free-standing.[51]

§ 4.4.1a Why are they "independent"?

There is no good evidence why Congress in 1889 decided to move the ICC from the Department of the Interior in order to make it "independent". Some have suggested that the fear of presidential domination was behind the move of the ICC out of an executive department, but that is pure speculation. One scholar has attributed Congress' creation of the independent agency to "historical accident". Whatever the historical record showed initially, however, the ICC soon came to be referred to as an "arm of Congress" with an independent status that could not be subject to executive control. By the time the FTC was created in 1914, the notion of insulating agencies from political influence had caught on in Congress.[52]

During the 1930s, several of the leading regulatory agencies were established as independent, an event that caused Louis Brownlow to make his famous "headless fourth branch" statement mentioned earlier.[53] His point was that these agencies were becoming "miniature independent governments" whose existence violated the basic theory of the American Constitution.[54] Nevertheless, independent agencies seem here to stay. In the 1970s alone, five independent agencies were created by Congress.

Why some, and not other, agencies are designated independent is a question that admits of no easy answer. From a functional viewpoint, executive agencies have responsibilities that are similar to independent agencies. The FDA, for example, adjudicates, just as does the FTC. Both kinds of agencies make policy through rulemaking as well. The pattern is certainly uneven, if not inexplicable.

51. A list of Cabinet departments, executive and independent agencies can be found in the Unified Agenda of Federal Regulations, 49 Fed.Reg. 15702 (1984).

52. *See* M. Bernstein, Regulating Business by Independent Commission 23 (1955); R. Cushman, The Independent Regulatory Commissions 60–61, 101, 190–93 (1941); Senate Comm. on Gov'n. Affairs, Vol. V.—Regulatory Organization, S.Doc. No. 95–91, 95th Cong., 2d Sess. 26–27 (1977); *see also* C. Miller, The Legislative Evolution of the Interstate Commerce Commission (1930).

53. *See supra* text accompanying note 4. In 1971, a report prepared for the President by a council headed by Roy Ash echoed the fourth branch criticisms of the Brownlow Committee. *See* President's Advisory Comm'n. on Executive Organization, Report on Selected Independent Regulatory Agencies 14–15 (1971).

54. *See also* FTC v. Ruberoid Co., 343 U.S. 470, 487 (1952) (Jackson, J. dissenting).

Perhaps all it shows is that Congress has not succumbed to the hobgoblin of foolish consistency.

A Senate Study on Federal Regulation stated the case for agency independence in terms that invite further study:[55]

> In our view, a certain degree of insulation from the popular political process is desirable and/or necessary for particular agencies to perform their functions. Those agencies with responsibility for deciding cases for licensing or establishing rates perform essentially judicial functions where considerable insulation is desirable. Whether the nonjudicial functions performed by the regulatory commissions justify a similar insulation from the popular political process is a question which has been debated for several decades.

According to the study, Congress establishes independent agencies for two reasons: to insulate them from executive control and to make them more susceptible to congressional control. Whether the first reason is consistent with the second, or whether either are consistent with the constitutional plan, are questions that will be explored.

§ 4.4.1b   The functional characteristics of independent agencies

There are several ways in which independent agencies can be functionally or structurally distinguished from executive agencies. Unlike their executive counterparts, independent agencies are organized as commissions consisting of five or seven members. This makes their deliberations and decisions the product of collegial decisionmaking, which is a process that has its closest analogue in the appellate judicial setting.[56] Further, commissioners are appointed

---

55.   Senate Study, *supra* note 52, at 8. As the Senate Study indicates, one of the prime reasons for independent agencies is that their adjudicative functions require them to emulate the independence found in the judicial system. But much of the current work of agencies involves policymaking, which is an executive and not a judicial function. This has led to a recent variation on the independent agency which separates the policymaking and judicial functions into two agencies. For example, the Occupational Safety and Health Administration (OSHA), which sets occupational safety and health policy, is located in the Department of Labor, while the Occupational Safety and

Health Review Commission (OSHRC), which adjudicates whether an employer has violated OSHA regulations, is an independent agency. This "split-enforcement" model has produced its own set of difficulties. *See* Shapiro & McGarity, *Rethinking OSHA: Rulemaking Reforms and Legislative Changes*, 6 Yale J. Reg. 1, 59–62 (1989) (discussing the difficulty of functionally separating adjudication from policymaking); Verkuil, *The Purposes and Limits of Independent Agencies,* 1988 Duke L.J. 257 (same).

56.   Collegial decisionmaking is meant to produce a different kind of decision than that which results from the usual

by the President and confirmed by the Senate to serve set terms which expire at staggered intervals. The terms vary in length from commission to commission, but most exceed the four-year term of the President.[57] The President can designate who will be the chairperson of independent agencies, with some notable exceptions, like the statutory four-year term of the Chairman of the Board of Governors of the Federal Reserve System.[58] By comparison, executive agency administrators (or Cabinet officers) are subject to dismissal at the pleasure of the President. Finally, the members of independent commissions are also required by statute to be selected on a bipartisan basis. The President is restricted to naming only a majority of the members from his own party; the remainder must be from the other party or be registered independents. There are no comparable restrictions on appointment of executive officials where party affiliation is a virtual precondition to appointment.

Each of these differences is designed to make commissioners, and their agencies, less susceptible to presidential control, and they undoubtedly have such an effect. But they cannot reduce the President's power entirely. One reason is that the appointment itself must be the President's, as *Buckley v. Valeo* has confirmed.[59] This power is of paramount importance even though it is leavened by the bipartisan requirement.[60] Another reason is that the terms of years requirement is usually ameliorated. First, members of independent commissions often do not serve the full terms to which they are entitled. Second, the power to appoint raises the corollary power to remove. This latter possibility is one of the most controversial aspects of the entire saga of independent agencies. The relationship between Congress and the President over the independent agencies has come to be explained through the exercise of the removal power.

single administrator format of the executive agency. *See* Jones, *Multitude of Counselors: Appellate Adjudication as Group Decision Making,* 54 Tul. L. Rev. 541 (1979). We will reconsider this point in terms of the Sunshine Act requirements. *See infra* § 9.4.

57. The terms are usually for five, six, or seven years, but the Board of Governors of the FRS is for 14 years. *See* Senate Study, *supra* note 52, at 35.

58. 12 U.S.C. § 242.

59. In *Buckley,* the Supreme Court held unconstitutional an attempt by Congress to place in itself the power to ap-

point some members of the Federal Election Commission. The Court held that any appointee exercising "significant" authority was "an Officer of the United States" whose appointment was exclusively an exercise of executive power under Article II. 424 U.S. 1, 125–26 (1976).

60. It does not appear difficult for the President to identify friendly members of the other party or eager-to-please independents to fill the minority positions. *See* Graham & Kramer, Appointments to the Regulatory Agencies; Federal Communications Commission and Federal Trade Commission (1949–1974) 385–86 (1976).

§ 4.4.2 *Myers* and *Humphrey's Executor*

If a President could simply imply from his exclusive power to appoint under Article II a concomitant power to remove, much of the discussion about independence would be pointless. Congress therefore has long sought to condition the President's removal power with varying degrees of success. The legality of these efforts is an issue that to this day is not completely resolved.

Since the power to remove, unlike the power to appoint, is not specifically mentioned in the Constitution, two conclusions about that authority are possible. It could be concluded that the Congress (through the Senate) shares the removal power, because it shares the appointment power, or that the power resides in the President alone.[61] Congress employed the first conclusion for many years until brought up short in *Myers v. United States*.[62] *Myers* involved a statute that provided postmasters were to be appointed and removed by the President with the Senate's concurrence and that, unless removed, were to serve four-year terms. President Harding ordered the removal of Myers, without senatorial concurrence, before his term expired. Myers sued for back pay in the Court of Claims and lost. The issue presented by the appeal to the Supreme Court was whether Article II prevented Congress from conditioning the President's power to remove executive officers. Chief Justice Taft, a former President, answered the question emphatically in the affirmative in a lengthy and far-reaching opinion. He distinguished between the role of the Senate in the removal and appointment settings:

> The power to prevent the removal of an officer who has served under the President is different from the authority to consent to or reject his appointment. When a nomination is made, it may be presumed that the Senate is, or may become, as well advised as to the fitness of the nominee as the President, but in the nature of things the defects in ability or intelligence or loyalty in the administration of the laws of one who has served as an officer under the President are facts as to which the President, or his trusted subordinates, must be better informed than the Senate, and the power to remove him may therefore be regarded as

---

61. Alexander Hamilton announced in regard to the Senate's role that "the consent of [that body] would be necessary to displace as well as appoint". The Federalist No. 77, at 485 (A. Hamilton) (B. Wright ed. 1961).

62. 272 U.S. 52 (1926). In his dissent, Justice Holmes, with characteristic conciseness, refused to read the President's duty of faithful execution of the laws as any greater than that which "Congress sees fit to leave within his power". *Id.* at 177.

confined for very sound and practical reasons, to the governmental authority which has administrative control.

But the decision did not confine itself to executive officials only. The Chief Justice went on to conclude:

> The imperative reasons requiring an unrestricted power to remove the most important of his subordinates in their most important duties must therefore control the interpretation of the Constitution as to all appointed by him.

The only limitations placed upon removal dealt with matters committed by Congress to the discretion of particular agency officials and with "quasi-judicial" matters. Concerning these activities, the Court thought that the power of removal could be conditioned by Congress only to the extent that removal was deferred until after the officials made their decisions. Taft reasoned that the President:

> may consider the decision after its rendition, as a reason for removing the officer, on the ground that the discretion regularly entrusted to that officer by statute has not been on the whole intelligently or wisely exercised. Otherwise he does not discharge his own constitutional duty of seeing that the laws be faithfully executed.

The broad scope of the *Myers* decision jolted Congress. For years thereafter, it ceased to include the removal restrictions in legislation establishing agencies as independent.[63] But the idea of agency independence from presidential removal was dramatically revived by the Court in a New Deal removal case involving the FTC.

When President Roosevelt decided to remove William Humphrey, an FTC commissioner, before his seven-year term expired, he did so without regard to the statutory restriction on removal contained in the act.[64] Later, when Humphrey's executor sued unsuccessfully for back pay in the Court of Claims and appealed to the Supreme Court, the United States defended on the basis of *Myers*. This time, in *Humphrey's Executor v. United States,* the Supreme Court sustained the statutory for-cause removal requirement.[65] Emphasis was placed on the quasi-judicial and quasi-legislative nature of the FTC's work. Justice Sutherland wrote for a unanimous Court:

63. Neither the Communications Act of 1934 nor the Securities Exchange Act of 1934 contained removal restrictions, although both were established as independent agencies.

64. The FTC Act provided that "any Commissioner may be removed by the President for inefficiency, neglect of duty or malfeasance in office". *See* 15 U.S.C. § 41. This Act was passed in 1914 before the decision in *Myers*.

65. Humphrey's Executor v. United States, 295 U.S. 602 (1935).

We think it plain under the Constitution that illimitable power of removal is not possessed by the President in respect of officers of the character of those just named. The authority of congress, in creating quasi-legislative or quasi-judicial agencies, to require them to act in discharge of their duties independently of executive control cannot well be doubted; and that authority includes, as an appropriate incident, power to fix the period during which they shall continue in office, and to forbid their removal except for cause in the meantime.

The Court took pains to limit *Myers* to executive agencies and it emphasized the concept of agency independence:

The power of removal here claimed for the President falls within this principle, since its coercive influence threatens the independence of a commission, which is not only wholly disconnected from the executive department, but which, as already fully appears, was created by Congress as a means of carrying into operation legislative and judicial powers, and as an agency of the legislative and judicial departments.

Humphrey's Executor is viewed by Congress as a triumph of the independent agency concept and it certainly fettered the President's removal power over officials performing certain kinds of functions. In later cases, the Court emphasized the importance of the quasi-judicial nature of an official's duties when the Executive sought to remove that person without cause.[66]

Humphrey's Executor did not entirely repudiate *Myers,* however. First, it did not reach executive officials. Second, even as to independent commissioners, the FTC removal statute did not go as far as the Tenure in Office Act struck down in *Myers;* it imposed only a for-cause requirement upon presidential removal, not a senatorial concurrence requirement. Thus, to satisfy *Humphrey's Executor,* a President would need only to assert cause for removal. The President would not need to ask the Senate to concur in a decision to remove. This is an important theoretical distinction between the *Myers* and *Humphrey's Executor* removal contexts if (as no President has yet done) cause for removal is asserted.

66. In Wiener v. United States, 357 U.S. 349 (1958), the Court prevented President Eisenhower from removing a member of the War Claims Commission without cause, even though the statute contained no restrictions upon removal. The adjudicative nature of the Commissioner's duties determined the need for some insulation from removal.

§ 4.4.3 *Morrison v. Olson*

The Supreme Court returned to the subject of agency independence in *Morrison v. Olson*,[67] where it affirmed the constitutionality of the independent counsel provisions of the Ethics in Government Act of 1978.[68] The Act, which has since expired, provided that in cases where the Attorney General determines there are "sufficient grounds" to investigate whether high ranking government officials have broken the law, a special three-judge court is authorized to appoint a special prosecutor. The Act restricts the Attorney General from removing the special prosecutor except for "good cause, physical disability, mental incapacity, or any other condition that substantially impairs the performance of such independent counsel's duties." In 1986, James McKay was appointed as a special prosecutor to determine whether Theodore Olson, an Assistant Attorney General in the Reagan Administration, had given false or misleading testimony to a congressional committee. After McKay was replaced by Alexia Morrison, she served Olson (and two other former Justice Department officials) with subpoenas. They moved to quash the subpoenas on several grounds including that the independent counsel provisions were unconstitutional and Morrison therefore had no authority to proceed.

One of the grounds that Olson and the others gave for the unconstitutionality of the independent prosecutor was that the Act restricted the president's authority to remove the special prosecutor. They argued that since the function of "prosecution" was an "executive function," and did not involve "quasi-legislative" or "quasi-judicial" powers, the *Myers* case was controlling. They contended that *Myers* forbid congressional restrictions on the president's supervision of officials performing purely executive functions, and that the removal restrictions were therefore unconstitutional.

The Court rejected this argument on two grounds. First, as noted in the previous section, the removal restriction struck down in *Myers* was a senatorial concurrence requirement. By comparison, "this case does not involve an attempt by Congress itself to gain a role in the removal of executive officials other than its established powers of impeachment and conviction."[69] Second, the Court reinterpreted *Humphrey's Executor* as constituting a "core function" test:

> We undoubtedly did rely on the terms "quasi-legislative" and "quasi-judicial" to distinguish the officials involved in *Hum-*

---

67. 487 U.S. 654 (1988).

68. 28 U.S.C. §§ 49, 591 et seq.

69. *Id.* at 686.

phrey's Executor and *Weiner* from those in *Myers,* but our present considered view is that the determination of whether the Constitution allows Congress to impose a "good-cause"-type restriction on the President's power to remove an official cannot be made to turn on whether or not that official is classified as "purely executive." The analysis contained in our removal cases is designed not to define rigid categories of those officials who may or may not be removed at will by the President, but to ensure that Congress does not interfere with the President's exercise of the "executive power" and his constitutionally appointed duty "to take care that the laws be faithfully executed" under Article II.[70]

The Court concluded that the "good cause" removal restriction did not intrude on the President's core functions for three reasons. First, the special prosecutor was an "inferior official" under the Appointments Clause since her office had limited jurisdiction and tenure, and she was not authorized to exercise policy-making or significant administrative authority. Second, although the special prosecutor exercised some discretion, the President's need to control the exercise of that discretion was not "so central to the functioning of the Executive Branch as to require as a matter of constitutional law that the counsel be terminable at will by the President."[71] Finally, the President retained sufficient power to supervise the independent counsel as an executive branch official because the President retained under the "good cause" provisions "ample authority to assure that the counsel is competently performing his or her statutory responsibilities in a manner that comports with the provisions of the Act."[72]

Justice Scalia, who filed the only dissenting opinion, vigorously protested that when Article II says that the "executive power shall be vested in a President," this statement "does not mean *some* of the executive power, but *all* of the executive power."[73] Since prosecution is an executive function, the dissent insisted that Article II grants the President exclusive control over the exercise of this power. The majority responded that "[t]his rigid demarcation—a demarcation incapable of being altered by law in the slightest degree, and applicable to tens of thousands of holders of office neither known or foreseen

---

70. *Id.* at 689–90.

71. *Id.* at 691–92.

72. *Id.* at 692. Although the Court did not define exactly what was encompassed with the term "good cause," it

cited the legislative history of the Act as including "misconduct" within that term.

73. 487 U.S. at 705.

by the Framers—depends upon an extrapolation from general constitutional language which we think is more than the text will bear.''[74]

During 1999, Congress debated whether to reenact the Independent Counsel Act, which was set to expire. The Clinton impeachment debacle seemed to lead both branches (and organized interests like the American Bar Association) to favor letting the Act expire and it did.

§ 4.4.4 The future of agency independence: The core function idea

The majority's willingness to accept Congress' decision to give the special prosecutor independence from the Attorney General (and therefore from the President) can be contrasted with the Court's unwillingness to accept other congressional attempts to limit the President's executive powers. In declaring unconstitutional the legislative veto[75] and congressional appointment of officials who perform executive functions,[76] the Court interpreted the Constitution in the same type of "formalistic" or "literal" manner that Justice Scalia applied in *Morrison*. As the Court's response to Justice Scalia suggests, the majority's more pragmatic approach—and its reliance on a core function test—is justified because the Constitution does not speak directly to the president's authority to remove officials. In the other cases, the Court was able to cite specific constitutional provisions which prohibited what Congress had done.[77]

Morrison expanded Congress' authority to establish "for cause" removal restrictions. Prior to *Morrison,* it had been assumed that Congress could not establish such restrictions for officials who performed "purely" executive functions. *Morrison* permits such restrictions as along as they do not unduly interfere with the President's capacity to execute the laws.

Morrison, however, could also open the door for the Court to narrow Congress' authority to enact such restrictions. Professor Strauss suggests that some congressional attempts to limit the president's supervision of agency policy-making could be unconstitutional under a "core-function" approach.[78] He argues for viewing agency

74. *Id.* at 690 n. 29.

75. INS v. Chadha, 462 U.S. 919 (1983).

76. Buckley v. Valeo, 424 U.S. 1 (1976).

77. *Cf.* Public Citizen v. United States Dept. of Justice, 491 U.S. 440

(1989) (Kennedy, J. concurring) (where Constitutional text is explicit, no balancing is appropriate, but where only general Article II interests are at stake, balancing process should be employed).

78. Strauss, *The Place of Agencies in Government: Separation of Powers and*

control as a form of "checks and balances," rather than a "separation of powers" problem, and proposes that so long as one branch does not jeopardize the "core function" of another, the courts should endorse executive and legislative controls of independent agencies. This proposition has obvious merit. Instead of trumpeting independence as a value in itself, the inquiry becomes whether, in a particular setting, it is a concept necessary to protect fundamental branch interests. If agency adjudication is involved, separation of functions (rather than *powers*) notions would forbid executive or legislative interference.[79] On the other hand, if agency policy-making is involved, both branches can have a role to play without jeopardizing the constitutional plan.[80] Thus, while the Congress may be able to condition removal by a for-cause requirement, the President should be able to meet it with an assertion of failure to follow administration policy.

There may be some instances, however, where the President should be denied such a removal power. For example, if the President attempted to remove the Chairman of the Board of Governors of the Federal Reserve system, or a member of the Federal Election Commission, on the basis that the person failed to follow administration policy, there would be valid concerns about executive branch over-reaching. Moreover, removal for poor policy-making can be a disguise for removal for adjudicative decisionmaking in those independent agencies where both roles are placed in the same commissioners.[81] Congress could attempt to respond to these valid concerns by narrowing the grounds for removal sufficiently to protect against executive displacement of core functions.

The Court may be headed in the direction that Professor Strauss recommends. *Mistretta v. United States,*[82] which upheld the constitutionality of the Sentencing Commission, although it was "an indepen-

the Fourth Branch, 84 Colum. L. Rev. 573 (1984).

79. Grounding of separation of powers analysis in separation of functions principles has historical significance. The underpinnings of the British separation of powers doctrine were in the natural justice notion that no man should be a judge in his own cause. *See* W.B. Gwyn, The Meaning of Separation of Powers 6–7 (1965); *see generally supra* § 2.1.2.

80. Strauss suggests, for example, that the President's extension of regulatory analysis requirements to indepen-

dent agencies would pose no constitutional difficulties under his analysis. Strauss, *supra* note 78, at 662. Alternatively, if Congress wants to restrict executive branch control over agency policymaking it can do so, but on the condition that it restrict its own access as well. Otherwise, one branch would threaten the core function of the other. *Id.* at 666–67.

81. *See* Verkuil, *Jawboning Administrative Agencies: Ex parte Contacts by the White House,* 80 Colum.L.Rev. 943, 954–55 (1980).

82. 488 U.S. 361 (1989).

dent agency in the judicial branch," relies on a balance of powers and checks and balances analysis much like that recommended by Professor Strauss. In adopting "a flexible understanding of separation of powers," the Court permitted Congress to authorize the President to remove Article III judges who sat on the Commission under certain limited circumstances because it constituted "negligible threat to judicial independence."[83]

Whether, however, the Court will actually use this approach to strike down congressional attempts to limit the president's control of agency policy-making remains to be seen. In the past, the Court has viewed agency policy-making as a joint activity between the President and Congress, and has recognized that "for cause" restrictions permit Congress to exercise more influence over agency policy-making than they would have if such provisions were unconstitutional.

§ 4.4.5 Illustrations of the politics of agency independence

If the independent agency is part of legal folklore, it is also central to congressional folklore and that fact is, for any President, of far more practical consequence. For example, when President Reagan met privately with the FCC Chairman, Mark Fowler, to discuss a pending rulemaking proceeding, a front-page story and outcries from Capital Hill were produced.[84] If such a meeting took place between the President and a cabinet or executive officer, it would have gone unnoticed. Thus, folklore or not, independent agencies are seen as the arms of Congress and that political reality constrains executive behavior.

When it comes to exercise of the appointment and removal power, Congress's notions about independence, even if not supported legally, shape executive behavior. The classic example involved the reorganized Civil Rights Commission. The Commission was established in 1957 in the Executive branch by President Eisenhower. It was composed of six members (only three from the same party) who served without prescribed terms.[85] On its face, it appeared to be an executive agency and its members typically submitted their resignations when a new President took office.

However, when President Reagan decided in 1983 to replace several of the incumbent members with others who shared his views

---

83. *Id.* at 410.

84. *See generally infra* § 9.3.3 (discussing White House ex parte contacts in rulemaking).

85. Civil Rights Act of 1957, 42 U.S.C. § 1975(b).

on matters like affirmative action, the issue of independence arose. The hold-over members refused to resign and the President was unable to get his new appointees confirmed. Much was made in the press, and on the Hill, about the need for policy-making "independence" in civil rights policy, even though the legal case for such a proposition was weak, at best.[86]

The confrontation between the President and Congress was compromised by the passage of new legislation, the United States Civil Rights Commission Act of 1983,[87] which reconstituted the Commission into a body of eight bipartisan members, four appointed by the President and four (two each) by the Senate and House, without the necessity for senatorial concurrence. The members are granted six-year terms. All reference to the Commission as an executive branch agency in the statute were eliminated.

The benefits from this political compromise may be small. The appointment of its members diluted the President's appointment power.[88] In return, he was able to break the political logjam and get his people on board. But the agency, which had been respected for its objectivity and moral authority, became an adversarial entity of dubious influence in Congress and in the White House. The lesson of this experience may just be that the political limits on the appointment power are far more profound than the legal ones.

Occasionally, the President and Congress react to calls for independence in ways that appear to defy both politics and tradition. Although it involves the President's power to make appointments, which is discussed in the next section, *Melcher v. Federal Open Market Committee*[89] is a good example of how the sides can switch. In *Melcher*, the government found itself supporting agency independence, and relying on an argument that undercut the President's authority to appoint agency officials. The case involved a challenge by

86. *See* Berry v. Reagan, 32 Empl. Prac. Dec. (CCH) & 33,898 (D.D.C. 1983), *dismissed as moot,* & 33,925 (D.D.C. Nov. 30, 1983) (asserting *Humphrey's Executor* claims).

87. Pub. L. No. 98–183, 97 Stat. 1301.

88. President Reagan accepted this limitation on his authority in a signing message which stated that Buckley v. Valeo, 424 U.S. 1 (1976), would not be offended so long as the Commissioners did not perform the duties of "Officers of the United States". Statement Accompanying Signing, Nov. 30, 1983. The *Buckley* definition of officer is whether he or she exercises "significant authority" under the laws of the United States. 424 U.S. at 126. It is arguable that Civil Rights commissioners, whose role is to investigate and report, exercise such authority. *See* Hannah v. Larche, 363 U.S. 420 (1960).

89. 644 F.Supp. 510 (D.D.C.1986), *aff'd on other grounds,* 836 F.2d 561 (D.C.Cir.1987), *cert. denied,* 486 U.S. 1042 (1988).

a member of the Senate that the membership of the Open Market Committee of the Federal Reserve Board was unconstitutional because five of the committee's twelve members were not appointed by the President pursuant to Article II.[90] The Open Market Committee sets and implements monetary policy by directing the Federal Reserve banks to purchase and sell securities.[91] The government defended this organization structure against an argument that it violated *Buckley v. Valeo*[92] by asserting that the Open Market Committee members are "inferior officers," not "Officers of the United States," because they operate under the authority of the Board of Governors of the Federal Reserve System. While Article II vests the appointment of "Officers of the United States" in the President, the Constitution provides that "inferior officers" may be appointed by the President, "Courts of Law," or the "Heads of Departments." One can, however, readily construct an argument that the policy decisions of the Open Market Committee are significant enough to qualify its members as "Officers of the United States." The fact that the President nevertheless supported agency independence, in apparent contradiction of the executive interest, suggests the complexity of the appointment power. The D.C. Circuit declined to reach the merits of the issue, holding that the doctrine of equitable discretion required for separation of powers reasons that a congressional plaintiff should properly seek relief through legislation.[93]

But just as the President occasionally supports agency independence, Congress sometimes supports executive control. Over the years legislation has been drafted to change the Nuclear Regulatory Commission's (NRC) status as an independent agency.[94] One Senate bill, which was supported by a majority of the Commission, placed the responsibility for the safety of nuclear power plants under a single administrator who would be appointed by the President with the advice and consent of the Senate. Once confirmed, however, the administrator would serve at the pleasure of the President.

90. Seven of the members of the Committee are governors of the Federal Reserve Board appointed by the President with senatorial concurrence. 12 U.S.C. § 263 (1982). The other five members are selected by the boards of directors of the various Federal Reserve banks on a regional basis. *Id.*

91. *See* 12 U.S.C. § 263(b) (1982); 12 C.F.R. Pt. 270 (1986).

92. 424 U.S. 1 (1976).

93. *Melcher v. Federal Open Market Committee,* 836 F.2d 561, 563 (D.C.Cir. 1987). The Court followed Riegle v. FOMC, 656 F.2d 873 (D.C.Cir.1981), *cert. denied,* 454 U.S. 1082 (1981). The Court made clear in *Melcher* that the inability of private plaintiffs to bring the same challenge made no difference to its analysis. *See id.* at 565.

94. *See, e.g.,* Nuclear Regulation, Reorganization, and Reform Act of 1988, S. 2443, 100th Cong., 2d Sess. (1988).

The impetus for Congress' switching to a single administrator was the weaknesses of the commission structure in the non-adjudicative context of safety regulation. A Senate report noted:

> In short, the committee found that the Commission structure is poorly suited to the task of regulating the commercial nuclear power industry. As a means of formulating decisions, the Commission decision making process is inefficient and, frequently, indecisive. . . . No single individual is responsible for a decision, once made.[95]

Supporters of the legislation also viewed the provision that the administrator would serve at the pleasure of the President as an important protection of the public. The expectation was that once the legislation was passed, the administrator would become an executive official with the status and power effectively to regulate nuclear safety—and more importantly, the President would then become responsible for nuclear safety. Although this proposal did not become law, it is an illuminating example of the cross cutting politics of independence.

§ 4.5 "Principal" versus "Inferior" Officers

The President's ability to supervise the government is also impacted by where Congress vests the power of appointment. The Appointments Clause of Article II requires "principal" officers to be appointed by the President with senatorial concurrence, but it permits Congress to vest the appointment of "inferior" officials "in the President alone, in the Courts of Law, or in the Heads of Departments."[96] For example, the Ethics in Government Act, discussed earlier,[97] required the appointment of an independent counsel by a special three-judge court. In *Morrison v. Olson*,[98] the Supreme Court approved this process because the special prosecutor was an "inferior officer," which meant that the prosecutor could be appointed "in the Courts of Law." The Court reached this conclusion because the independent counsel, subject to removal by a higher officer (the Attorney General), performed only limited duties and had limited jurisdiction and tenure.

Edmond v. United States[99] indicates that the dividing line between a "principal" and "inferior" officer remains unclear despite

---

95. S. Rep. No. 364, 100th Cong., 2d Sess. 15 (1988).

96. U.S. Const., Art. II, § 2.

97. *See supra* § 4.4.3.

98. 487 U.S. 654 (1988).

99. 520 U.S. 651 (1997).

Morrison. Edmond, who was convicted by a court-martial, challenged the makeup of the Coast Guard Court of Criminal Appeals, which had affirmed his conviction. He argued that because the President had not appointed the civilian members of the appeals court, their service was unconstitutional, which negated the court's decision to affirm the court martial. Because the Coast Guard operates as a branch of the Department of the Treasury during peace-time, the civilian members had been appointed by the Secretary of the Treasury. Edmond argued that the military judges were not "inferior" officials because two of the criteria in *Morrison* did not apply: the military judges were not limited in tenure or jurisdiction. The Court replied that *Morrison* did not "purport to set forth a definitive test for whether an officer is 'inferior' under the Appointments Clause."

The Court acknowledged that the judges exercised "significant authority", but this fact was not determinative. Instead, the "exercise of 'significant authority pursuant to the laws of the United States' marks, not the line between principal and inferior officer for Appointments Clause purposes, but rather ... the line between officer and non-officer." By comparison, the dividing line between a "principal" and "inferior" officer depends on whether a person has a "superior" who directs and supervises the officer's performance. This is the key consideration because it preserves political accountability. The President must appoint "principal" officers and "inferior officials" are limited to those persons who report to a "principal" officer. The judges on the appeals court were "inferior" officers because their decisions were subject to review by additional officials. The fact that such review was deferential did not matter. According to the Court, the significant fact was that the court of appeals had "no power to render a final decision on behalf of the United States unless permitted to do so by other executive officers."

In a concurring opinion, Justice Souter warned that the existence of a supervisor did not necessarily mean that a person is an "inferior" officer. In some cases, such as this one, the officer is subject to "substantial supervisory authority", but this condition may not exist in other cases. Nevertheless, Justice Souter thought that a person still might be an "inferior officer" because the person has limited powers and duties. Justice Souter noted that in *Morrison* the independent counsel was not subject to close supervision by the Attorney General and that a crucial reason why the independent counsel was an "inferior officer" was the person's limited powers and jurisdiction.

Freytag v. Commissioner of Internal Revenue[100] presented a different problem concerning the appointment of "inferior" officials. The issue was whether the Chief Judge of the Tax Court, an Article I or administrative court, could appoint "special judges" (whose powers are similar to magistrates in the federal district courts). Five members of the court characterized the Tax Court as a "Court of Law" and sanctioned the appointment on that basis. The concurring Justices construed the Tax Court as a "Department" which allowed the Chief Judge to undertake the appointments as the department "head". The difficulty with the majority decision is that inferior officials in many independent agencies are not appointed by the "Heads of Departments" because the agencies are free-standing and not located in an executive department. The majority's unwillingness to construe the Tax Court as a "department" would seem to make it difficult for the Court to sanction these appointments.

These cases indicate the difficulty of reconciling the complex structure of the administrative state with a Constitution written for a far simpler government. By and large, the Court has found ways to reconcile modern government with constitutional dictates, although it may not accept every innovation that Congress attempts.

§ 4.6   Other Limitations on Executive Control

The President's power to control agency discretion is bounded not only by the concept of independence, but also by legal constraints operating upon him and his staff. These range from the decision of Congress to place legal authority for agency decisions in subordinate officials to the tort liability of the President and his aides resulting from failed attempts to discipline agency officials. In addition, the executive power to control agency officials is effectively circumscribed by the rules and regulations governing the protected civil service.

§ 4.6.1   The congressional decision to locate responsibility in subordinates

While under Article II the executive power resides in the President, Congress has the ability through specific delegations either to enhance or reduce that power. Congress enhances it when it makes a delegation of authority directly to the President, leaving it to the President to decide when, how, and if to delegate operational authority to subordinates. Alternatively, Congress may seek to place final decisional authority directly in subordinates themselves. Congress has chosen this latter method for the implementation of most regula-

---

100. 501 U.S. 868 (1991).

tory schemes by delegating the power to act to the heads of independent agencies or cabinet departments.[101]

The Supreme Court has held that Congress can insulate decision-making power from the final authority of the President by delegating it to others. While the proposition could in extreme applications[102] undermine the executive power in Article II, Attorneys General have long advised their Presidents to acquiesce in the congressional decision to locate authority in subordinates.[103] After the fact, the President can always exercise his executive will by ordering the offending official to be fired, but even that power is not absolute, as President Nixon learned during the Watergate prosecution.[104]

Undoubtedly, the power of the President to control subordinates can be hedged by congressional delegations. But the President still has techniques available to preserve his executive power. Removing nontenured personnel is one. Harsh talks in the Oval Office is another. Nevertheless, presidents quickly learn that there are limits to their authority. President Truman predicted that the biggest shock of moving from the military to the civilian world for his successor, Dwight Eisenhower, would be the realization of how hard it was to

101. *See* Kendall v. United States, 37 U.S. (12 Pet.) 524 (1837) (over the President's objection, Postmaster General ordered to pay a sum of money under a special statute). Of course, Marbury v. Madison, 5 U.S. (1 Cranch) 137 (1803), had already held that the Court could direct the performance of a non-discretionary duty placed in the President by Congress. *See generally,* Monaghan, *Marbury and the Administrative State,* 83 Colum.L.Rev. 1 (1983).

102. *See* E. Corwin, *supra* note 9, at 80–81.

103. The classic situation arose when Andrew Jackson ordered the district attorney to discontinue condemnation proceedings on behalf of the United States concerning the jewels of the Princess of Orange. The jewels had been imported into the United States without payment of duty and, while condemnation proceedings were pending, the President learned that they had been stolen from the House of Orange and decided to return them. In an opinion by Attorney General Taney, it was said that the President, under his power faithfully to execute the laws, could order the attorney to dismiss the prosecution and return the jewels. The district attorney might ignore this order at his peril, but the President could not, however, order the dismissal himself. 2 Op.Att'y Gen. 482, 489 (1831).

104. President Nixon ordered the Attorney General, and then the Deputy Attorney General, to fire Archibald Cox, the Watergate prosecutor. When they resigned rather than so act, the Solicitor General, Robert Bork, complied. It was later determined that the policy was illegal because a valid Department of Justice regulation limited discharge to the grounds of "extraordinary impropriety" which were not alleged. Nader v. Bork, 366 F.Supp. 104 (D.D.C. 1973). In reaction to these events, Congress passed legislation that requires the appointment of a "special prosecutor" in cases involving possible legal violations by high governmental officials. The President is restricted from firing the special prosecutor except for the reasons specified in the legislation. *See supra* § 4.4.3.

get subordinates to carry out presidential orders.[105]

§ 4.6.2   Tort liability of the President and his staff

Dismissal or demotion of agency policy-making officials by the President can be an effective tool of administration only so long as it does not lead to burdensome private litigation. There is no doubt that the President enjoys protection against private actions on the basis of privilege, which is constitutionally based.[106] His staff, however, has less freedom of action in this regard.

In *Nixon v. Fitzgerald,* the Court held 5 to 4 that the President's "unique position in the constitutional scheme" grants him absolute immunity from suit by (in this case) a civil servant who alleged he was vindictively dismissed for "whistle blowing".[107] The dissenters were prepared to relegate the President to the same qualified immunity they held applicable to Presidential staff aides and department officials in *Harlow v. Fitzgerald.*[108] Moreover, even the majority did not rule out the possibility that Congress might narrow the President's absolute immunity by statute. This latter suggestion is a troubling one constitutionally since the Court has earlier held that legislators and judges enjoy absolute immunity "because of the special nature of their responsibilities."[109]

The question of absolute versus qualified immunity for high government officials raises competing interests that have long been debated. The tension is between the necessity to insulate high officials from civil consequences for their actions in order to encourage effective and bold management of government[110] and the danger that such insulation will invite arbitrary and unconstitutional government action.[111] The most that need be noted here is that in recent years the scope of constitutional torts had been expanded and the

---

105. "He'll sit right there, and he'll say, 'Do this! Do that!' and nothing will happen. Poor Ike—it won't be a bit like the army. He'll find it very frustrating." The Truman Wit 59–60 (A. Goldman, ed. 1966).

106. United States v. Nixon, 418 U.S. 683, 713 (1974), confirmed the existence of a constitutional privilege of confidentiality between the President and his staff which could be forced to yield only to legitimate interests of the "adversary system of justice" (there a subpoena in a criminal case).

107. 457 U.S. 731 (1982).

108. 457 U.S. 800 (1982).

109. *See* Butz v. Economou, 438 U.S. 478, 511 (1978).

110. *See* Gregoire v. Biddle, 177 F.2d 579, 581 (2d Cir.1949), *cert. denied* 339 U.S. 949 (1950) (Hand, J.) (absolute immunity for Attorney General because litigation "would dampen the ardor of all but the most resolute ... ").

111. *See* Scheuer v. Rhodes, 416 U.S. 232 (1974) ("good faith" immunity for governors under § 1983).

scope of absolute immunity has been contracted.[112] This makes the possibility of tort liability at least a factor in an executive decision of how far to go in exercising control over the bureaucracy.

The immunity discussed here refers to immunity concerning actions taken by officials pursuant to their public duties. In *Clinton v. Jones*,[113] the Supreme Court refused to grant President Clinton temporary immunity from a civil action brought by Paula Jones for damages arising out of events that occurred before the President took office. The President had sought to postpone the litigation, which was based on a claim of sexual harassment, until after he left office. Distinguishing *Harlow*, the majority noted that the "principle rationale for affording certain public servants immunity from suits for money damages arising out of their official acts is inapplicable to unofficial conduct." The majority was not impressed with arguments by the President that defense of such a lawsuit would hobble his ability to carry out his constitutional duties or that the lack of immunity would pose a serious risk of a large volume of politically motivated harassing and frivolous litigation. In a concurring opinion, Justice Breyer announced he was less "sanguine" about the potential that "individual district court procedural rulings could pose a significant threat to the President's official functions." He would have required the President to provide the District Court with a "reasoned explanation" of why the immunity is needed. Justice Breyer's concurrence in *Clinton v. Jones*, much like Justice Scalia's dissent in *Morrison v. Olson* became prescient after President Clinton's impeachment problems emerged.

§ 4.6.3   Civil service considerations

When the Court held in 1886 that constitutionally Congress could restrict the removal of inferior officers in executive departments by statute,[114] it effectively paved the way for the "protected" civil service. Today, the President's control over the appointment process is limited to that top group of officials who in number represent about one percent of the federal government's almost 3 million civilian workforce.[115] They include about 675 presidential appointees, whose appointments require senatorial advice and consent, and a like number, who can be appointed by the President

---

112. *See generally,* P. Schuck, Suing Government (1983).

113. 520 U.S. 681 (1997).

114. *See* United States v. Perkins, 116 U.S. 483 (1886).

115. *See* N.Y. Times, Aug. 12, 1984 (listing Bureau of the Census employment statistics as of Oct. 1983 including total federal, state and local government employment of 16 million).

without advice and consent.[116] Other policy level officials are part of the "Senior Executive Service," established by the Civil Service Reform Act of 1978.[117] These employees, who exercise "important policy-making, policy-determining, or other executive functions," are protected against direct presidential control, but they can be selected and reassigned by the secretaries or department heads involved. Arguably, the presence of the Senior Executive Service expands the President's control over the government.[118]

The President's powers over the normal civil service are greatly circumscribed. He can partially shape civil service policy through his authority to appoint, with senatorial concurrence, the director of the Office of Personnel Management, which is designated as an independent agency within the executive branch.[119] He also has the authority to appoint, again with senatorial concurrence, the three members of the Merit Systems Protection Board,[120] whose task it is to adjudicate matters under the Civil Service Reform Act of 1978. But these officials are largely independent of presidential direction and control.

The civil service protections established by Congress not only severely limit a president's ability to discipline and replace protected employees, but they even curtail his ability to reduce the size of the government payroll.[121] It has been suggested therefore that the "real" fourth branch of government is not the independent agency, but rather the civil service.[122]

The problems an entrenched civil service pose for the President's powers of control and supervision run far beyond the White House.

116. *See* 5 U.S.C. §§ 5312–5317 (Executive Levels I–V). There are also about 1,665 "schedule C" political appointees in Grades 1 to 15 who are excepted from the normal civil service appointment process because of the confidential and policy determining character of their positions. *See* 5 C.F.R. § 6.2.

117. *See* 5 U.S.C. §§ 3131–3132 (establishing and defining the senior executive service; there are about 800 members of the SES).

118. *See* L. Fisher, The Politics of Shared Power 126–28 (1981).

119. 5 U.S.C. § 1101. The director is appointed for a 4–year term. *Id.* at § 1102.

120. The Board is comprised of 3 members, no more than 2 from the same party, who serve 7 year terms and can be removed only "for inefficiency, neglect of duty or malfeasance in office". *Id.* at §§ 1201, 1202.

121. In National Treasury Employees Union v. Reagan, 663 F.2d 239 (D.C.Cir. 1981), the court rejected a broad class action claim bought by those offered federal jobs who had been caught in a hiring freeze ordered by President Reagan upon assuming office in January 1981. It left open, however, proof of claims on remand by those sought to be employed by the Veterans Administration for whom Congress had mandated a "funded personnel ceiling" that it was beyond the President's power to affect.

122. *See* K. Meier, Politics and the Bureaucracy: Policy–Making in the Fourth Branch of Government (1979).

Top political appointees at the agency level, including independent commissioners, also feel the frustrations of civil service insularity. In a memorable phrase, Professor Glen Robinson, once an FCC commissioner, complained about the problem of "staff capture".[123] His concern was that the permanent staff were working on their own agenda and might possibly skew the presentation of information to the Commission so as to achieve their own view of the public interest.

There are many stories in Washington along these lines and it is undoubtedly true that the transitory political appointees and the permanent civil service may view each other with skepticism, if not distrust.[124] To some extent that is the intention of the civil service system. The existence of the civil service limits the President's ability to make government more accountable at the same time it assures against making the government more political.

§ 4.7 Executive Control at the State Level

Governors face policy control problems not dissimilar to those confronting the President. Indeed, the problem of independence versus accountability at the state level is of a greater order of magnitude than it is at the federal level. State executive branch officials have agendas that are in many ways as critical as those facing their federal counterparts. Energy policy is a shared responsibility, as is improvement in the quality of public education. Additional state policy responsibilities are appearing daily as the federal government unloads important assignments upon states for health and welfare by the use of block grant programs and by deregulation of other federal programs.[125] These responsibilities make state policy control a matter of acute national interest.

§ 4.7.1 Separation of powers and the elected official problem

States generally follow the tripartite branch structure of the federal constitution. But when it comes to agency coordination and control, the separation of powers issues are far more complicated than they appear on the surface of state constitutions. The primary problem is that agency independence has achieved constitutional

123. Robinson, *The Federal Communications Commission: An Essay in Regulatory Watchdogs,* 64 Va. L. Rev. 169, 227–30 (1978). *See also* Hercules, Inc. v. EPA, 598 F.2d 91, 127 (D.C.Cir.1978) (questioning whether staff *advocates* should be able to participate in the drafting of a rule).

124. *See* H. Heclo, A Government of Strangers: Executive Politics in Washington (1977).

125. *See* Gray, *Regulation and Federalism,* 1 Yale J. Reg. 93 (1983).

status in many states. For example, in at least twelve states, public utility commissioners are elected and the trend in that direction seems to be accelerating. Similarly, in at least seventeen states, the chief education officer is an elected official.[126]

When agency officials are elected, their agencies in effect are administrative entities with policy roles co-equal to those of the traditional policy-making branches. The consequences of this constitutional and political agency independence for coordination of critical state policy are almost certainly negative.[127] Policy balkanization is substituted for policy coordination. Independent elected officials are in effect political rivals of the elected officials of the executive and legislative branches. As rivals, they have a difficult time achieving the political and budgetary support necessary to accomplish their assigned tasks. Moreover, because of the presence of elected officials in agencies, governors and legislatures are in a position to avoid responsibility for the missions assigned to those agencies. In effect, the true policy-making branches can pass the political buck to these agencies without supporting them financially. The outcome could easily be less coherent and effective state policy-making.[128]

The potential for this type of conflict applies to all but a few states. In forty-five states, for example, the Attorney General is a constitutionally established, elective office.[129] In those states, the Attorney General is likely to be a political rival, rather than a policy-making confidant of the chief executive, as he or she is at the federal level. Such a relationship seems inevitably designed to frustrate

126. *See* Council of State Governments, The Book of States (1980–1982) 196–97 (1980); Harris & Navarro, *Does Electing Public Utility Commissioners Bring Lower Electric Rates?*, Pub. Util. Fortnightly, Sept. 1, 1983, at 23.

127. Legal constraints follow from granting agencies constitutional status. In Louisiana, for example, it has been held that the legislature cannot alter the responsibilities of the constitutionally created Public Service Commission by mere statutory directions. *See* Louisiana Consumers' League, Inc. v. Louisiana Public Service Commission, 351 So.2d 128 (La.1977) (refusing to apply the state APA to the PSC); Force & Griffith, *The Louisiana Administrative Procedure Act,* 42 La. L. Rev. 1227, 1228–29 (1982).

128. It is difficult to prove this point empirically. In terms of performance of public utility commissions, the evidence suggests that elected commissions do no better than appointed commissions in setting the level of rates. *See* Harris & Navarro, *supra* note 126. In terms of performance on educational matters, one might compare expenditures per capita in those states with elected officials. The evidence in this regard is not conclusive. Of 17 states with elected education officers, 10 had educational expenditures per capita below the median level of states including states ranked 49, 48, 46, 44, 43, and 41 in expenditures. However, three of the states with elected officials were ranked in the top ten expenditures per capita. *See* USA Today, January 5, 1984, at 3A.

129. *See* The Book of States, *supra* note 126, at 195.

policy coordination. Many policy issues are, at their heart, legal issues. An attorney general who works on a personal agenda, rather than the governor's, is invariably going to conflict with the policy choices that the executive branch has to make.[130]

A paradox emerges from this analysis. While we all applaud democracy, too much democracy, such as the direct election of all policy-makers, can frustrate executive decisionmaking. To support this hypothesis, one need only consider the effect that direct public policy-making, in the form of ballot issues, has had upon the State of California. A state government the size and complexity of California's (or even Rhode Island's) cannot be run by the electorate acting as a committee of the whole. While the initiative process has its defenders (and even proponents, like Jack Kemp, who at one time wanted to make it a national option), the more convincing argument is that government by initiative is likely to produce incoherent responses to critical problems. One observer has labeled the outcome "electoral roulette".[131] Of course, initiatives in California have now been trumped by recalls, in particular the replacement of Governor Davis with Governor Schwarzenegger.

§ 4.7.2 Techniques for achieving policy control at the state level

States exhibit a concern for separation of powers issues and a flexibility about solutions to policy control that offer lessons to the federal government. States seem capable of reorganizing themselves constitutionally so as to restore the discipline of tripartite government. In New Jersey, for example, the only elected officials are the governor and the members of the legislature.[132] In New Jersey and

130. Governor Cuomo of New York once faced that problem with his Attorney General. *See* "Governor, Abrams engaged in Battle," N.Y. Times, Jan. 23, 1984, at 10, col. 1. The Attorney General refused to follow Governor Cuomo's request to defend the Governor's plan to introduce sports betting. The Governor fought back on political grounds, as one might predict. He is quoted as follows: "If he has less legal work to do, that's something to consider," Mr. Cuomo said. "He might need less resources."

131. *See* D. Maglebey, Direct Legislation (1984). Professor Maglebey explains

that in the initiative process the proposals are often written so unclearly that they cannot be comprehended by the vast majority of voters. That is certainly a problem. But even if they *were* written clearly, how could a voter who devotes a few minutes to the process be expected to understand the meaning and implications of initiatives upon critical state priorities. State legislatures who spend their full time in the process are often criticized for failing to understand the implications of their legislative actions.

132. *See* The Book of States, *supra* note 126, at 195–97.

four other states, the governor, with the advice of the legislature (Senate and/or House), appoints the Attorney General and almost all other important agency officials.[133] The states have also produced an ambitious and instructive set of legislative initiatives and judicial opinions on the separation of powers issues that have arisen from their activities.[134]

Another state executive-legislative policy control technique may offer a workable alternative to OMB efforts at the federal level. The Office of Administrative Law (OAL) was established by the California legislature in 1979 as a quasi-independent agency within the executive branch. The agency's purpose is to review all new and existing agency rules for clarity, consistency, authority and necessity. The OAL has the power to reject agency rules outright, which it does usually on the basis of failure to meet a "necessity" requirement. An agency can either accept the disapproval, or rewrite the rule and resubmit it to the OAL. The agency will negotiate with OAL over the language of the rule on an off-the-record basis. If no accommodation can be reached, the agency can appeal to the governor to have the rule reinstated.[135]

The OAL director is appointed by the governor and confirmed by the Senate for a four-year term. The governor may remove the director only for cause; this is what establishes the quasi-independent status of the OAL. Thus, it is an agency within the executive branch whose director does not serve at the pleasure of the governor. The for-cause removal restriction upon executive officials is surely a critical aspect of the California legislation.[136]

133. *Id.*

134. *See, e.g.,* General Assembly of New Jersey v. Byrne, 90 N.J. 376, 448 A.2d 438 (1982); Advisory Opinion In re Separation of Powers Opinion of the Justices, 305 N.C. 767, 295 S.E.2d 589 (1982); State ex rel. McLeod v. McInnis, 278 S.C. 307, 295 S.E.2d 633 (1982). *Compare supra* § 4.3.2 (impact of *Chadha* on federal reorganization policy).

135. West's Ann. Cal. Gov't Code §§ 11340.1, 11349; *see* Cohen, *Regulatory Reform: Assessing the California Plan,* 1983 Duke L.J. 231, 244 n. 68, 265. While the OAL enjoyed a rocky relationship with the agencies at the onset, it has since become an accepted institution in California. *See* M. Asimow, A. Bonfield & R. Levin, State and Federal Administrative Law 504–505 (2d. ed. 1998).

136. At the federal level congressional willingness to cede policy-making power to the executive branch is hampered precisely because OMB is viewed as a White House enclave. The power to share in the appointment (and condition the removal) of OMB's director may be one way to bring the executive and legislative branches closer together. But while this effort may make the agency more accountable, it would raise questions under *Myers* and *Humphrey's Executor* as to whether the President's Article II power was improperly invaded.

§ 4.7.3 Concluding Note: Are All Cabinet Members Equal?

Could some cabinet members have their removal conditioned by Congress? Certainly attempts to condition the removal of the Secretaries of State, Defense or Treasury would run afoul of Article II and *Marbury's* admonition that some positions are inherently executive and political; their appointment must be at the pleasure of the President and may not be conditioned. But would the same limitations apply to the Secretaries of Veterans Affairs or Transportation, for example? These offices are not inherently political and oversee duties that were subject to independent agency control in the past (e.g., ICC authority was transferred to DOT). One might contemplate these duties being transferred to other entities less executive in the future.[137] While few in Congress have given thought to putting for cause removal restrictions on cabinet officials, the ability to do so may not necessarily be foreclosed in all such cases. It is fair to ask whether, once Congress chooses to make an office one of cabinet level significance, its authority to condition the removal of those officials has been conceded.

137. At one time, for example the Postmaster General was a cabinet official, but now much of that office's duties are performed by the Postal Rate Commission, an independent agency.

Chapter Five

JUDICIAL CONTROL OF AGENCY DISCRETION—THRESHOLD ISSUES

§ 5.1   The Role of Judicial Review

It is possible to construct a theory of judicial review of agency action that is entirely consistent with the Constitution's separation of powers between the executive, legislative and judicial branches of government. Granting that Congress has the exclusive power to make the laws and the President has the exclusive power to implement and enforce the laws, the courts have two vital roles in administrative law. First, courts confine agency actions within boundaries established by the Constitution. In this role, the courts exercise power largely independent of that granted by Congress.[1] The judiciary has the power to hold not only that a particular agency action lies impermissibly beyond constitutional boundaries, but also that Congress acted unconstitutionally in purporting to grant an agency the power to take some types of actions. Second, courts limit agency discretion within boundaries established by legislation. In this role, courts assist Congress in implementing policies the legislative branch has chosen to reflect in statutory standards. As long as those standards are within the limits set by the constitution, they are binding on the executive branch, independent agencies, and the courts.

Courts typically review three aspects of agency decisions—conclusions of law, findings of fact, and procedures used in the decision-making process. Each of these components of judicial review serves important purposes linked to the dual goals of assuring that agencies act within constitutional limits and assuring that agency actions are consistent with policy decisions made by the legislature.

§ 5.1.1   Conclusions of law

When Congress grants power to an agency to act in a particular area, it couples that grant of power with statutory limits on the

---

1. Marbury v. Madison, 5 U.S. (1 Cranch) 137 (1803). To some extent, Congress may retain power even over judicial resolution of some constitutional law issues through its power to control the jurisdiction of federal courts. *See* L. Tribe, American Constitutional Law § 3–5 (2d ed. 1988).

circumstances in which the agency is empowered to act and the type of action the agency is permitted to take. Thus, any agency action must be premised on one or more legal conclusions—most frequently, agency interpretations of statutes. The agency's action is consistent with the policy decisions made by the legislature only if the agency's action is based on an accurate determination of the intent of the legislature when it authorized the agency, for instance, to prohibit "undue discrimination" in rates charged for transactions "in interstate commerce",[2] or to establish "discharge standards" that provide "an ample margin of safety".[3] An agency action that is premised on an incorrect interpretation of statutory provisions represents a departure from the policies established by Congress. In this sense, courts aid Congress by insuring that agencies stay within the substantive boundaries established by Congress.

Occasionally, Congress authorizes an agency to act in a manner that is arguably unconstitutional. For instance, Congress' direction to FCC that it cancel a broadcast license because members of Congress were displeased with the views expressed by the licensee violated the First Amendment.[4] In this situation, judicial review of the agency's legal conclusion must proceed through a two step process in order to serve both purposes of judicial review. First, the court must determine whether the agency's interpretation of its statutory authority is correct in order to insure that the agency is not acting in a manner inconsistent with the legislature's determination of national policy. Second, assuming that the agency accurately determined legislative intent, the court must decide whether the action Congress authorized the agency to take is consistent with the Constitution. In some cases, a court will reverse this analytical sequence for prudential reasons. If an agency action raises a serious constitutional issue, a court will strain to interpret the relevant statutory provisions in a manner that does not permit the agency to take the constitutionally questionable action.[5] If it is clear, however, that Congress has authorized an agency to engage in unconstitutional actions, a court will hold the statute authorizing such actions unconstitutional.[6]

---

2. Natural Gas Act, 15 U.S.C. § 717; Federal Power Act, 16 U.S.C. §§ 791–828c.

3. Clean Water Act, 33 U.S.C. § 1317(a).

4. *See* News America Publishing, Inc. v. FCC, 844 F.2d 800 (D.C.Cir.1988).

5. *See* McNary v. Haitian Refugee Center, Inc., 498 U.S. 479 (1991); Johnson v. Robison, 415 U.S. 361 (1974); Ashwander v. Tennessee Valley Authority, 297 U.S. 288, 341, 346–348 (1936) (Brandeis, J., concurring).

6. *See* Buckley v. Valeo, 424 U.S. 1 (1976).

§ 5.1.2 Findings of fact

Legislative delegations of power invariably are accompanied by one or more factually based limits on agency discretion. An agency can act only if specified facts exist or only if its action will cause specified changes in facts. For example, the Food and Drug Administration cannot approve a food additive that is found "to induce cancer in man or animals",[7] and the Environmental Protection Agency must establish water quality criteria that make waters fishable and swimmable.[8] When agencies take actions based on inaccurate factual predicates, they depart from legislative policy just as much as when their actions are based on erroneous interpretations of statutory provisions. In practice, it is often impossible to separate these two forms of agency departure from legislative policy. Agency applications of statutory provisions to specific disputes usually require a combination of statutory interpretation and fact finding that is not easily disentangled. Thus, courts assist the legislative branch when they review an agency finding of fact to insure that the agency has not based its action on inaccurate factual predicates.

Agency fact finding occasionally implicates constitutional law issues. For instance, an agency can regulate the distribution of pornography, but whether a particular publication constitutes pornography or speech protected by the First Amendment is a question of fact. When a court reviews an agency finding with respect to a fact on which the constitutionality of the agency's action depends, it is exercising its independent power to confine all government actions within the boundaries established by the Constitution.

§ 5.1.3 Choice of procedures

The legislature almost invariably couples any grant of power to an agency with procedural safeguards the agency is required to use in deciding whether and how to exercise that power. To some extent, these procedural safeguards are linked to the substantive policy decisions of the legislature through the fact-finding process. If Congress has decided as a matter of substantive policy that an agency should act only on the basis of specified factual predicates, it may also decide that adherence to those factual predicates is so important to substantive goals that the agency should not act unless it is relatively certain that those factual predicates exist. Mandating specific procedural safeguards that reduce the likelihood of erroneous

---

7. Food, Drug, and Cosmetics Act, 21 U.S.C. § 360(d)(1)(H).

8. Clean Water Act, 33 U.S.C. §§ 1251(a)(2), 1313(c)(2).

findings of fact thus can be viewed as an aspect of substantive policy making by the legislative branch.

The procedures Congress requires an agency to use in its decisionmaking also reflect legislative policy decisions of another type. All procedural safeguards involve at least an implicit trade off between fact finding accuracy and factors such as delay in decisionmaking, amount of government and private party resources required in the decisionmaking process, and fairness to individuals potentially affected by agency actions. As Roger Cramton stated years ago, the potential benefits of administrative procedure—fairness and accuracy—must be balanced against the "efficient disposition of agency business."[9] Congress is responsible, at least in the first instance, for selecting the proper balance of costs and benefits of potentially available procedural safeguards. Thus, when courts enforce procedural mandates imposed by Congress, they are once again assisting the legislative branch in implementing its policy decisions.

The Due Process Clause of the Constitution is the source of minimum procedural safeguards that must be provided when a government agency takes an action that deprives a person of life, liberty, or property. When a court reviews an agency action to determine whether the agency provided the minimum safeguards required by due process, it is exercising the independent judicial power to require the government to act within constitutional limits.

§ 5.1.4   Scope of review

Judicial review of agency conclusions of law, findings of fact, and procedures plays two important roles in the administrative process. In some cases, it is essential to permit the courts to confine government discretion within limits set by the Constitution. In almost all cases, judicial review confines agency discretion within limits set by Congress. Thus, where constitutional issues are not implicated, judicial review of agency action is supportive of the efforts of the legislative branch to establish and implement policy through legislative delegation of power. The fact that judicial review serves this critical purpose, however, says little about the desired scope of judicial review of agency actions.

Cases are rare in which the language of a statute can support only one interpretation or the available evidence can support only one finding of fact. Scope of review refers to the extent to which

9. Cramton, *A Comment on Trial-* *Type Hearings in Nuclear Power Plant*   *Siting,* 58 Va. L. Rev. 585, 591 (1972).

reviewing courts defer to agency interpretations of statutes, findings of fact, and choice of procedures. The concept of scope of review is so critical to the administrative law system that it will be discussed in considerable detail in the chapters dealing specifically with review of law, facts, and procedure. For now, it is important only to recognize the reasons courts frequently conclude both that they should review agency actions and that they should give agencies some measure of deference in the review process.

Courts describe their role in reviewing agency findings, conclusions, and procedures as limited. One standard formulation of the test to be used in court review of agency actions calls for affirmance of the agency if its action has a "rational basis".[10] There are several reasons for the deference typically accorded to agency actions. First, Congress frequently indicates its intention to allow agencies a measure of discretion to interpret statutory provisions, resolve factual controversies, and select procedures. To some extent, Congress manifests this intent explicitly through statutory provisions that require use of a deferential standard for review of agency findings and conclusions or that give agencies a choice of procedures to use in resolving disputes. To some extent, however, the legislative intent to accord agencies' discretion is implicit in the congressional choice of statutory language and decisional standards that are susceptible to several different interpretations. Where Congress has indicated its intent to give an agency a measure of discretion, courts engaging in nonconstitutional review of the actions of that agency are bound by that legislative policy decision just as they are bound by legislative policy decisions with respect to the substantive standards or procedures an agency must use.

Second, reviewing courts tend to defer to agencies because agencies often have superior knowledge of the wide range of factors that should be considered in making decisions. The agency's comparative advantage may lie in any or all of the following areas: (1) the subject matter of the dispute, e.g., the EPA is likely to know more about pollution than a judge; (2) the relationship of the specific issue before the agency to the agency's overall statutory mandate and goals; and, (3) the resources available to the agency and the most effective ways of using those scarce resources. The traditional "expertise" rationale for regulation through the use of specialized agencies has fallen into disfavor in recent years in response to the contention of many

10. Camp v. Pitts, 411 U.S. 138 (1973); NLRB v. Hearst Publications, Inc., 322 U.S. 111, 131 (1944).

observers of the process that agencies often do not have a good understanding of their areas of responsibility.[11] This contention might well support efforts to improve the quality of agency decision-makers or even to reduce the amount of government intervention in the economy. It does not support, however, a movement toward granting agencies less deference on judicial review. Such a change could only be supported by studies demonstrating that generalist judges, who may be called upon to review a particular dispute in a specialized area once or twice a year, have a knowledge of that area superior to agency decision makers who are required to resolve hundreds of similar and related disputes each year. This case has never been made.

Third, courts defer to agencies in part because of a recognition that the institutional role of the courts limits their power to effectuate government policies. When a court reverses an agency, the result of that reversal rarely is to substitute immediately a better decision for the agency's flawed decision. Rather, the typical opinion reversing an agency requires the agency to begin the decisionmaking process again, with a better understanding of the substantive standards or procedures Congress required the agency to use. Courts have the power to block agency actions based on any of several possible errors committed by the agency, and the ultimate effect of such court reversal may be an improvement in the agency's action on remand. The immediate effect of court reversal, however, often is to delay implementation of any regulatory policy.[12] In this situation, many courts have an understandable tendency to affirm agency actions that are premised on less than an ideal evaluation of the relevant factual and legal issues in order to avoid the social costs of delaying agency action to obtain only a slight improvement in decisionmaking quality. Courts often remand a rule to an agency without vacating the rule if the court concludes that the agency is likely to be able to respond adequately to the court's objections to the rule. Commentators and judges are debating the legality of this approach.[13]

11. *See generally* S. Breyer, Regulation and Its Reform 342–345 (1982).

12. For instance, the Fifth Circuit reversed seven consecutive orders of the Federal Power Commission and its successor, the Federal Energy Regulatory Commission, attempting to establish a policy for allocation of a natural gas shortage experienced by a pipeline. As a result, while the proceedings began in 1973, there was still no policy in effect in 1983 that a reviewing court had found legally acceptable. In the absence of a policy established by the agency and affirmed by a court, the shortage was allocated according to policies unilaterally determined by the pipeline itself. *See* Southern Natural Gas Co. v. FERC, 714 F.2d 424 (5th Cir.1983).

13. See Levin, *"Vacation" at Sea: Judicial Remedies and Equitable Discretion in Administrative Law*, 53 Duke L.J. (2003)(describing the cases and the debate).

§ 5.1.5 Consistency and rationality as limits on discretion

For all of the reasons stated above, courts permit agencies considerable discretion in all aspects of decisionmaking—fact finding, interpreting statutes, and selecting procedures. The existence of this substantial discretion within agencies explains in part another set of concerns that motivates courts that are called upon to review agency actions. Where discretion exists, there is always the potential for its abuse. This danger is particularly acute where the substantive standards established by the legislature are vague, or the factual predicates for agency action are uncertain. Agency decisionmakers could exercise their discretion in any of several ways that are inimical to the public welfare and inconsistent with the intent of Congress. Agency discretion could be exercised for corrupt reasons, to help political allies or to punish political foes, or it could simply be exercised in a sloppy manner.

Some of the tests used by courts to review agency actions are rooted in large part in a desire to minimize the potential for abuse of agency discretion. The best single example of this force at work in the process of judicial review is the recurrent emphasis on rationality and consistency in agency decision making. Reviewing courts scrutinize agency actions in an effort to detect irrationality and unexplained inconsistency of various types. They search for (1) internal consistency and rationality in the agency's reasoning process; (2) interdecisional consistency—are similar cases being resolved in a similar manner; and, (3) intertemporal consistency—is the agency applying the same decisional standards over time. Consistency serves many valuable purposes. It is one of the central principles of distributive justice. It provides an automatic check on corruption and political partisanship in decision making, and it provides notice of what conduct is permissible or impermissible. To the extent that the legislative branch has failed to assure consistent agency decisionmaking by confining agency discretion within narrow statutory limits, courts search for some other means of requiring agencies to be consistent. For this purpose they refer most frequently to the agency's own statements in its rules, pronouncements of policy, its prior or contemporaneous decisions in other cases, and its other statements in the agency action that is subject to court review.

In the chapters that follow, the major cases in administrative law will be analyzed with reference to this theory of judicial review of agency action. Generally, the court opinions are consistent with the theory, but many cases illustrate the difficulty of applying the theory consistently, and several suggest that courts sometimes succumb to the understandable temptation to assume a role greater than that allocated to the judiciary in the Constitution and applicable statutes.

§ 5.2   The Constitutional Basis for Judicial Review

In some cases, an aggrieved party has no right to judicial review of an agency action at all or that right is significantly circumscribed. Until 1988, for instance, most decisions of the Veteran's Administration were not subject to judicial review.[14] A party attempting to obtain judicial review of an agency action must find a right to judicial review either in a statute governing the action or in the Constitution.

There is no constitutional right to judicial review of an agency action unless that action arguably infringes upon a constitutional right. Thus, if Congress indicates clearly its intent that a certain type of agency action not be reviewed by courts, courts defer to that legislative decision as long as the agency action does not implicate constitutional issues.[15] This principle is consistent with, and arguably required by, the constitutional separation of powers. Setting aside constitutional issues, the role of the judiciary is to enforce the policy decisions of the legislative branch. The legislative branch has the power to make those policy decisions, including decisions that judicial review of certain types of agency actions would do more harm than good because of the attendant delays in implementing agency actions, the potential that the decentralized judiciary will introduce inconsistencies in the agency's decisionmaking process, and the burdens on the agency of having to defend its actions in court.

The issue of whether a party has a constitutional right to judicial review of an agency action arises infrequently because the legislature usually provides an explicit statutory right to judicial review. When legislative intent is not clear, courts presume that Congress intended to provide a right to judicial review of an agency action.[16]

Courts go to extreme lengths to determine that Congress intended to permit judicial review of constitutional issues raised by agency actions in order to minimize direct conflicts between the legislative and judicial branches.[17] For this reason, cases specifically holding

---

14. *See* Stichman, *The Veterans Judicial Review Act of 1988: Congress Introduces Courts and Attorneys to Veterans' Benefits Proceedings*, 41 Admin.L.Rev. 365 (1989).

15. *See, e.g.,* Briscoe v. Bell, 432 U.S. 404 (1977).

16. Abbott Laboratories v. Gardner, 387 U.S. 136, 141 (1967).

17. *See* Webster v. Doe, 486 U.S. 592 (1988); Johnson v. Robison, 415 U.S. 361 (1974).

that there is a constitutional right to judicial review of constitutional issues raised by agency actions are exceedingly rare. Despite the dearth of case law on the issue, dicta in several cases[18] and scholarly analysis[19] suggest strongly that there is a constitutional right to judicial review of constitutional issues raised by agency actions.

Agency actions can implicate at least two different types of constitutional issues—violation of substantive rights and violation of procedural rights. The Supreme Court's decision in *Johnson v. Robison*[20] illustrates both. Robison, a conscientious objector who had served two years of alternate service, applied for and was denied veteran's benefits. He sought judicial review of the denial on two grounds: (1) denial of veteran's benefits to a conscientious objector who provides alternate service violates the First Amendment right to freedom of religion, and (2) denial of veteran's benefits without providing sufficient procedural safeguards violates the Fifth Amendment right to Due Process. The Court held that Robison was entitled to judicial review of both issues based on its interpretation of legislative intent. Congress had specifically forbidden judicial review of VA decisions concerning eligibility for benefits for two reasons: (1) to assure uniformity in eligibility decisions, and (2) to avoid burdening VA and the courts with expensive and time consuming court challenges. The Court concluded that Congress had not intended to prohibit judicial review of constitutional questions raised by VA actions because court review of this limited nature did not create either of the problems Congress sought to avoid by prohibiting judicial review. The Court pointed out that a different interpretation of legislative intent would raise serious issues concerning the constitutionality of the statute.

Judges and Justices disagree on two issues that arise in this area. First, there is a difference of opinion with respect to the propriety of interpreting a statute that appears to preclude all judicial review of a class of agency actions as a statute that permits judicial review of constitutional issues raised by an agency action. Thus, for instance, the Justices divided on this issue in *Webster v. Doe*.[21] The CIA Director fired an employee as a security risk. The

18.　*E.g., Id.*

19.　*See* Hart, *The Power of Congress to Limit the Jurisdiction of Federal Courts: An Exercise in Dialectic,* 66 Harv. L.Rev. 1362 (1953).

20.　415 U.S. 361 (1974). A seven-Justice majority reaffirmed the approach

taken in Johnson v. Robison in McNary v. Haitian Refugee Center, Inc., 498 U.S. 479 (1991).

21.　486 U.S. 592 (1988). *See also* Demore v. Hyung Joon Kim, 538 U.S. 510 (2003) (holding six-to-three that a statute that seemed to preclude all judicial re-

employee sought judicial review of that action, claiming that it violated both a statute and the Constitution. The Court unanimously interpreted the statute to reflect a congressional decision that a court should not review such an agency decision to determine whether it violates a statute. A six-Justice majority then applied the canon of construction that requires a court to interpret a statute in a manner that avoids raising a serious question with respect to the constitutionality of the statute. Through application of that canon, the majority attributed to Congress an intent not to prohibit judicial review of the constitutionality of the agency's action. Two Justices dissented on that issue. They saw no evidence in the statute that Congress intended to allow courts to consider constitutional attacks on the validity of the CIA Director's decision to fire an employee as a security risk. They interpreted the statute as evidencing congressional intent to preclude the courts from engaging in any form of review of such decisions. They also expressed the view that such a congressional prohibition on judicial consideration of the arguable unconstitutionality of an agency action did not raise any serious constitutional question, at least in the context of this class of agency actions— CIA decisions to fire employees as security risks.

Second, there is a difference of opinion concerning the types of constitutional challenges that a court should consider when the language of a statute suggests that Congress intended to preclude judicial review of a class of agency actions. This difference of opinion is apparent in the opinions issued by the divided en banc Seventh Circuit in *Czerkies v. Department of Labor.*[22] A federal employee sought judicial review of a decision of the Office of Workers Compensation Programs that denied him benefits to which he thought he was entitled. The judges unanimously interpreted the statute as evidencing congressional intent that courts not review such decisions. An eight-judge majority held, however, that the employee could obtain review of his claim that the procedures the agency used violated due process, even though the language of the statute seemed to forbid review on any basis. Three judges wrote a separate opinion in which they drew a distinction between a claim that an agency engaged in an isolated violation of the Constitution in a particular case and a claim that an agency was engaged in a systematic violation of the Constitution in an entire class of cases. They argued that a court has the power to consider only the latter type of alleged violation of the

view of a class of agency actions did not preclude review of constitutional claims.)

22. 73 F.3d 1435 (7th Cir. en banc 1996).

Constitution in the face of a statute that seems to forbid all judicial review of the agency action at issue.

There may be another type of issue that falls within the scope of the constitutional right to judicial review. In *Wayne State University v. Cleland,*[23] the Sixth Circuit strongly suggested that there is a constitutional right to judicial review of actions that are claimed to be ultra vires, that is, beyond the statutory power of the agency. The Sixth Circuit's conclusion is suspect, however, since ultra vires is not an issue of constitutional law.[24] Ultra vires actions do not appear to violate any constitutional prohibition. They are simply unlawful because they are not authorized by statute. In addition, it would be difficult to limit the scope of a constitutionally based right to judicial review of actions claimed to be ultra vires,[25] since a clever lawyer can turn any argument that an agency committed an error into an argument that it acted beyond its statutory power.

Judicial recognition of a constitutional component to judicial review of agency action creates the need to address two subsidiary issues: (1) can Congress place any limits on the exercise of the constitutional right to judicial review of constitutional issues, and (2) can the courts grant some measure of deference to agency findings with respect to facts with constitutional implications. The courts have answered both questions in the affirmative.

§ 5.2.1 Legislative limits on judicial review of constitutional questions

Congress has the power to limit in some ways the exercise of the constitutional right to obtain judicial review of constitutional issues raised by agency actions. For instance, the legislature frequently limits the time in which a constitutional issue raised by an agency action can be the subject of court review. Two cases indicate that courts will defer to such temporal limits imposed by the legislature.

Yakus v. United States[26] involved an attempt to challenge the validity of price control regulations in a criminal proceeding initiated to enforce those regulations against Yakus. A majority of the Court held that Yakus was precluded from challenging the regulations in the enforcement proceeding because: (1) Congress had provided a prior opportunity to challenge the validity of the regulations in the pre-enforcement context; (2) Yakus had not availed himself of that

---

23. 590 F.2d 627 (6th Cir.1978).

24. *See, e.g.,* Carter v. Cleland, 643 F.2d 1, 7 (D.C.Cir.1980).

25. *See* Verkuil, *Congressional Limitations on Judicial Review of Rules,* 57 Tul.L.Rev. 733, 751–753 (1983).

26. 321 U.S. 414 (1944).

opportunity; (3) the 60 day time period provided by Congress for pre-enforcement judicial review of the regulations had expired; and, (4) Congress had explicitly limited review of the validity of the regulations to the period 60 days after their promulgation. The Court reasoned that, since Congress had provided an adequate alternative method of judicial review, it could prohibit review of the regulations in a later enforcement action.

Three characteristics of *Yakus* suggest the need for caution in interpreting the Court's decision. First, it arose in the context of wartime price controls where the need for expeditious final resolution of issues of validity of regulations was particularly apparent, perhaps even at the sacrifice of some legal rights that courts normally grant criminal defendants during conditions of peace. Second, even in that context, Justice Rutledge wrote a spirited dissent. Third, the majority specifically noted that it was not presented with a challenge to the constitutionality of the regulations.

Adamo Wrecking Co. v. United States[27] involved a more recent attempt to obtain judicial review of a regulation in an enforcement proceeding outside the special context of wartime regulations. EPA had promulgated an emission standard under the Clean Air Act that required persons engaged in demolition of buildings to follow specified procedures to limit the pollutants entering the atmosphere as a result of demolition. The Clean Air Act provided a right to judicial review of an emission standard, but limited the exercise of that right to the 30 day period following the promulgation of the standard. Adamo did not seek judicial review of the regulation applicable to its activities within that period. EPA subsequently charged Adamo with criminal violation of the regulation, and Adamo attempted to challenge the regulation in the enforcement proceeding.

The Court held that Congress had permissibly limited the time in which Adamo could challenge the regulation to the thirty day period following its promulgation. Thus, a court could not review the regulation by pursuing any of the traditional inquiries into the procedural or substantive adequacy of the regulation. The Court did permit Adamo to pursue a much more limited type of judicial review in which a court could conclude that the regulation was invalid on definitional grounds, that is, a court could conclude that the regulation was not valid because it was not an "emission standard" at all. Since the regulation at issue required a wrecking company to abate asbestos emissions potentially resulting from demolition of a building

27.   434 U.S. 275 (1978).

through use of specific procedures, there was a serious question whether the regulation actually met the statutory definition of an "emissions standard". The Court permitted this form of judicial review based on its conclusion that the legislature had not intended to limit this narrow type of definitional review exclusively to the 30 day period provided by the statute.

Adamo did not allege that the Clean Air Act limit on judicial review was unconstitutional, and only one Justice explicitly discussed that issue. In a concurring opinion, Justice Powell expressed serious reservations concerning the constitutionality of the legislative limit on judicial review. He questioned whether it was realistic to assume that 30 days was an adequate period for the many contractors affected by the regulation to become aware of its existence and to initiate judicial review proceedings. He suggested that *Yakus* was distinguishable because of its wartime context.

It is risky to attach too much significance to *Yakus* and *Adamo*. Neither involved a direct challenge to a legislative provision that limited judicial review of the constitutionality of an agency action, and both provoked some disagreement among the Justices. It seems likely, however, that courts will defer to reasonable time limits imposed by the legislature on the right to judicial review of constitutional issues raised by agency actions in most contexts. There are many circumstances, apart from the exigencies of war, in which prompt, final resolution of all issues concerning the validity of agency actions will yield substantial benefits to the public. Those benefits can include greater certainty concerning permissible conduct and reduced costs of agency enforcement efforts. Thus, the decision to impose reasonable time limits on exercise of the right to judicial review of constitutional issues is one of those policy decisions that should be allocated to the legislative branch.

There is one context, however, in which a court can be expected to review a constitutional question raised by an agency action even if such a question is first brought to a court's attention after the time period provided by the legislature. Sometimes the scope of an agency regulation is not clear at the time the agency initially promulgates the regulation. The regulation may not raise any serious constitutional issues in its most obvious applications. Yet, the agency may apply the regulation at some later time in an unexpected manner that does raise serious constitutional issues. Courts almost certainly will review such an "as applied" challenge to the constitutionality of an agency action even if the challenge is brought after the time permitted by the legislature. It seems patently unfair to require a party to forego a constitutional right merely because it failed to assert that right at a time when it had no reason to believe that the right was in jeopardy.[28] In this situation, however, a court is likely to use one of two traditional methods of avoiding a direct confrontation with the legislature. Either the court will interpret the agency regulation in a manner that renders the regulation inapplicable to the situation in which it raises serious constitutional issues,[29] or it will interpret the statutory limit on judicial review in a manner that renders that limit inapplicable to constitutional challenges to the agency's regulations.[30] Indeed, courts routinely interpret statutory time limits on judicial review not to begin to run until after the issue a petitioner seeks to raise is ripe for review.[31]

§ 5.2.2   Review of issues of constitutional fact

Sometimes the constitutional validity of an agency action depends upon whether a particular fact exists. For instance, when a firm is subject to rate regulation, the rates set for the firm can be so low that they violate the Fifth Amendment prohibition against taking property without "just compensation".[32] Thus, the constitutionality of the rates set for the firm by an agency depends in part on the accuracy of the agency's findings with respect to facts such as the value of the firm's assets and the amount of costs it incurs. In the context of a challenge to the constitutionality of rates established by an agency, these become issues of "constitutional fact."

In *Ohio Valley Water Co. v. Ben Avon Borough*,[33] the Court held that the Due Process Clause requires that any constitutional fact must be subject to de novo review by a court. That is, a reviewing court must retry the issue as if the agency had not addressed it at all. This holding was broadened in *Crowell v. Benson*[34] to require de novo review of any "fundamental" or "jurisdictional" fact, that is, a fact

---

28. *See* Verkuil, *supra* note 25, at 749–751.

29. *See, e.g.,* Phelps Dodge Corp. v. Federal Mine Safety and Health Review Comm'n, 681 F.2d 1189 (9th Cir.1982) (refusing to apply regulation to Phelps because regulation did not give Phelps fair warning that Phelps' conduct was prohibited).

30. *See, e.g.,* Johnson v. Robison, 415 U.S. 361 (1974) (interpreting statutory provision prohibiting judicial review not

to preclude review of constitutional issues).

31. *E.g.,* Atlantic States Legal Foundation v. EPA, 325 F.3d 281, 285 (D.C. Cir. 2003); Baltimore Gas & Electric Co. v. ICC, 672 F.2d 146, 149 (D.C. Cir. 1982). See section 5.7.3 for discussion of the ripeness doctrine.

32. *See* Railroad Commission Cases, 116 U.S. 307, 331 (1886).

33. 253 U.S. 287 (1920).

34. 285 U.S. 22 (1932).

whose existence is essential to the agency's statutory power to take the challenged action.

The Court has never explicitly overruled *Ben Avon* and *Crowell v. Benson,* but the Court[35] and commentators[36] seem to agree that the doctrine of de novo review of constitutional and jurisdictional facts is now moribund. Modern courts accord to agency findings of facts of this type the same degree of deference they accord to other findings of fact on which the validity of the agency's action depends. Thus, constitutional and jurisdictional facts usually are subject to the "substantial evidence" or "arbitrary and capricious" standards of review incorporated in the Administrative Procedure Act.[37]

The demise of the *Ben Avon* doctrine can be attributed to a number of changes in judicial attitude: (1) abandonment of attempts to find substantive economic content in the Due Process Clause;[38] (2) recognition that agencies are at least as capable as courts of making accurate factual findings;[39] and, (3) recognition that de novo review of findings of fact eliminated many of the efficiency-enhancing advantages of delegating decisions to specialized agencies.

§ 5.3　The Statutory Basis for Judicial Review

Congress has expressly provided a statutory right to judicial review of most agency actions, either by including such a right in the organic act that authorizes the agency to take the challenged action or by making the agency's action subject to the judicial review provisions of the Administrative Procedure Act (APA).

Most final agency actions are subject to judicial review in accordance with the provisions of the APA. Section 701 of the APA provides a right to judicial review "except to the extent that—(1) statutes preclude judicial review; or (2) agency action is committed to agency discretion by law." The first exception is relatively straight forward. If Congress has specifically prohibited judicial review of an agency action, courts defer to that legislative prohibition. If Congress

35. *See* Northern Pipeline Constr. Co. v. Marathon Pipe Line Co., 458 U.S. 50, 82 n. 34 (1982).

36. *See* P. Strauss, T. Rakoff, and C. Farina, Administrative Law 973–978 (10th ed. 2003).

37. *See* section 7.3, *infra.*

38. *See* Verkuil, *supra* note 25, at 746. This explanation is consistent with the continuing judicial practice of engaging in de novo review of constitutional facts in circumstances where the agency action has the potential to infringe upon a noneconomic constitutional right. For instance, courts engage in de novo review of an agency finding that a book or film is pornographic. *See* L. Tribe, *supra* note 1, at 1054.

39. *See* Dickinson, *Crowell v. Benson: Judicial Review of Administrative Determinations or Questions of "Constitutional Fact,"* 80 U.Pa.L.Rev. 1055 (1932).

has not explicitly addressed the issue of judicial review or if it has addressed that issue in an ambiguous manner, courts frequently determine that Congress intended that the action be subject to judicial review. In interpreting statutes, the courts presume that Congress intended to provide a right to judicial review.[40] A trio of Supreme Court decisions in the 1980s suggests, however, that the presumption of reviewability is not as strong as it once was.[41]

The second exception in APA section 701 is more troublesome. Taken literally, it could foreclose almost all judicial review, since most statutes that authorize agencies to take actions also confer on those agencies considerable discretion. The legislative history of section 701 indicates that the second exception was intended to limit judicial review of agency action where "statutes are drawn in such broad forms that in a given case there is no law to apply".[42] This legislative history provides some additional guidance, since it focuses attention on the extent of the discretion granted the agency rather than the existence of any discretion. It suggests that a court should decline to review an agency action only when Congress has declined to provide any judicially enforceable statutory limit on an agency's discretion.

Even with this additional guidance, however, the agency discretion exception to the APA right to judicial review is problematic. Congress frequently delegates authority to act bounded by standards so vague or inherently in conflict that a court could conclude that Congress gave the agency complete discretion.[43] The Supreme Court responded initially to this problem by interpreting the second exception in section 701 in a narrow manner. Recently, however, the Court has shown less reluctance to hold that an action is committed to agency discretion.

Citizens to Preserve Overton Park, Inc. v. Volpe[44] provides the starting point for analyzing the agency discretion exception. *Overton Park* involved a challenge to a decision by the Secretary of Transportation to provide federal aid to permit construction of a highway through a public park. The statutes authorizing such federal funding

40. Abbott Laboratories v. Gardner, 387 U.S. 136, 141 (1967).

41. Webster v. Doe, 486 U.S. 592 (1988); Heckler v. Chaney, 470 U.S. 821 (1985); Block v. Community Nutrition Institute, 467 U.S. 340 (1984).

42. S.Rep. No. 752, 79th Cong., 1st Sess., 26 (1945); *see, e.g.* International Union, United Automobile, Aerospace &

Agricultural Implement Workers v. Donovan, 746 F.2d 855, 863 (D.C.Cir.1984) (lump-sum appropriation which provided no direction for distribution gave Secretary unreviewable discretion).

43. *See infra* §§ 7.4–7.5.

44. 401 U.S. 402 (1971).

prohibited federal aid to highways through public parks unless "there is no feasible and prudent alternative". The Secretary argued that his action was not subject to judicial review because Congress authorized him to exercise wide discretion concerning the routing of federally funded highways. The Court concluded that the statute limited the Secretary's discretion in ways that were capable of judicial enforcement. Thus, it declined to apply the committed to agency discretion exception to the APA right of judicial review, characterizing that exception as applicable only "in those rare instances where ... there is no law to apply".

The narrow interpretation of APA § 701(a)(2) announced in *Overton Park,* combined with the presumption of reviewability reaffirmed in *Overton Park*, allowed courts to assert the power to review almost any agency action. Directionally, *Overton Park* had that effect. Yet, circuit courts sometimes declined the Court's apparent invitation to review virtually all types of agency actions.

Two appellate court opinions involving the same issue illustrate the tendency of courts to decline to review some types of agency actions in the absence of a statutory provision authorizing review notwithstanding the Court's holdings in *Overton Park*. In *Hahn v. Gottlieb,*[45] the First Circuit was asked by a tenant's group to review a rent increase authorized by the Federal Housing Administration (FHA) for a privately owned, but federally financed and subsidized, low income housing project. The court declined to review the FHA action, holding that rent increases granted by FHA fall within the committed to agency discretion exception of the APA. The statute did not prohibit judicial review, and it provided a decisional standard at least as capable of judicial application as the "just and reasonable" and "public interest" standards routinely applied by reviewing courts in other contexts. Under the FHA statute, rent increases were authorized to assure "a reasonable return on investment consistent with providing reasonable rentals to tenants".

The First Circuit based its holding on three factors: (1) the appropriateness of the issues raised for review by the courts; (2) the need for judicial review to safeguard the interests of the plaintiffs; and, (3) the impact of review on the effectiveness of the agency in carrying out its assigned role. With respect to the first factor, the court concluded that it could not contribute intelligently to the process of determining rents because that process requires consideration of complicated economic, financial, and accounting issues. The

45. 430 F.2d 1243 (1st Cir.1970).

court recognized that the second factor suggested a need for judicial review, since tenants of low income public housing projects have a strong interest in maintaining low rents. It went on, however, to allude to the possibility that judicial review of rent increase decisions might hurt tenants in the long run because: "Delay, the frictions engendered by the process of litigation, and the possibility—seldom discussed—of landlord appeals from FHA decisions in favor of tenants may lead to higher rentals immediately and ultimately to less participation [in low income housing projects] by private investors."

The court seemed to consider the third factor dispositive; it concluded that judicial review of FHA approvals of rate increases would impair the agency's effectiveness in fulfilling its mission for two reasons. First, FHA has frequent occasion to consider requests for rate increases, and judicial review would force FHA to use more formal decision making in all such cases. The court feared that judicial review, therefore, would be inconsistent with constant congressional pressure for increased simplification and expedition in "essentially managerial decisions". Second, judicial review would expose private investors in low income housing to increased delay and risk in receiving a return on their investment. This, in turn, would discourage investment in low income housing when Congress indicated its intent to encourage such investment.

The First Circuit's opinion in *Hahn* is problematic on at least two grounds. First, FHA approval of rent increase requests seems precisely analogous to the ratemaking functions of scores of federal agencies—both the issues on review and the implications of review are identical. Yet, courts routinely review agency actions approving rate increases involving utilities, railroads, trucks, buses, etc. Second, the First Circuit's broad interpretation of the agency discretion exception seems inconsistent with the Supreme Court's characterization of that exception in *Overton Park* as "very narrow" and as applicable only in "rare instances".

The Second Circuit had occasion to consider precisely the same issue in *Langevin v. Chenango Court, Inc.*[46] It declined to follow the First Circuit's precedent in *Hahn,* noting that courts frequently review agency actions functionally identical to FHA grants of rent increase requests. Significantly, however, the Second Circuit also found this class of agency actions unreviewable, but on different grounds. It found the statute ambiguous concerning the right to judicial review, and interpreted it to preclude judicial review. The

46.   447 F.2d 296 (2d Cir.1971).

Second Circuit's conclusion that the legislature intended to preclude judicial review of FHA rent increase approvals was based primarily on two factors: (1) the large number of rent increase actions that would be subject to review, and (2) the "managerial nature of the responsibilities confided to the FHA".

The Second Circuit's opinion in *Langevin* is as difficult to reconcile with *Overton Park* as the First Circuit's opinion in *Hahn*. The *Overton Park* Court held that the separate APA exception to the right to judicial review based on statutory preclusion of review is applicable only when there is "clear and convincing" evidence that Congress sought to prohibit judicial review. The evidence of such legislative intent cited by the Second Circuit seems to fall far short of the "clear and convincing" standard.

There are too many other decisions refusing review on similar grounds to permit summary dismissal of *Hahn* and *Langevin* as mere idiosyncratic aberrations. In several contexts, the courts seem not to follow the Supreme Court's holding in *Overton Park* that nonreviewability is the rare case. These cases seem to have in common the factors principally relied upon by the *Hahn* and *Langevin* courts: (1) statutes that are ambiguous on the issue of judicial review; (2) a large number of agency actions potentially subject to review; (3) imprecise decisional standards; and, (4) issues that are complicated and difficult for courts to understand. In addition, these cases seem to arise in two decisionmaking contexts in which courts are particularly reluctant to participate—"managerial" decisions[47] and decisions that have foreign relations or military implications.[48]

In a trio of cases decided in 1985, 1988, and 1994, the Court legitimized the approach taken in cases like *Hahn* and *Langevin*, broadened its interpretation of the "committed to agency discretion" exception to judicial review, and both narrowed and weakened the presumption of reviewability. In *Heckler v. Chaney*,[49] the Court held unreviewable FDA's refusal to take enforcement action against states that used drugs that have not been proven "safe and effective" for the purpose of implementing capital punishment by lethal injection.

---

47. *See, e.g.,* Kletschka v. Driver, 411 F.2d 436 (2d Cir.1969) (grant decisions and personnel transfer decisions of VA are unreviewable); Ferry v. Udall, 336 F.2d 706 (9th Cir.1964) (decisions concerning use of public lands are unreviewable).

48. Panama Canal Co. v. Grace Line, Inc., 356 U.S. 309 (1958) (decisions on rates for use of Panama Canal are unreviewable); Dalehite v. U.S., 346 U.S. 15 (1953) (decisions concerning method of shipping goods in foreign aid program are unreviewable); U.S. ex rel. Schonbrun v. Commanding Officer, 403 F.2d 371 (2d Cir.1968) (military decisions are unreviewable).

49. 470 U.S. 821 (1985).

More broadly, the Court announced a presumption of unreviewability of agency decisions not to prosecute or enforce. The Court concluded that such decisions are presumptively committed to agency discretion because they require an agency to balance a number of factors peculiarly within its expertise in the process of determining how to allocate its scarce resources. The Court referred to two possible ways of rebutting the presumption of unreviewability of agency inaction: (1) by reference to a statute that requires an agency to act in specified circumstances; or, (2) by reference to a legislative rule in which the agency itself has committed to act in specified circumstances.

In *Webster v. Doe,*[50] the Court held unreviewable the CIA Director's decision to terminate an employee. The statute authorized the Director "in his discretion" to terminate an employee "whenever he shall deem such termination necessary or advisable in the interest of the United States." The Court held that termination decisions under this statutory standard are "committed to agency discretion" because: (1) the language "fairly exudes deference to the Director"; (2) there was "no law to apply", since the statute provided "no meaningful standard against which to judge the agency's exercise of discretion"; and, (3) the discretionary power to discharge employees seemed to follow logically from the agency's national security mission. Significantly, the Court did not hold that an agency decision that is "committed to agency discretion" is insulated from judicial review on all grounds. Rather, the Court held only that such decisions are insulated from statutory review under the APA. Thus, a six-Justice majority of the Court permitted Doe to attempt to establish that his termination violated the Constitution.

In *Dalton v. Specter,*[51] the Court held unanimously that none of the actions taken in closing military bases through use of the procedures prescribed in the Defense Base Closure and Realignment Act of 1990 are subject to judicial review. That statute created the Base Closing Commission and authorized it to prepare a report recommending the closure of military bases. The Act required the closure of the bases the Commission recommended for closure if, but only if, the report of the Commission was approved by the President and was not the subject of a joint congressional resolution of disapproval. Neither the President nor Congress could change the report in any way. The statute gave the President only the choice of complete approval or complete disapproval of the report and gave

50.   486 U.S. 592 (1988).   **51.**   511 U.S. 462 (1994).

Congress only the choice of implicit acquiescence or complete disapproval. The Commission issued a report that recommended the closure of many bases, and the President approved that report and submitted it to Congress. Senator Specter sought judicial review of both the Commission's report and the President's approval of that report. A five-Justice majority held that the Commission's report is not reviewable because it does not qualify as "final agency action," and that the President's approval of the report is not reviewable because the President is not an "agency."[52] Four concurring Justices expressed the view that it was unnecessary to address those issues. The Court was unanimous in holding that the statute implicitly precluded judicial review of base closing decisions. The Court referred to several features of the statutory procedures for closing bases that provided circumstantial evidence that Congress did not want the courts to review any of the actions that ultimately produced a decision to close a base. Those features included: Presidential and Congressional review of the Commission's report, the all or nothing nature of the potential Presidential and Congressional actions, tight and rigid action deadlines, and statutory provisions specifically authorizing judicial review of some post-closure actions taken in implementing the statute. The Court concluded that the circumstantial evidence of an intent to preclude review of base closure decisions was sufficient to rebut the "strong presumption that Congress did not mean to prohibit all review."

The circuit courts have experienced some difficulty applying the new standards for reviewability announced in *Chaney*, *Doe*, and *Dalton*. Those opinions unquestionably have reduced the classes of agency actions that are reviewable under the APA, however.[53]

§ 5.4 Standing to Obtain Judicial Review of Administrative Action

Not everyone can invoke the power of a court to review an agency action. A court will review an agency action only at the behest of a party who has standing to challenge that action. The two part test for resolving the standing question first announced by the Court in *Association of Data Processing Service Organizations, Inc. v. Camp*[54] provides the starting point for analyzing standing issues: (1) "[t]he first question is whether the plaintiff alleges that the chal-

52. See infra § 5.7.1 for a discussion of "final agency action."

53. *See* Levin, *Understanding Unreviewability in Administrative Law,* 74 Minn.L.Rev. 689 (1990).

54. 397 U.S. 150 (1970).

lenged action has caused him injury in fact, economic or otherwise"; (2) the second question is "whether the interest sought to be protected by the complainant is arguably within the zone of interests to be protected or regulated by the statute or constitutional guarantee in question".

The first part of the test is based on Article III of the Constitution. That Article limits the power of federal courts to the resolution of "cases" and "controversies". The second part of the *Association of Data Processors* test is statutory. It asks the question whether Congress intended to allow parties in plaintiff's situation to obtain judicial review of the type of agency action challenged. By imposing this second requirement, the Court recognizes that it is up to Congress to decide as a matter of policy the parties that have the power to obtain judicial review of an agency action,[55] except in unusual cases where the agency action arguably violates the party's constitutional rights[56] or where Congress has violated Article III by authorizing a court to resolve a dispute that does not qualify as a "case or controversy."[57]

The articulation of the test for standing in *Association of Data Processors* is deceptively simple. In fact, standing may be the most arcane and bewildering concept in administrative law. The Court applies the test to determine standing in several different ways that produce seemingly inconsistent results.

It is impossible to understand the major cases on standing without recognizing that the Court uses the standing doctrine to serve many different purposes. Commentators have identified several unstated purposes that the Court has tried to further through its decisions on standing.[58] In addition to the articulated goals of implementing the case or controversy limitation of Article III and effectuating congressional intent, the Court sometimes uses standing: (1) to avoid deciding issues it does not want to decide; (2) to allow it to decide issues it does want to decide; (3) to avoid deciding issues that it believes should be decided by other branches of government; (4) to avoid deciding issues that should be decided by state governments; (5) to reflect implicitly the subjective values the Court assigns to various constitutional and statutory rights; (6) to limit the ability of judges to become involved in policy disputes that are governed only

55. *See* Consumer Federation of America v. FTC, 515 F.2d 367 (D.C.Cir. 1975).

56. *See supra* § 5.2.

57. *See infra* § 5.4.2.

58. *See* Nichol, *"Re–Thinking Standing,"* 72 Cal.L.Rev. 68 (1984). *See generally* L. Tribe, *supra* note 1, at §§ 3–14 to 3–21.

by vague constitutional standards; and (7) to avoid judicial involvement in cases where the plaintiff's claim has little merit. The Court has ignored the near unanimous pleas of commentators to unravel the many strands of the overburdened standing doctrine and to assign to other doctrines those concerns that have no relationship to the central question of *who* should have access to the courts to challenge a government action that arguably violates the law. Thus, the student of administrative law has no choice but to try to understand a series of cases that defy explanation solely on the basis of the decisional factors identified by the Court. It is easiest to begin this process through an historical approach.

§ 5.4.1   The history of the constitutional test for standing

In its modern standing decisions, the Court routinely applies the "Case or Controversy" Clause of Article III as a constitutionally-based limit on standing. The Court interprets Article III to require a plaintiff who has suffered an "injury-in-fact" that was "caused" by the challenged action and that can be "redressed" by a judicial decision reversing the challenged action. The Court defines "injury-in-fact" to include only certain types of injuries, e.g., "concrete," "particularized," and "imminent" injuries. The Court discusses this constitutional limit on standing as if it inevitably follows from a reading of Article III and as if it had always existed. Numerous scholars have searched in vain, however, for support for the proposition that Article III limits standing to plaintiffs who have suffered an "injury-in-fact."[59] Until the twentieth century, no U.S. court suggested that Article III limited the types of plaintiffs who could bring suit. The early Congresses enacted several statutes that authorized actions brought by parties who had not suffered an "injury-in-fact," and U.S. courts regularly decided cases brought by "strangers" and "informers." The only limit the courts imposed on such actions was reflected in the doctrine of damnum absque injuria. That doctrine required dismissal of a suit if the plaintiff lacked a cause of action rooted in the common law, equity, or a statute. Thus, any plaintiff who brought an action authorized by a statute could avoid dismissal of the action based on damnum absque injuria.

---

59. See Sunstein, *What's Standing After Lujan–Of Citizen Suits, "Injuries," and Article III*, 91 Mich. L. Rev. 163 (1992); Winter, *The Metaphor of Standing and the Problem of Self–Governance*, 40 Stan. L. Rev. 1371 (1988); Berger, *Standing to Sue in Public Actions: Is It a Constitutional Requirement?* 78 Yale L. J. 816 (1969); Jaffe, *Standing to Secure Judicial Review: Public Actions*, 74 Harv. L. Rev. 1265 (1961).

The constitutional component of standing law has a remarkably short history. The first opinion that refers to Article III as a limit on standing was issued in 1944.[60] The first opinion that refers to "injury-in-fact" as a constitutional limit on standing was issued in 1970.[61] Over the following three decades, the Court issued over one hundred opinions that applied the "injury-in-fact" test as a requirement of Article III. In those opinions, the Court used many adjectives to distinguish between injuries that do and do not qualify as "injury-in-fact" and added the requirements that the "injury-in-fact" must be "caused" by the challenged action and must be "redressable" by a court. Until 1992, however, all of the Court's lengthy discussions of the Article III limits on standing qualified only as dicta, since those discussions appeared only in cases in which the plaintiff had no statutorily-conferred cause of action. The first decision holding that Article III precludes a plaintiff from litigating a statutorily-authorized cause of action was issued in 1992.[62]

Until 1992, the Court's many decisions denying standing based on Article III were easy to explain as illustrative of one of several techniques the Court used to reduce the opportunities for activist courts to engage in creative reasoning to interfere with decisionmaking by politically accountable institutions. Thus, for instance, the Court relied on Article III reasoning to deny standing to a taxpayer who claimed that the Constitution prohibits a member of Congress from serving as a member of the military reserves,[63] a taxpayer who claimed that the Constitution requires publication of the details of the CIA budget,[64] a poor person who claimed that the Constitution prohibits localities from making zoning decisions that have the effect of placing housing beyond the means of poor people, and to citizens who wanted to challenge IRS decisions that were favorable to particular classes of taxpayers.[65] Congress had not authorized any of those lawsuits. By contrast, when the Court was convinced that Congress had authorized the plaintiff's lawsuit, the Court adopted a broad interpretation of the "injury-in-fact" test and deferred to the congressional intent to allow the case to proceed.[66]

60. Stark v. Wickard, 321 U.S. 288 (1944).

61. Barlow v. Collins, 397 U.S. 159 (1970).

62. Lujan v. Defenders of Wildlife, 504 U.S. 555 (1992), discussed *infra* § 5.4.2.

63. Schlesinger v. Reservists Committee to Stop the War, 418 U.S. 208 (1974).

64. U.S. v. Richardson, 418 U.S. 166 (1974).

65. Allen v. Wright, 468 U.S. 737 (1984); Simon v. Eastern Kentucky Welfare Rights Organization, 426 U.S. 26 (1976).

66. *See* Havens Realty Corp. v. Coleman, 455 U.S. 363 (1982); Trafficante v.

In its 1992 decision in *Lujan v. Defenders of Wildlife*,[67] a six-Justice majority of the Court held for the first time that the Article III limits on standing precluded a plaintiff from obtaining judicial resolution of a dispute in circumstances in which Congress clearly had conferred a cause of action on the plaintiff. Specifically, the Court held that Article III prohibits Congress from authorizing "any person" to bring an action to enforce a statute or rule. The Court held that Article III limits the class of permissible plaintiffs to those who have suffered a "concrete," "particularized," and "imminent" "injury-in-fact." Because the Court concluded that the plaintiff had not suffered such an injury, the plaintiff lacked standing to bring the enforcement action.

Six years later, in *Steel Co. v. Citizens for a Better Environment*,[68] a six-Justice majority held that another statute that purported to confer standing on "any person" was unconstitutional as applied. The Court held that the plaintiff lacked Article III standing because, even though he suffered an "injury-in-fact" that was caused by the conduct he sought to challenge, his injury was not "redressable" by a court. We discuss *Defenders of Wildlife* and *Steel Co.* in greater detail in sections 5.4.2 and 5.4.4.

The Court's decisions in *Defenders of Wildlife* and *Steel Co.* obviously are not motivated by the concerns that originally induced the Court to create a constitutional law of standing. They do not reduce the opportunities for activist judges to engage in creative reasoning to interfere with the performance of politically accountable institutions. They have the opposite effect. They authorize judges to engage in creative reasoning to interfere with the performance of a politically accountable institution—Congress. It is difficult to identify the Court's reasons for taking this dramatic step based solely on the language of the opinions issued in *Defenders of Wildlife* and *Steel Co.* It is relatively easy to infer the Court's motive from the extrajudicial writings of one of the Justices, however. Justice Scalia authored both the majority opinion in *Steel Co.* and the plurality opinion in *Defenders of Wildlife*. Justice Scalia also authored a 1983 law review article in which he described his approach to constitutional standing disputes.[69] Justice Scalia believes that the Take Care Clause in Article II precludes anyone but the Executive Branch from enforcing a federal law. His opinions in *Defenders of Wildlife* and *Steel Co.* follow

Metropolitan Life Ins. Co., 409 U.S. 205 (1972).

67. 504 U.S. 555 (1992).

68. 523 U.S. 83 (1998).

69. Scalia, *The Doctrine of Standing as an Essential Element of the Separation of Powers*, 17 Suffolk L. Rev. 881 (1983).

logically from that belief. At the time he wrote the 1983 article, Justice Scalia's interpretation of the Constitution was considered idiosyncratic. As a result of his opinions in *Defenders of Wildlife* and *Steel Co.*, his view has now become the law of the land, at least for the present. Justice Scalia's effort to reshape the law of standing suffered a major setback, however, in *Friends of the Earth v. Laidlaw Environmental Services.*[70] In subsequent sections, we will provide detailed descriptions of the doctrinal elements of the constitutional component of the test for standing.

§ 5.4.2 The nature of the required injury

Since 1970, the Court has stated consistently that Article III limits the class of constitutionally permissible plaintiffs to those who have suffered an "injury-in-fact" caused by the challenged action. The Court has experienced considerable difficulty distinguishing among the types of "injuries" that motivate an individual to file a lawsuit, however. In a sense, every citizen is injured by an unlawful act, since every citizen has an interest in maintaining the integrity of the legal system. That type of injury alone does not qualify as an "injury-in-fact." The Court has often stated that an "abstract" injury, an "undifferentiated" injury, or an injury that is "common to all members of the public" does not qualify as an "injury-in-fact."[71] These adjectives are difficult to apply in many contexts, however. The problematic nature of the "injury-in-fact" test, and the highly variable jurisprudence defining and applying that test, can be illustrated by reference to the Supreme Court's decisions with respect to four of the many types of injuries that have been the subject of frequent disputes—economic injuries, informational injuries, environmental injuries, and procedural injuries.

The Court has consistently applied the injury-in-fact test in a broad, permissive manner when a plaintiff claims to have suffered an economic injury. The unanimous opinion in *Association of Data Processing Service Organizations v. Camp,*[72] illustrates the Court's approach to economic injuries. The plaintiff, an association of firms that provide data processing services, sought judicial review of a decision by the Comptroller of the Currency that allowed banks to provide data processing services to their customers. The Court held that the plaintiff had alleged an economic injury that qualified as an

---

70. 528 U.S. 167 (2000).

71. *See, e.g.,* U.S. v. Richardson, 418 U.S. 166 (1974).

72. 397 U.S. 150 (1970). *See also* Clarke v. Securities Industry Assn., 479 U.S. 388 (1987); Investment Company Institute v. Camp, 401 U.S. 617 (1971).

"injury-in-fact" for standing purposes. The economic injury obviously was indirect, probabilistic, and somewhat speculative in nature. In order for any particular data processing firm to suffer an economic injury as a result of the issuance of the challenged decision, a bank would have to decide to offer data processing services to one of the firm's clients at a price lower than the price charged by the firm, thereby forcing the firm to choose between lowering its price or losing a customer.

In its 1998 decision in *Clinton v. New York*,[73] a seven-Justice majority seemed to apply an even broader and more permissive version of the "injury-in-fact" test in the context of an economic injury. Congress enacted a statute that included a provision that conferred tax benefits on anyone who sold a food processing facility to a farmers cooperative. The President "vetoed" that provision. The plaintiff, a farmers cooperative, sought review of the President's veto on the basis that the statute authorizing the veto was unconstitutional. The plaintiff alleged that it was in the process of negotiating to purchase a food processing facility at the time of the veto and that the veto of the statutory provision that would have conferred tax benefits on the seller of the facility had an adverse effect on its negotiations. The majority held that the veto of the tax provision "inflicted a sufficient likelihood of economic injury to establish standing under our precedents." In resolving the constitutional standing issue in *Clinton*, the majority appeared to be influenced by the language of the statute that purported to authorize the plaintiff to challenge the veto decision. The majority began its discussion of standing by referring to "an unmistakable congressional interest in a prompt and authoritative judicial determination of the constitutionality of the Act" that purported to grant the President the power to veto certain tax provisions.[74]

The Court's decisions applying the "injury-in-fact" test in the context of informational injuries are more difficult to interpret and to reconcile. In its 1974 decision in *United States v. Richardson*,[75] the Court held that a group of voters did not have standing to obtain judicial review of the CIA's refusal to make its budget public, an arguable violation of the constitutional requirement that "a regular statement and account of the ... expenditures of all public money

73.   524 U.S. 417 (1998).

74.   *See* section 4.3.3, for a discussion of the important issue on the merits that the Court resolved in *Clinton*.

75.   418 U.S. 166 (1974).

shall be published from time to time."[76] The voters argued that they were injured by the agency's refusal because they lacked access to data that would help them decide how to vote. The Court held that the voters' injury was too "abstract," "generalized," and "undifferentiated" to qualify as "injury-in-fact" sufficient to support standing.

In its 1982 decision in *Havens Realty v. Coleman*,[77] the Court held that a "tester"—a black person who pretended to want to rent an apartment for the sole purpose of detecting racial discrimination— had standing to sue a landlord for falsely informing him that there was no apartment available in a building. The Court held that the informational injury suffered by the plaintiff qualified as "injury-in-fact." The Court emphasized that Congress had enacted a statute that prohibited a landlord from providing false information for the purpose of engaging in racial discrimination. The Court seemed to accept the logical proposition that Congress can create a judicially-cognizable "injury-in-fact" by enacting a statute that creates a right. The violation of such a statutory right then constitutes an "injury-in-fact."

In its 1998 decision in *Federal Election Commission v. Akins*,[78] a six-Justice majority held that a group of voters had standing to obtain review of an agency decision that an organization was not a "political committee." If the agency had decided that the organization was a "political committee," the organization would have been required to report to the agency a lot of information about its activities, and the agency would have been required to make that information available to the public. Thus, the voters argued that they had suffered an indirect informational injury as a result of the agency's decision not to classify the organization as a "political committee." The majority held that the voters' informational injury qualified as "injury-in-fact." The majority reasoned that the voters suffered a judicially-cognizable injury because they were deprived of "information [that] would help them ... to evaluate candidates for public office, especially candidates that received assistance from" the organization that the agency had refused to classify as a "political committee." The majority recognized that the injury suffered by the voters was a "generalized grievance" that was "shared in substantially equal measure by all or a large class of citizens." In several prior cases, the Court had used those characterizations to describe injuries that do not qualify as an "injury-in-fact." The majority

76. U.S. Constitution, Art. 1, § 9, cl. 7.

77. 455 U.S. 363 (1982).

78. 524 U.S. 11 (1998).

distinguished those cases as involving injuries that were also "abstract . . . For example, harm to the common concern for obedience to law." By contrast, the majority concluded that the informational injury suffered by the voters in *Akins* was "concrete." Thus, even though the injury was "widely shared," it qualified as "injury-in-fact." The majority distinguished *Richardson* as a case in which the voters had no statutory right to the information of which they were deprived. By contrast, in *Akins*, "there is a statute which . . . does seek to protect . . . [voters] from the kind of harm they say they have suffered."

The informational standing cases can be reconciled on only one basis—the presence or absence of a statute that gives people in plaintiffs' class a right to the information at issue. In the absence of such a statute, the Court applies a version of the "injury-in-fact" test so demanding that no plaintiff can meet it. In the presence of such a statute, the Court adopts a broad, permissive version of the "injury-in-fact" test that anyone in the class of beneficiaries of the statute can meet. This distinction makes sense. Congress clearly has the power to create judicially-enforceable rights by enacting a statute, and any violation of such a statutory right should qualify as a judicially-cognizable injury.

The Court's decisions applying the "injury-in-fact" test to environmental injuries are problematic. They cannot be reconciled either with each other or with the Court's decisions with respect to other types of injuries. The Court has long recognized that "injury-in-fact" can include injuries to "aesthetic, conservational, and recreational values."[79] Five of the Court's decisions demonstrate, however, the highly variable manner in which the Court applies the "injury-in-fact" test to environmental injuries.

Sierra Club v. Morton[80] involved a challenge to a Forest Service decision to allow construction of a large Walt Disney Enterprises recreational complex in the previously pristine Mineral King Valley of California. Sierra Club sued as a membership organization with a special interest in conservation. It alleged that the Forest Service action "would destroy or otherwise adversely affect the scenery, natural and historical objects and wildlife of the park and would impair the enjoyment of the park for future generations". The Court accepted these forms of harm as sufficient to meet the injury in fact test for standing:

79. *See, e.g.*, Association of Data Processing Service Organizations v. Camp, 397 U.S. 150 (1970).

80. 405 U.S. 727 (1972).

"Aesthetic and environmental well-being, like economic well-being, are important ingredients of the quality of life in our society, and the fact that particular environmental interests are shared by the many rather than the few does not make them less deserving of legal protection through the judicial process."

The Court held that Sierra Club did not have standing, however, because it did not allege that any of its members "use Mineral King for any purpose, much less that they use it in any way that would be significantly affected by the proposed actions of respondents". A "mere interest in a problem" in the abstract by a "representative of the public" is not sufficient to confer standing on a group. A group has standing only to the extent that its members have standing, and its members have standing only if one or more can show personal injury.

Sierra Club was considered by many a simultaneous victory for environmental interests and for advocates of careful pleading. That interpretation was confirmed by the Court's decision in *United States v. Students Challenging Regulatory Agency Procedures* (SCRAP).[81] There, a group of law students challenged an ICC order permitting an increase in the rail rates applicable to recyclable materials. The group alleged that its members would be harmed by the ICC action in their capacities as users of natural resources, since higher freight rates applicable to recyclable materials would yield greater use of natural resources and increased air pollution throughout the country. The Court recognized that every resident of the United States could make credible allegations identical to those of the students. Yet, by a 6–3 margin, the Court held the environmental injuries alleged by the students sufficient to give them standing:

"But we have already made it clear that standing is not to be denied because many people suffer the same injury."

SCRAP establishes an extremely low threshold for the nature and magnitude of the injury sufficient to obtain standing. If the Court had retained the approach it took in SCRAP, almost anyone would have standing to obtain review of almost any action that has an adverse effect on the environment.

The Court's decision in *Duke Power Co. v. Carolina Environmental Study Group*[82] indicated the Court's continuing sensitivity to environmental harm, but it also suggested that there may be limits to the Court's willingness to find sufficient injury-in-fact even to envi-

81. 412 U.S. 669 (1973).   **82.** 438 U.S. 59 (1978).

ronmental interests. *Duke Power* involved a challenge to the constitutionality of a statute that allegedly enabled Duke to construct two
nuclear power plants. The statute was challenged by individuals and
groups representing individuals who live in proximity to the two
plants. Those individuals claimed to have standing based on a
lengthy list of injuries. The Court held that the individuals and
groups had standing based on some of the injuries alleged, but it
suggested that some of the other injuries would not be adequate
alone to support a holding of standing. Specifically, the Court found
sufficient two of the "immediate" adverse effects alleged: thermal
pollution of two lakes and emission of small quantities of non-natural
radiation. It questioned whether two other forms of injury would
have been sufficient: the possibility of a nuclear accident and the
present apprehension created by that possibility.

The Court's decision in *Lujan v. National Wildlife Federation*[83]
reinforced both *Duke Power's* suggestion that the Court will impose
some limit on the nature of the environmental injury sufficient to
support standing and *Sierra Club's* suggestion that standing often is
dependent on careful compliance with the rules of procedure. *National Wildlife Federation* involved an attempt to challenge DOI's "program" for reclassifying public lands in ways that permit them to be
used for mining. The Federation attempted to support its claim of
injury by submitting affidavits of members who stated that their
recreational and aesthetic enjoyment of their use of public lands was
injured by the agency's "program" of reclassification. The Court
recognized that recreational and aesthetic injuries can support standing, but it held five-to-four that the affidavits did not allege injuries
sufficiently specific to withstand the government's motion for summary judgment. The five-Justice majority reasoned that: (1) the only
agency actions subject to potential challenge were decisions to reclassify specific tracts of land, since the agency had chosen to implement
its "program" through a series of separate classification decisions;
and, (2) the affidavits did not allege a sufficiently specific injury
because the affiants stated only that they used lands "in the vicinity
of" large areas that included the relatively small tracts of land the
agency reclassified. The *National Wildlife Federation* majority also
called into question the continuing validity of the reasoning in
SCRAP. It referred to that reasoning as an "expansive expression of
what would suffice ... [for standing that] has never since been
emulated by this Court.... "

83. 497 U.S. 871 (1990).

The Court made an abrupt departure from its prior approach to "injury-in-fact" in *Lujan v. Defenders of Wildlife*.[84] The plaintiffs sought judicial review of a decision authorizing federal funding of a project that they claimed to violate the Endangered Species Act (ESA). That Act forbids a government agency from acting in a way that reduces the habitat of an endangered species unless the agency first goes through a statutorily-proscribed procedure. The agency had not followed that procedure, and the federally-funded project would have obvious adverse effects on the habitat of an endangered species. ESA, like most federal environmental statutes, authorizes "any person" to bring an action to enforce the statute, so there was no question that Congress had authorized the plaintiffs to obtain review of the challenged action. The plaintiffs included a biologist who studies the species whose habitat would be endangered by the agency action. A six-Justice majority held that the plaintiffs lacked standing because they had not suffered an "injury-in-fact."

The decision in *Defenders of Wildlife* is difficult to interpret. The Court divided four-two-three. The plurality opinion includes detailed reasoning, but the concurring Justices expressed vague reservations about the reasoning in the plurality opinion without disclosing much about their own reasoning.

The plurality held that Article III precludes Congress from conferring standing on "any person." Congress can confer standing only on someone who has suffered an "injury-in-fact." The plaintiffs claimed to have suffered "injury-in-fact" on four different theories. The first three were "ecosystem nexus," "animal nexus," and "professional nexus." "Ecosystem nexus" refers to the complicated relationships among the species that share an ecosystem. Under that theory, which is widely accepted by biologists, anyone who shares an ecosystem with another species is injured by the extinction of that species. The "animal nexus" theory asserts that the extinction of any species injures anyone who derives pleasure from observing members of that species anywhere, e.g., in a zoo. "Professional nexus" refers to the argument that anyone who makes his living by studying a species is injured by its extinction. The plurality rejected all three nexus theories as "beyond all reason" and as "pure speculation and fantasy."

The plaintiffs submitted an affidavit of one of its members to support a fourth claim of injury. The affiant stated that she was a professional biologist who studies the endangered species at issue;

84. 504 U.S. 555 (1992).

that she had visited the habitat of the species in the past to study it; that she planned to make similar visits in the future; and that she would be injured by the extinction of the species because she would not be able to study it in its habitat in the future. The plurality seemed to recognize that the affiant described a form of injury that might qualify as an "injury-in-fact." The plurality held, however, that the affidavit was inadequate because it did not describe an "imminent injury." To meet the "imminent injury" element of the "injury-in-fact" test the plaintiff was required to prove that she planned to observe the species in its habitat at a date certain in the near future. The dissenting Justices accused the plurality of mounting "a slash-and-burn expedition through the law of environmental standing."

It is impossible to reconcile the reasoning and holding in *Defenders of Wildlife* with many of the Court's prior standing opinions. It is inconsistent with the many cases like *Clinton*, *Akins*, and *Havens*, in which the Court deferred to Congress and adopted broad, permissive versions of the "injury-in-fact" test when a statute specifically authorized the plaintiff to bring the action in question. It is also inconsistent with the many cases, including all of the economic injury cases, in which the Court applied a broad, probabilistic version of the "injury-in-fact" test. Thus, for instance, the Court has never required a market participant to prove that it would suffer a "particularized" and "imminent" loss of a customer as a result of a challenged agency decision that would permit a new class of firms to enter a market. The Court has always considered it sufficient that the issuance of such an order probably would harm a firm in some uncertain way at some uncertain time in the future.

The plurality opinion in *Defenders of Wildlife* also includes a discussion of "injury-in-fact" that is helpful in describing the Court's approach to another type of injury. A high proportion of administrative law disputes that courts resolve involve procedural injuries, i.e., the plaintiff alleges injury attributable to an agency's failure to follow a procedure that is required by a statute or by the Due Process Clause, e.g., a hearing, adequate notice, or an environmental impact statement. The plurality opinion in *Defenders of Wildlife* includes the Court's first discussion of the circumstances in which a plaintiff has standing attributable to a procedural injury. The plurality characterized procedural rights as "special." It held that "an individual [can] enforce procedural rights ... so long as the procedures in question are designed to protect some threatened concrete interest of his that is the ultimate basis of his standing." Thus, for instance, if the substantive outcome of a proceeding has the potential to cause a plaintiff to suffer a substantive "injury-in-fact," the plaintiff has standing to challenge the agency's failure to provide a statutorily-mandated hearing even though it is by no means certain that provision of the hearing will change the substantive outcome of the proceeding.

At the time the Court decided *Defenders of Wildlife*, its meaning was unclear. The four-Justice plurality opinion contained a lot of reasoning that was new and that represented an abrupt change in direction for the Court. If the Court had continued to apply that reasoning, it would have had significant effects on the law of standing. Generally, it would have reduced dramatically the circumstances in which anyone would be able to establish standing to challenge any action that had an adverse effect on environmental or informational interests. Adoption of the reasoning in the plurality opinion would have had those effects through the combination of judicial refusal to accept most environmental or informational injuries as sufficiently concrete and particularized to qualify as injuries in fact and by eliminating judicial deference to congressional decisions to confer standing on large numbers of people by creating statutory rights the violation of which qualify as injuries-in-fact. Only four Justices joined in the plurality opinion, however. The two concurring Justices stated that they were concurring in the result but that they did not agree with all of the reasoning in the plurality opinion.

The Court clarified the meaning and scope of *Defenders of Wildlife* in its 2000 decision in *Friends of the Earth v. Laidlaw Environmental Services*.[85] A seven-Justice majority adopted an extremely narrow interpretation of *Defenders of Wildlife*, returned to the Court's prior liberal approach to environmental standing, and implicitly rejected Justice Scalia's theories that were the basis for the plurality opinion in *Defenders of Wildlife*.

Laidlaw was an action for injunctive relief and for civil penalties brought by an environmental group against a firm that was illegally discharging excess amounts of mercury into the Tyger River. Friends of the Earth claimed standing derivative of the standing of several of its members. (See § 5.4.6 for discussion of the standing of membership organizations.) The members submitted affidavits in which they stated that they curtailed activities such as fishing and swimming in the Tyger River downstream of Laidlaw's point of discharge because of their belief that Laidlaw's illegal discharges were having adverse

85. 528 U.S. 167 (2000).

effects on water quality. At the beginning of the proceeding, the district court relied on those affidavits as the basis for its finding that Laidlaw's illegal discharges were causing petitioners injury-in-fact sufficient to support standing. Later in the proceeding, however, the district court conducted an evidentiary hearing in which Laidlaw presented expert testimony that the illegal discharges could not possibly cause injury to either fish or people. The district court found that testimony persuasive and concluded that Laidlaw's illegal discharges had caused no damage to the quality of the water in the Tyger River. Based on that conclusion, plus the court's finding that Laidlaw had stopped engaging in illegal discharges, the district court declined to grant injunctive relief, though it did impose civil penalties on Laidlaw.

The Fourth Circuit relied on the district court's finding of no injury to water quality and its refusal to grant injunctive relief as the bases for its holding that the petitioner's action was moot. Since the Supreme Court had often referred to mootness as "the doctrine of standing set in a timeframe," the court concluded that the petitioners no longer could maintain an action against Laidlaw once the district court made its finding of no harm to water quality and declined to grant injunctive relief.

The Supreme Court reversed the Fourth Circuit. It held, inter alia, that the injury-in-fact test was satisfied by an individual's changes in behavior based on "reasonable concerns" that the conduct he seeks to challenge is producing harmful pollution even if it turns out that the challenged conduct is not actually causing any harm to the environment. More broadly, the majority stated that courts should accord significant deference to Congress in deciding whether a petitioner has standing. In a dissenting opinion, Justice Scalia accurately described the effect of the majority opinion in *Laidlaw*: "If there are permit violations, and a member of a plaintiff environmental organization lives near the offending plant, it would be difficult not to satisfy today's lenient standard."

As significantly qualified by *Laidlaw*, the restrictions on environmental standing previously announced in *Defenders of Wildlife* and *National Wildlife Federation* apply only when a petitioner's "concern" about the adverse effects of a defendant's conduct is "unreasonable" because the petitioner lacks geographic proximity or temporal proximity to a potential source of pollution or other environmental degradation. Thus, for instance, a petitioner would lack standing to challenge Laidlaw's illegal discharges if it used only parts of the Tyger River that are upstream of the Laidlaw point of discharge or hundreds of miles downstream of that point, or if it planned to use the Tyger River only at some uncertain time in the future.

§ 5.4.3 The relationship between the injury and the interest asserted

The Court sometimes requires a close relationship or "nexus" between the injury that the party alleges as a basis for standing and the interest that the party is attempting to vindicate through judicial review. The process of linking injury sustained with interest asserted involves difficult problems of characterization.[86] Four taxpayer standing cases illustrate the manner in which the Court sometimes applies the nexus requirement.

Flast v. Cohen[87] establishes that a taxpayer has standing to challenge the constitutionality of a government expenditure where the expenditure arguably violates a constitutional provision that was intended to limit the government's power to spend—in *Flast,* the First Amendment's prohibition on "establishment" of a religion. In three other cases, however, the Court has denied standing to taxpayers who attempted to challenge the constitutionality of federal expenditures. In *Frothingham v. Mellon,*[88] the taxpayer claimed that a federal grant program violated the Tenth Amendment reservation of residual rights to the states. In *United States v. Richardson,*[89] a taxpayer challenged the CIA's failure to account for its expenditures of funds on the basis that the CIA's practice violated the "regular Statement of Account" requirement of Article I, Section 9, Clause 7. In *Schlesinger v. Reservists Committee to Stop the War,*[90] a taxpayer claimed that congressmen who retained their military reserve status violated the prohibition in Article 1, Section 6, Clause 6 against holding any office in the executive branch while serving in the legislature.

The Court did not distinguish these cases based on the nature of the injury alleged; indeed, the injury in each case was to the complaining party's interest as a taxpayer. Rather, the Court concluded that only the complaining party in *Flast* had standing because only she was able to establish an adequate nexus between her injury (damage to her religious values) and the interest she sought to protect (the prohibition on government "establishment" of religion).

---

86. *See* Scott, *Standing in the Supreme Court—A Functional Analysis,* 85 Harv. L. Rev. 645, 664 (1973). *See generally* L. Tribe, *supra* note 1, at § 3–19.

87. 392 U.S. 83 (1968).

88. 262 U.S. 447 (1923).

89. 418 U.S. 166 (1974).

90. 418 U.S. 208 (1974).

In the other three cases, the Court concluded that there was an insufficient link between the miniscule injury to the complaining party as a taxpayer (a few pennies in tax liability) and the constitutional interest that the party wanted the Court to recognize.

The nexus requirement is not part of the constitutional test for standing. It is variously described as a policy based extension of the Article III requirement that is intended to filter out cases brought by officious intermeddlers,[91] and as part of the statutory "zone of interest" test that is intended to place control of legal issues in the hands of those most directly affected by their resolution.[92]

Whatever may be the basis for the nexus requirement, the Court does not apply it in a uniform manner. For instance, the Court frequently uses the nexus requirement as a means of precluding one party from asserting before a court the interests of another party. Yet, in many cases it allows petitioners standing to assert the rights of others.[93] The lack of consistency in the Court's use of nexus as a prerequisite for standing suggests that the Court may be using the nexus requirement as a means of furthering goals unrelated to the stated purposes of the standing doctrine.

Two Supreme Court decisions help to clarify the scope, purpose, and nature of the nexus requirement. First, in *Federal Election Commission v. Akins*,[94] the Court held that a plaintiff had standing in circumstances remarkably similar to those in which the Court had held that the plaintiff lacked standing in *U.S. v. Richardson*.[95] The majority in *Akins* characterized *Richardson* as a case in which the Court denied standing because it perceived a need to find a logical nexus between the plaintiff's injury and the values that the provision of the Constitution at issue was intended to protect. By contrast, the majority saw no need to impose such a nexus requirement in *Akins* because the plaintiff sought to enforce a statute that Congress had enacted to benefit people with the plaintiff's interests. Second, in *Powers v. Ohio*,[96] a seven-Justice majority held that a litigant has standing to assert the rights of a third party when: (1) the third party suffered an "injury-in-fact;" (2) the third party had a close relationship with the plaintiff; and, (3) there was "some hindrance" to the third party's assertion of the right.

---

91. L. Tribe, *supra* note 1, at § 3–19.

92. Nichol, *supra* note 58, at 95–97.

93. *See* L. Tribe, *supra* note 1, at § 3–19.

94. 524 U.S. 11 (1998).

95. 418 U.S. 166 (1974).

96. 499 U.S. 400 (1991).

§ 5.4.4 Causality and redressability

Once the Court created the "injury-in-fact" requirement for constitutional standing in 1970, it was inevitable that the Court would add the requirement that the plaintiff prove that the action it is challenging "caused" its "injury-in-fact." It was equally predictable that the Court would add the requirement that the plaintiff's "injury-in-fact" must be "redressable" through some action that a court can take. The Court added those logical corollaries to the "injury-in-fact" test in its 1973 decision in *Linda R.S. v. Richard D.*[97] Since then, it has issued scores of decisions in which it has applied the causality and redressability requirements to determine whether a plaintiff has constitutional standing. In the vast majority of cases, the same factors that influence a court to conclude that there was or was not a causal relationship between the defendant's action and the plaintiff's injury also influence the Court's decision that the injury is or is not redressable by a court. Thus, with one important exception, the Supreme Court's reasoning and conclusion with respect to redressability is functionally indistinguishable from its reasoning and conclusion with respect to causation. We will postpone discussion of that notable exception—the Court's 1998 decision in *Steel Co. v. Citizens for a Better Environment*[98]—until the end of this section. We will begin with a discussion of a few of the Court's many decisions that resolve causation issues.

As all students of tort law know, causation can be a slippery and malleable concept. The Court has not applied the causation requirement in a uniform and consistent manner.

Two cases illustrate particularly vividly the Court's tendency to manipulate the causation requirement to further other goals. *Warth v. Seldin*[99] involved a challenge to the restrictive zoning practices of Penfield, New York. Those practices were alleged to violate the Equal Protection Clause of the Fourteenth Amendment by making it impossible to construct low cost housing and, as a result, making it impossible for any poor people, including most members of minority groups, to live in Penfield. In an impressive effort to overcome any potential standing hurdle, four different types of parties challenged the zoning practices: (1) low income individuals who claimed that they were injured by their inability to buy low-priced housing; (2) builders of low-priced housing who alleged injury as a result of their inability to construct such housing; (3) a non-profit organization

---

97. 410 U.S. 614 (1973).

98. 523 U.S. 83 (1998).

99. 422 U.S. 490 (1975).

whose main purpose was to address issues of social concern in Penfield; and, (4) taxpayers in a nearby community who alleged injury resulting from a reduced tax base attributable to the high proportion of low-priced housing that their community was required to absorb because of Penfield's refusal to permit any low-priced housing.

The Court had little difficulty concluding that the third and fourth groups had no standing, principally because of the lack of sufficient nexus between their alleged injury and the legal interests (of third parties) they were attempting to assert.[100] The homebuilders presented a somewhat stronger case for standing, but the Court concluded that they lacked standing because they had no pending proposals for housing projects that were jeopardized by Penfield's zoning practices. The low income individuals who expressed a desire to move to Penfield had the most compelling argument for standing. They were able to establish injury resulting from their inability to find a place to live in Penfield, and they were attempting to assert a legal interest directly related to that injury. The Court concluded, however, that they did not have standing because they could not establish that the unavailability of low-priced housing in Penfield was a result of Penfield's zoning practices. Three dissenting Justices protested vigorously that the majority had erected an insurmountable barrier to standing; ironically, no party could obtain standing to challenge the zoning practices unless it was first able to devise a way to circumvent those practices. The majority opinion says more about the Court's unwillingness to allow the judiciary to become enmeshed in difficult cases involving the relationship between the Equal Protection Clause and millions of local zoning decisions than it says about the law of standing.

In *Simon v. Eastern Kentucky Welfare Rights Organization*,[101] the Court was presented with an attempt by poor people to obtain judicial review of an IRS ruling. The Internal Revenue Code exempts from federal income taxes non-profit organizations, including hospitals, that operate "exclusively for ... charitable ... purposes". For 13 years prior to the challenged ruling, IRS had interpreted this provision to require hospitals, as a necessary condition of their tax exempt status, not to "refuse to accept patients in need of hospital care who cannot pay for such services." The challenged ruling modified this interpretation dramatically. It allowed hospitals to retain tax exempt status if they provided emergency services to poor

---

100. *See supra* § 5.4.3.

101. 426 U.S. 26 (1976); *see also* Allen v. Wright, 468 U.S. 737 (1984).

people, even if they regularly turned away poor people who sought non-emergency treatment.

In *Simon,* as in *Warth,* the petitioners could establish injury (each had been denied medical treatment at a hospital because of poverty), and the injury was closely related to the interest the poor people were attempting to vindicate. Moreover, the interests of poor people in medical care would seem to fall within the zone of interests Congress was trying to protect through enactment of the Internal Revenue Code provision exempting charitable organizations from federal taxes. The Court held that the poor people had no standing to challenge the IRS ruling, however, because they failed to establish a causal relationship between their injury (inability to obtain medical services) and the agency action (allowing hospitals to remain tax exempt even if they refuse to provide non-emergency medical service to poor people). In the Court's words:

> "So far as the complaint sheds light, it is just as plausible that the hospitals to which respondents may apply for service would elect to forego favorable tax treatment to avoid the undetermined financial drain of an increase in the level of compensated services."

If the Court applied the *Warth/Simon* approach to the causation requirement in every case where standing is contested, it would revolutionize the law of standing. At least in the absence of a lengthy preliminary hearing focusing on causation, many parties who now routinely are permitted to obtain judicial review of agency actions would be precluded from doing so. For instance application of the *Warth/Simon* approach would change the result of all of the economic injury cases discussed in § 5.4.2. In each of those cases, the Court engaged in logical, probabilistic assessment of the likely causal relationship between the agency action and the injury alleged. It did not require "concretely demonstrable" evidence of a causal relationship. As with some of the "nexus" cases, *Warth* and *Simon* can only be explained as attempts to further goals independent of the stated goals of the standing requirement.[102] In *Simon,* the Court obviously feared that a grant of standing would expose thousands of interpretive rulings addressed to individual taxpayers to potential judicial review at the behest of competitors, thereby greatly complicating IRS' pursuit of its vital mission.

In *Clinton v. New York*[103] the Justices seemed to agree on a probabilistic approach to causation issues. All nine Justices agreed

102. *See* Nichol, *supra* note 58, at 79–82.

103. 524 U.S. 417 (1998).

that a plaintiff has Article III standing if it is "likely" that the challenged action caused, or will cause, the plaintiff "injury-in-fact." The Justices differed, however, in the results of their application of that standard. Seven Justices concluded that it was "likely" that a prospective purchaser of an asset suffered an economic injury when the President vetoed a statutory provision that would have provided tax benefits to the owner if it sold the asset to the prospective purchaser. Two dissenting Justices characterized that causal relationship as "speculative" and, at best, merely "plausible."

In most cases, the redressability analysis is functionally redundant, in the sense that a court almost always concludes that an injury is judicially redressable if it was caused by the conduct of the defendant that is the focus of the plaintiff's claim on the merits. In its 1998 decision in *Steel Co. v. Citizens for a Better Environment*,[104] however, the Court held for the first time that a plaintiff that suffered an "injury-in-fact" caused by defendant's conduct lacked Article III standing because the injury could not be redressed by a court.

The plaintiff brought an action to enforce the Emergency Planning and Community Right-to-Know Act. That Act, like most federal environmental statutes, specifically authorizes "any person" to bring an action to enforce the Act. The plaintiffs alleged that the defendant had violated the Act by failing to report its emissions and inventories of hazardous substances. The plaintiffs lived or worked near the defendant's plant. They claimed to be injured by the defendant's failure to report because they use information about emissions and inventories of hazardous substances in the process of formulating their emergency response plans. The six-Justice majority assumed, without deciding, that the plaintiffs had established that the defendant's violation of the law had caused them "injury-in-fact." Yet, the majority held that the plaintiffs lacked Article III standing because the statute did not authorize a court to provide any remedy that would redress the plaintiff's injury. The statute authorized three types of remedies: declaratory and injunctive relief, civil penalties, and award of plaintiff's costs. The majority held that declaratory and injunctive relief would not redress plaintiffs' injury because it applies in the future, while plaintiffs' suffered their injury in the past. The majority held that civil penalties would not redress plaintiffs' injury because they would be awarded to the government, rather than to the plaintiffs. Finally, the majority held that award of plaintiffs' costs of investigation and prosecution would not redress plaintiffs' injury

104. 523 U.S. 83 (1998).

because "a plaintiff cannot achieve standing . . . by bringing suit for the cost of bringing suit."

Three Justices wrote a concurring opinion in *Steel Co.* They concurred, instead of dissenting, because they interpreted the statute not to authorize a cause of action in the circumstances presented. The concurring Justices expressed the view that the plaintiffs had standing. They noted that the Court had never before relied on redressability alone as a basis to deny a plaintiff Article III standing. They questioned whether Article III requires redressability. They also criticized the majority for applying the redressability requirement in a "mechanistic" way in which the outcome depended solely on whether the plaintiff would receive "a peppercorn." Finally, the concurring Justices criticized the majority for ignoring the lessons of history "that punishment or deterrence can redress an injury" by reducing the likelihood that "the wrongdoer will . . . repeat the injurious conduct that prompted the litigation."

In its 2000 opinion in *Laidlaw*, discussed in § 5.4.2, the Court greatly limited the scope of its holding in *Steel Co.* and made it much easier for environmental plaintiffs to establish both causality and redressability. In *Laidlaw*, the Court held that a petitioner who changes his behavior based on "reasonable concern" that the challenged conduct is having an adverse effect on the petitioner's environment has satisfied the injury-in-fact requirement of standing. This new definition of "injury-in-fact" makes it much easier for a petitioner to establish a causal relationship between the defendant's challenged conduct and the petitioner's injury. The facts of *Laidlaw* illustrate the dramatic difference in the relative ease of establishing causation. After *Laidlaw*, a petitioner must establish only that: he previously used the Tyger River downstream of Laidlaw's plant for fishing or swimming; he no longer uses it for that purpose; and, his change in behavior was based on his reasonable belief that illegal discharge of a highly toxic substance like mercury had an adverse effect on water quality in the Tyger. That is easy to establish in a brief affidavit. Before *Laidlaw*, the petitioner was required to establish that the conduct at issue—illegal discharges of small quantities of mercury—had adverse effects on water quality in the river that increased the health risks of swimming in the river or of eating fish caught in the river. That could only be established in an extremely expensive and time-consuming hearing in which competing experts on hydrology and toxicology testified. Few, if any, environmental petitioners had the resources required to establish a causal relationship between the defendant's conduct and the petitioner's injury when injury-in-fact was defined in that manner.

Laidlaw had a more direct effect on redressability. In *Steel Co.*, the Court strongly suggested that civil penalties can *never* redress an injury suffered by a petitioner because the penalties are paid to the government, rather than to the injured individual. When the Fourth Circuit applied that interpretation of *Steel Co.* in *Laidlaw* the Court reversed. It held that *Steel Co.* applied only to "wholly past" violation of statutes. Where the conduct at issue is continuing when the petitioner brings the action, the Court held that civil penalties can redress the injury by deterring similar conduct in the future even if the defendant ceases the challenged conduct during the pendency of the case. The *Laidlaw* majority also instructed courts to defer to Congress when it enacts a statute that authorizes imposition of remedies like civil penalties that Congress reasonably believes will redress an injury. Justice Scalia wrote a dissenting opinion in which he criticized the *Laidlaw* majority for allegedly misinterpreting *Steel Co.*

It is impossible to read the complicated and conflicting opinions issued in the Court's over one hundred cases resolving standing disputes without drawing the inference that the Justices are greatly influenced by their personal political and ideological values and beliefs. The concepts of injury-in-fact, causality, and redressability are extraordinarily malleable. The Justices can, and do, manipulate those concepts to obtain results they prefer on political and ideological grounds. Some Justices are sympathetic to environmental plaintiffs, while others are not. Lower court judges follow the Justices' lead in this respect. An empirical study of all circuit court decisions that resolved environmental standing disputes between 1993 and 1998 produced disturbing results. A Republican judge is four times as likely as a Democrat judge to deny standing to an environmental plaintiff.[105]

§ 5.4.5   The statutory test for standing

The modern law of standing requires a plaintiff to establish that: (1) it has suffered an "injury-in-fact" that was caused by the challenged action of the defendant and that is redressable by a court; and, (2) the interest it is asserting is arguably within the zone of

105. Pierce, *Is Standing Law or Politics*, 77 North Carolina Law Review 1741   (1999).

interests to be protected or regulated by the statute in question.[106] The first part of the test is based on the Court's interpretation of Article III of the Constitution, while the second part is based on the Court's interpretation of statutes. It is important to recognize, however, that the Court's application of the constitutional part of the test is greatly influenced by its interpretation of statutes relevant to the dispute. Thus, as discussed in § 5.4.2, if Congress has not addressed the standing issue, the Court often applies a demanding version of the "injury-in-fact" test that produces a holding that the plaintiff lacks Article III standing. Conversely, if Congress has clearly indicated its intent to authorize the plaintiff to sue, the Court usually applies a broader, more permissive version of the "injury-in-fact" test that produces a holding that the plaintiff has Article III standing. This relationship between the two tests makes sense, since Congress has the power to create legally-cognizable rights and interests by statute. In fact, until its 1992 decision in *Defenders of Wildlife* and its 1998 decision in *Steel Co.*, the Court had never held that a plaintiff who had statutory standing lacked constitutional standing.

Difficult statutory standing disputes arise with considerable frequency because Congress often declines to address standing clearly and explicitly when it enacts a statute. In the absence of a statutory provision that explicitly addresses the standing issue, a court must construct and apply some test that will allow it to make a judgment with respect to the likely intent of Congress.

Before Congress enacted the APA in 1946, courts could rely only on the statute that authorized the challenged agency action as the basis for its judgment that Congress did, or did not, intend to authorize the plaintiff to challenge the agency action in court. In the pre-APA world, the courts used dramatically different tests to resolve statutory standing disputes, depending on the characteristics of the statute that authorized the challenged agency action. If the statute was silent on the standing issue, the Court applied a narrow "legal right" test, but, if the statute explicitly authorized a broader class of plaintiffs to challenge the agency action, the Court deferred to Congress and applied a much more liberal test of statutory standing. Two famous opinions, both authored by Justice Brandeis, illustrate the "legal right" test.

The *Chicago Junction Case*[107] involved an attempt by six competing railroads to obtain judicial review of an ICC order approving New

---

106. *See* Association of Data Processing Service Organizations v. Camp., 397 U.S. 150 (1970).

107. 264 U.S. 258 (1924).

York Central's acquisition of two previously independent terminal railroads that controlled a high proportion of rail traffic in the Chicago area. The six competitors alleged that the acquisition would provide New York Central a substantial advantage and subject its competitors to serious disadvantages and prejudice in access to traffic. ICC and New York Central argued that the six competitors did not have standing to obtain judicial review of the ICC order.

The Court held that the six competitors had standing to obtain judicial review. It found that the ICC action had the effect of diverting traffic unfairly from competitors to New York Central by denying the competing railroads equality of treatment. Since the Interstate Commerce Act entitled all carriers to equal treatment, the competing carriers had standing to obtain judicial reversal of the ICC's denial of that statutory right.

Alexander Sprunt & Son, Inc. v. United States,[108] decided six years after *Chicago Junction,* also involved an appeal of an ICC order. Based on complaints from shippers, the ICC initiated an investigation into the rates charged to ship cotton to Houston. ICC found the pre-existing rate relationship unduly discriminatory because the ship-side rate was lower than the city-delivery rate. It ordered the railroads to eliminate the discriminatory relationship by equalizing the two rates. The railroads complied with the ICC order and declined to seek judicial review. Alexander Sprunt & Son owned a ship-side warehouse. It sought judicial review of the ICC order, claiming that the order and the resulting change in rate relationships caused it to lose business and that the ICC erred in concluding that the pre-existing rate relationship was unduly discriminatory.

The Court recognized that the ICC action caused economic harm to Alexander Sprunt & Son, but it held that Alexander Sprunt & Son had no standing to obtain judicial review of the ICC order on two grounds. First, the Court found that the Act conferred upon shippers a legal right "only to reasonable service at reasonable rates and without unjust discrimination." Alexander Sprunt & Son was not asserting a violation of that right. Only carriers had the legal right to maintain specific rates in effect, and Alexander Sprunt & Son could not assert that right on behalf of the carriers that had chosen not to assert that right in court. Second, the Court concluded that judicial reversal of the ICC order would be an exercise in futility, since the carriers would remain free to keep the newly equalized rates in effect on a voluntary basis even if a court held that ICC could not force the

108.   281 U.S. 249 (1930).

carriers to maintain such a rate relationship. This reasoning reflected the Court's willingness to look only at the formal legal effects of an agency action and its unwillingness to look at the practical effects of the action. Since the carriers had chosen to employ the rates that favored Alexander Sprunt & Son before the ICC held those rates unlawful, there was good reason to expect the carriers to return to the use of those rates if a court reversed the ICC order. The Court concluded that Alexander Sprunt & Son's sole remedy was to file a new complaint with ICC alleging that the new rates are unreasonable or unduly discriminatory.

Chicago Junction and *Alexander Sprunt & Son* illustrate the "legal right" approach to the standing issue: if the agency action violates a legal right of the complaining party, that party has standing to obtain judicial review; if the agency action does not violate the party's legal right, the party has no standing to obtain review. The legal right approach was criticized on many grounds.[109] Perhaps the most telling criticism was based on its confusion of the issue of access to the courts with the issue of whether a party should prevail on the merits of a dispute. Under the legal right approach, a court must effectively determine whether the petitioner's claim has merit in order to decide whether the petitioner is entitled to have the merits of its case considered by the court. This circular reasoning process is unnecessary to the determination of the threshold question of access to judicial review, and it can force a court to determine the merits of a claim at such an early stage that the court does not focus enough attention on the merits. Thus, considering the merits of a party's claim as part of the process of determining whether the party has standing to assert that claim invites poorly reasoned summary judicial disposition of the merits of the claim.

The modern law of standing is more liberal than the legal right approach reflected in *Chicago Junction* and *Alexander Sprunt & Son.* Yet, some aspects of those decisions may retain vitality today. In particular, some recent decisions of the Court reflect an apparent reinvigoration of the second basis for the holding in *Alexander Sprunt & Son*—a party does not have standing to obtain judicial review of an agency action unless judicial reversal of that action would benefit the party by eliminating some legally recognized harm to the party.[110]

109. *See, e.g.,* Davis, *The Liberalized Law of Standing,* 37 U.Chi.L.Rev. 450 (1970).

110. *See supra* § 5.4.4.

The Court's 1940 decision in *Federal Communications Commission v. Sanders Brothers Radio Station*[111] seemed to indicate an abandonment of the legal right approach. Sanders Brothers owned a radio station in East Dubuque, Illinois. Another party applied for an FCC license to operate a radio station in Dubuque, Iowa. The FCC granted the license over the objection of Sanders Brothers that a second station would erode its market and revenue base. Sanders Brothers sought and obtained judicial review of the FCC order. The court of appeals granted judicial review on the theory that FCC was required to consider allegations of potential economic injury to competitors in the process of deciding whether to grant a broadcast license to a new applicant. The applicant asked the Supreme Court to reverse the court of appeals because the statute did not make harm to competitors a basis for denial of a license, and, therefore, the FCC grant of the license did not deny Sanders Brothers any legal right.

The Supreme Court affirmed the court of appeals, but on an entirely different basis. The Court agreed with the applicant that potential harm to competitors was not a factor to be considered by FCC in granting or denying a license. It held, however, that Sanders Brothers had standing to obtain judicial review of the FCC order despite the fact that the order did not violate any legal right of Sanders Brothers. Congress provided an explicit statutory right to judicial review to any person aggrieved or adversely affected by an FCC order granting or denying an application for a broadcast license. The Court concluded that Congress established this permissive standard for access to the courts in recognition of the fact that competitors often are the only persons with sufficient incentive "to bring to the attention of the appellate court errors of law in the action of the Commission in granting the license". Thus, while Sanders Brothers could not argue on the merits that grant of the license impermissibly caused it economic harm, it could use that economic harm as the basis for standing, and then argue on the merits that the FCC action was unlawful on some other basis.

The Court's theory in *Sanders Brothers* was "explained" in subsequent court of appeals' opinions applying that theory. Most notably, the Second Circuit's opinion in *Associated Industries of New York State v. Ickes*[112] provides an expanded rationale for the *Sanders Brothers* approach. The Second Circuit reasoned that, since Congress had the right to authorize the Attorney General to obtain judicial

111. 309 U.S. 470 (1940).

112. 134 F.2d 694 (2d Cir.1943), *reversed on other grounds*, 320 U.S. 707 (1943).

review of any agency action in order to protect the interests of the general public, Congress could designate by statute any other party "as a private attorney general" to vindicate the interests of the public. By specifically conferring standing on all parties adversely affected or aggrieved by the agency action, Congress had done just that. Indeed, unless competitors have standing to review agency decisions granting licenses, most licensing decisions are unlikely to reach a court. Since Congress provided for judicial review of agency grants of licenses, it is reasonable to assume that Congress intended to confer standing on the class of people who are most likely to seek judicial review.

Congress enacted the APA in 1946. Section 702 provides that: "A person suffering legal wrong because of agency action, or adversely affected or aggrieved by agency action within the meaning of a relevant statute, is entitled to judicial review thereof." Initially, circuit courts differed in their interpretations of this provision of the APA. Some courts interpreted it as simply codifying the prior judicial approach to statutory standing disputes. Under that interpretation, a party had statutory standing based only a showing of "adverse affect" if, but only if, the statute that authorized the agency action explicitly authorized a suit by a party who was adversely affected. Conversely, if the statute was silent on the standing issue, a plaintiff had standing only if the agency action violated the plaintiff's "legal right." Other courts interpreted the "adversely affected or aggrieved" language of APA § 702 more broadly to authorize anyone to obtain review of any agency action that adversely affects the plaintiff. The Court resolved this interpretive dispute in its 1970 decision in *Association of Data Processing Service Organizations v. Camp.*[113]

The Court began by explaining the relationship between the constitutional and statutory components of the standing test: Congress can resolve the standing "question one way or another, save as the requirements of Article III dictate otherwise." The Court described the "adversely affected or aggrieved" language of the APA as symptomatic of a "trend ... toward enlargement of the class of people who may protest administrative action." It then noted that the APA requires a plaintiff to be "adversely affected ... within the meaning of a relevant statute." The Court interpreted that phrase as requiring a judicial inquiry into the relationship between the interests of the plaintiff that were "adversely affected" by the agency action and the interests that were protected by the statute that the plaintiff relied upon as the basis for its claim on the merits. The

113.   397 U.S. 150 (1970).

Court framed the statutory standing question as "whether the interest sought to be protected by the complainant is arguably within the zone of interests to be protected ... by the statute ... in question."

The Court has applied the zone of interests test ever since it decided *Association of Data Processors*, but its interpretation and application of the test has differed significantly from time-to-time. The Court's use of "arguably" to describe the required relationship between the plaintiff's interest and the zone of interests "arguably" protected by a statute suggested that the Court was going to take a liberal approach to defining the zone of interests. That approach was apparent in the manner in which the Court applied the test in *Association of Data Processors*. The data processors sought review of a decision of the Comptroller of the Currency that allowed banks to offer data processing services to their customers. The data processors wanted to argue on the merits that the Comptroller's decision violated the Bank Service Corporation Act and the National Bank Act. Those statutes restrict the range of activities of banks. It was clear, however, that the primary purpose of the restriction was to protect the deposits of bank customers, rather than to protect competitors of banks. Still, the Court found enough evidence in the structure of the statutes and their legislative history to support an inference that Congress probably was motivated in part by its consideration of the interests of competitors of banks. Thus, the plaintiff's interest was "arguably" within the zone of interests Congress intended to protect.

The Court's 1984 decision in *Block v. Community Nutrition Association*[114] raised serious questions about the continuing validity of the broad interpretation of the zone of interests test apparent in *Association of Data Processors*. The Agriculture Marketing Agreement Act required the Department of Agriculture to issue market orders designed to eliminate "destabilizing competition" among dairy farmers. DOA issued an order under the Act that required milk processors to pay a higher price for reconstituted milk if that milk was used for any purpose other than to manufacture surplus milk products. The effect of the DOA order was to increase the price of milk to consumers. Several consumers and groups of consumers sought judicial review of the order.

The Court recognized the existence of a presumption in favor of allowing judicial review of agency actions by parties adversely affected by those actions. The Court held, however, that the language and history of the statute provided evidence of Congress' intent to pre-

---

114.   467 U.S. 340 (1984).

clude judicial review at the behest of consumers sufficient to overcome the presumption. Throughout the Act and its history, Congress emphasized that the process of regulating milk prices was complicated and delicate, and that DOA has to be able to issue market orders in an expeditious manner. The statute contained no provision authorizing consumer participation in the regulatory process or authorizing consumers to obtain judicial review. The Act permitted milk processors to participate in the regulatory process, but it severely limited the nature of their participation and made it very difficult for processors to obtain judicial review of market orders. The Court found this evidence sufficient to establish congressional intent to limit severely the participation of individuals other than milk producers in the process of stabilizing milk prices in order to avoid the potential disruptive effect of judicial review proceedings brought by non-producers. This general intent to limit participation, combined with the absence of any statutory provision permitting consumer participation, was sufficient to support the Court's unanimous holding that Congress intended to preclude consumers from challenging milk market orders on judicial review.

In the wake of the Court's decision in *Block*, circuit courts began to adopt differing interpretations of the zone of interests test. Some continued to apply the original, permissive version of the test that was apparent in *Association of Data Processors*, while others interpreted *Block* as supporting a more narrow and more demanding version of the test. The Court resolved this split among the circuits in 1987 in its six-to-three decision in *Clarke v. Securities Industry Ass'n.*[115] The majority stated that "the test is not meant to be especially demanding," and that it is intended only to exclude a party "if the plaintiff's interests are so marginally related to or inconsistent with the purposes implicit in the statute that it cannot reasonably be assumed that Congress intended to permit the suit." Three concurring Justices rejected the majority's characterization of the test. They agreed that the plaintiff had standing but only because a "close examination of the Act and its history" revealed evidence that Congress specifically intended to protect the interest asserted by the plaintiff.

The expansive definition of the "zone of interest" test adopted by the *Clarke* majority has many virtues.[116] By broadening the range of interests that can challenge agency actions in court, it broadens

115. 479 U.S. 388 (1987).

116. *See* Pierce, *The Role of the Judiciary in Implementing an Agency Theory of Government,* 64 NYU L.Rev. 1239, 1280–84 (1989).

the range of interests that can participate effectively in agency decisionmaking processes. This, in turn, reduces the potential that factionalism will dominate an agency's decisionmaking process through the phenomenon of "capture" of the agency by a single powerful interest group. It also reflects accurately the nature of the process of statutory enactment. Almost all major statutes are a product of compromise among a large number of affected interests. Congress rarely intends to exclude completely consideration of any affected interest.

The Court cut back on the expansive approach it took in *Clarke,* however, in *Air Courier Conference v. American Postal Workers Union.*[117] A six-Justice majority held that postal employees lacked standing to obtain review of a Postal Service rule that permitted private couriers to engage in international remailing activities. The employees challenged the rule on the basis that it violated the postal monopoly provisions of the Private Express Statute of 1792. They claimed standing, however, based on a statute enacted in 1970 in which Congress dealt extensively with the relationship between the Postal Service and its employees. The Court held that postal employees were not even arguably within the zone of interests protected by the Private Express statute. The Court found no evidence that Congress considered the interests of potential future postal employees to any extent when it enacted that statute in 1792. The Court then held that the interest in protecting postal employees evidenced by Congress when it enacted the 1970 statute was irrelevant for purposes of determining whether such employees have standing to challenge an action as a violation of the 1792 statute. The 1970 statute did not purport to amend the 1792 statute. The Court held that the "zone of interests" relevant for standing purposes encompasses only those interests arguably protected by "the statute whose violation is the gravamen of the complaint." The Court also held that a plaintiff must prove that Congress intended to protect its interest in order to fit within the "zone of interests"—a significant departure from the broad, permissive version of the zone test the Court had applied in cases like *Association of Data Processors* and *Clarke.*

The Court did not adhere to the strict version of the zone test apparent in *Air Courier Conference* for long, however. A five-Justice majority abandoned that version of the test and returned to the permissive version of the test in the Court's 1998 decision in *National Credit Union Administration v. First National Bank & Trust Co.*

117.   498 U.S. 517 (1991).

(NCUA).[118] Banks sought review of an order issued by the National
Credit Union Administration in which it authorized a credit union to
broaden its membership by enrolling members who do not have a
common employer or a common vocation. The banks wanted to argue
that the order violated a provision of a statute that authorizes credit
unions to enroll as members only individuals who have a "common
bond." The banks alleged that they were injured by the order
because they would lose some of their customers to credit unions.
Thus, the banks were asserting an interest in protecting themselves
from the arguably unlawful competition authorized by the order. The
banks had a serious problem, however, in satisfying the zone of
interests test. There was no evidence of any kind that Congress was
trying to protect banks or other competitors of credit unions when it
enacted the statute that contained the "common bond" requirement.
All of the evidence indicated that Congress was motivated solely by a
desire to protect customers of credit unions. Thus, if the Court had
applied the demanding version of the zone of interests test it applied
in *Air Courier Conference*, it would have held that the banks lacked
standing. Instead, the five-Justice majority in *NCUA* said that the
lack of evidence that Congress intended to protect competitors of
credit unions was "irrelevant." It reasoned that, since enforcement of
the "common bond" requirement would protect the interests of
banks, those interests fall within the zone of interests protected by
the statute whether or not Congress intended to protect the interests
of banks. The four dissenting Justices argued that the majority
opinion "eviscerates the zone-of-interests requirement" by adopting
an interpretation of the test that any plaintiff can always satisfy.

Given the extreme vacillation apparent in the Supreme Court's
opinions interpreting and applying the zone of interests test, it is
difficult to predict the version of the test that the Supreme Court or
any lower court will apply in any case. Since Congress rarely provides
clear indications of the interests it intends to protect when it enacts a
statute, the choice of which version of the zone of interests test to
apply usually determines the outcome of a standing dispute.

§ 5.4.6   Associational standing

In *Hunt v. Washington Apple Advertising Com'n,*[119] the Court
established a three-part test to determine whether an association has
standing:

118.   522 U.S. 479 (1998).   **119.**   432 U.S. 333, 347 (1977).

"[A]n association has standing to bring suit on behalf of its members when: (a) its members would otherwise have standing to sue in their own right; (b) the interests it seeks to protect are germane to the organization's purpose; and (c) neither the claim asserted nor the relief requested requires the participation of individual members in the lawsuit."

In its 1986 opinion in *UAW v. Brock*,[120] the Court rejected the government's attack on the concept of associational standing derivative of a member's standing and reaffirmed the *Hunt* test. Conferring standing on associations is an important means of reducing the impact of a major problem in our political system—a small group each of whose members has a large amount at stake enjoys significant advantages over a large group each of whose members has a small amount at stake.[121]

§ 5.5   Standing to Participate in Agency Action

A person can participate in an administrative proceeding in two circumstances. The person can require or request an agency to hold a proceeding in connection with taking some action or the person can ask to participate in a proceeding that the agency is already obligated, or obligates itself, to hold.

An agency will initiate a proceeding on request in three circumstances. First, an agency may be required to hold a hearing before making a certain type of decision. The Federal Communications Commission (FCC), for example, is required to hold a hearing before denying an application for a broadcast license.[122] Besides a statutory right to initiate, there may also be a constitutional right to a hearing. An agency must grant such a hearing as a matter of due process if its action deprives an individual of life, liberty, or property.[123]

Second, an agency may be required to hold a comparative hearing concerning multiple licensing applications whenever there is a possibility that the agency will not approve all of the applications. The doctrine originated in *Ashbacker Radio Corporation v. FCC*,[124]

---

120. 477 U.S. 274 (1986).

121. *See* Pierce, *supra* n. 116, at 1284–85; M. Olsen, The Logic of Collective Action: Public Goods and the Theory of Groups, 53–65 (1965).

122. 47 U.S.C. § 309(e); *see also* 21 U.S.C. § 355(c) (hearing required for FDA to approve or disapprove an application to market a new pharmaceutical drug).

123. U.S. Const. Amend. 5. *See infra* § 6.3.

124. 326 U.S. 327 (1945); Pierce, *Obtaining Agency Consideration of a Competing Proposal: Alternatives to Ashbacker*, 26 Kan.L.Rev. 185, 186–89 (1978).

where the Supreme Court reviewed an FCC decision to grant a license to a competitor of Ashbacker. The two licenses were mutually exclusive because a second radio station run by Ashbacker would have caused too much electrical interference for the first station. In those circumstances, the Court decided that the grant of the license to Ashbacker's competitor in effect was a denial of one to Ashbacker. Since the denial violated the FCC's obligation to hold a hearing before it denied any license, the Court ordered the FCC to hold a comparative hearing at which the merits of both applications could be considered.

Third, an agency may start a proceeding in response to a "petition". "Petitions" of this type are authorized both by the APA and individual enabling acts. The APA requires "[e]ach agency to give an interested person the right to petition for the issuance, amendment, or repeal of a rule".[125] Enabling acts, like that for the FCC, authorize petitions for various purposes, such as denying a license application.[126] Many agencies have clarified the receipt, consideration, and disposition of petitions by promulgating procedural rules to govern them.[127]

An agency can use its rulemaking authority to promulgate procedural or substantive rules that affect the scope of the previous initiation rights.[128] A prominent procedural limitation, for example, conditions the right to a hearing on whether there is some genuine and substantial factual issue that requires a hearing to resolve. Thus, although the Food and Drug Administration (FDA) is obligated to hold a hearing before it forbids the sale of a pharmaceutical drug, the right to a hearing is conditioned on whether the drug's manufacturer can present any responsible scientific evidence that the drug is safe and efficacious for the purposes for which it is used.[129]

Agencies can establish substantive rules to avoid deciding some issue each time it comes up in a hearing. For example, the Atomic Energy Commission (AEC) used a rulemaking proceeding to determine the environmental effects of the storage or reprocessing of nuclear fuel. It then used those results in subsequent licensing hearings for nuclear power plants to determine the overall cost-

---

125.   5 U.S.C. § 553(e).

126.   47 U.S.C. § 309(d)(1).

127.   *See, e.g.,* 21 C.F.R. § 10.30 (FDA citizen's petition). *See* Luneburg, *Petitioning Federal Agencies for Rulemaking,* 1988 Wis.L.Rev. 1.

128.   *See generally infra* § 6.4.7.

129.   *See* 21 C.F.R. § 12.24(b); Weinberger v. Hynson, Westcott & Dunning, Inc., 412 U.S. 609 (1973).

benefit balance of those proposed projects. Because the AEC had made that determination in the rulemaking proceeding, it excluded the issue from consideration in any licensing proceeding.[130]

The existence and scope of the right to intervene is determined initially by the type of proceeding. The APA requires every agency to give "interested parties" the opportunity to participate in informal rulemaking "through the submission of written data, views, or arguments with or without the opportunity for oral presentations".[131] An agency can avoid this responsibility only if the APA authorizes it to dispense with the use of rulemaking procedures altogether.[132] For certain agencies, Congress has provided participants with additional procedural protections.[133] These can include the right to make oral presentations or to present and cross-examine witnesses.

The right to intervene in adjudications and formal rulemaking is usually controlled by agency enabling acts and agency rules. These sources typically extend eligibility to "any person,"[134] to "parties in interest",[135] or to "affected" persons.[136] Eligibility, however, can be qualified in either of two ways. In some cases, a statute indicates only that an eligible person *"may be "*allowed to intervene.[137] In other cases, eligibility to intervene is conditional on whether it will be in the "public interest,"[138] will not unduly delay a proceeding,[139] or will be for "good cause".[140] Some agencies have specified by procedural rules how they will use the discretion created by these two types of statutory provisions.[141]

---

130. *See* Vermont Yankee Nuclear Power Corp. v. Natural Resources Defense Council, 435 U.S. 519 (1978); *see infra* § 6.4.7 (discussion of the effects of legislative rules in adjudicatory proceedings).

131. 5 U.S.C. § 553(c).

132. *See* 5 U.S.C. § 553(b), (d); *see generally supra* § 6.4.4d.

133. For a description and discussion of these "hybrid" rulemaking schemes, *see infra* § 6.4.9.

134. *See, e.g.,* 15 U.S.C. § 45(b) (Federal Trade Commission); 29 U.S.C. § 160(b) (National Labor Relations Board); 21 C.F.R. § 12.45 (Food and Drug Administration).

135. *See, e.g.,* 47 U.S.C. § 309(d)(1) (Federal Communications Commission).

136. *See, e.g.,* 15 U.S.C. § 45(b) (Federal Trade Commission); 29 U.S.C. § 160(b) (National Labor Relations Board).

137. *See, e.g.,* 16 U.S.C. § 825g(a) (Federal Energy Regulatory Commission); 17 C.F.R. 201.9(e) (Securities Exchange Commission).

138. *See, e.g.,* 13 C.F.R. § 109.10(b) (Small Business Administration); *see also* 49 C.F.R. § 1112.4 (intervention allowed in Interstate Commerce Commission hearings if it will not "unduly broaden the issues raised in the proceeding").

139. *See, e.g.,* 15 U.S.C. § 45(b) (Federal Trade Commission).

140. *See, e.g.,* 47 C.F.R. § 1.223 (Federal Communications Commission).

141. *See, e.g.,* 16 C.F.R. § 3.14 (Federal Trade Commission).

Unlike persons statutorily eligible to initiate a proceeding, an intervenor's participation in a proceeding can be limited in either or both of two ways. The intervenor can be restricted to litigating only one or several of the issues the agency will consider. The intervenor can also be limited to the use of only certain procedures. Intervenors, for example, might be allowed only to submit written evidence or comments.

§ 5.5.1   Eligibility to intervene as an "interested" or "affected" person

The definition of who can intervene as an "interested" or "affected" person has been influenced by who has standing to appeal final agency decisions as an "aggrieved" person. When standing was extended to persons whose economic interests were aggrieved by an agency decision, the same class of persons was declared eligible to intervene. Similarly, when standing was extended to persons whose aesthetic, conservational, or recreational interests were aggrieved by an agency decision, the same classes of persons were declared eligible to intervene.

Eligibility to intervene on the basis of an adverse economic interest followed the Supreme Court's decision in *FCC v. Sanders Brothers*.[142] The Court held that a competitor of a business firm granted a Federal Communications Commission license qualified as a person aggrieved because among other reasons the competitor likely would be "the only person having a sufficient interest to bring to the attention of the appellate courts errors of law in the action of the Commission in granting the license". In a subsequent case, *Associated Industries of New York State v. Ickes,* the rationale of *Sanders Brothers* was explained as the creation of "private attorney generals" who could call to the court's attention errors of fact and law made by an agency.[143] Based on this rationale, businesses now commonly qualify as intervenors when they have an economic stake in the outcome of an adjudication.[144] So do public interest groups whose members have an economic interest in the outcome.[145]

---

142.   309 U.S. 470 (1940). For a more complete analysis of *Sanders Brothers* and its influence on standing doctrine, *see supra* § 5.4.5.

143.   134 F.2d 694, 704 (2d Cir.1943), *dismissed as moot* 320 U.S. 707 (1943).

144.   *See, e.g.,* Virginia Petroleum Jobbers Ass'n v. FPC, 265 F.2d 364, 367–68 (D.C.Cir.1959) (competitors of natural gas distributor qualified as intervenors in FPC licensing proceeding); Philco Corp. v. FCC, 257 F.2d 656, 658–59 (D.C.Cir. 1958) (competitor of applicant for broadcast license is a "party in interest" for intervention).

145.   *See, e.g.,* Scenic Hudson Preservation Conference v. FPC, 354 F.2d 608, 616 (2d Cir.1965) (forest trails built by

The eligibility to intervene based on a noneconomic interest followed a series of Supreme Court cases that granted standing to environmental and conservation groups.[146] *Office of Communication of United Church of Christ v. FCC* held that the FCC was required to allow intervention by responsible and representative community groups in a broadcast licensing hearing.[147] Four reasons were offered in support of the decision. First, in the similar situation of standing, the courts had long granted participation rights to such parties. Second, there was no indication that Congress intended to restrict participation only to persons with a financial interest in the outcome.[148] Third, the agency could better represent the interests of the public if it allowed them to participate. When the FCC objected that it would be overrun by intervenors and that intervention therefore would not be helpful, the court noted that the Commission could restrict participation in the ways described earlier.[149] Fourth, the court reasoned by analogy to *Sanders Brothers* that unless "listeners—broadcast consumers—can be heard, there may be no one to bring programming deficiencies or offensive overcommercialization to the attention of the Commission in an effective manner". The last point was influential because the church organization sought to intervene to argue that a television broadcasting license should not be renewed because of racist programming.

Finally, when the Supreme Court extended standing to situations where there was no express statutory provision for it, a similar extension was made for intervention. In *Barlow v. Collins*[150] and *Association of Data Processing Service Organization v. Camp*,[151] the Court held that the test for standing without express statutory authorization was whether the person seeking review had a personal stake and interest that would impart concrete adversariness and whether the person sought to protect interests that were arguably within the "zone of interests" to be protected or regulated by the statute in question. Again, the rationale in part was that Congress must have intended that those persons whose interests were taken

conservation group would be inundated by construction of public dam).

146. *See, e.g.,* United States v. Students Challenging Regulatory Agency Procedures, 412 U.S. 669 (1973); Sierra Club v. Morton, 405 U.S. 727 (1972); *see generally supra* § 5.4.2.

147. 359 F.2d 994 (D.C.Cir.1966); *see also* Scenic Hudson Preservation Conference v. FPC, 354 F.2d 608, 620 (2d Cir. 1965).

148. Although the court did not rely upon it, the economic stake of listeners was cited by the court as the "huge aggregate investment in receiving equipment." 359 F.2d at 1002.

149. *See supra* § 5.5.

150. 397 U.S. 159 (1970).

151. 397 U.S. 150 (1970).

into account in the process of enacting a statute could appeal an agency decision because otherwise no one might bring to the attention of the courts errors by an agency.

National Welfare Rights Organization v. Finch has made a similar extension of intervention rights.[152] The court held that the Department of Health, Education, and Welfare (HEW) should have allowed the welfare rights organization to intervene in a hearing it held to determine whether or not two states had complied with regulations for the funding of welfare programs. The court explained that *Barlow* and *Data Processing* should apply because standing and intervention cases were often used interchangeably, that the purpose behind both rights was to increase public input, and that the ability of the interest group to appeal would be enhanced if they had some opportunity to help make the record on which the appeal would be based. The court concluded the group was sufficiently adversarial because its members as welfare recipients had an economic stake in the outcome of the hearing. The court also found that the interests of the welfare recipients were within the "zone of interests" that the statute was intended to protect.

The court had another possible basis for intervention that it overlooked. The APA provides that "[s]o far as the orderly conduct of public business permits, an interested person may appear before an agency or its responsible employees for the presentation, adjustment or determination of an issue, request, or controversy in a proceeding, whether interlocutory, summary, or otherwise, or in connection with an agency function."[153] Although the APA has been used as a basis for intervention rights,[154] some commentators argue that an agency has complete discretion to decide whether to allow intervention because the section uses the words "may appear".[155] Other commentators disagree. Professor Davis, for example, notes that the Attorney General's Manual on the APA allows an agency to refuse intervention by an "interested person" only if the "orderly conduct of business" requires it.[156]

Because of the interrelated and parallel development of standing and intervention, courts and legal commentators have assumed that

152. 429 F.2d 725 (D.C.Cir.1970).

153. 5 U.S.C. § 555(b).

154. Ecee, Inc. v. FERC, 645 F.2d 339, 349–50 (5th Cir.1981); Easton Utilities Com'n v. AEC, 424 F.2d 847, 850–52 (D.C.Cir.1970); American Communications Ass'n v. U.S., 298 F.2d 648, 650–51 (2d Cir.1962).

155. *See* Shapiro, *Some Thoughts on Intervention Before Courts, Agencies and Arbitrators,* 81 Harv.L.Rev. 721, 766 (1968).

156. 3 K. Davis, Administrative Law Treatise § 14.15 (1980); *see* Attorney General's Manual on the APA 63 (1947).

eligibility under each was the same.[157] Although standing cases have been applied to intervention, no court has held that everyone qualified as an intervenor must also qualify for standing. The reason is that standing must take into account that Article III restricts the judiciary to entertaining "cases" and "controversies".[158] Thus, standing must test for whether a person has an adversarial interest in making an appeal. Because agencies have no similar restraint, Congress or an agency can authorize a person without such an interest to intervene.[159]

The difference between intervention and standing may be of some importance because of recent limitations imposed on standing by the Supreme Court.[160] As explained earlier, the reasons for these limitations are somewhat in doubt. One possible source, however, is an attempt by the Court to police the requirement that a person be sufficiently adversarial that Article III is satisfied. If this is the case, these developments would have no logical relationship to intervention and the case law they produce should not be applied to intervention.

§ 5.5.2   Agency discretion to control intervention

When the right to intervene is subject to qualifications in addition to limited eligibility, agencies have considerable, or even complete, discretion to decide the fate of particular requests.[161] Some agencies have claimed that they have unreviewable discretion to determine whether an eligible person or group can participate in a specific case when intervention is sought pursuant to a statute that provides only that intervenors "may" participate.[162] An agency is likely to prevail with this claim unless the APA obligates the agency to allow intervention[163] or the statute indicates that the agency's decision is subject to judicial review.

When courts review agency decisions whether a person or group has the necessary qualifications, agencies are still accorded "substantial discretion".[164] The reason is that agencies are believed to be in

---

157. *See, e.g.,* ACLU v. FCC, 523 F.2d 1344, 1346–48 (9th Cir.1975); Martin–Trigona v. Federal Reserve Bd., 509 F.2d 363, 366 n. 10 (D.C.Cir.1974).

158. U.S. Const. Art. III, § 2.

159. *See* Koniag, Inc., Village of Uyak v. Andrus, 580 F.2d 601, 606 (D.C.Cir. 1978).

160. *See supra* § 5.4.

161. *See supra* § 5.5.

162. *See, e.g.,* Firestone Tire & Rubber Co., 77 F.T.C. 1666, 1668–69 (1970) (intervention is a matter of privilege and not right).

163. *See supra* § 5.5.1.

164. *See, e.g.,* BPI v. AEC, 502 F.2d 424, 425–27 (D.C.Cir.1974); Cities of Statesville v. AEC, 441 F.2d 962, 976–77 (D.C.Cir.1969); Palisades Citizens' Ass'n v. CAB, 420 F.2d 188, 192–93 (D.C.Cir. 1969); Office of Communication of Unit-

the best position to determine the usefulness of intervention because of their more intimate knowledge of the nature of a case, its parties, and the potential for inefficiency and duplication. Professor Davis, however, has cautioned that courts may be too quick to support an agency's decision to deny intervention entirely.[165] He argues that the court should always consider whether the agency could have benefitted from some sort of limited intervention. Because participation by submission of written briefs and other written materials poses little burden, Professor Davis sensibly concludes that denials of intervention should normally be limited to denial of participation in oral processes.

§ 5.5.3   Reform of intervention

Broad participation by diverse interest groups in agency proceedings has been heralded as an important reform of the administrative process.[166] One reason is that the process is most democratic when all interests affected by a decision can and do participate in influencing its outcome. Another reason is that a more rational decisionmaking process results when a multiplicity of viewpoints and evidence is considered. A final reason is that it checks the tendency of agencies to favor the industries they regulate when no one else participates in decisionmaking.

Some commentators have warned, however, that those benefits only accrue in certain types of proceedings and with the participation of certain types of intervenors. They note that broad participation often causes delay and expense and can lead to ineffective law enforcement. To determine the value of the intervention in a given case, the Administrative Conference has recommended that five factors be considered: the nature of the contested issues, the intervenor's precise interest in the subject matter or outcome, whether other parties will represent that interest, the ability of the proposed intervenor to present relevant evidence and arguments, and the effect of the intervention on the agency's implementation of its statutory mandate.[167]

ed Church of Christ v. FCC, 359 F.2d 994, 1005–1006 (D.C.Cir.1966).

165. 3 K. Davis, *supra* note 156, at § 14.16.

166. *See, e.g.,* Council for Public Interest Law, Balancing the Scales of Justice: Financing Public Interest Law in America (1976); Trubek & Trubek, *Civil Justice Through Civil Justice: A New* *Approach to Public Interest Advocacy in the United States,* in Access to Justice in the Welfare State 122–23 (M. Cappelletti ed. 1981); Lazarus & Onek, *The Regulators and the People,* 57 Va.L.Rev. 1069, 1092–93 (1971).

167. Administrative Conference of the United States, Public Participation in Administrative Hearings (Recommenda-

Public interest advocates have resisted these attempts to limit intervention. They claim that the limitations invite agencies to favor regulated industries by eliminating intervention, ignore the fact that agency decisions have greater legitimacy when affected parties have participated, and overestimate the delay and other costs imposed by such participation.[168]

This debate concerning the value of intervention is created in part by the fact that each side is viewing the administrative process from a different perspective. Broad participation recognizes the pluralistic nature of our polity and decreases the risks of factional domination of an agency's decisionmaking process, but it also creates the risk of adding significant delay and cost to a decisionmaking process that is already plagued by those problems.[169]

Ways must be found to accommodate these values. The most practical suggestion is that of Professors Davis and Shapiro.[170] There should be a presumption in favor of participation by persons and groups that are significantly affected by a decision. Problems of delay and increased cost should be minimized by limiting intervention to certain issues or procedures. In this manner, an open system of decisionmaking can be maintained, but without imposing costs that render it ineffective.

§ 5.5.4 Public financing of intervention

Vigorous debate surrounds another reform proposal to increase the breadth of participation in agency proceedings. Public interest advocates contend that governmental financing of public interest advocacy ensures that the interests of consumers and others are adequately presented. They note that many public interest groups are thinly financed and that as a result they often lack sufficient funds to participate in prolonged controversies.[171]

Government responded to these claims by establishing several

tion No. 71–6), 1 C.F.R. §§ 305.71–6; *see generally* Cramton, *The Why, Where and How of Broadened Participation In the Administrative Process*, 60 Geo.L.J. 525, 527–35 (1972).

168. *See, e.g.,* Lazarus & Onek, *supra* note 166, at 1074, 1097.

169. *See supra* § 1.10.

170. *See supra* text accompanying note 155.

171. *See, e.g.,* Council for Public Interest Law, *supra* note 164; Tobias, *Of Public Funds and Public Participation: Resolving the Issue of Agency Authority to Reimburse Public Participants in Administrative Proceedings,* 82 Col.L.Rev. 906, 907–09 (1982). A related reform would be for the government to lower or absorb some of the costs of participation. *See* Gellhorn, *Public Participation in Administrative Proceedings,* 81 Yale L.J. 359, 388–98 (1972).

methods of support for public interest intervention.[172] Some agencies, which were statutorily entitled to do so, funded public interest groups to participate in rulemaking proceedings.[173] Other agencies attempted such funding without express statutory authorization, leading to a split in the courts concerning whether the funding was legal.[174] In addition, lawyers in some agencies were designated to represent consumers in agency proceedings and oppose recommendations of the agency's staff if they were considered not to be in the consumer's best interests.[175] Some states established Offices of Public Counsel to represent consumers, usually in utility ratemaking proceedings. These offices functioned in the same manner as the previous groups of lawyers, but they were independent of the agency in whose proceedings they participated.[176] Congress considered establishing a Consumer Protection Agency with broad powers to intervene in agency proceedings on behalf of consumers, but the bill did not pass.[177]

Critics of federal funding of public interest advocacy contend that in a pluralistic society, the government should play a neutral and detached role between competing interest groups. They note that the ability to raise sufficient funds is a test of the legitimacy of a public interest organization because it measures whether there is any significant public support for the point of view espoused. They argue that in many instances, public funding ends up supporting a class of public advocates who have little public support and who could not afford participation but for federal financial support. These critics also question the extent of any benefits available from funded participation because of the abstract nature of the benefits and because of

172. *See generally* Murphy & Hoffman, *Current Models for Improving Public Representation in the Administrative Process,* 28 Ad.L.Rev. 391 (1976).

173. *See* Tobias, *supra* note 171, at 910–81.

174. *Compare* Greene County Planning Bd. v. FPC, 559 F.2d 1227 (2d Cir. 1976), (en banc), *cert. denied* 434 U.S. 1086 (1978) (FPC could not reimburse intervenors absent express statutory authority to do so) *with* Chamber of Commerce v. United States Department of Agriculture, 459 F.Supp. 216 (D.D.C. 1978) (USDA could rely on implied statutory authority for reimbursement).

175. *See* 39 U.S.C. § 3624(a) (Postal Rate Commission); Bloch & Stein, *The*

Public Counsel Concept in Practice: The Regional Rail Organization Act of 1973, 16 Wm. & Mary L.Rev. 215 (1974) (ICC Office of Rail Public Counsel).

176. *See* Penn, *Advocate From Within,* Trial, Febr. 1976, at 20 (description of New Jersey Department of Public Advocacy); Note, *The Office of Public Counsel: Institutionalizing Public Interest Representation in State Government,* 64 Geo. L.J. 895 (1976).

177. *See* Staff of Senate Comm. on Government Operations, Vol. III—Public Participation in Regulatory Agency Proceedings, 95th Cong., 1st Sess. 65–71 (Comm.Print 1977).

the difficulty of their measurement. In conclusion, opponents of funding believe that it encourages unproductive litigation, increases cost and delay in the administrative process, and underwrites lobbying for ideological causes or values with which most taxpayers would disagree.[178]

Supporters of intervention argue that the critics have ignored evidence that weakens their arguments. For example, studies have shown that the reason public interest groups have trouble raising money is the economics of the group organizing process. As explained earlier, public interest groups face free rider problems that do not similarly affect smaller groups such as industry trade organizations.[179] Other studies have purported to establish that funded intervention has been helpful to the agencies that have used it.[180] Supporters also argue that funded intervention does not favor particular interests over other interests if funding is administered by the use of neutrally constructed and applied criteria of eligibility.

§ 5.6 Jurisdiction and Venue

Some agency actions are subject to judicial review in district courts, while other actions are subject to direct review by circuit courts. If Congress does not address the jurisdictional issue, review is available in a district court under the broad grant of federal question jurisdiction in 28 U.S.C. § 1331. If Congress confers jurisdiction on circuit courts, that jurisdiction is exclusive.

Congress frequently addresses issues of jurisdiction to review explicitly in the statutes that authorize agencies to act. Courts frequently must resolve difficult jurisdictional issues, however. Congress often provides that certain types of agency actions are subject to district court review, while other types of actions taken by the same agency are subject to exclusive review in circuit courts. Frequently, however, the congressional intent to divide review responsibility is implicit. Viewed as an issue to be resolved through formal legal analysis, when Congress provides that only certain types of agency actions are subject to circuit court review, it has indicated by its silence that all other actions taken by that agency are subject to district court review. This method of statutory drafting can give rise to difficult characterization problems, since many agency actions are susceptible to more than one characterization, and there is often reason to doubt that Congress actually intended what its silence

---

178. *See* M. Breger, *Halting Taxpayer Subsidy of Partisan Advocacy* (1983) (Heritage Foundation Lecture).

179. *See supra* § 1.7.

180. *See, e.g.,* Tobias, *supra* note 171, at 939–55.

implies. Sometimes the allocation of review jurisdiction Congress *seems* to have chosen by its silence is inconsistent with practical considerations concerning the advantages of review in district courts and review in circuit courts. In such cases, courts have an understandable tendency to conclude that Congress actually intended the more logical allocation of jurisdiction.

Exclusive circuit court review makes sense when an agency action is subject to review based solely on the record made by the agency and when the agency action involves issues of policy on which consistency and uniformity are highly desirable. Circuit court review enhances uniformity and consistency because: (1) circuit courts are less numerous than district courts; (2) they decide cases through the use of three-judge panels; (3) they have access to an en banc procedure for minimizing intracircuit conflicts; and, (4) their decisions are directly reviewable by the Supreme Court, which has responsibility to minimize intercircuit conflicts. By contrast, district court review makes sense for actions: (1) that are so numerous that direct circuit court review would strain the resources of circuit courts; (2) that tend to focus primarily on factual disputes unique to a specific case, rather than on broad policy disputes; and, (3) that arise under a statute that authorizes the reviewing court to conduct evidentiary hearings to supplement the record compiled by the agency.

Congress usually allocates review jurisdiction in a manner consistent with the comparative advantages of district courts and circuit courts. When Congress' intent is unclear, courts usually resolve jurisdictional disputes in a manner consistent with courts' perception of the comparative advantages of review in circuit courts and district courts. Two cases illustrate this tendency particularly well.

In *Investment Co. Institute v. Board of Governors of Federal Reserve System,*[181] the D.C. Circuit held that the agency's regulations were subject to exclusive circuit court review. The statute provided only for circuit court review of "orders." Congress' silence with respect to regulations could support an inference that "regulations" were subject to district court review. The court declined to draw such an inference, however, for two reasons. First, rules and regulations are the kinds of actions most suitable for exclusive review in circuit courts because they usually involve broad issues of national policy. Second, Congress' failure to provide for circuit court review of regulations was probably attributable to an oversight rather than to an intentional decision to allow district court review of regulations.

181.   551 F.2d 1270 (D.C.Cir.1977).

At the time Congress provided for circuit court review of "orders", the agency could act only by issuing orders. When Congress amended the statute to authorize the agency to issue "regulations," it made no change in the judicial review provisions of the statute.

In *Telecommunications Research and Action Center v. FCC*,[182] the D.C. Circuit held that circuit courts have exclusive jurisdiction to consider claims that an agency has "unreasonably delayed" an action, in violation of APA § 706(1), when the action at issue ultimately is subject to review in a circuit court. The Communications Act provides for exclusive circuit court review of "final orders," but a claim of unreasonable delay in taking an action is not a petition to review a "final order." The court based its holding primarily on policy grounds—circuit courts that exercise exclusive jurisdiction to review all "final orders" issued by an agency develop expertise concerning the agency that is valuable in assessing a claim that the agency has "unreasonably delayed" an action.

Occasionally, Congress provides for exclusive review in a particular district court or a particular circuit court. EPA actions under the Clean Air Act, for instance, are subject to review only in the D.C. Circuit. In most statutes, however, Congress confers review jurisdiction on all circuit courts or all district courts and addresses the question of which district court or circuit court should review an action in a generally worded venue provision.

Venue provisions for the circuit courts are of three types. The first allows a petitioner to bring suit in the circuit in which that person resides and either in which the person's principal business is located,[183] or in which the particular activity under review took place.[184] In addition, suits are sometimes allowed in the District of Columbia Circuit whether or not venue would have otherwise been proper there.[185] A second category includes the same forum choices as the first, except that a petitioner need only transact some business in the circuit in order for there to be venue.[186] A third category requires the appeal to occur in the circuit where the subject matter of the

---

182. 750 F.2d 70 (D.C.Cir.1984).

183. *See, e.g.,* 29 U.S.C. § 655(f) (judicial review of OSHA standards).

184. *See, e.g.,* 8 U.S.C. § 1105a(a)(2) (review of Immigration and Naturalization deportation and exclusion orders).

185. *See, e.g.,* 15 U.S.C. §§ 77i(a), 79x(a), 80a–42(a), 80b–13(a) (Securities and Exchange Commission orders); 15

U.S.C. § 2618(a)(1)(A) (Environmental Protection Agency regulations for toxic substances); 28 U.S.C. §§ 2342(4), 2343 (orders of Nuclear Regulatory Commission).

186. *See, e.g.,* 7 U.S.C. § 136n(b) (Environmental Protection Agency orders for pesticides); 15 U.S.C. § 45(c) (FTC orders); 33 U.S.C. § 466g (EPA actions concerning water pollution).

regulation is located or where the effects of the regulation will be felt.[187]

Venue provisions for the district courts usually provide for four possible locations.[188] First, a suit can be brought in the district court in which the defendant agency and its officials reside, which for most agencies includes at least the District of Columbia. Second, a suit can be brought where the cause of action arose. For example, a motion to quash an administrative subpoena can be brought in the district where the search was to take place.[189] Third, a suit can be brought where any real property involved is situated. A suit to evict federal personnel from privately owned land, for example, might be brought where the land is located. Finally, a suit can be brought where the plaintiff resides if no real property is involved. For this purpose, corporations reside where they are incorporated.[190] Congress has provided for more restrictive venue provisions in a few instances, such as an appeal of an Interstate Commerce Commission order concerning the collection of money or fines.[191]

§ 5.6.1   The problem of forum shopping

The availability of multiple forums creates an opportunity for forum shopping. Current venue rules allow a party to take advantage of, or avoid, precedent in a particular circuit, act on a belief that the judges in a particular circuit are more sympathetic than the judges in other circuits, or attempt to create a conflict between circuits in order to obtain an ultimate resolution of the dispute by the Supreme Court.[192]

Critics contend that such forum shopping is unseemly, threatens judicial comity, endangers agency attempts to apply policy uniformly across the country, is biased against thinly financed public-interest groups, and makes business planning more difficult because of uncer-

---

187. *See, e.g.,* 33 U.S.C. § 921(c) (orders concerning benefits under Longshoremen's and Harbor Workers' Compensation Act reviewable only in circuit in which injury occurred); 15 U.S.C. § 766(c) (Department of Energy regulations reviewable only in "appropriate" circuit within which regulations have an effect).

188. 28 U.S.C. § 1391(e).

189. *See generally* Wood, *Federal Venue: Locating the Place Where the Claim Arose,* 54 Tex.L.Rev. 392 (1976).

190. *See* Suttle v. Reich Bros. Const. Co., 333 U.S. 163, 166–68 (1948).

191. 28 U.S.C. § 1398 (venue limited to district in which person resides or has principal office).

192. *See generally* Brecher, *Venue in Conservation Cases: A Potential Pitfall for Environmental Lawyers,* 2 Ecology L.Q. 91, 94 (1972).

tainty about the ultimate outcome of an issue.[193] They also contend that forum shopping raises the cost of judicial appeals when litigation results concerning which of several eligible courts of appeal will hear a matter.[194]

If more than one appeal is filed in different circuits, Congress originally provided that the first filed would be the one to go forward.[195] In several prominent cases, however, the courts have discovered that appeals were filed simultaneously. In fact, parties in those cases were so anxious to obtain the circuit of their choice that they employed radios and open telephone lines to file within seconds of a final decision. This technique became known as a "race to the courthouse".

The Third and Fifth Circuits were involved in one of these races to the courthouse in *United Steelworkers v. Marshall.*[196] Both the Lead Industries Association (LIA) and the United Steelworkers of America appealed an occupational exposure rule for lead, promulgated by OSHA. The LIA petition was filed at 8:45 a.m. eastern standard time in the Third Circuit and the Steelworkers petition was filed simultaneously at 7:45 a.m. in the Fifth Circuit. The Third Circuit declared the race to the courthouse to be a "dead heat" and it noted that "[u]nlike racetracks . . . courts are not equipped with photoelectric timers, and we decline the invitation to speculate which nose would show as first in a photo finish."

To determine which court would entertain the lawsuit, the Third Circuit relied upon its statutory authority to transfer cases to another circuit if a transfer would be for the "convenience of the parties" and in the "interests of justice".[197] The court ordered the case transferred to the District of Columbia Circuit because that circuit was already considering a case that raised similar issues and because the circuit was convenient for the parties. The court dismissed the arguments of both parties in favor of the circuits in which they filed on the ground that they were makeweight.

193. *See* McGarity, *Multi-Party Forum Shopping for Appellate Review of Administrative Action,* 129 U.Pa.L.Rev. 302, 312–18 (1980); Note, *Venue for Judicial Review of Administrative Actions: A New Approach,* 93 Harv.L.Rev. 1735, 1741–42 (1980) [cited hereinafter as *Administrative Venue*].

194. McGarity, *supra* note 193, at 307–12; *Administrative Venue, supra* note 193, at 1742–43.

195. 28 U.S.C. § 2112(a).

196. 592 F.2d 693 (3d Cir.1979); *see also,* American Public Gas Ass'n v. FPC, 555 F.2d 852 (D.C.Cir.1976).

197. *See* 28 U.S.C. § 2112(a) (circuit court transfer); *see also,* 28 U.S.C. § 1404(a) (district court transfer). Intervenors usually cannot take advantage of these transfer provisions. Sunstein, *Participation, Public Law and Venue Reform,* 49 U.Chi.L.Rev. 976, 981 n. 19 (1982).

§ 5.6.2   Reform of venue provisions

Forum shopping could be eliminated entirely if appeals were limited to a particular court, but the Supreme Court would lose its opportunity to see how several circuits have resolved difficult issues and some litigants would be forced to appeal in an inconvenient forum.[198] A more moderate reform has eliminated merely those problems associated with the race to the courthouse. Congress has correctly chosen a lottery as the appropriate solution.[199] If petitions are filed in more than one court that meets the venue requirements, a lottery is conducted to determine which court would hear the case. The lottery has all of the simplicity of the first-to-file rule with none of its disadvantages. It has eliminated costly litigation concerning discretionary transfers when more than one appeal has been filed. It has also eliminated any litigation over which appeal was filed first. Further, it is a better method to resolve which circuit will hear a case because meaningful criteria to transfer cases are difficult to create.[200] Finally, it is unlikely to work a hardship on any of the parties because their participation is limited to the filing of briefs and an oral argument.

§ 5.7   Timing of Judicial Review

Assuming that a party has a right to obtain judicial review of an agency action at all,[201] it is entitled to such review only at specific times. Temporal limits on judicial review of agency action result from the application of four principles: (1) a party can obtain review only of final agency actions; (2) a party can obtain judicial review of an agency action only after it has exhausted its administrative remedies; (3) a party can obtain judicial review of an agency action only when that action is ripe for review; and, (4) Congress can limit the time in which an agency action can be subjected to judicial review.

The fourth principle was discussed previously.[202] Congress can establish a deadline by which judicial review must be sought in order to further the policy goals of allowing the agency and the parties affected by its policies to know within a reasonable period of time whether the agency's actions are lawful.

Deadlines for seeking review of agency actions create serious problems in one recurring situation—when the issues potentially

---

198. *See* McGarity, *supra* note 193, at 356–60.

199. 28 U.S.C. § 2112.

200. McGarity, *supra* note 193, at 371–75.

201. *See supra* §§ 5.2 and 5.3.

202. *See supra* § 5.2.1.

raised by the agency action are not appropriate for judicial resolution by the time of the deadline. Thus, for instance, the Solid Waste Disposal Act requires a petition to review a rule to be filed within ninety days of EPA's issuance of the rule. Yet, a court will dismiss a petition for review filed by the deadline if the court concludes that the rule is not ripe for pre-enforcement review. (See § 5.7.3 for a discussion of ripeness.) Courts address this problem by holding that the statutory time limit for review of an agency action does not begin to run until the issues the petitioner seeks to raise are ripe for review.[203] Thus, for instance, if EPA issues a rule to implement the Solid Waste Disposal Act on January 1, 2003; a court concludes that the rule is not ripe for pre-enforcement review; and, EPA first applies the rule to the petitioner on January 1, 2006, the petitioner has until March 31, 2006 to file a petition to review the rule. As a practical matter, however, the petitioner has no choice but to attempt to obtain pre-enforcement review of the rule by filing a petition for review by March 31, 2003 to avoid the risk that a court will dismiss a subsequent petition to review as untimely based on the court's conclusion that the rule was ripe for pre-enforcement review.

The other three principles have the effect of forcing parties to wait until an agency has completed all of the steps in the administrative process necessary to formulate, and sometimes to implement, a policy before any aspect of the agency's action can be subjected to judicial review. The severe limit on premature judicial intervention in the administrative process that results from application of these three related principles has important practical consequences. Agency proceedings often are expensive and time-consuming. Depending upon the nature of the issues presented to the agency and the procedures the agency employs to address those issues, effective participation by a party in an agency proceeding can require expenditure of hundreds of thousands or even millions of dollars, and final resolution of the issues may require many years.[204] An agency typically acts through a multi step decision making process, beginning with a notice or order initiating a proceeding, and extending through many intermediate stages before it issues an order resolving the issues before it on a final basis. Generally, courts will not intervene in this process until it has been completed.

203. *E.g.*, Atlantic States Legal Foundation v. EPA, 325 F.3d 281, 285 (D.C. Cir. 2003).

204. *See* Pierce, *The Choice Between Adjudicating and Rulemaking for Formulating and Implementing Energy Policy*, 31 Hastings L.J. 1 (1979).

All participants in the administrative process find the delay inherent in the process and the high cost of participation in the process frustrating, but these features are particularly troublesome in two recurring situations. First, sometimes an agency initiates a proceeding to consider whether to take an action it does not have the power to take. Parties potentially adversely affected by the threatened action understandably become upset upon discovering that they must devote substantial resources to participation in the agency proceeding for several years even though they are virtually certain that the agency ultimately will be precluded by the courts from taking the threatened action. Second, sometimes an agency takes an inordinate amount of time to act in a way that it eventually must act. The agency's delay in this situation can cause considerable harm to both private and public interests. The major cases applying the principles of finality of agency action, exhaustion of administrative remedies, and ripeness for judicial review help to explain why courts are reluctant to intervene in the administrative process before the agency decisionmaking process has been concluded and why, despite such reluctance, courts sometimes are willing to intervene in the process when steps remain to be taken by the agency.

§ 5.7.1   Final agency action

Section 704 of the Administrative Procedure Act provides that only "final" agency actions are subject to judicial review.[205] Sometimes a statute authorizing an agency to act specifies the agency actions that are subject to judicial review and the steps that must be taken within the agency as a condition precedent to obtaining review of that action. In the absence of specific statutory authority to the contrary, APA section 704 limits judicial intervention in the administrative process to review of "final agency action." During the course of the judicial proceeding to review that final action, the court can consider alleged errors committed by the agency in earlier stages of the process, assuming that the party has preserved its right to

---

205. The full text of section 704 provides: Actions reviewable. Agency action made reviewable by statute and final agency action for which there is no other adequate remedy in a court are subject to judicial review. A preliminary, procedural, or intermediate agency action or ruling not directly reviewable is subject to review on the review of the final agency action. Except as otherwise expressly required by statute, agency action otherwise final is final for the purposes of this section whether or not there has been presented or determined an application for a declaratory order, for any form of reconsideration, or, unless the agency otherwise requires by rule and provides that the action meanwhile is inoperative, for an appeal to superior agency authority.

judicial review of those alleged errors by raising them at the appropriate stages of the agency decision making process.

Courts are often required to decide whether an agency action is "final" in circumstances in which the appropriate characterization of the action is debatable. A representative sample of the Supreme Court's decisions resolving finality disputes illustrates the factors courts consider in deciding whether an action is final.

In *Dalton v. Specter*,[206] the Court held that a report issued by the Base Closing Commission was not reviewable because it was not final agency action. The report recommended the closure of many military bases. It was final action, in the sense that the Commission planned to take no further action in the case. The Court held that it was not final action in a more important sense, however. The Court concluded that the report "carries no direct consequences" because no base could be closed unless and until the President approved the report.

By contrast, in *Bennett v. Spear*,[207] the Court held that an agency action was final, even though it would have effects only through the subsequent action of another agency. The plaintiffs sought review of a "biological opinion" issued by the Fish & Wildlife Service. The opinion concluded that an irrigation project operated by another agency posed a danger to the habitat of an endangered species. The opinion recommended that the agency reduce the amount of water it made available for irrigation purposes. The Court held that the biological opinion was a final agency action even though it did not directly require a reduction in the amount of water made available to the plaintiffs. The Court noted that agencies and their employees can be punished for acting in a manner inconsistent with a biological opinion. Thus, the issuance of the opinion "altered the legal regime" applicable to the irrigation project in a way that rendered it highly likely that the agency that controls the project would reduce the amount of water it makes available to plaintiffs. The Court announced a two-step test for determining whether an agency action is final:

> First, the action must mark the 'consummation' of the agency's decisionmaking process. Second, the action must be one by which 'rights or obligations have been determined' or from which 'legal consequences will flow'.

Two cases illustrate the difficult characterization problems that can arise when the same agency has two opportunities to address the

206. 511 U.S. 462 (1994). *See also* discussion in § 5.3 *supra.*

207. 520 U.S. 154 (1997).

same issue. In *ICC v. Locomotive Engineers*,[208] the Court held that an ICC order is not final when the agency still has pending before it a timely-filed motion to reconsider the order. However, in *Stone v. INS*,[209] the Court held that an INS deportation order was final and immediately reviewable even though the agency still had before it a timely-filed motion to reconsider the order. The Court distinguished *Locomotive Engineers* based on its conclusion that Congress had expressed its strong desire that courts expedite review of deportation orders, rather than await the outcome of the agency's process of reconsidering a deportation order.

The requirement of final agency action as a prerequisite to judicial review is designed to avoid premature judicial involvement in the agency decision making process. Judicial intervention in the administrative process before that process has concluded often has the effect of taking from the agency much of the initial decision making power the legislature intended to grant the agency. A reviewing court is supposed to give some degree of deference to an agency's decision. It cannot defer to the agency's decision if the agency has not yet made a final decision. In addition, it is difficult as a practical matter for a court to review an agency action before the agency has reached a final decision. The court often does not have before it a complete statement of the reasons for the agency's action or a complete record of pleadings and evidence that can be used as the basis for judicial review. Indeed, a court cannot even discern the precise nature of the dispute between the party seeking judicial review and the agency until after the agency has taken final action in the proceeding before it. In some cases, the final agency action requirement may have a constitutional component, since there is no "case" or "controversy" within the court's decisionmaking power under Article III until the agency has taken actions sufficient to create "concrete adverseness" between it and the party seeking judicial review. For all these reasons, courts rarely review agency actions that are not final. A pair of court of appeals cases involving pesticide registration show, however, that the final order rule is subject to rare exceptions.

A pesticide must be registered under the Federal Insecticide, Fungicide, and Rodenticide Act (FIFRA)[210] in order to be shipped in interstate commerce. If a pesticide is found to be unsafe, the agency[211] must cancel its registration. Cancellation must take place

208. 482 U.S. 270 (1987).

209. 514 U.S. 386 (1995).

210. 7 U.S.C. § 135.

211. During the period in which this dispute was litigated, Congress shifted responsibility in this area from the De-

through a complicated multi-phase process that begins with a notice of cancellation, and proceeds through consideration by an advisory committee and a public hearing before the agency can cancel the registration. During the pendency of the cancellation proceeding, the agency can suspend the registration if it finds suspension "necessary to prevent an imminent hazard to the public."

Environmental Defense Fund, Inc. v. Hardin[212] involved an attempt by EDF to obtain judicial review of the agency's failure to take sufficient action in response to an EDF request that the agency initiate a cancellation proceeding with respect to all uses of DDT and suspend the registration of DDT during the pendency of the cancellation proceeding. The agency issued a notice beginning a cancellation proceeding with respect to four uses of DDT, solicited comments with respect to all other uses, and took no action in response to the suspension request. EDF asked the D.C. Circuit to order the agency to issue a cancellation notice with respect to all uses of DDT and to suspend DDT's registration. The agency argued that the court could not review its action, or more accurately its inaction, because it had issued no final order. The D.C. Circuit recognized that a court rarely intervenes in the administrative process before an agency has taken final action, but it found the agency's action reviewable because "exigent circumstances render it equivalent to a final denial of petitioner's request."

The court recognized that the final agency action rule is based on important policy considerations. It concluded, however, that:

> "No subsequent action can sharpen the controversy arising from the decision by the Secretary that the evidence submitted by petitioner does not compel suspension or cancellation of the registration of DDT. In light of the urgent character of petitioner's claim, and the allegation that delay itself will cause irreparable injury, the controversy is as ripe for judicial consideration as it can ever be.

> . . .

> "[W]hen administrative inaction has precisely the same impact on the rights of the parties as denial of relief, an agency cannot preclude judicial review by casting its decision in the form of inaction rather than an order denying relief."

The court then proceeded to the challenging task of devising an appropriate judicial remedy for agency inaction. It could not reverse

partment of Agriculture to the EPA. We will refer to both as the agency.

212.   428 F.2d 1093 (D.C.Cir.1970).

any agency action because the agency had not acted. Moreover, the court could not identify a basis for reversal, since the agency did not state any factual or legal basis for its failure to act. The court finally ordered the agency: (1) to decide whether or not to suspend DDT's registration and to state reasons for its decision; and, (2) to decide whether or not to begin a proceeding to cancel DDT's registration or to state its reasons for deferring that decision.

On remand, the agency refused to suspend DDT's registration on the basis that the evidence before it at that stage did not warrant summary suspension. It refused to initiate a cancellation proceeding with respect to the other uses of DDT on the basis that the agency was in the process of investigating the safety of DDT in its other uses. EDF again requested the D.C. Circuit to review the agency's failure to act. Again, the agency argued that the court could not review its failure to act because it was not final agency action. The agency was able to support its argument with the Seventh Circuit's decision in *Nor–Am Agricultural Products, Inc. v. Hardin.*[213] There, the Seventh Circuit was asked to review an order of the agency suspending the registration of a pesticide and initiating a cancellation proceeding. The court refused to do so on the bases that: (1) the agency's decision to suspend a registration is not reviewable because it is not final agency action; and, (2) the agency's decision to begin a cancellation proceeding is not reviewable because it is not final agency action. Yet, in *Environmental Defense Fund, Inc. v. Ruckelshaus,*[214] the D.C. Circuit held that both the agency's decision not to suspend and its decision to defer initiation of a cancellation proceeding were reviewable.

The D.C. Circuit reasoned that the decision not to suspend DDT's registration was reviewable because, once that decision was made, the issue of the "imminence" of the threat to public health allegedly posed by DDT had been finally resolved. The balance of the proceeding would continue to focus on the public health threat, but not on its imminence. The D.C. Circuit dealt with the contrary decision of the Seventh Circuit on the nonreviewability of suspension orders in two ways. First, it expressed its disagreement with that decision, principally because it felt that the imminence of a public health threat is an issue separate and distinct from the existence and magnitude of the threat itself. Second, it distinguished the Seventh

213. 435 F.2d 1151 (7th Cir.1970) (en banc), *cert. dismissed* 402 U.S. 935 (1971). *Accord* Dow Chemical Co. v. Ruckelshaus, 477 F.2d 1317 (8th Cir. 1973); Pax Co. v. United States, 454 F.2d 93 (10th Cir.1972).

214. 439 F.2d 584 (D.C.Cir.1971).

Circuit's decision as dealing only with the reviewability of a decision to suspend, rather than a decision *not* to suspend. The Seventh Circuit had concluded that the harm to the registrant resulting from an arguably unjustified order to suspend was tolerable; by contrast, the D.C. Circuit held that the harm to the public resulting from an arguably unjustified decision *not* to suspend was intolerable.

The D.C. Circuit concluded that the agency's decision to defer initiation of a cancellation proceeding until after it had concluded its preliminary investigation also was reviewable. It found in the legislative history of FIFRA an intent that the agency begin a cancellation proceeding whenever it concludes "that there is a substantial question about the safety of a registered item. . . . " The court interpreted the agency's findings to include such a conclusion. The D.C. Circuit distinguished the Seventh Circuit's contrary holding on the unreviewability of the agency's decision to initiate a cancellation proceeding. It agreed with the Seventh Circuit that a decision to initiate cancellation proceedings is not reviewable, but found that holding entirely consistent with its holding that a decision *not* to initiate a cancellation proceeding is reviewable.

In *EDF v. Ruckelshaus,* as in *EDF v. Hardin,* the court was presented with a serious problem of devising appropriate relief for an agency failure to act. It ordered the agency to begin the cancellation proceeding, rather than remanding that issue to the agency for further action. A court order directing an agency to take an action of this type is unusual and arguably inappropriate, since Congress gave the agency the exclusive authority to begin a cancellation proceeding. The court was not willing to dispose of the suspension issue through such an extraordinary remedy. It concluded that the suspension decision was a mixed question of law and fact that the agency should have approached through a two-step process: (1) determine the legal standard for suspension; and, (2) apply that standard to the evidence. The court ordered the agency on remand to make an immediate decision on the suspension issue through that process.

The D.C. Circuit opinions in the pesticide cases represent sharp departures from the typical judicial approach to the final agency action requirement. The cases have not been consistently followed, and they may have been overruled by the Supreme Court.[215] Two

215. In FPC v. Transcontinental Gas Pipe Line Corp., 423 U.S. 326, 333 (1976), and again in Vermont Yankee Nuclear Power Corp. v. NRDC, 435 U.S. 519, 544–545 (1978), the Court admonished the D.C. Circuit to cease its prior practice of dictating to agencies the procedures to use in addressing issues and the "time dimension of the needed inquiry . . . . " In Heckler v. Chaney, 470 U.S.

inferences can be drawn from the DDT cases. First, no matter how important a legal rule may be, courts at least try to find ways of circumventing a rule when presented with a factual situation that is uncommonly compelling. The D.C. Circuit opinions read as if they were written by a judge who was outraged by what he thought the agency was doing. He characterized the health hazards posed by DDT as so large that "even a temporary refusal to suspend results in irreparable injury on a massive scale". The judge also may have believed that the agency was dragging its feet solely because of pressure from constituents in the agricultural community and among pesticide manufacturers.

The second lasting importance of the DDT cases may lie in their underlining of the importance of final agency action as a prerequisite for judicial review. The D.C. Circuit experienced great difficulty in its attempts to review the agency's failure to take final action. It had no order before it to review. It had no agency interpretations of law, statements of reasons, or findings of fact to consider on review. It was unable to devise any form of relief consistent with the traditional limited role of courts in reviewing agency actions. Once the court decided to intervene before the agency had acted, it had little choice but to exercise some of the initial decisionmaking power that the legislature had granted the agency. Thus, the major lesson of the EDF cases may be that courts rarely, if ever, should interject themselves in the administrative process before it has been concluded. Of course, any court will be tempted to intervene in a case involving a public health hazard that the court is willing to characterize as "massive".

§ 5.7.2 Exhaustion of administrative remedies

Generally, a court requires a party to exhaust all remedies available to it within the administrative process before it will take jurisdiction to review the agency's action. The exhaustion doctrine is related to, but distinct from, the final agency action requirement.[216] While the final agency action requirement is based on statutes—APA section 704 and comparable provisions of agency organic acts—the exhaustion doctrine is a prudential rule created by the courts to enable them to allocate responsibilities efficiently between agencies and courts.[217]

821 (1985), the Court held agency inaction presumptively unreviewable. *See supra* § 5.3.

216. Association of National Advertisers, Inc. v. FTC, 627 F.2d 1151

(D.C.Cir.1979), *cert. denied* 447 U.S. 921 (1980) (Leventhal, J., concurring).

217. *Id.* Statutes sometimes require exhaustion of specified agency remedies, however. *See, e.g.,* 15 U.S.C. § 717r ("No

The Supreme Court's opinion in *Myers v. Bethlehem Shipbuilding Corp.*[218] illustrates the operation of the exhaustion doctrine. The National Labor Relations Board (NLRB) is empowered to prohibit unfair labor practices engaged in by employers to the extent that those employers are engaged in interstate and foreign commerce. The NLRB initiated a hearing to determine whether Bethlehem's labor practices at one of its plants were unfair. Bethlehem sought and obtained a federal court injunction against NLRB, prohibiting it from holding the hearings on the basis that Bethlehem's practices were not within NLRB's jurisdiction. Bethlehem contended, and the district court found, that Bethlehem's plant did not operate in interstate or foreign commerce. The Supreme Court reversed, holding that the district court had no power to enjoin the NLRB hearings because Bethlehem had not exhausted its remedies before NLRB. The Court concluded that Congress intended NLRB to have the exclusive power to determine whether an unfair labor practice had been committed in interstate or foreign commerce, including the power to determine initially whether the employment situation was in interstate or foreign commerce. Thus, Bethlehem was required to argue to NLRB, rather than to a court, its contention that its plant did not operate in interstate commerce. If it was dissatisfied with the NLRB's resolution of that jurisdictional issue, it could obtain judicial review of the issue after it had exhausted all its remedies before NLRB.

Bethlehem argued that the NLRB decision to subject its labor practices to a hearing caused it unjustified irreparable harm. The irreparable harm consisted of the expense of having to participate in the hearing and potential labor unrest resulting from the conduct of the hearing. According to Bethlehem, these injuries were totally unjustified because any future finding by NLRB that Bethlehem's plant was in interstate commerce would be groundless. The Court responded that the expense and inconvenience of litigation did not constitute irreparable harm sufficient to justify circumvention of the exhaustion rule. The Court added: "Lawsuits also often turn out to have been groundless; but no way has been discovered of relieving a defendant from the necessity of a trial to establish that fact.... "

While the Court's analogy to lawsuits is apt, its flat statement that groundless lawsuits cannot be halted before their conclusion is an oversimplification of the complicated rules governing appeals from

proceeding to review any order of the [Federal Energy Regulatory] Commission shall be brought by any person unless such person shall have made application to the Commission for a rehearing thereon.")

218.   303 U.S. 41 (1938).

interlocutory rulings by trial judges.[219] The exhaustion doctrine of administrative law is subject to pragmatically based exceptions similar to the exceptions to the prohibition against appeals of interlocutory orders of trial judges. Indeed, other cases interpreting the exhaustion doctrine suggest that the result in *Myers* would have been different with only subtle changes in the context in which the exhaustion issue was presented in that case.

In *AMP, Inc. v. Gardner,*[220] for instance, the Second Circuit agreed to review a determination of the Food and Drug Administration (FDA) that a surgical instrument was a "drug" at the beginning of FDA's proceeding to determine whether AMP should be allowed to market the instrument. If FDA's determination was correct, AMP would be required to conduct years of expensive tests before it could market the instrument. The holdings in *Myers* and *AMP* appear superficially inconsistent, but Professor Mashaw and Dean Merrill suggest that *Myers* and *AMP* can be distinguished based on three factors:[221] (1) the burden the party would have to bear if it were required to participate in the administrative proceedings—FDA proceedings to determine whether a new drug can be marketed are notoriously long and expensive, while NLRB unfair labor practice hearings are similar to a routine civil trial; (2) the need for further agency proceedings to resolve the issue raised—FDA had already classified the instrument as a drug and stated its reasons for doing so, while NLRB had not yet made a definitive finding on whether Bethlehem operated in interstate commerce; and, (3) the importance of the legal issue raised on appeal independent of the factual record the agency was developing—FDA's determination was based on only a few facts it had already assessed, while NLRB's determination necessarily would be based on evaluation of numerous facts that would be presented to the agency in the hearings Bethlehem had attempted to enjoin.

Sometimes even the identical issue is subject to different treatment under the exhaustion doctrine. Two D.C. Circuit decisions involving the issue of whether an agency decisionmaker should be disqualified from participation in a proceeding on the basis of the decisionmaker's alleged bias illustrate this point. In *SEC v. R.A. Holman & Co.,*[222] the D.C. Circuit held that a court did not have the power to decide the disqualification issue until after the agency had

---

219. *See* C. Wright, Law of Federal Courts § 102 (1983).

220. 389 F.2d 825 (2d Cir.1968), *cert. denied,* 393 U.S. 825 (1968).

221. J. Mashaw, R. Merrill, and P. Shane, The American Public Law System 980 (5th ed. 2003).

222. 323 F.2d 284 (D.C.Cir.1963).

completed its actions in the proceeding. In *Association of National Advertisers, Inc. v. FTC,*[223] the same court held that it could resolve the disqualification issue before the agency had completed its actions in the case. The court distinguished its seemingly inconsistent holding in *Holman* on the basis of the relative importance of evidence of bias in the two cases and the status of the issue before the agency at the time review was sought. In *Holman,* the agency had not yet addressed the disqualification issue, and the court concluded that extensive evidentiary hearings would be necessary to permit the agency and a reviewing court to resolve that issue. In *Association of National Advertisers,* by contrast, the agency already had before it the single item of evidence relevant to the disqualification decision, and the agency had already rejected the disqualification claim on the basis of that evidence. Thus, *Holman* and *Association of National Advertisers* also can be explained through application of the three factors suggested by Professor Mashaw and Dean Merrill.

The Supreme Court's opinion in *McKart v. United States*[224] contains the Court's most comprehensive discussion of the exhaustion doctrine. McKart claimed to be exempt from the draft as a sole surviving son. McKart's local Selective Service Board rejected his claim and classified him as I—A (eligible for the draft). Selective Service System regulations provided McKart a right to appeal his classification to an appeals board. He declined to exercise this right within the time provided. McKart was ordered to report for a pre-induction physical and failed to report. In his subsequent criminal prosecution for failure to report, McKart attempted to raise the defense that the local Selective Service Board had classified him erroneously as eligible for the draft when he was ineligible as a sole surviving son. The United States argued that McKart was precluded from raising this defense because he had failed to exhaust the previously available administrative remedy of an appeal of his classification to an appeals board.

In assessing the government's argument, the Court compiled an impressive list of important functions served by the exhaustion doctrine. First, and most important, the legislature creates an agency for the purpose of applying a statutory scheme to particular factual situations. The exhaustion doctrine permits the agency to perform this function, including in particular the opportunity for the agency to apply its expertise and to exercise the discretion granted it by the legislature. Second, it is more efficient to permit the administrative

223.   627 F.2d 1151 (D.C.Cir.1979).   224.   395 U.S. 185 (1969).

process to proceed uninterrupted and to subject the results of the process to judicial review only at the conclusion of the process than to permit judicial intervention at each phase of the process. Three, agencies are not part of the judicial branch; they are autonomous entities created by the legislature to perform a particular function. The exhaustion doctrine protects that agency autonomy. Fourth, judicial review of agency action can be hindered by failure to exhaust administrative remedies because the agency may not have an adequate opportunity to assemble and to analyze relevant facts and to explain the basis for its action. Fifth, the exhaustion requirement reduces court appeals by providing the agency additional opportunities to correct its prior errors. Sixth, allowing some parties to obtain court review without first exhausting administrative remedies may reduce the agency's effectiveness by encouraging others to circumvent its procedures and by rendering the agency's enforcement efforts more complicated and more expensive.

Notwithstanding this recitation of convincing reasons for requiring exhaustion of administrative remedies, the Court excused McKart from the exhaustion requirement and held that he was improperly classified. As a result, he was acquitted of the criminal charges. The Court based its holding on several factors. First, application of the exhaustion doctrine in a criminal prosecution "can be exceedingly harsh". Second, some of the reasons for the exhaustion doctrine do not apply when the administrative remedy that was not exhausted is no longer available and the administrative process is at an end. Third, some of the purposes served by the exhaustion requirement are not implicated when the question requires only statutory interpretation, as opposed to expert evaluation of facts or exercise of discretion. Fourth, excusing McKart from the requirement of exhaustion is not likely to encourage others to circumvent the remedies available in the Selective Service System because, "we doubt whether many registrants will be foolhardy enough to deny the Selective Service System the opportunity to correct its own errors by taking their chances with a criminal prosecution and a possibility of five years in jail."

It also would be "foolhardy" to rely on the Court's holding in *McKart* as a basis for predicting successful avoidance of the exhaustion requirement in a case that was missing any of the four factors the Court relied upon. In particular, the fact that the issue in *McKart* did not require any application of the agency's expertise or discretion and did not require any evaluation of evidence by the agency may have been critical to the Court's holding. In footnotes, the Court carefully distinguished any alleged misclassification based on facts not properly presented to the agency or based on arguable errors in the agency's exercise of its expertise or discretion. Moreover, the Court has applied the exhaustion doctrine in other cases where the "exceedingly harsh" result was conviction for a crime.[225]

One of the standard corollaries to the exhaustion doctrine is the rule that a party can only raise on judicial review issues that were properly preserved in the proceedings before the agency by continuing to raise them at each point in the process where the agency had an opportunity to consider or to reconsider those issues. Despite occasional appellate court decisions to the contrary, courts generally apply this corollary unless they conclude that the party should be excused entirely from the exhaustion requirement. However, in *Sims v. Apfel,*[226] the Court held this rule inapplicable to Social Security Administration disability proceedings because those proceedings are not adversarial in nature.

Most of the law of exhaustion is judge-made. Congress has the power to specify the requirements of exhaustion by statute, however, and it sometimes does so. Two cases illustrate the potential effects of statutory exhaustion rules. In *Heckler v. Ringer,*[227] beneficiaries of the Medicare program sought review of an agency ruling that had the effect of disallowing reimbursement for a particular surgical procedure. The Court held that none of the beneficiaries could obtain judicial review of the ruling because none had yet complied with the detailed exhaustion requirements that the Medicare statute made prerequisites to the exercise of court jurisdiction over any agency decision involving eligibility for Medicare reimbursement. The statutory exhaustion requirements the Court applied in *Ringer* had the effect of rendering the duty to exhaust more demanding and less flexible than the judge-made duty to exhaust. When Congress specifies the remedies a party must exhaust as a jurisdictional prerequisite to judicial review of a class of agency actions, courts do not have discretion to excuse a party's failure to exhaust one of those statutorily-prescribed administrative remedies.

In *Darby v. Cisneros,*[228] the Court relied on section 704 of the APA as the basis for a holding that a party was not required to

---

225. *See, e.g.,* McGee v. United States, 402 U.S. 479 (1971); Yakus v. United States, 321 U.S. 414 (1944).

226. 530 U.S. 103 (2000).

227. 466 U.S. 602 (1984).

228. 509 U.S. 137 (1993); *see* Duffy, *Administrative Common Law in Judicial Review,* 77 Tex. L. Rev. 121, 152–62 (1998) (viewing *Darby* as a triumph of statutory judicial review (§ 704) over common law judicial review).

exhaust an available administrative remedy. The petitioner was the subject of an adverse decision by an Administrative Law Judge (ALJ). The agency's rules provided that an ALJ's decision becomes final in thirty days unless the agency decides to review the decision. The rules went on to permit a party to seek review of an ALJ decision by a higher authority within the agency. The petitioner sought judicial review of the ALJ decision without first seeking review from the higher agency authority. The Court rejected the agency's argument that the petitioner was required to exhaust the available intra-agency review procedure as a prerequisite for judicial review of the ALJ decision. The Court relied on the following language in APA section 704. "Agency action otherwise final is final for the purposes of this section ... whether or not there has been ... an appeal to superior agency authority" "unless the agency otherwise requires by rule and provides that the action meanwhile is inoperative.... " Since the agency did not make its intra-agency review process mandatory by rule, the Court held that the petitioner was not required to exhaust that remedy. Thus, APA section 704 allows an agency to decide by rule whether to make an intra-agency review process mandatory or permissive. If it makes the review process mandatory, a petitioner must exhaust it as a prerequisite for judicial review. If it is permissive, however, a petitioner can choose not to pursue the intra-agency appeal and can instead go directly to court.

§ 5.7.3   Ripeness of administrative action for judicial review

The modern law governing the "ripeness" of an agency action for judicial review is based on the Supreme Court's 1967 decision in *Abbott Laboratories v. Gardner.*[229] In that opinion, the Court explained the basis for the judicially created ripeness limitation on judicial review. "[I]ts basic rationale is to prevent the courts, through avoidance of premature adjudication, from entangling themselves in abstract disagreements over administrative policies, and also to protect the agencies from judicial interference until an administrative decision has been formalized and its effects felt in a concrete way by the challenging parties." In *Abbott Laboratories,* the Court established a two part pragmatic test for resolving the ripeness issue. Prior to that decision, the Court vacillated between a pragmatic and a formalistic approach to ripeness.

---

229. 387 U.S. 136 (1967); *see, e.g.* American Trucking Ass'ns v. ICC, 747 F.2d 787, 789 (D.C.Cir.1984); Air New Zealand Limited v. CAB, 726 F.2d 832, 835 (D.C.Cir.1984).

The majority and dissenting opinions in *Columbia Broadcasting System, Inc. v. United States*[230] illustrate the competing approaches to ripeness that antedated *Abbott Laboratories*. CBS sought judicial review of an FCC regulation that purported to authorize cancellation or non renewal of the license of any radio station that was a party to a contract that attached any of several conditions to the station's ability to broadcast programming made available by a network. Many of the provisions of the contracts between CBS and its radio station affiliates violated the FCC regulation. The radio station affiliates of CBS refused to enter into new contracts with CBS and threatened to cancel or repudiate their existing contracts because of fear that FCC would revoke their licenses pursuant to the challenged regulation. FCC argued that its regulation was not ripe for review because it was not self-executing, that is, it did not actually cancel any license or impose any other sanction.

A majority of the Justices held the FCC regulation ripe for judicial review because failure to comply would penalize FCC licensees and, indirectly, CBS. Since the regulation was binding on all licensees, they could be expected to conform their conduct to the regulation, with inevitable adverse consequences to CBS. The three dissenting Justices took an entirely different view of the ripeness issue. Since the FCC regulation did not formally determine the rights either of CBS or of its station affiliates and did not require either CBS or any station to take any action, the dissenting Justices thought that judicial intervention was inappropriate. Presumably, they would have been willing to review only an order implementing the regulation by cancelling or declining to renew a license.

Columbia Broadcasting System could have been a landmark case if the Court had applied the reasoning of the majority in subsequent cases. Instead, however, the majority opinions of the Court reflected the formalistic approach of the Justices who dissented in *Columbia Broadcasting System* intermittently until the Court's 1967 landmark decision in *Abbott Laboratories*. No decision of the Court since that time has adopted the formalistic approach—for good reason. If the view of the dissenting Justices in *Columbia Broadcasting System* were adopted, many important agency rules—almost certainly including the rule challenged in that case—would never be subject to judicial review. It is totally unrealistic to assume that a radio station would risk the loss of its most valuable asset—its license to operate— by refusing to comply with the FCC regulation. In the absence of noncompliance by any station, the courts would never be presented

230. 316 U.S. 407 (1942).

with an appeal of an FCC action that met the dissenting Justices' standard of ripeness.

Abbott Laboratories involved an attempt to obtain judicial review of an FDA regulation before FDA applied that regulation to any party. The regulation required manufacturers of prescription drugs to include on all labels and in all advertisements the generic name of a drug every time the proprietary name of the drug was mentioned. Abbott claimed that FDA did not have the statutory authority to impose this requirement. FDA countered with the argument that its regulation was not appropriate for judicial review because FDA had not yet applied the regulation in an enforcement proceeding.

The Court began by analyzing the statutes applicable to the FDA to determine whether Congress intended to preclude preenforcement review of FDA regulations. Finding no "clear and convincing evidence" of such a congressional intent,[231] the Court concluded that it was free to review the challenged regulation. This did not end the Court's inquiry into the appropriateness of preenforcement judicial review of the regulation, since:

> "A further inquiry must, however, be made. The injunctive and declaratory judgment remedies are discretionary, and courts traditionally have been reluctant to apply them to administrative determinations unless these arise in the context of a controversy 'ripe' for judicial resolution.... The problem is best seen in a twofold aspect, requiring us to evaluate both the fitness of the issues for judicial decision and the hardship to the parties of withholding court consideration."

Applying the first part of the test, the Court held the issues appropriate for preenforcement review. Abbott and FDA agreed that the sole issue was whether Congress intended to authorize FDA to require the generic name to appear *every time* the proprietary name appeared. FDA planned no further proceedings with respect to this legal issue, and no evidence was necessary to resolve the issue.

The Court also found that Abbott would suffer significant hardship if the Court refused to review the regulation in advance of its enforcement. Abbott would be forced to choose between compliance at considerable cost and noncompliance at the risk of criminal and civil penalties. The Court summarized its reasoning succinctly:

> "Where the legal issue presented is fit for judicial resolution, and where a regulation requires an immediate and significant

231. *See supra* § 5.3.

change in the plaintiffs' conduct of their affairs with serious penalties attached to noncompliance, access to the courts under the Administrative Procedure Act and the Declaratory Judgment Act must be permitted, absent a statutory bar or some other unusual circumstances, neither of which appears here."

Three Justices dissented in *Abbott Laboratories*, primarily on the basis that permitting preenforcement review of regulations would impair the ability of agencies to protect the public. As the dissenters saw it, preenforcement review would allow any of hundreds of district judges to enjoin important agency actions for long periods of time pending judicial determination of their validity. The majority countered this objection in two ways. First, it emphasized that the standards for obtaining a judicial stay of an agency action are so high that agencies would be able to continue to enforce most challenged regulations during the pendency of judicial review proceedings. Second, the majority believed that allowing preenforcement review in appropriate cases would enhance the efficacy of agency efforts to protect the public: "If the Government prevails, . . . the industry is bound by the decree; if the government loses, it can more quickly revise its regulation."

Many years of experience with *Abbott Laboratories'* relatively permissive approach to preenforcement review of agency regulations has demonstrated that the Justices in the majority were better predictors of the impact of preenforcement review than the dissenting Justices. Indeed, Congress now frequently limits judicial review of the validity of regulations to the preenforcement context in order to enhance an agency's effectiveness.[232] Yet, there is some support for the dissenting Justices' prediction as well. Routine preenforcement review of agency rules has greatly increased the cost of the rulemaking process and is deterring agencies from acting by rule.[233] At least one prominent commentator has called for the abolition of preenforcement review, arguing that it is substantially to blame for the ossification of the rulemaking process.[234]

The dissenting Justices in *Abbott Laboratories* also identified a broader problem potentially created by judicial review of agency actions that have significant impacts on the nation. If judicial review of such actions is authorized in district courts, a party that objects to a particular agency action often can select from among the hundreds of district judges the one judge who is likely to be least sympathetic

---

232. *See supra* § 5.2.1.

233. *See infra* § 6.4.6b.

234. J. Mashaw, *Greed, Chaos, & Governance: Using Public Choice to Improve Public Law* 181 (1997).

to the agency's action. If, for instance, the agency's action adversely affects the tobacco industry, the industry might choose to challenge the action in a district court located in the heart of the tobacco growing region. This flexibility in choice of review forum can have undesirable effects. A single district judge, perhaps with aberrational views on the issue, can delay significantly the government's pursuit of a major national goal by holding an agency action invalid.

To reduce the potential adverse effects of this power of a party to select the most favorable of several hundred forums for judicial review, Congress should, and usually does, provide that the actions of agencies that frequently establish significant national policies are subject to judicial review exclusively in federal circuit courts of appeal. In order to avoid the difficulties posed by *Abbott Laboratories* that result from judicial review by hundreds of district court judges, federal judges have increasingly held that the circuit court judicial review provisions are exclusive. At the same time, these judges permit early review at the circuit court level through generous interpretations of the ripeness doctrine.

Congress typically limits the scope of potential forum shopping still further by specifying that judicial review is available only in courts that have some connection with the agency action or with the parties affected by that action. As we discussed in an earlier section, these legislative directives do not eliminate completely the problems caused by forum shopping.[235] Private parties usually retain some flexibility to choose from among several potential reviewing courts, and even circuit courts sometimes take very different approaches in reviewing some types of agency actions. Still, limiting review of agency actions with national impact to circuit courts reduces considerably the potential problems created by permitting review in any of hundreds of district courts. The limited number of circuit courts and the use of three judge panels to decide cases decreases substantially the degree of variation in the views expressed by circuit courts in comparison with the extreme variability that often exists in the views of district judges.

The Court's opinion in *Abbott Laboratories* also had a significant collateral effect on judicial review of rules that was not discussed by any of the Justices. Before *Abbott Laboratories,* an agency rule almost invariably was subject to judicial review only in the context of an attempt by the agency to apply its rule to a particular factual situation. As a result, a reviewing court had no reason to require that

---

235.   *See supra* § 5.6.

an agency actually develop an evidentiary record in a rulemaking proceeding in order to permit the court to determine whether a rule was appropriate for the factual contexts in which it was likely to be applied. The reviewing court could use the facts surrounding the circumstance in which the agency was attempting to apply the rule as the basis for this aspect of judicial review. After *Abbott Laboratories,* however, a high proportion of agency rules were subjected to judicial review in the abstract preenforcement context. As a result, courts found it necessary to impose new procedural requirements in rule-makings so that they could review the factual underpinnings of a rule on the basis of an evidentiary record of some type. Thus, *Abbott Laboratories* indirectly required substantial changes in the procedures used in rulemaking and in the method of conducting judicial review of the substance of rules. We will discuss these changes in some detail in subsequent parts of the book.[236]

The *Abbott Laboratories* test for ripeness is much more permissive than the formalistic approach often used by the Court before *Abbott Laboratories.* It does not permit preenforcement review of all agency regulations, however, as the Court's opinion in the companion case of *Toilet Goods Ass'n v. Gardner*[237] demonstrates. Toilet Goods Association challenged an FDA regulation that authorized the Commissioner to suspend the certification of any color additive based on a finding that the manufacturer had refused to permit FDA employees "free access to all manufacturing facilities, processes, and formulae involved in the manufacture of color additives. . . . " The Court applied the two part *Abbott Laboratories* test and held this FDA regulation was not ripe for review.

The Court found that the issue presented was not appropriate for immediate review even though it could be framed as a purely legal issue—whether FDA has the statutory power to condition certification of color additives on a manufacturer's denial of free access to FDA inspectors. The Court pointed out that the regulation was permissive rather than mandatory. It did not compel the Commissioner to suspend certification; it only purported to authorize him to exercise a discretionary power to do so. Thus, the legal issue conceivably could arise in a wide variety of contexts, depending upon the Commissioner's subsequent determination of what constitutes free access and his determination of the circumstances that justify use of the sanction of suspension. The right of "free access" asserted by FDA was not self-defining. The Court could only speculate about the

236. *See infra* §§ 6.4.6, 7.3.   **237.** 387 U.S. 158 (1967).

manner in which FDA would define and apply this vague standard. The Court felt that its ability to address this legal issue adequately would be enhanced greatly in the context of a specific attempt to enforce the regulation. It could then consider such contextual facts as the reason for the inspection and the manufacturer's justification for limiting the inspector's access to facilities, processes, or formulae.

Turning to the second part of the test, the Court found the hardship imposed on additive manufacturers as a result of a decision to decline preenforcement review less severe than the hardship to drug manufacturers in *Abbott Laboratories*. If a manufacturer refuses access to an FDA inspector, and if the Commissioner chooses to exercise the discretionary authority granted in the regulation, the sanction would consist "only" of suspension of certification, and the Commissioner's decision to impose that sanction would then be subject to judicial review.

The Court's analysis of the "appropriateness" issue in *Toilet Goods* seems sound; it might have been better advised to rest its holding entirely on this part of the test in the circumstances. Its treatment of the "hardship" issue seems disingenuous. As the three concurring Justices pointed out, suspension of certification of a color additive is a severe sanction, since it forces a manufacturer to cease production of the additive until the conclusion of a lengthy court proceeding reviewing the Commissioner's action. We interpret *Abbott Laboratories* and *Toilet Goods* as standing for the proposition that, once a party is able to demonstrate some substantial hardship as a result of a judicial decision declining to engage in preenforcement review of a regulation, the court will focus on the appropriateness of the issues for immediate review. If the court concludes that the agency action raises issues that can be addressed intelligently in the abstract, it will do so. If the court concludes that the resolution of the issues raised depends on facts not properly before the court, it will defer judicial treatment of the issues until the agency attempts to apply the regulation in a specific case.

The D.C. Circuit's decision in *National Automatic Laundry and Cleaning Council v. Shultz*[238] illustrates how far the ripeness analysis has shifted since the Court abandoned the formalistic approach. The Council attempted to obtain judicial review not of a regulation, but of a letter from the Administrator of the Federal Wage and Hour Administration. In his letter, the Administrator interpreted the Fair Labor Standards Act to apply to employees of coin operated laun-

238.   443 F.2d 689 (D.C.Cir.1971).

dries. Based on this interpretation of the Act, operators of coin laundries would be bound by the minimum wage law and related provisions concerning payment of overtime. In a thoughtful opinion, Judge Leventhal held that the letter met both parts of the *Abbott Laboratories* test. Refusal to review the letter would impose hardship on the employers, since they would be forced to choose between paying the minimum wage and risking civil and criminal penalties. The issue of scope of coverage of the Act was appropriate for immediate review notwithstanding the relatively informal nature of the agency action, because: (1) the letter was signed by the agency head and its context indicated that it represented a final and authoritative resolution of a legal issue; and, (2) a court can restrict its ruling to a legal issue that is susceptible to resolution in the abstract without addressing other issues that may arise in the context of subsequent attempts to apply a rule or statutory interpretation to a particular set of facts.

The 1990 opinion for a five-Justice majority in *Lujan v. National Wildlife Federation*[239] suggests that some Justices may be inclined to make significant changes in ripeness doctrine to reduce what they perceive to be the tendency of some judges to assume an unduly broad role in government policymaking. The Federation attempted to challenge the legality of the Department of Interior's "land withdrawal review program." That "program" consisted of hundreds of adjudicatory decisions in which DOI reclassified many tracts of public land in ways that made them potentially available for mining operations.

The majority concluded that the "program" was not reviewable because there was no legally cognizable "program." The only potentially reviewable agency actions were each of the discrete reclassification decisions. The majority then suggested that even those individual decisions were not ripe for review because reclassification does not inevitably lead to mining; rather, DOI must grant a permit to authorize mining even if land is classified in a manner consistent with mining.

A five-Justice majority narrowed the scope of the permissive *Abbott Laboratories* test for ripeness in *Reno v. Catholic Social Services*.[240] Petitioners sought judicial review of two rules in which the INS limited the classes of individuals who were eligible for a statutorily-authorized amnesty program applicable to certain illegal immigrants who had lived in the U.S. for a long time. The Court held

239. 497 U.S. 871 (1990).   **240.** 509 U.S. 43 (1993).

that preenforcement review was not available for rules that prescribe eligibility requirements for government benefits. The majority distinguished between regulatory rules and benefit eligibility rules on the basis of its application of the second part of the *Abbott Laboratories* test. In the view of the majority, many regulatory rules satisfy the second part of the test because deferral of their review will require a regulatee to suffer the hardship of having to choose between changing its behavior to comply with an arguably invalid rule or violating the rule at the risk of incurring severe penalties. By contrast, the majority saw no analogous hardship attributable to deferring review of a benefit eligibility rule until an individual has been the subject of a decision denying his application for the benefit through application of the eligibility rule.

In *Thunder Basin Coal Co. v. Reich*,[241] the Court reduced the strength of the *Abbott Laboratories* test even in the context of attempts to obtain preenforcement review of regulatory rules. The Court held that a mine owner could not obtain preenforcement review of an agency rule that authorized employees to designate a union representative to accompany a government inspector when he inspects a mine. The Court reasoned that, since Congress had provided an alternative means through which a mine owner could obtain review of the rule in an enforcement proceeding, Congress had implicitly precluded preenforcement review of the agency's rule. If the Court had applied that reasoning in *Abbott Laboratories*, it would have held that the petitioner in that case also could not obtain preenforcement review of the rule at issue in that case, since the petitioner in *Abbott Laboratories* also had access to a statutorily-authorized alternative means of obtaining review of the rule in an enforcement proceeding.

The decisions in *Catholic Social Services* and *Thunder Basin* seem to be part of a broader movement by the Court to apply the ripeness requirement in a more demanding manner that reduces the opportunities to obtain preenforcement judicial review of agency rules. The Court is continuing to move in that general direction by reducing the scope and effect of the *Abbott Laboratories* case. In *Shalala v. Illinois Council on Long Term Care*,[242] a five-Justice majority held that rules issued to implement the Medicare Act are not subject to preenforcement review. More broadly, all of the Justices suggested that the presumption of preenforcement review of

241. 510 U.S. 200 (1994).   **242.** 529 U.S. 1 (2000).

rules that was one of the bases for the Court's decision in *Abbott Laboratories* is either non-existent or weak.

In *National Park Hospitality Association v. Department of Interior*,[243] a six-Justice majority held that a rule issued by the National Park Service (NPS) that purported to exempt NPS concession contracts from the scope of the Contracts Dispute Act (CDA) was not ripe for preapplication review. The majority stated persuasive reasons that were specific to the case: The rule was a non-binding statement of policy rather than a legally-binding legislative rule, and NPS does not even have responsibility to implement the CDA. However, the majority also included in its opinion broad reasoning that could foreshadow further narrowing of the scope of the *Abbott Laboratories* test:

> Absent [a statutory provision providing for immediate judicial review], a regulation is not ordinarily considered the type of action 'ripe' for judicial review ... until the scope of the controversy has been reduced to more manageable proportions and its factual components fleshed out, by some concrete action applying the regulation to the claimant's situation in a fashion that harms or threatens to harm him. (The major exception, of course, is a substantive rule which as a practical matter requires the plaintiff to adjust his conduct immediately....)

> [The rule] does not create "adverse effects of a strictly legal kind," which we have previously required for a showing of hardship.... [It] does not command anyone to do anything or to refrain from doing anything; it does not grant, withhold, or modify any formal legal license, power, or authority; it does not subject anyone to any civil or criminal liability; and it creates no legal rights or obligations....

> Moreover, [it] does not not affect [petitioner's] primary conduct....

§ 5.7.4   A postscript on the tactical implications of the ripeness doctrine

Preenforcement review of regulations is often available at present unless a court concludes that there is no issue that is appropriate for consideration in the abstract. Failure to obtain judicial reversal of a regulation in a preenforcement review proceeding does not necessarily foreclose subsequent opportunities to obtain judicial review of the same regulation as it is applied in a particular case, since the

---

243. 538 U.S. 803 (2003).

factual context in which the regulation is applied may raise issues distinct from those resolved in the prior preenforcement review proceeding.[244] In many circumstances, however, a party displeased with a regulation would prefer to wait and to challenge all aspects of that regulation in a proceeding in which that regulation is applied. It is often more difficult to convince a court to find a flaw in a regulation in the abstract than to convince a court to reverse the regulation when it is applied to a specific situation. In addition, while "as applied" challenges to regulations often are theoretically available even after a court has affirmed a regulation on preenforcement review, many parties believe that initial judicial affirmance of a regulation in the abstract gives the regulation an intangible momentum that helps the agency defend it against subsequent challenges on separate grounds.

There are two important limits to a party's discretion to defer a judicial challenge to a regulation until that regulation is applied—one legal and one a countervailing tactical consideration. The legal constraint lies in the statutory time limits on judicial review of regulations contained in many statutes. As discussed in section 5.2.1, Congress increasingly imposes strict time limits on the availability of judicial review of regulations, and the Court has upheld such limitations. Where they exist, time limits on judicial review of regulations force parties to seek preenforcement judicial review or to forego all opportunity for judicial review, except to the extent that the party challenges the regulation on a basis that was not appropriate for review in the preenforcement context.

The countervailing tactical consideration that sometimes makes preenforcement review desirable to a challenging party lies in the possibility that preenforcement review will yield an interpretation of an ambiguous agency action that is beneficial to parties displeased with that agency action. In short, sometimes parties challenging an agency action are delighted when a court refuses to review that action on ripeness grounds. The D.C. Circuit's opinion in *Pacific Gas & Electric Co. v. FPC*[245] illustrates this point.

The Federal Power Commission issued an order designated as a "general statement of policy". The order contained a set of priorities for provision of natural gas service during periods of shortage. Pacific Gas & Electric, as an electric utility, was placed in a low priority. It sought court review of the order on a variety of procedural and substantive grounds. FPC argued that the order was not ripe for

---

244. *See, e.g.,* Pennell v. City of San Jose, 485 U.S. 1 (1988).

245. 506 F.2d 33 (D.C.Cir.1974).

review. The order was ambiguous in several important respects—perhaps intentionally. One part of the order, for instance, stated that it shifted the burden of proof, while another part of the order suggested that it had no such effect. By challenging the order prior to its application, Pacific Gas & Electric placed FPC in a tactical dilemma. It could avoid preapplication review only by arguing that the ambiguous order had no effect on any party. The court resolved the ambiguities in favor of FPC and held that the order was not ripe for review. This result, however, served Pacific Gas & Electric's needs well. Once the court held that FPC intended that the order have no binding effect in any subsequent proceedings, Pacific Gas & Electric and the other parties displeased with the order were free to ignore it, and the agency was powerless to use it for any purpose other than as a general indication to the public concerning the agency's tentative policy preference.

§ 5.7.5 The relationship between finality, exhaustion, and ripeness

Analytically and formally, the requirements of final agency action, exhaustion of administrative remedies, and a dispute ripe for review are discrete doctrines. Functionally, the three doctrines serve similar purposes, however, and a pattern of facts that supports application of one of the three often will support as easily application of the other two. The D.C. Circuit's multiple opinions in *Ticor Title Insurance Co. v. FTC*[246] illustrate the close functional relationship among the three doctrines.

FTC brought an action against Ticor alleging that it was engaged in unfair trade practices. Rather than defending against this action, Ticor petitioned the D.C. Circuit for a declaratory order that FTC could not constitutionally exercise a prosecutorial function because prosecution is committed exclusively to the Executive Branch and FTC is an agency "independent" of the Executive Branch. *Ticor* was decided before the Supreme Court held that "independent" agencies can exercise a prosecutorial function,[247] and at a time when that issue was the subject of considerable disagreement among scholars and judges.

The Supreme Court has sometimes considered facial challenges to the constitutionality of an agency's decisionmaking process before the agency has completed that process under an exception to the normal requirements of finality, exhaustion, and ripeness, but the

---

246. 814 F.2d 731 (D.C.Cir.1987).

247. Morrison v. Olson, 487 U.S. 654 (1988), discussed *supra* § 4.4.2b.

scope of that exception is not clear. The three judges that decided *Ticor* agreed that Ticor's constitutional challenge was not appropriate for judicial decision in advance of the completion of FTC's decisionmaking process, but each judge relied on application of a different doctrine to support that conclusion.

Judge Edwards concluded that Ticor had not exhausted its administrative remedies and was not excused from doing so in the circumstances. He identified two potential bases for excusing a party's failure to exhaust administrative remedies: (1) when an agency's assertion of jurisdiction violates a clear right conferred in a specific statute or constitutional provision; or, (2) when postponement of review would cause irreparable harm. He held both exceptions inapplicable.

Judge Williams concluded that review was unavailable because the agency had not yet taken a "final" action. He noted that finality is a jurisdictional prerequisite to review, while exhaustion and ripeness are judge-made prudential doctrines. He recognized that the finality requirement was subject to an exception when an agency's course of action would violate a clear statutory or constitutional right, but he concluded that petitioner's asserted right to be prosecuted only by the Executive Branch was "far from clear."

Finally Judge Green concluded that the agency's action was unreviewable at the time because Ticor had not established hardship attributable to delaying review sufficient to meet the *Abbott Laboratories* test of ripeness. She disagreed both with Judge Edwards' reasoning and with Judge Williams' reasoning because of her belief that exhaustion and finality are doctrines sufficiently flexible to permit review of the agency's action in the circumstances.

The three opinions in *Ticor* illustrate the close functional relationship among the three doctrines. They also expose differences of opinion concerning the scope and content of the three doctrines. It is notable, however, that each judge identified the superficial strength or weakness of the petitioner's case on the merits as an important factor in deciding whether to consider an issue at an early stage in an agency's decisionmaking process.

§ 5.8   Primary Jurisdiction

The doctrine of primary jurisdiction typically is raised, not in a proceeding before an administrative agency, but in litigation before a court. Agency and court jurisdiction to resolve disputes and issues frequently overlap. Primary jurisdiction is a concept used by courts to allocate initial decisionmaking responsibility between agencies and courts where such overlaps exist.

If a court concludes that a *dispute* brought before the court is within the primary jurisdiction of an agency, it will dismiss the action on the basis that it should be brought before the agency instead. If a court concludes that an *issue* raised in an action before the court is within the primary jurisdiction of an agency, the court will defer any decision in the action before it until the agency has addressed the issue that is within its primary jurisdiction. The court retains jurisdiction over the dispute itself and all other issues raised by the dispute, but it cannot resolve that dispute until the agency has resolved the issue that is in its primary jurisdiction.

Primary jurisdiction is conceptually analogous to exhaustion of administrative remedies.[248] Both are prudential rules created by the courts to allocate between courts and agencies the initial responsibility for resolving issues and disputes in a manner that recognizes the comparative advantages of agencies and courts. There is no "fixed formula" for determining whether an agency has primary jurisdiction over a dispute or an issue raised in a dispute.[249] In making such determinations, courts consider several factors, including: (1) the extent to which the agency's specialized expertise makes it a preferable forum for resolving the issue; (2) the need for uniform resolution of the issue; and, (3) the potential that judicial resolution of the issue will have an adverse impact on the agency's performance of its regulatory responsibilities.

The question of whether an issue is within the agency's primary jurisdiction is different from, but closely related to, the question of whether the agency actually has statutory jurisdiction to resolve an issue. Determination of a question concerning the scope of an agency's statutory jurisdiction requires detailed analysis of statutory provisions and, in many cases, of the factual context in which the issue arises. By contrast, determination of the agency's primary jurisdiction involves a more pragmatic evaluation of the advantages and disadvantages of allowing the agency to resolve an issue in the first instance. Indeed, courts frequently hold that an agency has primary jurisdiction to determine whether an issue is within the scope of its statutory jurisdiction where the determination of the scope of the agency's statutory jurisdiction depends in part upon expert evaluation of facts that are more accessible and understanda-

248.　See *supra* § 5.7.2.

249.　United States v. Western Pacific Railroad Co., 352 U.S. 59 (1956).

ble to the agency than to a court.[250] In this situation, the court may determine that the issue of the scope of the agency's statutory jurisdiction is within the agency's primary jurisdiction,[251] yet the agency or a reviewing court may subsequently determine that the dispute is not within the scope of the agency's statutory jurisdiction.[252]

A holding that an agency has primary jurisdiction to resolve an issue raised in a judicial proceeding has two important consequences. First, it transfers some of the power to resolve that issue to the agency. The extent of that transfer of decisionmaking power varies. A reviewing court still has the power to reverse the agency's initial resolution of the issue, but the agency's decision is entitled to more or less deference from a reviewing court depending on the nature of the issue.[253] Second, if the issues referred to the agency as within its primary jurisdiction are critical to judicial resolution of the underlying dispute, the court cannot proceed with the trial of the case until the agency has resolved those issues and the agency's decision has been either affirmed or reversed by a reviewing court.[254] This process may delay considerably judicial resolution of the underlying dispute.

§ 5.8.1 The origin of the doctrine

The Supreme Court first applied the primary jurisdiction doctrine in *Texas & Pacific Railway Co. v. Abilene Cotton Oil Co.*[255] Abilene sued the Texas & Pacific for damages in a state court, alleging that the Texas & Pacific had charged it an unreasonable rate for shipping several carloads of cotton seed. The Texas & Pacific defended on the basis that only the ICC could determine that a freight rate was unreasonable. The Court began by recognizing that before the passage of the Interstate Commerce Act, Abilene had a common law right to obtain damages from a railroad that charged it unreasonable rates. That Act gave ICC the power to prohibit unreasonable rates and unduly discriminatory rates. The Act also included a provision that preserved all preexisting common law causes of action. Despite the existence of such a saving provision, the Court

---

250. *E.g.,* FPC v. Louisiana Power & Light Co., 406 U.S. 621, 647–648 (1972).

251. J.M. Huber Corp. v. Denman, 367 F.2d 104 (5th Cir.1966) (question of whether royalty payments to mineral lessors are sales of natural gas is within primary jurisdiction of FPC).

252. Mobil Oil Corp. v. FPC, 463 F.2d 256 (D.C.Cir.1971) (reversing FPC order concluding that royalty payments to mineral lessors are sales of natural gas).

253. *See infra* chapter 7.

254. Mississippi Power & Light Co. v. United Gas Pipeline Co., 532 F.2d 412, 421–422 (5th Cir.1976).

255. 204 U.S. 426 (1907).

concluded that ICC had primary jurisdiction to resolve all disputes concerning the reasonableness of freight rates as a result of passage of the Act.

The Court premised its holding in *Abilene* principally on the need for uniformity with respect to decisions concerning the reasonableness of rates. It concluded that uniformity was unlikely to be achieved if many different courts retained the power to determine the reasonableness of rates. Lack of uniformity in such determinations would frustrate the agency's efforts to further the goals of the Act. The Act prohibited unduly discriminatory rates, and rates that varied because of differing court decisions inevitably would be discriminatory.

Abilene provides an illustration of what would be considered today an easy case for application of the primary jurisdiction doctrine. If courts and ICC each had the power to determine the permissible level of freight rates, conflicts between ICC and trial courts would be inevitable. Indeed, *Abilene* could have been treated as a case of federal preemption of state law under the Supremacy Clause, since decisions of state courts in cases determining the proper level of freight rates would have interfered with ICC's power to pursue goals contained in a federal statute. Any time primary jurisdiction is raised in a state court proceeding, the primary jurisdiction analysis is entangled with preemption analysis and issues of federalism.[256] More generally, primary jurisdiction is conceptually and functionally analogous to the abstention doctrine, except that abstention cases raise analytical difficulties unique to federalism that complicate the resolution of abstention issues.[257]

§ 5.8.2 The current approach to primary jurisdiction

In *United States v. Western Pacific Railroad Co.,*[258] the Court addressed a more challenging primary jurisdiction question. The government refused to pay a freight bill tendered by Western Pacific on the basis that Western Pacific had billed under its tariff provision applicable to "incendiary bombs," while the government maintained that the fuseless napalm bombs shipped were eligible for the lower tariff rate applicable to gasoline. Western Pacific sued in the Court of Claims, where both parties and the court assumed that the court had the power to interpret the tariff and to determine which rate applied.

---

256. *See, e.g.,* Motor Coach Employees v. Lockridge, 403 U.S. 274 (1971).

257. *See* Shapiro, *Abstention and Primary Jurisdiction: Two Chips off the*

Same Block?—A Comparative Analysis, 60 Cornell L.Rev. 75 (1974).

258. 352 U.S. 59 (1956).

The Supreme Court raised the question of primary jurisdiction to interpret Western Pacific's tariff sua sponte, and held that issue to be within ICC's primary jurisdiction. As a result, while the Court of Claims retained ultimate power to resolve the overall dispute between Western Pacific and the government, it was required to suspend its decisionmaking process and to refer to ICC the issue of which tariff provision applied to the government's shipment.

The Court based its holding in *Western Pacific* primarily on the greater expertise of the ICC in interpreting freight tariffs in the circumstances presented. In prior cases, the Court had held that courts have the power to interpret tariffs in the first instance because tariff interpretation is an issue solely of law and, hence, is within traditional judicial competence. The Court concluded, however, that the interpretive issue raised in *Western Pacific* should be resolved initially by ICC because that agency originally had determined the appropriateness of the tariff classifications and corresponding rates based on detailed evaluation of the costs of shipping different categories of freight. The agency thus had a specialized knowledge of the factors that caused it to draw the distinctions reflected in the tariff. That same knowledge would be useful in determining which rate in the tariff applies to a particular type of good. The Court stopped short of holding that all issues of tariff interpretation are within the primary jurisdiction of the agency that approved the tariff. It distinguished between interpretive issues like that presented in *Western Pacific,* where the agency's specialized knowledge of the reasons underlying the tariff is very useful in interpreting the tariff, and interpretive issues "where the question is simply one of construction" or where the agency "has already construed the particular tariff at issue or has clarified the factors underlying it". The first type of interpretive issue is in the agency's primary jurisdiction, while the second is within the initial decisionmaking power of a court.

The Court's decision in *Western Pacific* was particularly significant for two reasons. First, it recognized the important link between the scope of an agency's primary jurisdiction and the scope of the agency's expertise. Second, it established a pragmatic test for applying the primary jurisdiction doctrine:

> "No fixed formula exists for applying the doctrine of primary jurisdiction. In every case the question is whether the reasons for existence of the doctrine are present and whether the purposes it serves will be aided by its application in the particular litigation."

§ 5.8.3 Primary jurisdiction and antitrust law

Courts frequently must decide whether they can resolve an antitrust controversy without referring some issues to the agency that regulates some of the practices of the defendant. Regulation is sometimes compatible with competition enforced through the antitrust laws, but sometimes it is not. Final resolution of the often difficult question of the compatibility of these two different legal regimes requires detailed analysis of the nature and purposes of the regulatory scheme and the nature and effect of the practice that is being challenged under the antitrust laws. The inquiry under the primary jurisdiction doctrine is whether and to what extent the agency should conduct this analysis in the first instance.

The Supreme Court's decisions in *Far East Conference v. United States*[259] and *Federal Maritime Board v. Isbrandtsen Co.*[260] illustrate the important distinction between the question of whether an agency has primary jurisdiction to consider the relationship between its regulatory role and the antitrust laws, and the final determination of the appropriate relationship between regulation and competition enforced by the antitrust laws.

Far East Conference originated as an action brought by the Justice Department alleging that a practice of the Conference violated the Sherman Act. The Conference was one of several associations of steamship companies engaged in foreign commerce whose practices were in part regulated by the Federal Maritime Board (FMB) under the Shipping Act of 1916. The Conference maintained a dual rate for shipment of goods in ships of any of its members. If a shipper agreed to ship all its goods exclusively in ships owned by members of the Conference, it was charged a lower rate than it was required to pay if it did not enter into such an agreement. The Justice Department claimed that this dual rate system violated the Sherman Act.

The Conference moved to dismiss the antitrust action on the basis that the FMB had primary jurisdiction to determine whether the dual rate structure was appropriate in light of the arguably inconsistent policies underlying the Sherman Act and the Shipping Act. The district court denied the motion to dismiss, but the Supreme Court reversed. It relied upon the FMB's superior expertise in interpreting and applying the Shipping Act and the need for uniformity in regulating the practices of the shipping industry as the basis for its holding that FMB had primary jurisdiction to determine the

259. 342 U.S. 570 (1952).   **260.** 356 U.S. 481 (1958).

legality of the dual rate structure challenged by the Justice Department,

> "Uniformity and consistency are secured, and the limited functions of review by the judiciary are more rationally exercised, by preliminary resort for ascertaining and interpreting the circumstances underlying legal issues to agencies that are better equipped than courts by specialization, by insight gained through experience, and by more flexible procedure."

After the Court's decision in *Far East Conference,* FMB determined that dual rate structures adopted by members of shipping conferences were appropriate measures to offset outside competition and were consistent with the Shipping Act. The Court reversed this agency determination in *Isbrandtsen* and held that the practice of maintaining dual rates constituted a violation of both the antitrust laws and the Shipping Act. Justice Frankfurter wrote a biting dissent contending that the majority's decision in *Isbrandtsen* was patently inconsistent with *Far East Conference.*

Justice Frankfurter's dissent reflects a lack of understanding of the nature and purpose of the primary jurisdiction doctrine. In *Far East Conference,* the Court held only that FMB had the power to address the dual rate issue initially. In ordering the antitrust action dismissed pending FMB's decision on that issue, the Court explicitly recognized that the judiciary retains ultimate power to decide the issue once the agency has addressed the issue in the first instance. In holding that FMB had primary jurisdiction to address the dual rate issue, the Court said:

> "This is so even though the facts after they have been appraised by specialized competence serve as a premise for legal consequences to be judicially defined."

Thus, *Far East Conference* and *Isbrandtsen* are entirely consistent and provide an excellent illustration of the potential value of the primary jurisdiction doctrine. By referring the issue to the agency with specialized knowledge of, and authority over, the practices of the shipping industry, the Court was able to obtain the valuable insights of that agency before resolving an important controversy affecting the industry regulated by FMB. The fact that the Court ultimately reversed the agency, even after according the agency's analysis of the dual rate practice appropriate deference, does not detract from the value to the Court of obtaining the agency's analysis of the relationship between dual rates and the agency's responsibilities under the Shipping Act.

Ricci v. Chicago Mercantile Exchange[261] also involved an arguable conflict between regulation and antitrust law. In a five to four decision, the Court provided particularly helpful guidance concerning the role of primary jurisdiction. The outcome of the case is not nearly as important as the decisional factors stressed by the Justices. Taken together, the majority and dissenting opinions identify all of the major considerations that should underlie any decision whether to invoke the primary jurisdiction doctrine.

Ricci filed a complaint alleging that the Exchange and one of its members had engaged in a conspiracy in violation of the Sherman Act that had the effect of temporarily excluding Ricci from membership in the Exchange and increasing the cost of his membership. The Seventh Circuit stayed judicial action on the complaint on the basis that it raised issues concerning membership in the Exchange that should first be resolved by the agencies that regulate the practices of the Exchange—the Department of Agriculture and the Commodities Exchange Commission. A majority of the Supreme Court agreed with the Seventh Circuit.

The majority premised its holding on the following reasoning:

> "The problem to which the Court of Appeals addressed itself is recurring. It arises when conduct seemingly within the reach of the antitrust laws is also at least arguably protected or prohibited by another regulatory statute enacted by Congress. . . .
>
> " . . . [W]e agree with the Court of Appeals that, given administrative authority to examine the Ricci Exchange dispute in the light of the regulatory scheme and exchange rules, the antitrust action should be stayed until the administrative officials have had opportunity to act. This judgment rests on three related premises: (1) that it will be essential for the Antitrust Court to determine whether the Commodity Exchange Act or any of its provisions are 'incompatible with the maintenance of an antitrust action'; (2) that some facets of the dispute between Ricci and the Exchange are within the statutory jurisdiction of the Commodity Exchange Commission; and (3) that adjudication of that dispute by the Commission promises to be of material aid in resolving the immunity question."

The majority's choice of words in this passage is very revealing. In order to invoke primary jurisdiction, an issue in the dispute must only "arguably" be within the agency's statutory jurisdiction, and a

261.   409 U.S. 289 (1973).

court must conclude only that the agency's resolution of that issue will be a "material aid" in ultimate judicial resolution of the dispute. The final determination of the issues referred to the agency, including the issue of the actual scope of the agency's statutory jurisdiction, is reserved for judicial resolution *after* the court has received the "material aid" it expects from the agency in the form of the agency's initial decision on the issues.

The dissenting opinion did not indicate disagreement with the "arguably protected or prohibited" standard or the related "material aid" standard used by the majority. Rather, the dissenting Justices believed that the agency's decision on the issues would not be a material aid to the judiciary because the dissenting Justices were confident that the issues were beyond the statutory jurisdiction of the agency. As Justice Powell saw the case:

> "The principle which should govern this case can be stated quite adequately in one sentence: An agency cannot have primary jurisdiction over a dispute when it probably lacks jurisdiction in the first place."

The dissenting Justices went on to describe the likely harmful consequence of application of the primary jurisdiction doctrine— substantial delay in judicial resolution of the dispute while the agency considers the issues referred to it. The dissenting Justices recognized that this unfortunate result was worthwhile in some cases:

> "Yet all this might be justifiable if either the Commission or the Secretary were likely to make a meaningful contribution to the resolution of this lawsuit. . . .

> "Thus, if the Commodities Exchange Commission had jurisdiction over some aspect of this suit and special expertise in the area of its jurisdiction, a case could, perhaps, be made for awaiting its decision."

Since the dissenting Justices believed that the issues were not within the agency's statutory jurisdiction, they saw inadequate justification for the substantial delay inevitably resulting from invocation of primary jurisdiction even though they recognized that "the commission might make findings of fact or statements as to the law within areas of its expertise which the Court might find helpful."

In conclusion, the dissenting Justices argued for more careful balancing of the competing considerations involved in decisions whether to invoke primary jurisdiction:

"Wise use of the doctrine necessitates a careful balance of the benefits to be derived from utilization of agency processes as against the costs in complication and delay."

Both opinions make good points. Close questions concerning an agency's statutory jurisdiction and power should be resolved by the agency in the first instance, but referral of issues to agencies frequently results in lengthy delay of litigation.[262] Thus, courts should consider this likely adverse result of holding an issue to be within an agency's primary jurisdiction in the process of deciding whether the issue "arguably" is within the scope of the agency's statutory power.

§ 5.8.4 Judicial reservations about primary jurisdiction

Sometimes the Court concludes that an issue involving interpretation of a regulatory statute is sufficiently clear that it is susceptible to judicial resolution without prior resort to the agency charged with responsibility to implement the statute. When this is the case, there is no need to force the petitioner to suffer the delay and complication that results from application of the primary jurisdiction doctrine. The court can expedite the process of dispute resolution by deciding the issue of statutory interpretation itself. Two cases decided by the Court in the mid–1970's illustrate this type of situation.

Gordon v. New York Stock Exchange, Inc.[263] was an antitrust action challenging the practice of charging fixed exchange commission rates. A recent statutory enactment conferred upon SEC plenary power to regulate exchange commission rates. The question before the Court was whether the regulatory power exercised by SEC immunized the exchange commission rates from attack under the antitrust law. The Court could have referred that issue of interpretation of the Securities and Exchange Act to the SEC under the doctrine of primary jurisdiction. Instead, the Court engaged in a painstaking analysis of the Act itself and held that the Securities and Exchange Act impliedly repealed the antitrust laws as those laws potentially applied to exchange commission rates. The result of this holding was to eliminate all judicial power to regulate such rates and to vest all such power in the SEC, subject only to court review of SEC's actions pursuant to the Securities and Exchange Act. This was not the result sought by the petitioner, but at least the Court provided a prompt resolution of the issue of statutory interpretation

262. *See* Pierce, *Reconsidering the Roles of Regulation and Competition in the Natural Gas Industry,* 97 Harvard L.Rev. 345, 364 n. 109 (1983).

263. 422 U.S. 659 (1975).

that gave petitioner and all similarly situated parties notice that the practice of which they complained could be controlled only by the agency.

Nader v. Allegheny Airlines, Inc.[264] began as an action for fraud. Ralph Nader was "bumped" from an Allegheny flight that was overbooked. He alleged that undisclosed intentional overbooking constituted common law fraud. The district court agreed, and a jury awarded Mr. Nader $25,000 in punitive damages. Allegheny appealed, and the D.C. Circuit reversed the district court on the basis that the Civil Aeronautics Board had primary jurisdiction to determine whether undisclosed intentional overbooking constitutes a fraudulent or deceptive practice.

The D.C. Circuit stated its belief that CAB had the statutory power to immunize carriers from common law liability for fraud by concluding that a practice was not fraudulent or deceptive. The Supreme Court analyzed the statute and resolved this issue without prior resort to the CAB. It held that CAB did not have the statutory power to immunize conduct that was otherwise fraudulent. Thus, the judiciary retained the power to entertain common law actions for fraud brought against regulated air carriers without referring any issues to CAB for its initial resolution.

The Court's decision with respect to the specific primary jurisdiction issue raised in *Nader* appears questionable. At the time the case was decided, CAB was conducting a rulemaking proceeding to consider possible changes in airline reservation systems. The Court's acquiescence in the use of common law tort remedies for overbooking may have interfered with the agency's efforts to identify and to implement other remedies for the problem superior to, and inconsistent with, judicial awards of punitive damages. Ordinarily, the Court invokes primary jurisdiction in these circumstances even if it ultimately rejects the agency's solution.[265] The Court's decision in *Nader* might be explained better as a visceral response of the Justices to the widespread frustration experienced by travelers with reservations who were "bumped" than as a careful application of the primary jurisdiction doctrine.

On a broader level, however, both *Gordon* and *Nader* stand for the proposition that the Court will not require a petitioner to suffer the substantial delay that results from application of the primary jurisdiction doctrine if it believes that the agency can provide only

264. 426 U.S. 290 (1976).

265. *See* Far East Conference v. United States, 342 U.S. 570 (1952).

limited assistance to a court that otherwise has the power and the competence to resolve a dispute. Thus, in the language of the majority in *Ricci,* if the issue is not even "arguably" within the agency's statutory jurisdiction, prior resolution of the issue by the agency will not be a "material aid" to the court, and the issue should not be referred to the agency as within its primary jurisdiction.

In *United States v. AT & T Co.,*[266] the court seemed to blend the concepts of exclusive and primary jurisdiction in a useful way. After first deciding that the *Gordon* approach with regard to SEC exclusive jurisdiction did not apply to the FCC's relationship to the government's antitrust suit against AT & T, the court went on to add that the issue of primary jurisdiction could be resolved at a later stage if discovery showed the FCC to have "special expertise." This approach allowed the case to move forward with minimum delay and ultimately (as it turned out) eliminated the need for any referral to the agency at all.

§ 5.9   The Problem of Agency Delay

Agency delay is a serious problem.[267] Agencies often require years to take an action, and that delay often causes significant harm to public and private interests. The existence and notoriety of administrative delay often distorts judicial applications of administrative law doctrines. Court decisions declining to refer an issue to an agency under the primary jurisdiction doctrine or excusing a petitioner from the requirements of finality, ripeness, or exhaustion often are influenced by the court's concern that an agency may require years to resolve a dispute.[268]

The Court's opinion in *Coit Independence Joint Venture v. FSLIC*[269] illustrates the tendency for notorious agency delay to induce courts to distort legal doctrines. The majority applied the exhaustion doctrine as the basis for its holding that a federal agency could preempt a class of state court actions if, but only if, the agency issued a rule providing that a state court can entertain such an action if the agency has not taken final action within a specified period of time. The majority opinion is inconsistent with all prior law concerning both the exhaustion doctrine and the Supremacy Clause. It can be explained only as a product of the Court's concern that

---

266.   461 F.Supp. 1314 (D.D.C.1978).

267.   *See* Senate Committee on Governmental Affairs, Study on Federal Regulation, Vol. IV, Delay in the Regulatory Process, S.Doc. No. 95–72, 95th Cong., 1st Sess. (1977).

268.   *See supra* §§ 5.7 and 5.8.

269.   489 U.S. 561 (1989).

conferring jurisdiction on a federal agency would yield unfair delay to private parties.

In order to evaluate any possible remedy for agency delay, it is first necessary to understand the root of the problem. Most agencies have severely constrained resources and enormous responsibilities. The Social Security Administration, for instance, must make 1.2 million disability determinations each year, while the EPA was required to issue fifty-five major rules over a twenty-four month period just to begin implementation of the Clean Air Act Amendments of 1990. Moreover, the institutions charged with responsibility to limit agencies' discretion—Congress, the courts, and the President's Office of Management and Budget—inadvertently interfere with agencies' attempts to use their resources efficiently by imposing procedural obligations that require significant time and staff resources to fulfill.[270]

On a broad basis, the solution to the problem of agency delay must come through efforts in which courts are only peripherally involved—increased funding and staffing, improved case management[271] and selection of more efficient decisionmaking procedures.[272] Moreover, agencies should engage in careful priority-setting in recognition of their inability to accomplish all of their assigned tasks in a timely manner.[273] On an individual case basis, the remedies are limited. Undoubtedly, the most frequent method used to expedite agency action in individual cases is informal action by the legislative branch—a call from a well-placed Congressman often causes a case to be placed higher on an agency's agenda. Oversight hearings by a legislative committee focusing on the agency's delay in resolving an issue can be even more effective. Agency heads are averse to congressional and public chastisement.

The courts sometimes prod an agency into prompt action through one to two methods. First, APA section 706(1) empowers courts to "compel agency action . . . unreasonably delayed. . . . " This section is always available as a potential basis for a court order directing an agency to act in a long-delayed matter by a date certain. Section 706(1) is rarely used successfully, however, for good reason. It is very difficult for a court to determine when agency delay is "unreasonable". A court can know only a small fraction of the

---

270. *See infra* § 6.4.6.

271. *See* J. Mashaw, Bureaucratic Justice (1983).

272. *See infra* § 6.4.

273. *See* Shapiro & McGarity, *Reorienting OSHA: Regulatory Alternatives and Legislative Reforms,* 6 Yale J.Reg. 1, 18–24 (1989).

elements that must enter into an agency's process of setting its agenda and allocating its resources among competing tasks. Any court order requiring an agency to expedite its decisionmaking in one matter is likely to produce corresponding delays in other matters. The Supreme Court has admonished the appellate courts repeatedly that agencies must be allowed to determine their own priorities.[274] The D.C. Circuit applies a deferential six-part balancing test to allegations of unreasonable delay.[275] Although the courts are generally reluctant to order agencies to respond more quickly than they are willing to do, judges will respond to egregious delays. The D.C. Circuit, for example, ordered OSHA to promulgate a rule protecting farm workers after a 14 year delay, describing the situation as a "disgraceful chapter of legal neglect."[276]

The second potential vehicle for judicial intervention to expedite agency action is through judicial enforcement of a specific statutory provision requiring an agency to resolve an issue or class of issues within a time specified by the legislature. In recent years, Congress frequently has included in legislation deadlines by which agencies must take particular actions. Almost all environmental legislation, for instance, couples the authority to take a particular action with a specific time within which that action must be taken.[277] EPA is subject to hundreds of statutory deadlines. It rarely is able to act within the specified time. At this point, if a citizen or group files an action against the agency, a court will order EPA to take the statutorily mandated action promptly. In this situation, the judiciary is fulfilling its institutional role by enforcing the legislature's policy of requiring action within a specified time, and the legislature certainly has the power to set priorities through specific statutory deadlines for the agencies it establishes. The only serious question is whether discrete decisional deadlines imposed by the legislature actually play a constructive role in reducing agency delay.

The legislature is far removed from the management problems of agencies. It has little understanding of the issues it delegates to

274. *See* Mobil Oil Exploration & Producing Southeast Inc. v. United Distribution, 498 U.S. 211 (1991); Heckler v. Chaney, 470 U.S. 821, 831–32 (1985).

275. TRAC v. FCC, 750 F.2d 70, 80 (D.C.Cir.1984).

276. Farmworker Justice Fund, Inc. v. Brock, 811 F.2d 613 (D.C. Cir. 1987); *see also* Public Citizen Health Research Group v. Chao, 314 F.3d 143 (3d Cir.

2002) (holding that OSHA's nine year delay in adopting a new workplace exposure limit for hexavalent chromium was excessive).

277. *See* Shapiro & Glicksman, *Congress, The Supreme Court, and the Quiet Revolution in Administrative Law,* 1988 Duke L.J. 879; S. Melnick, Regulation in the Courts (1983).

agencies and even less understanding of the problems agencies encounter in allocating their scarce resources among a wide variety of
tasks. The fact that agencies rarely meet legislatively imposed decisional deadlines underlines congressional lack of understanding of
the administrative process and presents the judiciary with significant
difficulties in enforcing legislative deadlines. When the agency misses
the statutory deadline, a court invariably imposes a new deadline.
When the agency misses that deadline, the court substitutes yet
another deadline. This process keeps the agency under constant
pressure to resolve a particular issue, but at considerable cost in the
form of reduced quality of decisionmaking and reduced resources
devoted to other important agency missions.[278] Moreover, Congress'
decision to impose hundreds of unrealistic deadlines on EPA has the
effect of conferring on individual private citizens the power to set the
agency's priorities by allowing individuals to decide which deadlines
to take to court. It is difficult to be optimistic about the potential
efficacy of any judicially or legislatively imposed deadlines for agency
decisionmaking. The solution to the problem of agency delay will
have to come from sources like increased staffing and funding,
improved management practices, and judicial and legislative acquiescence in the use of less cumbersome agency decisionmaking procedures, rather than from statutory or judicial deadlines.

278. *See* Pierce, *Judicial Review of Agency Actions in a Period of Diminishing Agency Resources,* 49 Admin. L. Rev. 61 (1996); Abbott, *Case Studies on the Costs and Benefits of Federal Statutory and Judicial Deadlines,* 39 Admin.L.Rev. 467 (1987).

Chapter Six

JUDICIAL CONTROL OF ADMINISTRATIVE DISCRETION— PROCEDURAL ISSUES

§ 6.1 Sources of Agency Procedural Requirements

There are five potential sources of procedural requirements that agencies must follow—agency rules, the Constitution, statutes, Executive Orders, and the common law. We will discuss the latter four sources in some detail in subsequent sections of this chapter, but the first—agency rules—is an important independent source of judicially enforceable procedural requirements.

If an agency has established in its regulations a procedure for dealing with a particular class of cases, it must follow that procedure even if the self-imposed procedure goes beyond that required by statute or by the Constitution.[1] In this situation, the agency has the power at any time to eliminate the self-imposed procedural requirement by amending its rule, but it cannot violate its own procedural rule while that rule is in effect. This distinction is crucial; it isolates the purpose of the requirement that an agency follow its own rules. When an agency adopts procedures more demanding than those imposed on it, the agency has made an implicit judgment that it places a higher value on accuracy and fairness in its decisionmaking process than Congress or the Constitution demand. The agency must remain free to reassess that initial judgment in light of its experience with the procedures it adopted and changes in the resources or time available to it to devote to that type of decisionmaking. When an agency chooses instead to deny in a particular case a procedural safeguard that it has decided generally to provide in similar cases, the almost inescapable inference is that the agency is trying to hide some aspect of its decisionmaking in the case. Permitting agencies to make these kinds of decisions would expose the administrative process to substantial risk of manipulation of procedural rules to further impermissible or even corrupt goals.

In some cases, the Due Process Clause of the Constitution is a source of required procedures. An agency action cannot deprive a

---

1. *See* United States v. Nixon, 418 U.S. 683, 694–696 (1974).

person of life, liberty, or property without due process of law. The Due Process Clause requires courts to resolve two different questions: When does an agency action trigger the requirements of due process by threatening interests in life, liberty, or property? How much process is required when the Due Process Clause applies?

Statutes are the most important single source of procedural requirements. An agency's choice of procedures in a given case may be affected by several statutes. There are generic statutes, like the Administrative Procedure Act (APA) and the National Environmental Policy Act (NEPA), that apply to broad classes of actions taken by many different agencies. In addition, each individual agency action is governed by one or more organic acts that simultaneously delegate authority to the agency and prescribe procedures for the exercise of that authority.

The common law is the final potential source of procedural requirements. Some federal courts routinely ordered agencies to add procedural safeguards not required by statute or by due process until the Supreme Court's 1978 decision in *Vermont Yankee Nuclear Power Corp. v. Natural Resources Defense Council, Inc.*[2] In that case, the Court prohibited any judicial imposition of procedures beyond those required by statutes or the Constitution.

§ 6.2   The Role of Procedures in Limiting Agency Discretion

Procedural safeguards adopted for agency decisionmaking can serve both an agency's own goals and the goals of the governmental institutions charged with responsibility to control the exercise of discretion by the agency—Congress, the Judiciary, and the President. Most of the discussion of procedures in this chapter will emphasize the external function of procedures; that is, the way in which an externally imposed requirement that an agency use a particular procedure limits an agency's discretion. It is important to remember, however, that each agency also has internal goals that are affected by its choice of procedures.

Frequently, the agency's internal goals are perceived as conflicting with the goals of Congress or the courts. An agency may attempt to avoid using a particular procedural safeguard, for instance, to disguise its efforts to benefit particular favored constituents, or to avoid public recognition that its policies are premised on questionable factual assumptions. In many cases, however, the agency's internal goals coincide with the goals of courts and the legislature. An agency

---

2.   435 U.S. 519 (1978).

often perceives its dominant goal as maximizing the accuracy and fairness of its decisionmaking process consistent with the resources available to it. In such circumstances, the agency may voluntarily choose decisionmaking procedures more demanding than those imposed by Congress or the courts. It is virtually impossible, however, for an outside observer to distinguish decisionmaking contexts in which the agency's own goals coincide with the goals of other governmental institutions from contexts in which those goals conflict. As a result, courts and Congress impose procedural requirements on agencies based on the assumption that agency internal goals conflict with the goals of the legislature or the judiciary. Viewed from this traditional perspective, externally imposed procedural requirements are a means of limiting agency discretion.

Procedural safeguards mandated to accompany an agency's exercise of delegated power can serve several important purposes. First, they can help keep an agency within the substantive boundaries of its authority. Substantive standards contained in legislation delegating power to agencies usually authorize the agency to act only if it finds that certain facts exist or that its action will create a specified factual situation in the future. For instance, certain NLRB powers are premised on the agency's first finding the existence of an "unfair labor practice," and the EPA must establish water pollution standards that ultimately will make rivers and lakes "fishable and swimmable". Procedural safeguards accompanying these substantive standards provide a means of assuring that the agency limits its actions to those consistent with these substantive standards. A court has little effective power to enforce substantive standards unless an agency is required to follow procedures that create a record that permits review of the factual predicates for the agency's action.

Second, procedural safeguards can increase the probability that an agency will select the most effective solution to a problem. If all parties potentially affected by an agency's action are permitted to participate in a meaningful way in the agency's decisionmaking process, there is less chance that an agency will base its action on an inaccurate understanding of the facts or an incomplete analysis of the problem and its possible solutions. Viewed in this manner, every additional procedural safeguard imposed on an agency improves the accuracy of the agency's decisionmaking process. The unfortunate corollary is that every additional procedural safeguard also increases the resources that must be devoted to the decisionmaking process and increases the amount of time required for an agency to make a decision. The Food and Drug Administration, for instance, once used procedures for determining the appropriate content of peanut butter that necessitated years of hearings and millions of dollars in litigating costs.[3] The enhanced accuracy resulting from this choice of procedures did not justify the extreme delay and cost in agency and private party resources. Thus, in every case some institution must balance the conflicting goals of accuracy, expedition, and conservation of decisionmaking resources in selecting the procedures appropriate for a particular type of agency decisionmaking.

Third, procedural safeguards can enhance the political and public accountability of agencies. Judges are not the only people who participate in the process of reviewing agency actions to assure that they remain true to externally imposed substantive goals or standards. The legislative branch, other parts of the executive branch, and many segments of the general public also participate actively in this process. If the factual predicates and reasoning process underlying agency actions are readily available to legislators, government analysts, reporters, and scientists, each of these groups can act as indirect checks on the exercise of agency discretion by exposing flaws in agency decisionmaking or in the statutes delegating power to agencies.

Fourth, procedures that open the agency decisionmaking process to outside scrutiny reduce the potential for the use of agencies as vehicles for political patronage or punishment. A high proportion of agency decisionmaking is inevitably political, in the sense that Congress frequently delegates to agencies the power to make decisions that affect the distribution of wealth among regions and among sectors of the population. Agency decisionmaking can become political in another, more invidious sense, however. Agencies often are importuned by legislators or executive branch officials to favor or disfavor particular individuals or companies because of past or expected future political and financial support or opposition. It is more difficult for agencies to respond to this type of political pressure if they are required to follow procedures that expose the basis of their decisions to public and judicial scrutiny.

Fifth, procedural safeguards enhance public acceptance of government decisions. The attenuated control of agency decisionmaking by politically accountable institutions raises serious questions concerning the political and constitutional legitimacy of agency deci-

---

3. *See* Hamilton, *Rulemaking on a Record by the Food and Drug Adminis-*   *tration,* 50 Tex.L.Rev. 1132 (1972).

sions.[4] In this situation, an apparently open and rational decision-making process may be an important element in gaining public acceptance of agency decisions.

§ 6.3 The Due Process Clause as a Source of Procedural Requirements

Some agency decisions have such a significant impact on the rights of individuals that they can be made only through the use of procedures that afford the affected individuals a constitutionally mandated minimum level of protection from potential arbitrary government action. If an agency action deprives an individual of life, liberty, or property, the Due Process Clauses of the Fifth and Fourteenth Amendments apply to that action, and a court must determine the minimum procedural safeguards the agency must provide in order to satisfy the Due Process Clause.

Relatively few administrative law procedural disputes are resolved on the basis of application of the Due Process Clause. The greatest proportion of procedural disputes are resolved through interpretation and application of statutory provisions or agency procedural rules. The Due Process Clause is far more important to an understanding of administrative procedures than a simple counting of cases invoking it suggests, however, for three reasons. First, courts interpret ambiguous statutory provisions in a manner that is designed to harmonize the procedures required by statute with those required by the Constitution. Thus, in many cases that appear to involve only controversies concerning the procedures required by a particular statute, a court's interpretation of a statute is based in large part on its analysis of the procedures required by due process.[5] Second, Congress selects procedural requirements to impose on various types of agency decisionmaking based in part on its understanding of judicial decisions interpreting and applying the Due Process Clause. Third, agencies base their procedural rules in part on their understanding of the requirements of due process. Because of this constant process of cross-fertilization between the Due Process Clause, statutorily required procedures and procedures required by agency rules, most procedural safeguards employed by agencies have their roots in the Due Process Clause.

Courts must answer three questions in a Due Process Clause analysis. Does the clause apply at all? If so, what procedures does it require? When must the agency make those procedures available?

---

4. *See supra* chapters 3 and 4.

5. *See, e.g.,* Califano v. Yamasaki, 442 U.S. 682 (1979); Greene v. McElroy, 360 U.S. 474 (1959).

Courts use a two step analytical process to determine what procedures, if any, are required by due process in making a particular type of decision. First, the court must determine whether the Due Process Clause applies at all. An agency's choice of procedures is constrained by due process only if the action it is taking has the effect of depriving an individual of "life, liberty, or property". Courts often experience considerable difficulty resolving this definitional threshold issue in due process analysis. For decades, the Court drew a wooden line between "rights" and "privileges," with "rights" protected by due process and "privileges" unprotected. In 1970, the Court rejected that distinction by including certain statutory welfare benefits within the scope of the property interests protected by due process.[6] It has attempted ever since, however, to find some alternative basis for distinguishing between interests that are or are not protected by due process. Its efforts to date have not produced a consistent basis for making this initial determination.

Second, if an agency action deprives an individual of life, liberty, or property, the Court determines what procedures the agency must use to comply with the Due Process Clause. Historically, the Court approached this question mechanically, with only two possible outcomes. If the agency decision affected protected interests of one or a few individuals on the basis of contested facts unique to those individuals, the agency was required to conduct a "hearing" in the process of making that decision. If instead, the agency action affected the interests of a large number of people on bases common to all members of the group, it was not required to conduct a "hearing". By "hearing," the Court traditionally meant the kind of proceeding normally conducted by a court in adjudicating a dispute between two private litigants, that is, a trial, accompanied by all the procedural safeguards usually made available in a judicial trial.[7] If the party was not entitled to such a "hearing," it was entitled to no constitutionally based procedural safeguards at all.

During the 1970s, the Court abandoned this all or nothing approach. It began to determine the nature of the procedures required by due process by evaluating several features of the particular type of agency action at issue—the nature of the contested issues of fact, the nature of the individual interest at stake, the risk of erroneous deprivation of that interest through the procedures used by the agency, the probable value of additional procedural safeguards, and the burden that would be imposed on the government if it were

---

6. Goldberg v. Kelly, 397 U.S. 254   **7.** *See infra* § 6.3.3.
(1970).

required to provide those additional safeguards.[8] While this reflects a far more realistic and pragmatic approach to due process issues, it makes prediction of the outcome of due process controversies difficult. Due process can require anything from an opportunity to complain informally to a responsible employee of the agency[9] to a formal trial,[10] depending upon the Court's evaluation of each of the factors in the due process calculus. Each of those decisional factors is difficult to evaluate. Some require careful consideration of the relationship between contested factual issues and specific procedural safeguards. Others require the Court implicitly to place a value on interests—such as a school child's interest in not being paddled for something he did not do—that are not easy to evaluate.

The required timing of procedures mandated by due process also varies under the modern approach. Sometimes the agency must provide all of the procedures before it acts;[11] in other circumstances, it can act on a summary basis as long as it provides the necessary procedural safeguards in a hearing conducted shortly after it acts.[12] The required timing depends on the Court's evaluation of the adverse impact on the individual whose interests are at stake that would result from delay in providing a hearing, versus the adverse impact on the government that would result from delaying the agency action until after all procedures required by due process have been provided.

§ 6.3.1   Interests protected by Due Process

The Due Process Clause provides, "No person shall ... be deprived of life, liberty, or property, without due process of law." The Court will not apply the Due Process Clause to an agency action at all unless it finds an interest in "life," "liberty," or "property" that the agency action places in jeopardy.[13] The Court analyzes each of these three concepts separately; unless an agency action threatens to deprive an individual of something that fits within one of these three categories, the procedures used by the agency are not subject to review under the Due Process Clause.

The Court did not have to adopt this interpretation of the Due Process Clause, and it could change its interpretation in the future. Respected scholars have urged alternative interpretations. Professor

---

8. *See, e.g.* Mathews v. Eldridge, 424 U.S. 319 (1976).

9. Memphis Light, Gas & Water Division v. Craft, 436 U.S. 1 (1978).

10. Goldberg v. Kelly, 397 U.S. 254 (1970).

11. *Id.*

12. Barry v. Barchi, 443 U.S. 55 (1979).

13. Ingraham v. Wright, 430 U.S. 651 (1977).

Davis argues that the Court should read "life, liberty, and property" together, instead of considering each as a separate concept. Under his interpretation, the phrase "life, liberty, and property" would encompass any important interest of an individual irrespective of whether that interest fits comfortably in one of the three categories included in the phrase. The Davis interpretation would result in application of the Due Process Clause to any agency action that imposes "a grievous loss on any person".[14] Professor Van Alstyne argues that the Court should emphasize the relationship between "process" and "liberty". "Liberty" should be defined broadly to encompass a substantive right to freedom from arbitrary government decision making procedures. Under his interpretation of the Due Process Clause, "government may not adjudicate the claims of individuals by unreliable means."[15]

If either Professor Davis' or Professor Van Alstyne's interpretation were accepted, the Court would not need to analyze the interests at stake in an agency action to determine whether they fit under one of the specific headings: life, liberty, or property. The Due Process Clause would apply to any agency action that has an important impact on an individual, and the Court could concentrate all its efforts on the challenging task of determining how much process is due in each case. While the Court sometimes describes the scope of the Due Process Clause in grand terms that suggest adoption of the Davis–Van Alstyne interpretation,[16] the Court continues to cling to its interpretation of "life," "liberty," and "property," as narrow, independent concepts. As a result, unless the Court is willing to characterize the interest affected by an agency action as "life," "liberty," or "property," the Constitution does not compel an agency to provide any procedural safeguards no matter how serious the adverse impact of the agency action on an individual.

Professor Davis illustrates this important, if unfortunate, characteristic of due process analysis by reference to the Court's opinion in *United States ex rel. Knauff v. Shaughnessy.*[17] In that case, the Court held the Due Process Clause inapplicable to a summary decision of an immigration officer denying entry into the United States to a foreign born spouse of a United States serviceman, where the effect of the decision was to force the serviceman to choose between separating

---

14. K. Davis, Administrative Law Treatise, § 11.14 (2d ed. 1979).

15. Van Alstyne, *Cracks in "The New Property", Adjudicative Due Process in the Administrative State,* 62 Cornell L.Rev. 445, 487 (1977).

16. *E.g.,* Mathews v. Eldridge, 424 U.S. 319, 333 (1976).

17. 338 U.S. 537 (1950).

permanently from his wife or separating permanently from his country. It is hard to imagine an agency action with more disastrous impact on an individual. Yet, the Court declined to apply the Due Process Clause because it did not find any deprivation of "life," "liberty," or "property".

The meaning of "life" is never subject to serious dispute in the administrative law context, because no agency has the power to deprive an individual of life. Most due process controversies in administrative law involve agency actions that arguably deprive a person of "liberty," "property," or both. The Court has vacillated between expansive and parsimonious interpretations of both concepts.

§ 6.3.1a Property interests

Until 1970, the Court employed a traditional common law definition of property. If an individual owned some object of value like a house or a car, he had a property "right" protected from arbitrary government deprivation by Due Process. Anything else an individual received from the government—a continuing government job or continuing welfare payments, for instance—was only a "privilege" that the government could take at any time for any reason. At its apogee, the distinction between protected "rights" and unprotected "privileges" was so extreme that it posed a serious threat to the substantive constitutional rights of any individual who was dependent to some extent on a continuing beneficial relationship with the government. Justice Holmes' famous or infamous opinion in *McAuliffe v. Mayor of New Bedford*[18] illustrates the most extreme version of the right/privilege distinction. A policeman complained that the Mayor had deprived him of his First Amendment right to freedom of speech by firing him solely because he expressed views on an issue of public importance contrary to those of the Mayor. Justice Holmes rejected the policeman's complaint on the basis that his government job was a mere privilege that was not subject to any constitutional protection. In Justice Holmes' words, the policeman "may have a right to talk politics, but he has no constitutional right to be a policeman".

Gradually, the most potentially damaging aspect of the right/privilege distinction eroded in the face of increasing judicial recognition that government officials could summarily revoke the constitutional rights of a substantial segment of the public if they remained free to condition the continued availability of important

18. 155 Mass. 216, 29 N.E. 517
(1892).

government benefits on the non-exercise of constitutional rights.[19] The Court adopted the doctrine of unconstitutional conditions. Under this doctrine, while an agency could withhold a government benefit for no reason, it could not condition the availability of a benefit on the recipient's agreement not to exercise a constitutional right. Thus, for instance, while a government employee could be summarily dismissed, she could not be dismissed "because she was a Democrat or a Methodist."[20]

Initially, the unconstitutional condition doctrine was not accompanied by any procedural safeguards. Thus, it applied only if the agency was foolish enough to state that its decision to deny a benefit was based on an individual's exercise of a constitutional right. Eventually, however, the Court recognized that the doctrine provided little protection unless the individual had a meaningful procedural opportunity to establish that the agency's action was based on the individual's exercise of a constitutional right when the agency either stated no reason for its action or stated a reason independent of the individual's exercise of a constitutional right. Thus, in *Perry v. Sindermann,*[21] for instance, the Court held that a professor at a state college had a due process right to a hearing on his claim that he was fired because he chose to exercise his First Amendment right to criticize the policies of the college administration, even if the professor had no right to his job. The Court today applies the Due Process Clause routinely in circumstances where an individual makes a claim that a government benefit of any type was withdrawn because of the individual's exercise of a constitutional right.[22]

The Court's adoption of the unconstitutional condition doctrine and its recognition of the need for due process protection of that doctrine need not have resulted in total abandonment of the right/privilege distinction. The Court could have been content to

---

19. *See* L. Tribe, American Constitutional Law § 10–7 (2d ed. 1988).

20. Cafeteria & Restaurant Workers Union v. McElroy, 367 U.S. 886 (1961).

21. 408 U.S. 593 (1972).

22. In limited circumstances, the government can restrict access to certain benefits based on an individual's agreement to refrain from conduct that would be an exercise of a constitutional right if the conduct were engaged in by someone who was not receiving such a benefit. Thus, for instance, a District Attorney can discipline an employee for certain

forms of speech that would be protected by the First Amendment if engaged in by members of the general public. Connick v. Myers, 461 U.S. 138 (1983). This is because, in rare circumstances, the government can establish a sufficient justification for such a restriction of First Amendment rights. The scope of the unconstitutional condition doctrine is unclear and subject to intense debate. *See, e.g.,* Baker, *The Prices of Rights: Toward a Positive Theory of Unconstitutional Conditions,* 73 Corn.L.Rev. 1185 (1990).

apply the Due Process Clause to government benefits only when procedural safeguards were necessary to protect the substantive constitutional rights of recipients of government benefits. Instead, in its 1970 decision in *Goldberg v. Kelly*,[23] the Court applied the Due Process Clause to certain types of welfare payments, thereby foreshadowing its subsequent decisions in several contexts announcing flatly that it had "fully and finally rejected the wooden distinction between 'rights' and 'privileges' . . . "[24]

Goldberg v. Kelly involved a claim by recipients of Aid to Families with Dependent Children (AFDC) that the procedures of the agency charged with responsibility to implement the AFDC program violated the Due Process Clause. The agency provided an opportunity for a judicial-type hearing to determine a recipient's continued eligibility for AFDC payments, but that hearing was available only after the payments were discontinued if the agency first decided on the basis of less formal procedures that the recipient was ineligible. If the Court had followed its traditional approach to determining property rights, it would have dismissed the complaint of the welfare recipients in a brief opinion stating that welfare benefits are mere privileges that are entitled to no due process protection. It would have added that the procedural safeguards surrounding the unconstitutional condition doctrine were not applicable, because the recipients of the benefits made no claim that the benefits were being denied because of their exercise of a constitutional right. Instead, the Court held that welfare payments were property interests within the scope of the Due Process Clause. Accordingly, the Court required the agencies that implement the AFDC program to provide a judicial-type hearing to determine a recipient's eligibility for AFDC payments before terminating those payments.

The Court reasoned that AFDC payments "are a matter of statutory entitlement for persons qualified to receive them." It quoted from an article by Professor Reich in which he argued that: (1) a high proportion of property in the United States consists of intangible entitlements to continuing benefits; (2) a high proportion of those entitlements flow from government; and, (3) the traditional legal approach to property protects the entitlements of the rich but not the poor.[25] Thus, for instance, the Court had long extended due

---

23.　397 U.S. 254 (1970).

24.　Board of Regents v. Roth, 408 U.S. 564, 571 (1972).

25.　Reich, *Individual Rights and Social Welfare: The Emerging Legal Issues,* 74 Yale L.J. 1245 (1965). *See also* Reich, *The New Property,* 73 Yale L.J. 733 (1964). *But see* Williams, *Liberty and Property: The Problem of Government Benefits,* 12 J.Leg.Studies 3 (1983).

process protection to the governmental benefit of a license to practice law, characterizing that benefit as a "right", while it consistently afforded no protection to benefits like welfare or government employment. Professor Reich's thesis was well-documented and presented a compelling case in support of judicial recognition that at least some government benefits are worthy of protection from arbitrary deprivation. Unfortunately, he did not suggest a basis for limiting the government benefits that should be protected or a basis for determining the type of procedures appropriate to protect the availability of the wide variety of government benefits that exist in the United States.[26] Yet the Court soon recognized that it had to limit the potential scope of its holding in *Goldberg* in some way.

Every agency decision concerning eligibility for every form of government benefit could not possibly be preceded by a mandatory judicial-type hearing. The government makes millions of decisions annually, some of which require resolution of complicated technical issues. Government could not continue to provide the wide range of benefits and public goods routinely supplied by the various agencies today if all of its decisions had to be made through use of judicial-type procedures. The Court's post-*Goldberg* decisions represent a continuing effort to limit the application of the broad principles announced in *Goldberg* in two ways: (1) limits on the types of government benefits included within the scope of the Due Process Clause, and (2) limits on the procedures required when an agency makes a decision with respect to a benefit that is protected by due process. We will defer detailed discussion of limits on required procedures until section 6.3.3.

§ 6.3.1b   The search for limits on property interests

Beneficial relationships with the government take many forms. The most significant post-*Goldberg* decisions have arisen in the context of welfare programs, government employment, prisoner's rights, education in state schools, utility services provided by government agencies, and government licenses. *Goldberg* arose in the welfare context, and the Court's subsequent decisions suggest that all statutory welfare benefits are subject to the Due Process Clause if the

---

26. Professor Reich has steadfastly adhered to his views concerning the necessity of connecting government benefits to full adjudicatory procedures. *See* Reich, *The Liberty Impact of the New Property*, 31 W. & M. L. Rev. 295 (1990). Yet, questions continually arise about who such liberty interests favor and how to limit the procedures necessary to implement them. *See* Verkuil, *Revisiting the New Property After Twenty–Five Years*, 31 W. & M. L. Rev. 365 (1990) (new property favors those on welfare roles over those trying to get on them).

statute creates an entitlement to benefits for individuals with specific characteristics. In *Mathews v. Eldridge*,[27] for instance, the Court held the Due Process Clause applicable to social security disability benefits. In that case, however, the Court held that eligibility decisions under the social security disability program could be made through the use of procedures far less demanding than the trial-type hearing required in *Goldberg*. Thus, it seems that the Court will limit the scope of its holding in *Goldberg* in the welfare context solely through limits on the procedures required to accompany decisions concerning eligibility for continuing welfare benefits, rather than through attempts to limit the type of welfare benefits to which due process applies at all.

In contexts other than welfare, the Court's decisions demonstrate that it is searching for limits on the scope of *Goldberg* in both ways—by requiring less burdensome procedures and by excluding some types of decisions concerning benefits from any due process protection. Four cases that arose in four different contexts illustrate the tension on the Court between the advocates of near universal application of due process to benefit decisions and the advocates of excluding some types of benefit decisions from due process protection entirely.

In *Goss v. Lopez*,[28] a five-Justice majority of the Court held that a public school's decision to suspend a student for ten days for disciplinary reasons deprived the student of property within the meaning of the Due Process Clause. Hence, the school was constitutionally compelled to provide some limited procedural rights. The four dissenting Justices argued that a ten day suspension was an interest too trivial to justify constitutional protection. Similarly, a six-Justice majority held in *Memphis Light, Gas & Water Division v. Craft*,[29] that a decision by the utility division of a municipality terminating service based on nonpayment of bills involved a deprivation of property subject to due process protection. Again, three dissenting Justices argued that this interest was too trivial to warrant constitutional protection.

The proponents of limiting the benefit decisions that are subject to due process prevailed in *O'Bannon v. Town Court Nursing Center*.[30] In that case, residents of a nursing home claimed that due process applied to an agency decision to revoke the authority of the nursing home to provide them care at government expense. The

27. 424 U.S. 319 (1976).

28. 419 U.S. 565 (1975).

29. 436 U.S. 1 (1978).

30. 447 U.S. 773 (1980).

revocation did not deprive the residents of the benefit of continued care at government expense, but it forced them to relocate to another home. The seven-Justice majority recognized that the agency decision caused the residents harm because of the trauma associated with relocation, but it held that due process did not apply because the agency decision caused the residents only "indirect" harm. Justice Brennan argued in a dissenting opinion that forcing residents of a nursing home to relocate deprived the residents of a property interest.

Some cases provoke no disagreement concerning the applicability of due process when the nature of the agency decision suggests a basis for disagreement. In *Barry v. Barchi*,[31] for instance, the Court unanimously held the Due Process Clause applicable to an agency's fifteen day suspension of a horse trainer's license. It seems incongruous that seven Justices believe that a nursing home resident has no property interest in avoiding forced relocation, four Justices believe that a student has no property interest in avoiding a ten day suspension, three Justices believe that a citizen has no property interest in continuing to receive utility service, but all nine Justices agree that a horse trainer has a property interest in avoiding a fifteen day suspension of his license.

These disparate attitudes toward government benefits can be explained in several ways. First, a majority of the Court continues to believe that at least some types of government benefits—the ability to remain in the nursing home of your choice, for instance—are not worthy of constitutional protection. Thus, while the Court says it has abandoned the distinction between "rights" subject to protection and "privileges" not subject to protection, it is actually in the process of changing the boundary that separates "rights" from "privileges". It probably will no longer call interests on each side of that boundary "rights" and "privileges," but it is continuing to draw a distinction with the same effect. Second, it is very difficult to draw principled distinctions between benefits subject to due process protection and benefits not subject to such protection. Each Justice's view is influenced by the subjective value each places on particular interests. Justice Rehnquist and Justice Brennan, for instance, obviously disagree on the importance of continued utility service. Third, the Court's opinions in this area continue to be influenced by its former characterization of particular government benefits as "rights" or "privileges". The otherwise inexplicable unanimity of the Court in holding a fifteen day suspension of a horse trainer's license subject to

31.   443 U.S. 55 (1979).

due process becomes much easier to understand upon discovery that the Court had long labelled occupational licenses "rights" under the old right/privilege distinction.[32] The significant difficulty the Court continues to experience in distinguishing between government benefits that are or are not property provides powerful support for adoption of the Davis–Van Alstyne approach—all government decisions with a significant adverse impact on an individual should be subject to due process.[33] Under this approach due process would require a hearing in each of the cases discussed above, and the only question the court would have to address is the nature of the hearing required.

The Court's decisions concerning the applicability of due process to the employment relationship between government and an individual provide a particularly good illustration of the difficulty the Court has encountered in distinguishing between protected and unprotected government benefits. Even before the Court's opinion in *Goldberg,* it had held certain government employment relationships protected by due process. Specifically, tenured professors at state colleges—those whose contracts specified that they can be fired only for cause—had a due process right to a hearing in which they could contest the college's contention that it had cause to fire them.[34] After *Goldberg,* the Court was required to decide a series of cases in which other government employees argued that *Goldberg* dictated expansion of the traditionally narrow property interest in continued government employment.

Board of Regents v. Roth[35] and *Perry v. Sindermann*[36]—companion cases decided on the same day—represented the Court's major post-*Goldberg* attempt to determine the scope of the Due Process Clause in the context of employment at a state college. Both Roth and Sindermann were professors at state colleges, and neither had tenure. The Court held that Sindermann's job was protected by due process, but Roth's was not.

Roth was hired for a fixed term of one year, and was not rehired for the following year. He expected to be rehired, but the college never gave him any assurance that he would be retained beyond the first year. The Court explained its holding that Roth's employment

---

32. *See* Schware v. Board of Bar Examiners, 353 U.S. 232 (1957).

33. *See supra* § 6.3.1.

34. Slochower v. Board of Higher Education, 350 U.S. 551 (1956).

35. 408 U.S. 564 (1972).

36. 408 U.S. 593 (1972).

relationship was not protected by due process in the following language:

> "To have a property interest in a benefit, a person clearly must have more than an abstract need or desire for it. He must have more than a unilateral expectation of it. He must instead have a legitimate claim of entitlement to it."

The Court held that Sindermann, unlike Roth, had "a legitimate claim of entitlement" to his job notwithstanding the absence of any formal tenure status at the college. The Court based its holding on Sindermann's reliance upon several statements contained in the college's publications that indicated the college's intent to retain indefinitely any employee who had taught at the college for more than seven years as long as the teacher's performance was satisfactory. The Court found Sindermann's reliance on these statements sufficient to transform what otherwise would have been an "unilateral expectation" into a "legitimate claim of entitlement":

> "A person's interest in a benefit is a 'property' interest for due process purposes if there are such rules or mutually explicit understandings that support his claim of entitlement to the benefit and that he may invoke at a hearing."

If the Court had been able to confine its due process decisions concerning employment relationships to teachers at state colleges, its jurisprudence in this area might have continued to evolve in a satisfactory manner. Protecting tenured professors from arbitrary dismissal could be defended as a logical extension of the unconstitutional condition doctrine, since the unique concept of academic tenure arguably is a prerequisite of academic freedom, which in turn is "a special concern of the First Amendment".[37] The distinction between tenured and untenured professors recognized generally in academia provided a convenient and defensible basis for determining which employment relationships justify due process protection. Unfortunately, the many other government employment relationships that the Court was required to address are not characterized by such clear bases for distinction.

§ 6.3.1c Property as a statutory right?

Arnett v. Kennedy[38] involved a dispute concerning the procedures used in a decision to dismiss an employee of the Office of Economic

---

37. Minnesota State Board for Community Colleges v. Knight, 465 U.S. 271, 296 (1984).

38. 416 U.S. 134 (1974).

Opportunity (OEO). The Justices divided three ways on the proper resolution of the issues presented. Four Justices (White, Marshall, Douglas and Brennan) believed that the agency could be compelled by due process to provide procedural safeguards greater than those set forth in the applicable statute *and* that the procedures required by statute were constitutionally inadequate. Two Justices (Powell and Blackmun) believed that the agency could be compelled by due process to provide greater procedural safeguards, *but* they also concluded that the statutory procedures followed by the agency were sufficient to satisfy due process. The other three Justices (The Chief Justice, Rehnquist and Stewart) expressed the opinion that the Court had no power under the Due Process Clause to require the agency to use procedures more demanding than those required by statute. The reasoning stated by Justice Rehnquist on behalf of those three Justices is both intricate and controversial.

Justice Rehnquist interpreted the statute governing Kennedy's employment relationship to permit his dismissal only if the agency could show cause. Thus, Justice Rehnquist recognized that Kennedy had a property interest in his job under *Roth* that was entitled to due process protection. Notwithstanding the existence of that protected property interest, Justice Rehnquist believed that the Court could not apply the Due Process Clause to require the agency to use procedures more demanding than those contained in the statute because the statute conditioned the property interest it created with the procedures it attached to that interest. He reasoned that, since no property interest could exist in the abstract, any property interest must have a specific source—either the common law or a statute. Where, as in *Arnett,* the property interest is created by the legislature, the legislature has the power to define the scope of the interest in any way it chooses. It can limit its duration or qualify it with reference to the employee's refraining from engaging in conduct that constitutes cause for dismissal. Since the legislature that created the property interest can limit its scope substantively, Justice Rehnquist reasoned that the legislature also had the power to limit the scope of the property interest by making it subject only to the procedural safeguards specified in the statute. Justice Rehnquist found that the legislature had engaged in just that form of permissible procedural limitation of the scope of a right it created when it included in the same statutory provision language creating a right to continued employment absent a finding of cause and language specifying the procedures accompanying that right.

While Justice Rehnquist's opinion appears first in the report of the case, his analysis is not a part of the holding of the case. His opinion appears first because two Justices concurred with the three Justices for whom Justice Rehnquist was writing, thereby creating a majority of five Justices who concluded that the procedures used by the agency did not violate due process. The two Justices whose separate opinion was necessary to constitute a majority in favor of affirmance concurred on grounds entirely different from those expressed by Justice Rehnquist, however. In particular, the concurring Justices disagreed with Justice Rehnquist's reasoning that the legislature could avoid judicial imposition of additional procedures under the Due Process Clause by imposing procedural limits on the scope of a right conferred by statute. Thus, the views expressed by the plurality for whom Justice Rehnquist wrote do not constitute the holding of the Court. Rather, the Court divided six to three on this issue, with the two concurring Justices and the four dissenting Justices expressing strong disagreement with Justice Rehnquist's analysis.

Despite their disagreement concerning other issues, the concurring Justices and the dissenting Justices responded to the plurality's approach in the same manner. The legislature can choose not to create a property interest at all. Once the legislature creates a property interest by statute, however, it is the Court rather than the legislature that must determine the nature of the procedures required by due process before an individual can be deprived of that property interest.

The theory espoused by Justice Rehnquist in *Arnett* was rejected by six Justices in that case, but it may have been accepted by five Justices in *Bishop v. Wood*.[39] Bishop, a city policeman, was fired summarily on the basis of insubordination, absenteeism, and conduct unsuited to an officer. City ordinances classified Bishop as a permanent employee who could be fired only for cause. Bishop argued that the City denied him due process by failing to make available any procedures that would permit him to rebut the charges against him. The five-Justice majority held that Bishop had no property interest protected by due process because he could be fired at will. They based this holding on reasoning similar to the reasoning of the three-Justice plurality in *Arnett*: "the ordinance may also be construed as . . . merely conditioning an employee's removal on compliance with certain specified procedures". The district court had construed the ordinance in precisely this way, and the majority accepted that

39. 426 U.S. 341 (1976).

interpretation of state law. Since Bishop's property interest could exist only as a function of state law, the majority reasoned that its scope also was a matter solely of state law.

The four dissenting Justices accused the majority of resurrecting the theory rejected by six Justices in *Arnett*. In their view, *Bishop* was controlled by *Arnett:*

> "The ordinance plainly gives petitioner a right to his job unless there is cause to fire him. Having granted him such a right it is the Federal Constitution, not state law, which determines the process to be applied in connection with any state decision to deprive him of it."

The majority denied this accusation, contending instead that it had merely deferred to the lower court's interpretation that the ordinance granted the City power to fire Bishop "at will".

Although *Bishop* appeared to adopt the theory of the plurality in *Arnett*, the Court subsequently rejected that interpretation of the case. In *Cleveland Board of Education v. Loudermill,* the Court decided that the *Bishop/Arnett* theory "misconceives the constitutional guarantee."[40] The Court held that a state employee could not be dismissed from a position in which he had tenure rights without a prior hearing. The Court concluded that " '[w]hile the legislature may elect not to confer a property interest in [public] employment, it may not constitutionally authorize the deprivation of such an interest, once conferred, without appropriate safeguards.' "

The Court was correct to conclude that the *Bishop/Arnett* theory "misconceives the constitutional guarantee." First, it is important to recognize the ultimate implications of acceptance of the theory. If the Court were to accept the *Bishop/Arnett* theory, the Due Process Clause would have no application to any interest in property created by a statute that also includes procedural provisions. Thus, the Court would be overruling almost all of its modern due process cases involving property interests, plus many of its older cases in which it had classified some types of statutory benefits as "rights".

This revolutionary result would not mark the limits of the implications of the *Bishop/Arnett* theory, however. According to that theory, all property interests have their source either in statutes or in the common law, and legislatures can circumscribe statutory property interests by statute. Legislators also have the power to modify the common law, however. Thus, carried to its logical con-

---

40.   470 U.S. 532 (1985).

clusion, the *Bishop/Arnett* theory would empower legislators to determine the procedural scope of all property interests—whether statutory or common law in origin. Thus, the *Bishop/Arnett* theory ultimately would have one of two effects—(1) elimination of Due Process Clause protection of property interests entirely; or (2) reversal of *Marbury v. Madison*, since the legislature rather than the Court would then be the ultimate source of interpretations of the Due Process Clause.

The Court apparently was motivated by these problems to reject the *Bishop/Arnett* approach. The Court explained that "[t]he categories of substance and procedure are distinct" because "otherwise the Clause would be reduced to a mere tautology." As a result, "once it is determined that the Due Process Clause applies, 'the question remains what process is due.'" The Court emphasized that the answer to what process is due "is not to be found in the Ohio statute" that gave the employee his job tenure rights.

The purpose of the Due Process Clause is to insure that *individuals* who have been given rights are not subject to *arbitrary* governmental deprivation of those rights. There is an important distinction between legislative action that limits the substantive scope of a right and legislative action that limits the procedural scope of a right. A legislative decision to impose a substantive limit on a right by, for instance, limiting its duration or conditioning it on appropriate behavior, affects all people potentially eligible for that right in the same way. Thus, as long as the substantive limit does not infringe on a substantive constitutional right, the Court can rely on the political process as an automatic and sufficient limit on potential excesses of the legislature in depriving a large group of people of a substantive property right.

The political process cannot be relied upon to the same extent as an automatic limit on procedural excesses by the legislature. If the legislature is permitted to create putative substantive rights that are not enforceable because they are not accompanied by procedural safeguards, an agency can ignore those rights, quite possibly by favoring political friends and disfavoring political enemies. Yet, the legislature can avoid accountability to the electorate for these results by pointing to the putative rights it granted by statute.

The Due Process Clause is supposed to limit the power of the legislature to authorize arbitrary deprivation of rights of individuals. Yet, under *Bishop/Arnett*, the legislature would have had sole power to determine the extent to which its actions are limited by due process. It could have conditioned interests on whatever procedural safeguards it chose to make available, or even on no procedural safeguards whatsoever. While the legislature should remain free to place substantive limits on rights, as long as those limits do not offend substantive provisions of the Constitution, the judiciary should retain the power to require the legislature to accompany its putative substantive standards surrounding rights granted to individuals with procedural safeguards that give real effect to the putative substantive standards.

Although the Supreme Court has now apparently rejected the *Bishop/Arnett* theory as a means of defining (or eliminating) property interests subject to due process protection, it will continue to encounter difficulty determining the scope of protected property interests. A majority of the Court apparently is unwilling to extend due process to all government benefit decisions, and the Justices disagree on which benefits should or should not be protected procedurally. No Justice has yet identified an objective basis for distinguishing protected and unprotected benefits that can be applied satisfactorily across the entire range of government benefit decisions. Professors Davis and Van Alstyne have proposed an excellent basis for making these decisions,[41] but the Court has not yet accepted their approach.

§ 6.3.1d   "New" property versus "old" property

There are increasing symptoms of both judicial and legislative misgivings about the concept of "new property," i.e., "property" interests in government benefits that are created by statutes and protected by due process. Two circuit court decisions illustrate ways in which the courts may reduce, or even eliminate, their recognition of statutory benefits as constitutionally-protected interests in property.

In *Schneider v. California Department of Corrections*,[42] the Ninth Circuit drew a sharp distinction between "old property," i.e., property recognized by the common law, and "new property," i.e., property created by a statute. The court noted that, "while an explicit statutory provision may ... be a sufficient condition to the creation of a cognizable property interest, ... it assuredly is not a necessary one." A common law property interest can exist independent of statutes. The court characterized common law property as "private property" that is protected from government deprivation by both the Due Process Clause and the Takings Clause. By contrast, since a statutory interest in "new property" exists solely as a function of its creation

---

41. *See supra* § 6.3.1.   **42.** 151 F.3d 1194 (9th Cir.1998).

by the legislature, it can be redefined or limited by legislative action. The *Schneider* opinion provides a potential foundation for additional judicial decisions that emphasize the difference between the high level of constitutional protection accorded to interests in "old property" and the lower level of constitutional protection accorded to interests in "new property."

In *Colson v. Sillman*,[43] the Second Circuit held that a state statute that authorized the payment of healthcare benefits to disabled children did not create a "property" interest that is protected by due process. The court noted that the statute did not create an unconditional right to receive the statutory benefits. Instead, the statute qualified the right to receive the benefits in two ways: it authorized the agency to exercise its "judgment" in deciding what benefits are needed, and it made payment of benefits contingent on the adequacy of the amount of money appropriated to provide benefits. The court held that the statute conferred no "property" interest on eligible beneficiaries because those two conditions on payment of benefits negated any potential inference that the legislature intended to create a "property" interest in the benefits authorized by the statute. The opinion in *Colson* emphasizes the potential importance of the precise language of a statute in the process of deciding whether a statute creates a "property" interest to receipt of a statutorily authorized benefit. A statute authorizing provision of a benefit does not create a "property" interest protected by due process unless the statute confers on each beneficiary an unconditional right to receive the benefit if the person meets the conditions of eligibility provided in the statute.

Read together, the opinions in *Schneider* and *Colson* invite legislatures to enact, or to amend, benefit statutes in ways that preclude courts from holding that those statutes create protected "property" interests. Many legislatures seem prepared to accept that invitation. Thus, for instance, in 1996 Congress enacted the Personal Responsibility and Work Opportunity Act.[44] In that statute, Congress abolished the AFDC program that was the subject of the Supreme Court's first decision recognizing the "new property" in *Goldberg v. Kelly*.[45] Congress replaced that program with a system of "block grants to states for temporary assistance for needy families." The part of the statute that describes the block grant program begins with the following provision: "No individual entitlement.—This part

---

43. 35 F.3d 106 (2d Cir.1994).

44. Pub. L. No. 104–193, (110 Stat. 2105).

45. 397 U.S. 254 (1970). See discussion in § 6.3.1a *supra*.

shall not be interpreted to entitle any individual ... to assistance
under any State program funded under this part." It is hard to
imagine that any court will hold that an individual has a protected
"property" interest in any benefits made available by this statute,
given the powerful evidence that Congress did not intend to create
any "property" interest when it enacted the statute.

The issuance of judicial decisions like *Schneider* and *Colson*,
combined with the enactment of statutes like the Personal Responsibility and Work Opportunity Act, may foreshadow the ultimate
demise of due process protection for the "new property."[46] Many
statutes continue to be drafted in a manner that seems to confer a
property right on eligible individuals, however, e.g., Social Security,
Medicare, and Medicaid. In the context of such statutes, courts
continue to apply, and even to extend, the holding and reasoning of
Goldberg v. Kelly. Thus, for instance, in *Grijalva v. Shalala*,[47] the
Ninth Circuit held that due process requires the Secretary of Health
& Human Services to issue, and to enforce, a set of procedural
safeguards that HMOs must use in the process of deciding whether to
deny a medical procedure to a Medicare beneficiary.

§ 6.3.1e   Liberty interests

The Due Process Clause protects individual interests in liberty as
well as property. The concept of liberty obviously encompasses freedom from arbitrary incarceration by the government.[48] The Court has
long recognized, however, that liberty is a concept much broader than
mere freedom from physical restraint. Thus, in its 1923 opinion in
Meyer v. Nebraska,[49] the Court characterized its prior cases defining
liberty for due process purposes in the following language:

> "While this Court has not attempted to define with exact-
> ness the liberty ... guaranteed [by Due Process], the term has
> received much consideration and some of the included things
> have been definitely stated. Without doubt, it denotes not merely
> freedom from bodily restraint but also the right of the individual
> to contract, to engage in any of the common occupations of life,
> to acquire useful knowledge, to marry, establish a home and

---

46. *See* Pierce, *The Due Process Counterrevolution of the 1990s?* 96 Colum. L. Rev. 1973 (1996). *But see* Farina, *On Misusing "Revolution" and "Reform": Procedural Due Process and the New Welfare Act*, 50 Admin. L. Rev. 591 (1998).

47. 152 F.3d 1115 (9th Cir.1998).

48. *See, e.g.,* Morrissey v. Brewer, 408 U.S. 471 (1972).

49. 262 U.S. 390, 399 (1923).

bring up children, enjoy those privileges long recognized ... as essential to the orderly pursuit of happiness by free men."

In recent years, the Court has experienced difficulties delineating the scope of liberty interests analogous to the problems it has encountered in defining property for due process purposes.

The Court began the decade of the 1970s with opinions defining liberty interests as expansively as it defined property interests in *Goldberg*. It was particularly sensitive to the liberty interest in avoiding arbitrary government imposition of a "badge of infamy". Thus, in *Wisconsin v. Constantineau*,[50] the Court held a Wisconsin statute unconstitutional under the Due Process Clause because it authorized a police chief to post notice in all liquor stores declaring an individual to be an habitual drunkard without providing that individual an opportunity to challenge the police chief's official characterization of the individual. The Court held that "posting ... is such a stigma or badge of disgrace that procedural due process requires notice and an opportunity to be heard".

Similarly, in *Goss v. Lopez*,[51] the Court held that public school students were deprived of a liberty interest when they were suspended from school for alleged misconduct without being provided an opportunity to challenge the charge of misconduct. The liberty interest implicated in *Goss*, as in *Constantineau*, was the individual's interest in a good reputation. The Court recognized that charges of misconduct "could seriously damage the students' standing with their fellow pupils and their teachers as well as interfere with later opportunities for higher education and employment.... " The Court emphasized that an individual's liberty interest in maintaining a reputation free of unfavorable characterizations arbitrarily imposed by government officials was independent of any arguable property interest simultaneously withdrawn by the government official. Four Justices dissented in *Goss*, but only on the basis that a ten day suspension for alleged misconduct did not cause the "serious damage" to reputation required to trigger due process protection. All nine Justices seemed to recognize the existence of a liberty interest in a reputation free of serious damage by arbitrary government labeling.

The Court's opinions since *Goss* seem to form a pattern of sporadic retreat from its prior broad interpretation of liberty.[52] The

50. 400 U.S. 433 (1971).

51. 419 U.S. 565 (1975).

52. *See, e.g.,* Ingraham v. Wright, 430 U.S. 651 (1977); *see generally* Herman, *The New Liberty: The Procedural Due Process Rights of Prisoners and Others Under The Burger Court,* 59 N.Y.U.L.Rev. 482 (1984).

Court's retreat has proceeded simultaneously along several analytical paths. A 1976 opinion illustrates those paths. *Paul v. Davis*[53] involved a due process challenge to a police chief's widespread circulation to merchants of names and photographs of "active shoplifters". Mr. Davis' name and photograph was circulated even though he had never been convicted of shoplifting and he had not been provided any opportunity to challenge the charge that he was an active shoplifter. Despite the obvious similarity of the case to *Constantineau*, a five-Justice majority of the Court held that Davis had not been deprived of any liberty interest. That holding was premised on three lines of reasoning.

First, the majority denied that reputation is encompassed in the concept of liberty at all. It characterized *Constantineau* as a property case only, where the effect of posting Mrs. Constantineau's name was to deprive her of her common law property right to purchase alcoholic beverages. Second, the majority reasoned that it was unnecessary to accord due process protection to an individual's reputation because state tort law provides sufficient protection for reputation interests. Finally, the majority stated that any property or liberty interest must have its source in either federal or state substantive law. It was unable to find any federal law source of a reputational right, and "Kentucky law does not extend to respondent any legal guarantee of present enjoyment of reputation. . . . "

Four Justices wrote a scathing dissent, calling the majority opinion "a short-lived aberration," and arguing that:

> "[T]he Court by mere fiat and with no analysis wholly excludes personal interest in reputation from the ambit of 'life, liberty, or property' under the Fifth and Fourteenth Amendments, thus rendering due process concerns never applicable to the official stigmatization, however arbitrary, of an individual."

The dissenting Justices may have been accurate in their characterization of the majority opinion in *Paul* as a poorly analyzed contraction of liberty interests, but so far their prediction that it represents "a short-lived aberration" has proven inaccurate. Since *Paul*, a bare majority of the Court has decided several additional cases in which it has used one or all of the three methods used in *Paul* to contract the scope of the concept of liberty—(1) the interest at stake is not within the literal meaning of liberty; (2) tort law remedies are sufficient to protect the interest at stake; (3) the interest is not recognized by federal or state common or statutory law. In particular, the Court has refused to require procedural safeguards under the Due Process

---

53.   424 U.S. 693 (1976).

Clause in two circumstances: (1) where a state does not recognize an arguable liberty interest by statute,[54] and, (2) where a state has made a conscious decision not to provide procedural safeguards even though a liberty interest is at stake.[55] We previously discussed the significant flaws in this approach to due process analysis in the context of the Court's decisions concerning the application of the Due Process Clause to property interests. Followed to its logical conclusion, this approach would eliminate all due process protection for all liberty interests.[56]

It is impossible to predict how far the Court will go in its apparent effort to limit the scope of due process protection accorded to interests that previously qualified as liberty. Indeed, it is difficult even to determine how far the Court has gone to this point. Most of its recent decisions in this area have been by votes of five-to-four, and its recent decisions do not consistently deny or provide procedural protection to reputational liberty interests.

The Court's inconsistent treatment of liberty and property interests is apparent from its 1980 decision in *Owen v. City of Independence*.[57] Owen, the police chief of Independence, was fired by the City Council. The Council stated no official reason for its action, but Owen was fired immediately after a councilman accused Owen of a range of conduct constituting malfeasance in office. A majority of the Court assumed, with no discussion, that Owen's discharge violated his due process right to notice and a hearing. Four Justices dissented, but on a basis independent of the violation of due process rights assumed by the majority. Thus, all nine Justices apparently agreed that the City had deprived Owen of an interest protected by due process.

The result in *Owen* is easy to explain, but the explanation does not make much sense. A government employee who has no statutory or contractual entitlement to his job has no property interest protected by due process. An individual also has no protected liberty interest in avoiding governmental damage to his reputation. Yet, the Court holds that the government deprives an individual of an interest protected by due process if it simultaneously makes a tangible change in the individual's legal status, e.g., it terminates an untenured

---

54. *E.g.*, Meachum v. Fano, 427 U.S. 215 (1976) (prisoner was not deprived of a liberty interest when transferred involuntarily from one prison to another because state statutes provided no right to remain at first prison).

55. *E.g.*, Ingraham v. Wright, 430 U.S. 651 (1977) (freedom from corporal punishment is a liberty interest, but Court will not require procedural safeguards where state legislature has decided not to require procedural safeguards).

56. *See supra* § 6.3.1c.

57. 445 U.S. 622 (1980).

employee or prohibits a person from buying alcohol, and officially injures the individual's reputation, e.g., by stating that the individual's legal status was changed because of some alleged wrongdoing. Of course, this strange combination of rules has the effect of encouraging government agencies not to state their reasons for taking adverse actions against individuals in many circumstances.

In its 1995 opinion in *Sandin v. Conner*,[58] the Court reduced dramatically the scope of the interests of prisoners that qualify as interests in liberty that are protected by due process. In the 1970s and 1980s, the Court issued a series of opinions that had the effect of creating a broad range of liberty interests of prisoners that were protected by due process.[59] A prisoner was held to have a liberty interest in anything that was governed by a prison rule. Since prisons typically have hundreds of rules that govern access to virtually all privileges and penalties, the result was to confer on prisoners hundreds of protected liberty interests. By the 1990s, prisoners were filing up to 50,000 court complaints per year in which they alleged that they were deprived of liberty interests without being accorded due process. A high proportion of the complaints involved trivial alleged violations of prison rules, e.g., a prisoner claimed that he had been deprived of a liberty interest when he was given a box lunch instead of a tray lunch.[60]

The Court greatly reduced the scope of the liberty interests of prisoners in *Sandin* by holding that a prisoner is deprived of a liberty interest only when prison authorities impose "an atypical and significant hardship on the inmate in relation to the normal incidents of prison life." The Justices then divided five-to-four in deciding whether the inmate had been subjected to such "atypical and significant hardship." The prisoner had been subjected to thirty days of solitary confinement. A five-Justice majority held that thirty days of solitary confinement did not qualify as deprivation of a liberty interest. Thus, in a single opinion the Court raised the threshold to qualify as a liberty interest from deprivation of a tray lunch to something more severe than thirty days of solitary confinement.

§ 6.3.1f   Summary of interests protected by due process

The Justices disagree sharply concerning the nature of the interests in life, liberty, or property protected by due process and

58.   515 U.S. 472 (1995).

59.   *See* Olim v. Wakinekona, 461 U.S. 238 (1983); Hewitt v. Helms 459 U.S. 460 (1983); Greenholtz v. Inmates of Nebraska Penal & Correctional Complex,

442 U.S. 1 (1979); Wolff v. McDonnell, 418 U.S. 539 (1974).

60.   *See* Burgin v. Nix, 899 F.2d 733 (8th Cir.1990).

concerning the basic analytical process appropriate to determine whether the stakes in a dispute between an individual and the government implicate a protected interest. Some Justices sometimes state that an interest is protected only if that interest is explicitly recognized by the common law or by statute. Some Justices have carried this analysis one step further by concluding that the legislature can limit procedurally any interest it creates, and thereby can eliminate the Court's power to require additional procedural safeguards. The Court rejected that approach in *Cleveland Board of Education v. Londermill*.[61] Some Justices sometimes conclude that the Court must determine independently of statutes or the common law whether an interest is protected by due process. These Justices have not provided any basis for determining whether an interest is protected. A larger number of Justices recognize that protected interests must have an independent substantive law source, but believe that the Court must determine the procedural safeguards accompanying those interests. Sometimes this view attracts a majority of Justices; sometimes it does not.

As a result of persistent strong disagreements among the Justices and inconsistency in the views expressed by each Justice, it is extremely difficult to predict the outcome of a dispute over whether an interest affected by a government action is subject to due process protection. Despite the fact that the Court consistently states that it has "fully and finally rejected the wooden distinction between 'rights' and 'privileges' ... ," the Court is much more likely to hold that due process applies to an interest traditionally classified as a right than to hold that due process applies to an interest traditionally classified as a privilege.[62] Beyond this generalization, it is possible to predict whether the Court will recognize an interest as protected by due process only by reading carefully the Court's most recent decisions concerning the particular interest at stake, e.g., welfare, employment, or punishment of school children. The Court's decisions are not linked by a consistent set of principles or by a consistent analytical approach.

The Court's unprincipled and unpredictable decisions concerning the scope of the interests protected by due process underline the value of the alternative approach proposed by Professors Van Alstyne and Davis—any government decision that has a significant adverse

---

61. 470 U.S. 532 (1985).

62. *See* Van Alstyne, *The Recrudescence of Property Rights as the Foremost* *Principle of Civil Liberties: The First Decade of the Burger Court,* 43 Law and Contemporary Prob. 66 (1980).

impact on an individual should be protected by due process.[63] Under this approach, the Court could focus all its energy on the challenging, but unavoidable, determination of the degree of procedural protection that must accompany each government action that has a significant adverse impact on an individual.[64] Unfortunately, no Justice has yet adopted the Davis–Van Alstyne approach.

§ 6.3.2 The Due Process Clause applies to individualized determinations

In determining whether the Due Process Clause requires use of any procedural safeguards, the Court considers the manner in which the government has deprived an otherwise protected interest. Government deprivation of an individual's protected interest creates due process concerns; deprivation of protected interests of a group of people does not. Two cases decided near the beginning of the century illustrate this important point.

Both *Londoner v. Denver*[65] and *Bi–Metallic Investment Co. v. State Board of Equalization*[66] concerned property tax assessments by the city of Denver. In *Londoner,* the Court held that individual property owners were denied due process when the city refused to grant a hearing to permit each property owner to challenge a special assessment and apportionment of taxes for street paving.

> "[W]here the legislature of a state, instead of fixing the tax itself, commits to some subordinate body the duty of determining whether, in what amount, and upon whom it shall be levied, and of making its assessment and apportionment, due process of law requires that at some stage of the proceedings before the tax becomes irrevocably fixed, the taxpayer shall have an opportunity to be heard. . . . "

In *Bi–Metallic* the property owner argued that the city's decision refusing to grant a hearing to permit challenges to an across-the-board forty per cent upward revaluation of all taxable real property also violated due process. Justice Holmes rejected this argument. He distinguished *Londoner* on the basis that there "[a] relatively small number of persons was concerned, who were exceptionally affected, in each case upon individual grounds." By contrast, in situations like that presented in *Bi–Metallic,* Justice Holmes held:

> "Where a rule of conduct applies to more than a few people it is impracticable that every one should have a direct voice in its

---

63. *See supra* § 6.3.1.

64. *See infra* § 6.3.3.

65. 210 U.S. 373 (1908).

66. 239 U.S. 441 (1915).

adoption. The Constitution does not require all public acts to be done in town meeting or an assembly of the whole. General statutes within the state power are passed that affect the person or property of individuals, sometimes to the point of ruin, without giving them a chance to be heard. . . . There must be a limit to individual argument in such matters if government is to go on."

The *Londoner/Bi–Metallic* distinction remains viable today. The Court continues to rely upon that distinction in many of its most important modern decisions.[67] In its 1984 opinion in *Minnesota State Board for Community Colleges v. Knight,*[68] for instance, the Court emphasized:

> "Moreover, the pragmatic considerations identified by Justice Holmes in *Bi–Metallic Investment Co. v. State Board of Equalization* are as weighty today as they were in 1915. Government makes so many policy decisions affecting so many people that it would likely ground to a halt were policymaking constrained by constitutional requirements on whose voices must be heard."

The principles announced in *Londoner* and *Bi–Metallic* lie at the core of administrative procedure. *Londoner* and *Bi–Metallic* form the basis for the modern relationship between agency rules and agency adjudications,[69] and they remain crucial to legislative and judicial determinations of the types of procedural safeguards that should be required in various decisionmaking contexts.[70]

The most important passage in the two opinions is Justice Holmes' statement in *Bi–Metallic* distinguishing *Londoner*. Londoner was entitled to a hearing while Bi–Metallic was not because in *Londoner*, "a relatively small number of persons was concerned, who were exceptionally affected, in each case upon individual grounds". Thus, the distinction he drew could have been based upon any or all of three factors: number of people affected, amount of effect on each person, and/or factual basis for determining the effect on each person. While all three factors are important for some purposes in due process analysis, we believe that the number of people affected or

---

67. *E.g.* Vermont Yankee Nuclear Power Corp. v. NRDC, 435 U.S. 519, 542 (1978); United States v. Florida East Coast Railway Co., 410 U.S. 224, 246 (1973).

68. 465 U.S. 271 (1984) (holding that the First and Fourteenth Amendments do not bar states from limiting the rights of non-union faculty members to "meet and confer" with college officials concerning policy decisions).

69. *See infra* § 6.4.

70. *See infra* §§ 6.4.2 and 6.4.5.

potentially affected is the dominant factor determining whether the Due Process Clause applies at all to an agency action that affects protected interests.

Two circuit court decisions emphasize the importance of focusing on the number of people potentially affected by an agency action, as opposed to the number of people immediately affected by that action. In *Anaconda Co. v. Ruckelshaus,*[71] Anaconda urged the Tenth Circuit to enjoin an attempt by EPA to promulgate a rule limiting emissions of sulfur dioxide at a particular Anaconda plant. Anaconda argued that EPA was required to conduct a trial-type hearing before issuing the rule because the rule would affect only Anaconda's plant. The court rejected Anaconda's argument. It pointed out that the rule was general in form and was intended to reduce sulfur dioxide concentrations in an entire area. The fact that Anaconda's plant was the only source of sulfur dioxide emission in the area was not dispositive of the due process issue, since many other people were potentially affected by the general rule.

The Second Circuit addressed a similar issue in *Air Line Pilots Association, Intern. v. Quesada.*[72] FAA promulgated a rule revoking the commercial license of all airline pilots over the age of sixty on the basis that airline pilots over that age pose an undue safety hazard to passengers. The Pilots' Association challenged the rule on the basis that the procedures used to revoke the licenses violated due process. The Association argued that FAA was required to provide each pilot a trial-type hearing to determine whether that pilot's age posed an undue safety hazard. The Association pointed out that there were only a few licensed airline pilots over sixty who were affected by the rule. Thus, it argued that the situation more closely resembled *Londoner* than *Bi–Metallic*. The Second Circuit rejected the Association's argument. The court emphasized that FAA's rule potentially affected 18,000 licensed airline pilots under sixty and many thousands of future airline pilots, most of whom eventually will reach sixty. Since the agency chose to act based on the general health characteristics of an entire class of people, and that class ultimately could be expected to include thousands of individuals, the court held the FAA action to be governed by *Bi–Metallic* rather than *Londoner*.

Both the policy considerations and the practical considerations that formed the basis for the *Bi–Metallic* decision apply whenever the government takes an action that potentially affects a large number of people. In such cases, there is much less need for due process

71. 482 F.2d 1301 (10th Cir.1973).

72. 276 F.2d 892 (2d Cir.1960), *cert. denied* 366 U.S. 962 (1961).

protection than when the government singles out an individual for particularly disadvantageous treatment. Moreover, it is far too cumbersome to permit large numbers of potentially affected individuals to present testimony and to cross-examine witnesses in agency proceedings that are intended to produce policy decisions that affect large numbers of people.

The critical passage in *Bi–Metallic* could be interpreted to reflect the Court's intention to distinguish *Londoner* and *Bi–Metallic* on two bases other than the number of people affected in each case—the amount of impact of the government action and/or the government's basis for its action. We do not believe that either of these distinguishing features alone was critical to the Court's decision, however.

Justice Holmes could not have intended to distinguish *Londoner* and *Bi–Metallic* based on the amount of impact of the two decisions. The forty per cent across-the-board tax increase imposed in *Bi–Metallic* almost certainly had a greater adverse impact than the selective assessments for street paving in *Londoner*. Moreover, Justice Holmes specifically acknowledged in *Bi–Metallic* that government acting through general measures could "affect the person or property of individuals, sometimes to the point of ruin, without giving them a chance to be heard.... " Justice Holmes' reference to the degree of impact on individuals is important in due process analysis, but only as one of the factors to be considered in determining the nature of the procedures required by due process in a particular class of cases[73] once the Court determines through other means whether due process applies at all.

Professor Davis argues that the number of parties affected by an agency action should not be determinative of the procedures the agency is required to use.[74] Instead, he argues that a court should focus on the basis for the action. We will return to Professor Davis' views in this area frequently in subsequent sections, so it is worth developing his thesis here. Professor Davis distinguishes between "legislative facts" and "adjudicative facts":

> "Adjudicative facts usually answer the questions of who did what, where, when, how, why, with what motive or intent; adjudicative facts are roughly the kind of facts that go to a jury in a jury case. Legislative facts do not usually concern the immediate parties but are the general facts which help the tribunal decide questions of law and policy and discretion.

73. *See infra* § 6.3.4a.   **74.** 2 K. Davis, *supra* note 14, at §§ 10.5, 12.6.

The decisions in 1908 and 1915 in the Londoner and Bi–Metallic cases ... can readily be explained in terms of the distinction. In Londoner, facts about the particular piece of property had to be found through trial procedure because those facts were adjudicative, but in Bi–Metallic, facts about all the property in Denver did not call for trial procedure because such facts were legislative."

The distinction Professor Davis draws between legislative and adjudicative facts is very valuable. It is reflected in many administrative law cases where the issue is whether controversy concerning the existence of a fact justifies use of particular procedures. We shall rely upon Professor Davis' approach heavily in that context. In *Londoner* and *Bi–Metallic,* however, the issue was whether due process applied to the government action at all to require the use of any procedures. We believe that the number of people affected by the action is the dominant factor in resolving that issue. If we are right, an agency or court frequently does not have to go through the often difficult task of determining whether a controverted fact is legislative or adjudicative if the agency action affects a large number of people.

The number of people affected by the government actions at issue in *Londoner* and *Bi–Metallic* is critical for two reasons: one practical and one theoretical. First, on the practical side, there is a high correlation between the number of participants in a proceeding and the cost of allowing each participant access to procedural safeguards. Indeed, the relationship between the number of participants and the cost of using many procedural safeguards is geometric rather than arithmetic. In the case of cross-examination, for instance, increasing the number of participants from two to ten probably increases the cost of resolving the dispute by a multiple that is closer to fifty to one than five to one.[75] As the number of people affected, and hence the number of participants, increases above some admittedly uncertain level, mandating the use of trial-type procedural safeguards becomes prohibitively expensive in the sense that government could no longer make such decisions. This is the problem Justice Holmes alluded to when he said in *Bi–Metallic:*

> "Where a rule of conduct applies to more than a few people it is impractical that everyone should have a direct voice in its adoption ... there must be a limit to individual argument in such matters if government is to go on."

75. *See* Pierce, *The Choice Between Adjudicating and Rulemaking for For-* *mulating and Implementing Energy Policy,* 31 Hastings L.J. 1 (1979).

The number of people affected by a government decision should be dispositive of the issue of whether due process applies to that decision for a second, more fundamental reason. The political and constitutional purpose of the Due Process Clause requires procedural safeguards only when a government decision singles out one or a few individuals to be treated in a particularly disadvantageous manner. To explain this point, we will borrow heavily from the theme of Dean Ely's *Democracy and Distrust*.

Dean Ely argues persuasively that the Constitution is principally concerned with providing process of two types:

> "[T]he document is overwhelmingly concerned, on the one hand, with procedural fairness in the resolution of individual disputes (process writ small), and on the other, with what might capaciously be designated process writ large—with ensuring broad participation in the processes and distributions of government."[76]

These two forms of process-oriented protection are complimentary, as the Pennsylvania Supreme Court recognized in 1851:[77]

> "[W]hen, in the exercise of proper legislative powers, general laws are enacted, which bear or may bear on the whole community, if they are unjust and against the spirit of the constitution, the whole community will be interested to procure their repeal by a voice potential. And that is the great security for just and fair legislation.

> But when individuals are selected from the mass, and laws are enacted affecting their property, ... who is to stand up for them, thus isolated from the mass, in injury and injustice, or where are they to seek relief from such acts of despotic power?"

The Court answered its own question by stating that the only refuge for an individual singled out for adverse treatment is in the courts.

The distinction drawn by Dean Ely and by the Pennsylvania Supreme Court has an easy analogy in administrative law. The political process can be trusted to protect large groups of people from agency actions adverse to their interests, subject only to two crucial caveats—(1) the judiciary must insure that the political process can work effectively by enforcing such political rights as freedom of speech and the process of representation; and, (2) the judiciary must protect insular minorities from the potential for systematic discrimi-

76. J. Ely, Democracy and Distrust 87 (1980).

77. Ervine's Appeal, 16 Pa. 256, 268 (1851).

nation by the majority by enforcing the Equal Protection Clause of the Fourteenth Amendment. Thus, there is no need to protect large numbers of people (other than insular minorities) through application of the Due Process Clause.

When, however, an agency singles out one or a few individuals for adverse action, the political process provides little protection from decisions designed to help a few preferred individuals at the expense of a few disfavored individuals. Individuals singled out for adverse action can be protected only by forcing the agency to use a decision-making process that insures fairness to the individual. That is the purpose of the Due Process Clause.

§ 6.3.3   Procedures required by Due Process

Once a court holds that the Due Process Clause applies to an agency decision because that decision deprives an individual of life, liberty, or property, it must determine the procedures required by due process. Until recent years, this part of due process analysis was simple. Due process required a "hearing," and the Court meant by hearing the kind of proceeding traditionally used by courts to litigate civil disputes.[78] Judge Friendly lists the procedural safeguards provided in a judicial hearing as follows:[79]

(1) An unbiased tribunal.

(2) Notice of the proposed action and the grounds asserted for it.

(3) Opportunity to present reasons why the proposed action should not be taken.

(4) The right to present evidence, including the right to call witnesses.

(5) The right to know opposing evidence.

(6) The right to cross-examine adverse witnesses.

(7) Decision based exclusively on the evidence presented.

(8) Right to counsel.

(9) Requirement that the tribunal prepare a record of the evidence presented.

(10) Requirement that the tribunal prepare written findings of fact and reasons for its decision.

---

78. Of course, as in a civil proceeding in a court, you are entitled to an oral evidentiary hearing only if there are contested issues of material fact. *See* § 6.3.4b

79. Friendly, *Some Kind of Hearing,* 123 U.Pa.L.Rev. 1267 (1975).

Most of the Court's major due process decisions of the first half of the century stopped at the point of concluding that due process required a hearing, on the assumption that everyone understood what the Court meant by a hearing.[80]

In *Goldberg v. Kelly*,[81] the Court departed from its tradition of simply requiring a hearing and assuming that hearing had a commonly understood meaning. *Goldberg* involved a challenge to the procedures used by New York welfare authorities in deciding whether to terminate benefits previously received by an individual under the federal program of Aid to Families with Dependent Children (AFDC). Before deciding to terminate benefits, the welfare unit supervisor notified the beneficiary of the agency's intent to terminate and the reasons for the proposed termination, and provided the beneficiary an opportunity to submit a written response challenging the reasons for the proposed termination. If the unit supervisor decided to terminate the benefits as a result of this process, the former beneficiary was entitled to an evidentiary hearing, but only after the benefits were terminated.

AFDC beneficiaries alleged that New York's procedures violated due process because they did not provide for a judicial-type hearing prior to termination of benefits. The Court agreed with the beneficiaries concerning the need for a pre-termination hearing because erroneous termination of AFDC benefits would place a beneficiary in an "immediately desperate" situation. It went on to say, however, "that the pre-termination hearing need not take the form of a judicial or quasi-judicial trial". The pre-termination hearing could be limited "to minimum procedural safeguards, adapted to the particular characteristics of welfare recipients, and to the limited nature of the controversies to be resolved."

The Court then proceeded to consider separately the need for each of the elements of a judicial-type hearing. It concluded that the nature of an AFDC termination decision was such that most of the ten elements of a judicial-type hearing should be made available. In particular, it held New York's procedures inadequate because they did not include the right to present evidence orally and the right to cross-examine adverse witnesses. The Court found these safeguards critically important because: (1) many AFDC beneficiaries have limited ability to communicate in writing, and (2) many AFDC termi-

---

80. *See, e.g.,* Ohio Bell Telephone Co. v. Public Utilities Commission, 301 U.S. 292 (1937); ICC v. Louisville & Nashville Railroad, 227 U.S. 88 (1913).

81. 397 U.S. 254 (1970).

nation controversies turn on issues of the veracity of witnesses. Thus, while the Court explicitly recognized in *Goldberg* that due process can require procedures less rigorous than those available in a judicial-type hearing, ultimately it required a judicial-type hearing for the specific type of decision at issue in *Goldberg*. Indeed, the only procedural safeguards rejected by the Court were the right to counsel provided at government expense and formal findings of fact.

The Court's decision in *Goldberg* provoked considerable controversy. It was the first case in which the Court applied the Due Process Clause to government benefits that were previously classified as mere "privileges," and it was the first case in which the Court considered in detail the elements of the "hearing" required by due process. Three critical evaluations of the *Goldberg* decision had a significant impact on the Court's post-*Goldberg* decisions—Justice Black's dissenting opinion, Judge Friendly's thoughtful essay on the nature of a hearing,[82] and Professor Mashaw's thorough study of decisions concerning eligibility for welfare.[83]

In his dissenting opinion, Justice Black argued that the majority's decision ultimately would harm rather than help people in need of welfare. By making it difficult and expensive to terminate welfare benefits, he predicted that the decision would have two adverse impacts. First, welfare authorities would be required to reallocate substantial amounts of money from the funds previously used to pay welfare benefits to the expensive new process required to determine whether beneficiaries remain eligible. Since the legislature was unlikely to increase the total funds available for welfare programs, the inevitable effect of this reallocation would be to reduce the amount of money available to those eligible for welfare. Second, by making it difficult and expensive for welfare administrators to remove ineligible individuals from the welfare system, the majority inadvertently created an incentive for welfare administrators to exercise much more caution in determining initial eligibility for welfare. As a result, many individuals with a "desperate need" for welfare would have to wait additional months before that need could be met. Justice Black's dissent provided the initial impetus for reevaluating the desirability of requiring judicial-type hearings in benefit termination cases.

Drawing upon several studies of the welfare system, Professor Mashaw documented some of the concerns expressed by Justice Black. New York City welfare authorities alone made 40,000 benefit

82. Friendly, *supra* note 79.

83. Mashaw, *The Management Side of Due Process: Accuracy, Fairness and* *Timeliness in Adjudication of Social Welfare Claims,* 59 Corn.L.Rev. 772 (1974).

decisions each month. After *Goldberg,* New York City was required to hire a group of highly paid lawyers to preside over hearings to determine continued eligibility. Professor Mashaw also questioned the beneficial effect of the hearing requirement imposed in *Goldberg.* He argued that welfare recipients were poorly positioned to make effective use of formal, trial-type hearings because they cannot afford lawyers, they do not have the educational level necessary to exercise their procedural rights effectively, and most are too vulnerable to informal pressures from welfare authorities even to demand that they be given a hearing. Professor Mashaw concluded that the accuracy of welfare eligibility decisions could be improved to a much greater extent by adoption of a series of relatively inexpensive internal management tools than by requiring expensive formal decision making procedures.

Finally, Judge Friendly used the Court's decision in *Goldberg* and several similar cases of the period as a starting point for discussion of what a "hearing" should be. He made two significant points. First, the judicial-type hearing so familiar to U.S. judges is only one of many ways of attempting to maximize accuracy in decisionmaking. It is not even the dominant method of resolving legal disputes in the courts of most other countries. While judicial-type hearings may be best-suited for some types of decisionmaking, they are inappropriate for others. Second, each procedural safeguard provided in a judicial-type hearing serves different functions. By analyzing the nature of particular types of disputes and the functions served by potential procedural safeguards, it is possible to devise procedures functionally equivalent to a judicial-type hearing, but without all of the expensive safeguards normally provided in such a hearing. For instance, Judge Friendly concluded that a neutral decisionmaker serves so many important functions that other procedures can be eliminated with little loss of accuracy if decisionmaking neutrality is ensured.

The post-*Goldberg* decisions of the Court reflect at least implicitly the criticisms of Justice Black, Judge Friendly, and Professor Mashaw. *Mathews v. Eldridge*[84] involved a decisionmaking context superficially analogous to *Goldberg.* Eldridge, a recipient of social security disability payments, challenged the constitutional adequacy of the procedures used by the Social Security Administration (SSA) to determine that he was no longer eligible for such benefits. SSA employed a multi-step procedure that relied principally upon questionnaires, several physical examinations by different doctors, notice

---

84.   424 U.S. 319 (1976).

of tentative determination of ineligibility, and an opportunity to contest in writing that tentative determination. Eldridge had a right to a post-termination evidentiary hearing, but he challenged the constitutional adequacy of the pre-termination procedures instead of pursuing that remedy. Eldridge cited *Goldberg* to support his contention that SSA's procedures violated due process by failing to provide an opportunity for a judicial-type hearing prior to termination of disability benefits. The Court distinguished *Goldberg* and held SSA's procedures adequate.

The Court began its discussion of the issue in *Mathews* by establishing the following analytical framework:

> " '[D]ue process,' unlike some legal rules, is not a technical conception with a fixed content unrelated to time, place and circumstances.... [O]ur prior decisions indicate that identification of the specific dictates of due process generally requires consideration of three distinct factors: First, the private interest that will be affected by the official action; second, the risk of an erroneous deprivation of such interest through the procedures used, and the probable value, if any, of additional or substitute procedural safeguards, and finally, the Government's interest, including the function involved and the fiscal and administrative burdens that the additional or substitute procedural requirement would entail."

It then proceeded to assess each of the factors identified in this balancing test.

The Court identified the private interest at stake as the beneficiary's interest in continuing to receive benefits for approximately one year—the average interval between the date of termination of benefits based on the procedures provided by SSA as the basis for its initial decision and the date when SSA could be expected to make a subsequent decision based on a post-termination evidentiary hearing. It recognized that "the hardship imposed upon the erroneously terminated disability recipient may be significant," and that the recipient's interest is similar to the AFDC recipient's interest at stake in *Goldberg*. It concluded, however, that a disability beneficiary's interest is less important than an AFDC beneficiary's interest because most disability beneficiaries have other sources of income and eligibility for disability payments does not depend on a showing of financial need.

The Court then proceeded to assess "the risk of an erroneous deprivation of such interest through the procedures used, and the probable value, if any, of additional or substitute procedural safeguards, ... '' The relevant comparison was between the written exchange of medical information provided by SSA and the judicial-type hearing requested by Eldridge. In holding SSA's procedures adequate, the Court emphasized two distinctions between the AFDC decision at issue in *Goldberg* and the disability decision at issue in *Mathews*—the nature of the most frequently disputed issues of fact and the nature of the participants in the decisionmaking process. The controversial factual issues in AFDC cases are likely to turn on the veracity of witnesses with conflicting stories concerning the beneficiary's activities. By contrast, the factual issues in dispute in disability cases involve conflicting medical diagnoses. Oral evidence and cross-examination are more important safeguards of the accuracy of the decisionmaking process when factual issues turn on veracity than when factual disputes are capable of resolution through application of relatively objective scientific criteria.

The dominant participants in the AFDC and disability decisionmaking processes also differ significantly. Because of the nature of the issues, AFDC beneficiaries typically must rely upon their own ability to present testimony and to cross-examine witnesses in an effort to establish their continued eligibility. Because of their relatively low educational levels, AFDC beneficiaries are poorly positioned to exercise procedural rights that rely upon effective written communication. By contrast, many disability disputes arise as a result of disagreements between government and private physicians who are used to communicating in writing.

Thus, the reliance upon written communications reflected in New York's AFDC termination procedures at issue in *Goldberg* produced much greater potential for error than did the reliance on written communications reflected in SSA's procedures for terminating disability benefits at issue in *Mathews*. Similarly, the substitution of oral procedures for written procedures could be expected to enhance substantially the accuracy of the fact-finding process in AFDC decisionmaking, but could be expected to provide only slight improvement in the accuracy of the fact-finding process in disability decisionmaking.

Finally, the Court evaluated the potential cost to the government that would result from a judicial determination that SSA must provide a judicial-type hearing before it terminates disability benefits. The costs would appear in the form of: (1) costs necessary to implement the hearing requirement; and, (2) costs of allowing beneficiaries to continue to receive benefits until a termination decision could be made based upon the record of a judicial-type hearing. The Court found these costs too high to justify imposition of a requirement of a pre-termination judicial-type hearing, particularly when the costs of the added procedures "may in the end come out of the pockets of the deserving since resources available for any particular program of social welfare are not unlimited," which was Justice Black's concern in *Goldberg*.

Application of the *Mathews* approach to a given class of disputes can yield any of a wide range of minimum procedural safeguards depending on the Court's assessment of the three factors encompassed in the *Mathews* balancing test. In *Goss v. Lopez*,[85] for instance, the Court held that a public school student was entitled to a hearing of some type before he could be suspended for ten days because, in the absence of a hearing, there was too great a chance that the student would be erroneously deprived of important property and liberty interests. It went on to conclude, however, that the required hearing could consist of an informal meeting between a school official and the student in which the student had an opportunity to tell his side of the story. The Court declined to require a judicial-type hearing because such a requirement "might well overwhelm administrative facilities in many places and, by diverting resources, cost more than it would save in educational effectiveness". Through similar reasoning the Court held in *Memphis Light, Gas & Water Division v. Craft*[86] that a governmental supplier of utility services could not terminate those services for nonpayment of bills without first providing the recipient an opportunity for an informal hearing (really just a meeting) before a government official with authority to make the decision.

The Court's approach in *Mathews* serves many valuable purposes. It allows the Court to recognize a wide range of interests protected from arbitrary government action without forcing government officials to adopt expensive, time consuming formal procedures in all decisionmaking contexts. It permits the Court to determine the minimum procedures mandated by due process in a way that reflects explicitly the social costs and benefits of providing particular procedural safeguards in particular classes of factual disputes.

The Court has not consistently followed the *Mathews* approach, however. In some cases, most notably *Ingraham v. Wright*,[87] a majority of the Court seems to have eschewed the *Mathews* approach in

85. 419 U.S. 565 (1975).   **87.** 430 U.S. 651 (1977).
86. 436 U.S. 1 (1978).

favor of an application of the Due Process Clause that gives near total deference to legislators. *Ingraham* involved a challenge to the procedures provided by Florida law before a student could be paddled. Florida provided *no* pre-paddling procedural safeguards. Five Justices declined to impose even the requirement of an informal hearing like that mandated in *Goss* and *Memphis,* principally because Florida's practice of declining to provide any procedural safeguards was the product of "a legislative judgment, rooted in history.... " Four dissenting Justices argued that the majority decision was inconsistent with *Mathews* and *Goss.*

The Justices are seriously divided between the *Mathews* approach and the "legislative judgment" approach reflected in the majority opinion in *Ingraham.* In most cases, a majority of the Court adopts the *Mathews* approach, but occasionally, as in *Ingraham,* a majority supports the legislative judgment approach. The tension among the Justices is illustrated well by the four way split among the Justices in *Arnett v. Kennedy.*[88]

Kennedy was fired from his civil service position as a regional representative of Office of Economic Opportunity (OEO) by OEO's Regional Director. Kennedy had a statutory right to keep his job subject only to the agency's right to fire him for cause. The Regional Director found cause to fire Kennedy because, according to the Regional Director, Kennedy had made false public accusations about the Regional Director. The statute under which Kennedy was employed provided only for a right to reply to the charges against him. Kennedy alleged that the statute violated his due process rights by failing to provide him a pre-termination judicial-type hearing before an impartial decisionmaker. Kennedy lost in a five-to-four decision, but the bases for the several decisions are more significant than the outcome of the case.

Three Justices (Marshall, Douglas and Brennan) applied a balancing test and concluded that Kennedy was entitled to a pre-termination judicial-type hearing before an impartial decisionmaker. Justice White used the same balancing test as the basis for his opinion that Kennedy was entitled to a decision by a neutral decisionmaker, but not to a judicial-type hearing. Two Justices (Powell and Blackmun) used the *Mathews* balancing test, but concluded that the statutory procedures met that test. The final three Justices (Burger, Rehnquist, and Stewart) concluded that the Court had no power to require procedures greater than those required by the legislature.

88.   416 U.S. 134 (1974).

Since the legislature was the source of Kennedy's property interest, those three Justices expressed the opinion that the legislature had total discretion to limit the scope of that interest by specifying the procedures that accompany the interest. Several Justices have urged adoption of the legislative judgment test in other cases, but it was explicitly rejected by an eight-Justice majority in *Cleveland Board of Education*.[89]

§ 6.3.4   Application of the *Mathews* criteria

Since most of the Court's recent decisions apply the balancing test in *Mathews* as the dominant method of determining the procedures required by due process, it is useful to consider the factors to be balanced in some detail. The *Mathews* test can be expressed in the form of the formula: $C = P \times V$, where C is the cost of providing an additional safeguard, P is the increased probability of an accurate finding on a contested factual issue resulting from provision of the additional safeguard, and V is the value of the individual interest at stake. The additional procedures should be required if, but only if, P times V equals or exceeds C. Viewed in this manner, the *Mathews* test is analogous to Learned Hand's famous formula for determining negligence[90]—the formula always produces the "right" result *if* only we know C, P, and V.

§ 6.3.4a   Private interest affected

The nature of protected interests adversely affected by agency decisions varies widely. Under *Mathews,* a court first must determine the amount of adverse impact on the individual affected, or the V term in the formula. Many adverse impacts of agency actions cannot be expressed easily in monetary equivalents. To illustrate some of the problems courts experience in applying *Mathews,* however, we will begin with the simplifying assumption that all adverse affects of agency actions have monetary equivalents.

Assume that each of three individuals alleges a violation of due process rights. The first, an electric utility, claims that it was arbitrarily deprived of ten million dollars through a decision of a regulatory agency. The second, a very successful jockey, alleges that the racing commission arbitrarily suspended him for fifteen days, thereby causing him to lose fifty thousand dollars. The third individual is an impoverished widow with four young children who argues

---

89. *See supra* § 6.3.1c.

90. *See* United States v. Carroll Towing Co., 159 F.2d 169 (2d Cir.1947).

that she was arbitrarily deprived of two hundred dollars in welfare payments.

In purely objective terms, the value of the interest at stake in the first example is two hundred times the value of the second and fifty thousand times the value of the third. We doubt, however, that most people would be comfortable with this objective method of valuing individual interests for due process purposes. Nor do we believe that courts do, or should, use this method. Rather, courts value the adverse impact of the agency action subjectively, that is, in terms of the adverse impact of the deprivation on the typical utility, jockey, or welfare recipient, respectively. Thus, some judges would consider the utility's interest greater than the interests of the jockey or the welfare recipient; some judges would consider the interests approximately equal; still others would consider the interests of the welfare recipient greater than the interests of the utility or the jockey. When we remove the unrealistic simplifying assumption that all interests can be expressed in monetary equivalents, the subjectivity of the valuation process becomes even more apparent. Judges must place implicit values on intangibles like a policeman's interest in a good reputation and a student's interest in not being paddled.

The subjective nature of the valuation of interests required by the *Mathews* test forms the basis for two frequent criticisms—the *Mathews* test requires judges to insert their own subjective values into constitutional decisionmaking and, since subjective values differ substantially among judges, the results of the *Mathews* test are predictable only within a relatively wide range of uncertainty. We will return to these two criticisms after we have discussed the other two criteria in the *Mathews* test.

§ 6.3.4b   The value of additional procedures

In the second part of the *Mathews* test, a court must determine "the risk of an erroneous deprivation of such interest through the procedures used, and the probable value, if any, of additional or substitute procedural safeguards". This part of the test requires a court to determine the nature of the factual issues that are most likely to be dispositive of a class of disputes between individuals and agencies, and then to estimate the marginal contribution to the accuracy of the resolution of those factual disputes that would result from requiring the agency to add one or more procedural safeguards, *e.g.,* more specific notice of reasons for a proposed action, rights to discovery, cross-examination. Two generally accepted principles are useful starting points in this process.

First, if there is no dispute concerning a material fact, the *Mathews* test requires no hearing safeguards. If the agency and the individual disagree only with respect to the way in which the law applies to an uncontroverted set of facts, additional procedures cannot possibly enhance the accuracy of the fact-finding process, simply because the agency does not need to resolve any factual controversies. This is a familiar principle that administrative law borrows from the concept of summary judgment in civil procedure. Of course, some procedures, like notice and an opportunity to respond, are necessary before an agency can determine whether there are controversies concerning material issues of fact.

The second principle that is useful as a starting point is Professor Davis' famous distinction between adjudicative facts and legislative facts. We cannot improve upon Professor Davis' description of this distinction and its significance to his analysis of procedural issues:

> "Adjudicative facts usually answer the questions of who did what, where, when, how, why, with what motive or intent; adjudicative facts are roughly the kind of facts that go to a jury in a jury case. Legislative facts do not usually concern the immediate parties but are the general facts which help the tribunal decide questions of law and policy and discretion.
>
> . . .
>
> Facts pertaining to the parties and their businesses and activities, that is, adjudicative facts, are intrinsically the kind of facts that ordinarily ought not to be determined without giving the parties a chance to know and to meet any evidence that may be unfavorable to them, that is, without providing the parties an opportunity for trial. The reason is that the parties know more about the facts concerning themselves and their activities than anyone else is likely to know, and the parties are therefore in an especially good position to rebut or explain evidence that bears upon adjudicative facts. Because the parties may often have little or nothing to contribute to the development of legislative facts, the method of trial often is not required for the determination of disputed issues about legislative facts."[91]

Professor Davis' extensive writings on the legislative-adjudicative fact distinction have had a major impact on judicial attitudes toward

---

91. 2 K. Davis, *supra* note 14, at § 12.3. *See also* R. Pierce, Administrative   Law Treatise § 9.2 (4th ed. 2002).

the need for judicial-type hearings to resolve factual controversies. The important distinction he draws is now reflected as well in the language of Federal Rule of Evidence 201. That rule implicitly authorizes federal judges to take judicial notice of legislative facts without providing parties a formal opportunity to challenge those facts.

A pair of polar examples illustrate the potential utility of the distinction between adjudicative and legislative facts. Consider first the issue of whether A or B struck the first blow in a fight. The issue is specific and unique to the litigation between A and B. The parties are particularly well-situated to assist the trier-of-facts in resolving the issue through testimony and cross-examination. This is a classic issue of adjudicative fact.

By contrast, consider the issue presented to, and resolved by, the Court in *Brown v. Board of Education*[92]—are separate educational facilities for racial minorities inherently unequal? This too was an issue of contested fact, but one of a very different nature. It was general. Its resolution was crucial to millions of people, rather than just to the specific parties. In resolving an issue of this type, no court or agency would or should limit itself to evidence presented by the parties. Rather, the decisionmaker relies principally upon the vast social science literature relevant to the issue. Oral testimony and cross-examination of witnesses is little help to a court or agency in resolving this type of issue and is not required by due process. This is a classic issue of legislative fact.

We agree completely with Professor Davis' conclusion that judicial-type hearings should not be required to resolve contested issues of legislative fact, and the courts seem to have embraced this part of his analysis. Professor Davis' approach does not produce a clear resolution of all questions concerning the procedures appropriate for resolution of contested issues of fact, however, for three reasons.

First, as Professor Davis recognizes, agencies frequently are called upon to resolve factual issues that are difficult to classify as legislative or adjudicative. For instance, agencies frequently confront controversies concerning such factual issues as the relative net economic benefits of alternative projects, the existence or non-existence of an active seismic fault, the ability of steel pipe of a given specification to withstand extreme ambient temperatures, and the degree of carcinogenic potential of a pesticide.[93] Each of these issues of fact is

92.   347 U.S. 483 (1954).   **93.**   *See* Pierce, *supra* note 75, at 48–53, 84.

more general than who struck the first blow in a fight, but more specific than whether separate educational facilities are inherently unequal. Similarly, each of these issues falls somewhere between the separate but equal issue and the who struck the first blow issue with reference to the extent to which oral testimony and cross-examination would enhance the accuracy of the fact-finding process. Thus, factual issues do not fall neatly into one of two categories. Instead, an agency or court must determine where each issue lies on a functionally defined continuum, that is, a continuum that is based on the extent to which additional procedures will enhance accuracy in finding that fact.

Second, not all controversies concerning adjudicative facts require use of a judicial-type hearing. In many cases, the nature of a contested adjudicative fact renders it subject to resolution with an acceptable degree of accuracy through the use of procedures less costly and time consuming than a judicial-type hearing. The *Mathews* case itself provides a good illustration of this point. Whether a social security recipient remains disabled is a classic issue of adjudicative fact. Yet, the Court held the procedural sequence of medical examinations, written reports, and written responses adequate to satisfy due process. The Court has long recognized that procedures other than a judicial-type hearing are appropriate for resolving some issues of adjudicative fact.[94]

Finally, the legislative-adjudicative fact distinction cannot be used alone to resolve most procedural issues, since the extent to which additional procedures will enhance the accuracy of fact-finding is only one of three factors a court must consider in deciding what procedures are required by due process. In *Mathews,* for instance, the Court did not conclude that oral testimony and cross-examination would not enhance accuracy at all. Rather, the Court concluded that the marginal contribution of those additional procedures to the accuracy of the fact-finding process was not sufficient to justify the large increase in costs resulting from the use of such procedures given the nature of the individual interest at stake.

The nature of the contested facts is an important component of the due process calculus established in *Mathews* because additional procedures enhance accuracy in finding some facts more than others. The legislative-adjudicative fact distinction is a useful starting point

---

94. *See, e.g.,* North American Cold Storage Co. v. Chicago, 211 U.S. 306 (1908) (permitting destruction of poultry determined by inspection to be putrid, subject only to the owner's right to file a subsequent tort action to establish that the poultry was not putrid).

because a judicial-type hearing is a virtually useless extravagance as a means of resolving classic issues of legislative fact. Formal procedures are likely to be more useful and less expensive when factual controversies are more specific and more directly tied to the parties. Even with respect to classic issues of adjudicative fact, however, the Court frequently does not require a judicial-type hearing as a matter of constitutional law because the costs of requiring such a procedure exceed its benefits as a means of assuring accuracy.

§ 6.3.4c   The cost of additional procedures

Some of the costs of providing additional procedural safeguards are readily apparent. Judicial-type hearings require, for instance, trial lawyers, administrative law judges, and stenographers. These direct personnel costs alone can be very high when an agency must resolve tens of thousands or even hundreds of thousands of factual disputes annually.

Formal procedural safeguards can impose even greater indirect costs on agencies, on society, and even on the class of individuals that are the putative beneficiaries of the procedures. The nature and magnitude of these indirect costs varies with the decisionmaking context. In the welfare benefit termination context, for instance, formal pre-termination procedures delay terminations of benefits to individuals no longer eligible, thereby increasing the welfare agency's cost of providing benefits. This, in turn, increases society's costs to the extent that the legislature increases total appropriations for welfare. To the extent the legislature does not increase total appropriations for welfare, all increased costs resulting from constitutionally imposed procedural safeguards inevitably reduce the total amount of benefits available to the entire class of eligible individuals.

In the regulatory context, use of formal procedures delays resolution of issues on which private investment decisions are predicated, thereby creating prolonged periods of uncertainty that harm society by retarding investment. Formal procedures also increase the cost of participating effectively in regulatory proceedings, thereby limiting the effective participation of poorly funded groups such as environmental organizations and consumer representatives.[95] Thus, the *Mathews* test requires a court to analyze with some care the decisionmaking context in order to identify all of the direct and indirect costs of requiring an agency to provide an additional or substitute procedural safeguard.

95. *See* Pierce, *supra* note 75, at 18–30.

The Seventh Circuit took an interesting approach to applying the *Mathews* test in *Van Harken v. Chicago.*[96] Courts usually engage only in crude verbal characterizations of the benefits and costs of a procedure urged by an individual who alleges that the procedures made available by an agency are unconstitutionally inadequate. In *Van Harken*, the court actually made quantitative estimates of the additional benefits and costs of the procedure at issue. Like many municipalities, the City of Chicago decriminalized its legal regime applicable to violations of parking rules. Chicago replaced the previously available full trial with a system in which a nonjudicial city employee conducts a hearing at which the parking ticket is given the same legal effect as the live testimony of the policeman who issued the ticket. If the nonjudicial employee finds that the ticketed individual committed the infraction, the individual can appeal to a court. Van Harken argued that the new system violates due process, and that the City was required to return to the earlier system of judicial adjudication of alleged violations of parking laws. The court estimated that adoption of the procedures urged by Van Harken would cost the City 134,000 police hours per year and would confer benefits of only $1.38 on each innocent recipient of a parking ticket. The court had no difficulty rejecting Van Harken's due process argument. Making quantitative estimates of the costs and benefits of the procedure at issue is useful, at least where the benefits of additional procedures are easy to quantify. In such cases, a court may discover that the costs of a procedure are enormous and the benefits are trivial.

§ 6.3.4d   Criticisms of the *Mathews* test

Critics of the balancing test set forth in *Mathews* emphasize the difficulty of identifying, implicitly quantifying, and then balancing three disparate factors: (1) significance of interest at stake, (2) extent to which additional procedures will enhance accuracy, and (3) cost of additional procedures. The difficulty of this task can lead to two problems. The first step—determining the significance of the interest at stake—requires each Justice to insert his or her subjective view concerning the relative value of welfare benefits, a fair rate of return, a government job, a person's reputation, access to government provided educational benefits, freedom from corporal punishment, and hundreds of other objectively incomparable interests that qualify as life, liberty, or property. Thus, the *Mathews* test forces each Justice

---

96.   103 F.3d 1346 (7th Cir.1997).

276 JUDICIAL CONTROL—PROCEDURAL ISSUES   Ch. 6

to determine the scope of a constitutional right by reference to his or her subjective values.

Second, since each Justice is likely to place a different value on these interests and is likely to come to different conclusions concerning the marginal contribution and the costs of providing additional procedures, the results of application of the *Mathews* test to a class of disputes is unpredictable within a wide range of possible procedures until the Court actually decides a case involving that class of disputes. We recognize these two shortcomings, but still prefer the *Mathews* approach to any alternative that has been identified to date.

The *Mathews* test requires each Justice to place a subjective value on particular protected interests, but in the context of a flexible outcome balancing test where differences in subjective values typically produce only modest differences in the required procedural safeguards. This seems far preferable to the Court's earlier right-privilege approach in which each Justice's subjective valuation of interests was sub rosa and the result was either a full judicial-type hearing or no procedural protection at all, depending on the subjective value the Justices attached to the interest at stake. Moreover, there is no apparent alternative to subjective judicial valuation of interests for due process purposes that would protect the values the Due Process Clause is intended to protect. Objective judicial valuation of protected interests is both impossible and inappropriate.[97] If the judiciary does not insert its subjective values, some other government institution must. If the judiciary defers to legislative or executive value judgments, as a plurality of the Court argued it should in *Arnett*, the result would be total emasculation of the Due Process Clause.[98]

It is difficult to predict the precise result of application of the *Mathews* test to a class of disputes until the Court decides a case within that class. Lack of predictable results is a disadvantage of the flexible balancing approach, since uncertainty may force conservative agencies to adopt formal procedures to avoid the risk of reversal on constitutional grounds. It is easy to make too much of this disadvantage, however, for two reasons. First, the results of the *Mathews* test will become more predictable over time as the Court decides more cases using that test. For instance, the Court's many post-*Goldberg* opinions now suggest strongly that welfare termination may be the *only* context in which due process compels an agency to provide a judicial-type trial before it takes an action that adversely affects an individual. Second, as long as the Court requires only the *minimum*

97. *See supra* § 6.3.4a.   **98.** *See supra* § 6.3.1c.

procedural safeguards justified by the *Mathews* balancing test, legislatures and agencies should experience little difficulty drafting statutory and regulatory provisions that provide procedures adequate to withstand an attack under the Due Process Clause without imposing excessive costs on the government.

The *Mathews* cost-benefit analysis compares the costs of adding procedures with the benefit those procedures provide only to adversely affected individuals. Legislatures and agencies, by contrast, should balance those same costs against the *total* benefits resulting from the use of additional procedures. Those total benefits encompass the often independent interests of society and government in an accurate decisionmaking process. Thus, as long as legislatures and agencies make a good faith effort to select procedures based δn a balancing of total costs and benefits, the procedures they choose rarely will be vulnerable to attack under the *Mathews* test. Application of the more narrow cost-benefit analysis required by *Mathews* will result in reversal only when the legislature or the agency has not made a good faith effort to provide adequate procedural safeguards or when the Court's subjective valuation of the interests at stake differs substantially from the implicit values of the legislature or the agency. Thus, the *Mathews* test serves the constitutional values that underlie the Due Process Clause—protection of individuals from arbitrary adverse actions by the government.

§ 6.3.5 Summary and postscript

The jurisprudence on the Due Process Clause is vast and not entirely consistent. In this section, we will summarize the current state of the law, distinguishing carefully between issues that have been clearly resolved, issues that are subject to continuing controversy among the Justices, and our own views on how the Court should resolve those issues.

The Court asks two questions in addressing any due process issue today—(1) Does the Due Process Clause apply to the agency action at all? (2) If so, what procedures are required by due process? The first question can be further divided into two parts. (1) Does the agency action adversely affect an interest protected by the Due Process Clause? (2) Does the agency action adversely affect the protected interests of an individual or relatively few individuals?

In answering the first part of the first question, the Court begins its analysis by deciding whether the interest affected is "life," "liberty," or "property". The Court has not adopted a consistent approach to determining whether an interest falls into one of these categories.

Although the Court claims that it no longer distinguishes between property "rights" recognized at common law, and government benefits that are mere "privileges," the Court's decisions of the past thirty years suggest that it is merely moving the traditional line dividing "rights" and "privileges" in order to encompass within the Due Process Clause some as yet uncertain proportion of government benefits conferred by statute. The scope of the concept of "liberty" similarly is not clear. Thus, for instance, an individual's interest in a reputation free of arbitrary stigmatization by government agencies sometimes is included in the concept of liberty, but sometimes it is not.

Some Justices had concluded that the Court did not have the power to compel an agency to provide procedural safeguards greater than those required by the legislature where the legislature has created a protected interest and simultaneously has circumscribed that interest with procedures provided by statute. In a few cases, a majority of the Court appeared to have accepted that approach. The Court, however, recently rejected that theory on the ground that it would emasculate the Due Process Clause. As a result, the Court will conclude that an interest either is or is not protected by due process by determining first whether that interest is recognized by the Constitution, the common law or statute, and second whether the interest is sufficiently important to justify constitutional protection through application of the Due Process Clause.

We find the Court's decisions categorizing interests as protected or unprotected by due process unsatisfactory. A shifting majority of the Court relies upon inconsistent methods of analysis from one case to another. Some of the decisions can only be explained as the product of largely unstated differences of opinion among the Justices concerning the subjective value each attaches to different types of interests. Several sets of cases decided in the past thirty years seem irreconcilable on the basis of any principled distinction. Specifically, in the area of government employment relationships, we are unable to reconcile *Arnett, Bishop,* and *Owen;* in the area of reputational interests, we are unable to reconcile *Constantineau, Paul* and *Owen;* and, in the area of the interests of students, we are unable to reconcile *Goss* and *Ingraham.*

We would like to see the Court begin to introduce a greater degree of consistency and principle in its decisions concerning the nature of interests that are entitled to due process protection. We believe that the Court could accomplish this by adopting the Davis-

Van Alstyne approach.[99] Under this approach, any agency decision that has a substantial adverse impact on an individual would be subject to due process protection. To date, however, the Court has declined to adopt this approach.

If the Court decides that the interest affected by the agency action is protected by due process, it still may decline to require the agency to adopt particular procedures to protect that interest. Whether the Court will require particular procedures depends on the number of people whose interests are affected and, perhaps, on the basis on which those interests are affected. In *Londoner* and *Bi–Metallic,* the Court distinguished between agency actions that affect "a relatively small number of persons . . . in each case upon individual grounds" and actions "where a rule of conduct applies to more than a few people". This distinction is fundamental to an understanding of administrative procedure. It means at least that the Court will not require a judicial-type hearing under the Due Process Clause when an agency acts in a way that affects a large number of people in the same general manner. At most, the Court will require an agency to provide an informal proceeding emphasizing notice and an opportunity to protest.

We believe that the *Londoner–Bi–Metallic* distinction should be interpreted even more broadly to mean that the Due Process Clause does not apply at all if the agency action deprives a large group of people of an otherwise protected interest. We base our argument on the belief that procedural safeguards are necessary only to protect individuals from arbitrary government action; the political process provides adequate protection for large groups of people. Some recent decisions suggest that the Court shares our view of this issue,[100] but some respected commentators interpret *Londoner* and *Bi–Metallic* to stand for the more limited proposition that judicial-type procedures are not required when agency actions with widespread effect are predicated on the resolution of general or "legislative" facts.

If the Court concludes that the Due Process Clause applies to an agency action, it must then determine the minimum procedures the agency must provide in deciding whether to take that action. The requirements of due process are flexible—due process can require procedures that vary along a spectrum from the formal judicial-type

---

99. *See supra* § 6.3.1.

100. *E.g.,* Minnesota State Board for Community Colleges v. Knight, 465 U.S. 271 (1984); Vermont Yankee Nuclear Power Corp. v. NRDC, 435 U.S. 519, 542 (1978); United States v. Florida East Coast Railway Co., 410 U.S. 224, 246 (1973).

hearing mandated in *Goldberg* to the informal exchange of views compelled in *Goss*.

Similarly, the timing of the required procedures can vary depending on the decisionmaking context. In some circumstances, all of the procedures must be provided in advance of the agency action, but in most cases an agency can base its action on summary procedures as long as it provides the adversely affected individual a reasonably prompt subsequent opportunity to contest the agency's action through the use of all the procedural safeguards required by due process. Thus, for instance, an agency cannot terminate certain types of welfare benefits without a pre-termination hearing because this type of action would place an individual in an "immediately desperate" situation.[101] On the other hand, an agency can terminate a government employment relationship without first providing all the procedures required by due process as long as it provides those procedures within a reasonable time after termination of the employment relationship.[102] In each case, the Court's determination of when the procedures must be provided depends on its evaluation of the detriment to the individual resulting from deferral of the procedures versus the costs to the agency resulting from deferral of the action until all procedures have been provided.

In most cases, the Court uses the three-part balancing test announced in *Mathews* as the basis for its determination of both the timing and the nature of the procedures required by due process:

> "[I]dentification of the specific dictates of due process generally requires consideration of three distinct factors: First, the private interest that will be affected by the official action; second, the risk of an erroneous deprivation of such interest through the procedures used, and the probable value, if any, of additional or substitute procedural safeguards, and finally, the Government's interest, including the function involved and the fiscal and administrative burdens that the additional or substitute procedural requirement would entail."

The first part of the test requires the Court to place a subjective value on each of the many interests that can be adversely affected by an agency action. The third part requires the Court to identify carefully all of the direct and indirect costs of requiring an agency to

---

101. Goldberg v. Kelly, 397 U.S. 254 (1970).

102. Gilbert v. Homar, 520 U.S. 924 (1997); Arnett v. Kennedy, 416 U.S. 134 (1974).

adopt procedures more demanding than those required by the legislature.

The second part of the *Mathews* test requires the Court to focus on the nature of the factual controversy and the extent to which additional procedural safeguards can enhance the agency's accuracy in finding facts of that type. Two general principles are helpful in the process of applying step two. First, if there is no factual controversy before the agency, the *Mathews* test does not require the use of any procedures. If due process requires any procedures in this circumstance, it requires only those procedures necessary to permit the agency to determine whether there is a factual controversy. Second, if the only factual controversy before the agency is with reference to a "legislative fact," as opposed to an "adjudicative fact," the agency is not required to provide any formal procedure for the resolution of that fact. Beyond these two helpful principles, it is difficult to generalize about the likely outcome of application of the *Mathews* test to a particular type of factual issue. The balancing process required by *Mathews* frequently does not compel an agency to use formal judicial-type procedures even when its action depends on its resolution of an adjudicative fact.

§ 6.4　Statutes as a Source of Procedural Requirements

Statutes are the dominant source of the procedures agencies must follow. An agency must refer to at least two statutory sources to determine the procedures it is required to use in a given case—the Administrative Procedure Act[103] (APA) and the organic act that authorizes the agency to take the action under consideration. The statutorily required procedures can be determined only by reading the relevant provisions of the two statutes together and analyzing the interrelationship between the two.

The APA sets forth four types of procedures potentially available to agencies—formal adjudication, informal adjudication, formal rulemaking and informal rulemaking. The APA was enacted in 1946 in response to the need to rationalize federal agency decisionmaking procedures and to provide greater uniformity and predictability in the procedures used by agencies. The New Deal had produced a dramatic increase in both the number of federal agencies and the breadth of the powers of those agencies. By 1946, scores of federal agencies had the power to take actions with substantial impacts on private rights and on public welfare. The organic acts that created each agency and empowered it to act in various ways typically said

---

103.　5 U.S.C. §§ 551–706, reproduced in Appendix.

little about the procedures the agency was required to use. As a result, each agency adopted its own idiosyncratic procedures. The procedures employed to perform similar functions varied widely from one agency to another and sometimes even from case to case in the same agency. This situation created concerns of two types. First, in some cases the procedures seemed inadequate to protect the private parties affected by agency actions from arbitrary deprivation of their rights and to insure agency decisionmaking that furthers the public good. Second, the lack of uniformity in federal agency decisionmaking procedures made it difficult for parties to participate effectively in agency proceedings because they often could not predict in advance the procedures an agency would use to make a particular decision. Passage of APA in 1946 culminated over a decade of consideration of the most appropriate response to the dual problems of inadequate agency procedures and lack of uniformity and predictability of agency procedures.[104]

Two of the four procedures described in APA have close analogues in the legal system. Formal adjudication looks very much like a judicial trial, complete with an independent Administrative Law Judge (ALJ) and oral presentation of evidence subject to cross-examination. It is designed to serve functions analogous to those of a judicial trial—resolution of factually based disputes between individuals whose conduct is regulated by an agency and between the agency and such individuals. Informal rulemaking closely resembles the process of enacting legislation. The agency is not required to use an independent ALJ or to provide an opportunity for oral testimony and cross-examination. It can act through the far less formal sequence of issuing a notice of its intent to act, providing an opportunity for individuals and groups to comment in writing on its proposed action, and accompanying its final action with a statement of basis and purpose. Functionally, informal rulemaking is well-suited to quasi-legislative tasks—establishing rules applicable to groups of people.

The procedures required for formal adjudication and for informal rulemaking differ dramatically in ways that parallel the functions of the two types of proceedings. In formal adjudication, as in a judicial trial, the emphasis is on procedural protection of the rights of the individuals participating in the proceeding. In informal rulemaking, as in the process of enacting legislation, the emphasis is on procedures that maximize the likelihood of establishing a rule that will best serve the public welfare. The third procedure described in APA—formal rulemaking—is a strange combination of the other two.

104. *See supra* §§ 2.2 and 2.3.

It requires an agency to provide almost all of the rigorous procedural safeguards usually associated with resolution of a factual dispute between individuals even though the agency is considering a rule applicable to a group of people.

The fourth procedure—informal adjudication—is used in more cases than any of the other three procedures. It is governed only by APA § 555, which provides for few procedural safeguards. There are three other potential sources of procedural safeguards applicable to an informal adjudication: the statute that authorizes the agency to take the action at issue, agency rules, and the Due Process Clause. In *Pension Benefit Guarantee Corp. v. LTV Corp.*,[105] the Court held that a court cannot require an agency to use procedures greater than those required by one of those sources of authority when an agency engages in informal adjudication. We will discuss the procedures applicable to informal adjudication in greater detail in § 6.4.10.

The APA describes the four procedures available to agencies, but it does not direct any agency to use a particular procedure. Instead, it refers to provisions of agency organic acts as the basis for determining which of the procedures described in APA an agency is required to use in taking particular types of actions. For instance, an agency is required to use formal adjudication only in the case of "adjudication required by statute to be determined on the record after opportunity for an agency hearing".[106] In addition, Congress sometimes supplements or modifies one of the generic procedures described in the APA in the context of particular types of actions taken by an agency through the procedural provisions it includes in an agency's organic act. Thus, the APA and agency organic acts must be read in *pari materia* in order to determine the procedures an agency must follow in a given case.

In the early years following passage of the APA, the Court seemed to read the Act as a codification of the requirement of a "hearing" rooted in the Due Process Clause. *Wong Yang Sung v. McGrath*[107] is the best example of these early interpretations. *Wong Yang Sung* involved a dispute concerning the adequacy of the hearing required to determine whether to deport a resident alien. Immigration authorities gave Wong Yang Sung a hearing before ordering his deportation, but that hearing did not include all the procedural safeguards required by APA for formal adjudication. Most significantly, the Immigration Service did not provide an independent judge to

105. 496 U.S. 633 (1990).
106. 5 U.S.C. § 554(a).

107. 339 U.S. 33 (1950), *modified,* 339 U.S. 908 (1950).

preside at the hearing—one of the procedural safeguards central to formal adjudication under the APA. As a result the outcome of the dispute between Wong Yang Sung and the government concerning the adequacy of the hearing depended on whether the APA provisions for formal adjudication applied to deportation cases.

The Immigration Service argued that it was not required to comply with APA procedures for formal adjudication because those procedures apply only to "adjudication required by statute to be determined on the record after opportunity for an agency hearing," and the statute authorizing deportation of aliens did not contain this requirement. The Court held the APA's procedures for formal adjudication applicable to deportation proceedings, however, based on an entirely different reasoning process. It noted that it had previously held the Due Process Clause applicable to deportation proceedings. It observed that: "When the Constitution requires a hearing, it requires a fair one, one before a tribunal which meets at least prevailing standards of impartiality." The Court then reasoned that the formal adjudication procedures prescribed by Congress when it enacted APA indicated the "prevailing standards of impartiality" that must be satisfied by any constitutionally compelled hearing. It followed from this reasoning that any agency action subject to due process protection at all had to be undertaken through use of the full judicial-type procedures required by APA for formal adjudication. For a brief period, the Court interpreted and applied *Wong Yang Sung* in this extremely broad manner, holding that a wide range of agency actions were subject to the APA's formal adjudication procedures whether or not the agency's organic act required those procedures.[108]

Within a few years, the Court abandoned this initial attempt to interpret APA as delineating the requirements of due process. Congress was unhappy with the results of the Court's decision in *Wong Yang Sung*. It passed legislation that specifically exempted deportation proceedings from the APA requirements for formal adjudication and prescribed separate decisionmaking procedures for deportation proceedings. In *Marcello v. Bonds*,[109] the Court upheld the new procedures under the Due Process Clause, thereby implicitly overruling that portion of its opinion in *Wong Yang Sung* that suggested that the formal adjudication procedures described in the APA represent the minimum procedural safeguards required for agency actions within the scope of protection of the Due Process Clause.

108. *See, e.g.* Cates v. Haderlein, 342 U.S. 804 (1951); Riss & Co. v. United States, 341 U.S. 907 (1951).

109. 349 U.S. 302 (1955); *see* Schuck, *The Transformation of Immigration Law,* 84 Colum.L.Rev. 1, 30–34 (1984).

In *Marcello,* the Court recognized that Congress often had good reasons for requiring different procedures for resolving different types of disputes because of the nature and context of the decisions to be made. Congress is free to establish different decisionmaking procedures for different agencies and different types of decisions as long as the procedures it establishes do not fall below the minimum procedures required by due process. Since *Marcello,* the Court determines the adequacy of the procedures used by an agency through independent analysis of the requirements of statutes and of the Constitution.[110] The Court has recognized that, in many circumstances, an agency hearing can be substantially less demanding than the formal adjudication procedures of the APA and still comply with due process. Indeed, the procedural safeguards embodied in APA formal adjudication exceed the maximum protection required by due process for almost all agency decisions.[111]

§ 6.4.1　Agency choice of rulemaking or adjudication

Adjudication is best-suited to one class of agency actions—resolution of factual disputes between individuals or between an agency and an individual. Informal rulemaking is best-suited to another class of agency actions—establishment of rules applicable to groups of people. The APA does not, however, limit an agency's power to select procedures in accordance with these functionally based distinctions.

An agency can use rulemaking to promulgate any "rule," and the APA defines rule to include an "agency statement of general or particular applicability and future effect designed to implement, interpret, or prescribe law or policy. . . . ''[112] Thus, an agency can use rulemaking procedures to resolve a factual controversy between individuals or between the agency and an individual. In taking such actions, an agency can use informal rulemaking procedures unless Congress has required it to use formal rulemaking or due process requires it to provide additional or substitute procedural safeguards. We will reserve detailed discussion of this topic until later in this chapter.[113]

Similarly, an agency can establish general rules applicable to large groups of people through an order issued in a proceeding

---

110. In cases where the procedures required by a statute are unclear, however, the Court continues to resolve the ambiguity in favor of an interpretation that eliminates the need to resolve the issue under the Due Process Clause. *See,* *e.g.,* Califano v. Yamasaki, 442 U.S. 682 (1979).

111. *See supra* § 6.3.3.

112. 5 U.S.C. § 551(4).

113. *See infra* § 6.4.5.

conducted as an adjudication. This power is entirely consistent with the analogy between adjudication and a judicial trial, since courts frequently resolve specific disputes by announcing generally applicable rules that affect large groups of people through the concepts of precedent and stare decisis. Congress can compel an agency to take a particular type of action either through adjudication or through informal rulemaking, but it rarely exercises that power. EPA and the Centers for Medicare and Medicaid Services(CMS) are notable exceptions. Their organic acts include numerous provisions that require them to address specific issues by issuing rules.

Since agencies, unlike courts, usually have a choice of using adjudication or rulemaking, they could be expected to use the procedure that seems functionally most appropriate to the decision the agency must make. Yet, agencies sometimes perceive their best interests to lie in the use of procedures that are functionally inappropriate. Professor Bernstein argues, for instance, that the National Labor Relations Board's (NLRB) notorious preference for formal adjudication as its primary vehicle for establishing general rules is based on its peculiar political vulnerability.[114] If the NLRB announces a general rule in a rulemaking, its action appears to be a major policy decision that it must defend in Congress against inevitable harsh attacks by important segments of the public. If, instead, a general rule just happens to emerge from NLRB's resolution of a specific factual controversy, its decision is less obviously based on policy considerations. It can defend its action more easily by referring to the mass of specific evidence before it that justified its application of the rule to the specific controversy before it at the time.

The near universal judicial and scholarly criticism of agency use of adjudication as a vehicle for formulating general rules is based on considerations that can be placed in four general categories: quality, efficiency, fairness and political accountability.[115] Formulation of a general rule through adjudication of a specific dispute produces low quality decisions for two reasons. First, participation in adjudication

114. Bernstein, *The NLRB's Adjudication—Rule Making Dilemma Under the Administrative Procedure Act*, 79 Yale L.J. 571, 598 (1970); *see generally* Scalia, *Back To Basics: Making Law Without Rules,* Regulation, July/Aug., 1981, at 25 (predicting agency return to use of adjudication to avoid White House oversight and hybrid rulemaking procedures).

115. *See* McCubbins, Noll & Weingast, *Administrative Procedures as Instruments of Political Control*, 3 J.L.Econ. & Org. 243 (1987); Shapiro, *The Choice of Rulemaking and Adjudication in the Development of Administrative Policy,* 78 Harv.L.Rev. 921 (1965). *See also* Robinson, *The Making of Administrative Policy: Another Look at Rulemaking and Adjudication and Administrative Procedure Reform,* 118 U.Pa.L.Rev. 485 (1970).

is limited by the doctrine of standing to those few people who are directly affected by the outcome of the adjudication.[116] As a result, the agency's decision is based on the views of only a small fraction of the total number of people affected by a general rule. By contrast, since the outcome of a rulemaking obviously has widespread impact, all parties potentially affected by the rule under consideration can participate. Second, decisionmaking through adjudication typically focuses on myriad facts unique to the dispute before the agency. This emphasis on what may well be idiosyncratic specific facts diverts the agency's attention from the broad policy implications of the rule under consideration. In a rulemaking, the agency must focus its attention instead on the issue of how alternative rules will affect national social welfare by shaping the future conduct of large numbers of people.

Determining broad rules through formal adjudication is inefficient for several reasons. First, when formal adjudication is used as a means of exploring the many effects of a proposed rule, a single proceeding can be very expensive and time-consuming. The technique of amassing evidence through oral testimony and cross-examination, that is so effective as a means of resolving discrete factual disputes between two parties, breaks down completely in multi-party, multi-issue agency adjudication. In these circumstances, a single adjudication can require more than a decade to complete at a cost of many millions of dollars in fees to lawyers and expert witnesses.[117] Second, the expensive process of formal adjudication may have to be repeated in subsequent cases. An agency cannot apply a fact specific rule of conduct derived from one adjudication in a second adjudication without providing the parties to the second proceeding an opportunity to establish that their factual situation supports a different rule. Third, rules of conduct extracted from an adjudication tend to be considerably less clear in scope and content than rules that result from rulemaking. A rulemaking is designed to produce a rule that can guide all conduct in the area, and the agency must strive for simplicity and clarity in expressing the rule. By contrast, deriving a rule from a lengthy opinion issued in a complicated adjudication is precisely analogous to determining the holding of a complicated court case. The resulting "rule" can be interpreted in very different ways by the many parties affected by the rule.

Making general rules of conduct through rulemaking enhances agencies' political accountability for their policy decisions in two

---

116. *See supra* §§ 5.4 and 5.5.　　　　**117.** *See* Pierce, *supra* note 75.

ways. First, the prior notice of a proposed legislative rule required by APA § 553 provides the most politically accountable institutions of government—Congress and the President—an opportunity to influence an agency's choice among alternative rules of conduct. Second, the policy decisions on which a rule is based are obvious to Congress and to the President when an agency announces a rule of conduct through rulemaking. If those politically accountable institutions disagree with the policy premises of the rule, they can influence the agency to change its rule, or they can mandate a change in the rule through statutory enactment. By contrast, when an agency announces a "rule" through a decision in an adjudication, the policy premises of the rule are often buried in a lengthy opinion dominated by discussion of the specific facts of a dispute. The agency can insulate its policies from Congressional and Presidential oversight by making the disingenuous claim that it makes no policy decisions; rather, it decides all cases based solely on the specific facts presented.

Finally, formulating general rules through adjudication is unfair in three ways. First, relying entirely on adjudication creates substantial potential for inadvertent or even intentional disparate treatment of similarly situated parties. The process of formulating and implementing a rule through adjudication must start with a specific case involving particular parties. The parties to the initial proceeding may be adversely affected by the rule many years before similarly situated parties, simply because of the sequence in which the agency conducts its proceedings. Second, determining and announcing rules of conduct through rulemaking provides potentially affected parties superior notice of prohibited and permitted conduct. If the agency chooses to proceed only through adjudication, affected parties have no way of determining the legality of their conduct in advance of an agency decision that may have retroactive effect. As a result, they may unwittingly violate the law for years until the agency finally tells them what the law is and acts against them for violating it. Third, determining general rules in an adjudication involving one or a few individuals deprives the many other parties affected by the rule of any opportunity to participate in the process of shaping the rule.

Given this impressive list of criticisms of agency reliance on adjudication to formulate general rules, it is not surprising that courts attempt to encourage agencies to place greater reliance on rulemaking. Courts use three indirect methods of encouraging agencies to use rulemaking. First, courts tend to hold that an agency has the power to issue substantive rules even when Congress has not clearly indicated its intent to grant such authority to the agency.

Second, courts have made it easier for agencies to issue rules by permitting agencies to use efficient procedures for promulgating rules.[118] Third, courts have encouraged agencies to use rulemaking by giving powerful legal effects to rules adopted through rulemaking.[119]

Despite these efforts to encourage rulemaking, some agencies still choose to rely almost entirely on adjudication. Courts occasionally have attempted to require agencies to select appropriate procedures, but their attempts to do so have not been marked by great success. The general rule is that courts cannot interfere with the near total discretion of agencies to choose whether to make rules by rulemaking or by adjudication procedures. The tension between some agencies and the courts in this area is so persistent that it has produced several important court decisions.

§ 6.4.1a   Agency power to make rules

An agency does not even confront the decision whether to act by rulemaking or by adjudication unless it has the power to promulgate rules with legislative effect. The leading case involving the power of an agency to promulgate legislative rules is the D.C. Circuit's opinion in *National Petroleum Refiners Ass'n v. Federal Trade Commission*.[120] The Federal Trade Commission (FTC) is charged with responsibility to enforce the FTC Act's prohibition against "unfair methods of competition in commerce and unfair or deceptive acts or practices in commerce". In an effort to make this vague mandate more specific in a particular context, FTC issued a rule that prohibited retail sales of gasoline without posting the octane rating of the gasoline. National Petroleum Refiners challenged the rule on the basis that Congress had not given FTC the power to issue binding rules at all.

The court's conclusion that Congress had granted FTC the power to issue legislative rules is not nearly as interesting as the reasoning process through which it reached that conclusion. The D.C. Circuit began its opinion by emphasizing that it could not decide the policy question of whether FTC should have rulemaking power, but only the legal question of whether Congress actually gave it that power. A fair reading of the entire opinion suggests, however, that the court's analysis of policy was far more important in explaining its holding than its analysis of congressional intent.

---

118.   *See infra* § 6.4.1.

119.   *See infra* § 6.4.7.

120.   482 F.2d 672 (D.C.Cir.1973), *cert. denied* 415 U.S. 951 (1974). *See also* American Hospital Ass'n v. NLRB, 499 U.S. 606 (1991) (holding that general grant of rulemaking power to NLRB was not limited by requirement that NLRB determine appropriate bargaining unit "in each case.").

The statute clearly gave FTC power to enforce the unfair trade practice prohibition through adjudication. The available evidence of congressional intent suggested that Congress had not given FTC power to enforce that prohibition through issuance of substantive rules. In one provision of the statute, Congress referred to FTC's power to make rules, but the placement and wording of that provision suggested that the reference was limited to procedural rules. The legislative history of the Act indicated that Congress never addressed the issue. That fact alone could have been held dispositive of the issue. Since it was unusual for Congress to grant an agency legislative rulemaking power in 1914 when Congress passed the FTC Act, it is fair to assume that Congress would not have given FTC that power without some discussion of the issue. The subsequent history of the statute both at FTC and in Congress also suggested that the agency did not have power to issue legislative rules to implement its unfair trade practice authority. For almost fifty years after the Act was passed, FTC had not attempted to exercise legislative rulemaking power, and on several occasions it had denied it had that power. In several instances, FTC also had informed Congress that it had no general rulemaking power. It had sought and obtained statutory amendments authorizing it to issue legislative rules with respect to areas of its authority other than unfair trade practices. Notwithstanding this cumulatively powerful evidence that Congress had not given FTC power to issue legislative rules, the court held that FTC had that power, largely because the opposite conclusion "would render the Commission ineffective to do the job assigned it by Congress".

The refiners argued that FTC could not have legislative rulemaking power because that power would be inconsistent with the enforcement procedures prescribed in the statute. The statute required a sequence consisting of: issuance of a complaint, a trial of the contested factual issues, and issuance of a cease and desist order. The court rejected this argument on the basis that the enforcement sequence would remain the same even if FTC exercised legislative rulemaking power. It would still have to go through the same steps. Of course, the trial part of the sequence would be very different in scope and purpose. In the absence of a legislative rule, the defendant could introduce evidence in an attempt to show that its practices were fair. If a party is accused of violating a valid legislative rule, however, the only issue to be tried is whether its conduct violated that rule.

The court then proceeded to describe the policy advantages of allowing an agency to act by legislative rule. Substantive rulemaking power allows an agency to conserve its resources by avoiding the need to relitigate the same issue in several proceedings. It eliminates the unfairness inherent in case-by-case adjudication in which the agency must focus on a single defendant when it attempts to establish a policy for an entire industry. Rulemaking provides all affected interests a "bright line" standard to guide their behavior. Rulemaking also reduces delay in implementation of regulatory policy. For all these reasons, the court concluded that, when faced with what it characterized somewhat disingenuously as ambiguous evidence of legislative intent, FTC should be held to have the power to promulgate legislative rules.

National Petroleum Refiners suggests that a court will hold that an agency has the power to promulgate legislative rules when a statute includes any language that will support such an interpretation. *National Petroleum Refiners* illustrates one of several ways in which courts have encouraged agencies to use rulemaking indirectly—in this case by making the procedure available to the agency at all.

In 1988, the Court reduced significantly the permissible scope of rules issued through the rulemaking process in its surprising opinion in *Bowen v. Georgetown University Hospital.*[121] The Court created a principle of statutory construction that an agency does not have the power to issue rules with retroactive effect unless Congress has explicitly conferred on the agency power to issue rules with retroactive effect. That rule of construction will be dispositive in its application to most agencies because Congress typically grants an agency plenary power to issue rules without specifying the permissible temporal scope of the rules.

The Court seems to have premised the rule of construction it adopted in *Georgetown* on four assumptions: (1) retroactive rulemaking is strongly disfavored in our legal system; (2) when Congress grants an agency plenary power to issue rules, it implicitly intends to limit the agency to issuance of rules with prospective effect only; (3) agencies rarely issue rules with retroactive effect; and (4) a prohibition on use of the rulemaking process to issue rules with retroactive effect will protect citizens from potential unfair treatment by agencies. The Court provided no support for any of these assumptions, and each is insupportable.

Courts routinely create "rules" with retroactive effect by announcing new doctrines in the course of deciding cases. Congress

121.   488 U.S. 204 (1988).

frequently creates rules with retroactive effect through the process of statutory enactment, and the Court regularly acknowledges Congress' power to do so.[122] The power to make retroactive rules is crucial to some agencies' ability to fulfill their statutory missions effectively, particularly in the areas of taxation and economic regulation, where notice of an agency's intent to issue a future rule with prospective effect only will distort private parties' temporal patterns of decisionmaking. Many agencies regularly issue rules with retroactive effect,[123] and the Supreme Court has even compelled an agency to issue a retroactive rule.[124] Moreover, prohibiting use of the rulemaking process to issue rules with retroactive effect will *increase* the risk of unfair agency actions, since agencies remain free to issue "rules" with retroactive effect through the process of informal adjudication, and that process is subject to fewer constraints on agency discretion than is the rulemaking process.[125]

The Court seemed to reduce the scope of the rule of construction announced in *Georgetown* in its unanimous 1996 opinion in *Smiley v. Citibank*.[126] The Court applied a legislative rule to two transactions that took place long before the agency issued the rule. That holding was obviously inconsistent with the rule of construction announced in *Georgetown*. The Court did not mention *Georgetown* or retroactivity in the text of its opinion. In footnote 3, however, the Court stated "there might be substance to" the petitioner's argument that the rule was impermissibly retroactive if the rule had "replaced a prior agency interpretation." The Court continued:

> Where, however, a court is addressing transactions that occurred at a time when there was no clear agency guidance, it would be absurd to ignore the agency's current authoritative treatment of what the statute means.

Thus, *Smiley* suggests that the prohibition on retroactive rulemaking announced in *Georgetown* applies only when an agency attempts to apply a legislative rule retroactively to govern transactions that were subject to a prior, inconsistent, legislative rule at the time they took place.

---

122. *See, e.g.,* Landgraf v. USI Film Products, 511 U.S. 244 (1994); PBGC v. R.A. Gray & Co., 467 U.S. 717 (1984); Baltimore & Susquehanna R. Co. v. Nesbit, 51 U.S. (10 How.) 395 (1850). *See generally* Hochman, *The Supreme Court and the Constitutionality of Retroactive Legislation,* 73 Harv.L.Rev. 692 (1960).

123. *See, e.g.,* American Public Gas Ass'n v. FPC, 567 F.2d 1016 (D.C.Cir. 1977), *cert. denied,* 435 U.S. 907 (1978).

124. Addison v. Holly Hill Fruit Products, 322 U.S. 607 (1944).

125. *See supra* § 6.4.1 and *infra* §§ 6.4.6 and 6.4.10.

126. 517 U.S. 735 (1996).

The Court seemed to reduce the scope of the *Georgetown* holding still further in its 1998 decision in *Regions Hospital v. Shalala.*[127] An agency applied a cost reimbursement rule it issued in 1989 as the basis to disallow some costs that were incurred in the prior three years. The petitioner argued that the agency's action violated the *Georgetown* prohibition on retroactive rules. The Court rejected that argument. It held that the rule was not given retroactive effect because the agency applied it only to future years and to the three prior years that were still open to audit by the agency.

The rule of construction announced in *Georgetown* creates a serious practical problem in many circumstances. The notice and comment procedure that agencies must use to issue most legislative rules can take years to complete. During the pendency of that rulemaking process, there often is no legislative rule that governs a class of transactions. Agencies have attempted to address this problem in various ways, with disparate reactions from courts.

Some agencies issue interpretative rules that purport to govern a class of transactions during the period prior to the agency's issuance of a legislative rule. See § 6.4.4 for a discussion of interpretative rules. The Fifth Circuit upheld that approach in *Carpenters District Council v. Dillard Department Stores.*[128] However, the D.C. Circuit held that the *Georgetown* prohibition on retroactive rules also applies to interpretative rules in *Health Insurance Ass'n v. Shalala.*[129]

Some agencies rely on the good cause exemption from the notice and comment procedure to justify issuance of an interim emergency legislative rule that will govern transactions that take place during the period in which the agency is conducting the notice and comment proceeding required to issue a permanent legislative rule. See § 6.4.4d for a discussion of the good cause exemption. Courts seem to have become more receptive to agency attempts to invoke the good cause exception for this purpose in light of the practical problems created by the *Georgetown* prohibition on retroactive rules.[130]

Of course, as discussed in § 6.4.1b, most agencies also have the discretion not to issue rules at all and simply to resolve all disputes in adjudicatory proceedings in which the agency adopts and applies particularized interpretations of the typically broad and ambiguous

---

127. 522 U.S. 448 (1998).

128. 15 F.3d 1275 (5th Cir.1994). *Accord* Cowen v. Bank United of Texas, 70 F.3d 937 (7th Cir.1995).

129. 23 F.3d 412 (D.C.Cir.1994).

130. *See, e.g.,* Service Employees International Union v. County of San Diego, 60 F.3d 1346 (9th Cir.1994); Hawaii Helicopter Operations Ass'n v. FAA, 51 F.3d 212 (9th Cir.1995).

language of the statute it is implementing. That approach produces far greater potential for unfairness, however, because it often produces decisions in which an individual or a firm is held to have violated a statute by engaging in conduct that it did not recognize to be a violation of the statute at the time it engaged in the conduct. Courts limit agencies' discretion to engage in this practice, however, by applying a multi-part balancing test that has the effect of filtering out cases in which an agency's retroactive interpretation of an ambiguous statute or rule would produce manifestly unfair results.[131]

The rule of construction announced in *Georgetown* also has induced courts to change their approach to the remedies they choose when they conclude that an agency has made a procedural error in the process of issuing a legislative rule. Prior to the issuance of the *Georgetown* opinion, circuit courts regularly vacated and remanded agency rules when they concluded that the agency had not complied with the notice and comment procedure in some respect or that the agency's decision to issue the rule was arbitrary and capricious because the agency had not adequately discussed an important issue. See § 6.4.6 for a discussion of rulemaking procedures and the application of the arbitrary and capricious test to rules issued through use of the notice and comment procedure. After *Georgetown*, however, a judicial decision vacating a rule would have the undesirable effect of creating a period of time in which no valid rule applies to a class of transactions. Circuit courts have reduced this potential adverse effect of the *Georgetown* opinion by changing the remedy they apply when they conclude that an agency has erred in the process of issuing a rule. In a high proportion of such cases, a circuit court now remands the rulemaking for additional agency proceedings, but it does not vacate the rule.[132] That practice is controversial, however. Two judges have expressed the view that a court is required to vacate an agency action when the agency committed a procedural error in taking the action or failed to provide adequate reasons to support the action.[133]

§ 6.4.1b Judicial oversight of agency choice of procedures

The first major dispute concerning agency choice of procedures reached the Supreme Court in *Securities & Exchange Commission v.*

---

131. *See, e.g.,* General Electric Co. v. EPA, 53 F.3d 1324 (D.C.Cir.1995); NLRB v. Majestic Weaving Co., 355 F.2d 854 (2d Cir.1966).

132. *See, e.g.,* Idaho Farm Bureau Federation v. Babbitt, 58 F.3d 1392 (9th Cir.1995); Allied–Signal, Inc. v. NRC, 988 F.2d 146 (D.C.Cir.1993).

133. Milk Train v. Veneman, 310 F.3d 747 (D.C. Cir. 2002); Checkosky v. SEC, 23 F.3d 452, 466 (D.C.Cir.1994).

Chenery Corp.[134] Chenery Corporation sought judicial review of a Securities and Exchange Commission (SEC) order disapproving as inequitable Chenery's proposed reorganization under the Public Utility Holding Company Act. SEC disapproved the reorganization because of certain stock transactions engaged in by the company's management during the process of reorganization. Chenery asked the Court to reverse the SEC order on the basis that SEC had not previously established any general standards for management stock trading during reorganization. Chenery argued that it was unfair for SEC to declare a practice improper retroactively in an adjudication without first issuing a general rule prohibiting the practice.

The Court recognized that it had previously encouraged agencies to use rulemaking whenever possible, and it reaffirmed its preference for rulemaking. It refused to reverse the SEC action, however, and declined to impose any "rigid requirement" that agencies establish general rules only by rulemaking. The Court's statement of its reasons for refusing to interfere with SEC's choice between adjudication and rulemaking in *Chenery* remains the best single explanation for the judicial reluctance to interfere with an agency's choice of procedures:

> "Not every principle essential to the effective administration of a statute can or should be cast immediately into the mold of a general rule. Some principles must await their own development, while others must be adjusted to meet particular, unforeseeable situations. In performing its important functions in these respects, therefore, an administrative agency must be equipped to act either by general rule or by individual order. To insist upon one form of action to the exclusion of the other is to exalt form over necessity.
>
> In other words, problems may arise in a case which the administrative agency could not reasonably foresee, problems which must be solved despite the absence of a relevant general rule. Or the agency may not have had sufficient experience with a particular problem to warrant rigidifying its tentative judgment into a hard and fast rule. Or the problem may be so specialized and varying in nature as to be impossible of capture within the boundaries of a general rule. In those situations, the agency must retain power to deal with the problems on a case-to-case basis if the administrative process is to be effective. There is thus a very definite place for the case-by-case evolution of

---

134.   332 U.S. 194 (1947).

statutory standards. And the choice made between proceeding by general rule or by individual, ad hoc litigation is one that lies primarily in the informed discretion of the administrative agency."

Thus, while courts have a strong preference for agency reliance on rulemaking, they recognize that many regulatory problems are not susceptible to resolution through rulemaking, because: (1) the agency could not foresee the problem; (2) the agency does not yet know enough about the problem to be confident of any generalized solution; or (3) the problem is so variable in nature or context that the agency needs to retain the flexibility to resolve it in different ways through case-by-case adjudication.

The next time the Court addressed the issue of an agency's choice between adjudication and rulemaking, the Justices divided three ways, indicating wide divergence in their approach to the issue. *National Labor Relations Board v. Wyman–Gordon Co.*[135] involved an attempt by NLRB to apply in one adjudication a general rule it had announced in an earlier adjudication. In *Excelsior Underwear,* NLRB had announced what it called the *Excelsior* rule, requiring employers to furnish to all unions involved in a representation election a list of the names and addresses of all employees eligible to vote in the election. NLRB had announced the *Excelsior* rule without applying it in the case in which it announced the rule. It then attempted to apply its *Excelsior* rule to Wyman–Gordon by issuing an order in an adjudication requiring that company to provide unions with employee names and addresses. Wyman–Gordon challenged the NLRB order on the basis that NLRB was attempting to enforce a rule that had not been promulgated in accordance with APA rulemaking procedures.

The four Justices who joined in the plurality opinion seemed to accept almost all of Wyman–Gordon's arguments. They concluded that the APA procedures for rulemaking were carefully designed to maximize fairness and adequate consideration of the factors important to the determination of a rule of general applicability, and that NLRB could not avoid those procedures by making general rules through adjudication. In particular, the plurality recognized that making rules through adjudication eliminated two major advantages of APA rulemaking—general notice of the proposed rule and opportunity for participation in the proceeding by all parties potentially affected by the rule. The plurality also recognized that an agency inevitably has the power to establish some general rules through

135.   394 U.S. 759 (1969).

adjudication if it announces its decision and the basis for that decision in one case and then uses that case as precedent to guide its decision in the next case, in the traditional manner of courts. The plurality concluded, however, that NLRB had not followed this permissible sequence in establishing its *Excelsior* rule because it had not even applied that rule to the parties to the proceeding in which it first announced the rule. Thus, the plurality felt that NLRB had attempted inpermissibly to engage in pure rulemaking without following rulemaking procedures.

At this point in the opinion, it would be logical to expect the plurality to hold the NLRB order invalid. Instead, the plurality affirmed the order because NLRB could have issued that order even in the absence of its announcement of its *Excelsior* rule in a prior adjudication.

Before discussing the very different approaches taken by the concurring and dissenting Justices, it is useful to focus on two features of the *Excelsior* rule and the order upheld in *Wyman–Gordon*. First, the rule announced in *Excelsior* was not the type of rule that depends for its validity on any particular findings of fact. It was a rule based purely on policy considerations. Subsequent cases indicate that this is an important distinction, since an agency cannot rely on a factually based rule developed in a prior adjudication as its basis for resolving the same issue in a later adjudication, without providing the parties to the later adjudication an opportunity to challenge the factual predicate for the rule.[136] By contrast, an agency can apply a factually based rule developed through rulemaking in an adjudication without permitting the parties to the adjudication to challenge the factual premises of the rule.

Second, NLRB did not rely on the *Excelsior* rule as a self-implementing rule of conduct that employers were required to follow at their peril without further agency action. Rather, NLRB issued an order prior to the election specifically directing *Wyman–Gordon* to furnish the list of employee names and addresses. The plurality emphasized that, while the NLRB order was valid, *Wyman–Gordon* had no duty to comply with the *Excelsior* rule in the absence of an agency order specifically directing it to supply the list contemplated by *Excelsior*. This is a second important distinction between a rule adopted through adjudication and a rule adopted through rulemaking. Only rules adopted through rulemaking can be self-implementing.

136. *See infra* § 6.4.7.

Three Justices concurred with the result reached by the plurality in *Wyman–Gordon,* but based their concurrence on a different process of reasoning. The concurring Justices objected to what they saw as inconsistent reasoning reflected in the plurality's dual conclusions that the procedures used by NLRB were improper, but that the order resulting from the use of those procedures was valid. Instead, the concurring Justices upheld the order on the basis that the NLRB followed permissible procedures in establishing a general rule in an adjudication. The concurring opinion reasoned that an agency can create a rule through adjudication as long as the rule is adopted as "a legitimate incident of a specific case before it, . . . " The concurring Justices were not troubled by NLRB's failure to apply its new rule in the very adjudication in which it announced that rule. They accepted NLRB's explanation that it declined to apply its rule retroactively to the conduct of the company involved in that litigation because retroactive application would penalize the company for engaging in conduct it reasonably believed to be lawful based on NLRB's prior decisions. As the concurring Justices pointed out, courts look with disfavor upon agency attempts to apply retroactively rules of conduct that constitute changes in announced agency policy. They will affirm retroactive application of such rules in adjudications only when they conclude that the regulatory necessity for the agency to apply its new policy retroactively is so great as to counterbalance the unfairness of penalizing a party for conduct it reasonably believed to be permissible.[137]

The two dissenting Justices took an entirely different view of the issue in *Wyman–Gordon.* They agreed with the plurality's conclusion that NLRB violated the APA by promulgating a rule without following rulemaking procedures, but thought the logical consequence of that conclusion had to be a holding that the order based on the rule was invalid. Since NLRB gave its *Excelsior* rule prospective effect only, and did not apply it to resolve the *Excelsior* dispute, the dissenting Justices concluded that it was a rule. As such, it was invalid because of NLRB's failure to follow APA rulemaking procedures. The dissenting Justices agreed that it would be unfair to apply the *Excelsior* rule retroactively to the parties to the *Excelsior* case, but thought this provided even greater support for their conclusion that NLRB should have used rulemaking procedures. They reasoned that: "it is precisely in these situations, in which established patterns

137. *Compare* Leedom v. International Atkinson Co., 195 F.2d 141 (9th Cir. al Bhd. of Electrical Workers, 278 F.2d 1952). 237 (D.C.Cir.1960), *with* NLRB v. Guy F.

of conduct are revolutionized, that rulemaking procedures perform
... vital functions.... "

The major explanation for the difference between the views of
the dissenting Justices and the majority Justices in *Wyman–Gordon*
lies in the implicit value they place on rulemaking procedures. The
Justices in the majority undoubtedly would have preferred that
NLRB use rulemaking procedures to adopt its *Excelsior* rule. They
recognized, however, that forcing an agency to use rulemaking as the
exclusive method of establishing general rules of conduct would
reduce the potential effectiveness of the agency. The agency's ability
to regulate conduct would be limited by its ability to foresee all
problems susceptible to resolution by general rule. They were not
willing to reduce agency regulatory power to that extent. The dissenting Justices placed such a high implicit value on rulemaking procedures that they were willing to mandate exclusive reliance on rulemaking as the source of general rules even though the result would
be a reduction in the effectiveness of agency regulation proportionate
to each agency's inability to foresee the need for general rules.

The Court's opinion five years later in *National Labor Relations
Board v. Bell Aerospace Co.*[138] suggested that the controversy over
agency choice of procedures evident in *Wyman–Gordon* had ended.
NLRB had long held that all "managerial employees" were outside
the scope of the National Labor Relations Act. It changed that
interpretation substantially in the course of an adjudication by holding that managerial employees are in the scope of the Act unless the
nature of their managerial responsibilities creates a conflict between
their interests as union members and their interests as managers.
The Second Circuit reversed the NLRB order on the basis that an
agency should use rulemaking procedures when it announces a
general change in a longstanding policy.

The Supreme Court reversed the Second Circuit and affirmed the
NLRB. Three Justices dissented on another basis, but the Justices
were unanimous in approving NLRB's use of adjudication to announce its general change in policy. The Court quoted extensively
from *Chenery* and held "that the choice between rulemaking and
adjudication lies in the first instance within the Board's discretion".
It added that "there may be situations where the Board's reliance on
adjudication would amount to an abuse of discretion or a violation of
the Act, ... " but it did not give any examples of such situations. The

138. 416 U.S. 267 (1974).

reluctance of courts to interfere with agency choice of procedures since *Bell Aerospace* suggests that such situations are rare.

Morton v. Ruiz[139] is the only case in which the Court actually reversed an agency action in part because it was based on a general policy that was developed through adjudication instead of rulemaking. Mr. Ruiz applied to the Bureau of Indian Affairs (BIA) for general assistance benefits. BIA refused to grant Mr. Ruiz' application on the basis of a policy stated in one of its internal manuals, and apparently developed through adjudication, that limited eligibility for such benefits to Indians that live on a reservation. The Court reversed the BIA action on the grounds that it was based solely on a rule that was not promulgated through use of APA rulemaking procedures.

The dispute in *Ruiz* has several unusual features that suggest that the holding in that case has precedential value only in very limited circumstances. First, the Court identified the major evil of BIA's action as its failure to provide public notice of its rule. Since the parties affected by the rule were not likely to have ready access to legal advice based on research of the internal manuals and results of prior adjudications of BIA, that failure to provide public notice created the clear potential for Indians to leave the reservation without realizing that they were relinquishing their right to benefits by doing so. Second, the adverse consequences of BIA's failure to provide public notice of its rule were severe—the potential to extinguish all rights to benefits otherwise available to members of a class of needy individuals. Third, BIA violated its own stated policy of publishing all eligibility requirements for benefits. Thus, the BIA action could have been held invalid solely on the independent ground that an agency must follow its own rules.[140]

Appellate court decisions reversing an agency's action because of its choice of procedures also are rare. Except for cases involving the special problem of retroactive application of changes in policy, *Ford Motor Co. v. Federal Trade Commission*[141] is one of the few cases in which a federal appellate court reversed an agency order on the basis that the agency should have acted by rulemaking instead of by adjudication. In *Ford,* the Ninth Circuit reversed an FTC order holding that a specific car dealer's repossession practices violated the FTC Act. It based its reversal on the Supreme Court's dictum in *Bell Aerospace* that an agency's decision to proceed by adjudication in-

---

139. 415 U.S. 199 (1974).

140. *See supra* § 6.1.

141. 673 F.2d 1008 (9th Cir.1981), *cert. denied* 459 U.S. 999 (1982).

stead of by rulemaking might constitute an abuse of discretion in some circumstances. The Ninth Circuit concluded that FTC had abused its discretion in the circumstances of the *Ford* case because: (1) FTC had a pending rulemaking to consider the same conduct that was at issue in the Ford adjudication; (2) the practice banned in *Ford* seemed to be widespread in the industry; (3) FTC decided the *Ford* case on a broad basis equally applicable to other dealers; (4) FTC was unfair in requiring a single dealer to defend an industry-wide practice; (5) rulemaking procedures were better suited to the legal and policy issues involved; and, (6) there was no obvious reason FTC could not proceed through rulemaking. The Ninth Circuit's decision in *Ford* almost certainly is an aberration. It has been severely criticized.[142] It is inconsistent with both *Chenery* and *Bell Aerospace*. Indeed, even the Ninth Circuit seems not to have followed it in subsequent cases.[143]

Rulemaking procedure offers so many obvious advantages as a vehicle for considering the adoption of general rules of conduct that courts will continue to be tempted to try to force agencies to use rulemaking for that purpose. Courts rarely will yield to that temptation, however, because of their recognition that no one but the agency involved can consider adequately all of the complicated factors relevant to its choice between rulemaking and adjudication.

Courts are willing to require an agency to act by rulemaking in one situation, however. Occasionally, Congress explicitly requires an agency to implement a statute, or a provision of a statute, by issuing legislative rules. In that situation, a court is required to enforce the statutory command. Thus, for instance, the Medicare statute requires the Secretary of Health and Human Services (HHS) to reimburse healthcare providers in accordance with methods prescribed by legislative rules issued through use of the notice and comment process. HHS has issued 620 pages of legislative rules that describe the basic principles it will use in resolving reimbursement disputes. Those rules do not clearly resolve all of the hundreds of issues that arise in reimbursement disputes, however. HHS has supplemented its legislative rules with thousands of pages of interpretative rules that provide more detailed guidance with respect to HHS reimbursement decisions. In *Shalala v. Guernsey Memorial Hospital*,[144] the Justices

142. *See, e.g.,* American Bar Association Administrative Law Section, Resolution and Report (1983); R. Pierce, *supra* note 91, at § 6. 9.

143. *See, e.g.,* Cities of Anaheim, Riverside, Banning, Colton and Azusa v.

FERC, 723 F.2d 656 (9th Cir.1984); Montgomery Ward & Co. v. FTC, 691 F.2d 1322 (9th Cir.1982).

144. 514 U.S. 87 (1995).

divided on the question whether HHS had complied with its statutory duty to issue legislative rules to govern issues that arise in reimbursement disputes. A five-Justice majority held that the HHS legislative rules were adequate, even though they left important details to be addressed in interpretative rules. The four dissenting Justices argued that HHS had not complied with its statutory duty because the HHS legislative rules left an important issue unresolved.

§ 6.4.1c Judicial incentives to use rulemaking

Courts can be expected to continue to encourage agencies to use rulemaking through indirect means—(1) by holding that agencies have rulemaking power in situations where the existence of that power is in doubt; (2) by making it less expensive and less time-consuming for agency's to use rulemaking procedures; and, (3) by giving powerful legal effect to rules adopted through rulemaking procedures. The D.C. Circuit's opinion in *National Petroleum Refiners* illustrates the first method.[145] We will discuss several illustrations of the second method in subsequent sections of this chapter.[146] The FTC's choice of adjudication over rulemaking that the Ninth Circuit found inexplicable in *Ford* shows how important it is for Congress and the courts to make rulemaking a reasonably rapid and inexpensive procedural option for an agency. FTC undoubtedly chose to proceed by adjudication in its attempt to regulate the repossession practices of auto dealers in part because its rulemaking proceeding on the same subject was progressing very slowly. This slow progress was attributable to a statutory amendment to the FTC's organic Act that required it to add expensive additional procedures to the efficient and expeditious APA procedures for informal rulemaking.[147]

The contrast between the Fifth Circuit's decision in *Shell Oil Co. v. Federal Energy Regulatory Commission*[148] and the Supreme Court's decision in *Heckler v. Campbell*[149] illustrates the third method by which courts indirectly encourage agencies to use rulemaking as the principal method of resolving general regulatory issues—by giving rules adopted through rulemaking greater effect than rules adopted through adjudication.[150] In *Wyman–Gordon,* the Court held valid a National Labor Relations Board order based solely on a general rule of conduct announced in a prior adjudication. The Court emphasized, however, that NLRB had the power to issue the order in

---

145. *See supra* § 6.4.1a.

146. *See infra* §§ 6.4.5 and 6.4.9a.

147. *See infra* § 6.4.9b.

148. 707 F.2d 230 (5th Cir.1983).

149. 461 U.S. 458 (1983).

150. *See also infra* § 6.4.7.

question independent of the rule it previously announced. NLRB had this power because its rule was based solely on policy considerations and not on the resolution of any factual issues. *Shell* demonstrates the significance of this limitation of the scope of the holding in *Wyman–Gordon*.

Shell involved an attempt by the Federal Energy Regulatory Commission (FERC) to apply in one adjudication a general rule it had adopted in a prior adjudication. The rule was that gas wells drilled through "sidetracking" do not qualify as "new wells".[151] The Fifth Circuit reversed FERC's order on the basis that the rule was premised on a finding of fact—sidetracking does not involve substantial drilling costs—and FERC had not provided Shell an opportunity to contest that fact in the adjudication. The court recognized in dicta that FERC could have relied on its rule without providing Shell an opportunity to contest the factual predicate for that rule in the adjudication if the rule had been validly adopted in a rulemaking proceeding. This recognition was based on a critical procedural distinction between rulemaking and adjudication. Shell could not have participated in the prior adjudication in which FERC announced its rule, but it could have participated in a rulemaking proceeding leading to adoption of the same rule. Thus, it would be fair to hold Shell bound by the results of fact-finding conducted in a rulemaking. It was not fair to hold the company bound by the results of fact-finding in a prior adjudicatory proceeding in which it could not participate.

Heckler v. Campbell provides an illustration of the importance of the dicta in *Shell*. The Department of Health and Human Services (HHS) used rulemaking procedures to establish a "matrix" showing the availability of jobs of different types in the economy. The purpose of the matrix was to eliminate the need to determine job availability in each adjudication concerning eligibility for disability benefits. HHS used the matrix rule as the basis for its finding in an adjudication that there were jobs available for which Ms. Campbell was qualified. HHS denied her application for disability benefits solely on this basis. The Second Circuit reversed, holding that HHS must provide each applicant an opportunity to contest each controverted factual issue in each adjudication. The Supreme Court reversed the Second Circuit and affirmed the HHS order. It held that an agency can apply a rule

---

151. "Sidetracking" is the process of drilling a well by using part of the bore of a preexisting well and then drilling on an angle from a point in the old well bore to a new completion location. Qualification of a well as a "new well" enabled a gas producer to charge a higher ceiling price for gas produced from that well.

to resolve a contested factual issue in an adjudication, as long as the rule was adopted through APA rulemaking procedures and the factual issues resolved in the rulemaking are general rather than specific to the individual.

The Court's decision in *Heckler* was based on its opinions in two famous earlier cases—*United States v. Storer Broadcasting Co.*[152] and *FPC v. Texaco, Inc.*[153] This trilogy of cases stands for the important proposition that agencies can apply rules adopted in rulemaking proceedings to eliminate the need to allow presentation of evidence on contested factual issues in subsequent adjudications. As a result, rules adopted through rulemaking have legal effects much more powerful than rules adopted through adjudication. An agency can adopt a general rule in an adjudication, but it cannot rely on that rule as a sufficient basis for resolving the same issue in a subsequent adjudication if the validity of the rule depends on the existence of contested facts. Instead, the agency must relitigate the issue and its factual predicate in each case.

§ 6.4.2   The requirement of formal adjudication

As the Court made clear in *Marcello v. Bonds,*[154] an agency is required to use APA formal adjudication only when Congress has directed it to do so.[155] In the APA, Congress directed agencies to use formal adjudication only in cases of "adjudication required by statute to be determined on the record after an opportunity for an agency hearing.... "[156] Thus, a court must address two issues in order to determine whether an agency is required to resolve a dispute through use of formal adjudication. First, is the agency action an adjudication? Second, did Congress require that adjudication "to be determined on the record after opportunity for an agency hearing"? The answer to this question is more important than the answer to the first question because the procedural requirements for informal adjudication are *less* demanding than the procedural requirements for informal rulemaking.[157]

Courts have taken two different approaches in determining whether an agency must use formal adjudication. The first approach, followed by a majority of circuits in the 1970s and early 1980s, is

---

152. 351 U.S. 192 (1956).

153. 377 U.S. 33 (1964).

154. 349 U.S. 302 (1955).

155. *See supra* § 6.4.

156. 5 U.S.C. § 554(a).

157. *Compare supra* § 6.4.6 *with supra* § 6.4.10.

illustrated by the First Circuit's opinion in *Seacoast Anti–Pollution League v. Costle.*[158]

Seacoast involved a challenge to a permit issued by the Environmental Protection Agency (EPA) authorizing the applicant to discharge heated water into an estuary. Seacoast argued that EPA violated APA by following procedures inconsistent with those governing formal adjudication. Thus, the court had to resolve the threshold issue of whether EPA was required by statute to comply with APA formal adjudication procedures.

The court's initial step in resolving this issue was to determine whether the agency action was adjudication at all. It used two lines of reasoning to determine that the EPA action was adjudication. First, the court referred to the APA definition of adjudication. The APA defines adjudication as the process for formulating an order.[159] APA defines order as the disposition of any matter other than by rulemaking but specifically including licensing.[160] Thus, the court concluded that the EPA action was adjudication because it was licensing. Second, to buttress this conclusion, the First Circuit considered the nature of the proceeding. The court concluded that the action was adjudication because it focused on resolution of factual disputes concerning a specific party, rather than policy issues underlying a general rule or standard. That conclusion was questionable, since the dispute focused on a generic scientific relationship—the impact of thermal pollution on marine life. The court's second level of analysis was not particularly important to the outcome in *Seacoast,* since the proceeding fell within the explicit definitional inclusion of licensing as adjudication. In many cases that do not involve licensing, however, the second level of analysis engaged in by the First Circuit is critical to a court's decision, because the definitional boundary between adjudication and rulemaking in the APA is not clear.

The court's conclusion that EPA's action was adjudication did not dispose of the issue of whether EPA was required to use APA formal adjudication proceedings. An agency is required to use APA formal adjudication only when adjudication is "required by statute to be determined on the record after opportunity for an agency hearing.... "[161] Cases interpreting this provision of APA can be divided into several categories. First, there are cases like *Marcello* in which Congress explicitly indicated that the agency is not required to use

---

158. 572 F.2d 872 (1st Cir.1978), *cert. denied,* 439 U.S. 824 (1978).

159. 5 U.S.C. § 551(7).

160. 5 U.S.C. § 551(6).

161. 5 U.S.C. § 554(a).

formal adjudication.[162] Second, there are cases where Congress explicitly indicated its intent to require an agency to use formal adjudication by including in the statute the precise language that triggers the APA formal adjudication provision—"on the record after opportunity for an agency hearing.... " Third, there are cases where the language of the agency's organic act does not include these magic words, but where the legislative history of the statute contains powerful evidence that Congress intended to require the agency to use formal adjudication.[163] In these three situations, the court's task is routine—it determines and defers to congressional intent.

There is a final, surprisingly large class of cases in which the court has a much more challenging task—where the agency's organic act includes ambiguous language such as "after hearing," and the legislative history of the act does not indicate the nature of the hearing Congress intended to require. The statute at issue in *Seacoast* fell in this category. It required a "public hearing," but it did not require that the hearing be "on the record". The court concluded that the ambiguous language of the statute reflected a congressional intent to require formal adjudication based entirely on the following reasoning:

> "We are willing to presume that, unless a statute otherwise specifies, an adjudicatory hearing subject to judicial review must be on the record."

The First Circuit's reasoning is troubling, since the Supreme Court has held consistently since 1972 that ambiguous statutory terms like "hearing" do not alone trigger the APA provisions requiring formal trial-type proceedings.[164] The First Circuit distinguished these cases as dealing only with the rulemaking context. In the context of an adjudication, the First Circuit believed that its presumption in favor of formal trial-type procedures was justified.

During the 1980s, courts increasingly rejected the First Circuit's approach in determining whether an agency must use formal adjudication procedures. The D.C. Circuit's 1989 opinion in *Chemical Waste Management, Inc. v. EPA*[165] illustrates the way in which a majority of circuit courts now resolve disputes concerning the need to use formal adjudication. *Chemical Waste Management* involved a challenge to the validity of a procedural rule in which EPA specifically declined to

---

162. *See supra* § 6.4.

163. *See, e.g.,* Independent Bankers Ass'n v. Board of Governors of the Federal Reserve System, 516 F.2d 1206 (D.C.Cir.1975).

164. *See infra* § 6.4.5.

165. 873 F.2d 1477 (D.C.Cir.1989).

use formal adjudication procedures to determine whether a party must take "corrective action" because it released hazardous waste into the environment. The court held that EPA was not required to use formal adjudication because Congress required only that EPA provide a "public hearing"; Congress did not use the statutory language that triggers a requirement of formal adjudication, "on the record after opportunity for agency hearing."

The language of the D.C. Circuit's opinion in *Chemical Waste Management* illustrates the extent to which judges' views concerning the desirability of formal adjudicatory process changed over the decade of the 1980's. The court stated that an informal exchange of written views was sufficient in "corrective action" proceedings because "the factual issues that . . . arise will relate almost entirely to technical (or policy) matters that create little need to establish witness veracity or credibility through observation of a witness's demeanor on cross-examination and therefore can just as easily (perhaps more effectively) be resolved through analysis of the administrative record and written submissions and oral statements of the parties." The *Chemical Waste Management* panel took the unusual step of circulating its opinion to all D.C. Circuit judges in order to make clear that the circuit was reversing unanimously and en banc its prior presumption that Congress intends an agency to use formal adjudication when it uses the term "hearing" in the context of an adjudication. The circuit expressed the view that prior circuit court opinions, including the First Circuit's opinion in *Seacoast* and the D.C. Circuit's own prior precedents, are inconsistent with the Supreme Court's 1984 opinion in *Chevron v. NRDC*,[166] holding that a court must accept an agency's reasonable interpretation of ambiguous language in an agency-administered statute.

The Supreme Court has not yet explicitly resolved the issue of when an agency is required to use formal adjudication. A sequence of four opinions issued between 1972 and 1990 suggests strongly, however, that the Court would adopt the D.C. Circuit's reasoning in *Chemical Waste Management,* rather than the First Circuit's reasoning in *Seacoast.* In its 1973 opinion in *United States v. Florida East Coast Ry Co.,*[167] the Court held that an agency could fulfill the statutory requirement of a "hearing" through use of an informal written exchange of data and views *in the context of a rulemaking.* In its 1978 opinion in *Vermont Yankee Nuclear Power Corp. v. NRDC,*[168]

---

166. 467 U.S. 837 (1984), discussed *infra* § 7.4.

167. 410 U.S. 224 (1973), discussed *infra* § 6.4.5.

168. 435 U.S. 519 (1978), discussed

the Court held that a court cannot compel an agency to use rulemaking procedures more demanding than those required by statute or by the Constitution. In its 1984 opinion in *Chevron v. NRDC,*[169] the Court held that a reviewing court must accept an agency's reasonable interpretation of ambiguous language in a statute the agency administers. Finally, in its 1990 opinion in *PBGC v. LTV Corp.,*[170] the Court upheld an agency's use of informal adjudication procedures to resolve a dispute involving hundreds of millions of dollars in liability. The Court supported its holding with the following reasons: (1) the "plain language" of the statute did not compel the agency to use formal adjudication; and, (2) *Vermont Yankee*'s prohibition on judicial imposition of procedures greater than those required by statute or by the Constitution applies to adjudications as well as to rulemakings.

§ 6.4.3 The elements of formal adjudication

There is a remarkable similarity between formal adjudication and the procedures traditionally used by trial courts. Almost all the procedural safeguards identified by Judge Friendly as characteristic of judicial trials have near perfect analogues in formal adjudication.[171] Specifically, a party to a formal adjudication is entitled to an unbiased decisionmaker, notice of the proposed action and the basis for that action, right to counsel, opportunity to present evidence orally and to make arguments, opportunity to know the opposing evidence and to cross-examine opposing witnesses, resolution of factual issues based exclusively on evidence admitted at trial, and written findings and conclusions.

§ 6.4.3a The central role of the Administrative Law Judge

All formal adjudications must be presided over by (1) the agency; (2) one or more members of the body which comprises the agency; or, (3) one or more Administrative Law Judges (ALJ).[172] As a practical matter, the presiding officer almost always is an ALJ, simply because most agencies have far too many cases to designate either the agency (usually a cabinet officer, commissioner or collegial body) or a member of the agency (usually one of several commissioners in a collegial body) to preside over any single adjudication.

---

infra § 6.4.9a.

169. 467 U.S. 837 (1984), discussed *infra* § 7.4.

170. 496 U.S. 633 (1990), discussed *infra* § 6.4.10.

171. *See supra* § 6.3.3.

172. 5 U.S.C. § 556(b).

The ALJ presides over the entire trial stage of an adjudication, with the agency assuming a role roughly analogous to that of an appellate court. The ALJ regulates the course of the proceeding, including scheduling, resolution of procedural and evidentiary disputes, and ultimate issuance of an initial decision.

Administrative law judges are almost entirely independent of the agencies at which they preside. Their pay is prescribed by the Office of Personnel Management independent of any evaluations or recommendations made by the agency.[173] An agency can take no action against an ALJ without convincing a separate agency that good cause exists for doing so. The agency must use a formal adjudicatory proceeding to resolve the good cause issue.[174] ALJs are assigned to cases by rotation, and an agency can omit the initial decision of the ALJ assigned to a case only if the ALJ becomes unavailable or the agency finds "that due and timely execution of its functions imperatively and unavoidably so requires".[175] Finally, an ALJ cannot be subject to supervision or direction by any agency employee with investigative or prosecutorial functions and cannot consult any person on any fact at issue in a proceeding without providing all parties notice and opportunity to participate.[176]

In short, ALJs are very nearly as independent of federal agencies as federal trial judges are of the executive branch. This high degree of independence of ALJs from agencies is designed to protect the rights of individuals affected by agency adjudicatory decisions from any potential sources of bias. The high degree of independence of ALJs also can cause serious problems of inter-ALJ inconsistencies in decisionmaking, however.[177]

Many agencies that are not required by statute to act through formal adjudication adopt decisionmaking procedures that are similar to formal adjudication, i.e., they designate individuals to preside over oral evidentiary hearings and to write initial decisions that resolve issues of law and fact based on the evidence presented in the hearing. Most agencies that choose this method of adjudication do not use ALJs as presiding officers, however. Instead, they designate individuals to serve as Administrative Judges (AJs) to preside at their hearings. Agencies rarely use ALJs as presiding officers when they have the discretion to use AJs because ALJs are expensive and are

173. 5 U.S.C. § 5372.

174. 5 U.S.C. § 3105.

175. 5 U.S.C. §§ 557(b)(2), 557(d), 3105.

176. 5 U.S.C. § 554(d).

177. *See* Pierce, *Political Control versus Impermissible Bias in Agency decisionmaking: Lessons from Chevron and Mistretta*, 57 U.Chi.L.Rev. 481 (1990).

not subject to any system of performance evaluation. There are about twice as many federal AJs as federal ALJs. Use of AJs as presiding officers creates a higher risk of biased decisionmaking, however, because AJs are not subject to the many statutory safeguards that insure the decisional independence of ALJs. The Administrative Conference of the United States commissioned a comprehensive study of this phenomenon in 1992.[178] The Conference recommended that Congress enact legislation that would require agencies to use ALJs in a higher proportion of cases, but that Congress also authorize each agency to appoint a Chief ALJ who would have responsibility to evaluate the performance of the agency's ALJs. Most ALJs were livid about the proposal to authorize evaluation of their performance. Congress did not act on the proposal, and two years later Congress abolished the Administrative Conference.

§ 6.4.3b Notice

All persons potentially affected by an agency's resolution of a formal adjudication must be given notice of the time and place of the hearing, the legal and jurisdictional authority for the hearing, and the matters of fact and law asserted.[179] Opposing parties then must be given an opportunity to indicate the factual and legal issues they intend to contest. Again, the analogy to a judicial trial is nearly perfect. The agency files a pleading in the nature of a complaint, and the respondent files a pleading in the nature of an answer.

§ 6.4.3c Presentation of evidence

A party to a formal adjudication can appear in person or through counsel and can present evidence in oral or documentary form.[180] A party must be permitted "to conduct such cross-examination as may be required for a full and true disclosure of the facts".[181] This language seems to provide an ALJ some flexibility to limit cross-examination of opposing witnesses, but in practice ALJs rarely exercise this authority for fear of reversal of the agency's final decision on procedural grounds.[182]

Agencies are not required to use the rules of evidence applicable to courts. Indeed, one of the reasons Congress allocates certain types of disputes to agencies instead of to courts is to eliminate some of the excessively technical aspects of court litigation. Compliance with all

---

178. Verkuil, Gifford, Koch, Pierce & Lubbers, *The Federal Administrative Judiciary* (1992).

179. 5 U.S.C. § 554(b).

180. 5 U.S.C. §§ 555(b), 556(d).

181. 5 U.S.C. § 556(d).

182. *See, e.g.,* Reilly v. Pinkus, 338 U.S. 269 (1949).

the technical formalities of proof would impose a substantial burden on agencies with large caseloads. Moreover, many of the rules of evidence are far more valuable in jury trials than in agency proceedings. Thus, for instance, agencies can admit and rely on hearsay evidence to a greater extent than courts.[183] In addition, agencies frequently permit or require parties to submit direct testimony in "canned" or pre-drafted written form.[184] An agency is not entirely unfettered in its discretion to admit or exclude evidence, however. It must "provide for the exclusion of irrelevant, immaterial, or unduly repetitious evidence."[185] In addition, it may not rely on evidence that a reasonably prudent person would not rely on in conducting his affairs.[186]

§ 6.4.3d Findings and conclusions based exclusively on the record

Upon conclusion of the evidentiary phase of a formal adjudication, the ALJ issues an initial decision that must include "findings and conclusions, and the reasons or basis therefor, on all the material issues of fact, law or discretion presented on the record, . . . "[187] That initial decision becomes the agency's decision unless there is an appeal to the agency or the agency elects on its own motion to review the decision. If an appeal is taken, the parties must be given an opportunity to submit to the agency exceptions to the initial decision and reasons in support of those exceptions.[188] Both the ALJ's initial decision and any subsequent decision by the agency on appeal must be based exclusively on the evidentiary record compiled during the hearing. The agency or ALJ can take official notice of a fact not appearing in the evidentiary record, however, as long as it gives an opposing party an opportunity to rebut that fact.[189] No agency employee involved in the investigation or prosecution of the proceeding can participate in any manner in the decisionmaking in a formal adjudication.[190]

The First Circuit's opinion in *Seacoast Anti–Pollution League v.*

183. *See, e.g.,* NLRB v. Remington Rand, 94 F.2d 862, 873 (2d Cir.1938), *cert. denied* 304 U.S. 576 (1938).

184. *See* Gellhorn, *Rules of Evidence and Official Notice in Formal Administrative Hearings,* 1971 Duke L.J. 1, 37.

185. 5 U.S.C. § 556(d). *See* Pierce, *Use of the Federal Rules of Evidence in Federal Agency Adjudications,* 39 Admin.L.Rev. 1 (1987).

186. *See* Richardson v. Perales, 402 U.S. 389 (1971).

187. 5 U.S.C. § 557(c).

188. 5 U.S.C. § 557.

189. 5 U.S.C. § 556(e).

190. 5 U.S.C. § 554(d).

Costle[191] illustrates some of the important features of formal adjudication under APA, as well as one of the errors courts frequently make in interpreting the APA provisions concerning formal adjudication. After concluding that an Environmental Protection Agency (EPA) proceeding to decide whether to grant a permit authorizing discharge of thermal pollution was a formal adjudication,[192] the court considered Seacoast's allegations that EPA violated APA formal adjudication procedures. The Administrator used a panel of EPA scientists to help him review the initial decision. That panel submitted a report to the Administrator that cited scientific literature concerning the thermal sensitivity of various biota. The Administrator relied on the advice of the panel, including its references to scientific literature, as part of the basis for his decision to grant the permit. Seacoast alleged two errors arising from this procedure: (1) the Administrator erred in relying on the panel's advice in his decisionmaking; and, (2) the Administrator erred in relying on the scientific literature cited by the panel as the basis for one of his findings of fact.

The First Circuit held that the Administrator did not err in relying on the advice of the panel of scientists. It described as one of the major advantages of administrative decisionmaking the ability of the government to apply to complex, multi-dimensional problems a range of scientific expertise far broader than that possessed by any individual decisionmaker. Thus, while the Administrator is charged with exclusive responsibility to make a decision, he can rely on competent subordinates to sift and analyze the evidence on which that decision should be based.

The court came to the opposite conclusion, however, concerning the Administrator's reliance on the panel's references to the thermal sensitivity of various biota. It drew a distinction between permissible reliance on staff to analyze evidence in the record and reliance on evidence not contained in the record. It concluded that agency staff personnel are free to provide evidence "as witnesses, but not as deciders". In this respect, the court made a serious, though relatively common, error.

The court confused disputes concerning adjudicative facts with disputes concerning legislative facts. As we discussed in some detail in the section concerning due process, Professor Davis has identified and developed this important distinction.[193] Adjudicative facts are

---

191. 572 F.2d 872 (1st Cir.1978).

192. *See supra* § 6.4.2.

193. *See supra* § 6.3.4b.

specific to the parties to a dispute, such as who did what and when. Accuracy in resolving disputed adjudicative facts is greatly enhanced by their presentation through oral testimony subject to cross-examination because of the parties' intimate and unique knowledge of those facts. Legislative facts are not unique to a particular dispute but are general facts that are useful in permitting informed interpretation and application of statutory and constitutional provisions. Courts frequently "find" legislative facts, such as whether racial segregation in schools hurts members of a minority race, based on extra record sources. Indeed, this method of proceeding has been enshrined through the concept of the Brandeis Brief and is authorized even in a trial governed by the Federal Rules of Evidence.[194] Courts are not, and should not, be limited to consideration of oral evidence introduced at trial when confronted with the need to resolve issues of legislative fact. It follows that agencies, with their less technical rules of evidence and greater ability to interpret scientific literature, should be free to rely on extra record sources in resolving disputes concerning legislative facts. Reliance on oral testimony subject to cross-examination as the exclusive basis for determining facts like the thermal sensitivity of various biota will produce hearings that are unnecessarily long and costly, combined with "findings" of legislative facts that are less accurate than if the agency was informed by a search of the scientific literature. Seacoast should have been entitled only to an opportunity to rebut in writing the legislative facts of which the Administrator took official notice.

§ 6.4.4   Rulemaking

Rulemaking is analogous to legislating. Indeed, most of this section will focus on the procedures an agency must use to promulgate a particular type of rule, referred to as a legislative rule, whose legal effect is virtually identical to that of a statute. Congress frequently delegates to an agency its power to issue rules of conduct in a specified area. The agency can exercise that power in accordance with the substantive and procedural standards established by Congress. The substantive standards vary in specificity from agency to agency, but many agencies are limited only by broad substantive standards that permit considerable exercise of discretion in agency rulemaking.

The procedures required for agency rulemaking are a product of a combination of the APA and each agency's organic act. Procedurally, the APA divides agency rulemaking into three categories: (1) rules

---

194. Fed.R.Evid. 201 advisory committee notes.

that can be adopted without any procedures; (2) informal rulemaking; and, (3) formal rulemaking. Agency organic acts can specify whether an agency must use formal rulemaking procedures or instead is free to use informal rulemaking procedures. Organic acts also can supplement or supplant the rulemaking procedures set forth in the APA. In addition, it is frequently necessary to compare a rule with the provisions of an agency's organic act in order to determine whether the rule fits within one of the categories for which the APA requires no procedures. Thus, the APA provisions governing rulemaking must be read in conjunction with an agency's organic act in order to determine the nature of the procedures the agency is required to employ in promulgating a rule.

The APA sets forth two alternative procedures for promulgating legislative rules, but it exempts several types of rules from both sets of procedural requirements. The exemptions apply to interpretive rules, procedural rules, general statements of policy, and legislative rules when the agency finds good cause for failing to follow the procedures normally required for legislative rulemaking. These labels are descriptive, but it is often difficult to determine in close cases whether a particular rule falls within one of the statutory exemptions. The APA also exempts rules relating to public property, loans, grants, benefits, contracts, and military or foreign affairs functions.

§ 6.4.4a   Interpretive rules

A legislative rule is binding on agencies, courts and private parties. It creates legally enforceable duties that did not exist before the rule was promulgated. By contrast, an interpretive rule is not binding on a court, although a court's interpretation of the law often is influenced by the existence of an agency's interpretive rule concerning the legal issue before the court. An interpretive rule interprets or clarifies the nature of the duties previously created by passage of a statute or promulgation of a legislative rule. It does not create new duties. An agency frequently has a choice of acting through legislative rule or through interpretive rule, but its choice has important procedural and substantive implications. Two D.C. Circuit decisions illustrate these implications.

Joseph v. United States Civil Service Commission[195] involved a challenge to a Commission rule that added the District of Columbia to the list of local jurisdictions in whose election process government employees could participate notwithstanding the general statutory prohibition on such activities by federal government employees. Mr.

---

195.   554 F.2d 1140 (D.C.Cir.1977).

Joseph asked the D.C. Circuit to reverse the rule on the basis that the Commission did not follow the procedures required to promulgate a legislative rule. The Commission defended the validity of the rule by arguing that it was interpretive and, as such, was exempt from APA rulemaking procedures. The Commission contended that the rule merely interpreted a statutory provision authorizing it to exempt from the statutory prohibition on political activities federal government employees who reside in localities in which the majority of voters are government employees.

The D.C. Circuit held the rule invalid. It concluded that the statutory provision authorized the Commission to act by legislative rule, and that the Commission intended that the challenged rule have the full force of law. Hence, the Commission was required to follow APA rulemaking procedures in promulgating its legislative rule. Since it did not do so, the rule was invalid.

The same court's opinion in *General Motors Corp. v. Ruckelshaus*[196] illustrates the contrasting disadvantage to an agency of acting through an interpretive rule. The Environmental Protection Agency (EPA) issued what it characterized as an interpretive rule requiring any auto maker to submit a plan to remedy defects discovered in a class of vehicles regardless of the age or mileage of the vehicles as long as the defect manifested itself during the useful life of the vehicle. EPA attempted to apply that rule to a class of vehicles manufactured by General Motors. The company challenged the rule and its application on two grounds: (1) it was a legislative rule and, as such, was invalid because EPA did not follow APA rulemaking procedures; and, (2) the rule was substantively invalid because its inclusion of vehicles of all ages was inconsistent with the intent of Congress in authorizing EPA to order remedial plans.

The court rejected General Motors' first argument, holding the rule interpretive rather than legislative. It described the distinction between the two as a product principally of the agency's intent in promulgating the rule. The D.C. Circuit found that EPA never intended its rule to have the force of law, but only to indicate EPA's interpretation of its organic act. Since it was only an interpretive rule, however, the rule could not have controlling effect in resolving the issue it addressed. An interpretive rule has only such persuasive power with a court as is inherent in the quality of the reasoning reflected in the rule itself. The court found the rule unpersuasive because it did not indicate a careful analysis of the issue. As a result,

196.   724 F.2d 979 (D.C.Cir.1983).

the court gave the rule little weight and proceeded to analyze the issue in depth independent of the rule. It concluded that Congress did not intend the interpretation of the statute reflected in EPA's interpretive rule. On that basis, the court held the rule substantively invalid and reversed EPA's order requiring General Motors to remedy defects in a class of relatively old vehicles.

The majority in *General Motors* added a dictum that helps to illustrate part of the significance of the distinction between a legislative rule and an interpretive rule. The majority suggested that EPA might be able to achieve the result it sought through its interpretive rule if it acted instead by legislative rule. The dissenting judge questioned this dictum because it seemed inconsistent with the majority's conclusion that the rule misinterpreted the statute. The majority's observation is both accurate and important. Courts review the substantive validity of legislative rules under a different, more deferential standard of review than they use in reviewing interpretive rules. Because of the many advantages resulting from an agency's use of legislative rulemaking and because of the procedural safeguards inherent in APA informal rulemaking procedures, courts reverse legislative rules only if they are arbitrary and capricious or reflect a statutory interpretation inconsistent with Congress' clearly expressed intention. We shall explore this topic in considerable detail in Chapter Seven.[197]

Courts have experienced considerable difficulty distinguishing between valid interpretative rules and procedurally invalid legislative rules. The D.C. Circuit's opinion in *American Mining Congress v. Mine Safety & Health Administration*[198] is particularly helpful in identifying factors that are useful in making this important distinction. The agency had previously used the notice and comment procedure to issue a legislative rule that required every mine operator to make a report whenever an occupational illness is "diagnosed" in one of its employees. The agency then issued a "Program Policy Letter," in which it stated that a chest x-ray with particular characteristics requires a "diagnosis" of an occupational illness that must be reported. American Mining Congress argued that the letter was an attempt to issue a legislative rule that was invalid because the agency had not used the notice and comment procedure. The agency argued that the letter was a valid interpretative rule.

The court held that the letter was a valid interpretative rule. The Court applied a four-part test:

197. *See infra* § 7.4.   **198.** 995 F.2d 1106 (D.C.Cir.1993).

[I]nsofar as our cases can be reconciled . . . , it is . . . on the basis of whether the purported interpretive rule has "legal effect," which in turn is best ascertained by asking (1) whether in the absence of the rule there would not be an adequate legislative basis for enforcement action or other agency action to confer benefits or ensure the performance of duties, (2) whether the agency has published the rule in the Code of Federal Regulations, (3) whether the agency has explicitly invoked its general legislative authority, or (4) whether the rule effectively amends a prior legislative rule. If the answer to any of these questions is affirmative, we have a legislative, not an interpretive rule.

Unfortunately, the D.C. Circuit changed one part of the excellent *American Mining Congress* test in *Paralyzed Veterans of America v. D.C. Arena.*[199] In *American Mining Congress*, the court held that an agency cannot change a *legislative* rule without going through the notice and comment procedure required to issue a legislative rule. In *Paralyzed Veterans,* the court held that an agency cannot change an *interpretative* rule or an interpretation of a legislative rule without issuing a legislative rule. The holding of *Paralyzed Veterans* is demonstrably wrong,[200] but it is the law in the D.C. Circuit at present.

Although the APA specifically exempts interpretive rules from rulemaking procedures, some agencies voluntarily use some variation of those procedures when they issue interpretive rules that have a significant impact. Agencies are always free to provide procedural safeguards greater than those required by statute or by the Constitution, and in many circumstances the additional procedures voluntarily adopted provide significant benefits to the public and to the agency by permitting more thorough consideration of the issue before the agency. A few courts have held, however, that an agency must provide procedures greater than those required by statute or by the Constitution when it issues interpretive rules with significant impacts.[201] Such decisions almost certainly were overruled by the Supreme Court's holding in *Vermont Yankee Nuclear Power Corp. v. Natural Resources Defense Council, Inc.*[202] that courts rarely have the

---

199. 117 F.3d 579 (D.C. Cir. 1997).

200. Pierce, *Distinguishing Legislative Rules from Interpretive Rules*, 52 Admin. L. Rev. 547 (2000)(relying on statutory language and numerous judicial decisions to demonstrate that the Administrative Procedure Act is simple and symmetrical in this respect—a legislative rule can only be amended or rescinded by issuing another legislative rule, while an interpretative rule can be amended or rescinded by issuing another interpretative rule).

201. *See, e.g.,* Independent Broker–Dealers' Trade Ass'n v. SEC, 442 F.2d 132, 144 (D.C.Cir.1971).

202. 435 U.S. 519 (1978).

power to require agencies to follow procedures more demanding than those required by statute or by the Constitution. We will reserve detailed discussion of that important case for a subsequent section of this chapter.[203]

§ 6.4.4b   General statements of policy

General statements of policy also are exempt from APA rulemaking procedures. The D.C. Circuit's opinion in *Pacific Gas & Electric Co. v. Federal Power Commission*[204] illustrates the traditional judicial approach to distinguishing between legislative rules and general statements of policy. Pacific Gas & Electric (PG & E) challenged an order in which FPC announced a set of priorities for allocating natural gas among customers in the event of a shortage. PG & E contended that the order was invalid because FPC had not followed APA procedures for promulgating a rule. FPC defended the validity of its order on the basis that it was a general statement of policy exempt from APA rulemaking procedures.

The D.C. Circuit affirmed the FPC order, accepting the agency's characterization of the order as an exempt statement of policy. As with the distinction between legislative and interpretive rules, the court relied principally on the agency's intention in taking its action. The court explained the distinction between a legislative (or substantive) rule subject to APA rulemaking procedures and an exempt general statement of policy in clear, concise language:

> "The critical distinction between a substantive rule and a general statement of policy is the different practical effect that these two types of pronouncements have in subsequent administrative proceedings. ... A properly adopted substantive rule establishes a standard of conduct which has the force of law. In subsequent administrative proceedings involving a substantive rule, the issues are whether the adjudicated facts conform to the rule. ... The underlying policy embodied in the rule is not generally subject to challenge before the agency.
>
> A general statement of policy, on the other hand, ... is not finally determinative of the issues or rights to which it is addressed. The agency cannot apply or rely upon a general statement of policy as law because a general statement of policy only announces what the agency seeks to establish as policy. A policy statement announces the agency's tentative intentions for the future. When the agency applies the policy in a particular

203. *See infra* § 6.4.9a.   **204.**   506 F.2d 33 (D.C.Cir.1974).

situation, it must be prepared to support the policy just as if the policy statement had never been issued. An agency cannot escape its responsibility to present evidence and reasoning supporting its substantive rules by announcing binding precedent in the form of a general statement of policy."

The D.C. Circuit then analyzed the order carefully in an effort to determine FPC's intent. It concluded that, while some of the language in the order was ambiguous, FPC intended that its order have the effect only of a general statement of policy. The court's conclusion then became a self-fulfilling prophecy. Since the order was only a general statement of policy rather than a rule, its only effect was to place affected parties on notice concerning FPC's policy preferences at the time it issued the order. FPC could not rely on the order in any subsequent proceeding to support a conclusion or finding of fact or even to shift the burden of proof in a manner consistent with its general policy preference. In short, the order was very nearly a legal nullity, although it had a significant practical effect on all participants in FPC proceedings conducted to allocate shortfalls in natural gas supply. By revealing FPC's approach to the issues, the order allowed parties to use FPC's tentative choice of methodology as a focal point for presentation of evidence and arguments either supporting or attacking the priorities announced in the order.

Unfortunately, the D.C. Circuit muddled the *Pacific Gas & Electric* test in *Appalachian Power Co. v. EPA*.[205] The court replaced the easy-to-apply "legally binding" test with a new "practically binding" test. Under the new test, the D.C. Circuit will refuse to accept an agency's characterization of a document as a statement of policy and will instead characterize it as a legislative rule if the court concludes that the agency is treating the document as if it "is for all practical purposes binding." This test is extremely difficult to apply and it often causes courts to conclude that a statement of policy is a legislative rule simply because agency employees usually adhere to the policy. As the Fifth Circuit recognized in *Professionals and Patients for Customized Care v. Shalala*,[206] the fact that agency employees routinely apply the policy announced in a document is "not particularly probative ... Indeed, what purpose would an agency's statement of policy serve if agency employees could not refer to it for guidance?" Professor Funk has argued persuasively that the *Pacific Gas & Electric* test is much more sensible and easier to apply than the *Appalachian Power* test—a court need only accept an

205. 208 F.3d 1015 (D.C. Cir. 2000).   **206.** 56 F.3d 592 (5th Cir. 1995).

agency's characterization of a document as a non-binding statement of policy and then prohibit the agency from using the document as if it were a legally binding legislative rule.[207]

§ 6.4.4c Procedural rules

Rules "relating to practice and procedure" also are exempt from APA rulemaking procedures. The D.C. Circuit's opinion in *Pickus v. United States Board of Parole*[208] provides a good illustration of the typical judicial method of distinguishing between substantive and procedural rules. Pickus challenged a rule adopted by the Board without complying with APA rulemaking procedures. The rule set forth a relatively mechanical formula for determining the time when any prisoner would be paroled. The Board intended the rule to be binding, but it argued that it was not required to follow APA rulemaking procedures because the rule was procedural.

The Parole Board's rule was procedural in the sense that it prescribed a decisionmaking procedure. The D.C. Circuit held, however, that the rule was substantive for APA purposes because it had "considerable impact on ultimate agency decisions." The court distinguished formalistic procedures, such as timing and format for presentation of evidence and arguments, from decisionmaking procedures that substantially affect the rights of parties. Since the Parole Board rule in *Pickus* fell in the latter category, it was invalid because of the Board's failure to follow APA rulemaking procedures. The distinction drawn by the court in *Pickus* is analogous to the Supreme Court's distinction in *Erie Railroad Co. v. Tompkins*[209] between procedural rules governed by federal law in diversity cases and substantive rules governed by state law in such cases. If a rule is likely to be outcome determinative through its impact on the merits of a case, a court will characterize the rule as substantive rather than procedural.

§ 6.4.4d The good cause exception

The APA exempts even some legislative rules from its rulemaking procedures. An agency is excused from complying with rulemaking procedures if it finds "good cause" for omitting those procedures. The good cause exception is narrowly confined to emergencies in which the exigencies of the situation require immediate action or in which advance notice of the action would harm the public. Even in

207. Funk, *When Is a "Rule" a Regulation? Marking a Clear Line Between Nonlegislative Rules and Legislative Rules*, 54 Admin. L. Rev. 659 (2002).

208. 507 F.2d 1107 (D.C.Cir.1974).

209. 304 U.S. 64 (1938). *See* J. Cound, J. Friedental, A. Miller & J. Sexton, Civil Procedure: Cases and Materials, 359–408 (7th ed. 1997).

such unusual cases, a court typically permits the agency rule to remain in effect only during the period required to replace it with a rule adopted through use of APA procedures.

The Temporary Emergency Court of Appeals' decision in *Nader v. Sawhill*[210] illustrates the limited scope of the good cause exception. Ralph Nader challenged the validity of a rule issued by the Federal Energy Administration (FEA) on the basis that FEA had not followed APA rulemaking procedures. The challenged rule permitted certain oil producers to charge a higher price than previously authorized. The rule was clearly legislative, but the court affirmed it under the good cause exception. The court accepted FEA's argument that the public would have been harmed by the agency's compliance with the notice and comment procedures normally required for legislative rulemaking because providing oil producers advance notice of a future price increase would have induced many producers to withhold oil until after the price increase went into effect, thereby aggravating the then-existing national shortage of oil. The court emphasized that the rule was valid only for the relatively brief period until FEA could replace it with a rule promulgated through APA notice and comment procedures.

As discussed in § 6.4.1a, the Supreme Court's decision in *Bowen v. Georgetown University Hospital*[211] created a serious practical problem. In *Georgetown*, the Court adopted a rule of statutory construction that had the effect of prohibiting most agencies from issuing legislative rules that have retroactive effects. Yet, a reviewing court often concludes that a legislative rule is invalid because the agency committed a procedural error or failed to discuss an important issue adequately. In that situation, *Georgetown* has the potential to create a legal environment in which there is no valid rule that applies to a class of transactions during the potentially long period required to issue a new rule through use of the notice and comment procedure. Courts have been receptive to agency attempts to use the good cause exception to fill the gap in legal authority that otherwise would result from a judicial decision holding a rule invalid because of flaws in the rulemaking process. Thus, for instance, in *Mid-Tex Electric Cooperative v. FERC*,[212] the D.C. Circuit upheld an agency's invocation of the good cause exception to justify its issuance of an interim rule to replace a nearly identical rule the court had previously held to be procedurally invalid. The court upheld the interim rule, even though

---

210. 514 F.2d 1064 (TECA 1975).
211. 488 U.S. 204 (1988).

212. 822 F.2d 1123 (D.C.Cir.1987). *See* discussion in § 6.4.1e.

the agency had not adopted it through use of the notice and comment process, for three reasons. First, the rule was an interim measure adopted in the continuing process of establishing a permanent rule. Second, even though the court had held the earlier rule invalid on procedural grounds, it had upheld the substance of the rule "in substantial measure." Third, the court was persuaded by the agency's argument that continuing its pre-rulemaking policy in effect during the lengthy period required to complete a new rulemaking would be "contrary to the public interest."

As Professor Jordan has documented, the good cause exemption from APA rulemaking procedures is the source of frequent, bitter disputes because it typically requires agencies and reviewing courts to balance two conflicting goals in contexts that implicate deeply held values.[213] The APA procedures for informal rulemaking are designed to serve the important goals of "accurate, well-informed decisionmaking and participant satisfaction with the way government operates." Sometimes emergencies arise in which these goals must be sacrificed in order to permit government to act expeditiously to further goals even more fundamental, *e.g.,* health and safety. Yet, the potential for harm resulting from an agency's inappropriate response to a problem, or a perceived problem, reaches its maximum when the agency believes that it is confronted with an emergency. Hence, the need for well-informed agency decisionmaking is particularly acute when an agency characterizes the situation as an emergency. In this area reviewing courts have little choice but to apply their own necessarily subjective values to determine whether the problem addressed by the agency is so exigent that accuracy and participant satisfaction must be sacrificed to permit an immediate response.

§ 6.4.5 The choice between formal and informal rulemaking

Any rule that has a significant, binding effect on the substantive rights of parties will be characterized as a legislative rule. The APA provides two different procedures for promulgating a legislative rule. The first, called informal rulemaking, consists of public notice of the proposed rule, an opportunity for affected members of the public to comment on the proposal, and publication of the final rule accompanied by a statement of its basis and purpose. Informal rulemaking resembles the process of legislating, but with somewhat more struc-

---

213. Jordan, *The Administrative Procedure Act's "Good Cause" Exemption,* 36 Ad.L.Rev. 113 (1984).

ture and with the resulting rule subject to judicial review. The alternative, formal rulemaking, is much more elaborate.

Formal rulemaking begins with the same step as informal rule-making—public notice of the proposed rule. After that step, however, the provision for public comment is replaced by procedures virtually identical to those required for formal adjudication.[214] The agency must conduct an evidentiary hearing presided over either by the agency head or by an ALJ. At the conclusion of this trial-type hearing, the agency must make findings and conclusions based solely on the record amassed at the hearing. As with formal adjudication, parties have a right to present evidence and to cross-examine opposing witnesses, except that in formal rulemaking an agency can adopt procedures to receive some or all of the evidence in written form if no party will be prejudiced by this procedure.[215] In short, formal rule-making procedure is nearly identical to formal adjudication.

The formal judicial type hearing that long has dominated the process of resolving specific factually-based disputes between individuals in common law courts functions reasonably well when it is transferred to resolution of similar disputes by agencies. Formal hearings perform poorly, however, as means of resolving the broad, complicated policy issues that are the focus of most agency rulemaking proceedings. The agency becomes so enmeshed in testimony concerning specific facts that its attention is diverted from the important policy considerations that should dominate the process of formulating general rules. Moreover, it is simply impossible for an agency to resolve many controversies concerning general rules within a reasonable time if it must use trial-type procedures.

Most rulemaking proceedings involve complicated and inherently uncertain relationships between many issues that have factual, legal and policy components. Most rulemaking proceedings involve consideration of rules that affect significantly the interests of hundreds or even thousands of parties. These two typical characteristics of agency rulemakings combine with trial-type procedures to produce a seemingly never-ending procedural morass. Each of scores, or even hundreds, of parties to the proceeding presents witnesses, each of whom addresses several issues. Each witness is subject to cross-examination on each issue by each of the lawyers representing parties with differing interests. The complicated sequence of direct testimony, cross-examination, redirect, recross, and cross-on-cross is repeated for each of one hundred or more witnesses. Agencies that choose to, or

214. *See supra* § 6.3.4.   **215.** 5 U.S.C. § 556(d).

are forced to, use this procedure for rulemaking typically discover that they do not have an evidentiary record sufficient to permit issuance of a rule even after spending a decade or more in the rulemaking process.[216]

The disastrous effect of requiring an agency to use formal rulemaking procedures is well known. Frequently, if an agency is required to regulate solely through the use of formal rulemaking procedures, it ultimately abandons its efforts to regulate entirely.[217] Indeed, this often is the intended effect of requiring agencies to regulate through formal rulemaking. Any experienced lobbyist knows that encumbering a regulatory agency with expensive, time-consuming procedural requirements is functionally equivalent to withdrawing the agency's substantive power to regulate.

The APA does not specify whether an agency must use informal or formal rulemaking. The APA makes informal rulemaking procedures applicable to agency promulgation of legislative rules except "[w]hen rules are required by statute to be made on the record after opportunity for an agency hearing, ... "[218] Thus, an agency is required to use formal rulemaking procedures only when its organic act requires it to do so. Until 1972, most observers of administrative law believed that an agency was required to use formal rulemaking if its organic act specified that it could take a particular type of action only after a "hearing". This widespread belief was based largely on the fact that both Congress and the courts traditionally had used the term hearing as a short-hand reference to the kind of evidentiary hearing provided in a judicial trial.[219] In two important cases, the Supreme Court abandoned almost completely the traditional equation of the term "hearing" with a judicial-type trial.

In *United States v. Allegheny–Ludlum Steel Corp.,*[220] the Court was presented with a challenge to an Interstate Commerce Commission (ICC) rule requiring users of freight cars to return those cars in the direction of their owners' tracks. The rule was intended to reduce the geographic maldistribution of railroad cars that exists in some seasons of the year. Allegheny–Ludlum challenged the validity of the rule on the basis that ICC refused to grant Allegheny–Ludlum's motion for a trial-type hearing even though the statute authorizing

216. *See* Pierce, *supra* note 75. *See also* Hamilton, *Rulemaking on a Record by the Food & Drug Administration,* 50 Tex.L.Rev. 1132 (1972).

217. *See* Hamilton, *Procedures for the Adoption of Rules of General Applicability: The Need for Procedural Innovation*

in Administrative Rulemaking, 60 Calif.L.Rev. 1276, 1311–13 (1972).

218. 5 U.S.C. § 553(c).

219. *See supra* § 6.3.3.

220. 406 U.S. 742 (1972).

issuance of the rule required ICC to provide a "hearing" before acting. The Court affirmed the rule, holding that "hearing" did not mean judicial-type hearing. ICC fulfilled the statutory requirement of a hearing by following the three step procedure set forth for informal rulemaking—public notice, opportunity for comments, and statement of basis and purpose.

One year after its decision in *Allegheny–Ludlum,* the Court was confronted with the need to resolve another procedural controversy involving ICC rulemaking directed at the problem of maldistribution of freight cars. *United States v. Florida East Coast Ry. Co.*[221] involved a challenge to an ICC rule that imposed a per diem charge on any railroad that retained possession of a boxcar owned by another railroad. Florida East Coast argued that the rule was invalid because ICC had refused its request for a judicial-type hearing. Superficially, the issue in *Florida East Coast* resembled closely the issue previously resolved in *Allegheny–Ludlum,* but the case was complicated by two distinguishing features. First, it arose under a different statutory provision that specifically directed ICC to base its action on consideration of several facts that were contested. Second, Florida East Coast raised a credible argument that ICC's failure to conduct a judicial-type hearing violated due process.

The statutory provision governing issuance of the ICC rule contested in *Florida East Coast,* like the provision at issue in *Allegheny–Ludlum,* required the agency to provide a "hearing" before acting. The statutory provision added, however, that ICC must consider several facts, such as the pattern of ownership of freight cars, in determining whether to assess a per diem charge. Florida East Coast argued that the statutory requirement that ICC resolve contested facts, when combined with the statutory requirement that ICC conduct a hearing, indicated that Congress intended to require ICC to conduct a formal evidentiary hearing. The Court rejected this argument on three grounds.

First, the Court denied that an evidentiary hearing provides the only appropriate vehicle for resolving contested issues of fact. It observed that informal notice and comment procedures could fulfill adequately an agency's duty to consider contested facts of the type ICC was directed to consider in deciding whether to issue a per diem rule.

Second, the Court observed that hearing is an ambiguous term that is sufficiently flexible to encompass both a judicial-type trial and an informal sequence of notice, comment and response. The Court

221. 410 U.S. 224 (1973).

stated that hearing should be given a meaning consistent with the context in which the term is used. Thus, in the *Florida East Coast* context, where the agency was considering adoption of a general rule based on consideration of general facts, hearing can mean notice and comments.

Finally, the Court pointed out that the APA required an agency to use formal rulemaking procedures only "when rules are required to be made on the record after opportunity for an agency hearing, . . . " Thus, the APA formal rulemaking requirements cannot be triggered by a statutory provision referring only to a hearing. Rather, the organic act must add to the requirement of a hearing either the magic words "on the record" or some equivalent verbalization that evidences the clear intent of Congress to require formal rulemaking.[222]

Two Justices dissented in *Florida East Coast*. It is difficult to determine whether the arguments in the dissenting opinion and the rejoinders in the majority opinion are premised principally on statutory interpretation or instead are based on application of the Due Process Clause. The two opinions provide a good vehicle to explore the murky relationship between the statutory requirement and the constitutional basis for requiring a judicial-type hearing.

The dissenting Justices argued that Florida East Coast was entitled to a judicial-type hearing because: (1) the ICC rule imposed potentially devastating charges on some railroads; and, (2) the procedures used by the ICC were inadequate to permit Florida East Coast to contest the ICC's factual assertions concerning the availability of freight cars of various types. The dissenting Justices concluded that Florida East Coast was entitled to a judicial-type hearing under the ICC Act and the APA, but the dissenting Justices did not reach that conclusion through statutory analysis. Rather, their reasoning process seemed to reflect due process analysis.

The majority responded to the dissent in a manner that also blurred the line between statutorily and constitutionally compelled procedures. The majority began by referring to the distinction drawn in the APA between rulemaking and adjudication, suggesting that a judicial-type hearing is appropriate only for adjudication unless Congress clearly and explicitly required the agency to provide a judicial-type hearing for rulemaking. Then, instead of attempting to define those divergent statutory concepts by reference to the provisions of the APA, the Court proceeded to define each by reference to its prior decisions under the Due Process Clause. The Court's decision to

222. *See supra* § 6.4.2.

eschew reliance on the APA definitions of rulemaking and adjudication seems sensible. As we discussed earlier in this chapter, the APA definitions of rulemaking and adjudication are so ambiguous that they provide little assistance to agencies and courts.[223]

The Court relied on its landmark due process decisions in *Londoner v. Denver*[224] and *Bi–Metallic Investment Co. v. State Board of Equalization*[225] as the basis to distinguish rulemaking from adjudication. As we discussed in some detail in the due process sections,[226] *Londoner* involved a classic case of adjudication because "a small number of persons 'were exceptionally affected, in each case upon individual grounds' ". The controversy at issue in *Bi–Metallic* was a classic rulemaking because the government action affected a large number of people in a similar manner. The Court required a trial-type hearing in *Londoner,* but not in *Bi–Metallic*. The Court found the government action in *Florida East Coast* analogous to the action in *Bi–Metallic* because ICC did not "single out any particular railroad for special consideration based on its own peculiar circumstances".

After *Florida East Coast*, the analysis to determine whether an agency must provide a judicial-type hearing in a rulemaking requires answers to the following sequence of questions. First, is the action subject to the APA at all? If not, the determination of required procedures must be premised entirely on interpretation of the agency's organic act and analysis of the action under the Due Process Clause. Second, assuming that the action is subject to the APA, is it rulemaking or adjudication? The Court answers this question by reference to the constitutionally based distinction drawn at the beginning of the century in *Londoner* and *Bi–Metallic*. If the agency action is rulemaking, the agency is required to provide a judicial-type hearing if Congress has explicitly directed it to do so by including in the agency's organic act the magic words "on the record" or some verbal equivalent. If the agency action is rulemaking subject to the APA, and Congress has not explicitly directed the agency to provide a judicial-type hearing in a rulemaking, a court will require an agency to provide only the three-step procedural sequence prescribed in the APA for informal rulemaking.

§ 6.4.6   Informal rulemaking procedure

Informal rulemaking consists of a sequence of three related steps. First, the agency must publish a general notice to the public in the Federal Register indicating its intention to issue a rule. The

223. *See supra* § 6.4.1.

224. 210 U.S. 373 (1908).

225. 239 U.S. 441 (1915).

226. *See supra* § 6.3.2.

public notice must specify the time, place and nature of the proceeding, the legal authority under which the agency proposes to act, and either the substance of the proposed rule or a description of the subject and issues involved in the rulemaking.[227] The purpose of the public notice is to permit members of the public to participate effectively in the rulemaking proceeding through the second step in the sequence—submission of written data, views or arguments concerning the proposed rule. Finally, the agency must publish the final rule in the Federal Register and must incorporate in that rule a concise general statement of its basis and purpose. The final rule is then subject to judicial review.

It is important to recognize the functional significance of the three-part procedural sequence to judicial review of rules. The agency's statement of basis and purpose accompanying its final rule provides the principal basis for judicial review of the substance of the rule. That statement consists largely of the agency's discussion of the public comments received in response to its notice of proposed rulemaking. Thus, without adequate notice there can be no meaningful opportunity to submit comments, and without such an opportunity, a court can have no basis for substantive judicial review of an agency rule.

Given the analogy between legislating and rulemaking, any procedural safeguards mandated for rulemaking seem initially superfluous. Legislative bodies are not ordinarily required to follow any externally imposed procedures in the process of enacting legislation. There is a crucial difference, however, between Congress and federal agencies to whom Congress delegates power to issue legally-binding rules of conduct. The constitutional and political legitimacy of congressional legislation is beyond dispute. By contrast, agencies are not directly accountable to the electorate, and their constitutional role as a quasi-legislative body is frequently challenged. As we discussed in some detail in Chapters Three and Four, agencies are politically accountable, but through a combination of ambiguous and attenuated forms of control exercised by Congress and the President. In order to enhance the legitimacy of agency rulemaking, Congress requires agencies to follow regularized procedures and makes agency rules subject to judicial review.

§ 6.4.6a Notice and comments

Notice is the core of the informal rulemaking procedure. The agency's notice of proposed rulemaking starts the process of framing

---

227. 5 U.S.C. § 553(b).

the issues in a rulemaking by giving interested members of the public a target for critical comments. The notice consists of two parts, the proposed rule itself (or its substance) and the agency's stated basis for proposing the rule. Interested members of the public need both parts to make effective comments on the proposal.

If the agency does not provide notice of the rule it actually implements, members of the public cannot even determine that they will be affected by the rule, much less submit comments to the agency setting forth their views concerning the reasons the rule should not be adopted. Hence, the notice of proposed rulemaking must bear a close relationship to the final rule. On the other hand, one of the major purposes of requiring an agency to consider comments on a proposed rule is to allow the agency to make changes in the proposed rule to reflect problems identified in the public comments. Thus, an agency must retain some flexibility to adopt a final rule that differs from the proposal described in its public notice. These two opposing considerations underlie many court challenges to the adequacy of agency notices of proposed rulemaking. *Wagner Electric Corp. v. Volpe*[228] and *South Terminal Corp. v. EPA*[229] illustrate the judicial approach to this aspect of the adequate notice controversy.

In *Wagner Electric,* the Third Circuit was confronted with a challenge to the adequacy of the Department of Transportation's notice proposing to modify its standards for testing turn signals and hazard warning flashers. The agency's terse notice referred only to its possible elimination of a test to determine maximum permissible failure rates of signals and flashers. Its final rule eliminated that test, but it also downgraded the performance criteria and durability standards applicable to signals and flashers. The court held the agency's notice inadequate to alert consumer groups and state agencies to the possibility that the agency would downgrade the performance criteria and durability standards. As a result, the agency also did not provide such groups an adequate opportunity to submit comments concerning the potential adverse affects of the action reflected in the agency's final rule.

The First Circuit's opinion in *South Terminal* fills in the other side of the equation. The court was asked to review the Environmental Protection Agency's (EPA) final rule implementing a Transportation Control Plan for the Boston Metropolitan Area. The plan was designed to reduce the level of pollutants emitted by automobiles in

228.   466 F.2d 1013 (3d Cir.1972).   **229.**   504 F.2d 646 (1st Cir.1974).

the Boston area. The final plan included an immediate freeze on, and ultimate reduction of, on-street parking, regulation of construction of new parking facilities, bus and car pool lanes on many streets, and auto emission controls. South Terminal challenged the final plan on the basis that it differed so radically from the plan described in the published notice that EPA had provided inadequate notice of, and opportunity to comment on, the rule it actually adopted.

The court recognized that EPA had changed the rule in many respects from the original proposal. The agency had dropped several features and added several others. The First Circuit pointed out that the notice and comment process is supposed to produce exactly this result—changes made in response to critical comments. As long as the parties were given fair warning concerning the general nature of the regulatory restrictions contemplated by the agency and the agency's willingness to consider functional alternatives to those restrictions, the court concluded that the public was sufficiently alerted to know what was at stake in the rulemaking.

Wagner Electric stands for the principle that an agency cannot issue a final rule that accomplishes changes in an area in which the agency's notice of proposed rulemaking gave no warning that it was considering changes. *South Terminal* holds that an agency's final rule can differ substantially from the proposed rule contained in its public notice of proposed rulemaking as long as the agency's notice fairly apprised the public of the possibility of changes of the type that occurred. Courts routinely apply two closely-related tests to determine whether a notice was adequate. A notice is adequate if it "sufficiently foreshadowed" the final rule or if the final rule was a "logical outgrowth" of the sequence of the notice and consideration of the comments received in response to the notice. If an agency is concerned that the changes it needs to make in its final rule extend beyond the scope of its public notice and therefore place its final rule in jeopardy of reversal under *Wagner Electric,* its only safe course of action is to issue a second notice of proposed rulemaking reflecting the nature of the changes it plans and then to provide an opportunity for submission of comments on that second proposal.

The appellate courts, led by the late Harold Leventhal of the D.C. Circuit, have expanded the concept of adequate notice under the APA to encompass notice of the factual and scientific basis for a proposed rule. Judge Leventhal's opinion in *Portland Cement Association v. Ruckelshaus*[230] best illustrates this expanded concept of

---

230.   486 F.2d 375 (D.C.Cir.1973). *See also* United States v. Nova Scotia Food Prods. Corp., 568 F.2d 240 (2d Cir.1977).

notice. Portland Cement challenged an EPA rule that set new standards for emissions from new and modified cement plants. EPA's notice of proposed rulemaking fairly apprised Portland of the nature of the rule it ultimately issued, but the notice said little about the basis for the proposed rule. EPA's notice stated only that its proposal was "based on stationary source testing conducted by the Environmental Protection Agency and/or contractors. . . . " EPA did not reveal to the public the nature of the tests and the methodology used in the tests until after the time had expired to submit comments on the proposed rule.

EPA adopted the proposed rule over Portland's objections. When EPA finally made available the description of test methodology and results, Portland's consulting engineer concluded in a detailed critique that the results were "grossly erroneous" due to serious deficiencies in sampling techniques. Because EPA already had promulgated the rule, Portland submitted the engineer's analysis and conclusions to the reviewing court rather than to the agency. The court remanded the rulemaking to EPA to permit the agency to respond to the engineer's criticisms, but EPA chose only to reaffirm the rule and to add the engineer's comments to the record for review. The court reversed, holding:

> "We find a critical defect in the decisionmaking process in arriving at the standard under review in the initial inability of petitioners to obtain—in timely fashion—the test results and procedures used in existing plants which formed a partial basis for the emission control level adopted, and in the subsequent seeming refusal of the agency to respond to what seem to be legitimate problems with the methodology of these tests."

The D.C. Circuit stated the basis for its reversal in *Portland Cement* in the form of a broad principle of general applicability: "It is not consonant with the purpose of a rule making proceeding to promulgate rules on the basis of inadequate data, or on data that, [to a] critical degree, is known only to the agency." One could argue that the expanded notice concept announced in *Portland Cement* is not consistent with, and hence did not survive, the Supreme Court's holding in *Vermont Yankee Nuclear Power Corp. v. Natural Resources Defense Council Inc.*[231] We will discuss that important decision in some detail in a subsequent part of this chapter.[232] For present purposes, it is sufficient to accept *Vermont Yankee* as standing for the

231. 435 U.S. 519 (1978).
232. *See infra* § 6.4.9a.

simple proposition that courts can not compel agencies to adopt procedures more demanding than those required by statute or by the Constitution. We believe that the concept of expanded notice announced in *Portland Cement* represents a substantial improvement in the rulemaking process and that the concept survives *Vermont Yankee* because it is premised on a valid interpretation of the informal rulemaking provisions of the APA.

It is easiest to understand the critical role of expanded notice in informal rulemaking by working backward through the three-step procedural sequence required by the APA. An agency's final rule must be accompanied by a statement of the basis and purpose of the rule. That statement and the rule it accompanies are subject to judicial review. The statement of basis and purpose must reflect the agency's consideration of all relevant comments. The agency must permit affected members of the public to include in their comments "data, views, or arguments". The sole basis on which the public can provide comments is the agency's public notice of proposed rulemaking. If the agency does not include in its public notice the factual and scientific basis for a proposed rule, the public has no basis on which to submit comments critical of the methodology and factual premises underlying the agency's proposal. Thus, if an agency proposes a rule with a factual or scientific basis and it does not make available to affected members of the public in a timely manner the facts and studies on which the proposal is based, the functional efficacy of permitting public comments on the proposal and of requiring the agency to respond to those comments is completely undermined.

Several types of information are indispensable to any effort to criticize or review the adequacy of an agency proposal predicated upon scientific analysis of facts. First, of course, are the results of any studies, experiments, mathematical models, or other analyses on which the agency based its proposal. Other essential information includes the names and qualifications of the individuals who performed the work for the agency, a description of the methodology used, identification of the sources of input data, a description of the statistical validity and reliability of the results of any calculations, and sensitivity data showing the extent to which the results of the calculations would change with various changes in input data. Depending upon the nature of the agency's methodology, reference to computer programs, mathematical formulae, and other calculational aids used by the agency staff also may be necessary.

Before *Portland Cement,* such data, although in theory readily accessible within the agency, rarely was made available to the public, reviewing courts, or even the responsible agency officials at the time a rule was proposed. The requirement that these data be made public in a timely manner in informal rulemaking proceedings has produced marked improvements in the quality of agency decisionmaking with very little added burden on the agency.

The expanded notice doctrine must be subject to pragmatic limits, however. It would be absurd, for instance, to require EPA to provide notice of the thousands of books, articles, and published studies that underlie each element of a proposed rule concerning the permissible level of emissions of sulfur oxides. Courts have strived to identify appropriate limits, but the decided cases do not yet provide a clear and consistent pattern of results. Two potential limits seem attractive. First, courts could exclude published books, articles, and studies from the scope of the agency's obligation based on the assumption that commentors are, or should become, familiar with the published literature on which any rule is based. Second, courts could limit the scope of the obligation by reference to the centrality of a study to the agency's proposed rule. Congress explicitly imposed such a limit in the context of EPA rulemaking under the Clean Air Act by requiring EPA to make publicly accessible documents "of central relevance" to the rulemaking.[233] Courts could apply this sensible limit in the process of determining the scope of the "notice" any agency must provide in a rulemaking.

§ 6.4.6b   Statement of basis and purpose

The APA requires an agency engaged in informal rulemaking to incorporate in its final rules "a concise general statement of their basis and purpose." As agencies increasingly have used informal rulemaking procedures to resolve complicated factual and scientific issues, reviewing courts have expanded the scope of the statement of basis and purpose that must accompany a rule. The D.C. Circuit described the modern requirement for a statement of basis and purpose accurately and candidly in *Automotive Parts & Accessories Ass'n v. Boyd.*[234] It cautioned against "an overly literal reading of the terms 'concise and general' ". It emphasized that the requirement of a statement of basis and purpose must be interpreted in a manner consistent with a reviewing court's need "to see what major issues of policy were ventilated by the informal proceedings and why the agency reacted to them as it did."

233. 42 U.S.C. § 7607(d).   **234.** 407 F.2d 330, 338 (D.C.Cir. 1968).

Reviewing courts also have given meaning to the APA requirement that agencies consider public comments on proposed rules through their interpretations of the requirement of a statement of basis and purpose. An agency's failure to respond in its statement of basis and purpose to well-supported arguments contained in public comments critical of the agency's proposed rule can form the basis for reversal of the agency's final rule.[235]

Most judicial decisions that set aside agency rules do so on the basis that the rule is "arbitrary and capricious" within the meaning of APA § 706(2)(A). The arbitrary and capricious test has undergone a major transformation over the decades. Seventy years ago, a reviewing court would uphold an agency rule under the arbitrary and capricious test as long as the rule had any plausible relationship to any permissible agency goal, even if the agency did not state the relationship between the rule and a permissible goal.[236] In *Securities & Exchange Commission v. Chenery Corp.*,[237] the Court modified that approach substantially by making it clear that a reviewing court can consider the validity of an agency action only on the basis of the reasons stated by the agency at the time it takes the action. If those reasons are inadequate or improper, a reviewing court must reverse the agency action even if it might affirm the same action based on a different set of reasons. In the rulemaking context, the reasons that form the basis for judicial application of the arbitrary and capricious test must be found in the agency's statement of basis and purpose.

The Court continued its transformation of the arbitrary and capricious test in *Citizens to Preserve Overton Park, Inc. v. Volpe*,[238] where the Court described the standard for review under the arbitrary and capricious test as requiring a judicial determination of "whether the decision was based on a consideration of the relevant factors and whether there has been a clear error of judgment." It went on to describe this exercise as "searching and careful", but it qualified its description by noting that: "[T]he ultimate standard of review is a narrow one. The Court is not empowered to substitute its judgment for that of the agency".

Overton Park authorized reviewing courts to consider the adequacy of the reasons given by an agency in support of its action, but its description of the appropriate scope of that review was confusing.

---

235. *See, e.g.,* Portland Cement Ass'n v. Ruckelshaus, 486 F.2d 375 (D.C.Cir. 1973).

236. *See* Pacific States Box & Basket Co. v. White, 296 U.S. 176 (1935).

237. 332 U.S. 194 (1947).

238. 401 U.S. 402 (1971).

A "searching and careful" inquiry does not sound like a "narrow" standard of review. In subsequent opinions, most notably *Camp v. Pitts*,[239] the Court omitted any reference to the need for a "searching and careful" inquiry.

In its 1983 opinion in *Motor Vehicle Manufacturers Association v. State Farm Mutual Automobile Insurance Company*,[240] the Court clarified the standard of review of agency reasoning in the following language:

> "Normally, an agency rule would be arbitrary and capricious if the agency has relied on factors which Congress has not intended it to consider, entirely failed to consider an important aspect of the problem, offered an explanation for its decision that runs counter to the evidence before the agency, or is so implausible that it could not be ascribed to a difference in view or the product of agency expertise."

In *State Farm*, the Court set aside an agency rule on the bases that: (1) the agency failed to consider at all an obvious alternative to the agency action that would have produced superior results as measured with reference to the agency's own findings and stated criteria for decisionmaking; and, (2) the agency did not adequately explain why it predicted that a safety device would be used less than five per cent of the time when the only available studies concluded that it would be used fifty per cent of the time.

Since the early 1970's, circuit courts have emphasized the "searching and careful" approach to judicial review of agency statements of basis and purpose authorized in *Overton Park*. By the time the Court decided *State Farm*, circuit courts routinely were requiring agencies to include in each statement of basis and purpose a discussion of each statutory goal and decisional factor, each dispute concerning the factual predicates for the rule, plausible alternatives to the action reflected in the rule, and each major issue raised in a comment submitted in the rulemaking. Moreover, courts often reverse agency actions even when the agency concededly has considered all decisional factors because the court finds the agency's consideration inadequate in some sense. In such cases, the court may reverse because the agency failed "to give full consideration" to a factor,[241] dismissed a factor with an "unconvincing assertion",[242] attempted

---

239. 411 U.S. 138 (1973).

240. 463 U.S. 29 (1983), discussed *infra* § 7.5.

241. Scenic Hudson Preservation Conference v. FPC, 354 F.2d 608, 617 (2d Cir.1965).

242. National Tire Dealers & Retreaders Ass'n, Inc. v. Brinegar, 491 F.2d

"to rely on generalized and conclusory policy consideration",[243] provided "abbreviated analysis" of an issue,[244] or failed to give "thoughtful consideration" to an issue.[245] These adverbs and adjectives used to characterize the adequate consideration test are extremely flexible, and reviewing courts apply the test with widely varying degrees of deference and stringency.

In the abstract, the burden imposed on agencies by the adequate consideration test may seem more manageable than it is in the real world of agency decisionmaking. Former Environmental Protection Agency Administrator Costle helped to put this burden in perspective by describing the scope of the duty in a typical case in which EPA attempted to issue a rule regulating an environmental hazard.[246] EPA received 192 comments that raised 400 separate issues, each of which required a response in the agency's statement of basis and purpose. That statement totaled 1600 pages. EPA's experience is not at all unusual. Recent rulemaking proceedings by other agencies have elicited as many as 10,000 separate comments.[247]

Numerous studies have documented the adverse effects of this demanding attitude of reviewing courts on the rulemaking process.[248] Promulgation of a single major rule often requires five to ten years and tens of thousands of agency staff hours. Even when an agency has completed this lengthy and arduous process, it cannot be confident that a court will uphold the resulting rule. Courts set aside about forty per cent of agency rules, usually on the basis that the rule is arbitrary and capricious because of some inadequacy in the agency's statement of basis and purpose.[249]

Excessively demanding judicial review has slowed the pace of rulemaking at all agencies, reduced agencies' incentives to use the rulemaking process, and even caused some major agencies to abandon

31, 40 (D.C.Cir.1974).

243. International Ladies' Garment Workers' Union v. Donovan, 722 F.2d 795, 818 (D.C.Cir.1983).

244. Id. at 826.

245. Telocator Network of America v. FCC, 691 F.2d 525, 544 (D.C.Cir.1982).

246. Costle, *Brave New Chemical: The Future Regulatory History of Phlogiston,* 33 Admin.L.Rev. 195 (1981).

247. *See* International Ladies' Garment Workers' Union v. Donovan, 722 F.2d 795, 804 (D.C.Cir.1983).

248. *See, e.g.,* Pierce, *The Unintended Effects of Judicial Review of Agency Rules: How Federal Courts Have Contributed to the Electricity Crisis of the 1990's,* 43 Admin.L.Rev. 7 (1991); J. Mashaw & D. Harfst, The Struggle for Auto Safety (1990); J. Mendeloff, The Dilemma of Toxic Substance Regulation (1988); Pierce, *Two Problems in Administrative Law: Political Polarity on the D.C. Circuit and Judicial Deterrence of Agency Rulemaking,* 1988 Duke L.J. 300.

249. Schuck & Elliott, *Studying Administrative Law: A Methodology for, and Report on, New Empirical Research,* 42 Admin.L.Rev. 519 (1990).

rulemaking entirely. Professor Mashaw and Harfst's careful study of the National Highway Traffic Safety Administration (NHTSA) illustrates the adverse effects of judicial review on an agency's incentive to use rulemaking.[250] Until 1972, NHTSA relied principally on rules as its means of furthering its statutorily assigned mission of improving highway safety. NHTSA rules reduced highway fatalities by thirty per cent. In 1972, however, a single court opinion convinced NHTSA to abandon rulemaking entirely.

In *Chrysler Corp. v. Department of Transportation,*[251] the Sixth Circuit set aside an NHTSA rule because the agency did not provide a sufficiently detailed, objective set of specifications for the dummies to be used in the tests required to implement the rule. The dummy specification issue had not been the focus of much attention in the rulemaking proceeding. The agency considered it far down the long list of issues raised in the proceeding in terms of its relative importance. Based on the *Chrysler* court's decision to set aside a rule based on an alleged inadequacy in the agency's discussion of a trivial issue, NHTSA drew the logical inference that it could issue a rule that would withstand judicial review only by devoting extensive additional staff resources to detailed discussion of *every* issue. The agency then concluded that its resources were inadequate to the task. It abandoned rulemaking entirely and devoted all of its resources to ad hoc adjudication of product recall cases. Unlike NHTSA's auto safety rules, its recall program has had no measurable effect on highway safety.

The Supreme Court seems to have recognized the adverse effects of excessively demanding judicial review on the rulemaking process. In two opinions issued in 1990 and 1991, the Court imposed limits on the power of reviewing courts to set aside agency actions based on alleged inadequacies in an agency's stated reasons for taking the action.

In *Pension Benefit Guaranty Corp. v. LTV Corp.,*[252] the Court held that an agency must discuss only the policy goals identified in the statute that authorized it to take the action at issue. A circuit court had set aside the agency's action because the agency did not discuss the relationship between its action and the policy goals Congress identified in a variety of other statutes closely related to the agency action. The Court expressed concern that:

250. J. Mashaw & D. Harfst, *supra* n. 248.

251. 472 F.2d 659 (6th Cir.1972).

252. 496 U.S. 633 (1990).

If agency action may be disturbed whenever a reviewing court is able to point to an arguably relevant statutory policy that was not explicitly considered, then a very large number of agency decisions might be open to judicial invalidation.

LTV involved judicial review of an action taken through informal adjudication, but its reasoning seems equally applicable to rules adopted through informal rulemaking.

In *Mobil Oil Exploration & Producing Southeast, Inc. v. United Distribution Co.,*[253] the Court imposed a second limit on the power of reviewing courts to set aside rules based on arguable inadequacies in an agency's statement of basis and purpose. The Fifth Circuit set aside a rule addressed to one problem because the agency did not adequately consider the potential adverse effects of the rule on another problem. The Supreme Court reversed, holding that an agency that chooses to address one problem by rule has no obligation to address a related problem, even if its attempt to solve one problem increases the severity of the other problem.

It remains to be seen whether the Court's opinions in *LTV* and *Mobil* will be sufficient to convince circuit courts to reduce the extent of the unrealistic demands they impose on the rulemaking process. The Court may need to issue an opinion that announces a more sweeping solution to this serious problem. At least one respected scholar and Supreme Court Justice has urged the Court to reverse *State Farm.*[254] It would experience no difficulty supporting such an opinion. The detailed and encyclopedic statements of basis and purpose demanded by many circuit courts bear little resemblance to the "concise, general statement of basis and purpose" Congress envisioned when it enacted APA § 553.[255]

Circuit courts have reduced the adverse effects of demanding judicial review of agency rules by changing their approach to their choice of remedies when they conclude that a rule is invalid because the agency made a procedural error in the rulemaking process or engaged in inadequate consideration of an issue raised in the proceeding. In most cases today, a court remands the rulemaking to the agency for further proceedings without vacating the rule.[256] As a result, the rule can remain in effect while the agency corrects the

---

253. 498 U.S. 211 (1991).

254. *See* Breyer, *Judicial Review of Questions of Law and Policy,* 38 Admin.L.Rev. 363 (1986).

255. *See* Shapiro, *APA: Past, Present, Future,* 72 Va.L.Rev. 447, 453–54 (1986).

256. *See, e.g.,* Idaho Farm Bureau v. Babbitt, 58 F.3d 1392 (9th Cir.1995); Allied–Signal v. NRC, 988 F.2d 146 (D.C.Cir.1993).

error in its decisionmaking procedures that was the basis for the court's opinion remanding the rulemaking to the agency.

During the mid–1990s, Congress considered enactment of several statutes that would have increased dramatically both the decision-making procedures agencies are required to use in a rulemaking and the stringency of judicial review of agency compliance with those procedural mandates. Congress enacted three statutes that impose modest additional procedures in some cases, but it failed to enact the statutes that would have imposed significant new requirements. We discuss this legislative debate and the three statutes it produced in § 9.5.

§ 6.4.6c Executive control of rulemaking

For over fifty years, scholars and Presidential commissions have complained that the President's ability to control the bureaucracy has become increasingly attenuated with increases in the size and scope of the administrative state.[257] The problem has components that span a broad spectrum from pragmatic—uncoordinated federal agencies frequently impose inconsistent duties—to conceptual—the questionable political and constitutional legitimacy of a rule issued by an agency with powers that are largely unconstrained either by statute or by the President. Each President has taken some steps designed to enhance the President's ability to coordinate and to control agency policymaking. Executive Order 12,291, issued in 1987, is the most ambitious effort to date.

E.O. 12,291 requires every Executive Branch agency to prepare a Regulatory Impact Analysis (RIA), including a cost-benefit-analysis (cba), in connection with every "major rule" the agency proposes to adopt. Agencies must use cba in the process of deciding whether to issue a rule and in determining the contents of a rule. The President's Office of Management and Budget (OMB) can exercise a variety of powers in an effort to influence agencies to comply with E.O. 12,291's mandate to rely on cba as the dominant decisionmaking criterion. OMB can require an agency to consider additional data or studies, to consult with other agencies, or to defer issuance of a rule until OMB has completed its evaluation of the agency's RIA.

E.O. 12,291's scope is limited in three important ways. First, it applies only to rules adopted through the rulemaking process. An agency can avoid OMB review entirely by adopting a general "rule"

---

257. *See, e.g.,* J. Landis, Report to the President–Elect 86 (1960); Report of President's Committee on Administrative Management 5–6, 16–25, 33–38, 51–53 (1937).

through the process of adjudication of cases. Second, it applies only to Executive Branch agencies. Third, E.O. 12,291 cannot be applied in any manner inconsistent with the statutes that govern agency decisionmaking. Thus, for instance, OMB cannot delay issuance of a rule beyond a statutory deadline,[258] and an agency cannot rely on cba as the basis for a decision when a statute requires the agency to use a decisionmaking criterion inconsistent with cba.[259]

There is evidence that E.O. 12,291 has had its intended effect of enhancing the President's ability to coordinate and to influence agency policymaking. That effect has come only at some cost, however, in the form of delay in the rulemaking process attributable both to the preparation of an RIA and to OMB review.[260] The requirement to prepare an RIA and the prospect of having to defend the RIA in potentially protracted negotiations with OMB may be deterring agencies from proposing some rules and may be encouraging agencies to use procedures other than rulemaking to make some major policy decisions.

President Clinton replaced E.O. 12,291 with E.O. 12,866. The Clinton Order retained the use of cba as an important decisionmaking tool, but it made several important changes in the scope of the order and in the OMB review procedures.[261] E.O. 12,866 imposed some obligations on "independent agencies," a class of agencies that prior Presidents had been unwilling to attempt to control for fear of adverse reactions from Congress.[262] The Clinton Order also responded to persistent criticisms of the secrecy and delay that attended the implementation of E.O. 12,291 by requiring that all communications between OMB and agencies be in writing, making those communications available to the public, and imposing time limits on OMB review. These changes eliminated most of the criticism of OMB's review process. They may also have reduced significantly the efficacy of the OMB review process, however. OMB seems not to have played a significant role in reviewing agency rules during the Clinton Administration. President Bush has continued to operate under E.O.

258. *See* EDF v. Thomas, 627 F.Supp. 566 (D.D.C.1986).

259. *See, e.g.,* Public Citizen v. Young, 831 F.2d 1108 (D.C.Cir.1987) (FDA must ban use of any color additive that causes cancer in man or animals even if use of additive would yield net benefits).

260. *See* McGarity, *Regulatory Analysis and Reform,* 65 Tex.L.Rev. 1243 (1987).

261. *See* Shane, *Political Accountability in a System of Checks and Balances: The Case of Presidential Review of Rulemaking,* 48 Ark. L. Rev. 161 (1995). See also § 9.5.2.

262. *See* § 4.4 for a discussion of "independent agencies."

12,866. Consistent with his more skeptical attitude toward the efficacy of government regulation, however, President Bush has used the OMB review process more aggressively to restrain agencies from issuing rules that he perceived to be unjustified.

§ 6.4.6d   Disincentives to use rulemaking

Notwithstanding the efforts of courts to encourage agencies to use rulemaking,[263] many agencies have reduced their reliance on rulemaking or have abandoned rulemaking entirely. Several factors help to explain this unfortunate trend. Since we discuss each factor in detail in other sections, we will simply list the factors here and refer to the sections in which each is discussed.

In some cases, Congress has created disincentives for agencies to use rulemaking by adding expensive and time-consuming supplemental procedural requirements to the APA's procedures for informal rulemaking.[264] Courts inadvertently have created powerful deterrents to the use of rulemaking by adopting expansive definitions of the "concise, general statement of basis and purpose" that must be incorporated in each legislative rule and of the duty to engage in reasoned decisionmaking an agency must meet to avoid judicial rejection of a rule as "arbitrary and capricious."[265] The President has contributed an additional deterrent to the use of rulemaking by subjecting the process to additional procedures and to review by OMB.[266] Finally, the Supreme Court's surprising 1988 opinion creating a presumption that agencies lack the power to issue rules with retroactive effect has created a disincentive to use rulemaking in many circumstances.[267] The effect of each of these factors is to reduce significantly the attractiveness of the rulemaking process and to give agencies powerful incentives to rely on other forms of administrative action, *i.e.*, adjudications and a variety of less formal means of announcing "rules", such as staff manuals and putatively nonbinding policy statements.

§ 6.4.6e   Interim rules on remand

A typical major rulemaking requires five to ten years to complete and tens of thousands of hours of agency staff work. At the end of that process, courts remand approximately forty percent of agency rules.[268] Most remands are based on a court's conclusion that the rule

---

263.　*See* § 6.4.1c *supra.*
264.　*See* § 6.4.9b *infra.*
265.　*See* § 6.4.6b *supra.*
266.　*See* § 6.4.6c *supra.*

267.　*See* § 6.4.1a *supra.*

268.　*See* Schuck & Elliott, *supra* note 249.

is arbitrary and capricious because the agency did not discuss "adequately" some decisional factor, comment, data dispute, or potential alternative to the action taken in the rule.[269] The inadequately discussed issue is often peripheral to the policy disputes at the core of the rulemaking. Yet, judicial remand of the rule usually requires the agency to choose between deferring action on the rule for the additional years required to complete a new rulemaking process that produces a statement of basis and purpose that is likely to satisfy a reviewing court, or abandoning the rulemaking entirely.

In 1987, the D.C. Circuit's opinion in *Mid–Tex Electric Power Cooperative, Inc. v. FERC*[270] provided agencies a more attractive third alternative. In many circumstances, an agency can issue an interim rule on remand from a judicial decision rejecting its permanent rule without first conducting a new rulemaking proceeding. An agency can issue an interim rule on remand from a judicial decision rejecting a permanent rule if: (1) the major elements of the rule were upheld; (2) the repromulgated rule is adopted only as an interim measure in an ongoing process to establish a permanent rule; and, (3) the agency includes features in the interim rule that represent a good faith effort to ameliorate the potential problems with the original rule that caused the court to set aside that rule. *Mid–Tex* is a constructive step toward reducing the policy paralysis that has been caused by excessively demanding judicial review of rules, but the ultimate solution to that problem can be found only in limiting the discretion of reviewing courts.

In *Allied–Signal, Inc. v. NRC*,[271] the D.C. Circuit provided agencies an even more attractive alternative to issuance of an interim rule on remand. The court announced that it would remand a rulemaking proceeding without vacating the resulting rule if it detects a procedural flaw in the rulemaking proceeding or inadequate reasoning to support the resulting rule, and it believes that the agency is likely to be able to correct that flaw on remand. Other circuits have followed the D.C. Circuit's lead in adopting remand without vacation as the preferred remedy for procedural errors made in a rulemaking.[272]

§ 6.4.6f Negotiated rulemaking

The high cost and years of staff work required to issue a rule through the informal rulemaking process has induced agencies to

269. *See supra* § 6.4.6b.

270. 822 F.2d 1123 (D.C.Cir.1987).

271. 988 F.2d 146 (D.C.Cir.1993). *See* discussions in §§ 6.4.1a & 6.4.4d.

272. *See, e.g.*, Idaho Farm Bureau v. Babbitt, 58 F.3d 1392 (9th Cir.1995).

search for alternatives to the rulemaking process. In the late 1980s, several agencies identified negotiated rulemaking, or Reg–Neg, as a potentially attractive option. As the name implies, Reg–Neg involves promulgation of a rule that is the product of agreement among representatives of all affected interests at the end of a negotiating process. Congress legitimated this process and provided a statutory framework for its implementation by enacting the Negotiated Rulemaking Act of 1990 and the Administrative Dispute Resolution Act.[273]

Reg–Neg offers two potential advantages. First, in some cases, agencies may be able to substitute Reg–Neg entirely for informal rulemaking. Rules that have only modest effects on a few interests are good candidates for this potential use of Reg–Neg. Second, in proceedings involving complicated rules with significant effects on many interests, agencies may be able to use Reg–Neg to reduce the scope of the contested issues the agency must address through the informal rulemaking process. Reg–Neg will never prove effective as a means of issuing a major rule that has disparate effects on many interests, however. No amount of negotiation can yield consensus with respect to such a rule. An empirical study of the use of Reg–Neg found that it does not save time, money, or resources, and that it does not reduce conflict or litigation.[274]

§ 6.4.6g   Obsolete rules and petitions for rulemaking

Rules often become obsolete over time. Some courts have reviewed a pre-existing rule and held that it had become obsolete, and thus arbitrary and capricious, even though it was valid at the time it was issued. The Court prohibited that practice in its unanimous opinion in *Auer v. Robbins*.[275] The Court held that a party that wants to challenge the continuing validity of an arguably obsolete rule must first file a petition for rulemaking pursuant to APA § 553(e). If the agency refuses to rescind or to amend the rule in response to that petition, the party can then seek review of that decision. The reviewing court is then in a position to evaluate the agency's reasons for deciding to retain the rule even in the face of changed circumstances.

273. 104 Stat. 4969, and 104 Stat. 2736.

274. Coglianese, *Assessing Consensus: The Promise and Performance of Negotiated Rulemaking*, 66 Duke L.J. 1255 (1997). *But see* Freeman & Langbein, *Regulatory Negotiation and the Legitima-* cy *Benefit*, 31 Env. L. Rep. 10811 (2001)(arguing that rules adopted through use of reg-neg have greater legitimacy and public acceptance.)

275. 519 U.S. 452 (1997).

§ 6.4.7   The effects of legislative rules in adjudicative proceedings

Statutes frequently provide individuals a right to formal adjudication of a dispute before an agency. An agency can significantly restrict the scope of such a statutory right to formal adjudication, however, by promulgating legislative rules that have the effect of eliminating the materiality of facts otherwise subject to resolution through formal adjudication. The Supreme Court's landmark decision in *United States v. Storer Broadcasting Co.*[276] illustrates this important relationship between legislative rules and formal adjudication. This is one of the ways courts indirectly encourage agencies to use rulemaking.[277]

The Federal Communications Act authorizes the Federal Communications Commission (FCC) to deny an application for a broadcast license only after first providing the applicant an opportunity to contest factual issues material to its application in a formal adjudication. FCC denied Storer's application without first conducting a formal adjudication. FCC acted on the basis of a newly promulgated legislative rule that prohibited common ownership of more than a specified number of broadcast stations. Storer conceded that it already owned the maximum number of stations permitted by the rule, but it argued that FCC violated its statute by denying Storer's application without first conducting a formal adjudicatory hearing. The Court recognized Storer's statutory right to a hearing, but it held that FCC had no duty to provide such a hearing when there were no material facts subject to resolution in such a hearing. By enacting a valid legislative rule, FCC had made one fact alone material to its action on Storer's application—Storer was ineligible for a license if it already owned more than the specified number of broadcast stations. Since Storer conceded that fact, it would be a waste of time to require FCC to provide Storer a formal adjudicatory hearing the outcome of which was predetermined by the valid legislative rule.

§ 6.4.8   Must agencies provide exceptions to rules?

Agencies frequently include in general rules provisions authorizing exceptions to those rules in certain circumstances. Providing for exceptions recognizes implicitly that any rule necessarily reflects only

276. 351 U.S. 192 (1956). *See also* Heckler v. Campbell, 461 U.S. 458 (1983), discussed *supra* in § 6.4.1c; Weinberger v. Hynson, Westcott & Dunning, Inc., 412 U.S. 609 (1973); FPC v. Texaco, Inc., 377 U.S. 33 (1964).

277. *See supra* § 6.4.1c.

a generalized evaluation of decisional factors whose precise contours and significance vary from case to case. An agency also may be able to enhance its chances of successfully defending the validity of a rule on judicial review if it explicitly provides for exceptions to the rule.[278] Occasionally, courts have suggested that an agency must provide for exceptions to rules, at least when the agency's statute requires it to provide an adjudicatory hearing before taking an action governed by a legislative rule. In *Storer Broadcasting,* for instance, the Court suggested that, while the FCC could eliminate the need for an adjudicatory hearing on some factual issues by legislative rule, the rule itself must provide some opportunity for an applicant to seek an adjudicatory hearing in an effort to justify an exception to, or waiver of, the rule.

In recent years, courts and scholars have recognized that, while it is often necessary for an agency to provide the safety valve of exceptions to rules, heavy reliance on an exceptions process can erode the major benefits of regulating by rule.[279] An agency that relies heavily on exceptions to general rules begins to look very similar to an agency that eschews rulemaking entirely in favor of ad hoc adjudication. The agency's decisions on exceptions soon become the source of general rules and its decisionmaking process is character- ized by all the disadvantages associated with formulation of general rules through adjudication—inefficiency, unfairness, and low quality policy decisions.[280]

In its recent decisions, the Supreme Court has retreated from its earlier dicta suggesting that agencies must provide exceptions to rules. In *FCC v. WNCN Listeners Guild,*[281] for instance, a majority of the Court rejected the argument of two dissenting Justices that FCC was required to provide for exceptions to its policy of allowing market forces to determine the programming of broadcast licensees. The language of APA supports the majority's position in *WNCN.* APA provides a right to petition for issuance, amendment, or repeal of a rule, but provides no right to petition for waiver of a rule.[282]

§ 6.4.9 Hybrid procedures

In the early 1970s, agencies, courts and Congress began to experiment with various hybrid procedures, that is, procedures that

---

278. *See* Note, *Regulatory Values and the Exceptions Process,* 93 Yale L.J. 938 (1984).

279. *See* Aman, *Administrative Equi- ty: An Analysis of Exceptions to Adminis- trative Rules,* 1982 Duke L.J. 277 (1982).

280. *See supra* § 6.4.1.

281. 450 U.S. 582 (1981).

282. 5 U.S.C. § 553(e). *See also supra* § 5.5.

are a cross between informal rulemaking and formal rulemaking. The impetus for hybrid procedures was the recognition that both formal and informal rulemaking procedures have inherent disadvantages as mechanisms for formulating general rules. We discussed in some detail the many disadvantages of formal rulemaking.[283] Many lawyers and judges believed, however, that informal notice and comment rulemaking was an unsatisfactory procedure for formulating rules whose wisdom or necessity was premised on contested facts. To many observers and participants in the administrative process who were accustomed to the judicial approach to fact-finding, it was heresy to allow agencies to resolve contested issues of fact without providing opponents an opportunity to cross-examine the proponents of those facts.

In some cases, agencies voluntarily add procedural safeguards, such as limited scope cross-examination, to the notice-comment-statement of basis sequence provided in informal rulemaking. Voluntary agency supplementation of informal rulemaking procedures presents no particular controversy. Presumably, an agency adds procedural safeguards voluntarily only when it concludes that the additional procedures will provide benefits, in the form of enhanced accuracy of fact-finding or greater public acceptance of the agency's rule, that exceed the costs of the added procedures. Since the agency is in the best position to make this assessment, other institutions of government are reluctant to second-guess an agency's decision to supplement notice and comment rulemaking with additional procedures. Judicial compulsion of agencies to add procedures not required by statute or by the Constitution presents a very different, and much more controversial, issue.

The D.C. Circuit issued a series of opinions in the 1970s in which it reversed agency rules because the agencies failed to provide procedures that the court believed necessary to resolve the issues before the agencies, even though the agencies had provided all procedures required by statute or by the constitution. *Mobil Oil Corporation v. Federal Power Commission* is illustrative of the D.C. Circuit's efforts to compel agencies to use hybrid procedures to promulgate legislative rules.[284] In *Mobil*, the court compelled an agency not otherwise required by statute to render decisions through formal procedures to " 'realistically tailor the proceedings to fit the issues before it, the formation it needs to illuminate those issues and the manner of

---

283. *See supra* § 6.4.5.

284. 483 F.2d 1238 (D.C.Cir.1973); *see generally* Scalia, *Vermont Yankee:*   *The APA, The D.C. Circuit, and the Supreme Court,* 1978 Sup.Ct.Rev. 345, 348–52.

presentation. . . .' " Specifically, the court held that although the FPC was not required by statute to act through formal proceedings, the policy questions before the agency were so "inextricably bound up with relatively specific factual issues" that "some sort of adversary, adjudicative-type procedures" were essential. To meet the additional procedural requirements imposed, the court suggested selective cross-examination on certain issues as well as other permissible means of providing "some mechanism whereby adverse parties can test, criticize and illuminate the flaws in the evidentiary basis being advanced regarding a particular point". Because almost all major agency policy decisions reflected in the outcome of a rulemaking proceeding are predicated on controverted facts, the D.C. Circuit's decision in *Mobil* was broad in scope.

§ 6.4.9a The impact of *Vermont Yankee*

The D.C. Circuit continued to apply its requirement that agencies use hybrid procedures in rulemakings involving contested issues of fact until the Supreme Court's 1978 landmark decision in *Vermont Yankee Nuclear Power Corp. v. Natural Resources Defense Council, Inc.*[285] The Atomic Energy Commission initiated a rulemaking proceeding to determine the manner in which potential environmental damage resulting from disposal of spent nuclear fuel should be reflected in deciding whether to license nuclear power plants. The agency provided all procedures required by its organic act and by the APA for informal rulemaking. It refused, however, to grant NRDC's request to cross-examine witnesses. The D.C. Circuit reversed the AEC rule because of this failure to adopt procedures needed for "thorough ventilation of the issues". The Supreme Court unanimously reversed the D.C. Circuit.

The Court noted that the agency had complied with the procedures for informal rulemaking required by the APA and applicable organic acts. It also recognized that the agency was not required by due process to use formal adjudicatory procedures because, quoting from its opinion in *Bi–Metallic Investment Co. v. State Board of Equalization*,[286] the agency did not single out a very small number of persons who are "exceptionally affected, in each case upon individual grounds, . . . " Thus, the only question before the Court was whether a court can compel an agency to provide procedures more demanding

285. 435 U.S. 519 (1978). Professor (now Justice) Scalia chronicled the decade long dispute between the D.C. Circuit and the Supreme Court concerning the procedures required for rulemaking and the significance of the APA as the legal framework for determining agency procedures. *See* Scalia, *supra* note 284.

286. 239 U.S. 441 (1915). *See supra* § 6.3.2.

than those required by statute or by the Constitution. The Court answered this question with an almost unequivocal no. It held that courts cannot impose upon agencies greater procedural requirements "[a]bsent ... extremely compelling circumstances.... " The Court provided no illustration of such circumstances.

The Court based its holding in *Vermont Yankee* on three reasons. First, if courts are allowed to dictate to agencies on an ad hoc basis the procedures they must use to tailor their procedures to the issues in each case, judicial review of agency choice of procedures will become unpredictable. As a result, conservative agencies would opt for the use of formal adjudicatory procedures in every case in order to eliminate the risk of judicial reversal, and all the advantages of informal rulemaking would be lost. Second, courts cannot second guess agencies by basing their procedural obligations on the record actually produced by use of the procedures chosen by the agency. Third, courts cannot require agencies that choose informal rulemaking procedures to produce records of hearing transcripts analogous to those that result from use of formal adjudicatory procedures. To these three related reasons, the Court could have added a fourth even more fundamental basis for its decision. The judiciary simply has no power independent of congressional enactments and the Constitution to compel a government agency to do anything.

§ 6.4.9b Legislative imposition of hybrid procedures

The Supreme Court's well-founded criticism of hybrid procedures that result from ad hoc decisions of reviewing courts has no application to hybrid procedures that result from congressional action. Congress has the power to require agencies to add procedures to those required by the APA for informal rulemaking, and it sometimes chooses to exercise that power. When it does, its action does not inherently create the problems that result from imposition of procedural requirements after the fact by reviewing courts. Congress can set forth the additional procedures required for a particular class of rulemakings in clear statutory language that avoids any difficulties associated with unpredictability or second-guessing. The most notable congressional effort at establishing hybrid procedures demonstrates, however, that, despite its institutional advantage as a source of procedures, Congress can do as poor a job as courts in selecting appropriate additional procedures to impose.

In 1974, Congress passed the Magnuson–Moss Warranty–Federal Trade Commission Improvement Act.[287] In that Act, Congress created

---

287. 15 U.S.C. § 557a.

a statutory hybrid procedure applicable to FTC rulemaking by adding selected procedural safeguards normally associated with formal adjudication to the relatively simple APA procedures for informal rulemaking. The major additions were (1) the requirement of an oral hearing and report by an independent presiding officer; (2) a right to cross-examine witnesses on disputed issues of material fact; and, (3) a right to submit rebuttal evidence concerning disputed issues of material fact. Congress seemed to recognize that a complete transformation of FTC rulemaking from informal to formal was functionally equivalent to removing the agency's power to make rules, so it attempted to add only selected elements of formal adjudicatory procedure. The rights to cross-examine and to present rebuttal evidence, for instance, were to be limited only to disputed issues of material fact, and the role of the presiding officer was to be limited to presiding and reporting, rather than actually deciding. In practice, these distinctions were far too subtle to create any meaningful difference between pure formal rulemaking, which has long proven virtually impossible to implement,[288] and the hybrid procedure constructed for FTC rulemaking.

Professor Boyer conducted a comprehensive empirical study of the FTC's experience with its hybrid procedure.[289] He assessed the effects of the additional procedures based on three criteria: accuracy, fairness and acceptability, and efficiency. He found no detectable increase in accuracy, or in fairness and acceptability, as a result of the added procedures, but he found that rulemaking proceedings conducted through use of the statutory hybrid were very expensive and protracted.

It may be that Congress ultimately will identify and enact a hybrid procedure that incorporates into informal rulemaking one or more features that will enhance the accuracy of the fact-finding process without sacrificing the obvious efficiency of informal rulemaking. We are skeptical, however. Certainly, Congress' one major effort of this type provides no basis for optimism. We think it more likely that APA informal rulemaking, interpreted to include Judge Leventhal's expanded concept of notice, will prove to be the most effective, fair and efficient procedure for promulgating general legislative rules.[290]

288. *See supra* § 6.4.5.

289. Boyer, *Report on the Trade Regulation Rulemaking Procedures of the Federal Trade Commission (Phase II),* 1979 ACUS Ann.Rep. 41; 1980 ACUS Ann.Rep. 33.

290. *See supra* § 6.4.6a; *see also* Scalia, *supra* note 284 at 405–09.

§ 6.4.10 Informal adjudication

Up to this point, our discussion has focused on the three generic agency procedures that dominate the literature on administrative law—formal adjudication, formal rulemaking and informal rulemaking. Many students will be surprised to learn that we have neglected entirely the category of agency decisionmaking that dominates administrative law in terms of the number of agency decisions that are based on each procedure. About ninety per cent of all agency decisions are made through the fourth category of informal adjudication.

The APA provides only a skeletal procedural framework applicable to agency informal adjudication. If an agency is not engaged in legislative rulemaking, it obviously is not required to use either formal or informal rulemaking procedures. If it is engaged instead in adjudication, the agency is required to use APA procedures for formal adjudication only when its organic act instructs it to do so. In a close case, a court may conclude that an agency is required to use formal adjudication when its organic act is not explicit in directing it to do so,[291] but in a high proportion of cases, an agency's organic act does not even arguably compel it to use formal adjudication to resolve a class of disputes. In this dominant class of cases, the APA contains only one brief section that describes applicable procedures. If, as frequently is the case, the agency's organic act contains no specification of the procedures it is required to provide, the agency is left with APA § 555 as its only source of statutorily prescribed procedures. That section provides only that: (1) a party can retain an attorney or other representative; (2) a party can obtain a copy of any data or evidence she provides; and, (3) a party is entitled to a brief statement of the grounds for denying any written petition.

If an agency is required to adjudicate a class of disputes without adequate statutory procedural requirements, its sole source of external guidance concerning its choice of procedures is the Due Process Clause. At this point it is useful to review briefly our previous extended discussion of the Court's decisions applying the Due Process Clause to agency actions.[292]

Due process can be the source of judicially imposed procedural safeguards only if an agency action deprives an individual of life, liberty or property. If the Due Process Clause applies to an agency action, it does not yield any particular set of required procedures. Rather, the procedural safeguards mandated by due process vary

---

291. *See supra* § 6.4.2.   **292.** *See supra* § 6.3.

substantially depending on the results of application of the three-part balancing test articulated most clearly in *Mathews v. Eldridge:*[293]

> "[I]dentification of the specific dictates of due process generally requires consideration of three distinct factors: First, the private interest that will be affected by the official action; second, the risk of an erroneous deprivation of such interest through the procedures used, and the probable value, if any, of additional or substitute procedural safeguards, and finally, the Government's interest, including the function involved and the fiscal and administrative burdens that the additional or substitute procedural requirement would entail."

This balancing test can produce a wide range of procedures. The requirement of formal adjudication that emerged from the Court's analysis of agency termination of Aid for Dependent Children is at one end of this spectrum. Because of the "immediately desperate" situation created by termination of this form of welfare and because of the dominance of specific factual disputes involving credibility and veracity in the AFDC termination decisionmaking process, the Court concluded in *Goldberg v. Kelly*[294] that welfare authorities could not terminate AFDC benefits without first conducting a formal adjudicatory proceeding that included each of the following procedural safeguards:

1. timely and adequate notice;

2. confronting adverse witnesses;

3. oral presentation of arguments;

4. oral presentation of evidence;

5. cross-examination of adverse witnesses;

6. disclosure to the claimant of opposing evidence;

7. the right to retain an attorney;

8. a determination on the record of the hearing;

9. a statement of reasons for the determination and an indication of the evidence relied on; and

10. an impartial decision maker.

At the other end of the spectrum are cases like *Goss v. Lopez,*[295] where the more modest impact of the government action on the individual's interests (a ten-day suspension from school) required a

---

293. 424 U.S. 319 (1976).

294. 397 U.S. 254 (1970). *See supra* § 6.3.3.

295. 419 U.S. 565 (1975). *See supra* § 6.3.3.

correspondingly less strict set of procedural safeguards. In *Goss,* the Court required the government to provide the individual only notice of the charges and evidence against him and an informal opportunity to explain his version of the facts.

The flexible outcome balancing test of due process analysis is unsatisfactory as the sole guide to agencies concerning the procedures they must use for informal adjudication. There is nothing wrong with the *Mathews* test itself; indeed, we have argued that it probably represents the best method available to determine the minimum procedures required by due process.[296] The difficulty lies in forcing agencies to select procedures based solely on their analysis of a highly subjective test, subject only to constitutional judicial review. It is not good policy to require agencies and reviewing courts to make thousands of relatively routine procedural decisions on a constitutional level. For over a decade, a group of scholars led by Warner Gardner has attempted unsuccessfully to improve the state of the law governing informal adjudicatory procedures by convincing Congress to amend the APA to add a provision specifying the procedures required for informal agency adjudication.[297]

In 1976, one of the authors conducted a theoretical and empirical study of the procedures required for informal adjudication.[298] The study yielded a surprising convergence of theoretical and empirical results. Theoretically, the study concluded that most agency informal adjudications could be fairly, accurately and efficiently conducted through provision of notice, an opportunity for written or oral comment, a statement of reasons, and a neutral decisionmaker. In the empirical part of the investigation, the author studied forty-two programs administered by four agencies. In only two of forty-two programs did the agency make available all ten of the procedural safeguards normally associated with formal adjudication. By far the largest group of programs—over one-half—were administered through use of a form of informal adjudication that consisted of notice, a statement of reasons, a neutral decisionmaker, and, in most cases, an opportunity to present arguments in either written or oral form. The relatively few programs that were administered through procedures that did not include these basic safeguards relied principally on physical inspection of products or premises as the basis for

---

296. *See supra* § 6.3.4.

297. *See, e.g.,* Gardner, *The Procedures by Which Informal Action Is Taken,* 24 Ad.L.Rev. 155 (1972).

298. Verkuil, *A Study of Informal Adjudication Procedures,* 43 U.Chi. L.Rev. 739 (1976). *See also* Verkuil, *A Study of Immigration Procedures,* 31 U.C.L.A.L.Rev. 1141 (1984).

regulatory action. In appropriate circumstances, inspection has always been considered an adequate substitute for more formal procedural safeguards.[299]

The policy implications of this study of informal agency adjudication seem obvious. The APA should be amended to require agencies to provide in all informal adjudications, other than those that rely upon physical inspection, the minimum procedural safeguards of notice, an opportunity to present views orally or in writing, a brief statement of reasons, and an impartial decisionmaker. Such an amendment would provide agencies helpful guidance concerning the procedures appropriate for informal adjudication and would eliminate the need for agencies and reviewing courts to attempt the difficult task of determining procedures appropriate for hundreds of types of adjudications through ad hoc application of the *Mathews v. Eldridge* constitutional test of procedural adequacy.

The Court provided at least a partial solution to the problem of inadequate statutory specification of informal adjudication procedures in *PBGC v. LTV Corp.*[300] The Court concluded that APA § 706(2)(A), which compels a court to set aside an agency action that is arbitrary or capricious, implicitly imposes on agencies a procedural requirement to provide an explanation for an action taken through use of informal adjudication. That requirement applies, however, only if and when a party seeks judicial review of the agency action. The Court also held that a court cannot compel an agency to use procedures beyond those required by statute or by the Due Process Clause.

§ 6.4.11   Prosecutorial discretion

We have saved until the end of our discussion of procedural controls the issue that Professor Davis has characterized as the most important unsolved problem in the United States legal system—control of prosecutorial discretion.[301] Every agency has the power to enforce many statutory prohibitions. No agency has resources sufficient to detect and to bring an action against every violation of every statutory provision it is empowered to enforce. As a result, each agency must have discretion to determine the circumstances in which it will devote substantial resources to enforcing legal obligations within its jurisdiction. Yet, an agency may be tempted to abuse this discretion because it does not believe in some of the laws it is required to enforce, or because of the political affiliations of individu-

---

299. *See e.g.* Ewing v. Mytinger & Casselberry, Inc., 339 U.S. 594 (1950).

300. 496 U.S. 633 (1990).

301. *See* Davis, *An Approach to Legal Control of the Police,* 52 Tex.L.Rev. 703 (1974).

als who stand to gain or lose as a result of its decision to proceed in a given case. Courts have attempted to respond to this recurrent problem in a number of ways—with markedly little success.

The Sixth Circuit's opinion in *Dunn v. Retail Clerks International Association*[302] provides a good introduction to the problem of controlling prosecutorial discretion. *Dunn* involved a suit brought by the owners of a grocery store alleging that a union committed a series of unfair labor practices by intimidating employees into voting for the union; that the owners presented documentary evidence of the unfair labor practices to the Regional Director of the National Labor Relations Board (NLRB); and that he refused to act against the union. The court characterized the situation as "pretty horrible," but concluded that it had no power to require any action because NLRB has exclusive jurisdiction over unfair labor practices and the NLRB's general counsel has wide discretion to decide whether to act on a complaint.

The only exception to the principle established in *Dunn* applies when the agency explicitly declines to prosecute on the basis of a stated reason that is clearly wrong. In *Southern California District Council v. Ordman,*[303] for instance, the NLRB's General Counsel sent a letter to the complaining party stating that he could not prosecute because the statute of limitations had run on an alleged unfair labor practice. The court reversed based on its conclusion that the statute of limitations had not run. It is not at all clear that *Southern California* is a constructive step in the direction of controlling agency prosecutorial discretion. The general counsel stated his reason for failing to prosecute pursuant to a rule voluntarily adopted by NLRB that required the general counsel to provide a statement of reasons. If NLRB wants to avoid potential future judicial control of its exercise of prosecutorial discretion after *Southern California,* it needs only to repeal its rule requiring a statement of reasons, thereby precluding both courts and the public from knowing why it declined to prosecute.

The Supreme Court took a modest step in the direction of controlling agency prosecutorial discretion in *Dunlop v. Bachowski.*[304] The Labor–Management Reporting and Disclosure Act confers upon the Secretary of Labor the power to bring an action to upset a union election if he finds election irregularities that affected the outcome of the election. The Secretary's power to challenge an election can be

---

302.   307 F.2d 285 (6th Cir.1962).   **304.**   421 U.S. 560 (1975).

303.   318 F.Supp. 633 (C.D.Cal.1970).

exercised only within sixty days after the election in order to provide prompt finality to union election results. The power to challenge an election is vested exclusively in the Secretary in order to save unions the expense of having to defend against expensive and debilitating election challenges.

Bachowski alleged that his opponent had engaged in several election irregularities that affected the outcome of the election; that the Secretary knew of the irregularities and their affect on the election; and, that the Secretary still declined to challenge the election results. The Third Circuit found the Secretary's action subject to judicial review and held that the Secretary must state his reasons for declining to bring an action challenging the results of the election.[305] The court then held that it had the power to review both the legality of the Secretary's reasons and the factual basis for his decision.

The Supreme Court agreed with the Third Circuit's holdings that the Secretary must state the reasons for his refusal to prosecute and that those reasons are subject to judicial review. It disagreed, however, with the court of appeals' holding that the factual basis for the Secretary's action was subject to judicial review. The Court concluded that the protracted evidentiary hearing required to determine the facts on which the Secretary premised his decision not to bring an action would interfere with the congressional desire to attain prompt finality in union elections and to allow unions to conserve their resources rather than expending them defending against frivolous litigation.

The Court's attempt to control prosecutorial discretion in *Dunlop* obviously is only a tentative first step. The remedy provided—a mandatory statement of reasons and judicial review of the legality of the reasons stated—can be circumvented easily by an agency intent on abusing its discretion. The agency need only state that its investigation produced inadequate evidence of conduct violative of the law, and the very limited judicial role created in *Dunlop* is at an end. It is difficult to devise, however, any more effective means of judicial control of agency prosecutorial discretion.

The solution initially adopted by the Third Circuit and rejected by the Supreme Court—an evidentiary hearing to determine the factual basis for the agency's decision not to prosecute—seems totally unworkable. It would require an inordinate expenditure of agency resources whenever a complaining party disagreed with an agency's decision not to prosecute. Courts then would experience great diffi-

305. Bachowski v. Brennan, 502 F.2d
79 (3d Cir.1974).

culty determining the factual circumstances in which an agency is required to prosecute. What if there is some evidence of violations of the law, but the agency does not think it has a good chance of proving those violations? What if the agency's decision is based in part on its limited investigative and prosecutorial resources and in part on the existence of several other cases in which it believes that the violations of law are more serious or more easily proven? These are relatively common reasons agencies decide not to prosecute. It is hard to envision a constructive judicial role in second-guessing these kinds of agency decisions. Indeed, an agency might soon find that its most frequent response to a judicial inquiry concerning its failure to prosecute is that its limited resources are devoted exclusively to responding to other judicial inquiries concerning its failure to prosecute.

In *Heckler v. Chaney*,[306] the Court recognized that most agency exercises of prosecutorial discretion are based on complicated consideration of factors uniquely within an agency's knowledge and expertise. The Court announced a presumption of unreviewability of agency inaction. The presumption can be rebutted either by the existence of a mandatory statutory duty to act in specified circumstances that are determinable by a reviewing court, or by the existence of such a duty imposed by the agency itself in a legislative rule.

Professor Davis has devoted considerable effort to the study of prosecutorial discretion. He believes that courts are inherently limited in their ability independently to control prosecutorial discretion because decisions to prosecute are based on many complicated factors that are beyond judicial ability to supervise. He sees as the primary answer to the problem of unlimited prosecutorial discretion agency promulgation of rules concerning its exercise of prosecutorial discretion. This solution follows logically from his well-documented belief that prosecutorial discretion should be limited, but that courts do not have sufficient understanding of the many factors underlying the exercise of prosecutorial discretion to establish useful rules or principles applicable to agency exercises of prosecutorial discretion.

Thus, agencies themselves are the only promising source of limits on their prosecutorial discretion. If they can be convinced to regularize their exercise of prosecutorial discretion through issuance of rules and statements of reasons, the courts can be of assistance in channeling each agency's exercise of prosecutorial discretion by enforcing the agency's own rules against it and by reviewing each

306. 470 U.S. 821 (1985). *See supra*
§ 5.3.2.

agency statement of reasons for consistency with the agency's rules and with its statements in other cases. In this sense, the Supreme Court's decisions in *Dunlop* and *Chaney* have some potential as a first step toward judicial control of prosecutorial discretion.

Courts are even more reluctant to review agency decisions to prosecute. The Supreme Court's opinion in *Moog Industries, Inc. v. Federal Trade Commission*[307] illustrates and explains this reluctance. FTC conducted a hearing in which it concluded that Moog's pricing practices were unfair and ordered Moog to cease and desist from those practices. Moog sought judicial review on the basis that the pricing practices in which it engaged were widespread in the industry and that it would go out of business if it were required to cease practices that were still available to its competitors. It asked the Court to hold FTC's cease and desist order in abeyance until the agency had issued similar orders against Moog's competitors. The Court declined to do so and affirmed the FTC's order.

The Court emphasized that an agency's decision whether to proceed simultaneously against an entire industry or instead to begin by prosecuting a single firm requires the agency to exercise specialized, experienced judgment unique to it. The agency is in the best position to determine whether a practice is widespread or concentrated in a few firms. Even if a practice is widespread, an agency may conclude that its most effective enforcement strategy requires it to move initially against a single firm that it believes to be engaging in the practice. Its selection of an initial target firm also is complicated by such considerations as the degree of difficulty it anticipates in establishing the nature and effect of each firm's practices. The Court indicated its unwillingness to interfere with an agency's exercise of its discretion to proceed initially against a single firm in the absence of a patent abuse of discretion—a standard that very few defendants can meet.[308]

In addition to Professor Davis' proposal to encourage agencies to adopt rules to govern their exercise of prosecutorial discretion, there is one other method through which Congress and the courts can be of assistance in encouraging agencies to proceed in an even-handed manner in enforcing laws within their jurisdiction. If an agency has available relatively inexpensive and rapid methods of acting against unlawful practices by general rule, it is much less likely to be tempted to proceed primarily through ad hoc or selective prosecution of individuals. Thus, judicial decisions such as *Vermont Yankee*,

307. 355 U.S. 411 (1958).

308. *See* FTC v. Universal–Rundle Corp., 387 U.S. 244 (1967).

which provide agencies the freedom to use informal notice and comment rulemaking as the basis for promulgating legislative rules, indirectly reduce the potential problems associated with agency exercise of prosecutorial discretion. On the other hand, statutes like the FTC Improvement Act, which make agency rulemaking extremely expensive and time-consuming, exacerbate the problem of agency exercise of prosecutorial discretion by virtually forcing agencies to regulate through ad hoc prosecution of individuals.[309]

There is one final serious problem in agency exercise of prosecutorial discretion—what can a court do if an agency chooses not to enforce at all a law subject to its exclusive jurisdiction. The Ninth Circuit confronted this challenging problem in *Rockbridge v. Lincoln*.[310] A statute gave the Secretary of Interior power to designate traders who could do business on the Navajo Indian Reservation and to "specify . . . the kind and quantity of goods and the prices at which such goods shall be sold to the Indians".[311] A group of Navajos brought an action against the Secretary alleging that he had refused completely to regulate the prices and practices of traders. The court began by analyzing carefully the language and legislative history of the statute. It concluded that the statutory grant of authority was not merely permissive; rather, Congress imposed a mandatory duty on the Secretary to regulate the prices and practices of traders. The court then ordered the Secretary to carry out that duty.

If a court concludes that an agency is subject to a duty to regulate some aspect of conduct, it can and will order the agency to fulfill that duty, but that order may just begin the process of judicial supervision of the agency's fulfillment of its regulatory duty. If an agency is reluctant to enforce a regulatory requirement, whether that reluctance is attributable to disagreement with the regulatory requirement or lack of resources, a judicial order simply directing the agency to enforce the regulatory requirement is unlikely to result in effective regulation. What does the court do, for instance, if the Secretary in *Rockbridge* sets ceilings on prices above the prevailing price levels on the reservation? What does the court do if the Secretary sets meaningful price ceilings, but does not enforce those ceilings? A court that attempts to coerce an agency into enforcing a regulatory requirement usually discovers that it cannot do so effectively through any action short of detailed supervision of every aspect of the agency's operations. Occasionally, a court attempts this type of

309. *See supra* §§ 6.4.1, 6.4.9a and 6.4.9b.

310. 449 F.2d 567 (9th Cir.1971).

311. 25 U.S.C. §§ 261, 262.

massive undertaking through issuance of an order specifying in detail the method and timetable on which the agency must proceed and indicating its willingness to maintain continuing jurisdiction over the agency to enforce each aspect of its mandate. This is an extreme step that should be reserved for extreme cases, however, since it requires a judge, in effect, to assume all of the resource allocation decisions of the agency head. Judges do not have the knowledge of agency resources or the administrative experience necessary to manage a major bureaucracy from a position outside the agency. During the 1990s, the Court has issued numerous opinions in which it has discouraged judges from attempting to exercise this form of control over agencies.[312]

§ 6.4.12 Private rights of action

In the previous section, we explored the problem of agency abuse of prosecutorial discretion and one potential solution to that problem—judicial intervention in agency decisions concerning enforcement of regulatory schemes. We concluded that courts could play only a very limited role in addressing the problem through this mechanism. Courts can do little more than to require agencies to state reasons for their prosecutorial decisions. In this section, we will consider an alternative method of responding to the problem of inadequate or uneven agency enforcement. A court can hold that a statute that delegates power to an agency to regulate the conduct of one class of individuals for the benefit of another class of individuals also confers on each beneficiary of the statute a judicially enforceable private right of action against anyone who violates the statute. Throughout this section, we will borrow heavily from the comprehensive treatment of this subject by Professors Stewart and Sunstein.[313]

The private right of action is much more effective as a potential response to inadequate agency enforcement than is judicial intervention in agency enforcement decisions. Conferring a private right of action on a beneficiary of a regulatory statute places all enforcement decisions in the control of the private party. The private right of action also avoids some of the most significant difficulties created by judicial intervention in agency enforcement decisions. Recognizing a private right of action does not require a court to attempt the near impossible, and arguably inappropriate, task of overseeing an agency's allocation of its enforcement resources.

312. *See, e.g.,* Blessing v. Freestone, 520 U.S. 329 (1997); Lewis v. Casey, 518 U.S. 343 (1996); Missouri v. Jenkins, 515 U.S. 70 (1995).

313. Stewart and Sunstein, *Public Programs and Private Rights,* 95 Harv. L.Rev. 1193 (1982).

Courts are asked to recognize private rights of action in many different contexts. Two circumstances should pose no particular difficulty. First, there is the situation, familiar to all students of tort law, in which a statutory standard is used to determine the level of reasonable care that is owed by one citizen to another.[314] This widely accepted doctrine of negligence per se does not require a court to conclude that a statute has created a new right of action, however; the right of action for harm caused by breach of the duty of reasonable care has long existed at common law. Applying the negligence per se doctrine requires only judicial recognition that the legislature can define reasonable care in a particular context by statute. The second easy case arises when the legislature has explicitly indicated its intent that a regulatory statute does, or does not, create a private right of action. In this situation, the court should simply defer to the legislative decision.

As discussed in detail in § 5.4, however, the Court has issued two decisions in which it has severely limited the availability of explicit private rights of action. In both cases, the Court relied on standing to limit both the range of individuals that can bring such an action and the circumstances in which anyone can bring such an action. In its 1992 decision in *Lujan v. Defenders of Wildlife*,[315] the Court held that only an individual who has suffered a "particularized," "concrete," and "imminent" injury caused by a defendant's conduct can bring a private right of action, even when Congress has explicitly authorized "any person" to bring such an action. In its 1998 decision in *Steel Co. v. Citizens for a Better Environment*,[316] the Court held that no one can bring an explicit statutory private right of action based on a "wholly past" violation of a statute or rule.

Hard cases arise frequently, however, where Congress has not clearly indicated whether it intended a statute administered principally by an agency to give rise also to a private right of action. Courts can take one of two general approaches to the private right of action issue in this difficult class of cases. Courts can approach the issue formalistically, recognizing a private right of action only when the legislature clearly indicated its intent to create such a right. Alternatively, courts can take a functional approach when the legislature is silent on the issue. Under the functional approach, the court implies a private right of action when such a right seems consistent with the nature and goals of the regulatory scheme created by the legislature.

---

314. *See* Thayer, *Public Wrong and Private Action*, 27 Harv.L.Rev. 317 (1914).

315. 504 U.S. 555 (1992).

316. 523 U.S. 83 (1998).

The Supreme Court has vacillated between these two approaches. Its recent decisions have reflected the formalistic approach. *Touche Ross & Co. v. Redington*[317] provides a good illustration of the formalistic approach. Touche Ross was retained by Weis, a brokerage firm, as an independent auditor of Weis' books and records. Weis' financial situation became precarious, and the district court appointed Redington as a trustee in the liquidation of Weis' business. Weis' assets proved to be insufficient to cover all of the claims of its customers and creditors. Redington sued Touche Ross on behalf of Weis' customers and creditors, alleging that Touche Ross was liable because of its alleged violation of section 17(a) of the Securities and Exchange Act. That provision imposes duties on independent auditors, enforceable by the Securities and Exchange Commission (SEC), to make reports and to provide opinions concerning the financial condition of brokerage firms.

The Court analyzed the language and legislative history of section 17(a) and found no evidence that Congress intended to create a private right of action to enforce the section. It concluded that the absence of evidence of such legislative intent was dispositive of the issue. In the language of the majority opinion: "The ultimate question is one of congressional intent, not one of whether this Court thinks it can improve upon the statutory scheme that Congress enacted into law."

The best illustration of the alternative, functional analysis, that dominated the Court's approach to the issue in the 1960's, is *J.I. Case Co. v. Borak.*[318] Borak owned shares of Case. Case proposed to merge with American Tractor Corporation. Borak sought to enjoin the merger on the basis that Case and some of its directors had violated section 14(a) of the SEC Act by including false and misleading statements in proxy statements related to the proposed merger.

The Court recognized that the language and legislative history of section 14(a) did not establish a specific congressional intent to create a private right of action for its violation. The Court held, however, that Congress implied a private right of action by alluding to statutory purposes, such as protection of investors, that would be furthered by recognition of a private right of action.

Stewart and Sunstein criticize the recent formalistic approach of the Court and urge the Court to return to its former functional approach to determining whether a regulatory provision creates a private right of action. They argue that the functional approach is

317. 442 U.S. 560 (1979).   **318.** 377 U.S. 426 (1964).

more consistent with the reality of the legislative process. Congress frequently enacts a statutory provision to further a general purpose without addressing specific subsidiary issues, such as whether the purpose of the provision would be furthered by making it the basis for a private right of action. In such circumstances, it is fair and proper for a court to draw the inference from the general purpose of the provision that Congress would have provided a private right of action if it had focused on that subsidiary issue.

Stewart and Sunstein also seem to recognize, however, that the Court's formalistic approach probably produces the right result most of the time, because the functional approach should yield recognition of a private right of action only in a narrow class of cases. A court should imply a private right of action based on a provision of a statute administered by an agency only when: (1) the provision creates a right-duty relationship between individuals analogous to relationships recognized by the common law; and, (2) the scope of the right-duty relationship is clear.

In the context of most regulatory statutes, creation of a private right of action can do far more harm than good. Most regulatory statutes confer authority on agencies in broad terms. As a result, agencies are granted the power to exercise their expertise and their discretion to determine the nature of the duties imposed by the statute. In performing this function, agencies are accountable, albeit in attenuated ways, to Congress and to the President.[319] In interpreting and applying broad regulatory provisions, agencies must make many basic policy decisions. Because they are more politically accountable than courts, agencies are better-suited to this policy making role than courts. The constitutional, political, and practical advantages of agencies as a source of policy decisions are recognized consistently in administrative law. Doctrines like the final order requirement, the duty to exhaust administrative remedies, and primary jurisdiction are designed to permit agencies to carry out their policy making role with a minimum of judicial interference.[320] The high degree of deference that reviewing courts are required to grant to many agency decisions also is based principally on recognition that agencies, rather than courts, must be the dominant source of policy decisions that Congress has chosen to delegate to agencies.[321]

Creating private rights of action to enforce broad regulatory standards administered by agencies forces courts to make policy

319. *See supra* Chapters 3 and 4.

320. *See supra* §§ 5.7 and 5.8.

321. *See infra* Chapter 7.

decisions in the process of interpreting imprecise statutory provisions and applying those provisions to the facts of the disputes brought before the courts. This result is destructive in three important ways. First, uniformity of regulation is impaired because courts can be expected to differ in their interpretations of broad statutory provisions. Second, the overall efficacy of the regulatory program is likely to suffer because courts have less understanding than a specialized agency of the facts relevant to regulatory disputes and of the relationships between the general purposes of a regulatory program and competing interpretations of particular statutory provisions. Third and most fundamental, unelected judges are not an appropriate source of non-constitutional policy decisions. Separation of powers requires that agencies retain the discretion to make policy decisions that Congress has entrusted to agencies.

Chapter Seven

JUDICIAL CONTROL OF ADMINISTRATIVE DISCRETION— SUBSTANTIVE ISSUES

§ 7.1   The Role of Substantive Review

When Congress grants an agency power to act in an area, it accompanies that grant of power with statutory limits on the type of action the agency can take and the factual circumstances in which it is empowered to act. Any agency action must be premised on an express or implied set of legal conclusions and pattern of facts. The major function of substantive judicial review of agency actions, apart from the independent role of the judiciary in enforcing the Constitution, is to ensure that agencies act only in ways that are consistent with the legislative policy decisions reflected in statutes that delegate power to agencies.

An agency's action is consistent with the policy decisions of Congress only if the agency's action is based on an accurate determination of legislative intent and an accurate determination of the factual predicates for the agency's action. Through substantive review, courts assist Congress in implementing the policies it has chosen to reflect in statutory provisions that establish legal standards applicable to agency actions and factual predicates on which agency actions must be premised.

The substantive standards through which Congress confines the exercise of agency discretion vary considerably in their precision. In some cases, Congress limits an agency's power to act through use of precise legal standards or by permitting an agency to act only if it first finds the existence of specific historic facts. The Natural Gas Policy Act of 1978, for instance, authorized the Federal Energy Regulatory Commission (FERC) to set a price ceiling of $1.75 per million British thermal units, escalated in accordance with a specific formula, for gas produced from a well drilled after April 20, 1977, if, but only if, that well is at least 2.5 miles from any well drilled between January 1, 1970, and April 20, 1977.[1] This degree of specificity is unusual, however. More frequently, Congress states the legal

---

1. 15 U.S.C. §§ 3301(3–5), 3312(b), 3312(c)(1)(B)(i).

standards applicable to agency actions in the form of a single broad standard, such as the Natural Gas Act's requirement that FERC approve construction of facilities only when they are consistent with the "public convenience and necessity",[2] or in the form of a lengthy list of often inconsistent goals that an agency is required to pursue. Similarly, the factual predicates for agency actions often are imprecise. The statutory limitation on the Occupational Safety and Health Administration's power to establish a rule for health and safety in the work place only when such a rule is "reasonably necessary or appropriate to provide safe or healthful employment" provides an illustration of the typically imprecise factual predicates for agency action.[3]

Judicial review of the substance of agency actions is essential to insure that each agency acts in a manner consistent with legislative policy decisions. It by no means follows, however, that a court should substitute its judgment for that of an agency. Indeed, it is part of the standard litany of judicial review of agency action that a reviewing court cannot substitute its judgment for that of an agency, but must instead assume a much more limited role. Reviewing courts accord agency decisions considerable deference for several reasons. First, an agency has a significant comparative advantage over a court with respect to most of its factual findings and legal conclusions because of the agency's superior expertise in a field, its better understanding of its overall mission and the way in which its action in a given case relates to that mission, and its greater familiarity with the facts and issues in a proceeding.

Second, courts defer to agencies because courts recognize that agencies, rather than courts, ultimately must make all decisions within their jurisdiction. A reviewing court may reverse and remand an agency's action many times, thereby forcing it to reconsider its decision. In the vast majority of cases, however, the agency remains free upon reconsideration to pursue the same action previously reversed by the court if it can base that action on a more solid evidentiary foundation, a somewhat different interpretation of its statutory mandate, or a more thorough discussion of the reasoning process through which it made its decision. A reviewing court always can delay a particular agency action, sometimes indefinitely, but a court can never take a specific action within an agency's jurisdiction or force the agency to take a specific action preferred by the court.

2. 15 U.S.C. § 717f(c).

3. *See* Industrial Union Dept. v. American Petroleum Institute, 448 U.S. 607 (1980).

Thus, the judicial role in administrative law is inherently limited, and a reviewing court often affirms an agency action based on a less than perfect evidentiary record and reasoning process because the court sees less potential harm as a result of allowing an imperfect agency action to go into effect immediately than would result from delaying that agency action for several years while the agency gathers additional evidence or considers additional decisional factors in an effort to remedy the imperfections that underlay its initial action.

Finally, courts defer to agencies because Congress has instructed them to do so. The evidence of congressional intent to accord to agencies some degree of deference on judicial review comes from two sources. First, in most cases Congress has explicitly directed courts to grant deference to some aspects of agency decisionmaking by providing for judicial review under an obviously deferential standard such as "substantial evidence" or "arbitrary and capricious". Second, in many cases Congress has implicitly evidenced its intent to confer upon agencies considerable discretion to interpret terms in statutes and to choose among several policy options by accompanying its grant of power to the agency with standards to guide the agency's exercise of that power that are so broad that they are susceptible to many different interpretations. A court cannot confine an agency's actions to the pursuit of a policy adopted by Congress when Congress has not reflected a policy decision in statutory language.

Congress' increasing tendency to delegate major policy decisions to agencies instead of making those decisions itself presents particular problems for courts engaged in substantive review of agency actions. Courts strive to limit agency discretion, but they experience great difficulty performing this mission when Congress declines to make the basic policy decisions that courts can use as a basis to channel agency exercises of discretion. In the all too frequent case of an agency whose statutory discretion is so broad that it can choose any of several policies to pursue, reviewing courts still can serve some valuable functions through substantive review. They can fairly infer from the general purposes of agency organic acts and from the legislative decision to make an agency's actions subject to substantive judicial review that Congress intended to limit agency discretion in two general ways. First, Congress intended to require the agency to engage in a rational decisionmaking process in which the agency considers all significant factors relevant to its decision and uses the best data available as the basis for its decision. Second, Congress intended to preclude the agency from making its decisions in a discriminatory manner based on the personal or political characteristics of the parties affected by the agency's action. By engaging in review of the rationality of the agency decisionmaking process—the evidentiary basis for the agency's findings and the reasoning used by the agency to proceed from its findings to its decision—and by comparing the agency action under review with the agency's actions in related proceedings for consistency, a reviewing court can fulfill these two functions even when Congress has provided little indication of the particular policy the agency is required to pursue.

In reviewing the rationality of agency decisionmaking, courts must be particularly careful not to go beyond their limited role in the administrative process. Outside the constitutional law context, the judiciary is the least appropriate branch of government to make policy decisions, since it is the least accountable to the electorate. Yet, judges charged with the responsibility to control agency discretion without adequate guidance from Congress concerning the way in which that discretion is to be exercised sometimes succumb to the temptation to interject into the process of substantive review their own views concerning the policies agencies should follow. Substantive review based putatively on the need to assure rationality and consistency can be transformed sub rosa into a means through which courts actually substitute their policy preferences for those of agencies. Since agencies are substantially more politically accountable than courts,[4] this is an inappropriate role for courts to assume. One of our principal goals in this chapter is to describe the limited role of judicial review of the substance of agency actions and to identify circumstances in which courts sometimes act in ways inconsistent with that limited role.

In our explication of substantive review of agency actions, we will discuss under separate headings various aspects of judicial review—review of findings of fact, review of interpretations of statutes, and review of the agency reasoning process. As we proceed through the discussion, however, it should become apparent that our division of judicial review into discrete categories is an oversimplification for pedagogical purposes. In practice, courts often are unable to respect the tidy lines we have drawn to separate aspects of judicial review. They look instead at the totality of the agency action, sometimes even blurring the distinction between procedural and substantive review of an agency action. Indeed, judicial review of an agency's reasoning process can be characterized as either substantive or procedural.

4. *See supra* Chapters 3 and 4.

§ 7.2 The Requirement of Findings of Fact and Conclusions of Law

The APA requires an agency to adopt in any formal adjudication or formal rulemaking a complete statement of its findings with respect to all material issues of fact and its conclusions concerning all legal issues presented.[5] The APA does not explicitly require findings and conclusions in the case of rules adopted through informal rulemaking, but it does require the agency to accompany its rule with a general statement of basis and purpose. The requirement for such a statement may be slightly less rigid than the requirement for specific findings and conclusions on each material issue that applies to formal adjudication and formal rulemaking. Yet, the statement of basis and purpose that an agency must incorporate in each rule adopted through informal rulemaking serves the same function as findings and conclusions—it provides the principal basis for substantive review of the agency action.

The APA does not explicitly require any findings, conclusions or statement of basis in the fourth, and largest, category of agency actions—informal adjudication. The Court eliminated this potentially significant impediment to substantive review of agency informal adjudicative action in its landmark decision in *Citizens to Preserve Overton Park, Inc. v. Volpe.*[6] Transportation Secretary Volpe had approved the route of a federally financed highway through a park over the objection of the citizens' group. The group challenged Volpe's decision under a statute that the Court interpreted to prohibit use of parklands for highways if a feasible and prudent alternate route exists. Volpe rendered his decision, however, without any findings of fact or statement of reasons, so the Court had no basis to determine whether his action was consistent with the statute. The Court rejected the argument of the citizens' group that Volpe's decision was invalid because of his failure to state any findings, conclusions or reasons, since neither the APA nor the agency's organic act required Volpe to provide any such statement in the case of an action taken through informal adjudication. The Court recognized, however, that a reviewing court must have some basis on which to engage in substantive review. It remanded the review proceeding to the district court with the suggestion that the court require the agency to explain the basis for its decision. This procedure would permit the court to obtain a statement it could then use as the basis for substantive review.

5. 5 U.S.C. § 557(c).   **6.** 401 U.S. 402 (1971).

The Court reaffirmed this part of its *Overton Park* holding in
PBGC v. LTV Corp.[7] The court held that APA § 706(2)(A) implicitly
authorizes a court to require an agency to provide a brief explanation
for an action taken through informal adjudication to enable the court
to determine whether the action is arbitrary or capricious.

In *Securities & Exchange Commission v. Chenery,*[8] the Court
announced an important corollary to the requirement that an agency
provide a statement of its basis for an action. The first time the
proceeding reached the Court, SEC had disapproved a corporate
reorganization of a public utility holding company on the basis of the
SEC's interpretation of several judicial decisions. The Court reversed
the SEC order on the basis that the agency had misinterpreted the
judicial decisions on which it relied.[9] SEC reconsidered its action in
light of the Court's opinion and issued a second order taking the
same action but premising that action on different reasoning. Chenery appealed SEC's second order, alleging that SEC was precluded
from taking the second action by the Court's earlier opinion reversing the same agency action.

The Court affirmed the SEC's second order in an opinion in
which it clarified the basis for its first opinion. It described its earlier
opinion as based upon "a simple but fundamental rule of administrative law". A court can review an agency action only on the basis of
the grounds stated by the agency. If those grounds are inadequate or
improper, as was the case with SEC's first order, the court must
reverse the agency action even if the action could be affirmed on a
basis not stated by the agency. A reviewing court cannot consider the
validity of an agency action on any basis other than the basis stated
by the agency. If the court were to rely on a reason not stated by the
agency, it would be improperly invading the exclusive province of the
agency. It follows that the Court could affirm the agency's second
order, even though its effect was identical to the first order, because
the second order was based on proper grounds.

§ 7.3 Review of Findings of Fact

In rare circumstances, agency findings of fact are specifically
made subject to de novo review by an agency organic act.[10] In all
other cases, agency findings are subject to review under either the

7. 496 U.S. 633 (1990). *See also,*
Camp v. Pitts, 411 U.S. 138 (1973); United States v. Morgan, 313 U.S. 409, 422
(1941).

8. 332 U.S. 194 (1947).

9. SEC v. Chenery, 318 U.S. 80
(1943).

10. *See* 7 U.S.C. § 2022; 5 U.S.C.
§ 706.

substantial evidence test or the arbitrary and capricious test. Traditionally, the substantial evidence test applied only to formal adjudication and formal rulemaking, while the arguably more deferential arbitrary and capricious test applied to informal rulemaking and informal adjudication. The APA reflects this dichotomy by mandating substantial evidence review only for findings adopted through formal rulemaking and formal adjudication.[11] In some cases, however, agency organic acts require review of findings of fact made through informal rulemaking under the substantial evidence test as well.[12] In addition, there is now a lively debate among judges and scholars as to whether there is a continuing difference between the substantial evidence test and the arbitrary and capricious test as they apply to findings of fact. We will return to these complications after we begin our discussion of judicial review of findings of fact by focusing on the context in which the state of the law is most clear—judicial review under the substantial evidence test of findings of fact adopted through formal procedures.

§ 7.3.1   The substantial evidence test

The Court first defined substantial evidence in *Consolidated Edison Co. v. NLRB:*

> "Substantial evidence is more than a scintilla. It means such relevant evidence as a reasonable mind might accept as adequate to support a conclusion."[13]

The Court clarified this definition in *Universal Camera Corp. v. NLRB*[14] by requiring that the evidence be "substantial" after the reviewing court takes into account "whatever in the record detracts from its weight". Thus, the evidence must be sufficient to support the conclusion of a reasonable person after considering the evidentiary record as a whole, not just the evidence that is consistent with the agency's finding.

Even with the qualification added in *Universal Camera*, the substantial evidence test accords considerable deference to agency findings of fact. The state of the evidentiary record concerning a disputed fact often is such that it would permit a reasonable person to reach more than one conclusion. In such cases, the agency's finding will be affirmed as long as it reaches any of those conclusions. Judicial deference to agency findings of fact is particularly appropriate. Agencies have a substantial comparative advantage over review-

---

11. 5 U.S.C. § 706(2)(E).

12. *See, e.g.,* 15 U.S.C. § 717r.

13. 305 U.S. 197, 229 (1938).

14. 340 U.S. 474, 488 (1951).

ing courts in finding facts because of their greater familiarity with the record and their specialized expertise in the areas in which they are required to resolve factual disputes.

Occasionally, courts have confused deference to agency findings with deference to findings by agency administrative law judges (ALJ). If an agency and an ALJ disagree with respect to a finding of fact, it is the agency's finding that is due deference on judicial review.[15] The ALJ's findings are only a part of the record to be considered by a reviewing court in determining whether the agency's finding is supported by the record as a whole. A finding by an ALJ is particularly influential with a reviewing court, however, when the finding is based largely on the credibility of witnesses, since the ALJ was actually present at the time the testimony was given.

In 1958, Professor Cooper conducted an extensive empirical study of judicial application of the substantial evidence test. He derived from this study the following seven rules of thumb that courts used in applying the test:[16]

(1) hearsay is not substantial evidence, at least if it is opposed by competent evidence;

(2) a finding contrary to uncontradicted testimony is not supported by substantial evidence;

(3) evidence that is slight or sketchy in an absolute sense is not substantial evidence;

(4) evidence that is slight in relation to much stronger contrary evidence is not substantial evidence;

(5) an Administrative Law Judge's finding contrary to an agency finding can be a significant factor leading a court to conclude that the agency finding is not supported by substantial evidence;

(6) dissenting opinions by members of the agency with respect to agency findings of fact have an effect on a reviewing court comparable to a contrary finding by an Administrative Law Judge;

(7) a court is more likely to reverse an agency finding if the agency has engaged in a consistent pattern of crediting the agency's witnesses and discrediting opposing witnesses.

15. *See, e.g.,* NLRB v. Brooks Cameras, Inc., 691 F.2d 912 (9th Cir.1982).

16. Cooper, *Administrative Law: The Substantial Evidence Rule,* 44 A.B.A.J. 945, 1002–3 (1958).

Only the first of these seven simple guidelines requires revision to reflect modern applications of the substantial evidence test. In recent years, courts have become more tolerant of hearsay evidence. In *Richardson v. Perales*,[17] for instance, the Court held that an agency can base a finding solely on hearsay evidence, even when the hearsay evidence was contradicted by non-hearsay evidence, if the hearsay evidence was of a type relied upon by a reasonably prudent person in conducting his affairs.

A six-Justice majority of the Court adopted and applied a surprisingly non-deferential version of the substantial evidence test in the 1998 opinion in *Allentown Mack Sales and Service v. NLRB*.[18] The NLRB found that an employer did not have "good faith objective reasonable doubt" that a union continued to enjoy the support of a majority of its employees. The employer argued that it had a reasonable basis for its doubt based on statements of non-support made to managers by ten of thirty-two employees. The agency discounted three of those statements based on a combination of their content and context. It then concluded that statements of non-support by seven of thirty-two employees were insufficient to provide the basis for a reasonable doubt that the union continued to enjoy the support of a majority of employees. The six-Justice majority reversed the agency finding on the basis that it was not supported by substantial evidence. The majority concluded that the three statements the agency discounted had "undeniable and substantial probative value on the issue of reasonable doubt." The majority also concluded that the agency was required to find that the employer had a basis for reasonable doubt based on the statements of non-support of the ten employees.

The dissenting Justices expressed the view that the agency's finding was supported by substantial evidence and adequate reasons. The dissenting Justices also criticized the majority for substituting its views of the facts for those of the specialized agency to which Congress had entrusted the fact-finding process.

The surprising opinion in *Allentown* seems to have been motivated by the Justices' broader concerns about the manner in which the NLRB is implementing the National labor Relations Act. The majority opinion accuses the NLRB of engaging in a combination of practices that are designed "to impede judicial review, and even political review, by disguising its policymaking as fact finding." Those practices include: refusing to issue rules that announce the agency's

17. 402 U.S. 389 (1971).   18. 522 U.S. 359 (1998).

policies and statutory interpretations; adopting a plausible but malleable statutory interpretation in the course of adjudicating a particular dispute and then gradually changing that interpretation in subsequent cases; and, adopting idiosyncratic evidentiary standards that have the effect of changing the meaning of the substantive standard the agency says it is applying.

When an agency acts through informal adjudication or informal rulemaking, APA does not subject its findings of fact to review under the substantial evidence test, but the agency's organic act sometimes does. The Federal Energy Regulatory Commission when it takes an action under the Natural Gas Act, for instance, must support each of its findings with substantial evidence no matter what procedure it follows in taking that action.[19] Some judges have suggested that the combination of informal decisionmaking procedures and substantial evidence review of findings of fact constitutes an irrational congressional compromise that renders substantive judicial review extremely difficult.[20] The principal problem they identify is the absence of an evidentiary record on which such review can be premised. We do not share this belief. Agencies today recognize that they must comply with the duty imposed by Judge Leventhal in *Portland Cement* to disclose the factual and scientific basis for any rule proposed for adoption through informal rulemaking in time for affected members of the public to comment on that basis.[21] The sequence of notice, comments and agency statement of basis then yields a record available to a reviewing court for application of the substantial evidence test. Many judicial opinions indicate that courts are able to apply the substantial evidence test to findings adopted on the basis of a rulemaking record consisting primarily of written exchanges of evidence and critiques of evidence presented by other parties.[22]

§ 7.3.2   The arbitrary and capricious test

If an agency acts through informal adjudication or informal rulemaking, and its organic act does not subject its findings to substantial evidence review, the APA authorizes judicial review of the agency's findings of fact under the arbitrary and capricious test. This

---

19.   15 U.S.C. § 717r.

20.   *See, e.g.,* Industrial Union Dept. v. Hodgson, 499 F.2d 467, 469 (D.C.Cir. 1974).

21.   *See supra* § 6.4.6a.

22.   *See, e.g.,* American Public Gas Ass'n v. FPC, 567 F.2d 1016 (D.C.Cir. 1977), cert. denied, 435 U.S. 907 (1978); *see generally* Gifford, *Rulemaking and Rulemaking Review: Struggling Toward a New Paradigm,* 32 Ad.L.Rev. 577 (1980).

ubiquitous test has undergone a dramatic transformation over the course of the last half century.

The original version of the arbitrary and capricious test was extraordinarily deferential to agencies. Indeed, it seemed not to envision judicial review of factual findings at all. The original version is illustrated by the Court's 1935 opinion in *Pacific States Box & Basket Co. v. White.*[23] A California manufacturer challenged the validity of an order issued by the Chief of the Oregon Division of Plant Industry prescribing the type, size and shape of containers to be used in the sale of raspberries and strawberries in Oregon. The Court affirmed the order solely on the basis that there was a plausible factual relationship between the order's stated purpose of avoiding consumer confusion and the provisions of the order. The Court described the standard for reviewing the agency's factual predicates in the following language:

> "[I]f any state of facts reasonably can be conceived that would sustain [the order], there is a presumption of the existence of that state of facts, and one who assails [that presumption] must carry the burden of showing ... that the action is arbitrary."

Students of constitutional law should recognize this formulation as descriptive of what has become known as the loose rational relation test. The Court continues to use this exceptionally deferential version of the arbitrary and capricious test in some important areas of judicial review—principally judicial review under the Fourteenth Amendment of the constitutionality of classifications contained in state statutes and state administrative actions that do not involve fundamental rights or suspect classifications.[24] The Court explicitly rejected use of this version of the test in 1983 in the context of statutory review of agency findings of fact.[25] The version of the arbitrary and capricious test regularly applied to findings of fact made by federal agencies whose actions are subject to statutory judicial review is much less deferential to the agency.

The Court's 1971 opinion in *Citizens to Preserve Overton Park, Inc. v. Volpe,*[26] illustrates the substantially less deferential version of the arbitrary and capricious test that modern courts apply to findings of fact made by federal agencies. In *Overton Park*, the Court described the arbitrary and capricious test as requiring "searching and

---

23. 296 U.S. 176 (1935).

24. *See* L. Tribe, American Constitutional Law §—16–1, 16–2 (2d ed.1988).

25. Motor Vehicle Manufacturer's Ass'n. v. State Farm Mut. Auto. Ins. Co., 463 U.S. 29 (1983).

26. 401 U.S. 402 (1971).

careful" inquiry into the facts that support the agency's decision. The D.C. Circuit's en banc opinion in *Ethyl Corp. v. EPA*[27] illustrates the potential result of applying this far more demanding version of the arbitrary and capricious test to findings adopted through informal rulemaking. Ethyl challenged the complicated factual basis for EPA's regulations requiring a reduction in the lead content of gasoline. Together, the majority and dissenting opinions in *Ethyl* devoted thirty-eight pages to a detailed analysis of the factual studies on which EPA premised its regulation.

The most definitive description of the modern version of the arbitrary and capricious test is contained in the Court's opinion in *Motor Vehicle Manufacturers Association v. State Farm Mutual Automobile Insurance Company*,[28] discussed in detail in §§ 6.4.6b and 7.5:

> Normally, agency [action] would be arbitrary and capricious if the agency has relied on factors which Congress has not intended it to consider, entirely failed to consider an important aspect of the problem, offered an explanation for its decision that runs counter to the evidence before the agency, or is so implausible that it could not be ascribed to a difference in view or the product of agency expertise.

In addition, an agency action is arbitrary and capricious if it represents a departure from agency precedent, and the agency does not acknowledge and explain the basis for its change in approach.[29]

§ 7.3.3 The arguable convergence of substantial evidence and arbitrary and capricious test

There is a lively debate among scholars and judges concerning the extent to which there is any meaningful difference between the modern version of the arbitrary and capricious test and the substantial evidence test. The Supreme Court has described the arbitrary and capricious test as "more lenient" than the substantial evidence test,[30] but it has never attempted to describe the difference between the two tests or to explain why one is more lenient than the other. Appellate courts increasingly treat the two tests as functionally identical, often referring to the tendency of the two to "converge"

27. 541 F.2d 1 (D.C.Cir.1976), *cert. denied*, 426 U.S. 941 (1976).
28. 463 U.S. 29 (1983).
29. *See* Atchison, Topeka, & Santa Fe R. Co. v. Wichita Board of Trade, 412 U.S. 800 (1973).

30. American Paper Institute v. American Electric Power Service Corp., 461 U.S. 402, 412 n. 7 (1983).

and to the distinction between the two as "largely semantic".[31] More broadly, empirical research has failed to detect a difference in reversal rates attributable to differences in the stated tests for reviewing findings of fact.[32]

Initially, judicial review of rules adopted through informal rulemaking was not based on a record of any type, so it would have been difficult for courts to apply the substantial evidence test to such agency actions. For two reasons, this justification for the distinction no longer exists. First, many agency organic acts now specifically require substantial evidence review of facts found through informal rulemaking. As a result, courts have gained considerable experience applying the substantial evidence test to informal rulemaking. Second, the Court's recent decisions make it clear that judicial review of the results of informal rulemaking must be based on the administrative record made in the rulemaking proceeding.[33]

The evidentiary records produced by formal and informal agency procedures differ. In the case of formal adjudication or formal rulemaking, the record consists principally of: (1) a transcript that contains the direct and cross-examination of all witnesses; (2) the briefs and pleadings of the parties; (3) the ALJ's initial decision; and, (4) the agency's final decision. In the case of informal rulemaking, the record consists principally of: (1) the agency's notice of proposed rulemaking, including any scientific studies or data compilations on which its proposal is based; (2) the data, critiques, and arguments contained in the public comments on the proposed rule; and, (3) the agency's statement of the basis and purpose of the final rule. Reviewing courts can and do apply the substantial evidence test to findings of fact adopted in informal rulemaking based on evaluation of administrative records of this type. The test remains the same—considering the record as a whole, is the evidence such that a reasonable person might accept that evidence as adequate to support the agency's finding?

We think that the time will soon come when reviewing courts agree that the arbitrary and capricious test, as that test is applied to

31. In 1984, the D.C. Circuit held that the substantial evidence test and the arbitrary and capricious test are identical as they apply to findings of fact. Association of Data Processing Service Organizations, Inc. v. Board of Governors, 745 F.2d 677 (D.C.Cir.1984); *see also* Pacific Legal Foundation v. DOT, 593 F.2d 1338, 1343 n. 5 (D.C.Cir.1979), *cert. denied* 444 U.S. 830 (1979); Associated Industries v. United States Dept. of Labor, 487 F.2d 342, 349–50 (2d Cir.1973).

32. Verkuil, *An Outcomes Analysis of Scope of Review Standards*, 44 William & Mary L. Rev. 679 (2002).

33. Vermont Yankee Nuclear Power Corp. v. NRDC, 435 U.S. 519, 549 (1978); Camp v. Pitts, 411 U.S. 138, 143 (1973).

findings of fact, is functionally indistinguishable from the substantial evidence test. Uniform application of the substantial evidence test to all agency findings of fact would eliminate some of the unnecessary confusion that now affects the law of substantive review of agency action. Courts have over fifty years of satisfactory experience applying the substantial evidence test. Over the past decade, they have developed considerable experience applying that test to findings adopted in informal rulemaking proceedings where the agency's organic act specifically mandates substantial evidence review. The substantial evidence test accords considerable deference to agency findings of fact. There is no apparent reason to provide greater deference to some types of actions by using what the Supreme Court has characterized as the "more lenient" arbitrary and capricious test.

§ 7.3.4 Judicial review of unknowable facts

Agencies frequently are required to predicate their actions on facts that cannot be "found" in the traditional sense of that term because they are on the frontiers of knowledge. In many circumstances, findings of fact of this type are critical to the action of the agency and, thus, are central to the process of judicial review of the agency action.

Professor McGarity argues that scientific questions that appear to raise issues of fact actually raise issues that fall somewhere on a spectrum between issues of pure scientific fact, in the sense that the question can be answered relatively easily through application of existing scientific methodology, to issues of pure policy, in the sense that the question cannot be answered at all though use of existing scientific methodology.[34] Most issues lie between these poles. For instance, it is theoretically possible for science to determine the carcinogenic potential of a substance in humans at low levels of exposure, but the experiments required to make this determination would be prohibitively time consuming, extraordinarily expensive, and morally unthinkable. Thousands of people would have to be exposed to low level doses of a suspected carcinogen under controlled conditions for decades. As a result, science can provide nothing better than an educated guess subject to substantial uncertainty.

Questions of this type raise issues more accurately characterized as policy issues than factual issues. The policy issue in each case is how to accommodate risk and uncertainty in government decision-

34. *See* McGarity, *Substantive and Procedural Discretion in Administrative Resolution of Science Policy Questions:* *Regulating Carcinogens in EPA and OSHA,* 67 Geo.L.J. 729 (1979).

making; given some degree of uncertainty concerning the existence and magnitude of the risks inherent in alternative decisions, which risks should the agency take? McGarity argues that these policy issues are appropriate for resolution as political questions rather than as scientific or factual questions. It follows that they should be resolved primarily by determining how Congress intended an agency to manage risks and uncertainties in a given context. We agree with McGarity entirely to this point in his analysis. As he recognizes, however, Congress frequently does not express itself clearly in this area. It is often impossible for an agency or a reviewing court to discern from the language of a statute or its legislative history how Congress intended an agency to resolve policy issues inherent in scientific uncertainty.

Three Supreme Court opinions illustrate particularly well the appropriate judicial approach to substantive review of agency findings with respect to unknowable facts. In *Federal Power Commission v. Florida Power & Light Co.,*[35] the Court was asked to overturn an FPC finding that electricity generated by FP & L and commingled with electricity from other sources, some of which commingled electricity admittedly was transmitted to another state, was transported in interstate commerce. That finding was supported by expert testimony based on one theory concerning the manner in which electricity flows, but was contradicted by expert testimony based on another theory. In fact, any honest physicist will admit that science does not yet know how electricity flows. Both of the theories relied upon by the experts are theoretical constructs that are useful for some purposes, but neither purports to describe the actual way in which electricity flows. The Court affirmed the agency's finding based on the following reasoning:

> "A court must be reluctant to reverse results supported by . . . considered and carefully articulated expert opinion. Particularly when we consider a purely factual question within the competence of an administrative agency created by Congress, . . . we recognize the relevant agency's technical expertise and experience, and defer to its analysis unless it is without substantial basis in fact."

In one sense, the Court's choice of language is unfortunate. The issue before the agency was not "a purely factual question" in the sense that courts usually think of issues of fact. Yet, the Court's deference to the agency with respect to its finding on this issue was appropriate

---

35.   404 U.S. 453 (1972).

on the two bases it relied upon: (1) the agency has expertise superior to that of a court with respect to issues such as the manner in which electricity moves; and (2) Congress directed the agency, not reviewing courts, to resolve such issues.

The Court's opinion in *Baltimore Gas & Electric Co. v. Natural Resources Defense Council, Inc.,*[36] also emphasizes the need for substantial judicial deference to agency resolutions of inherently uncertain scientific facts. NRC issued a rule stating that licensing boards should assume that permanent storage of nuclear waste will have no adverse affect on the environment for purposes of deciding whether to grant a license to any particular nuclear power plant. The D.C. Circuit reversed the NRC rule on the basis that its "finding" of no adverse environmental effect was arbitrary and capricious. The Supreme Court unanimously reversed the D.C. Circuit and affirmed the NRC rule. NRC recognized explicitly that its assumption of no adverse affect was surrounded by uncertainty because of the chance that no appropriate permanent storage site would be found and the chance that water might enter a site and transport radioactive material outside the site. NRC confronted these uncertainties directly and determined that they were insufficient alone to affect the outcome of individual plant licensing proceedings. The Court thus concluded that NRC had done exactly what Congress directed it to do—it explored the uncertain risks associated with a policy decision and then made the decision to confront those risks. In the Court's words:

> "Resolution of these fundamental policy issues lies . . . with Congress and the agencies to which Congress has delegated authority. . . .
>
> . . .
>
> "[A] reviewing court must remember that the commission is making predictions, within its area of special expertise, at the frontiers of science. When examining this kind of scientific determination, as opposed to simple findings of fact, a court must generally be at its most deferential."

In *Federal Communications Commission v. WNCN Listeners Guild,*[37] the Court was asked to hold invalid an FCC rule stating the agency's intent not to consider a licensee's entertainment format in license renewal and transfer cases. The FCC's rule was based on its "finding" that the marketplace can be more effective in serving viewer interests in diverse entertainment than can the agency's

---

36. 462 U.S. 87 (1983) (*Vermont Yankee* II).

37. 450 U.S. 582 (1981).

subjective judgments in licensing proceedings. The Court deferred to this finding on the basis that it would be inappropriate for a reviewing court to interfere with an agency's "forecast of the direction in which the future public interest lies".

The substantial deference accorded to agency findings of unknown facts in *Louisiana Power & Light, Baltimore Gas & Electric* and *WNCN* is appropriate on two grounds. First, to the extent that those findings were based on the specialized expertise of the agency involved, the agency has a significant comparative advantage vis a vis a generalist court in resolving such issues. Second, to the extent that these findings involved instead major policy decisions, agencies are far more appropriate institutions than courts for the resolution of policy issues. Congress is, of course, the most appropriate institution to make nonconstitutional policy decisions. Its constitutional legitimacy as principal policy maker is beyond question, and it is the governmental institution that is most directly accountable to the electorate. When Congress chooses not to make those decisions, but to delegate them to agencies, the choice is narrowed to agencies or courts as the principal source of policy decisions. Since agencies are far more politically accountable than courts,[38] courts should defer to agency resolutions of policy issues in the absence of a clear indication from Congress that the agency's policy is inconsistent with the intent of Congress.

Reviewing courts do not consistently follow the Supreme Court's lead in deferring to agency policy decisions premised on assumptions concerning facts that cannot be proven or disproven. Two decisions of the D.C. Circuit illustrate well the tendency of reviewing courts occasionally to refuse to accept agency actions that reasonably resolve issues of fact/policy based on necessarily inconclusive or ambiguous evidence.

In *Public Citizen v. Steed,*[39] the D.C. Circuit was confronted with a challenge to a rule issued by the National Highway Traffic Safety Administration (NHTSA) that suspended an earlier rule requiring tire manufacturers to label each tire with a grade indicative of its treadwear. NHTSA suspended the treadwear labelling rule on the bases that the rule necessitated high compliance costs and the grades assigned each tire were affirmatively misleading to consumers because of wide variations in actual treadwear of tires bearing the same grade label. In NHTSA's judgment, the agency's original policy of attempting to provide consumers some information concerning tread-

---

38.   *See supra* Chapters 3 and 4.   **39.**   733 F.2d 93 (D.C.Cir.1984).

wear did not justify a costly and affirmatively misleading treadwear labelling system.

NHTSA based its finding that the treadwear labelling system was misleading on treadwear test results that indicated that retests of tires with identical treadwear labels produced a variation of up to 80 points on a scale that recorded results in a range of 100 to 300 points. The court reversed NHTSA's action on the basis that NHTSA previously had found similar variations in test results insufficient to justify a refusal to issue the treadwear rule, and a reviewing court had affirmed that finding.

The D.C. Circuit's opinion in *Public Citizen* betrays a serious misunderstanding of the nature of the substantial evidence test. That test requires affirmance of an agency finding when the evidence is sufficient to permit a reasonable person to find as the agency did. Under the test, if the evidence before the agency would permit a reasonable person to find either way on an issue, the court must affirm either agency finding.

Evidence of a forty percent variation in test results for identical grade tires is sufficient to permit a reasonable person to conclude that the grading system is misleading to consumers. The fact that a prior reviewing court had affirmed NHTSA's earlier finding that such a variation in test results did not constitute a fatal defect in its labelling rule is totally irrelevant to the question of whether the agency's current finding was supported by substantial evidence. The agency simply changed its policy based on evidence that was sufficiently ambiguous to support either policy. The D.C. Circuit went beyond the permissible limits of judicial review by substituting its policy judgment for that of the agency.

International Ladies' Garment Workers' Union v. Donovan[40] involved a challenge to a Department of Labor rule that permitted members of the knitted outerwear industry to employ people to perform some tasks in the home. ILGWU challenged the agency's action on the basis that permitting homework would allow employers to circumvent the minimum wage law because of the difficulty of enforcing those laws in the homework context. The agency countered with a determination that the enforcement techniques available to it were sufficient to permit it to enforce the minimum wage laws against employers of homeworkers. The evidence concerning enforcement efficacy was in conflict. The agency relied upon two studies that concluded that the incidence of violations of minimum wage laws was

40.   722 F.2d 795 (D.C.Cir.1983), *cert. denied* 469 U.S. 820 (1984).

about the same for employers of homeworkers as for employers in industries in which homework was restricted. Several state enforcement officials submitted affidavits, however, alleging that homeworkers typically are paid subminimum wages. The court candidly recognized that "this is a case where only a limited amount of hard data exists," and that it was dealing with a predictive judgment "within the agency's field of discretion and expertise." Yet, the court reversed the agency on the basis that "the record contains substantial evidence suggesting that homeworkers will be paid subminimum wages."

The D.C. Circuit's opinion in *ILGWU,* like its opinion in *Public Citizen,* indicates a misunderstanding of the substantial evidence test. When the nature of the fact/policy issue is such that "only a limited amount of hard data exists," and that data is ambiguous, the reviewing court must defer to the agency's resolution of the issue. Whether there is also substantial evidence to support a contrary finding is completely irrelevant, as long as there is substantial evidence to support the agency's finding. In the case of a predictive judgment concerning the likely future efficacy of its own enforcement techniques, two studies conducted by the agency indicating that its enforcement efforts are likely to be effective are sufficient to permit a reasonable person to find as the agency did. Once the court reaches that conclusion, its limited role in reviewing agency findings of fact is concluded. The D.C. Circuit went beyond the bounds of judicial review in *ILGWU* by substituting its preferred resolution of a fact/policy dispute for that of the agency.

§ 7.4 Review of Agency Statutory Interpretations

Agencies frequently must adopt interpretations or constructions of the statutes they are required to implement. Until 1984, the Supreme Court maintained two inconsistent lines of cases that purported to instruct courts concerning the proper judicial role in reviewing agency interpretations of agency-administered statutes.

The Court's decision in *National Labor Relations Board v. Hearst Publications,*[41] illustrates one of the pre–1984 approaches. Hearst challenged NLRB's conclusion that newspaper vendors with particular types of relationships with a newspaper qualified as "employees" subject to all of the protections provided in the National Labor Relations Act. A court of appeals independently examined the question and decided that newsboys did not fit within the statutory

---

41. 322 U.S. 111 (1944).

term "employees". The Supreme Court reversed the appellate court and affirmed the agency.

The Court noted that the term employee is broad, has no precise and uniform meaning, and was not specifically defined by Congress. The Court concluded that Congress intended that the term take "color from its surroundings", that is, the meaning of the term should depend on its relationship to the statute in which it appears and the broad purposes of that statute. In this case, Congress intended the statute to substitute an orderly regime of collective bargaining for the labor strife that tends to typify some types of economic relationships. Since NLRB is the agency charged by Congress with that broad responsibility, and since it has superior expertise in determining whether a relationship has the characteristics that cause it to be a likely source of labor strife that can be avoided through collective bargaining, the Court concluded that NLRB, rather than reviewing courts, should be the primary source of interpretation and application of the statutory term "employee." It followed that an NLRB determination that people with particular economic relationships to a newspaper are employees should be affirmed as long as the agency considered the proper factors in making that determination. In the Court's language, "the Board's determination . . . is to be accepted if it has warrant in the record and a reasonable basis in law".

Prior to 1984, however, the deferential rational basis test coexisted simultaneously with its polar opposite. Thus, for instance, in *NLRB v. Bell Aerospace*,[42] the Court did precisely what it reversed the circuit court for doing in *Hearst* in the context of interpretation of the same term in the same statute. When NLRB determined that buyers are "employees" for federal labor relations purposes, the Court reversed NLRB and substituted its own construction of the term for the agency's construction.

The Court allowed these two inconsistent lines of cases to exist for forty years without making any attempt to reconcile or distinguish the two. In any case that raised an issue concerning the construction of an agency-administered statute, the Court simply applied one line of cases and ignored the opposite line of cases, alternating between the two with no apparent basis for its choice in each case.

The Court announced the abandonment of its traditional practice of arbitrary and inconsistent treatment of agency constructions of

42.   416 U.S. 267 (1974).

agency-administered statutes in *Chevron v. Natural Resources Defense Council.*[43] Henceforth, it would apply a two-step test in reviewing all agency constructions of agency-administered statutes:

> When a court reviews an agency's construction of the statute it administers, it is confronted with two questions. First, always, is the question of whether Congress has directly spoken to the precise question at issue. If the intent of Congress is clear, that is the end of the matter; for the court, as well as the agency, must give effect to the unambiguously expressed intent of Congress. If, however, the court determines Congress has not directly addressed the precise question at issue, the court does not simply impose its own construction on the statute, as would be necessary in the absence of an administrative interpretation. Rather, if the statute is silent or ambiguous with respect to the specific issue, the question for the court is whether the agency's answer is based on a permissible construction of the statute.

The Court has applied the *Chevron* two-step in over one hundred cases decided since 1984, and circuit courts have applied it in thousands of cases.

The single issue in *Chevron* was the proper interpretation of the term "source", as that term is used in the 1977 Amendments to the Clean Air Act. That Act requires any company that proposes to create a major new source of air pollutants to go through an elaborate "new source review" process. The Environmental Protection Agency (EPA) originally interpreted "source" in a way that subjected any significant addition or modification of a plant, such as addition of a boiler, to the new source review process, as long as the addition or modification produced emissions of pollutants above a relatively low threshold. In 1981, EPA changed its interpretation of "source" to refer to an entire plant. Under this much broader definition, a company was required to go through the new source review process only if the net effect of all additions or changes proposed at a plant would be an increase in emissions above the specified threshold. Thus, a company could avoid the new source review process by simultaneously increasing emissions through an addition to a plant while reducing emissions by a corresponding amount through other modifications to the same plant. This change in statutory interpretation was part of the EPA's movement to the "bubble concept", which is intended to give company management greater control over specific decisions affecting

43. 467 U.S. 837 (1984).

air quality as long as the total impact of a plant on air quality is not affected negatively by those decisions.

Natural Resources Defense Council (NRDC) appealed EPA's new interpretation of "source". The D.C. Circuit recognized that the language and legislative history of the statute did not indicate conclusively how "source" was to be defined. The court itself had adopted different interpretations of the term in different contexts in its prior opinions. The D.C. Circuit reversed EPA's interpretation in the present context, however, because EPA did not submit any studies to rebut NRDC's contention that EPA's new interpretation of source would produce less improvement in air quality than its old interpretation. The court held that an agency cannot change its policy without documenting the effect of such a change. The court seemed untroubled by the fact that EPA's old interpretation, and the policy underlying that interpretation, also were not supported by studies demonstrating the effect of various statutory interpretations. Indeed, there was no evidence available concerning the air quality impact of the two competing interpretations, and experts disagree concerning the likely effect of each.

The Supreme Court unanimously reversed the D.C. Circuit and affirmed EPA's new interpretation of "source" based on the following reasoning. The language of the statute and its legislative history indicated that Congress never addressed the issue of whether "source" was to be interpreted to mean each part of a plant or an entire plant. EPA's new interpretation furthered one of the two principal goals of the 1977 amendment—permitting industrial growth. There was no evidence available concerning the impact of the new interpretation on Congress' other major goal—improving air quality. Hence, EPA's choice of interpretations reflected a pure policy decision in an area in which Congress delegated EPA power to make such policy decisions.

The Court used exceptionally strong language in rebuking the D.C. Circuit for the expansive role it assumed in reviewing EPA's policy decision. In the Court's words, the D.C. Circuit "misconceived the nature of its role". "Federal Judges—who have no constituency— have a duty to respect policy choices made by those who do". The Court noted that judges are neither experts in the field nor members of "either political branch of government". By contrast, agencies are politically accountable experts to whom Congress has delegated a policy making role. "While agencies are not directly accountable to the people, the Chief Executive is, and it is entirely appropriate for this political branch of the Government to make such policy choices—

resolving the competing interests which Congress itself either inadvertently did not resolve, or intentionally left to be resolved by the agency charged with the administration of the statute in light of everyday realities." The Court concluded with the unequivocal statement that: "The responsibility for assessing the wisdom of such policy choices and resolving the struggle between competing views of the public interest are not judicial ones".

Chevron has increased significantly the degree of deference courts accord agency constructions of the statutes they are required to administer. If Congress has not "directly spoken to the precise question at issue," any agency construction must be affirmed as long as it is "reasonable". Courts still must determine whether Congress has "directly spoken" to the question at issue, however. The Justices do not always agree concerning either the answer to that question in a given case or the appropriate method of applying step one of *Chevron.*

In *K Mart Corp. v. Cartier Corp.,*[44] for instance, a four-Justice plurality stated that a court should use "traditional tools of statutory construction" when called upon to review an agency's construction of its statute. The plurality continued by applying several of these "traditional tools", *e.g.,* the structure of the statute, inferences of intent derived from statements of statutory goals, various canons of interpretation, and statements from legislative history. This potential approach to applying *Chevron* step one raises a series of troubling questions. Which of the many "traditional tools" should a court use when, as often is the case, different tools suggest different constructions? To what extent are the "traditional tools" of statutory construction methods of determining Congress' intent? Conversely, to what extent are they means through which courts have made judicial policy decisions in the absence of any clear congressional resolution of a policy dispute? To the extent that courts have used the "traditional tools" for the latter purpose, rather than for the former purpose, their use in applying *Chevron* step one seems entirely inconsistent with the Court's reasoning in *Chevron:* "If, however, Congress has not directly addressed the precise question at issue, the court does not simply impose its own construction on the statute, as would be necessary in the absence of an administrative interpretation."

The Justices appear to be sharply divided in their assessments of the value and legitimacy of various "traditional tools of statutory

44.   486 U.S. 281 (1988).

construction." This difference of opinion is apparent in many of the cases in which the Court must adopt a construction of a statute without the benefit of an agency construction. The five-to-three division of the Justices in *Public Citizen v. United States Department of Justice*[45] is illustrative. The five-Justice majority relied on a combination of statements in legislative history and application of canons of interpretation to support a particular construction of a statute. The three dissenting Justices accused the majority of using these traditional tools "to substitute their personal predilections for the will of Congress." The dissenting Justices then applied their preferred "traditional tool" of construction; according to the dissent, the "plain language of the statute" must be both the starting point and the stopping point in the process of statutory interpretation.

The wide disagreement among scholars and judges concerning the appropriate methods of interpreting ambiguous statutory language provides additional support for the highly deferential *Chevron* test. Deferring to all reasonable agency constructions of ambiguities in agency-administered statutes will enhance uniformity in the implementation of national regulatory and benefit systems.[46]

Interestingly, circuit courts seem to take *Chevron* more seriously than does the Supreme Court. Empirical studies of circuit court decisionmaking have found remarkable consistency in circuit court applications of *Chevron*.[47] Yet, studies of Supreme Court applications of *Chevron* have found a high degree of inconsistency.[48]

Moreover, the Supreme Court has never fully resolved whether *Chevron* applies to questions of law that expand an agency's jurisdiction.[49] The conceptual problem of whether jurisdictional matters can

---

45. 491 U.S. 440 (1989); *see also*, AT & T Corp. v. Iowa Utilities Board, 525 U.S. 366 (1999) (Justices divide 5–3 over whether, under *Chevron*, the FCC reasonably interpreted its authority under the telecommunications Act of 1996).

46. *See* Strauss, *One Hundred Fifty Cases Per Year: Some Implications of the Supreme Court's Limited Resources for Judicial Review of Agency Action*, 87 Colum.L.Rev. 1093 (1987).

47. *See, e.g.*, Kerr, *Shedding Light on Chevron: An Empirical Study of the Chevron Doctrine in the U.S. Courts of Appeals*, 15 Yale J. on Reg. 1 (1998); Revesz, *Environmental Regulation, Ideology, and the D.C. Circuit*, 83 Va. L. Rev. 1717, 1747–48 (1997).

48. *See* Pierce, *The Supreme Court's New Hypertextualism: An Invitation to Cacaphony and Incoherence in the Administrative* State, 95 Colum. L. Rev. 749 (1995); Merrill, *Textualism and the Future of the Chevron Doctrine*, 72 Wash. U.L.Q. 351 (1994).

49. In Mississippi Power and Light Co. v. Mississippi, 487 U.S. 354 (1988), Justices Scalia and Brennan disagreed over whether *Chevron* deference should apply to an agency interpretation of its own jurisdiction and the Court has never explicitly resolved the issue. See Comment, *Chevron Deference to Agency Interpretations that Delimit the Scope of the Agency's Jurisdiction*, 61 U. Chi. L. Rev. 957, 961 (1994).

be effectively isolated from nonjurisdictional ones is a challenging one that even divides the authors of this treatise.[50]

There is also uncertainty with respect to the circumstances in which the *Chevron* doctrine applies. All courts agree that *Chevron* deference applies to an agency interpretation of a statute announced in a legislative rule or in a formal adjudication. Courts are divided, however, on the question whether *Chevron* deference applies to agency statutory interpretations announced in interpretative rules and other less formal pronouncements.[51]

Until 2000, the uncertainty with respect to the scope of *Chevron* deference was attributable to the Supreme Court's silence on the issue. In the absence of any discussion of the scope issue by the Supreme Court, circuit courts differed with respect to whether *Chevron* applied to interpretative rules, statements of policy, informal adjudications, briefs, and letters. Circuit courts also differed with respect to the question whether some less powerful form of deference applies to an agency statutory construction announced in a format that is not entitled to *Chevron* deference. Between 2000 and 2003, the Court addressed the scope of *Chevron* issue in five cases. Unfortunately, the Justices are so badly divided on the issue that their many inconsistent and confusing opinions have created almost as much uncertainty on the scope issue in 2004 as existed before they first addressed the issue in 2000.

The Court first addressed the scope of *Chevron* issue in *Christensen v. Harris County.*[52] The Department of Labor announced a construction of the Fair Labor Standards Act in an opinion letter. A five-Justice majority recognized that *Chevron* deference applies to constructions of agency-administered statutes announced in legislative rules or formal adjudications, but it held that *Chevron* deference does not apply to a statutory construction announced in an opinion letter. The majority reasoned that opinion letters, like "policy statements, agency manuals, and enforcement guidelines" are not entitled to *Chevron* deference because they "lack the force of law." The majority also held, however, that statutory constructions announced in opinion letters and other less formal agency documents that lack

50. *Compare* Gellhorn & Verkuil, *Controlling Chevron Based Delegations*, 20 Cardozo L. Rev. 989 (1999) (arguing for non-*Chevron* deference in situations involving agency jurisdictional expansions) *with* R. Pierce, Administrative Law Treatise § 3.5 (4th ed. 2002) (arguing that *Chevron* applies to jurisdictional disputes).

51. *Compare* Harris v. H & W Contracting Co., 102 F.3d 516 (11th Cir. 1996), *with* Massachusetts v. FDIC, 102 F.3d 615 (1st Cir.1996).

52. 529 U.S. 576 (2000).

the force of law are still entitled to the weaker and more contingent form of deference the Court described and applied in its 1944 opinion in *Skidmore v. Swift & Co.*:[53]

> We consider that the . . . interpretations . . . of the Administrator. . . . while not controlling upon the courts by reason of their authority, do constitute a body of experience and informed judgment to which courts and litigants may properly resort for guidance. The weight of such a judgment . . . will depend upon the thoroughness evident in its consideration, the validity of its reasoning, its consistency with earlier and later pronouncements, and all those factors which give power to persuade, if lacking power to control.

The majority opinion in *Christensen* suggested that the Court would use a bright-line test to determine the scope of *Chevron* deference—legislative rules and formal adjudications are entitled to *Chevron* deference because they have the "force of law", while all less formal agency pronouncements are entitled only to *Skidmore* deference because they lack the force of law. The disparate views expressed by the other four Justices in two dissenting opinions suggested the possibility, however, that the clear and simple test announced in the majority opinion would be short-lived. In his dissenting opinion, Justice Scalia urged adoption of a different bright-line test. He urged application of *Chevron* deference to any agency construction of an agency-administered statute announced in any format, including an interpretative rule, opinion letter, statement, or agency brief, as long as the announced construction represented the agency's "fair and considered judgement on the issue", rather than a tentative construction or a construction adopted by a member of the agency's staff. Justice Scalia also argued that *Skidmore* deference was an anachronism that had no place in a post-*Chevron* world. In a separate dissenting opinion on behalf of three Justices, Justice Breyer urged adoption of a more open-ended test—*Chevron* deference should be accorded to constructions of agency-administered statutes that are announced in relatively informal documents like opinion letters and briefs except "where one has doubt that Congress intended to delegate interpretive authority to the agency." Justice Breyer's dissenting opinion also contained a discussion of degrees of deference and reasons for deference that suggested that he saw only a modest difference between *Skidmore* and *Chevron* deference.

53. 323 U.S. 134 (1944).

The Court addressed the scope issue next in *United States v. Mead*.[54] An eight-Justice majority held that *Chevron* deference does not apply to statutory constructions announced in classification ruling letters issued by the Customs Service. The majority gave persuasive reasons for its refusal to confer *Chevron* deference on this class of agency documents. The 46 offices of the Customs Service issue 10,000 to 15,000 classification rulings per year. The rulings contain no reasons, have no effects on third parties, and have no precedential effect. The majority disavowed any bright-line test for determining the scope of *Chevron* deference, however. The Customs Service classifications to which the majority refused to defer are informal adjudications, but the majority strongly suggested that it would confer *Chevron* deference on some informal adjudications. The *Mead* majority held that *Chevron* deference applies both to agency constructions adopted through use of "a relatively formal administrative procedure" like "notice and comment rulemaking or formal adjudication" and to constructions adopted through use of less formal procedures if there is "some other indication of a comparable congressional intent" to give the agency announcement the force of law. The majority left open the nature of the "indication of a comparable congressional intent" required to justify conferral of *Chevron* deference on a less formal agency document. In a dissenting opinion, Justice Scalia criticized the test announced in the majority opinion as "wonderfully imprecise," "virtually open-ended," and "utterl[y] flabb[y]."

The Court has addressed the scope of *Chevron* issue several times since *Mead*, but its subsequent opinions merely illustrate the murky nature of the *Mead* test and the continued existence of widely differing views among the Justices. In *Edelman v. Lynchburg College*,[55] a seven-Justice majority stated that *Chevron* deference "does not necessarily require an agency's exercise of express notice-and-comment rulemaking power." Two concurring Justices criticized the majority for failing to explain why they were conferring *Chevron* deference on the rule at issue. The concurring Justices stated that they were conferring *Chevron* deference on the rule at issue partly because it fell within the procedural rule exemption to the otherwise required notice-and-comment procedure and partly because the agency repromulgated the rule in a notice-and-comment proceeding anyway. In *Barnhart v. Walton*,[56] an eight-Justice majority included dicta at the end of its opinion in which it stated that it would have conferred *Chevron* deference on the agency's statutory construction

54.   533 U.S. 218 (2001).   **56.**   535 U.S. 212 (2002).
55.   535 U.S. 106 (2002).

even if it had been announced only in a ruling, a manual addressed to state decisionmakers, and a letter, rather than in a legislative rule. In *Clackmas Gastroenterology Associates v. Wells*,[57] a seven-Justice majority cited *Christensen* to support the broad proposition that *Chevron* deference is not due to "policy statements, agency manuals, and enforcement guidelines." The *Clackamas* majority ignored the contradictory language and reasoning in *Mead, Edelman, and Barnhart*.

§ 7.5 Review of Agency Reasoning Process

An agency rarely can support an action based solely on a simple list of findings of facts and conclusions of law. Typically, the agency's findings and conclusions must be linked to the action it takes through a chain of reasoning. Whether an agency acts through rulemaking or through adjudication, the agency must state its reasons in support of its action, and those reasons are subject to judicial review through application of the arbitrary and capricious test.[58] Functionally, judicial review of the agency reasoning process is the most important aspect of judicial review of agency action at present. Chief Judge Wald of the D.C. Circuit conducted an empirical analysis of the 600 agency actions reviewed by her court during the period June 1981 to June 1982.[59] The largest number of judicial remands were based on what the court determined to be an inadequacy in the agency's reasoning process.

When a court reverses an agency action based on inadequate reasoning, it invariably relies on the Supreme Court's 1983 decision in *Motor Vehicle Manufacturers Ass'n v. State Farm Automobile Insurance Co.*[60] In *State Farm*, the Court reversed the National Highway Traffic Safety Administration's (NHTSA) revocation of a rule that would have required manufacturers to equip all new cars with passive restraints. The rule revoked by NHTSA required manufacturers to install either air bags or automatic seat belts in all cars. The agency originally estimated that the rule would prevent 12,000 deaths and 100,000 injuries annually. It rescinded the rule on the sole basis that it had reason to believe that the manufacturers would elect the automatic seat belt option almost exclusively and, therefore, that the life-saving potential of the air bag option would not be

---

57. 538 U.S. 440 (2003).

58. *See* PBGC v. LTV Corp., 496 U.S. 633 (1990); Motor Vehicle Manufacturers Ass'n v. State Farm Mutual Automobile Insurance Co., 463 U.S. 29 (1983); Camp v. Pitts, 411 U.S. 138 (1973); Citizens to Preserve Overton Park, Inc. v. Volpe, 401 U.S. 402 (1971); SEC v. Chenery, 332 U.S. 194 (1947). *See supra* § 6.4.6b.

59. Wald, Remarks to the Administrative Conference of the United States (July 7, 1983).

60. 463 U.S. 29 (1983).

realized. The Supreme Court affirmed a D.C. Circuit opinion reversing NHTSA's rescission of its passive restraint rule.

The Court's opinion in *State Farm* is so significant that we will
analyze that opinion in some detail. At the outset, we wish to make it
clear that we agree with the Court's result and with most of the
reasoning it used to reach that result. Unfortunately, the opinion
contains a few passages that, when taken out of context, can and
have been relied upon by lower courts as a basis for disguised
substitution of policies preferred by appellate judges for policies
chosen by agencies. Thus, our criticism is limited to the effect *State
Farm* seems to be having on reviewing courts rather than to the
Court's decision in that case. Because of that unfortunate effect, we
see a continuing need for the Court to issue additional opinions in
which it firmly establishes the limited role of appellate courts engaged in substantive review of agency action.

In *State Farm,* the Court was presented with a threshold issue of
some importance. Should an agency's rescission of a rule be treated
as analogous to an agency decision not to act, in which case the
agency's action would be virtually unreviewable, or should it instead
be subjected to the same scope of review as an agency's initial
promulgation of a rule? The Court held that revocation of a rule is
subject to the same standard of judicial review as promulgation or
amendment of a rule. It noted that the statute under which NHTSA
acted equated revocation and promulgation. It also identified sound
policy reasons in support of that equation and against the analogy
suggested by NHTSA between agency inaction and agency revocation
of a rule. The Court found implicit in the many statutes making
agency actions subject to judicial review a congressional policy to
impose on agencies some burden to support the need for any change
in settled policy. Since revocation of a rule, like promulgation or
amendment, involves such a change in policy, the Court held that
revocation of a rule is subject to judicial review under the same
arbitrary and capricious standard as promulgation of a rule.

Next, the Court described this scope of review as "narrow". A
reviewing court must not substitute its judgment for the agency's,
but it must insure that the agency examined the relevant data and
established a "rational connection between the facts found and the
choice made". The agency's action should be set aside if it:

> "relied on factors which Congress has not intended it to consid-
> er, entirely failed to consider an important aspect of the problem,
> offered an explanation for its decision that runs counter to the

evidence before the agency, or is so implausible that it could not be ascribed to a difference in view or the product of expertise."

In applying this standard of review to NHTSA's revocation of its passive restraint rule, the Court reversed the agency's action on two different bases. All nine Justices joined in the Court's opinion reversing the agency on the first ground—the agency was arbitrary and capricious in revoking the rule without considering at all the alternative of amending the rule to require installation of air bags only in all new cars. The agency's reasoning in support of revocation was simple. The rule as written permitted manufacturers to comply by installing either air bags or passive seat belts. The agency recognized that air bags would save 12,000 lives and prevent 100,000 injuries per year, but it believed that the rule as written would not produce nearly this improvement in highway safety because manufacturers would elect to install ineffective passive seat belts rather than demonstrably effective air bags. The Court unanimously rejected this reasoning because NHTSA did not even consider the obvious alternative of modifying the rule to eliminate the passive seat belt option. Based on the agency's own findings and reasoning, the air bag only alternative would be totally effective in advancing the agency's life-saving mission.

It is easy to see why all nine Justices agreed that the agency's failure to consider at all an obvious alternative that the agency continued to find effective and feasible was arbitrary and capricious. Even with respect to this basis for reversal, however, the Court emphasized that NHTSA might be able to provide good reasons for rejecting the air bags only option on remand; judicial reversal was predicated on the agency's failure to consider the alternative at all.

The second basis for reversal in *State Farm* was the subject of a five-to-four vote of the Justices and was characterized even by the majority as a "closer" issue. The majority reversed as arbitrary and capricious the agency's subsidiary finding that passive seat belts would be ineffective because their uniform availability in cars would produce less than a five per cent increase in seat belt use. The agency based this finding entirely on its expectation that drivers would detach passive seat belts. The majority based its reversal of this finding primarily on the fact that the agency's own studies showed a doubling of seat belt use when passive belts are installed in place of manual belts. The majority conceded that NHTSA might be able to explain on remand how the results of these studies are consistent with its finding of a less than five per cent increase in seat belt use, but it did not find the agency's stated reasons adequate to explain such a wide disparity between the evidence before the agency and its finding.

Four Justices dissented briefly only with respect to the majority's reversal and remand of NHTSA's finding concerning the ineffectiveness of passive seat belts. The dissenting and concurring Justices concluded that the agency's explanation for the large disparity between the evidence produced by its own tests and its finding "while by no means a model, is adequate". After expressing this relatively minor disagreement with the majority, the dissenting and concurring Justices made a much more fundamental point. They noted that the agency's changed view of the passive restraint issue was related to the election of a new President with different political views than his predecessor. Their explication of the relationship between politics and administrative law bears repeating:

> "A change in administration brought about by the people casting their votes is a perfectly reasonable basis for an executive agency's reappraisal of the costs and benefits of its programs and regulations. As long as the agency remains within the bounds established by Congress, it is entitled to assess administrative records and evaluate priorities in light of the philosophy of the administration."

Both the majority and the dissenting opinions in *State Farm* are well-reasoned. The majority opinion carefully limits the scope of substantive review and recognizes the deference due to agencies charged with making hard policy decisions in conditions of uncertainty. The single unanimous basis for reversal announces a principle that is easy to accept—an agency action is arbitrary and capricious if the agency failed to consider at all an obvious alternative demonstrated to be both feasible and effective by the agency's own studies and findings.

The second basis for reversal, although it produced a five-to-four division, is also based on a principle that is easily defended. The majority went to great pains to emphasize the high degree of deference that should be accorded to an agency finding with respect to the probable future effect of an agency action when that future effect necessarily is uncertain. Thus, the majority emphasized that an agency action based on predictions of the uncertain future would not be arbitrary and capricious "simply because there was no evidence in direct support of the agency's conclusion". An agency must be free to make policy decisions based on probabilities subject to substantial uncertainties. The majority also emphasized that "a reviewing court must be most hesitant to intrude" on an agency's resolution of a policy issue that is surrounded by factual and predictive uncertainty.

In reversing the agency's predictive finding, the majority held only that, where there is a very large gap between such a predictive finding (less than five per cent increase in seat belt use) and the only empirical evidence available to the agency as the basis for its prediction (studies showing a one hundred per cent increase in seat belt use), the agency must provide a good explanation for the disparity in order to avoid reversal.

The caveat stated at the conclusion of the opinion of the four concurring and dissenting Justices makes an extremely important point concerning the respective roles of Congress, the President, agencies, and reviewing courts. Courts have long held that agencies can change their policies, within the usually broad limits set by Congress, only if they recognize explicitly that they are changing a prior policy and only if they explain the basis for the change.[61] *State Farm* properly holds that this requirement applies whether the change of policy is accomplished through adjudication, promulgation of a rule, amendment of a rule, or revocation of a rule.

The traditional duty to explain changes in policy is supportable on two grounds. First, Congress has at least implicitly dictated this course by subjecting all forms of binding agency action to judicial review under the arbitrary and capricious test. Second, requiring agencies to recognize and to explain the basis for their changes in policy helps to avoid potential discriminatory application of the law by agencies and ensures reasoned decisionmaking. An agency whose actions are subject to judicial review should not be free to change its policies for no reasons or based on factual predicates that are inconsistent with the evidence before the agency. The majority in *State Farm* reaffirms this principle in the relatively new and unfamiliar context of agency efforts to reduce regulation.

The principle reaffirmed by the majority must be qualified, however, by the more fundamental principle emphasized by the concurring and dissenting Justices in *State Farm*. Agencies must remain free to change their policies as long as: (1) the new policy is not outside the usually broad boundaries established by Congress; (2) the new policy is based on factual predicates that withstand application of the substantial evidence test; and, (3) the agency provides a plausible reason for changing its policy. Traditionally, the reasons

61. *See, e.g.,* Atchison, Topeka & Santa Fe Ry. Co. v. Wichita Board of   Trade, 412 U.S. 800 (1973).

given by agencies and found acceptable by courts have consisted of such things as the agency's discovery of new facts or its better understanding of the nature of a problem or the results of its prior attempts to respond to a problem.

Reviewing courts must recognize that an agency's change of policy also can be supported solely on the basis that a new agency decisionmaker sees different policy implications based on the same ambiguous facts and arguments that formed the basis for a predecessor's contrary resolution of the policy issue. As long as the conflicting policy decisions of both agency heads are within the substantive boundaries established by Congress and are supported by substantial evidence, as frequently will be the case, a reviewing court must affirm the new policy just as it affirmed the old policy. This result follows as a matter of constitutional law. It is not the place of the judiciary to interfere with policy decisions made by agency heads whose policy perspectives differ from their predecessors because of the results of a presidential election. That is why the Constitution provides for election of Presidents and reposes in the President the exclusive power to appoint agency heads.

Too often, judges whose policy preferences differ from those of a President forget that nonconstitutional policy-making is assigned by the Constitution to elected officials and their delegates, not to courts. The sometimes successful efforts of judges to block the New Deal policy initiatives of President Roosevelt, and thereby to frustrate the will of the electorate, provide a notorious and unfortunate example of the tendency of judges on occasion to usurp the policy making power of elected officials and, ultimately, of the people themselves. Some judges continue to misunderstand the limited role of the judiciary in reviewing agency policy decisions.

In section 6.4.6b, we described the ways in which circuit courts have caused considerable damage to the agency policymaking process by adopting expansive interpretations of the *State Farm* requirement of reasoned decisionmaking. The Court has taken two steps to reduce the power of circuit courts to set aside agency actions based on judicial application of an open-ended requirement of reasoned decisionmaking. In *PBGC v. LTV Corp.,*[62] the Court held that an agency is required to discuss only the relationship between its action and the policy goals stated in the statute that authorized its action. An agency is not required to discuss the relationship between its action and the policy goals stated in other statutes, even if the agency's

----

62.   496 U.S. 633 (1990).

action will have an obvious effect on attainment of those goals. In *Mobil Oil Exploration & Producing Southeast v. United Distribution Co.,*[63] the Court held that an agency is not required to discuss the effects of an action on problem B when the agency action is designed to address problem A, even if the action has an obvious adverse effect on problem B. An agency is free to address one problem at a time.

§ 7.6   A Digression on the Appropriate Role of Judicial Review

Two related debates are ongoing at present concerning the manner in which reviewing courts can be most constructive in guiding agency decisionmaking. At one level, the proponents of intense procedural review argue that substantive review must be limited, while the proponents of intense substantive review argue that procedural review alone is ineffective. At another level, proponents of substantive deference argue that attempts at vigorous review are counterproductive, while proponents of stringent substantive review argue that it is essential. We will summarize both debates before adding our own views.

The differing opinions of three D.C. Circuit judges in that court's en banc decision in *Ethyl Corp. v. Environmental Protection Agency*[64] illustrate the nature of the debate concerning the relative efficacy of procedural versus substantive review. The court ultimately affirmed EPA's lead additive rule by a five-to-four vote, but only after it engaged in careful scrutiny of the substantive basis for the rule. Between them, Judge Wright for the majority and Judge Wilkey for the dissenting judges, devoted almost forty pages to a detailed discussion of EPA's highly technical method of assessing the conflicting evidence concerning the health hazards associated with the use of lead additives in gasoline. In a concurring opinion, Judge Bazelon questioned the efficacy of the approach taken in both the majority and dissenting opinions:

> "Because substantive review of mathematical and scientific evidence by technically illiterate judges is dangerously unreliable, I continue to believe we will do more to improve administrative decisionmaking by concentrating our efforts on strengthening administrative procedure."

Judge Bazelon made two related arguments in his concurrence in *Ethyl* and in his other writings. First, he argued that judges are experts in procedure and that they can improve the administrative

---

63.   498 U.S. 211 (1991).   **64.**   541 F.2d 1 (D.C.Cir.1976), *cert. denied* 426 U.S. 941 (1976).

process substantially by using this expertise to compel agencies to adopt procedures that will expose important substantive aspects of their decisionmaking to scrutiny by reviewing courts, Congress, scientists, the public, and even the agency decisionmakers. There is merit to this argument. Judges can enhance the accuracy of the decisionmaking process by insuring that agencies comply with statutory procedures that force agencies to expose the scientific and factual bases for their actions to public criticism.[65]

Judge Bazelon both overestimated the potential efficacy of procedural review and underestimated the potential disruptive effect of judicially-imposed procedures, however. As Professor McGarity has established, procedural safeguards can only identify the existence of the scientific uncertainty that underlies many agency actions; additional procedures cannot eliminate that uncertainty or contribute to management of the societal risks inherent in scientific uncertainty.[66] Moreover, as the Supreme Court concluded in *Vermont Yankee,* ad hoc addition of procedures by reviewing courts has the potential to add intolerably to the cost in time and resources required for agency regulation by rulemaking.[67] In any event, the Court's opinion in *Vermont Yankee* limited substantially the potential application of Judge Bazelon's theory by holding that reviewing courts do not have the power to compel agencies to adopt procedures other than those required by statute or by the Constitution.

Judge Bazelon's second argument is that intensive judicial scrutiny of the substantive basis for an agency action premised on complicated analysis of scientific facts is likely to be ineffective at best and quite possibly counterproductive. Generalist judges have neither the training nor the experience necessary to understand, much less to review effectively, the methods used by an agency to analyze scientific data. Thus, Judge Bazelon urged vigorous procedural review combined with deferential substantive review. The Supreme Court has greatly limited the availability of Judge Bazelon's approach to procedural review, but it has not yet addressed in a definitive manner his argument that reviewing courts should not engage in detailed scrutiny of the substantive basis for agency actions that are based on scientific studies. That issue is the subject of continuing debate among judges and scholars, with the "hard look" doctrine at the center of the debate. The "hard look" doctrine requires a court to attempt to understand and to assess in detail the data and methodology an agency used to address a complicated scientific issue.

65. *See supra* § 6.4.6a.

66. *See* McGarity, *supra* note 34.

67. *See supra* § 6.4.9a.

Professor Rodgers' is one of the most outspoken proponents of "hard look" review.[68] He supports detailed substantive review on two related grounds. First, political controls are not adequate to assure that agencies make wise policy decisions. Congress is good at delegating power to agencies to address issues, but it is not good at confining agency discretion through use of specific statutory standards. When agencies act under broad delegations of power, courts can help to assure good policy decisions only by subjecting the agency reasoning process to close scrutiny.

Second, agencies do not function well in the absence of external discipline that forces them to consider policy issues seriously through a rational decisionmaking process. In the absence of detailed judicial review of the agency reasoning process, agencies often fail to understand the area in which they are acting and adopt policies that are poorly reasoned and predicated on a misunderstanding of the underlying facts. They also take actions based on improper motives—either decisional factors prohibited by statute or the desire to assist some individual or group for political reasons. Forcing agencies that have a natural tendency to make careless or result-oriented decisions to focus their opinions on statutory decisional factors, correct analysis of data, significant public comments, and plausible alternatives requires agencies to consider such factors in their actual decisionmaking process. The result is some improvement in the quality and objectivity of agency policy decisions. Professor Rodgers also links vigorous substantive review functionally with activist procedural review. He argues that the two serve similar purposes and that the Supreme Court's attempt in *Vermont Yankee* to impose severe limits on procedural review will have little effect because reviewing courts will continue to accomplish the same purposes through "hard look" review of the agency reasoning process.

Professor (now Justice) Breyer has developed forcefully the arguments against "hard look" review.[69] Justice Breyer frames the question as: "[W]hat is a reviewing court to do when it is uncertain whether an agency has dealt adequately with a complex and important scientific or technical issue?" He agrees with Rodgers' view that procedural and substantive review are functionally linked, and that the Supreme Court's decision in *Vermont Yankee* will have little practical significance if the Court leaves reviewing courts free to exercise "hard look" review of the agency reasoning process. He

68. *See* Rodgers, *A Hard Look at Vermont Yankee: Environmental Law Under Close Scrutiny,* 67 Geo.L.J. 699 (1979).

69. *See* Breyer, *Vermont Yankee and the Courts' Role in the Nuclear Energy Controversy,* 91 Harv.L.Rev. 1804 (1978).

argues, however, that the Court should follow *Vermont Yankee* with an opinion that rules out "hard look" review in favor of a much more deferential standard of "reasonableness".

Justice Breyer's argument is simple but compelling. Agency decisions, such as whether to proceed with the licensing of nuclear power plants, are policy decisions. The nation has a limited number of options, each of which is fraught with risks of uncertain magnitude. The risks attendant to decisions to build nuclear power plants are well known. There are similar grave risks associated with any other option however. Building coal-fired plants will cause increased air quality problems, increased acid rain, and perhaps the potentially catastrophic results of the greenhouse effect. Building no new power plants risks future blackouts and brownouts, severe economic recession, and increased potential for global strife attributable to future reliance on oil from parts of the world that are constantly on the brink of war.

The use of additional procedures or a more detailed consideration of decisional factors and alternatives cannot eliminate the need to make policy judgments in favor of one cluster of uncertain risks or another. Further, in many cases, additional procedures or a more detailed consideration of the issues will not improve the quality of decisionmaking. The choice between the various options is often unclear because of lack of data, the difficulty of the decision, and a lack of agency resources. In these cases, the use of additional procedures or more consideration will only lead to delay because the agency will not be in a better position to make the required policy judgment than it was before the additional work was undertaken.

By forcing delay in the implementation of one policy, the court effectively has chosen one of the alternative policies. The courts, however, usually fail to consider the merits of that policy decision, and they are probably unable to do so. The judiciary lacks the scientific expertise to assess the relative significance of delaying implementation of one policy and adopting another policy.

We are sympathetic with Professor Rodgers' concern that agencies do not always do an acceptable job and that the political system does not always control agencies adequately. Nevertheless, we believe that on balance the "hard look" doctrine can do more mischief than good for four reasons. First, it gives the courts a false impression about the precision of agency decisionmaking, and it can lead to substantial delay in the implementation of any policy choice. Besides the delay created by the time it takes an agency to respond to a judicial remand, agencies are slowed in the promulgation of rules by the necessity of preparing a justification for the rule that will survive the most intrusive judicial review.[70] Second, our strong impression is that the failure of any agency to engage in a more extensive explanation derives more times from the difficulty of the choices that must be made and the lack of evidence to make them than from disregard for the factors to be considered. Third, the "hard look" test inevitably invites judges to invoke their own views about the merits in reaching their decisions. Empirical studies of circuit court decision-making have found major inconsistencies in judicial applications of the hard look doctrine.[71] Fourth, even if agencies are imperfectly accountable, they are still more politically accountable than unelected federal judges.

We agree with Justice Breyer's position concerning the appropriate role of courts in reviewing the agency reasoning process. Like Justice Breyer, we would like to see the Supreme Court issue a decision specifying clearly the limited role of courts engaged in substantive review of agency actions taken pursuant to broad statutory delegations of power.[72]

More broadly, many scholars and judges overestimate the potential beneficial effects of judicial review and underestimate the costs of judicial review. An agency action can be reversed on any of four grounds—a procedural error, lack of adequate evidentiary support for a finding of fact, an inadequate statement of reasons, or an error in interpreting a statute. The fourth category probably is the smallest. Yet, it is the only class of cases in which judicial reversal frequently precludes an agency from taking the same action on remand following a judicial reversal. If reversal is based on the agency's failure to provide a procedure mandated by a statute or by the Constitution, the agency is free on remand to take the same action after adding the procedural safeguard. The presence of the safeguard may change the outcome of the case, but usually it does not. Similarly, if reversal is based on inadequate evidentiary support for a finding of fact, the agency can take the same action on remand if it is able to bolster its evidentiary support for that finding. Finally, in the case of the largest category of judicial reversals—those based on perceived inadequacies

---

70. *See* McGarity, *The Courts and Ossification of Rulemaking: A Response to Professor Seidenfeld*, 75 Tex. L. Rev. 525 (1997); McGarity, *Some Thoughts on "Deossifying" the Rulemaking Process*, 41 Duke L.J. 1385 (1992).

71. *See, e.g.*, Revesz, *supra* note 47, at 1763.

72. Verkuil, *Waiting for Vermont Yankee II*, 55 Tul.L.Rev. 418 (1981); *but see* Wald, *Making Informed Decisions on the District of Columbia Circuit*, 50 G.W.L.Rev. 135 (1982).

in the agency's reasoning process—the agency obviously has the freedom on remand to take the identical action as long as it considers adequately the second time whatever decisional factor it did not adequately consider the first time.

The effect of a particular instance of judicial reversal usually is unclear at the time the court reverses the agency. Often the agency has difficulty determining the basis for reversal and, therefore, the actions it must take on remand to satisfy the court. Will the court be satisfied with the addition of one more procedural safeguard or additional evidentiary support for a finding? How much additional consideration of decisional factors will be sufficient to satisfy the court? Or, is this a case in which the court so strongly disagrees with the agency action that it is never likely to find the agency's procedures, evidentiary support and stated reasons sufficient to affirm that action?

Even if a judicial opinion reversing an agency action is reasonably clear in identifying the basis for reversal, the agency almost invariably has several options on remand. It can correct the error identified by the court and take the same action a second time. It can correct the error and take a somewhat different action on remand. In either of these cases its action on remand may be affirmed, or it may be reversed on the basis of an error that was not raised in the review proceeding concerning the original action. Finally, the agency often can choose not to act in the area at all on remand. The parties affected by the agency's action can only guess the manner in which the agency will react to reversal on remand, the timing of that reaction, and whether the agency's action on remand will be affirmed or reversed in a later judicial review proceeding.

During the typically protracted period between judicial reversal of an agency action and ultimate affirmance of the agency's action on remand, neither the agency nor the parties affected by the agency's action have a good basis for predicting the policy the agency will be able to implement. This uncertainty has significant costs. The agency frequently cannot intelligently determine the actions it should take concerning related issues and in related proceedings until it knows the ultimate disposition of the action that was the subject of the initial judicial reversal. Similarly, private parties cannot make informed decisions without knowing the nature of the policy the agency eventually will be able to effectuate. If the agency action that was reversed involved an environmental control device that must be incorporated in new plants, for instance, parties considering construction of such plants have no good basis for determining what, if any, device they must include in the construction of such a plant during the several year period between initial judicial reversal of the agency action and the outcome of proceedings for judicial review of the agency's action on remand. They will either build the plant based on a set of assumptions concerning the agency's ultimate policy, and will be forced to incur large expenses for retrofitting if their assumption is wrong, or they will defer a decision to build the plant. Either way, society suffers a substantial net loss in social welfare.

Circuit courts have reduced significantly, however, the social cost of the delay and uncertainty potentially created by judicial applications of the duty to engage in reasoned decisionmaking. As we discussed in detail in § 6.4.6b, courts have made an important change in their choice of remedies in cases in which they conclude that an agency has failed to give adequate consideration to one or more issues. In most such cases, a circuit court will remand the case to the agency without vacating the agency action, thereby leaving the action in place while the agency addresses the inadequacies in its reasoning process.

The inherent costs of judicial reversal of an agency action, as a result of delay and uncertainty, help to explain the tendency of reviewing courts to defer to an agency even when its performance falls well short of excellence. These substantial costs of reversal also form part of the basis for our contention that courts should become even more tolerant of imperfect agency performance, particularly with respect to the open-ended and amorphous duty of an agency to consider adequately all decisional factors and available alternatives.

Confined to an appropriately narrow scope, judicial review also can yield substantial benefits, however. Agencies should not be permitted to ignore legislative policy decisions or legislative procedural mandates, and, of course, they should not be allowed to violate the constitutional rights of the parties affected by their actions. Reviewing courts have a duty to confine agencies within statutory and constitutional boundaries, and they must fulfill that responsibility even if by doing so they often produce attendant delay and uncertainty.

Reviewing courts also may be able to improve the general quality of the agency decisionmaking process through occasional reversals of agency actions on the basis of inadequacies in the agency's reasoning process. This is the area, however, in which we believe that the costs of judicial reversal often outweigh the benefits. An agency should be reversed on this basis only if its reasoning process is grossly inadequate.

§ 7.7 The Controversy Over Non-acquiescence in Judicial Decisions

In determining the appropriate scope of judicial review, courts also should recognize that their role necessarily is only negative. Courts can delay, or sometimes even block, an agency action, but they cannot act on behalf of an agency or implement the policies they prefer in place of the policies selected by an agency. Only the legislative branch of government has the power to direct agencies to further specific policies. A bitter dispute between the Department of Health and Human Services (HHS) and the Ninth Circuit illustrates starkly this fundamental limitation on the power of the courts.

Under President Reagan, HHS embarked on a project to attempt to eliminate from the roles of recipients of federal disability payments those individuals who are not in fact disabled. HHS attempted to accomplish this goal by conducting proceedings in which it made a finding based on medical evidence as to whether an individual is presently disabled. HHS took the position that if it made a finding, based on proper procedures, that a current recipient of disability aid is not disabled, and that finding was supported by substantial evidence, HHS had the power to remove the individual from the roles of eligible recipients of disability payments.

In two important circumstances, the Ninth Circuit expressed its strong disagreement with HHS' interpretation of its power and reversed specific HHS determinations of ineligibility. In *Finnegan v. Matthews*,[73] the Ninth Circuit held that, by amending the Social Security Act to provide that a recipient of state disability payments was eligible for federal disability payments "so long as he is continuously disabled," Congress intended to bind HHS to prior state determinations of disability status. Thus, if a person previously was found to be disabled by a state agency, HHS could hold that person ineligible only by finding, based on substantial evidence, that the person had experienced a material improvement in condition since the state determination was made. Under this interpretation, an HHS finding that the person is not presently disabled would have no legal effect.

Similarly, in *Patti v. Schweiker*,[74] the Ninth Circuit held that an HHS finding of disability at a particular point in time gives rise to a presumption of continuing disability that can be rebutted only by evidence of a material change in condition. Thus, if a person previously was found to be disabled by HHS, the agency's subsequent

---

73. 641 F.2d 1340 (9th Cir.1981).   **74.** 669 F.2d 582 (9th Cir.1982).

finding that the person is not disabled, even if supported by substantial evidence, would not be sufficient to render the person no longer eligible for disability payments.

HHS reacted to these two court decisions by indicating that, while it would follow the mandate of the Ninth Circuit in the case of the two individuals whose determinations of ineligibility were reversed in *Finnegan* and *Patti,* it did not consider itself bound by those decisions in the case of all other eligibility determinations. Since it believed that the Ninth Circuit's decisions were erroneous, it continued to declare ineligible any person that it found not to be disabled even if that person was the subject of a prior state or federal finding of disability and even if HHS had no evidence that the person's condition had materially improved. HHS took the position that it was bound to modify its procedures to conform to a Supreme Court decision, but that it was not required to change its procedures to conform to circuit court decisions. In the case of decisions of circuit courts or district courts, HHS took the position that it was obligated only to comply with the court's mandate in the specific case before the court.

The dispute intensified at this point. Numerous judges expressed publicly their outrage at what they characterized as unprecedented, lawless conduct of an agency.[75] Passing for the moment the issue of the legality of the HHS decision to decline to follow the decisions of a circuit court, that conduct by HHS was far from unprecedented. The Internal Revenue Service routinely declines to follow the decisions of circuit courts when it disagrees with those decisions and hopes to elicit more favorable decisions from other circuits or from the Supreme Court.[76] Other agencies also follow this procedure when they have doubts concerning the merits of a decision of a circuit court.[77] An agency policy of acquiescence in all circuit court decisions would create severe problems, since circuit courts often issue conflicting opinions. Federal regulatory and benefit programs should be implemented on a uniform national basis, not with significant regional variations based on the differing views of judges.[78]

75. New York Times, Feb. 23, 1984, at A14.

76. *See, e.g.,* IRS Action on Decision 1983–051 (Dec. 8, 1983) (explicitly declining to follow a decision of the Second Circuit); Rev.Rul. 80–26, 1980–1 C.B. 66 (explicitly declining to follow a decision of the First Circuit).

77. For instance, the Federal Energy Regulatory Commission declined to follow two decisions of the Fifth Circuit until after the D.C. Circuit issued two opinions indicating its agreement with the Fifth Circuit on the issue. *See* North Carolina v. FERC, 584 F.2d 1003 (D.C.Cir.1978).

78. *See* Estreicher & Revesz, *Nonac-*

The Ninth Circuit may have been particularly concerned about the HHS policy because of the context in which it arose. In most contexts, a party who is dissatisfied with an agency decision can be expected to have ready access to counsel. As a result, the party can always appeal an agency decision inconsistent with the prior decisions of a circuit court. Through this process of repeated appeals, individuals can continue to assert their right to judicial review, and the agency can continue to attempt to vindicate its position by trying to persuade other circuits and ultimately the Supreme Court to accept the agency's position. The Supreme Court then has the benefit of several circuit court opinions on the issue. The limited resources of most recipients of disability benefits precludes easy recourse to this traditional method of attempting to assert the right to judicial review of adverse agency actions.

The judges in the Ninth Circuit did not limit their objections to HHS' policy of nonacquiescence in judicial decisions to public protestations. In *Lopez v. Heckler,*[79] a district judge in the Ninth Circuit issued an order in a class action requiring HHS to reinstate as eligible persons all residents of the Ninth Circuit whose disability benefits had been terminated by HHS as a result of its nonacquiescence in the Ninth Circuit's decisions in *Patti* and *Finnegan.* The district court did not explain the basis for its order, but referred briefly to separation of powers, to due process, and to *Marbury v. Madison.* The Ninth Circuit refused to reverse the district court's order.[80] Like the district court, the circuit court provided little explanation of the legal basis for the district court's order other than a general reference to the unconstitutionality of the HHS policy of nonacquiescence. A concurring opinion referred to *Marbury v. Madison* and separation of powers. The concurring judge suggested a close analogy between the HHS policy and the pre-Civil war policy of southern states to refuse to recognize federal law. This analogy is strained to say the least, since HHS is not a state but the federal government. This dispute was between the President and the judges of a federal circuit, not between federal and state governments.

HHS then sought and obtained a stay of the district court order from the Supreme Court Justice assigned to the Ninth Circuit, Justice Rehnquist.[81] He based his grant of a stay of the district court order primarily on one of the very constitutional law doctrines that

quiescence by Federal Agencies, 98 Yale L.J. 679 (1989).

79. 572 F.Supp. 26 (S.D.Cal.1983).

80. Lopez v. Heckler, 713 F.2d 1432 (9th Cir.1983).

81. 463 U.S. 1328 (1983).

the district court and the Ninth Circuit relied upon as the basis for the order—separation of powers. Quoting from the Court's decision in *Federal Communications Commission v. Pottsville Broadcasting Co.*,[82] he referred to the fundamental distinction between the pervasive powers of superior courts to control the decisionmaking of lower courts and the limited powers of courts to control the decisionmaking of agencies exercising power delegated by Congress. He referred also to the Court's repeated emphasis on the principle that agencies must be left free by reviewing courts to make all initial decisions, subject only to judicial review of those decisions to determine whether they are within the boundaries established by Congress and the Constitution. In Justice Rehnquist's view, the district court's order exceeded the limited constitutional authority of the judicial branch by resolving thousands of disputes that fall within the exclusive original jurisdiction of the executive branch. Justice Rehnquist's analysis seems correct. Yet, the context in which the issue arose is troubling, given the vulnerable position of most recipients of disability benefits.

The Supreme Court never addressed the merits of the nonacquiescence dispute between HHS and the Ninth Circuit. Congress rendered that dispute moot by amending the statute in ways that clarified the standards for decisionmaking. Independent of the outcome of the controversy underlying Justice Rehnquist's order and opinion, the broader point he makes is fundamental. Courts can review agency actions and policies to insure that each action is within statutory and constitutional boundaries. Courts cannot take actions that have been assigned to agencies or make policy decisions that have been delegated to agencies by Congress.[83] If agencies have too much discretion to make policy or they make unsatisfactory policy decisions, the remedy must be found in political rather than judicial forums. Congress can control agency discretion within narrow boundaries by making policy decisions and reflecting those decisions in meaningful statutory standards. When Congress chooses not to make policy decisions, but opts instead to delegate that power to agencies, the choice is simple—should agencies or courts make those policy decisions? Under our constitutional system of government, the answer is evident—since agencies are far more accountable to the

---

82. 309 U.S. 134 (1940).

83. The Court emphasized this important point again in its unanimous summary reversal of a Ninth Circuit decision in INS v. Ventura, 537 U.S. 12 (2002). The Court criticized the Ninth Circuit for intruding "upon the domain which Congress exclusively entrusted to an administrative agency" by instructing an agency to reverse its decision in a case. The Court explained that "the proper course" for a reviewing court that perceives an error in an agency decision is "to remand to the agency for additional investigation or explanation."

electorate than courts, they must be allowed to make those policy decisions that Congress has chosen to delegate to them.

Chapter Eight

ACCESS TO PRIVATE AND PUBLIC INFORMATION

§ 8.1 The Role of Government Information Policies

Governments annually acquire millions of forms, documents, and other types of information from private parties for three functions.[1] Information is acquired to determine whether existing laws or rules have been violated or whether new laws or rules are necessary, to assist economic and social development, and to facilitate the regulation of products and services by licensing.

The Federal Trade Commission's (FTC) acquisition of information illustrates the government's "investigatory" function. The FTC investigates firms to determine whether they have violated a statutory provision, a trade rule promulgated by the Commission, or a cease and desist or consent order. Thus, the FTC can seek to determine whether a firm's sales practices are "unfair or deceptive," whether they violate a rule that has specified what types of practices are "unfair or deceptive," or whether they violate an agreement between the firm and the agency that the firm will not engage in certain types of practices in the future. The FTC also investigates firms in order to make reports to Congress about the need for new legislation or to determine the need for new trade rules under its existing authority.[2]

Census information is an example of "data collection" by the government. Census information, which offers a statistical basis from which government and private planning can take place, would not be collected and sold by a private party because of its public goods character. Its use by one customer would not necessarily diminish its value to other customers. As a result, anyone who purchased the information could immediately resell it in order to recoup at least some of the purchase price. No firm could make a sufficient number

---

1. *See* Commission on Federal Paperwork: Final Summary Report (1977); H. Kaufman, Redtape: Its Origins, Uses and Abuses (1977). *See also A Blackletter Statement of Administrative Law*, 54 Ad. L. Rev. 1, 76 (2002) (Verkuil, Duffy & Herz eds.) (describing government information policies).

2. *See* 15 U.S.C. § 46(a)–(d) (authority to gather and compile information, require reports, investigate compliance with final decrees, and investigate and make reports to Congress); *see also id.* at § 49 (authority to subpoena information for law enforcement purposes and to carry out investigatory responsibilities).

of sales in such a situation to recover the considerable costs of collecting census information. Other employment, financial, and economic statistics are collected by governments for the same reason.[3]

The information obtained by the Food and Drug Administration (FDA) is an example of the licensing function. A manufacturer of a new pharmaceutical drug is required to prove the safety and efficacy of the product before it can be marketed. To do so, the manufacturer engages in elaborate tests of the drug both in animals and humans to determine its therapeutic characteristics. The information derived from this process is submitted to the FDA for their review and judgment. The regulation of food and color additives, pesticides, and other consumer products operate under similar licensing and testing restrictions.[4]

Access to the information collected by the government is constantly sought by private individuals for three purposes. First, access is sought to "monitor" the performance of government. Newspapers, authors, politicians, and citizens seek information in order to determine what government has done and why. For example, access to the testing information submitted by FDA has been sought to determine whether FDA has made a proper judgment in approving drugs and medical devices for marketing.[5] Second, access is used for "commercial" purposes. Business firms and others seek information as an inexpensive way of gathering data economically useful to them. Business firms, for example, seek the type of data collected by FDA and the Environmental Protection Agency (EPA) to evaluate the technical nature of the products being produced by their competitors.[6] Finally, access is used for purposes of litigation. Persons involved, or who might become involved, in lawsuits with an agency or other private individuals will seek information to allow them to

3. *See* Greenawalt & Noam, *Confidentiality Claims of Business Organizations* in Business Disclosure: Government's Need to Know 398–400 (H. Goldschmid ed. 1979). The problem could be avoided if customers would agree contractually to keep the information they purchased secret, but there is no realistic way to make and enforce such agreements with very many purchasers. *See* Demsetz, *Information and Efficiency: Another Viewpoint,* 12 J. Law & Econ. 1, 12–13 (1969).

4. *See* 7 U.S.C. § 136 (pesticide regulation); 15 U.S.C. § 2603(a) (toxic substances regulation); 21 U.S.C. § 355 (new drug regulation); *id.* at § 376 (color additive regulation); *id.* at § 348 (food additive regulation); *see generally* Shapiro, *Limiting Physician Freedom to Prescribe a Drug for Any Purpose: The Need for FDA Regulation,* 72 N.W.U.L. Rev. 801, 802–07 (1978) (description of FDA testing and licensing regulations).

5. *See* McGarity & Shapiro, *The Trade Secret Status of Health and Safety Testing Information: Reforming Agency Disclosure Policies,* 93 Harv. L. Rev. 837, 840–45 (1980).

6. *Id.* at 849–51.

better assess and present their point of view. A tort lawyer representing an Air Force pilot, for example, might seek copies of the government report that evaluated the causes of the pilot's plane crash. Among other uses, the lawyer could utilize the information to determine whether to file a lawsuit against the manufacturer of the plane for negligent design.[7]

The public acquisition of private information has one characteristic in common with the private acquisition of public information. In both cases, the person or institution possessing the information may be unwilling to voluntarily give it up because its disclosure would be disadvantageous in some way. Private individuals often are unwilling to disclose information to the government because they fear it may be disclosed to competitors, or that it may assist the government in acting adversely to their interests. The government is often unwilling to disclose information voluntarily because it believes that disclosure would allow circumvention of government regulations or harm to the public interest in some way.

The extent to which both private individuals and the government must give up information to each other is controlled by a framework of statutes, legal precedents, and, in the case of government seizure of information, constitutional limitations. All of these sources of law have been influenced by difficult trade-offs. The government's ability to function depends on good information, but acquisition of that information can offend the right to privacy or other similar concerns. An individual's right to acquire information often serves the values of open government, but it can also be inconsistent with the efficient operation of the government. The following sections describe the law applicable to the acquisition and dissemination of governmental information and the policies that have shaped that law.

§ 8.2   Government Access to Private Information

The owners of information can voluntarily submit it to the government, but most agencies are statutorily authorized to compel its production if necessary. There are three forms of such compulsion. First, an agency can compel individuals or firms to answer questionnaires or submit other types of reports or forms. The census form is an obvious example, but agencies like the FTC are also authorized to use this means of data collection. Second, an agency can subpoena information and thereby require its production at a certain time and

---

7. *See* Tomlinson, *Use of the Freedom of Information Act for Discovery Pur-* poses, 43 Md. L. Rev. 119 (1984).

place. The FTC, for example, normally acquires investigatory information in this fashion. Finally, an agency can inspect the premises of a firm or individual, including inspection of the documents kept there. The Occupational Health and Safety Administration (OSHA), for example, will inspect factories to determine compliance with the health and safety laws and regulations it enforces.

As mentioned, firms often seek to avoid orders to produce information for various reasons including that it is considered unnecessary for legitimate government functions, it is too costly to produce, or its production could lead to a prosecution for violation of a law or rule.[8] The extent of an agency's authority to compel the production of information is determined by the nature of its statutory authority and by the Fourth and Fifth Amendments. Despite those limitations, however, most agencies are able to acquire the information they seek. The statutory authority under which they operate normally is quite expansive and, in most cases, the constitutional constraints are either easily met or not applicable.

§ 8.2.1 Statutory authority to compel disclosure

Most agencies have expansive authority to obtain information because Congress has authorized them to collect any data relevant and necessary to meeting their substantive responsibilities.[9] Since those responsibilities are usually stated in a broad and vague fashion,[10] they offer only the most general type of limitation on the agency's authority to compel the production of information. Further, an agency has no obligation under the Administrative Procedure Act (APA) to hold any type of proceeding prior to issuing an order to produce information, although agencies sometimes do so.[11]

In re FTC Line of Business Report Litigation illustrates the expansive power of agencies to acquire information and the reasons for that power.[12] The FTC is authorized "[t]o require by general or special orders, persons, partnerships, and corporations ... to file with the Commission in such forms as the Commission may prescribe annual or special, or both annual or special, reports...." The Com-

---

8. *See generally* Benston, *An Appraisal of the Costs and Benefits of Government Required Disclosure: SEC and FTC Requirements,* 41 Law & Contemp. Probs. 30 (1977).

9. *See, e.g.,* 15 U.S.C. § 49 (FTC).

10. *See supra* § 3.1.

11. In re FTC Line of Business Report Litigation, 595 F.2d 685, 695–96

(D.C.Cir.1978) *cert. denied,* 439 U.S. 958 (1978); *see also* Superior Oil Co. v. FERC, 563 F.2d 191, 198 (5th Cir.1977) (Federal Energy Regulatory Commission was authorized to procure any information "essential" to effective rate making).

12. 595 F.2d 685 (D.C. Cir. 1978).

mission can seek in those reports "such information as it may require as to the organization, business, conduct, practices, management, and relation to [other businesses] of the [party] filing such reports...."[13] Utilizing this authority, the FTC sought to have the nation's largest companies report certain business statistics on a "line of business" basis or by type of business. For example, General Motors would report its profits on the basis of each of the types of business in which it was engaged, such as the manufacture of cars, trucks, spare parts, and so on. Business firms vigorously resisted the FTC program on the grounds that since data was not kept by them in that form it would be costly to generate and that its benefit to the FTC was not worth the cost.[14] Despite the vigor of these objections, the District of Columbia Circuit dismissed a legal attack on the FTC's authority to require the reports in a short per curiam opinion.

The court considered the matter to be covered by Section 555 of the APA which states that "process, requirement of a report, inspection, or other investigative act or demand may not be issued, made, or enforced except as authorized by law".[15] Because of this section, the court dismissed the two major grounds on which the FTC was attacked. First, the court rejected the contention that the FTC was obligated to hold a rulemaking or other proceeding before it could adopt the reporting requirement. The court reasoned that since Section 555 covered such reporting requirements, they were not agency "actions" of the type that were subject to the other requirements of the APA. Second, the court rejected the contention that the FTC's actions were to be judged by the criteria of whether they were arbitrary and capricious.[16] Again, the court reasoned that since Section 555 applied, it furnished the grounds for appeal. The court noted that since the section required only that the agency's actions be "authorized by law," the only constraint on the agency was that the reports be within its statutory authority and within applicable constitutional limitations. As a result, the court refused to consider whether the costs of the FTC program exceeded its benefits. Instead, the opinion merely observed that the FTC's actions were clearly within the statutory authority quoted earlier.

University of Pennsylvania v. EEOC indicates that the Supreme Court continues to reject arguments that are not based on an

---

13.   15 U.S.C. § 46(b).

14.   *See generally* Benston, *supra* note 8.

15.   5 U.S.C. § 555(c).

16.   *See* 5 U.S.C. § 706(2)(A) (agency "action" shall not be "arbitrary" or "capricious").

agency's statutory authority as grounds for a subpoena.[17] The EEOC had subpoenaed faculty peer review evaluations used by the university in its tenure process to investigate charges of discrimination. The school had asked the Court to require the EEOC to give specific reasons why this information was necessary since this requirement would recognize the university's interest in maximizing the confidentiality of such reports. A unanimous Supreme Court rejected the university's argument. Congress had authorized the Commission to "have access to . . . any evidence of a person being investigated . . . that relates to unlawful employment practices covered by the [Act] and is relevant to the charge under investigation. The Court noted that Congress only required the EEOC to indicate the general relevance of the documents it sought and that requiring a 'specific reason' for disclosure would impede the EEOC's mission."

§ 8.2.2   Paperwork Reduction Act

In addition to an agency's statutory mandate, the Paperwork Reduction Act, originally enacted in 1980 and amended in 1996, limits an agency's authority to compel private parties to disclose information.[18] The Act applies any time that an agency seeks to impose a reporting or record keeping requirement on 10 or more persons. As interpreted by the Supreme Court,[19] the 1980 legislation applied only to disclosures to the government and not to third parties, but Congress overruled this interpretation in 1996. The Act now applies when agencies mandate a disclosure to the government or to members of the public. It requires agencies to establish offices to oversee their information collection activities, to use the procedures specified in the Act to obtain public comment on any proposal to obtain information (unless the agency uses APA rulemaking procedures to require disclosure of the information), and to certify that the agency meets a series of tests established by the legislation, including that the information is necessary for the agency's proper performance and it is not unnecessarily duplicative of information already reasonably available to the agency. Finally, the agency must submit its proposed data collection to the Office of Information and Regulatory Affairs (OIRA) in the Office of Management and Budget (OMB) for its approval. The Act specifies a series of procedures concerning the submission of a proposed data collection to OIRA and OIRA subsequent actions concerning the request. Although OIRA can dis-

---

17.   493 U.S. 182 (1990).

18.   44 U.S.C. §§ 3501–3520. For a more detailed discussion of the Act, *see infra* § 9.5.3.

19.   Dole v. United Steelworkers, 494 U.S. 26 (1990). For a discussion of this case, *see infra* § 9.5.3.

approve of a request, it appears that it seldom exercises this authority. Instead, it obtains concessions from an agency concerning the nature and scope of information to be collected. An independent regulatory agency is authorized to override OIRA's disapproval of a proposed data collection by a majority vote of the members.

Once OIRA approves of a data collection, it assigns it a control number that must appear on any reporting form or in agency regulations or orders referring to the collection requirement. If an agency does not comply with this requirement, the Act forbids penalizing any person who fails to comply with the collection requirements. The courts have held, however, that this prohibition does not apply if the data collection requirement is imposed by a statute, rather than by a regulation or agency order.[20]

§ 8.2.3 Fourth Amendment protections against government searches

The exact contours of the principal constitutional protection against government searches, the Fourth Amendment, were left by the framers in an ambiguous state.[21] The Amendment provides:

> The right of the people to be secure in their persons, houses, papers, and effects, against unreasonable searches and seizures, shall not be violated, and no Warrants shall issue, but upon probable cause, supported by Oath or affirmation, and particularly describing the place to be searched, and the person or things to be seized.

> The first clause clearly grants a general right to be free from "unreasonable" searches and seizures and the second clearly specifies the conditions under which a warrant can be obtained. But the amendment does not indicate whether a search can be conducted without a warrant, and if so, under what conditions it will be reasonable.

In the traditional search for evidence of a crime, the Supreme Court has long expressed a preference for use of a search warrant. The warrant process " 'interposes an orderly procedure' involving 'judicial impartiality' whereby 'a neutral and detached magistrate' can make 'informed and deliberate determinations' of probable cause."[22] In the absence of an exception, such as the hot pursuit of a

20. W. Funk, S. Shapiro & R. Weaver, Administrative Practice & Procedure 591 (2d ed 2001).

21. U.S. Const. Amend. 4.

22. 1 W. LaFave, Search and Seizure: A Treatise on the Fourth Amendment § 3.1(c), at 548–49 (2d ed.1987) (quota-

suspect, the search of a premises without a warrant is per se unreasonable.[23] This and other evidence seized in violation of the Fourth Amendment could be excluded from judicial proceedings where it could otherwise have been used.[24]

Exceptions to the requirement of a warrant are justified on the ground that the first clause of the Fourth Amendment establishes a power to search that is in addition to the use of the warrant process. Such searches, however, are generally "reasonable" only if the government has probable cause for them.[25] The reason is that it would make no sense to apply a lesser standard for the government's right to search when the government, instead of a neutral magistrate, determines the propriety of the search. Thus, the government is subject to the same requirement of probable cause whether or not a warrant must be obtained.[26]

To obtain a warrant, or to justify a search without one, the government must establish with probable cause that the items sought are in fact seizable by virtue of being connected with a crime and that the items will be found in the place to be searched.[27] To have probable cause, the government's evidence must satisfy a reasonable person that the previous facts are true.[28]

In the last twenty years, the Court has recognized that the Fourth Amendment is implicated in many governmental activities that are functionally different from the traditional search for criminals or evidence of a crime. In recognition of that distinction, the Court has balanced the need for the government's search with the level of intrusion it causes to arrive at the proper level of justification required of the government. For example, the Supreme Court in a pair of 1989 opinions determined that regulations requiring federal employees to undergo drug testing were constitutional. *National Treasury Employees Union (NTEU) v. Von Raab* upheld a United States Custom Service policy that required drug testing as a condition of appointment or promotion to jobs related to drug interdiction

tion marks and citation numbers deleted).

23. *See, e.g.,* Mincey v. Arizona, 437 U.S. 385, 390 (1978); Katz v. United States, 389 U.S. 347, 357 (1967).

24. *See* Mapp v. Ohio, 367 U.S. 643 (1961); *see also* Ker v. California, 374 U.S. 23, 30–31 (1963).

25. 1 W. LaFave, *supra* note 22, at § 3.1(a).

26. *See* Vale v. Louisiana, 399 U.S. 30, 34 (1970); Wong Sun v. United States, 371 U.S. 471 (1963).

27. Zurcher v. Stanford Daily, 436 U.S. 547, 554–56 (1978); *see generally* 1 W. LaFave, *supra* note 22, at § 3.1(b).

28. Terry v. Ohio, 392 U.S. 1, 21, 22 (1968); *see generally* 1 W. LaFave, *supra* note 22, at § 3.2(b).

and carrying firearms.[29] *Skinner v. Railway Labor Executives' Association* upheld Federal Railroad Administration regulations requiring railroads to conduct drug testing of employees involved in certain types of accidents.[30] Although the Court conceded that the testing constituted a "search," it rejected allegations that the Fourth Amendment had been violated despite the fact that neither regulation conditioned testing on "probable cause" of drug use or any similar standard. In both cases, the Court balanced the degree of the invasion of an employee's privacy—which the Court characterized as limited—against the government's interest in the testing—which the Court characterized as substantial. For example, *NTEU* found that the "Government's compelling interests in preventing the promotion of drug users to positions where they might endanger the integrity of our Nation's borders or the life of the citizenry outweigh the privacy interests of those who seek promotion to these positions, who enjoy a diminished expectation of privacy by virtue of the special, and obvious, physical and ethical demands of the positions." *Skinner* concluded, "In light of the limited discretion exercised by the railroad employers under the regulation, the surpassing safety interests served by toxicological tests in this context, and the diminished expectation of privacy that attaches to information pertaining to the fitness of covered employees, we believe that it is reasonable to conduct such tests in the absence of a warrant or reasonable suspicion that any particular employee may be impaired."

Administrative reports, subpoenas, and inspections implicate the Fourth Amendment, but in a way distinct from the investigation of a crime. As a result, the Supreme Court has indicated that the application of the Fourth Amendment must be adjusted to that distinction. The adjustment has occurred recently for reports and subpoenas and is still in the process of being determined for inspections. Nevertheless, it is still clear that the government has considerable power with which to obtain the information it seeks.

§ 8.2.4   Subpoenas and required reports

Before the 1940s, the judiciary refused to give administrative agencies the power to obtain information through the use of a subpoena or required report. One court typically maintained that any "intrusion into, and compulsory exposure of, one's private affairs and papers, without judicial process, or in the course of judicial proceedings ... is abhorrent...."[31] The combined effect of these holdings

---

29. 489 U.S. 656 (1989).

30. 489 U.S. 602 (1989).

31. In re Pacific Railway Commission, 32 Fed. 241, 251 (C.C.N.D. Cal. 1887).

"was to protect business against effective administrative investigation into business records". The Constitution thus became "a bulwark against government interference with free enterprise".[32]

The most outstanding of these cases was *FTC v. American Tobacco Co.,* authored by Justice Holmes.[33] The FTC was attempting to investigate whether two tobacco companies had committed unfair methods of competition when they controlled the resale prices at which their jobber customers resold their products. The FTC had subpoenaed from each "all letters and telegrams received by the Company from and sent to all of its jobber customers" for a specified period of time. The FTC had refused to disclose the nature or source of the complaints it had received about the tobacco companies on the ground that it had "an unlimited right of access to the respondent's papers" for purposes of investigation. The Court disagreed because it thought that interpretation of the agency's authority violated the Fourth Amendment.

Justice Holmes explained the Court's holding on the ground that "[a]nyone who respects the spirit as well as the letter of the Fourth Amendment would be loath to believe that Congress intended to authorize one of its subordinate agencies ... to direct fishing expeditions into private parties on the ground that they might disclose evidence of a crime." As a result, an agency is not allowed to "call for all documents in order to see if they contain [evidence]". The agency instead must have "some ground" for "supposing that the documents called for do contain it". The gravamen of Justice Holmes' argument thus was that the FTC failed to meet the traditional requirement in criminal matters that the government must establish with probable cause that the items sought are in fact seizable by virtue of being connected with a legal violation.[34]

In *Endicott Johnson Corporation v. Perkins,* a 1943 case, the Court began its retreat from *American Tobacco,* but in an indirect manner.[35] The Secretary of the Department of Labor had subpoenaed information from Endicott Johnson, a shoe manufacturer, concerning possible violations of the Walsh–Healy Act, which required all government contractors to observe minimum standards concerning wages, hours of labor, employment of children, and other working conditions. The company had refused to comply on the ground that the information was sought not from the plants where the shoes were

32. 1 K. C. Davis, Administrative Law Treatise § 4.1, at 228 (2d ed. 1978).

33. 264 U.S. 298 (1924).

34. *See supra* text accompanying notes 32–33.

35. 317 U.S. 501 (1943).

made, but from other related facilities, such as cardboard carton and tanning plants, that did not have any contracts with the government. The company therefore argued that before the Labor Department could subpoena information from those plants, it had to establish that they could be liable for a violation of the Act. The Court disagreed and held that as long as the evidence sought "was not plainly incompetent or irrelevant to any lawful purpose of the Secretary in the discharge of her duties under the Act . . . it was the duty of the District Court to order its production for the Secretary's consideration."

The Court explained that a contrary holding "would require the Secretary in order to get evidence of a violation either to allege she had decided the issue of [jurisdiction] before the hearing [on a possible violation], or to sever the issues for a separate hearing and determination." The Court thought that the "former was of dubious propriety, and the latter of doubtful practicality". Instead, the Court decided Congress wanted the issue of jurisdiction to be decided by the Secretary as the investigation proceeded. After the Secretary had made a final determination of jurisdiction, the company would be entitled to appeal it.

Endicott-Johnson was clearly inconsistent with *American Tobacco*. The justices in *Endicott* apparently perceived no Fourth Amendment problem in enforcing a subpoena against a party over whom the Department may have lacked jurisdiction to find a violation. Yet, in *American Tobacco,* the FTC was required to establish that it had probable cause to believe the documents it sought were relevant to whether the tobacco companies had committed a violation. The Court offered no explanation of why it was unimportant whether an agency "probably" had jurisdiction over a party, but it was important whether the documents being sought "probably" were relevant to finding a violation.

Oklahoma Press Publishing Co. v. Walling eliminated the discrepancy between the two previous cases by, in effect, overruling *American Tobacco.*[36] The Wage and Hour Administrator had subpoenaed documents from a newspaper concerning payroll data, the sources of its advertisement and news, and the nature of the distribution of newspapers outside of Oklahoma. With the information, the administrator intended to determine whether the newspaper had violated legislation that required businesses affecting interstate commerce to meet minimum wage and hour standards. The company

36.   327 U.S. 186 (1946).

refused to comply on the ground that it was not obligated to reply because of the First Amendment, and that in any event, no reason existed for supposing that it had violated the statute. The Court rejected the first argument, concerning lack of jurisdiction, on the basis of *Endicott Johnson*. The Court rejected the second, concerning the lack of probable cause, by concluding that it was not necessary.

The Court explained that probable cause was not necessary because Congress had not required it as a statutory matter and the Fourth Amendment did not require it as a constitutional one. The Court defended the second judgment on the ground that the invasion of privacy involved when documents are subpoenaed is less than when there is an actual search of a premises. In the latter case, the materials being sought are brought to the government at its offices. Two other considerations also seemed to influence the Court. First, the opinion noted that historically corporations have been treated differently from individuals concerning their right to privacy because they are entities that are created by governments. Second, the Court noted that the right to privacy must be balanced against the interests of the state. If the Amendment were interpreted to require probable cause, the Court was afraid it "would stop much if not all of investigation in the public interest at the threshold of the inquiry...."

In light of these considerations, the Court adjusted the application of the amendment in three ways. First, it decided that no specific crime needed to be charged, as in the case of a warrant, but it was sufficient that "the investigation be for a lawfully authorized purpose, within the power of Congress to command". Second, because no specific crime had to be charged, probable cause to suspect the commission of a crime was unnecessary. Instead, the "requirement of 'probable cause, supported by oath or affirmation' literally required in the case of a warrant is satisfied ... by the court's determination that the investigation is authorized by Congress, is for a purpose that Congress can order, and the documents sought are relevant to the inquiry". Third, the requirement of the warrant clause that the persons or things to be seized be "particularly" described requires only that subpoenas contain "a specification of the documents to be produced adequate, but not excessive, for the purposes of the relevant inquiry". The Court warned that what is "relevant," "adequate," and "not excessive" would vary in relationship to the nature, purpose, and scope of an investigation.

In *United States v. Morton Salt Co.,* the Court extended the previous case to the forced disclosure of information through required reports.[37] The FTC had ordered twenty salt producers to file special reports with the Commission that would indicate they were in compliance with a cease and desist order entered against them for engaging in unfair methods of competition. The Court rejected the producers' arguments that the Commission lacked statutory authority to order the reports and that the order violated the Fourth Amendment. In responding to the last argument, the Court accepted the producers' claim that the Commission was engaged in a "mere 'fishing expedition' to see if it can turn up evidence of guilt" and said that it did not matter. Since the FTC met the tests created in *Oklahoma Press,* the Court concluded the Commission could make its investigation.

The Court explained that Justice Holmes' notion that agencies could not engage in "fishing expeditions" was misguided for two reasons. First, the idea confused subpoenas issued by the judiciary, pursuant to the trial of a case, with those issued by administrative agencies, pursuant to an investigation. The latter was regarded as "a power of inquisition, which is analogous to the Grand Jury," and which "does not depend on a case of controversy for power to get evidence. . . . " An agency therefore can "investigate merely on the suspicion that the law is being violated, or even just because it wants assurance that it is not". Second, the Court reiterated the argument that corporations, as government-created institutions, have only a qualified constitutional right to conduct their affairs in secret. The Court concluded that this status means that "law-enforcing agencies have a legitimate right to satisfy themselves that corporate behavior is consistent with the law and the public interest".

The judiciary's complete about face from abhorrence of "fishing expeditions" to approval of them caused Professor Davis to observe, "What a flexible Constitution we have!"[38] The flexibility comes from the ambiguity of the amendment itself and its designation of "reasonableness" as the crucial element in approving searches without a warrant. When the Court appreciated the necessity of administrative investigations, it was able to balance, within the concept of reasonableness, the need for a search against the invasion of privacy that occurred. The invasion was discounted because no actual search occurred and because the recipients were corporations entitled to a lesser Fourth Amendment privilege. In this manner, agencies were

---

37. 338 U.S. 632 (1950); *see also* FTC v. Crafts, 355 U.S. 9 (1957).

38. 1 K. Davis, *supra* note 32, § 4.2, at 232.

freed from the traditional application of the amendment and subjected to a doctrine created specifically for them.[39]

§ 8.2.5 Anatomy of a subpoena

The effect of *Oklahoma Press* can be illustrated by considering the route by which subpoenas are created, served, and enforced.[40] The staff of the FTC, for example, will ask the Commission for a formal declaration of an investigation in order to obtain authority to subpoena information. If a majority of the five commissioners agree, they will issue a "resolution" that will state the Commission's statutory authority to investigate, and the reasons stated in general terms why the investigation has been started. Authority to issue the actual subpoena has been delegated by the Commission to the leadership of its staff. A subpoena will be sent by registered mail to the recipient indicating the time and location for compliance, a "specification" of the documents sought, and a copy of the resolution authorizing the investigation.[41]

The recipient of a subpoena has several options. The firm or person can comply or not respond at all. In the latter case, the FTC will seek an order from a district court compelling compliance.[42] Under the FTC's procedural rules, the firm or person can also negotiate with the Commission's staff to see if they will voluntarily change the subpoena, or even withdraw it, or a motion can be made to the Commission itself to quash or modify the subpoena. If the outcome of either or both of these options is not satisfactory to the recipient, the person or firm can await enforcement by court action.

The recipient will attempt before the Commission and the District Court to argue that the subpoena exceeds the bounds set by *Oklahoma Press*. The first of those is that the investigation must be authorized by Congress, for a purpose Congress can order, and that the documents sought are relevant to the inquiry. As previously explained, the statutory authority of the FTC to investigate, as well

---

39. The Court has also decided that the Fourth Amendment does not apply when information is revealed to a third party and the information is obtained from that third party. *See* United States v. Miller, 425 U.S. 435 (1976) (banks may disclose records of depositor accounts without obligation to notify depositor because Fourth Amendment does not apply); California Bankers Ass'n v. Shultz, 416 U.S. 21 (1974) (statutory obligation of banks to microfilm customers' checks

and disclose films when subpoenaed not prevented by Fourth Amendment).

40. *See generally* Cooper, *Federal Agency Investigations: Requirements for the Production of Documents,* 60 Mich. L. Rev. 187 (1961).

41. *See generally* Lemke, *The Federal Trade Commission's Use of Investigational Subpoenas,* 1 Loyola U.L.J. 15 (1970).

42. *See* 15 U.S.C. § 49.

as the authority of most agencies, is as broad as their mandate, which is also broad. As a result, challenges to an agency's statutory authority do not usually succeed. Further, Congress' authority to order the investigations is seldom in doubt because of the expansive definition given its power to control interstate commerce.[43]

The last ground for attack in the first set of tests would be to argue that the documents being sought are not relevant to the investigation. To make that determination, a court will ask whether the documents, as described in the specifications, could "possibly" inform the investigation, as defined in the FTC's resolution. For that reason, the FTC will have stated its purpose in the resolution in broad terms thereby qualifying most, if not all, of the documents it seeks as relevant. The courts have been generous in allowing agencies to state their purpose in a broad manner and, as a result, this ground of attack will usually also be largely unfruitful.[44]

The other test mandated by *Oklahoma Press* is whether the documents being sought are "adequately" described and are not "excessive" for the purposes of the inquiry. Vague and ambiguous specifications will not be enforced, but an agency can avoid that pitfall by careful drafting. Further, whether an agency's demands are excessive will depend on the nature of the investigation and the recipient's financial resources.[45] For example, an agency can more easily defend a demand for a large number of documents when the investigation is of a highly complex matter, rather than a simple one, and it is of a large and wealthy company, rather than a smaller and less well-off one. The resources of the company are important because a firm's ability to pay compliance costs has a bearing on whether the demand is excessive.

Even if a recipient is successful in establishing that some requests are irrelevant, imprecise, or excessive, the Commission or the courts usually respond by ordering that the subpoena be modified to eliminate the offending problems. As a result, except in the unlikely case that the entire subpoena is defective, a firm is unlikely to avoid substantial compliance on Fourth Amendment grounds. Consequently, many recipients use the tactic of attempting to delay enforcement by availing themselves of all the opportunities to negotiate and

43. *See supra* § 8.2.1.; FTC v. Ken Roberts Co., 276 F.3d 583 (D.C. Cir. 2001) (subpoena enforced even though agency's jurisdiction challenged).

44. *See, e.g.*, EEOC v. Dillon Cos., 310 F.3d 1271 (10th Cir. 2002)(relevancy limitation "not especially constraining").

45. *See, e.g.*, Genuine Parts Co. v. FTC, 445 F.2d 1382, 1391 (5th Cir.1971); Adams v. FTC, 296 F.2d 861, 866 (8th Cir.1961), *cert. denied*, 369 U.S. 864 (1962).

contest the subpoena. They are facilitated by the fact that usually there are no penalties for failure to comply unless there is a court order to do so. Where such penalties exist, the courts have been reluctant to enforce them until they order compliance.[46]

§ 8.2.6 Inspections

The Supreme Court's treatment of inspections has been similar to the cases concerning subpoenas and required reports in that the Court has recognized they are to be treated differently than a search of a premises for evidence of a crime. The Court, however, has been unable to decide what type of adjustments should be made as a result. As a consequence, it has developed two lines of authority. One requires a warrant to be obtained for inspections, although the requirements to obtain the warrant have been changed from those applicable to the traditional search. The other allows warrantless inspections as long as they are reasonable.

The line of authority requiring a warrant begins with *Camara v. Municipal Court.*[47] Mr. Camara was prosecuted for his failure to allow a city inspector to enter his premises. In the course of a routine inspection, the inspector had sought to verify a complaint that Mr. Camara's use of his premises was not allowed by the San Francisco city regulations. All city employees were authorized "to enter, at reasonable times, any ... premises to perform any duty imposed by the Municipal Code." The Code required housing inspections, of the type in which the inspector was engaged, "at least once a year and as often thereafter as may be deemed necessary". The Court held that the city ordinance was unconstitutional because it provided for warrantless searches.

The Court's opinion had two parts. First, the Court disagreed with an earlier case, *Frank v. Maryland,*[48] which had held Fourth Amendment interests in an inspection were merely "peripheral," because it had ignored the fact that individuals have a "very tangible interest" in the privacy of their premises. Second, the Court held that probable cause that a crime had been committed was not necessary in order to secure a warrant because cities would thereby be prohibited from making periodic area-wide inspections of buildings to determine the owner's compliance with city regulations. Instead, the Court adjusted the definition of probable cause to reflect a

---

46. *See, e.g.,* 15 U.S.C. § 60 (failure to comply with FTC subpoena punishable by fine and imprisonment); *see generally* P. Strauss, T. Rakoff & C. Farina, Gell-horn & Byses' Administrative Law: Cases and Comments 1067–68 (10th ed. 2003).

47.   387 U.S. 523 (1967).

48.   359 U.S. 360 (1959).

balancing between the city's interests and the degree of invasion of privacy that was caused. The Court held that " 'probable cause' to issue a warrant to inspect must exist if reasonable legislative or administrative standards for conducting an area inspection are satisfied with respect to a particular dwelling."

The Court extended the requirement of a warrant to commercial buildings in *See v. City of Seattle*.[49] The Court deemed its reasoning in *Camara* equally applicable in *See* because a "businessman, like the occupant of a residence, has a constitutional right to go about his business free from unreasonable official entries upon his private property". But the Court warned that it did not "question such accepted regulatory techniques as licensing programs which require inspections prior to operating a business or marketing a product." According to the opinion, Fourth Amendment challenges in that situation were to be resolved "on a case-by-case basis under the general Fourth Amendment standard of reasonableness".

The Court soon relied on the exception it created by the previous language. In *United States v. Biswell,* the Court upheld a federal statute that authorized warrantless inspections of licensed fire arms and ammunition dealers.[50] The Court offered four reasons for its decision. One was that the industry had long been subjected to close government scrutiny including inspection as a means of regulation. Another was that effective regulation required warrantless inspections because the searches, to be an effective deterrent, had to be unannounced. The third reason was that a dealer should have only a limited expectation of privacy since the person voluntarily chose to engage in a pervasively regulated business. The final reason was that the statute authorized inspections only for a limited purpose, time, and place and as a result, the dealer "is not left to wonder about the purposes of the inspector or the limits of his task".

Two recent cases involve the two lines of authority created by *See* and *Biswell*. In one, *Marshall v. Barlow's, Inc.,* the Court held that Congress could not constitutionally authorize the Occupational Health and Safety Administration (OSHA) to make warrantless inspections of a business premises to determine compliance with the agency's regulations.[51] The Court attempted to distinguish *Biswell* and similar cases on the grounds that they concerned "pervasively" or "closely" regulated businesses that were "long subject to close

---

49.   387 U.S. 541 (1967).

50.   406 U.S. 311 (1972); *see also* Colonnade Catering Corp. v. United States, 397 U.S. 72 (1970) (warrant unnecessary for inspection of the business premises of a liquor licensee).

51.   436 U.S. 307 (1978).

supervision and inspection" and that as a result no reasonable expectation of privacy could exist for such enterprises. Barlow's, an electrical and plumbing contractor, did not run that type of business.

When the government objected that a warrant requirement would make inspections less effective, the Court countered that only a few businesses were likely to deny entry and in those cases OSHA could obtain a warrant and appear unannounced on another occasion. The Court also doubted that the burden of obtaining warrants under the alternative probable cause standard developed in *Camara* would "exceed manageable proportions". The Court pointed out that a warrant "showing that a specific business has been chosen for an OSHA search on the basis of a general administrative plan for the enforcement of the Act derived from neutral sources, such as, for example, dispersion of employees in various types of industries across a given area, and the desired frequency of searches in any of the lesser divisions of the area, would protect an employer's Fourth Amendment rights."

In the second case, *Donovan v. Dewey,* the Court refused to declare unconstitutional a provision of the Federal Mine Safety and Health Act of 1977 that authorized the Secretary of Labor to make warrantless inspections of the nation's mines.[52] The justification for the decision was that cases like *Biswell* had made it clear that "a warrant may not be constitutionally required when Congress has reasonably determined that warrantless searches are necessary to further a statutory scheme and the federal regulatory presence is sufficiently comprehensive and defined that the owner of a commercial property cannot help but be aware that his property will be subject to periodic inspections undertaken for specific purposes". The Court noted that the OSHA statute reviewed in *Barlow's* did not meet that test for two reasons. It failed first to "tailor the scope and frequency of such administrative inspections to the particular health and safety concerns posed by the numerous and varied businesses regulated by the statute". It also did not "provide any standards to guide inspectors either in their selection of establishments to be searched or in the exercise of their authority to search".

The Court's description of the *Biswell* line of authority differed from its characterization of that precedent in *Barlow's*. In *Barlow's*, the Court had noted that a "long tradition of close government supervision" militated against imposition of a warrant requirement. In *Biswell*, the Court decided instead it was the "pervasiveness and

52. 452 U.S. 594 (1981).

regularity" of the federal regulation that determined whether a warrant was necessary for an inspection to be reasonable. The Court explained its shift on the ground that if the length of the regulation were the only criteria, new or emerging industries, such as nuclear power, could never be subjected to warrantless searches even if a statute otherwise met the restrictions imposed by *Biswell.*

In *New York v. Burger,*[53] which upheld a New York statute that authorized warrantless searches of automobile junkyards, the Court interpreted *Dewey* as establishing a three-part test to determine when a warrantless search is valid in a pervasively regulated industry. First, there must be a substantial government interest in the regulatory scheme supported by the warrantless searches. New York had a substantial interest in regulating junkyards because the industry is implicated in the problem of automobile theft. Second, the warrantless searches must be "necessary" to further the regulatory scheme. As in *Dewey,* the Court found that unannounced inspections were crucial to deterring the behavior the Act was intended to prevent. Finally, the government's inspection program must provide a constitutionally adequate substitute for a warrant in terms of the "certainty and regularity of its application." The New York statute met the last test because it contained time, place, and scope restrictions on the nature of the searches that were authorized.

The Court also rejected an argument that the statute was unconstitutional because it had no administrative purpose, but was instead designed to give the police an expedient means of enforcing penal sanctions for possession of stolen property. The Court said that it was legitimate for the government to address the same problem— stolen cars—by way of both an administrative and a penal sanction. The Court also declared that an administrative scheme is not unconstitutional simply because an inspector may discover evidence of a crime in the course of enforcing it.

After these cases, three conclusions are possible. First, probable cause in the traditional sense of a reasonable belief that a crime has been committed is unnecessary for a government inspection. Second, a warrant will be required unless warrantless searches are reasonably necessary to effectuate the purposes of regulation and the regulation is so pervasive that a business will have little expectation that its affairs are private. Third, if a warrant must be obtained, the warrant can be issued pursuant to a general administrative plan which specifies which sites will be inspected by the use of specific

53.   482 U.S. 691 (1987).

neutral criteria. If a warrant is unnecessary, an agency's statutory authority to inspect must be narrowly restricted in time, place, and purpose.

§ 8.2.7   Exceptions to the warrant requirement

Besides the exception to the warrant requirement for pervasively regulated businesses, the Court has recognized three other exceptions.[54] One is for consent. The other two are for emergencies and public view. *Michigan v. Tyler*[55] illustrates the exception for emergencies. The Court considered the extent to which fire officials could inspect a premises for evidence of arson after they had entered the premises without a warrant to put out a fire. Although numerous opinions were filed, a majority of the justices agreed that a burning building clearly presents an exigency of sufficient proportions to render a warrantless entry "reasonable," and that officials need no warrant to remain in a building for a reasonable time to investigate the cause of a blaze after it is extinguished.

In *Dow Chemical Co. v. United States,*[56] the Court applied the public view exception in the context of administrative law. The Environmental Protection Agency (EPA) inspected a plant owned by Dow by means of aerial photographs and the company claimed its Fourth Amendment rights had been violated. Chief Justice Burger concluded that an aerial observation of the visible areas of a business was not a "search" because it fell within the open fields exception to the warrant requirement. The Court rejected Dow's argument that the inspection fell within the "curtilage" provision, which protects open areas around private dwellings from warrantless inspections, because a corporation has a lesser expectation of privacy than individuals.

§ 8.2.8   Privilege as a limitation on administrative searches

In addition to Fourth Amendment constraints, agency searches can be subject to claims of privilege not to disclose based on the Fifth Amendment and common-law privileges such as the "lawyer-client" privilege. Claims that documents are highly confidential, however, will not prevent their disclosure to the government.

54. For a complete description, *see* K. Davis & R. Pierce, Jr., Administrative Law Treatise § 4.3 (1994).

55. 436 U.S. 499 (1978).

56. 476 U.S. 227 (1986); *see also* Air Pollution Variance Bd. v. Western Alfalfa Corp., 416 U.S. 861 (1974) (company has no reasonable expectation of privacy concerning observation of smoke emitted).

The Fifth Amendment provides that no person "shall be compelled in a criminal case to be a witness against himself. . . . "[57] It is, however, inapplicable to corporations,[58] and only partially applicable to individuals. In *Shapiro v. United States,* the Supreme Court created an exception to the privilege against self-incrimination, but the exact limits of it are still uncertain.[59] Mr. Shapiro had been convicted of violating wage and price restrictions based in part on records that he was required to keep. The Court upheld the conviction by deciding that records required to be kept by appropriate legislation, having an unquestioned relevance to a lawful purpose, acquire a public aspect that means they are not protected from disclosure by the Fifth Amendment.

In *Albertson v. Subversive Activities Control Board,* the Court attempted to clarify the extent of the "required records" exception.[60] It declared unconstitutional a statute that required communists to register with the government because the act was self-incriminating. The Court considered three factors to be relevant concerning whether required records implicate the Fifth Amendment. The Court asked whether a statute was directed at a specific group, whether the group was inherently suspect of criminal activity, and whether the statute was in an area permeated with criminal statutes. The Court noted that the statute aimed at the communists was directed at a specific group suspected of criminal activity and it was not in an essentially noncriminal and regulatory area.

The *Albertson* standards have been widely applied in deciding the scope of the "required records" exception.[61] In *California v. Byers,*[62]

57. U.S. Const. Amend. 5.

58. Hale v. Henkel, 201 U.S. 43 (1906). The privilege is unavailable because corporate records are believed not to contain the requisite degree of privacy or confidentiality necessary for the privilege to attach. *See* Bellis v. United States, 417 U.S. 85, 88 (1974); *cf.* United States v. Morton Salt, 338 U.S. 632, 651–52 (1950).

59. 335 U.S. 1 (1948); *see also* Braswell v. United States, 487 U.S. 99 (1988) (custodian of corporate records may not refuse to obey a subpoena on the ground disclosure could incriminate him); United States v. Sullivan, 274 U.S. 259 (1927) (use of income tax report in tax fraud prosecution does not violate Fifth Amendment).

60. 382 U.S. 70 (1965); *see generally* McKay, *Self-Incrimination and the New Privacy,* 1967 Sup.Ct.Rev. 193; Mansfield, *The Albertson Case: Conflict Between the Privilege Against Self–Incrimination and the Government's Need for Information,* 1966 Sup.Ct.Rev. 103.

61. *See, e.g.,* Marchetti v. United States, 390 U.S. 39 (1968) (registration and occupational tax laws applicable only to gamblers unconstitutional under *Albertson* tests); *see generally* C. Whitebread & C. Slobogin, Criminal Procedure: An Analysis of Constitutional Cases and Concepts § 15.05 (1986).

62. 402 U.S. 424 (1971).

however, a plurality of the Supreme Court proposed a modification of it. The plurality held that a California statute requiring a person to report any traffic accidents in which they were engaged was not a violation of the Fifth Amendment. The plurality used the *Albertson* tests, but for the purpose of determining whether there was a "substantial hazard" of self-incrimination. The fifth member of the majority rejected the *Albertson* standards altogether and the four dissenting justices applied the standards without the "gloss" used by the plurality.

In addition to possible Fifth Amendment claims, some testimonial privileges, such as that for lawyer-client communications, have been recognized. The source and extent of these privileges, however, are shrouded in confusion. These privileges are the product of state statutes, which are built on a common-law base. There is no federal statutory limitation that requires agencies to abide by them. Nevertheless, both federal courts and agencies have assumed that at least some of the privileges, especially the lawyer-client one, are applicable.[63]

Although some testimonial privileges may exist, there is no privilege based on a right to privacy in the information being sought. Information sought by the government is often kept confidential by its owners because of its sensitive business or personal nature. Nevertheless, the government is entitled to obtain it, although access may be conditional on whether proper precautions will be taken to keep it confidential.[64] Those precautions include both arrangements for the physical security of the information and for its confidential treatment in public investigations and hearings. When the normal practice would be to disclose the information to third parties, however, the owner of the information, or the government, has the burden of persuasion that it should be kept confidential. This burden is applicable both in open hearings and under the Freedom of Information Act.[65]

§ 8.2.9 Summary and assessment

An agency's authority to compel the disclosure of information is only broadly limited by relevant statutory and constitutional constraints. The statutory authority is normally quite expansive and the

---

63. *See generally* P. Strauss, et.al., *supra* note 46, at 903–04; Peterson, *Attorney-Client Privilege in Internal Revenue Service Investigations*, 54 Minn. L.Rev. 67 (1969).

64. *See, e.g.,* FTC v. Owens–Corning Fiberglas Corp., 626 F.2d 966 (D.C.Cir. 1980).

65. *See infra* § 8.3.1.

constitutional constraints are either easily met or not applicable. As a result, an agency can usually obtain most of the information it seeks. In some circumstances, an agency will need OIRA's approval to collect information, but agencies will normally be able to jump over this hurdle as well.

The government has been able to obtain such ample access to private information because it has been deemed necessary to effectuate the many regulatory programs that have been created. Congress has made that judgment by granting agencies broad statutory powers to acquire information. The Supreme Court has made that judgment by refusing to apply literally the dictates of the Fourth and Fifth Amendments. Instead, in various guises, the Court has balanced the government's need for the method of disclosure sought with the degree of intrusion of privacy or self-incrimination it involves. Further, the Court has struck its balance heavily in favor of the government thereby allowing it considerable freedom to acquire information.[66]

Ultimately, the public suffers the burdens of a broad investigatory power in order to obtain its benefits. The realm of privacy has been reduced so that the efficacy of regulation can be improved. The relevant issue therefore is not whether there is too little privacy, but whether there is too much regulation. Without information, regulation will not work. Hence, when the country chooses to regulate, its citizens will need to make the necessary trade-off in terms of their privacy.

§ 8.3   Private Access to Public Information

The government's obligation to make information available to private parties depends on the status of the person seeking access. In some cases the government is obligated to give access to "any person" and in others the person must have some special qualification. The Freedom of Information Act (FOIA) requires the government to disclose any "record" within its possession to "any person" upon request.[67] States have similar requirements of open records and of open meetings.[68] Two types of obligations are owed to "special"

---

66. *See* K. Davis & R. Pierce, Jr., *supra* note 54, § 4.6.

67. 5 U.S.C. § 522. There are two acts related to the FOIA. The Sunshine Act, 5 U.S.C. § 552(b), requires any agency headed by a multi-member board or commission to meet in public. Similarly, the Federal Advisory Committee Act

(FACA), 5 U.S.C. App., requires federal advisory committees to meet in open session. These acts are discussed *infra* § 9.4.

68. *See* 2 J. O'Reilly, "Federal Information Disclosure: Procedures, Forms, and the Law" §§ 27.01–05 (1990) (de-

requestors. Various statutes and agency rules require the disclosure to litigants of information relevant to a court or administrative proceeding as part of the discovery process.[69] The Privacy Act requires an agency to divulge any record to a person that is filed for purposes of retrieval under that person's name.[70]

Access under all of the previous provisions is subject to numerous exceptions, however. Litigation concerning the application of those exceptions, especially for the FOIA, has been voluminous. This text will not attempt to chronicle the nature of all of that litigation.[71] Instead, various illustrative controversies will be explored to highlight the contending policies involved.

§ 8.3.1 Disclosure under the FOIA

The FOIA requires, unless an exemption applies, the disclosure of two types of materials.[72] First, an agency is required to disclose its adjudicatory opinions, nonpublished policy and interpretive statements, and staff manuals and instructions. These materials must be disclosed whether or not they are requested because Congress intended to prevent agencies from operating according to "secret" laws unavailable to the general public. Second, an agency is required to disclose any other "record" that might be requested. By this residual category, Congress intended to establish as the norm that government information was public information.

The current FOIA is the product of years of reform efforts.[73] Prior to the APA, agencies were under no statutory obligation to disclose information and were apparently instead authorized to withhold it in their discretion. The 1946 APA had a freedom of information provision, but it was so riddled with expansive exceptions that agencies for the most part were still able to avoid disclosures. The present FOIA was passed in 1967 and amended subsequently three times. Each time the intent was to overrule a judicial decision that limited the degree of disclosure or to close procedural loopholes that agencies were able to exploit to avoid disclosures.

---

scription of state open-records and open-meeting laws).

69. *See infra* § 8.3.6.

70. 5 U.S.C. § 552a.

71. For a more exhaustive review, *see* K. Davis & R. Pierce, Jr., *supra* note 54, § 5.2; 2 J. O'Reilly, *supra* note 68. For an older, but still valuable source, *see* Litigation Under the Federal Freedom of Information Act and Privacy Act (A. Adler ed. 1990).

72. 5 U.S.C. at § 552(a) (1) (3).

73. *See generally* H. Cross, The People's Right to Know: Legal Access to Public Records and Proceedings (1953); Davis, *The Information Act: A Preliminary Analysis,* 34 U.Chi.L.Rev. 761 (1967).

The campaign for an expansive FOIA has always been put on the basis that it serves democratic values.[74] Open government facilitates interaction by politicians, interest groups and journalists. It also counteracts political corruption, such as that in Watergate, or financial corruption, such as in the case of bribes. The FOIA is used, however, by individuals and groups for many other purposes. Information is sought in order to gain a commercial advantage over business rivals or the government itself, to avoid government regulation, or to have advance warning of imminent government plans and acts.

Congress recognized these other motives and sought to protect the ability of government to function in light of them. It created nine exemptions for information concerning national defense and foreign affairs, internal personnel rules and practices, trade secrets and other commercial data, inter-agency and intra-agency memoranda, personnel and medical files, investigatory records, the regulation of financial institutions, geological and geophysical data and for information that is required to be kept confidential by some other statute.[75] The exemptions are an attempt to balance the benefits of disclosure against the particular disadvantages to the government or the economy if the information were released.

Although Congress recognized exceptions, it still created a four-prong "tilt" towards disclosure. First, the requestor need not establish why the information has been requested. Disclosure is obligated, unless an exception applies, for any reason. Second, the requestor must satisfy only two minimal requirements to gain access. There must be a "reasonable" description of the information sought and the request must correspond to the agency's published rules concerning the "time, place, fees (if any), and procedures to be followed".[76] Third, exemptions from disclosure, with one exception, are not mandatory, which enables agencies to disclosure exempted material if they so choose. Fourth, if the agency denies the request, or fails to act within the statutorily specified time period, the requestor can seek a district court order to compel disclosure. The agency has the burden of establishing that it is entitled to an exemption, or that the records do not exist, and the court uses a *de novo* scope of review to judge the agency's arguments.[77]

---

74. *See, e.g.,* Clark, *Holding Government Accountable: The Amended Freedom of Information Act,* 84 Yale L.J. 741 (1975); Nader, *Freedom from Information: The Act and the Agencies,* 5 Harv. C.R.—C.L.Rev. 1 (1970).

75. 5 U.S.C. at § 552 (b) (1) (9).

76. *See* 5 U.S.C. at § 552 (a) (3).

77. To justify its decision, an agency will file detailed affidavits. In response, the requestor, who has not seen the in-

Although Congress tilted the FOIA in favor of disclosure, Presidents have attempted to impact the extent of the tilt. In October, 2001, Attorney General Ashcroft issued a memorandum that directed agencies making discretionary decisions under the FOIA to consider carefully values as national security, effective law enforcement, and personal privacy. It stated DOJ would defend an agency's decision to withhold information as long as there was a "sound legal basis" for its decision under the FOIA. This memorandum replaced one issued by Attorney General Reno in 1993 that required agencies to resolve discretionary decisions to achieve "maximum reasonable disclosure." Under the Reno policy, DOJ defended an agency's withholding information if it reasonably foresaw that disclosure would harm an interest protected by an exemption. This flip-flop has occurred before. The Reagan administration, for example, adopted policies similar to those in the Ashcroft memorandum, which reversed the Carter administration policy, which was similar to the policies of the Clinton Administration. According to the GAO, such changes in policy do have an impact on the extent of FOIA disclosure.[78]

The last prong of the tilt is the most important because it established that the federal courts were to regulate closely government attempts to withhold information. The role of the federal courts in implementing the FOIA has been extended in another way. Many of the exemptions are written in a vague and ambiguous fashion. As a result, judicial interpretation is necessary to implement them. By their interpretation, the courts have influenced the degree of disclosure and secrecy that will occur.

Critics have charged that the implementation of the FOIA has produced an expensive and burdensome regulatory program. One estimate is that the FOIA has spawned more litigation and has increased the cost of operating the government more than any other single regulatory program.[79] The litigation results from the need for further judicial definition of the exemptions and from judicial regulation of use of the exemptions by agencies. The costs of operating the program result from both litigation costs and the costs of maintain-

formation and therefore has little basis for challenging the affidavits, normally requests that the court order the agency to file a *Vaughn* index that summarizes the withheld records, states the statutory basis on which each document, or a part of a document, is withheld, and cites the applicable affidavits that explain why the statutory exemption is applicable. The index is named for Vaughn v. Rosen, 484

F.2d 820 (D.C.Cir.1973), which was the first case to employ the use of such an index.

78. *See* GAO, Freedom of Information Act: Agency Views on Changes Resulting From New Policy (2003).

79. G. Robinson, E. Gellhorn & H. Bruff, The Administrative Process 521 (2d ed. 1980).

ing within each agency a system of locating records and determining whether they are to be disclosed. The value of the FOIA has been questioned in light of these costs. The act may be used far more by business firms and attorneys for commercial and legal purposes than by others, such as politicians, newspapers or citizens, for political purposes.[80]

These types of criticisms have had an impact. For a time, the Supreme Court construed open government legislation in a manner that increased the amount of information available to the public, and in the few cases where the Court narrowed the FOIA, Congress passed amendments to overrule it. Lately, however, the trend has been reversed and both the Court and Congress have generally acted to protect government information. This trend, however, should not obscure the considerable extent to which the legislation has opened up government processes; this trend has been accelerated by the 1996 Electronic FOIA amendments which replace an agency's "paper" reading rooms with agency sites on the World Wide Web.

However, after the events of 9/11 FOIA requests are being given careful scrutiny. Both Attorney General Ashcroft's October 2001 statement on FOIA policy[81] and the Critical Infrastructure Act of 2001[82] potentially change the balance of production in many agencies. The question now being posed is whether production might also inhibit or jeopardize national security efforts.

§ 8.3.2   Scope of disclosure

The language in 5 U.S.C. 551(1)–(3) raises three issues when the government refuses to disclose information. First, is the unit from which the documents are sought an "agency" subject to the FOIA? Second, are the documents sought "records" or other materials that the FOIA requires to be disclosed unless an exemption applies? Finally, does an exemption apply? This section examines the first two issues. The next section explores the third issue.

§ 8.3.2a   Definition of agency

The FOIA adopts the definition of agency used in the APA generally, but it also states that "agency" includes "any executive department, military department, Government corporation, Government controlled corporation, or other establishment in the executive

---

80. *See* Koch & Rubin, *A Proposal for Comprehensive Restructuring of the Public Information System,* 1979 Duke L.J. 1.

81. *See* DOJ, Office of Information and Privacy, Freedom of Information Act

Guide & Privacy Act Overview (May 2002 Edition) (discussing Ashcroft statement) [hereafter DOJ 2002 FOIA Guide].

82. *See* discussion *infra* at § 8.4.

branch of the Government (including the Executive Office of the President), or any independent regulatory agency."[83] The APA defines agency as "each authority of the Government of the United States, whether or not it is within or subject to review by another agency...."[84]

Although most government units fall within the FOIA's broad definition of agency, the courts have not included agencies whose "sole function" is to give advice to the President. In *Kissinger v. Reporters Committee for Freedom of the Press,*[85] for example, a reporter requested transcripts of telephone calls taped by Henry Kissinger at the time that he served as the National Security Advisor to President Nixon and was located in the Office of the President. The Supreme Court held the FOIA's legislative history clearly indicated that the "Office of the President" was not an agency within the FOIA definition because its only function is to advise the President. It therefore affirmed the government's refusal to release the transcripts of telephone conversations taped at the time Kissinger worked in the Office of the President.

The merit of the "sole function" test is that by excluding units that have no significant decisionmaking authority because they only "advise" other officials, it protects the deliberative process from intrusive public scrutiny. But the test is also overinclusive: for example, it protects purely factual information or ancillary aspects of an office's function that are not advisory in nature. Nevertheless, this "sole function" test offers a "bright line" rule to distinguish which agencies are not subject to the FOIA.

Although the FOIA applies only to government "agencies," the litigant in *Forsham v. Harris*[86] argued that the Act applied to records held by private parties if the government had a legal right to obtain the records. In rejecting this argument, the Court noted the FOIA's legislative history "indicates unequivocally that private organizations receiving financial grants are not within the definition of 'agency.'" It emphasized that the "FOIA applies to records which *in fact* have

---

83. 5 U.S.C. § 552(e); *see generally,* Meyer, *Agency Records,* in Litigation Under the Federal Freedom of Information Act & Privacy Act, *supra* note 71, at 169–172.

84. *Id.* § 551(a).

85. 445 U.S. 136 (1980); *see also Soucie v. David,* 448 F.2d 1067 (D.C.Cir. 1971) (White House Office of Science & Technology (OTS) is within the "Execu-

tive Office of the President," which is subject to the FOIA); *but see* Rushforth v. Council of Economic Advisers, 762 F.2d 1038 (D.C.Cir.1985) (Council of Economic Advisers (CEA) is not an agency for purposes of the FOIA because, unlike the OTS, it only advises the President and has no independent authority to initiate and support research).

86. 445 U.S. 169 (1980).

been obtained and not to records which merely *could have been* obtained."

§ 8.3.2b   Definition of record

An agency's obligation to disclose information is also conditioned on whether the information is located in a "record." A document is a "record" if it is generated and used by the agency and it is within its possession and control. As noted in the last section, *Kissinger v. Reporters Committee for Freedom of the Press,* held that the government did not have to disclose transcripts of telephone calls that Kissinger had with President Nixon because the transcripts were located in the Office of the President, which was *not* an agency within the meaning of the FOIA. Kissinger, however, had moved some of the transcripts to the State Department at the time he became Secretary of State. The Court also affirmed the government's refusal to disclose these transcripts. It held that they remained records of the Office of the President even though they were physically located at the State Department at the time they were requested. They were not records of the State Department because they were not within the State Department's control at any time, were never entered in the department's files, and were not generated or used by it.

Applying the criteria identified in *Kissinger,* the D.C. Circuit held that appointment materials, such as desk calendars and telephones logs "that are created solely for an individual's convenience, that contain a mix of personal and business entries, and that may be disposed of at the individual's discretion" were not agency records.[87] The court rejected the government's argument that if an employee was free to dispose of material, it was not a record for FOIA purposes. The court said that while this information was relevant, the actual use of the material must also be taken into account.

§ 8.3.3   Exemptions from disclosure

An "agency" may not withhold "records" that are not exempted from disclosure. Thus, the Court held that district court opinions

---

87. Bureau of National Affairs v. Department of Justice, 742 F.2d 1484 (D.C.Cir.1984); *see also* Washington Post Co. v. United States Department of State, 840 F.2d 26 (D.C.Cir.1988) (typewritten transcriptions of documents compiled by the staff of the Secretary of State were agency records because the documents (i) were generated by the agency opposing disclosure, (ii) had been placed in its files, (iii) were within its control, and (iv) had been used by it for an agency purpose); *see generally,* Meyer, Adler, & Goldman, *Agency Records,* in Litigation Under the Federal Freedom of Information Act & Privacy Act, *supra* note 71, at 173–184.

received by the Department of Justice as a litigant had to be disclosed to the requester, a weekly tax service, even though the opinions were publicly available from the district courts that had issued them.[88] The requestor had apparently sought the opinions from the government because of the difficulty of obtaining them from the individual district courts. The Court explained that the government's obligation to disclose the materials was not satisfied by the fact that they were available elsewhere because the FOIA does not permit the government to refuse to disclose records unless there is an applicable exemption.

Exemptions, however, are not mandatory. Unless a record falls within exemption (b)(3), which concerns records that another statute requires to be kept secret, the FOIA gives the agency the choice of whether to claim an exemption and resist disclosure. *Chrysler Corp. v. Brown*[89] illustrates this point. Chrysler sued to enjoin the Defense Department from complying with a FOIA request for information that the Department had obtained concerning the company's employment of women and minorities. Chrysler claimed that the Department was barred from releasing the information by exemption (b)(4), which applies to confidential commercial and financial information, and by the Federal Trade Secrets Act.[90] The Court held that the FOIA exemptions were not absolute and that an agency has discretion to release information within an exemption. The Court recognized, however, that the Department would not have discretion to release the documents if they were protected by the Trade Secrets Act. The Federal Trade Secrets Act establishes criminal penalties for the disclosure of proprietary information, including trade secrets, unless such disclosure has been authorized by law.

§ 8.3.3a Exemption (b)(1): National defense and foreign affairs

The exemption for information concerning national defense and foreign affairs was created to replace an earlier similar, but less precise, provision. Although Congress recognized the necessity of protecting national security and foreign affairs secrets, it was at the same time worried about executive abuse of such an exemption. When the Supreme Court in *EPA v. Mink* seriously limited the

88. United States Department of Justice v. Tax Analysts, 492 U.S. 136 (1989).

89. 441 U.S. 281 (1979); *see also infra* note 116 and accompanying text (discussion of case).

90. 18 U.S.C. § 1905.

judicial oversight of the use of this exemption,[91] Congress amended the FOIA to increase judicial regulation. Nevertheless, the executive retains considerable discretion to choose what materials to withhold.

In *EPA v. Mink,* the Court reviewed a decision by President Nixon to deny an FOIA request by Congresswoman Patsy Mink for a report given to him concerning the advisability of a proposed underground nuclear test. The exemption at that time was for materials that are "specifically required by Executive order to be kept secret in the interest of the national defense or foreign policy." The Supreme Court reached two conclusions about the scope of the exemption. First, the Court held that the clear language of the exemption, supported by its legislative history, limited judicial review to the issue of whether the documents being sought had been classified as secret. Since they had been, they were not available for disclosure. Second, the Court held that the court of appeals had erred when it ordered the district court to inspect the documents *in camera,* or in secret, to determine whether their secret portions could be severed from their nonsecret portions for purposes of disclosure. The Court reasoned that since the language of the FOIA clearly did not authorize such a procedure, it was beyond the power of the courts.

In response, Congress amended the exception to cover matters that are "specifically authorized under the criteria established by an Executive order to be kept secret in the interest of national defense or foreign policy" and that "are in fact properly classified pursuant to such Executive order." Congress also provided that a district court could examine the contents of any agency record *in camera* "to determine whether such records or any part thereof shall be withheld under any of the exemptions" in the act. Taken together, the changes authorized a district court to determine whether the documents requested are within the scope of an Executive secrecy order, including whether some portions of the documents can be released without violation of that order.[92]

Although Congress augmented the role of the courts, the President still has substantial discretion to withhold information. One reason is that the scope of the exemption is tied directly to the scope of secrecy set by Executive Order and a President has discretion concerning the extent of secrecy that is required. For example, President Reagan established a secrecy policy that was broader and

91. 410 U.S. 73 (1973).

92. 5 U.S.C. at § 552(a)(4)(B), (b)(1); *see* Adler, Halperin & Stern, *National Security Information,* in Litigation Under the Federal Freedom of Information Act and Privacy Act, *supra* note 71, at §§ 44–46; 2 J. O'Reilly, *supra* note 68, at §§ 11.01–.13.

more extensive than that used by his predecessors.[93] The Reagan order created new classifications categories, eliminated a presumption against classification contained in President Carter's order and increased the duration of classifications. By comparison, in 1995 President Clinton promised disclosure of previously unavailable national security information by establishing a ten-year limit on newly classified information and by automatically declassifying most information that is more than 25 years old.[94] The wisdom of these decisions cannot be litigated because the only question relevant for judicial review is whether a document falls within the boundaries of the Executive Order. Another reason is that courts use a highly deferential scope of review when considering government claims that certain records are within the scope of an Executive secrecy order.[95] While the government has lost some cases in the district courts and has settled others, no final judgment has ever been entered against the government that documents must be disclosed. The courts thus seem unwilling to second guess government secrecy claims.

§ 8.3.3b Exemption (b)(2): Personnel rules and practices

The Act's second exemption is for matters that "are related solely to the internal personnel rules and practices of the agencies".[96] The exact scope of the exemption was left in doubt because the Senate and House reports describing it differed remarkably.[97] The Senate report gives examples of rules concerning employee parking, sick leave and lunch hours. The rationale was that these are matters internal to the agency and presumably of small concern to the public. The House report gives examples of audit guidelines, manuals and investigation procedures. The apparent rationale was to avoid disclo-

---

93. *Compare* Exec. Order No. 12,356, 47 Fed.Reg. 14,874 (1982) (Reagan order), *with* Exec. Order No. 12,065, 3 Fed. Reg. 190 (1979), *reprinted in* 50 U.S.C.§ 401 App. (Carter order); Exec. Order No. 11,652, 37 Fed. Reg. 5209 (1972), 3 C.F.R. Pt. 678, *reprinted in* 3 U.S. Code Cong. and Ad. News 5513 (1972) (Nixon order); *see generally* Note, *Developments Under the Freedom of Information Act 1982*, 1983 Duke L.J. 390, 394–401.

94. Exec. Order No. 12958, U.S.C. sec. 435 note (2000), as amended, March 25, 2003 (http://www.whitehouse.gov/news/releases/2003/03/20030325-11.html.

95. *See, e.g.,* Salisbury v. United States, 690 F.2d 966, 970 (D.C.Cir.1982); Gardels v. CIA, 689 F.2d 1100, 1104–05 (D.C.Cir.1982); Taylor v. Department of the Army, 684 F.2d 99, 109 (D.C. Cir. 1982).

96. 5 U.S.C. at § 552(b)(2); *see generally* Adler, English & Meyer, *Internal Agency Rules, in Litigation Under the Federal Freedom of Information Act and Privacy Act, supra* note 71, at 47; 1 J. O'Reilly, *supra* note 68, at § 12.01–06.

97. *Compare* S.Rep. No. 813, 89th Cong., 1st Sess. (1965), *with* H.R.Rep. No. 1497, 89th Cong., 2d Sess. (1966).

sure of staff instructions that would aid persons to avoid compliance with regulations.

The Supreme Court, in *Department of the Air Force v. Rose*,[98] attempted to sort out the confusion created by the two reports. The case arose when the Air Force Academy refused to divulge case summaries of disciplinary proceedings with the names and other identifying material of the students deleted. The Court ordered that the summaries could be disclosed because there was a genuine and significant public interest in obtaining them and there was no risk that disclosure would allow someone to circumvent agency regulations. The Court thought that the "general thrust of the exception is simply to relieve agencies of the burden of assembling and maintaining for public inspection matters in which the public could not reasonably be expected to have an interest". The Court, however, did honor the House report by reserving for a later decision the possibility that the exemption might also permit "withholding of matters of some public interest ... where necessary to prevent the circumvention of agency regulations that might result from disclosure to the subjects of regulation of the procedural manuals and guidelines used by the agency in discharging its regulatory function." The courts of appeal that have considered the question left open in *Rose* have agreed that the government is entitled to protection for agency enforcement manuals when disclosure might lead to circumvention of regulations.[99]

In light of the events of September 11, 2001, the need to protect agency manuals has become a matter of homeland security and withholding of "critical infrastructure" information has now become essential.[100]

§ 8.3.3c Exemption (b)(3): Other statutory exemptions

In passing the FOIA, Congress intended to give recognition to its previous judgments concerning secrecy. It therefore established an

---

98. 425 U.S. 352 (1976).

99. *See, e.g.* Schiller v. NLRB, 964 F.2d 1205 (D.C.Cir.1992) (guidelines on implementing Equal Access to Justice Act exempt); Dirksen v. U.S. Dept. Of HHS, 803 F.2d 1456 (9th Cir.1986) (Medicare claims processing guidelines exempt); Crooker v. BATF, 670 F.2d 1051 (D.C.Cir.1981) (en banc) (BATF training manual concerning surveillance techniques exempt). Some circuits have protected manuals under section 552(a)(2)(C) of the Act. *See, e.g.*, Cox v. Department of Justice, 601 F.2d 1 (D.C. Cir.1979); Stokes v. Brennan, 476 F.2d 699, (5th Cir.1973); Hawkes v. IRS, 467 F.2d 787 (6th Cir.1972).

100. *See* USA Patriot Act of 2001, 42 U.S.C.A. § 519 (2002) (describing "critical infrastructure"; *see also* DOJ 2002 FOIA Guide, *supra* note 81 at 126–27 (describing the impact on Exemption two information).

exemption for matters that are "specifically exempt from disclosure by statute". Congress, however, found it necessary to revise the exemption because of the result in *FAA v. Robertson.*[101]

In *Robertson,* the Court considered a FOIA request for System Worthiness Analysis Program reports prepared by the Federal Aviation Administration (FAA) concerning the maintenance and performance of commercial airplanes. The agency had refused the request on the ground that the FAA act authorized the administrator to withhold any information that in his judgment would "adversely affect the interests of the objecting party" and "is not required in the interests of the public".

The court of appeals had held that the FAA statute was not an "exempting statute" within the meaning of the FOIA because the FOIA required that a statute "specifically" exempt material from disclosure. The court interpreted that requirement to mean that a statute had to specify or categorize the information to be withheld in order to qualify. According to the court, the FAA statute failed to do so because it delegated broad authority to the administrator under a "public interest" statute.

The Supreme Court reversed on the ground that neither the legislative history nor the language of the exemption justified the reading given to it by the lower court. The Court held that there was no requirement that a statute had to specify standards or the degree of discretion to qualify as an exemption statute.

The FAA statutory provision was reminiscent of the type of broad and imprecise exemption that had existed before the FOIA was passed and that caused Congress to pass the FOIA. As a result, Congress amended the exemption to prevent the FOIA from being overridden by outdated secrecy provisions. The exemption now applies only if another statute "requires that matters be withheld from the public in such a manner as to leave no discretion on the issue" or if it "establishes a particular criteria for withholding or refers to particular types of matters to be withheld."[102]

After the amendment, numerous statutes have been certified as Exemption 3 statutes because they require "matters to be withheld from the public in such a manner as to leave no discretion on the issue".[103] For example, the Central Intelligence Act of 1949 provides

101. 422 U.S. 255 (1975).

102. 5 U.S.C. at § 552(b)(3).

103. *See generally,* Adler, Glitzenstein & Plesser, *Information Exempted*

From Other Statutes, in Litigation Under the Federal Freedom of Information Act and Privacy Act, *supra* note 71, at 59–73.

in part that "the Agency shall be exempted from the provisions of . . . any other law which require[s] the . . . disclosure of the organization, functions, names, official titles, salaries, or numbers of personnel employed by the Agency."[104] Other examples of similar statutory provisions concern other CIA functions[105] and Internal Revenue Service[106] and Census documents.[107]

Other statutes have been certified as Exemption 3 statutes because they establish "particular criteria for withholding" or they refer "to particular types of matter to be withheld." In *Consumer Product Safety Commission v. GTE Sylvania,*[108] for example, the Supreme Court held that a section of the agency's enabling act which regulated the "public disclosure of information" by the Commission, qualified as an Exemption 3 statute.[109] The statute imposed several requirements including that the Commission had to take reasonable steps to assure that disclosures were accurate and that they were "fair in the circumstances and reasonably related to effectuating the purposes" of the Commission. The Court rejected the argument that the section applied to public disclosures of information other than FOIA disclosures on the ground that the legislative history failed to support such a distinction.

Several statutes, by comparison, have failed to qualify as Exemption 3 statutes under either test. *American Jewish Congress v. Kreps* provides the method by which such statutes can be distinguished.[110] The case held that the Commerce Department could not refuse, on the basis of Exemption 3, to disclose reports filed by American companies documenting requests by foreign governments that they boycott trade with other countries. The department had justified nondisclosure on the basis of the Export Administration Act of 1969 which provided that confidential information submitted to the Commerce Department could not be disclosed "unless the . . . agency determines that the withholding thereof is contrary to the national interest." To qualify under the first test of Exemption 3, the court required that a statute incorporate a congressional mandate of confidentiality that is "absolute and without exception". To qualify under

104. 50 U.S.C. § 403g; *see, e.g.,* Baker v. CIA, 580 F.2d 664 (D.C.Cir.1978); National Com'n on Law Enforcement & Social Justice v. CIA, 576 F.2d 1373 (9th Cir.1978).

105. 50 U.S.C. § 403(d)(3) (1982); *see* CIA v. Sims, 471 U.S. 159 (1985); Phillippi v. CIA, 655 F.2d 1325 (D.C. Cir. 1981).

106. 26 U.S.C. § 6103; *see* Comment, *Developments Under the Freedom of Information Act 1981,* 1982 Duke L.J. 423, 444–47.

107. 13 U.S.C. §§ 8(b), 9(a); *see* Baldrige v. Shapiro, 455 U.S. 345 (1982).

108. 447 U.S. 102 (1980).

109. 447 U.S. 102 (1980).

110. 574 F.2d 624 (D.C. Cir.1978).

the second alternative, the court required that a statute must be the "product of congressional appreciation of the dangers inherent in airing particular data and incorporates a formula whereby the administrator may determine precisely whether disclosure in any instance would pose the hazard Congress foresaw." The court found that the statute obviously failed the first test and that it failed the second because the criteria used, "national interest," was not sufficiently particular. The court buttressed the latter conclusion by noting that Congress had overruled the result in *Robertson,* where the statute had used a similarly vague concept of "public interest".

When a court finds that a statutory provision qualifies as an Exemption 3 law, it must still determine whether the documents requested under the FOIA fall within the confidentiality requirements of that provision. For example, in *Baldrige v. Shapiro,* the Supreme Court considered whether the confidentiality provisions of the Census Act covered a "master address register," which was composed of such information as addresses, householders' names, number of housing units and similar data.[111] The Court first held that since the census statute explicitly provided for nondisclosure of certain census data without any discretion on the part of the Census Bureau, the statute qualified as an Exemption 3 act. The Court then held that the "address register" fell within the scope of those confidentiality provisions. The two cities that had sought the census information had argued that the requirement of confidentiality did not extend to summaries of census data if their requests did not ask for individual names. But the Court found that both the language of the statute and the legislative history clearly anticipated that raw data was to be absolutely protected.

§ 8.3.3d   Exemption (b)(4): Trade secrets and commercial or financial information

Exemption 4 is for "trade secrets and commercial or financial information obtained from a person and privileged or confidential".[112] The exemption recognized that some of the information obtained by the government is of considerable proprietary value to its owners because they alone possess it. The disclosure of proprietary information by the government could have at least two disadvantages. First, the disclosure could be inefficient if it discouraged useful business competition and enterprise. Second, disclosure could discourage firms

---

111.   455 U.S. 345 (1982).

112.   5 U.S.C. at § 552(b)(4); *see generally* Vladeck & Adler, *Trade Secrets,* in Litigation Under the Federal Freedom of Information Act and Privacy Act, *supra* note 71, at 75–84; 2 J. O'Reilly, *supra* note 68, at §§ 14.01–.02.

from submitting the information to the government, especially on a voluntary basis.

Protection of proprietary information, however, can also be disadvantageous. Outsiders often have a difficult time assessing whether a government program is properly constituted and implemented without access to the information on which the program was based. The Food and Drug Administration (FDA), for example, licenses new pharmaceutical drugs and medical devices on the basis of research information submitted to it for that purpose. Without access to the testing information, which is considered a trade secret, no outsider can evaluate successfully whether FDA's judgment that a drug is safe and efficacious is correct.[113]

Congress balanced these contending values and decided to protect proprietary information, but it left unresolved several issues. First, it was unclear whether information had to be "trade secrets" and "commercial or financial" to be withheld. In *National Parks and Conservation Association v. Morton,* the D.C. Circuit resolved these language problems.[114] It held that "trade secrets" and "commercial or financial" information were separate categories of information, each eligible for nondisclosure. Further, it held that "commercial or financial" information could be withheld only if it were "privileged or confidential".

A second issue was how "confidential" should be defined. The *National Parks* court held that for commercial or business information to be considered "confidential," it must meet one of two tests. Disclosure of the information must be likely to "impair the government's ability to obtain the necessary information in the future," or to "cause substantial harm to the competitive position of the person from whom the information was obtained." To meet these tests, an agency had to demonstrate that secrecy either "encouraged cooperation with the government by persons having information useful to the officials" or that "[i]t protects persons who submit ... data ... from the competitive disadvantages which would result from its ... publication." The court reasoned that these "objective" tests of confidentiality were necessary; otherwise, a business would, in effect, be its own judge for the necessity of nondisclosure. If a business could insulate information from disclosure by merely treating the information as secret, the business, and not the judiciary, would determine

---

113. *See* McGarity and Shapiro, *supra* note 5.

114. 498 F.2d 765 (D.C. Cir.1974), affirmed in part and reversed in part sub nom, National Parks and Conservation Ass'n v. Kleppe, 547 F.2d 673 (D.C.Cir. 1976).

whether the exemption would apply. The court held that disclosure would not adversely affect the cooperation of the information providers because they were required by statute to provide the information. The court remanded the case back to the district court for further findings on competitive harm.

National Parks was considered to be the prevailing test for defining commercial and financial information until two subsequent cases. In *9 to 5 Organization for Women Office Workers v. Federal Reserve Board*,[115] the First Circuit reversed the district court's decision that Exemption 4 was inapplicable to a survey of salary information obtained by the Boston Federal Reserve Board as part of its function to review and approve the salaries paid to employees of the Federal Reserve Bank. The circuit court explained that the district court had erred because it assumed the two-part test in *National Parks* was the exclusive test concerning whether the exemption applied. The court held that *National Parks* imposed no such limitation. As a result, "if it can be demonstrated that a specific private or governmental interest will be harmed by the disclosure of commercial or financial information, the Government [is] not ... precluded from invoking the protection of Exemption 4 merely because the asserted interest is not precisely one of those two identified in *National Parks*...." The court identified a governmental interest in the "ability of the Government to make intelligent, well-informed decisions" and concluded that disclosure of the salary data would harm that interest.

The D.C. Circuit also distinguished the *National Parks* case in *Critical Mass Energy Project v. NRC*.[116] Judge Buckley's opinion rejected the request by a public interest group for safety reports voluntarily provided to the Nuclear Regulatory Commission (NRC) by a nuclear industry safety group. He noted first that the circuit had shifted its approach since *National Parks* in cases where information was required to be submitted to the government. Despite this requirement, there was still an issue of whether disclosure would reduce the reliability of the information that is submitted. He then noted that it was obvious that individuals would not voluntarily submit information they regarded as confidential if it were to be disclosed by the government. Because of this reality, Judge Buckley announced a categorical rule to determine the confidentiality of information not submitted under compulsion. According to the new rule, "financial or commercial information provided to the govern-

---

115. 721 F.2d 1 (1st Cir. 1983).   **116.** 975 F.2d 871 (D.C. Cir.1992) (en banc).

ment on a voluntary basis is 'confidential' for purposes of Exemption 4 if it is of a kind that would customarily not be related to the public by the person from whom it was obtained."

The last two cases introduced a more elastic definition of "confidential" commercial and financial information and result in a broader exemption. The *Critical Mass Energy Project* decision, however, goes further. It is no longer necessary for an agency to demonstrate that disclosure would in fact cause significant harm to some relevant private or governmental interest because such harm is presumed. Unlike *9 to 5*, this step eliminates judicial oversight because, as the dissenters in *Critical Mass Energy Project* noted, "it will do for an agency official to agree with the submitter's ascription of confidential status." By comparison, although *9 to 5* recognizes an additional government interest in confidentiality, there is still a judicial determination whether that interest exists in a given case.[117]

A third issue is how to define "trade secrets," because the Act itself does not do so. Most courts have adopted the Restatement of Torts definition of "any formula, pattern, or device, or compilation of information which is used in one's business and which gives him an opportunity to obtain an advantage over competitors who don't know or use it".[118] Courts have not uniformly followed the Restatement definition, however. In *Public Citizen Health Research Group v. FDA (Public Citizen I),* the District of Columbia Circuit Court defined a trade secret for purposes of the FOIA as any "commercially valuable plan, formula, process or device that is used for the making, preparing, compounding or processing of trade commodities and that can be said to be the end product of either innovation or substantial effort".[119] The court thought that because the Restatement definition was tailored to protecting business from breaches of contract and confidences by departing employees and others under fiduciary obligations, it was "ill-suited to the public law context in which the FOIA determinations must be made". In the public law context, the court found that the "interests of the public in disclosure and the protection of innovation incentives pose important considerations which the common law definition was not designed to handle". The court noted

---

117. In Public Citizen Health Research Group v. FDA, 185 F.3d 898, 904 (D.C. Cir. 1999), the court declared that the "public interest side of the balance is not a function of the identity of the requester," thereby removing the court from balancing judgments sought by requesters in individual cases.

118. Restatement of Torts § 757, Comment b at 5 (1939).

119. 704 F.2d 1280, 1288 (D.C. Cir. 1983).

that none of the courts that had adopted the Restatement definition had critically considered its propriety in light of this distinction.

Under its definition, the court rejected the holding of the district court that the information being sought was a trade secret. The request was for the testing data submitted to the FDA for a medical device, an intraocular lens implanted in the eye after cataract surgery. The court concluded the data do not qualify because "[t]he relationship of the requested information to the productive process is tangential at best...."

The *Public Citizen I* approach has the advantage of giving some weight to the value of open government by adopting a more restrictive definition of trade secret than provided in the Restatement. The decision therefore is more consistent with the "tilt" in the FOIA toward disclosure wherever it is reasonable. The only effect of the decision, however, may be to shift the basis for the nondisclosure of confidential information from the trade secrets portion of the exemption to the commercial and financial information portion. In fact, such a shift in emphasis occurred in *Health Research Group*. The court of appeals found that although the documents did not contain trade secrets, most of them did, or could, contain confidential commercial information and thus were exempt from disclosure.[120]

A fourth issue is how the exemption relates to the federal Trade Secrets Act and to other statutory provisions which also define the treatment of trade secrets. The Trade Secrets Act establishes criminal penalties for the disclosure of proprietary information, including trade secrets, unless such disclosure has been authorized by law.[121] In *Chrysler Corp. v. Brown,* the Supreme Court determined the relationship between the FOIA, the Trade Secrets Act and the provisions regarding disclosure in specific regulatory statutes.[122]

In *Chrysler,* the Chrysler Motor Corporation sued to enjoin the Defense Department from releasing information about Chrysler's employment of women and minorities pursuant to an FOIA request for disclosure of the information. Chrysler claimed that the information was proprietary and that the FOIA and the Trade Secrets Act prohibited its release. The Court held that Chrysler enjoyed no direct private right of action to enjoin a violation of the Trade Secrets Act, but that violation of the Act could be enjoined under section 10 of the

120. But even where the exemption applies, it may be necessary to decide whether to disclose redacted materials "in order to avoid application of Exemption 4." Trains-Pacific Policing Agree-ment v. United States Custom Service, 177 F.3d 1022 (D.C. Cir. 1999).

121. 18 U.S.C. § 1905.

122. 441 U.S. 281 (1979).

APA, which provides that a reviewing court shall "hold unlawful and set aside agency action . . . not in accordance with law".[123] The Court reasoned that "any disclosure that violates [the Trade Secrets Act] is 'not in accordance with law' within the meaning of the [APA]".

The Court opened the door to greater governmental disclosure by holding that the FOIA exemptions are not absolute and that an agency has discretion to release information within an FOIA exemption. The Court also held, however, that information that falls within the Trade Secrets Act may not be released. The Court rejected the government's argument that since the FOIA exemptions are discretionary, the FOIA itself authorizes regulations which permit the release of the information within the "authorized by law" proviso of the Trade Secrets Act. In rejecting this interpretation, the Court reasoned that since materials exempt from disclosure under the FOIA are outside that Act's mandate that information *must* be disclosed, the government could not rely on the FOIA as congressional authorization for the release of such information.

The government also argued that the provision commonly referred to as the "housekeeping statute,"[124] which provides that an executive department may prescribe such regulations as are necessary to carry out its business, provided the authorization to release the information. Again, the Court disagreed with the contention and found instead that Congress intended that provision to authorize only "procedural" rules concerning the organization of an agency and not "substantive" rules permitting the release of proprietary information.

The *Chrysler* court served notice that for an agency's disclosure regulation to satisfy the Trade Secrets Act there must be some identifiable "nexus" between the disclosure regulation and the delegation of legislative authority for its promulgation. Two kinds of statutory authorizations conceivably can satisfy the Court's criteria. First, Congress occasionally has given an agency explicit authority to release particular kinds of information that otherwise might be subject to a trade secrecy claim. For example, both the Toxic Substances Control Act (TSCA) and the Federal Insecticide, Fungicide and Rodenticide Act (FIFRA) explicitly authorize the release of health and safety data and thus meet the *Chrysler* criteria.[125] Second, Congress often gives an agency general rulemaking authority beyond that which the housekeeping statute confers. Arguably, such individ-

---

123. 5 U.S.C. at § 706 (2) (A).
124. 5 U.S.C. § 301.

125. 15 U.S.C. § 2613(b) (TSCA); 7 U.S.C. § 136h(d)(1) (FIFRA).

ual grants of authority would meet the Court's criteria, but this is a much closer question under the "nexus" test than cases in which explicit disclosure authority is given.[126]

The *Chrysler* court was correct in holding the APA available to plaintiffs aggrieved by threatened agency disclosure. In enacting the FOIA, Congress did not affirmatively remove the constraint of the Trade Secrets Act upon agencies. But to make the constraint anything more than academic, it must be enforceable. Given the draconian nature of the criminal penalties provided by the Trade Secrets Act for its violation, it was appropriate for the Court to effectuate another means of enforcement. By recognizing the applicability of the APA's "in accordance with law" provision, the Court held that one who submits the information to the government may act to enforce administrative compliance with the Trade Secrets Act.

Chrysler and similar attempts by private parties, usually corporations, to block the disclosure of information they submitted to the government are known as "reverse-FOIA" suits. In these cases, the parties argue, as did Chrysler, that the government should have invoked an exemption, usually the one for trade secrets and commercial information, to deny the FOIA request.[127]

§ 8.3.3e   Exemption (b)(5): Inter-agency and intra-agency memoranda

Congress has also provided an exemption for "intra-agency or inter-agency memoranda or letters that would not be available by law to a party other than the agency in litigation with the agency."[128] The purpose was to prevent the reduction in government effectiveness that would occur if employees were forced to "operate in a fishbowl" where all of their written comments to each other could be disclosed to the public. Like many of the other exemptions, however, Congress also left the exact scope of the exemption in doubt.

In *EPA v. Mink,* also discussed earlier, the Court considered the difficulty of determining whether documents concerning underground nuclear testing, which did not qualify for the national defense

126. *See* Schroeder & Shapiro, *Responses to Occupational Disease: The Role of Markets, Regulation and Information,* 72 Geo. L.J. 1231, 1282–88 (1983) (discussing whether the Occupational Health and Safety Administration can release trade secrets under their general rulemaking powers).

127. For a discussion of reverse FOIA cases, *see* section 8.3.3i *infra.*

128. 5 U.S.C. at § 552(b)(5); *see generally* Adler, Hitchcock & Lynch, *Agency Memoranda,* in Litigation Under The Federal Freedom of Information Act and Privacy Act, *supra* note 71, at 97–114; 2 J. O'Reilly, *supra* note 68, § 15.01–19.

exemption, were exempt as interagency memoranda.[129] The Court noted that the language of the exemption "clearly contemplates that the public is entitled to all such memoranda or letters that a private party could discover in litigation with the agency". Thus, *Department of Justice v. Julian*,[130] ruled that a criminal defendant was entitled under the FOIA to have access to the pre-sentencing reports compiled by his probation officer because although pre-sentencing reports are not available to third parties under the discovery rules, they are available to criminal defendants themselves.

In *United States v. Weber Aircraft Corp.*,[131] the Court held that the privileges listed in the legislative history of this exemption were not an exclusive list, but that Exemption 5 incorporates well-known statutory and common law privileges. To date, the Supreme Court has recognized as incorporated under Exemption 5 a privilege for government deliberations (executive privilege), attorney-work product, attorney-client communications, confidential commercial information, and sensitive governmental information.

Government Deliberations: In *Mink*, the Court noted that the rules governing discovery recognize an "executive privilege" for information the release of which would constrain "open frank discussions between subordinate and the chief concerning administrative action," but the Court also noted that the "executive privilege" did not extend to memoranda consisting entirely of "factual material" or factual material that could be severed from deliberative information. The privilege for governmental deliberation, however, applies only to pre-decisional documents, or documents involved in the process by which an agency reaches a decision, as *NLRB v. Sears, Roebuck & Co.*[132] explains.

Sears sought to obtain documents exchanged between the General Counsel of the National Labor Relations Board (NLRB) and its Regional Directors. Sears asserted that the FOIA required the disclosure of the information because it consisted of "statements of policy and interpretations which have been adopted by the agency and are not published in the Federal Register".[133] The agency claimed that the information qualified as intra-agency memoranda that are not discoverable when it is sued. The Court ordered disclosure of the

129. 410 U.S. 73 (1973); *see also* § 8.3.3(a).

130. 486 U.S. 1 (1988).

131. 465 U.S. 792 (1984).

132. 421 U.S. 132 (1975); *see also* Mead Data Central, Inc. v. U.S. Dept. of the Air Force, 566 F.2d 242 (D.C.Cir. 1977) (government has burden of establishing that documents are attorney work-product and that nonexempt material is not segregable).

133. *See* 5 U.S.C. at § 552(a)(2)(B).

memoranda because Exemption 5 did not apply to communications made after a decision and designed to explain it. This decision is consistent with the general FOIA policy to prohibit "secret" law. As noted earlier, the FOIA requires the publication of agency legal interpretations because Congress did not want agencies operating according to "secret" laws unavailable to the persons subject to them.

Some circuits have eschewed the fact/opinion distinction used in *Mink* and in these circuits purely factual material qualifies for protection if its release would expose the deliberative process. For example, the D.C. Circuit sitting en banc held that the Department of Health and Human Services (HHS) was justified in withholding agency logbooks that indicated which rulemaking proposals had won the approval of the Office of Management and Budget (OMB).[134] The court rejected the "fact/opinion" test as the exclusive test because in some circumstances "even material that could be characterized as 'factual' would so expose the deliberative process that it must be covered by the privilege." Instead, the court asked whether disclosure of the information could affect the government's deliberative process. It held that disclosure of the logs could reveal crucial aspects of the nature of the government's deliberations to the requester and thereby permit the requester to interfere with that process.

Attorney-Client Work Product: Records prepared by an attorney in contemplation of litigation may be withheld under an "attorney work-product" privilege if disclosure would reveal the theory and litigation strategy of a case, but the circuits are split concerning whether purely factual material is protected.[135] For example, *Sears* refused to order the release of a memorandum written by the General Counsel of the National Labor Relations Board (NLRB) that concerned the decision to prosecute a case. The Court noted that "[w]hatever the boundaries of the attorney's work-product rule are, the rule clearly applies to memoranda prepared by an attorney in contemplation of litigation which set forth the attorney's theory of the case and his litigation strategy." As noted earlier, the memoranda concerning decisions not to prosecute were not protected by an attorney-client privilege. They were not protected because the memoranda were not litigation advice to the agency, but instead constituted a decision by the agency not to prosecute.

134. Wolfe v. Department of Health and Human Services, 839 F.2d 768 (D.C. Cir.1988); *see also* National Wildlife Federation v. United States Forest Service, 861 F.2d 1114 (9th Cir.1988).

135. *Compare* Martin v. Office of Special Counsel, 819 F.2d 1181 (D.C.Cir. 1987) *with* Robbins Tire & Rubber Co. v. NLRB, 563 F.2d 724 (5th Cir.1977).

Agencies are entitled to withhold attorney work-product regardless of whether litigation is on-going or pending because work-product is not discoverable at any time. In *FTC v. Grolier, Inc.*,[136] the Court reversed a decision by the District of Columbia Circuit that documents cannot be withheld on the basis of the attorney work-product rule unless an agency can show that litigation related to the documents exists or potentially exists. The Court reasoned that since most courts protected work-product documents from discovery without regard to whether litigation was ongoing or pending, such documents were not "routinely" available in litigation. Accordingly, the Court concluded that under Exemption 5, attorney work-product is exempt from mandatory disclosure without regard to the state of the litigation for which it was prepared.

Attorney-Client Communications: Records, including facts, may be withheld as "attorney-client communications" if the communication is based on confidential information provided by the client. In *NLRB v. Sears, Roebuck & Co.*, discussed earlier, the Court recognized that Congress intended for Exemption 5 to include "documents which would come within the attorney-client privilege if applied to private parties." In the FOIA context, this privilege protects an agency's communications with its attorney if they are pursuant to obtaining legal advice. This privilege would include information which is *not* generated by the attorney and therefore which is not attorney work-product.

The court in *In re Grand Jury Subpoena Duces Tecum*[137] took note of the attorney-client privilege under FOIA in deciding whether the White House could refuse to comply with a subpoena issued by the "Whitewater" Independent Counsel. The prosecutor had subpoenaed two sets of notes created during meetings attended by Mrs. Clinton, her private lawyers, and two lawyers from the Office of the President who were government employees. Mrs. Clinton could not claim attorney-client privilege concerning the notes because the government attorneys did not work for her. The issue therefore was whether the Office of the President had such a privilege. The court acknowledged that a government agency, as distinct from an individual, could claim the privilege. It noted that such a privilege had been routinely found to exist under the FOIA and that the Supreme Court had held that corporate entities could invoke an attorney-client privilege. The court, however, refused to block the subpoena in this case. It observed that no case recognized an attorney-client privilege

---

136. 462 U.S. 19 (1983).

137. 112 F.3d 910 (8th Cir.), *cert. denied*, 521 U.S. 1105 (1997).

for agencies in the context of a grand jury subpoena, and that a federal statute requires executive branch employees, including attorneys, to report to the Attorney General any criminal activity by other government employees, which suggested to the court that Congress did not intend for government attorneys to be able to claim a privilege in this context. The court also justified its refusal on the basis of *United States v. Nixon*,[138] in which the Supreme Court found a constitutionally-based executive privilege to exist, but ruled that it did not bar disclosure of information relevant to a criminal prosecution. Finally, the court stated its refusal to recognize the privilege in this context would not significantly limit its use in other contexts which did not involve a grand jury subpoena, such as the FOIA.

Sensitive Information: Finally, records may be withheld under Exemption (b)(5) as "sensitive" information if disclosure would inflict harm on the government. *Federal Open Market Committee v. Merrill*[139] recognized this aspect of Exemption 5 when it affirmed the government's decision not to disclose a Federal Reserve Board (FRB) document.

The Federal Open Market Committee (FOMC) is the policymaking organ of the FRB that issues directions to the agency's employees through a document entitled the "Domestic Policy Directive". Because the document was published on a delayed basis, a FOIA request was filed for immediate access. The FRB refused on the ground that Exemption 5 protected against " 'premature disclosure which would impugn the effectiveness of government operations' ".

The Court recognized that the Domestic Policy Directive did not fit within the concept of executive privilege, developed in *Mink*, or within the concept of attorney's work-product, developed in *Sears, Roebuck & Co.* Further, the Court refused to accept the NLRB's argument that "[E]xemption 5 confers general authority upon an agency to delay disclosure of intra-agency memoranda that would undermine the effectiveness of the agency's policy if released immediately". The Court was afraid that "such an interpretation ... would appear to allow an agency to withhold any memoranda, even those that contain final opinions and statements of policy, whenever the agency concluded that disclosure would not promote the 'efficiency' of its operations or otherwise would not be in the 'public interest' ".

Instead, the Court adopted by analogy the privilege recognized in discovery for trade secrets and commercial information.[140] The Court

---

138.   418 U.S. 683 (1974).

139.   443 U.S. 340 (1979).

140.   For a further explanation of this and other discovery privileges, *see infra* § 8.3.6.

held that "the sensitivity of the commercial secrets involved, and the harm that would be inflicted upon the government by premature disclosure, should continue to serve as the relevant criteria in determining the applicability of this Exemption 5 privilege". The Court thought that this type of privilege had been contemplated by Congress when it passed this exemption.

The Court also spoke to the future scope of the exemption, but it left the scope in doubt. In response to an argument by the FRB that the Domestic Policy Directive would fall within any of the three privileges recognized in the discovery process, the Court warned that "it is not clear that Exemption 5 was intended to incorporate every privilege known to civil discovery". The Court was hesitant to reach that conclusion because several of the discovery privileges were duplicated by several of the other eight FOIA exemptions. Because of this overlap, the Court said new claims that a privilege is covered by Exemption 5 "must be viewed by caution."

In *United States v. Weber Aircraft Corporation,* the Court said that the previous case should not be interpreted to narrowly limit Exemption (b)(5).[141] An aircraft manufacturer had filed a FOIA request for Air Force safety investigation documents after it was denied access to those documents through the discovery process in a lawsuit. The court of appeals held that Exemption (b)(5) did not apply to the documents, despite the fact they were unavailable through discovery, because the exemption reached only those privileges explicitly recognized in the legislative history of the FOIA. The circuit court found that the legislative history recognized an executive privilege for pre-decisional documents containing advice, opinions or recommendations, but no privilege for official government information.

The Court reversed on the grounds that the information was not available through discovery and that Exemption (b)(5) therefore applied. The Court explained that *Federal Open Market Committee* held that a privilege that was mentioned in the legislative history is incorporated by the exemption, but the decision did not mean that all privileges not mentioned were excluded. Further, the Court noted that the dictum in *Merrill* that Exemption (b)(5) did not incorporate "every privilege known to civil discovery" did not support the court of appeal's decision. The Court said that "[i]t is one thing to say that recognition under Exemption 5 of a novel privilege, or one that has found less than universal acceptance would not fall within Exemption

---

141.   465 U.S. 792 (1984).

5 if not discussed in its legislative history," but that "[i]t was quite another to say that [the executive privilege] which has been well-settled for some two decades need be viewed with the same degree of skepticism".

In *Department of the Interior v. Klamath Water Users Protective Ass'n*,[142] the Supreme Court held unanimously that Exemption 5 did not encompass certain communications from third parties submitted to government. At issue were records submitted to DOI by Indian Tribes from "outside consultants." The Court drew a distinction between those consultant documents submitted pursuant to agency requests, which might qualify for attorney work-product or deliberate process privileges, and those "seeking a Government benefit at the expense of other applicants" which would not. By limiting its holding to self-interested outside consultant reports, the Court preserved aspects of the exemption for outside reports, such as those from Congress, state agencies, or non-self interested consultants.

§ 8.3.3f   Exemption (b)(6): Personnel and medical files

Another exemption is for "personnel and medical files and similar files the disclosure of which would constitute a clearly unwarranted invasion of personal privacy."[143] This definition raises three issues. First, is a record a "personnel" or "medical" file or a "similar" file? Second, would release invade personal privacy? Finally, would release constitute an "unwarranted" invasion of privacy?

Similar File: In *United States Department of State v. Washington Post Co.*,[144] the Court held a record falls within the definition of "similar" agency records if the information can be identified as applying to a particular individual. It rejected a circuit court's interpretation that the term "similar" raised an issue of whether the information being sought was similar to the type of information contained in medical and personnel files. The Supreme Court felt that the circuit court's interpretation would put some persons at risk of embarrassment if information that was not contained in medical, personnel, or functionally equivalent files, was released. The Court noted that since Congress' intent was to minimize such embarrassment, judicial review should focus on whether disclosure would constitute a clearly unwarranted invasion of personal privacy.

Invasion of Personal Privacy: In *Department of the Air Force v. Rose*,[145] which involved the claim by the Air Force Academy that

---

142.   532 U.S. 1, 12–16 (2001).

143.   5 U.S.C. at § 552(b)(6).

144.   456 U.S. 595 (1982).

145.   425 U.S. 352 (1976).

disciplinary records were absolutely exempt from disclosure, the Court noted that the legislative history indicated that the exemption was intended for "threats to privacy interests more palpable than mere possibilities". Further, the Court endorsed the technique of deleting personal references as a satisfactory method to avoid nondisclosure. The Court admitted that such deletions would not eliminate the danger of an invasion of personal privacy in all cases since the identity of a person could be disclosed by the context of the document in light of other information. Nevertheless, the Court concluded that disclosure could be made because the exemption only protects against "clearly unwarranted invasions of privacy" and not "incidental invasions".

Unwarranted Invasion of Privacy: Four factors are commonly employed to determine whether the release of information "would constitute a clearly unwarranted invasion of personal privacy": the degree of invasion of privacy, the public interest in disclosure, the requestor's interest in disclosure, and any other factors, such as statutory policies concerning confidentiality, that might affect the balance.[146]

When courts engage in balancing, however, they may not weigh the factors used in the same fashion. For example, *American Federation of Government Employees v. United States* held that there was a strong privacy interest in keeping home addresses confidential.[147] The court therefore supported the refusal of an agency to disclose names and addresses to a government union. Other decisions have concluded that the exemption applied only to "intimate details of a highly personal nature" and that names and addresses did not qualify as such.[148] The latter decisions are more consistent with the Court's admonition in *Rose* that incidental invasions of privacy are not covered and that a mere possibility that a harm would occur is not sufficient to invoke the exemption.

In *U.S. Department of Defense v. FLRA*,[149] the Supreme Court clarified two aspects of this exemption. The issue was whether an agency could refuse to disclose to a union the home addresses of government employees because such disclosure would be an "unwar-

146. *See* Carome & Adler, *FOIA Exemption for Privacy,* in Litigation Under the Federal Freedom of Information Act and Privacy Act, *supra* note 71, at 119–131; *see generally* 2 J. O'Reilly, *supra* note 68, at §§ 16.01–.14. *See also* Department of Justice v. Reporters Committee for Freedom of the Press, 489 U.S. 749 (1989) (applying similar standards to Exemptions 7(c) and 6); § 8.3.3g *infra*.

147. 712 F.2d 931 (4th Cir.1983).

148. Robles v. EPA, 484 F.2d 843 (4th Cir.1973); Getman v. NLRB, 450 F.2d 670 (D.C.Cir.1971).

149. 510 U.S. 487 (1994).

ranted invasion of privacy" according to the FOIA. First, the Court held that whether an invasion of privacy was warranted could not turn on the purpose for which the request for information was made. Thus, the identity of the requesting party has no bearing on the application of this exemption. Second, the " 'only relevant public interest' to be weighed is the extent to which disclosure would serve the 'core purpose of the FOIA,' which is 'contribut[ing] significantly to public understanding of the operations or activities of the government.' " Since the union only wanted the names to further union business, there was no public interest in the disclosure, and the Court reversed a lower court's decision ordering the agencies to release the names.[150]

§ 8.3.3g   Exemption (b)(7): Investigatory records

Exemption (b)(7) applies to "records compiled for law enforcement purposes, but only to the extent that the production of such law enforcement records (A) could reasonably be expected to interfere with enforcement proceedings; (B) would deprive a person of a right to a fair trial or an impartial adjudication; (C) could reasonably be expected to constitute an unwarranted invasion of privacy; (D) could reasonably be expected to disclose the identity of a confidential source ... and, in the case of a record compiled by a criminal law enforcement investigation, or by an agency conducting a lawful national security intelligence investigation, information furnished only by a confidential source; (E) would disclose investigatory techniques and procedures; or (F) could reasonably be expected to endanger the life or physical safety of law enforcement personnel." The 1986 FOIA Reform Act expanded the exemption to include "records or information." The previous exemption included only "investigatory records." Congress also substituted "could reasonably be expected" for "would" as the standard for risk of harm concerning interference with law enforcement proceedings, unwarranted invasion of personal privacy, disclosure of the identify of a confidential source, and endangerment of the life or physical safety of law enforcement personnel.

After these amendments, this exemption involves two issues. First, are the records sought "records compiled for law enforcement

---

150. While the agency is ordinarily not required to determine whether an individual has died or his activities have become public, thereby negating the exemption, several courts faced with old documents have refused to presume that the individuals are still alive. *See, e.g.,* Davin v. United States Department of Justice, 60 F.3d 1043, 1059 (3d Cir. 1995).

purposes"? Second, would release of the records cause one of the six harms listed in section (b)(7)?

In *John Doe Agency v. John Doe Corp.*,[151] the Supreme Court interpreted the term "compiled for law enforcement purposes" in a manner that expanded the scope of this exemption. It held that a record is "compiled" for law enforcement purposes if it is obtained by the government for the purpose of law enforcement, or if it is assembled for law enforcement purposes from records originally obtained by the government for some other purpose. The case concerned a request by a federal contractor for documents compiled by the government during an audit of the company. When the FBI began an investigation of the company for possible fraudulent practices, the documents were transferred by the agency which had compiled them to the FBI. The company argued the documents were *not* compiled for law enforcement purposes because at the time they were created, the company was not under criminal investigation. Since the documents had been collected by the FBI pursuant to its law enforcement purposes, however, the Court responded that the records fit within the plain meeting of this exemption.

The Court, by comparison, was less accommodating in *Department of Justice v. Landano*.[152] The issue was the definition of "confidential source" in section (b)(7). Prior decisions had established that a record was furnished by a "confidential source" when a particular person had spoken with a law enforcement agency with an understanding that the communication would remain confidential. In this case, the FBI asked the Court to presume that any person who cooperated with the Bureau in a criminal investigation intended for the FBI to keep confidential all information that the person furnished. The Court replied that neither the language of the exemption nor its legislative history supported an exemption of all FBI criminal investigative sources. It was willing, however, to recognize narrower generic circumstances in which an implied assurance of confidentiality could be inferred, such as any information furnished by a paid informant. The Court remanded the case for a determination whether such a circumstance existed in this case.

United States Department of Justice v. Reporters Committee for Freedom of the Press,[153] illustrates the second issue under this exemption. The Justice Department had refused to disclose "the rap sheet" of an organized crime figure under the section (b)(7)(C), which

---

151.   493 U.S. 146 (1989).   **153.**   489 U.S. 749 (1989).
152.   508 U.S. 165 (1993).

protects persons against an "unwarranted invasion of privacy." A "rap sheet" is a record containing an individual's criminal history including such publicly available items as arrests and charges. The request had been for information contained in the rap sheet that was publicly available in other locations such as court records. On this basis, the requester argued that disclosure could not constitute an unwarranted invasion of privacy.

First, the Court determined that release of the rap sheet would be "an invasion of privacy" by applying the dictionary definition of privacy which is "not fully available to the public." It reasoned that one can have a privacy interest in protecting information which, although available elsewhere, is unlikely to be disclosed because of the time and expense of acquiring it.

Second, the Court held that whether release of the rap sheet was an "unwarranted" invasion of privacy depended on the nature of the requested document and its relationship to subjecting agency performance to public scrutiny. The Court characterized the purpose of the FOIA as promoting the citizen's right to be informed about the performance of government agencies. It concluded that information in the rap sheet would not shed any light on an agency's performance of its statutory duty.

Finally, the Court adopted a "categorical" approach by holding that rap sheets could not be obtained through the FOIA pursuant to this or any other request. In other words, the Court abandoned the case-by-case approach normally used in FOIA matters which obligates a court to determine whether the specific documents requested must be disclosed. The Court justified its categorical approach on the ground that no rap sheet would contain information relevant to the purpose of shedding light on the government's performance.

Reporters Committee is noteworthy because the Court was willing to find an invasion of privacy even though the information contained in the rap sheet was publicly available in other locations. This interpretation gives more protection to privacy rights. Exemptions 6 and 7 both concern unwarranted invasions of privacy, but Exemption 6 concerns a "*clearly* unwarranted invasion," while Exemption 7 requires only an "unwarranted invasion." This difference apparently signals Congress' intent to give greater protection to criminal records than to medical and personnel records. The Court's unwillingness in this case to require the Justice Department to disclose information that was publicly available elsewhere may reflect this legislative intent.

Reporters Committee is also noteworthy because the Court relied on two acts of interpretation that could be used in the future to narrow the amount of information disclosed under the FOIA under this and other exemptions. In *Mink,* discussed earlier, the Court declared the Act's purpose to create a "broad right of access to 'official information.'" By comparison, *Reporters Committee,* the Court cites with approval the suggestion that the FOIA was not intended "'for a broader purpose such as making the government's collection of data available to anybody who has any socially useful purpose for it'" and distinguishes between "details to include in a newspaper story" and "the kind of public interest for which Congress enacted the FOIA." In addition, the Court for the first time in the context of an FOIA privacy dispute adopted the position that "categorical decisions may be appropriate and individual circumstances disregarded when a case fits into a genus in which the balance characteristically tips in one direction."

§ 8.3.3h   Summary of Exemptions 8 and 9.

Exemption 8 protects matters that are contained in bank examination reports. This exemption has received an expansive interpretation from the courts,[154] so much so that banks are not even being required to segregate materials in reports unrelated to financial conditions. A provision of the Federal Deposit Insurance Corporation does, however, explicitly limit the applications of Exemption 8 to all federal banking agencies inspector general's reports.[155]

Exemption 9 covers "geological and geophysical information and data, including maps, concerning wells." This exemption is rarely invoked or interpreted.

§ 8.3.3i   Reverse—FOIA Actions

As has been discussed above, in connection with the *Chrysler Corporation* case, it is also possible to prevent agency production of information submitted by third parties when the agency chooses not to exercise an available exemption from disclosure. These challenges are brought directly under the APA.[156] The plaintiff bears the burden of non-disclosure under the relevant exemption (usually Exemption 4

---

154. *See, e.g.,* Public Citizen v. Farm Credit Admin., 938 F.2d 290, 293–94 (D.C. Cir. 1991) (holding reports submitted to FCA by National Consumer Cooperative Bank protected by Exemption 8 even though FCA does not regulate NCCB).

155. 12 U.S.C. § 18310 (K) (2000) (Banking agencies shall disclose such reports).

156. *See* § 8.3.3d *supra.*

or 7(c)). Review on the record is deferential, i.e., has there been a clear error of judgment.[157] Nonetheless, success rates of plaintiffs' reverse cases have been higher than those in FOIA cases, where the review standard is *de novo*.[158]

Administrative practice in reverse-FOIA cases is controlled by Executive Order 12,600.[159] This order requires executive agencies to establish pre-disclosure notification procedures that will facilitate objections by submitters at the agency level and to preserve the status quo pending litigation.[160]

§ 8.4   Critical Infrastructure Information and the FOIA

The Homeland Security Act of 2002,[161] enacted by Congress in response to the terrorist attacks of Sept. 11th, includes a provision, the Critical Infrastructure Information Act (CIIA) of 2002, which may have a significant impact on the availability of information under the FOIA. The CIIA provides that "critical infrastructure information (including the identity of the submitting person or entity) that is voluntarily submitted" to the government for purposes of homeland security is exempt from disclosure under the FOIA if it is accompanied by an "express statement" that the information qualifies as critical infrastructure information.[162] In order to qualify, the statement must say: "This information is voluntarily submitted to the Federal Government in expectation of protection from disclosure as provided by the provisions of the Critical Infrastructure Information Act of 2002."[163]

The potential impact of the CIIA depends on how the courts eventually interpret the definition of "critical infrastructure information," which potentially includes a very broad range of information.

157. *See* Campaign for Family Farms v. Glickman, 200 F.3d 1180, 1187 (8th Cir. 2000).

158. *See* Verkuil, *An Outcomes Analysis of Scope of Review Standards*, 44 W & M L. Rev. 679, 719 (2002) (documenting a 20% reversal rate in reverse-FOIA cases).

159. 3 C.F.R. 235 (1998), *reprinted in* 5 U.S.C. § 552 note (2000).

160. However, an agency need not provide administrative appeal procedures nor record based fact-finding procedures. *See* Pacific Architects & Engineers v. United States Department of State, 906 F.2d 1345, 1348 (9th Cir. 1990) (written procedures provided by agency before disclosures were adequate).

161. H.R. 5005, 107th Cong. (2002), Pub. L. No. 107–296 (2002), 116 Stat. 2135 (2002).

162. *Id.* § 214(a)(1). The potential scope of the CIIA is of interest beyond its impact on the FOIA. The Act also prohibits the government from using critical infrastructure information that is voluntary submitted to it for any other purpose, including holding companies liable for civil damages or penalties under federal, state and local law. *Id.*

163. Id. § 214(a)(2).

The CIIA does not define "critical infrastructure information." If the courts adopt the same definition as is used in the USA Patriot Act, information is "critical infrastructure information" if it is not "customarily in the public domain" and it relates to a series of factors,[164] some of which, if read literally, could qualify information for nondisclosure even if national security is not at stake.[165]

The potential impact of the CIIA also depends on the government's capacity to verify that information in fact qualifies for the exemption. Under the FOIA, persons who submit information that is stamped as "confidential business information" are asked to provide "any information the disclosure of which the submitter claims could reasonably be expected to cause substantial competitive harm."[166] The CIIA, however, exempts information from disclosure under (c)(3) of the FOIA, not (c)(4), which covers confidential business information. FOIA advocates express concern that "unless and until either the President issues a new Executive Order requiring submitters to bear the burden of proving that information is in fact CII, or the HSD promulgates regulations to that effect, it is unclear how the government will determine whether a confidentiality claim is justified."[167]

§ 8.5   The Privacy Act and the FOIA

The Privacy Act regulates the acquisition, maintenance and disclosure of information to prevent its improper use.[168] The Act applies to any "group of records under the control of an agency from which information is retrieved by the name of the individual...." It defines an agency's responsibility to acquire and maintain accurate records, and it limits disclosure of the records to eleven situations. These include disclosure when it is required by the FOIA and when it is requested by other governmental entities. Finally, an individual is given access "to his record or to any information pertaining to him which is contained in the system...." The individual can request that a record be amended to correct any errors and a procedure, including judicial review, is provided to contest an agency's refusal to do so.

---

164. 6 U.S.C. §§ 131(3),(6).

165. *See* Steinzor, *Democracies Die Behind Closed Doors: The Homeland Security Act and Corporate Accountability,* 12 Kan. J. L. & Pub. Pol. 641 (2003).

166. Exec. Order 12,600, 52 Fed. Reg. 23781 (1987).

167. Steinzor, *supra* note 165, at 655.

168. 5 U.S.C. § 552(a); *see generally* Adler, Glitzenstein & Hammitt, *The Privacy Act,* in Litigation Under the Federal Freedom of Information Act and Privacy Act, *supra* note 71, at 251–288.

The government is exempted from the Act's restrictions and obligations in two ways.[169] Under a general exemption, the CIA and law enforcement agencies are not required to meet most of the previously mentioned requirements of the Act. Under seven specific exemptions, agencies are not required to meet some of those provisions. These exemptions cover most records kept for purposes of national security, law enforcement, census and Secret Service activities, and government employment. Under both the general and specific exemptions, an agency can avoid disclosure of records to individuals who seek access. To exempt a system of records under either type of exemption, an agency must hold a rulemaking proceeding for that purpose.

The relationship between the FOIA and the Privacy Act is complicated. Suppose, for example, that a person filed a request for documents under each act. The FOIA would *require disclosure* unless one of its nine exemptions could be applied. The Privacy Act would *forbid disclosure* unless one of its eleven exemptions applied. Each act is related to the other because of an interconnection in their exemptions.

The Privacy Act contains an exemption for documents that are sought under the FOIA. The exemption authorizes the disclosure of documents protected by the Privacy Act if no FOIA exemption is applicable to the documents.[170] If a FOIA exemption does apply, an agency must withhold the information from disclosure. Normally, an agency has discretion whether or not to withhold documents because of a FOIA exemption. If those documents are protected by the Privacy Act, however, they cannot be disclosed because the Privacy Act authorizes disclosure only when no FOIA exemption applies.

Department of Defense v. FLRA,[171] discussed earlier,[172] illustrates the interaction of the Privacy Act and the FOIA. The Court upheld the refusal by several agencies to disclose to a union the home addresses of government employees because such disclosure would be an "unwarranted invasion of privacy" according to the FOIA. The agencies, however, had argued that the disclosure was prohibited by the Privacy Act. The Court linked this argument with the FOIA as follows: "The employee addresses sought by the unions are 'records' covered by the broad terms of the Privacy Act. Therefore, unless the FOIA would require release of their addresses, their disclosure is 'prohibited by law,' and the agencies may not reveal them to the

---

169. 5 U.S.C. at § 552a(j)–(k).

170. *Id*. at 552a(b)(2).

171. 510 U.S. 487 (1994).

172. *See supra* note 140 & accompanying text.

unions." Because exemption (b)(6) (personnel records) applied, for the reasons discussed earlier, the FOIA did not "require" the release of the information. Moreover, because of the Privacy Act, the agencies did not have an option whether or not to assert exemption (b)(6).

One FOIA exemption is for information the disclosure of which is prohibited by some other statute.[173] At one time, the courts had disagreed whether the Privacy Act was intended by Congress to be such an "exempting statute". If the Privacy Act is an exempting statute, an agency could refuse to give a person access to his or her own records pursuant to a FOIA request even though no other FOIA exemption would apply. If the Privacy Act is not an exempting statute, an individual would be entitled to obtain records, not otherwise exempted under the FOIA, although the same person would not be entitled to obtain the records under the Privacy Act.

Attempts to qualify the Privacy Act as an exempting statute were criticized because such qualification would increase the level of government secrecy and decrease public accountability. Congress agreed with these criticisms. It amended the Privacy Act to indicate that "[n]o agency shall rely on any exemption [in the Act] to withhold from and individual any record which is otherwise accessible to such individual under the provisions of [the FOIA]."[174]

§ 8.6 Discovery and the FOIA

The third means by which information can be obtained from the government is by use of the discovery process during the pendency of a lawsuit or agency proceeding. Discovery in a civil lawsuit is available usually only for the period of time prior to trial and only for the documents relevant to a pending matter. Discovery is available on the same basis for some agency adjudications, but it is more limited, or even nonexistent, for others. To avoid the limitations of discovery processes, the FOIA is used as a supplemental source of discovery. This use has been controversial and has prompted proposed amendments of the FOIA.

Discovery from the government is available both when it is a party to a lawsuit and when it is not. If the government is a party, a fellow litigant is entitled to "obtain discovery of any matter, not privileged, which is relevant to the subject matter involved in the pending action." If the government is not a party, a litigant is

173. 5 U.S.C. at § 552(b)(3).

174. CIA Information Act, Pub.L. No. 98–477, § 2(c), 98 Stat. 2209, 2211 (1984); *see* Provenzano v. United States

Dept. of Justice, 717 F.2d 799 (3d Cir. 1983); judgment vacated 469 U.S. 14 (1984).

entitled to obtain a subpoena for "documentary evidence". The government can avoid compliance if the subpoena is "unreasonable and oppressive". In both situations, the government has a "privilege" not to disclose information under certain conditions that have been recognized and developed by the federal courts. Some of these privileges, like those for business information, attorney-client communications and matters affecting the public interest, are available to any litigant. Others, like those for state secrets, the identity of informers and for "official information," are available only to the government.[175]

The privilege for "official information" is illustrative of the effect of the government's privileges. Like other government privileges, it was developed by the federal courts to apply even in situations where there is no statutory provision forbidding disclosure. The privilege, which covers investigatory files and inter-agency and intra-agency memoranda, was created based on the belief that the "optimal efficiency in the governmental decisionmaking process may depend on a free flow of ideas between subordinate and chief".[176] The application of the privilege is also similar to that of the others. The courts will balance whether the positive effect of withholding the information outweighs the undesirable effects on the administration of justice. To make that determination, the court can use an *in camera* inspection procedure. If necessary, a court can order information released under a protective order. The order will indicate how the litigant can use the information and to whom it can be shown.[177]

For some agencies, the discovery process operates in adjudications in a substantially similar fashion to civil discovery. For other agencies, a party will be limited to disclosure of the exhibits, or evidence, that the agency staff intends to use in the adjudication. For a small number of agencies, there are no provisions for discovery. Discovery is unusual in most rulemaking proceedings.[178]

Because of differences in the discovery process and the FOIA, litigants will use the FOIA to supplement discovery in a variety of

---

175. Fed. R. Civ. P. 26(b), 34, 45; Fed. R. Evid. 501.

176. *See* Note, *Discovery of Government Documents and the Official Information Privilege,* 76 Colum. L. Rev. 142, 143 (1976).

177. *See* Fed. R. Civ. P. 26(c).

178. *See* Tomlinson, *Discovery In Agency Adjudication,* 1971 Duke L.J. 89;

Comment, *Discovery in Federal Administrative Proceedings,* 16 Stan. L. Rev. 1035 (1964); *see also* Koch, *Discovery In Rulemaking,* 1977 Duke L.J. 295; Toran, *Information Disclosure in Civil Actions: The Freedom of Information Act and Federal Discovery Rules,* 49 Geo. Wash. L. Rev. 843 (1981); Tomlinson, *supra* note 7; Koch & Rubin, *supra* note 80.

circumstances.[179] The FOIA may be used before a lawsuit has been started and therefore before discovery is available. For example, a person may try to obtain information contained in a government report to determine whether to file a lawsuit. The FOIA may also be used when an agency limits discovery or when it does not allow discovery. Further, the FOIA may be used to avoid the "relevancy" limitation of discovery. For example, a FOIA request can seek information concerning whether members of the agency have engaged in ex parte contacts. Courts may regard such information as "irrelevant" to a lawsuit. Finally, the FOIA may be used to obtain information that the government would not have to disclose in discovery because it is privileged. For example, a court may protect all of an agency's intra-agency memoranda under the "official information" exemption. By comparison, portions of the same information may be available under the FOIA. The exemption for intra-agency memoranda does not include purely factual material that can be severed from nonfactual material.[180]

Government lawyers and others argue that private litigants have abused the FOIA as a discovery tool. One alleged abuse is the use of the FOIA to divert agency lawyers from the legal matter in which the requestor is engaged. According to this complaint, private litigants make massive FOIA requests to divert the agency's attention from prosecuting a lawsuit to defending the agency's refusal to accede to the FOIA request. Another alleged abuse is the use of the FOIA to duplicate discovery requests. The duplicate requests are made in the hope that agency FOIA employees will produce different documents than the agency lawyers will produce in the discovery process. The requests are also made in the hope that the FOIA employees will accidentally give up exempt, or arguably exempt, materials. Litigants attempt to increase the likelihood of those occurrences by failing to notify agency attorneys of the duplicative requests in the hope they will not supervise the FOIA search.[181]

To end the abuses, Professor Tomlinson recommends a requirement that a party in litigation with the government must notify government counsel of all discovery-motivated FOIA requests made on behalf of a party.[182] If government counsel receives such notice, the danger of surprise at a trial or hearing, when a private party introduces documents obtained by the FOIA, is eliminated. Further, notice would allow counsel to coordinate FOIA and discovery

---

179. *See* Tomlinson, *supra* note 7.

180. *See supra* § 8.3.2(e).

181. Tomlinson, *supra* note 7, at 154–91.

182. *Id.,* at 194–200.

searches for the same records. While abuse of the FOIA for discovery purposes is a problem, the magnitude of the problem is not that great. In keeping with the FOIA policy of maximum feasible disclosure, any amendment intended to alleviate discovery abuse should be narrowly tailored to fix whatever problem might exist.

Finally, it should be noted that discovery is sometimes sought in FOIA suits themselves, but is rarely permitted. Discovery in such circumstances will surely be denied if it can be shown that it is a "fishing expedition" to gain information related to separate lawsuits.[183]

§ 8.7 Privately Initiated Correction of Public Information

The Freedom of Information Act (FOIA) allows the public to obtain information held by government. But under FOIA you take the information as you find it (or as the government produces it). What if that information is false, faulty or otherwise unreliable. Can it be "corrected"? Congress recently required the Office of Management and Budget (OMB) to provide "policy and procedural guidance to Federal agencies for ensuring and maximizing the quality, objectivity, utility, and integrity of information (including statistical information) disseminated by Federal agencies."[184] In response, OMB required each Federal agency to (1) issue its own specific guidelines within a year after OMB issued its guidelines, (2) establish administrative mechanisms allowing affected persons "to seek and obtain correction" of information maintained and disseminated by the Federal agency that "does not comply" with the OMB government-wide guidelines, and (3) report periodically to OMB on the complaints received and agency resolution of the complaints.[185] Agencies have now issued their own agency-specific guidelines,[186] which can be accessed from each agency's website.

183. *See* RNR Enterprises v. SEC, 122 F.3d 98 (2d Cir. 1997) (no abuse of discretion in denying discovery in FOIA action seeking files exempted for investigatory purposes).

184. Treasury and General Government Appropriations Act for Fiscal Year 2001, Pub. L. No. 106, § 515 (2001). While this statute does not have a codified title, it is commonly referred to as the "Data Quality Act" or "Information Quality Act," hereinafter referred to as "IQA."

185. Office of Management and Budget, Guidelines for Ensuring and Maxim-

izing the Quality, Objectivity, Utility, and Integrity of Information Disseminated by Federal Agencies, 67 Fed. Reg. 8452 (2002).

186. *See, e.g.,* Guidelines for Ensuring and Maximizing the Quality, Objectivity, Utility, and Integrity of Information Disseminated by the Environmental Protection Agency, 67 Fed. Reg. 63657 (2002); Guidelines for Ensuring and Maximizing the Quality, Objectivity, Utility, and Integrity of Information Disseminated by the Department of Labor, 67 Fed. Reg. 61669 (2002); Department of Commerce, Guidelines for Ensuring

The Information Quality Act was passed as an appropriations rider, buried in a 500–page appropriations bill, without the benefit of hearings or debate, or probably the knowledge of members of Congress except its sponsor. Further, since the legislation itself is very brief, constituting but two paragraphs, Congress gave limited guidance as to how the goal of information quality was to be accomplished, and how it was to be balanced with the regulatory goals of agencies. In light of this background, and the fact that the rider was written by an industry lobbyist, it is not surprising that interest groups representing environmentalists and other citizens and industry trade associations have clashed over OMB's attempts to implement the IQA.[187]

§ 8.7.1 OMB Guidelines to The Information Quality Act

In publishing the OMB data quality guidelines, OMB stressed, in the preamble, three underlying principles. First, OMB designed its government-wide guidelines in recognition that they apply to a wide variety of government information dissemination activities that may range in importance and scope. The guidelines were not prescriptive nor did they require a "one-size-fits-all" approach.[188] Second, OMB designed its government-wide guidelines so that agencies could apply them in a common-sense and workable manner, without imposing unnecessary administrative burdens.[189] As a result, many agencies chose to incorporate requests for correction into existing agency processes, as appropriate. Third, OMB designed its government-wide guidelines to ensure that agencies met basic information quality standards. OMB recognized that some government information might need to meet higher or more specific information quality standards than those that would apply to other information. The more important the information, the higher the quality standards to which it should be held. The OMB guidelines also recognized that high quality comes at a cost, and encouraged agencies to weigh the costs and benefits of higher information quality in the development of information.[190]

---

and Maximizing the Quality, Objectivity, Utility, and Integrity of Disseminated Information, 67 Fed. Reg. 62685 (2002).

187. *See* Shapiro, *The Information Quality Act and Environmental Protection: The Perils of Regulatory Reform by Appropriations Rider*, 28 W. & M. Env. L. & Pol. Rev. 339 (2004). For a general introduction to the IQA, some of which has been cited herein, consult www.theCRE.com (Center for Regulatory Effectiveness). Com.

188. 67 Fed Reg. at 8452/3.

189. *Id*. at 8453/1.

190. *Id*. at 8452/3—8453/1.

§ 8.7.2   Scope of Information Quality Act

Federal agencies subject to the Paperwork Reduction Act are obligated to comply with OMB's government-wide data quality guidelines.[191] This includes independent regulatory commissions and boards as well as executive agencies. The Data Quality Act directs OMB to establish quality standards for "information" that is "disseminated" by Federal agencies.[192] It is the definition of these two words that establishes the basic scope of the Data Quality Act.[193]

OMB defines "information" to include "any communication or representation of knowledge such as facts or data." OMB further explains that this definition "does not include opinions, where the agency's presentation makes it clear that what is being offered is someone's opinion rather than fact or the agency's views."[194]

OMB defines "dissemination" to include "agency initiated or sponsored distribution of information to the public."[195] OMB explains this definition in greater detail in the preamble to its guidelines. OMB includes information which has the appearance of representing agency views: "In addition, if an agency, as an institution, disseminates information prepared by an outside party in a manner that reasonably suggests that the agency agrees with the information, this appearance of having the information represent agency views makes dissemination of the information subject to these guidelines." It is on this basis that OMB explicitly makes certain "third-party" information—e.g., academic scientific research—subject to data quality standards. On the other hand, if the information does not have the appearance of representing agency views, or of being relied upon or used by an agency in support of, *e.g.*, a rulemaking or of a risk assessment, then the agency is not considered to be disseminating that information.

OMB also excludes from its definition of "dissemination" certain specific kinds of information—correspondence with individuals or persons, press releases, archival records, public filings, subpoenas or adjudicative process. This last exception—for adjudicative processes—is controversial because it exempts information used by agencies to approve licenses and permits, which largely involve information that

191. 44 U.S.C. § 3502(1); *see* OMB Guidelines, *supra* note 185, § II.

192. IQA, *supra* note 184, §§ 515(a) & (b)(2)(A).

193. The IQA also states that the OMB guidelines "apply to the sharing by Federal agencies of, and access to, infor-

mation disseminated by Federal agencies." *Id.*, § 515(b)(1)).

194. OMB Guidelines, *supra* note 185, § V.5; *see* discussion at 66 Fed. Reg. 49718, 49723/1 (September 28, 2001).

195. OMB Guidelines, *supra* note 185, § V.8.

originates with regulated industries. Given the incentive of companies seeking a license or government permission to interpret information in a light most favorable to them, such industry information can
be unreliable, yet OMB has exempted it completely from the IQA.[196]

§ 8.7.3   Substantive Standards of Quality

The IQA directed OMB to ensure and maximize "the quality,
objectivity, utility, and integrity" of information.[197] OMB was to do so
"in fulfillment of the purposes and provisions of chapter 35 of title
44, United States Code, commonly known as the Paperwork Reduction Act."[198] These terms are integrated[199] into the overall agency
responsibilities for information resources management embodied in
the Paperwork Reduction Act.[200] While, as noted, the IQA itself is a
terse statement of OMB's legislative authority and agency responsibilities, Congress presumably viewed it as a statement of substantive
policy and agency administrative procedures that was to be integrated into the overall policy structure of the Paperwork Reduction Act,
which has been interpreted and implemented by OMB for many
years.

The OMB guidelines define "quality" as an encompassing term
embracing "objectivity, utility, and integrity."[201] The substantive
quality standards in OMB's government-wide guidelines are set forth
in OMB's definitions for these three terms.

The OMB definition of "objectivity" is the most detailed and
elaborate of OMB's substantive definitions, encompassing a number
of different, mutually reinforcing concepts. "Objectivity" involves
both presentation and substance.[202]

In addition, OMB establishes higher standards for what OMB
defines as "influential" information.[203] As to this influential information, OMB provides standards relating to reproducibility and transparency, and adds more specific standards for agency analysis of risks
to human health, safety and the environment.[204] The last requirement has drawn strong opposition on the ground that OMB has
sought to replace standards that Congress has established in individ-

---

196. *See* Shapiro, *OMB's Dubious
Peer Review Procedures*, 34 Env. L. Rev.
10064, 10071 (2004).

197. IQA, *supra* note 184, § 515(a).

198. *Id.*

199. *See, e.g.*, 44 U.S.C. §§ 3502(11),
3504(c)(4), 3504(e)(1)(B), 3506(b)(1)(C),
3506(d)(1)(B), & 3506(e)(1).

200. 44 U.S.C. 3502 (13), *see* § 9.5.3
infra.

201. OMB Guidelines, *supra* note
185, § V.1.

202. *Id.*, § V.3.a & b.

203. *Id.*, § V.3.b.ii.

204. *Id.*, § V.3.b.ii.A, B & C.

ual environmental and other statutes regarding the analysis of risks with its own its own policy views concerning how agencies should interpret risk information.[205] Less controversial is OMB's requirement that federal agencies are to present information "in an accurate, clear, complete, and unbiased manner." OMB stresses that such information has to be presented in a proper context, and that on occasion, other information may have to be disseminated as well to ensure an accurate, clear, complete, and unbiased presentation.

As a substantive matter, agency information is to be "accurate, reliable, and unbiased." OMB makes a distinction here between "original and supporting data" and the "analytic results related thereto," a foreshadowing of the same distinction OMB makes in its discussion of "influential."[206] Specifically, "[i]n a scientific, financial, or statistical context, the original and supporting data shall be generated, and the analytic results shall be developed, using sound statistical and research methods."[207] OMB includes, under its discussion of substantive matter, its standards for peer review. OMB states a presumption favoring formal, independent, external peer review and therefore a presumption of "acceptable objectivity." An example of formal, independent, external peer review is the review process used by scientific journals. "However, this presumption is rebuttable based on a persuasive showing by the petitioner in a particular instance."[208] OMB subsequently proposed another set of guidelines that would supplement procedures under the IQA by requiring peer review of regulatory information and by specifying the procedures under which that review would take place.[209] Like OMB's initial guidelines, the peer review guidelines have drawn support from industry trade associations and opposition from public interest groups, the latter alleging that the proposal would slow the government's dissemination of information without an appreciable improvement in the quality of information.[210]

In addition, given the detailed guidelines applicable to scientific, financial, and statistical information—both in the OMB government-wide guidelines and in the agency-specific guidelines—it is clear that OMB believes it important that scientific, financial, and statistical information be subject to higher standards of quality in general.

205. *See* Shapiro, *supra* note 187, at 354–57.

206. *Compare* OMB Guidelines, *supra* note 185, § V.3.b, *with* § V.3.b.ii.A & B.

207. *Id.* § V.3.b.

208. *Id.* § V.3.b.i.

209. Proposed Bulletin on Peer Review and Information Quality, 68 Fed. Reg. 54023 (2003); *see also* Revised Information Quality Bulletin on Peer Review, 69 Fed. Reg. 23230 (2004).

210. *See* Shapiro, *supra* note 196, at 10064.

OMB made it clear that "reproducibility" does not require replica-tion.[211] Rather, reproducibility means that "the information is capa-ble of being substantially reproduced, subject to an acceptable degree of imprecision."[212]

§ 8.7.4   Administrative Review and Appeal Mechanisms

The IQA states that the agencies shall develop a process that allows "affected persons" to file complaints about the quality of information. OMB's guidelines require each agency to "establish administrative mechanisms allowing affected persons to seek and obtain, where appropriate, timely correction of information main-tained and disseminated by the agency that does not comply with OMB or agency guidelines." "The focus of the complaint process should be on the merits of the complaint, not on the possible interests or qualifications of the complainant."[213] "OMB originally opined that 'affected persons' should be defined as 'people who may benefit or be harmed by the disseminated information.'" The guide-lines also direct agencies to establish "appropriate time periods" for decisions on whether and how to correct the information, and to reconsider the issue if the complainant sought reconsideration of the agency's initial decision. OMB also decided that, while the substan-tive data quality standards were to continue to apply to an agency's dissemination of information, an agency could meld the IQA com-plaint procedures with other public notice statutes.[214]

211. As OMB stated: "It is not OMB's intent that each agency must re-produce each analytic result before it is disseminated." 67 Fed. Reg. at 8456/2.

212. OMB Guidelines, *supra* note 185, § III.3. "To be consistent with the OMB guidelines," OMB directed each agency to "explicitly refer complainants to all of the applicable guidelines—the OMB, department, and departmental component's guidelines—as the applica-ble information quality standards." Memorandum for President's Manage-ment Council from John D. Graham

(June 10, 2002), at 11. For a general discussion of the complaint and appeal process, *see* 66 Fed. Reg. at 49718, 49721/1–3, 67 Fed. Reg. at 8458/1–2, and June 10 Memo, *supra*, at 12.

213. June 10 Memo, *supra*, note 212, at 11.

214. The IQA's concerns with data quality should be compared with efforts to improve regulatory science through a "Regulatory *Daubert*" approach. *See* Symposium, 66 Law & Contemp–Probs. 1 (2003).

Chapter Nine

FAIRNESS AND POLITICAL ACCOUNTABILITY

§ 9.1 The Relationship Between Fairness and Political Accountability

Two of the most important concepts of government legitimacy concern "fairness" and "political accountability." Fairness emanates from the Due Process Clause; it is an inherently individualistic, process-oriented idea. Political accountability is a concept which springs from the nature of our democracy. Accountability of actors in the political setting, be they elected officials or bureaucrats, is a matter that can be legal but is ultimately controlled by the public remedy of the ballot. Political accountability is thus an inherently collective, substance-oriented idea.

In the administrative process, the two concepts are intertwined. Administrative law has been called a "surrogate political process",[1] which means administrative decisionmakers must respect both concepts. This has led to overlap and occasional merger of the two ideas. Obligations of fairness are seen as alternatives and supplements to political accountability as a method of bureaucratic control. Similarly, political accountability has come to include an obligation to be fair in the administration of government.

Despite these connections, the proper nature of the relationship between fairness and political accountability is not easily defined. Professor Ely understood the relationship to consist of those judicially-imposed mechanisms that are necessary to make the political system work.[2] Professor Tribe goes further and even postulates a "due process of lawmaking."[3] Still, it is difficult to see how the concept of fairness can be transferred wholesale into the political process. In a democracy, the unrestrained use of due process by unelected judges to strike down legislation or regulation[4] is decidedly

1. Stewart, *The Reformation of American Administrative Law,* 88 Harv. L. Rev. 1667, 1670 (1975).

2. J. Ely, Democracy and Distrust 181 (1983).

3. *See* L. Tribe, *American Constitutional Law* § 17–3 (2d ed. 1988) (explaining due process of lawmaking and law applying).

4. *See, e.g.,* Lochner v. New York, 198 U.S. 45 (1905). *Cf.* Sunstein, *Free Mar-*

inferior to political accountability as a method of bureaucratic control.

Administrative law has not yet worked out a comfortable relationship between fairness and political accountability. In the sections that follow, certain statutory, constitutional and executive formulae are examined that all have as their purpose the assurance of fairness or accountability in the political process. In each instance, however, the question arises whether the particular bureaucratic control device offered frustrates or enhances the goals sought. Ultimately, the inquiry becomes whether the processes designed to ensure fairness are transferable to settings that rely for their legitimacy upon more general notions of political responsiveness. Fairness principles must be modified when they contradict efforts to make the bureaucracy more politically accountable. It is in this sense that the *Chevron* doctrine,[5] which divides power between the "political" and judicial branches, seeks an accommodation between the two concepts.

§ 9.2   The Requirement of a Neutral Decision–Maker

As a general proposition, there can hardly be a more important component of fair procedure than the requirement that the decider be neutral or unbiased towards the parties and the issues before him or her.[6] The proposition that no person should be the judge in his or her own cause has been an integral part of natural justice in England since the Seventeenth Century and it is a basic underpinning of the concept of separation of powers.[7] Nevertheless, the concept of decider neutrality remains one of the most complex aspects of administrative practice.[8]

§ 9.2.1   Neutrality as a due process imperative

Although neutrality is viewed as a due process imperative, the exact obligations it creates are unclear. For example, a decisionmaker is clearly prohibited from having a direct or indirect financial interest in a proceeding.[9] The presence of such an interest violates the

---

kets and Social Justice, 240 (1997) (arguing that the Supreme Court's decision in *Buckley v. Valeo* invalidating aspects of campaign financing reform "is the modern analogue to the discredited case of *Lochner* ... ").

5. *See* supra § 7.4

6. *See* Friendly, *Some Kind of Hearing,* 123 U.Pa.L.Rev. 1267 (1975) (listing impartial decisionmaker at the top of a

hierarchy of procedural ingredients). *See supra* § 6.3.

7. *See supra* § 2.1.2.

8. *See* Arnett v. Kennedy, 416 U.S. 134 (1974) (White, J. concurring and dissenting); Van Alstyne, *Cracks in "The New Property": Adjudicative Due Process in the Administrative State,* 62 Corn. L.Rev. 445, 461 (1977).

9. Thus arrangements that allow judicial officials to benefit from the fines

concept of due process because it denies those who are regulated the right to a fair hearing.[10] However, the protection is not absolute. Officials who merely administer a statutory scheme, whereby penalties assessed reimburse the agency for the costs of administration, are not impermissibly biased in a due process sense as long as their actions can be said to be more prosecutorial than judicial.[11]

The right to a fair hearing is also denied where an administrator can be shown to have pre-judged the issues that will be litigated during a hearing.[12] But this protection is also not absolute. For example, the courts have largely rejected claims that pre-judgment results from an administrator performing both investigative and judicial functions.[13] Nevertheless, the matter is not free from doubt.[14] In *Goldberg v. Kelly,* the Supreme Court implied that separation of the investigative and decision functions in the welfare setting could be mandated as an aspect of due process.[15]

The obligations of decider neutrality concerning prejudgment are also complex because two situations must be distinguished. If a decisionmaker has actually pre-judged an issue, the person should be disqualified from any ruling concerning it. Often, however, decisionmakers will have reached judgments about issues without having closed their mind to other points of view. In fact, it would be unusual for judges and policy-makers not to have thought about issues that are involved in their jobs and to have reached some judgments concerning them. Thus, an appropriate standard by which prejudgment is determined must distinguish between these two situations which may involve the distinction between rulemaking and adjudica-

---

they impose are forbidden. *See* Ward v. Village of Monroeville, 409 U.S. 57 (1972); Tumey v. Ohio, 273 U.S. 510 (1927).

10. *See* Gibson v. Berryhill, 411 U.S. 564 (1973); *but see* Friedman v. Rogers, 440 U.S. 1, 18–19 (1979) (plaintiff must show bias in actual proceedings not just one-sided composition of board members).

11. *See* Marshall v. Jerrico, Inc., 446 U.S. 238 (1980) (interpreting § 16(e) of the Fair Labor Standards Act, imposing penalties for employing child labor).

12. *See* Texaco, Inc. v. F.T.C., 336 F.2d 754 (D.C.Cir.1964), vacated and remanded on other issues, 381 U.S. 739 (1965).

13. *See* Withrow v. Larkin, 421 U.S. 35 (1975).

14. *See* Wong Yang Sung v. McGrath, 339 U.S. 33 (1950); Hortonville Joint School Dist. No. 1 v. Hortonville Educ. Ass'n, 426 U.S. 482 (1976) (dissenting opinion).

15. 397 U.S. 254 (1970). In *Goldberg* the Court stated: "We agree with the District Court that prior involvement in some aspects of a case will not necessarily bar a welfare official from acting as a decisionmaker. He should not, however, have participated in making the determination under review."

tion.[16]

In *Laird v. Tatum,* Justice Rehnquist considered whether Supreme Court Justices should recuse themselves from hearing a case because of previous statements concerning some legal issue that it involved. Judicial standards of disqualification urge recusal where personal bias exists or where impartiality is in question.[17] In rejecting a challenge to his impartiality based on previous congressional testimony on constitutional issues then before the Court, Justice Rehnquist articulated the principles he thought should apply in that type of situation. Justice Rehnquist was careful to note that "[p]roof that a Justice's mind was a *tabula rasa* in the area of constitutional adjudication would be evidence of lack of qualifications, not lack of bias."[18]

In the Supreme Court, the decision whether a Justice should disqualify himself or herself is discretionary and unreviewable.[19] This proposition does not carry over to deciders in the administrative setting. As a result, the rules of decider neutrality at the agency level, even though more explicit, have caused considerable litigation and confusion.

§ 9.2.2   Neutrality under the APA

Section 556(b) of the APA requires decisionmakers in formal adjudication or formal rulemaking to conduct hearings in an "impartial manner" and it provides:

> A presiding or participating employee may at any time disqualify himself. On the filing in good faith of a timely and sufficient affidavit of personal bias or other disqualification of a presiding or participating employee, the agency shall determine the matters as a part of the record and decision in the case.

This impartiality requirement has been applied to agency commissioners and ALJs. Testifying before Congress on matters in litiga-

---

16. For example, provisions of the APA which deal with matters like separation of functions between prosecutors and ALJs apply to formal adjudication, but not to rulemaking. See 4 U.S.C. § 554.

17. *See* 28 U.S.C. §§ 144, 455; Note, *Disqualification of Federal Judges for Bias or Prejudice,* 46 Chi. L. Rev. 236 (1978).

18. Laird v. Tatum, 409 U.S. 824, 901 (1972).

19. Justice Scalia has felt political heat for his now famous duck hunting venture with Vice President Cheney while a case involving the Vice President was pending before the Court. *See Scalia, Cheney Duck Hunt While Energy Case Is Pending,* L.A. Times, Jan. 17, 2004; Cheney v. United States Dist. Court, 541 U.S. ___, 124 S.Ct. 1391 (2004) (memorandum of Scalia, J.), which concludes, based on a historical review of related situations, there is no

tion can be a perilous venture, as one FTC commissioner learned,[20] as can giving speeches before industry groups, as another FTC commissioner later came to regret.[21] In both instances, the commissioners were charged by litigants with prejudgment because of the statements that were made. The critical inquiry in these cases was whether the issue involved prejudgment of broad policy matters or of specific facts.[22] The courts disqualified the commissioners in question only in the latter situation.

The distinction drawn by the courts between judgments concerning broad policy matters or specific facts reflects the same concern expressed by Justice Rehnquist. Administrators should not be expected to have a mind that is a *"tabula rasa"* in the substantive areas in which they regulate. In fact, as noted in Chapter 4, administrators are often chosen precisely because of the views concerning certain policy questions. Nevertheless, a litigant ought to have the opportunity to attempt to change the mind of the administrator. Thus, the courts require that an administrator not reach a decision prior to a proceeding concerning whether a particular party has violated some statutory responsibility. If such a judgment has been made concerning the facts of a given case, the courts will hold that an unacceptable prejudgment has occurred.

Occasionally, the bias or prejudgment charges are asserted against all or a majority of commissioners. In this case, a situation of decisional necessity may make it imperative that the offending members participate in the process if there is to be any decision at all.[23] At some point, the doctrine of necessity must yield to the demands of due process and a proceeding before a manifestly closed-minded decisional body will have to be dismissed rather than continued.[24]

In many of these cases, however, the respondent's actual objection may go more to the organization of independent commissions

impartiality issue and that recusal would "harm the court."

20. *See* Pillsbury Co. v. FTC, 354 F.2d 952 (5th Cir.1966).

21. *See* Texaco, Inc. v. FTC, 336 F.2d 754 (D.C.Cir.1964), vacated and remanded on different issues, 381 U.S. 739 (1965). *See also* Kennecott Copper Corp. v. FTC, 467 F.2d 67 (10th Cir.1972) (rejecting bias charge against commissioner who publicly explained theory of FTC complaints).

22. *See* Koch, *Prejudgment: An Unavailable Challenge to Official Administrative Action*, 33 Fed. Bar J. 218 (1974).

23. *See* FTC v. Cement Institute, 333 U.S. 683 (1948); Ash Grove Cement Co. v. FTC, 577 F.2d 1368 (9th Cir.), *cert. denied*, 439 U.S. 982 (1978).

24. The doctrine of necessity can be avoided if another body can be found to render the decision. *See* International Harvester Co. v. Bowling, 72 Ill.App.3d 910, 29 Ill.Dec. 9, 391 N.E.2d 168 (1979). This is not possible of course with decisions by federal independent commissions like the FTC.

than to the specific issues at hand. By combining in one entity the authority to issue, investigate, and adjudicate complaints, agencies depart from the traditional mode of judicial decisionmaking and are often criticized on that basis. But once this form of administrative process received judicial legitimization and acceptance, that kind of objection ceased to be controlling. Prejudgment charges in this context are often seen as the product more of "dilatory tactics" than genuine grievances.[25]

The APA further enhances neutrality of ALJs by leaving to the Office of Personnel Management matters having to do with their appointment and compensation and by providing for separation of functions and insulation from ex parte contacts, which are discussed in the next section. The independence of judgment of ALJs is also ensured by protecting them from removal by the agency except where "good cause" is established.[26] This determination is made by the Merit Systems Protection Board only after formal APA adjudication.[27]

§ 9.2.3   Neutrality in informal adjudication: The ALJ's "three-hat" role

These protections do not mean that the ALJ cannot serve multiple roles in the informal decision process, as the "three hat" assignment in social security disability proceedings indicates. Even though presided over by an ALJ, social security disability hearings are informal since the formal adjudication provisions of the APA do not apply. In fact, these hearings are called "non-adversary."[28] In *Richardson v. Perales*[29] the Court considered whether requiring the ALJ in effect to represent the government, to represent the claimant, and to act as impartial decider resulted in a violation of due process. In concluding that multiple roles were permissible in this mass justice setting, the Court acknowledged that the clearly defined roles con-

---

25. Grolier Inc. v. FTC, 699 F.2d 983, 987 (9th Cir.1983). The *Grolier* court rejected a bias charge against an ALJ who had earlier been an attorney-advisor to an FTC Commissioner, after permitting affidavits to be filed on the issue. It refused to grant respondent's delaying request for discovery on the matter of the ALJ's prior knowledge of the case.

26. *See* Ramspeck v. Federal Trial Examiners Conf., 345 U.S. 128 (1953); Benton v. United States, 488 F.2d 1017 (Ct.Cl.1973).

27. 5 U.S.C. § 7521.

28. *See* Bloch, Lubbers & Verkuil, *Developing A Full And Fair Evidentiary Record In A Nonadversay Setting: Two Proposals For Improving Social Security Disability Adjudications*, 25 Car. L. Rev. I (2003).

29. 402 U.S. 389, 410 (1971) (the Court permitted multiple roles as a matter of necessity in disability decisionmaking, but emphasized that the ALJ does not "act as counsel" for the government).

templated by the adversary model could not define due process in all adjudicatory contexts. Subsequent cases have interpreted *Perales* not only to permit the multiple role assumed by Social Security ALJs, but to require it as a component of due process in cases where the claimant is unrepresented.[30] One problem with using a nonadversary, three-hat model is that the presence of claimants' representatives can imbalance the decider's role. In the SSA disability situation, claimants now have representatives in about 70 percent of all cases.[31] Since the right to counsel is assumed even in informal adjudications, the ALJ must now often balance what amounts to two-hats, that of impartial decider and representative of the government's interests. ALJs are uncomfortable with this imbalanced role and prefer to be seen exclusively as neutral deciders. This has led to suggestions that the government be separately represented which would free the ALJ to be a more passive, if not more objective, decider. Of course, the value of nonadversariness, or informality, would have to be jettisoned in the process. And in any event, the three-hat role of the ALJ would be still preserved in those situations where the claimant was not represented.[32]

§ 9.2.4 The special problem of decision quotas and reversal rates

The social security disability system has monumental decisional burdens placed upon it. The Social Security Administration (SSA) must manage the output of more than 1,200 ALJs and over 500,000 cases.[33] In the 1980s, SSA resorted to a system of decision quotas in order to manage the dockets of ALJs. The ALJs argued that their neutrality was threatened by these requirements and by related SSA management control techniques which selectively reviewed decisions of ALJs who decide in favor of a claimant in more than 50% of their cases.[34] Selectively reviewing judges with high allowance rates is a controversial practice that the SSA has since abandoned.

---

30. In Lashley v. Secretary of Health & Human Services, 708 F.2d 1048, 1052 (6th Cir.1983), the court held that "the ALJ's failure to fulfill his duty to develop *fully* the record denied Lashley a full and fair hearing." *Accord* Broz v. Schweiker, 677 F.2d 1351, 1364 (11th Cir.1982) (ALJ has a "duty of inquiry"); McConnell v. Schweiker, 655 F.2d 604 (5th Cir.1981); Smith v. Harris, 644 F.2d 985 (3d Cir. 1981). *See also* Heckler v. Campbell, 461 U.S. 458 (1983) (Brennan, J. concurring).

31. *See* Bloch, Lubbers & Verkuil, *supra* note 28 at 6.

32. *See id.* at 59–62 (proposing a nonadversarial counselor position rather than a government attorney).

33. Social Security Administration, Office of Hearings and Appeals, *Key Workload Indicators* (Fiscal Year 2002), at 1.

34. *See* J. Mashaw, Bureaucratic Justice (1983); Senate Comm. on Governmental Affairs, The Role of the Adminis-

Productivity rates also raise possible due process concerns. A work load of better than two hearings and decisions per working day (it takes about 20 days to complete the required 45 cases) may be feasible; apparently most ALJs were able to meet or better that standard. But at some point the requirement that ALJs fully develop the record at hearing, which has achieved due process recognition,[35] will come into conflict with the case-load burden imposed by the agency. When the values of fairness and efficiency clash, the courts will seek a resolution under the balancing approach to due process used in *Mathews v. Eldridge*.[36] The SSA currently does not engage in selective review of ALJs or set decision quotas.[37]

The SSA's management techniques stimulated a reassessment of the status and organization of ALJs.[38] In 1992, the Administrative Conference of the United States (ACUS) adopted a recommendation that attempted to balance the need to protect the independence of ALJs as fact-finders and the legitimate interest of agencies in the management of their employees, including ALJs.[39] ACUS recommended that agencies appoint a chief ALJ who would develop case processing guidelines in conjunction with other agency ALJs, agency managers, and others. The Chief ALJ would then evaluate an ALJ's performance based on these guidelines along with other factors, including judicial comportment and demeanor. Based on the review, the Chief ALJ would provide appropriate professional guidance to ALJs, including reprimands if necessary.

§ 9.2.4   Neutrality in the rulemaking setting

As was discussed earlier, agency officials have been criticized for prejudgment of factual issues in speeches or testimony before Con-

---

trative Law Judge in the Title II Social Security Disability Program, 98th Cong., 1st Sess. (1983). The selective review of allowance rates is undertaken pursuant to Social Security Disability Amendments of 1980, P.L. 96–265, 42 U.S.C. § 1305, which requires SSA on its motion to review ALJ decisions. SSA required 27 case dispositions per month in 1979 and raised it to 45 in 1983. SSA has also proceeded before the Merit Systems Protection Board to dismiss for "good cause" those ALJs whose productivity fall below 20 cases per month. *Id.* at 2, 21.

35. *See supra* note 29.

36. 424 U.S. 319 (1976); *see supra* § 6.3.4.

37. *See* Bloch, Lubbers & Verkuil, *supra* note 28, at 28–30.

38. *See* Koch, *Administrative Presiding Officials Today*, 46 Admin. L. Rev. 271 (1994); Verkuil, *Reflections upon the Federal Administrative Judiciary*, 39 U.C.L.A. L. Rev. 1341 (1992); Simeone, *The Function, Flexibility and Future of United States Judges of the Executive Department*, 44 Admin. L. Rev. 159 (1992).

39. Administrative Conference of the United States, 1992 Recommendations and Reports 35–37, 41.

gress. Those cases involved agency adjudication. The same kind of prejudgment neutrality should not be expected of commissioners when the discussions questioned revolve around matters to be resolved in rulemaking proceedings.[40] Rulemaking requires agency heads affirmatively to collect information and ventilate views concerning appropriate standards of behavior in any given industry or activity. Rulemaking is also characterized by different procedural rules for the collection of information than is adjudication.

In *Association of National Advertisers (ANA) v. FTC,* the differences between rulemaking and adjudication were a critical distinction for the court, which held, by divided vote, that the statements of Chairman Perschuk, indicating strong views on the need for regulating television advertising aimed at children, did not disqualify him from participating in a rulemaking proceeding on that subject.[41] Judge Tamm, for the majority in *ANA,* limited disqualification in rulemaking to those situations where "there has been a clear and convincing showing that [the decider] has an unalterably closed mind on matters critical to the disposition of the proceeding."[42]

The APA disqualification requirements of section 556(b) do not apply to informal rulemaking and no agency has adopted disqualification regulations for factual prejudgment, as opposed to conflicts of interest.[43] After careful study, the Administrative Conference has recommended adoption of the "closed mind" standard for disqualification advocated by the *ANA* court.[44] The fact that this test appears difficult to surmount is appropriate. It serves as recognition of the legislative nature of the rulemaking process and it brings to mind Justice Holmes' proposition in *Bi–Metallic* that in such matters it is primarily to the political process that one must turn for relief.[45]

40. *See supra* § 3.6., *infra* § 9.3.2. *See, e.g.,* Cinderella Career & Finishing Schools, Inc. v. FTC, 425 F.2d 583 (D.C.Cir.1970).

41. 627 F.2d 1151 (D.C.Cir.1979), *cert. denied,* 447 U.S. 921 (1980). The district court had concluded that since prejudgment in the adjudicatory context would be disqualifying, and since the FTC conducted rulemaking pursuant to the adversary procedures of the Magnuson–Moss Act, the decider impartiality standards of adjudication should apply to FTC rulemaking. ANA v. FTC, 460 F.Supp. 996 (D.D.C.1978) (Gesell, J.).

42. 627 F.2d at 1181. Judge MacKinnon, in dissent, argued that disqualifying partiality could be established by a preponderant showing of substantial prejudgment on any critical fact. *Id.* at 1183.

43. *See* Strauss, *Disqualifications of Decisional Officials in Rulemaking,* 80 Colum. L. Rev. 990, 1027 (1980).

44. *See* ACUS Rec. 80–4, 1 C.F.R. § 305.80–4 (also describing disqualifications rules for conflicts of interest in rulemaking). The recommendation is based on Strauss, *supra* note 43.

45. *See* Bi–Metallic Investment Co. v. State Bd. of Equalization, 239 U.S. 441, 445 (1915).

Thus, different standards for disqualification are in effect another distinction between the procedures required for agency rulemaking and adjudication.[46]

The judicial standards of disqualification developed for adjudication and rulemaking indicate a different balance has been struck concerning the relationship of fairness and political accountability in each instance. Fairness requirements need not be applied equally to adjudication and rulemaking because political accountability is likely to be a more appropriate and more effective method of agency oversight in the latter type of proceeding. For example, the process of regulatory analysis, which has as one of its purposes political accountability,[47] is available to bring agency rulemaking under the supervision of the White House. Such techniques would be unavailable in connection with adjudicatory matters because they would involve inappropriate ex parte contacts, as will be explained in the next section. Moreover, agency officials, who discuss their views on the proper resolution of a rulemaking proceeding, do not pre-judge matters in the same sense as they would in a discussion concerning the outcome of a specific adjudicatory decision. They are not deciding whether an individual party has violated some statutory standard. Instead, they are discussing whether a rule would serve the purposes for which a statutory standard was created. Although the latter judgment includes an assessment concerning the effect of the rule on the persons who would be regulated, the judgments are being reached for a purpose different than the type of factual assessment that occurs in the context of adjudication. For these reasons, rulemaking is properly recognized to be a part of the political process, even though it is conducted in the administrative setting.

§ 9.3   The Problems of Ex Parte Contacts

Fairness and political accountability are both directly implicated when bureaucratic decisionmakers are importuned on an ex parte basis about matters before them. In judicial proceedings, approaches by counsel or parties to the judge before whom a matter is pending, without notice to the other side, have long been forbidden. In administrative proceedings, ex parte contacts likewise can be forbidden, but the scope and application of such rules are complicated by the distinction between rulemaking and adjudication and by the nature of the person seeking to make the private contact.

46. *See* Linde, *Due Process of Lawmaking,* 55 Neb. L. Rev. 197, 229 (1976) (questioning whether administrative officials should have the same scope of political discretion as legislators because of their duty to render a rational decision).

47. *See infra* § 9.5.

§ 9.3.1 The APA restrictions

Since its enactment in 1946, section 554(d)(1) of the APA has forbidden ALJs to "consult a person or party on a fact in issue, unless on notice and opportunity for all parties to participate". This restriction, narrowly drawn to relate only to facts in issue in formal adjudication, was expanded by amendment in 1976 in several respects.[48] The subject matter of the contact was defined more broadly as "ex parte communication relevant to the merits of the proceeding". A process was established to put in the public record any improper written communications and the substance of any oral communications. Sanctions, including dismissal of the proceedings, were created. Finally these provisions, by virtue of being placed in section 557, were made applicable to formal rulemaking, as well as formal adjudication.

The Federal Labor Relations Board ran afoul of the APA restrictions in *Professional Air Traffic Controllers Organization (PATCO) v. Federal Labor Relations Authority*.[49] The Board revoked recognition of PATCO as a union for air traffic controllers after it called a nationwide strike against the Federal Aviation Administration. Board members had received ex parte contacts, including one by Albert Shanker, president of a teachers' union, who urged a board member not to punish PATCO severely for its actions. The Court held that Shanker's communication (and others) came within the APA prohibition of ex parte contacts from an "interested person," which it defined as " 'any individual ... with an interest in a proceeding that is greater than the interest the public as a whole may have.' " Nevertheless, the court declined to void the Board's decision because the ex parte communications did not so "irrevocably taint" the decisionmakers that their "judgment was unfair, either to an innocent party or the public interest that the agency was obligated to protect." The court considered the gravity of the communications and whether the Board's ultimate judgment was influenced, a party benefited from improper contracts, the contents of the communications were known to opposing parties, and a remand for a new proceeding would serve a useful purpose. Among other reasons, the court did not void the decision because of Shanker's communication because the Board's ruling was adverse to PATCO, whose interests Shanker championed.

---

48. *See* Sunshine Act Amendments of 1976, Pub. L. No. 94–409, § 4, 90 Stat. 1241 (1976).

49. 685 F.2d 547 (D.C.Cir. 1982).

The definition of "interested person" was also at issue in *Portland Audubon Society v. The Endangered Species Committee*,[50] which concerned a formal adjudication under the Endangered Species Act. The Act prohibits a federal agency from taking any action that would jeopardize a species that has been listed as endangered unless it obtains an exemption from a high-level seven member committee, whose members include the Secretary of the Departments of Interior and Agriculture and the Environmental Protection Agency (EPA) administrator. After the Committee by a 5–2 vote granted an exemption for timber sales in Oregon that threatened the Northern Spotted Owl, an environmental group alleged on appeal that some committee members received ex parte communications from a representative of the President. The court rejected the government's argument that the President was not an "interested person" within the meaning of the APA prohibition. Among other reasons, the court noted that the government's position would "destroy the integrity of all federal agency adjudications" because it would permit the President to influence formal adjudication. The decision was remanded to the committee with an order to hold, with the assistance of an ALJ, a hearing to determine the nature and extent of the ex parte contacts.

Both of these cases were of considerable political interest and importance at the time that they were decided. Nevertheless, because Congress required formal adjudication, the APA banned lobbying by representatives of interest groups, as in the PATCO case, or by presidential aides, as in the Spotted Owl case. This may reduce political input and accountability, but it preserves the fairness of the adjudication, by helping to ensure that decisionmakers take into account only the evidence and arguments presented in the hearing process. If Congress wants to open a process to such political intervention, it can do so by refusing to require that an agency use formal adjudication. As you will read next, the APA permits ex parte communications in informal rulemaking, which facilitates political input and accountability.

§ 9.3.2 Ex parte contacts and informal rulemaking

Informal rulemaking is unbounded by APA ex parte contact constraints and for many years the practice has been for participants in rulemaking proceedings privately to approach members of the agency before, during, and after the notice and comment period. In effect, participants and agencies treated rulemaking proceedings like the legislative process, where lobbyists approach members of Con-

---

50.   984 F.2d 1534 (9th Cir. 1993).

gress without restrictions. Since there are no parties in rulemaking, only public participants, it is understandable that the *ex parte* concept might be thought to be applicable only to adjudication.

Occasionally, the courts have imposed restraints upon private contacts when a rulemaking proceeding functionally resembled adjudication or licensing. In *Sangamon Valley Television Corp. v. United States*, the court forbid ex parte contacts in a rulemaking proceeding in which the Federal Communications Commission (FCC) chose the method by which UHF and VHF television licenses would be transferred.[51] The court concluded that, despite the format of the proceeding, "basic fairness requires such a proceeding to be carried on in the open". The court was influenced to extend the ex parte prohibition to this type of rulemaking because it resolved "competing claims to a valuable privilege".

Sangamon Valley's special facts limited its application to rulemaking proceedings that had a similar effect of allocating valuable privileges. In *Home Box Office (HBO) v. FCC*, however, the prohibition was extended.[52] The rulemaking proceeding in *HBO* involved the revision of pay cable television rules. Almost all of the participants appeared to have made separate and numerous approaches to the FCC commissioners. In remanding the rule to the FCC to determine the effect of those contacts on the propriety of the rulemaking proceeding, the District of Columbia Circuit drew some hard lines:

> Once a notice of proposed rulemaking has been issued ... any agency official or employee who is or may reasonably be expected to be involved in the decisional process of the rulemaking proceeding should "refus[e] to discuss matters relating to the disposition of a [rulemaking proceeding] with any interested private party, or an attorney or agent for any such party, prior to the [agency's] decision.... " If *ex parte* contacts nonetheless occur, we think that any written document or a summary of oral communication must be placed in the public file established for each rulemaking docket immediately after the communication is received so that interested parties may comment thereon....

In the panel opinion, Judge Wright supported the decision with references to due process interests and other statutory provisions, including the 1976 APA amendments, but he ultimately based the court's reasoning on the necessity that an agency establish a com-

51. 269 F.2d 221 (D.C.Cir.1959). Among the ex parte contacts recorded were personal meetings with members of the FCC and dinners and Christmas tur- keys provided by the president of one of the stations to the commissioners.

52. 567 F.2d 9 (D.C.Cir.), *cert. denied*, 434 U.S. 829 (1977).

plete record, including any ex parte contacts, for purposes of judicial review.

A short time later, another panel in the District of Columbia Circuit decided *Action For Children's Television (ACT) v. FCC,* which held that an ex parte prohibition applied only to rulemaking proceedings that involved "competing claims to a valuable privilege".[53] The panel, however, refused to rest its holding on a flat disagreement with *HBO* and instead expressly held "only that *Home Box Office's* broad proscription is not to be applied retroactively in the case *sub judice* as it constitutes a clear departure from established law".

The court explained that the problem of whether to prohibit ex parte contacts is "obviously a matter of degree and the appropriate line must be drawn somewhere". The court recognized that the determination of whether a rulemaking proceeding involved the allocation of a "valuable privilege" would be difficult,[54] but it thought that it was the correct standard nevertheless. The court favored that line because "[i]t is at that point where the potential for unfair advantage outweighs the practical burdens, which we imagine would not be insubstantial, that such a judicially-conceived rule would place on administrators". The panel explained that it was leery of creating a prohibition, like that of *HBO,* that would require a rulemaking record that "reflect[ed] every informational input that may have entered into the decisionmaker's deliberative process."

In *United States Lines, Inc. v. FMC,* the District of Columbia Circuit extended the ex parte contacts prohibition to one type of informal adjudication.[55] The case concerned an order of the Federal Maritime Commission (FMC) that granted an exemption from the antitrust laws for an agreement between ocean shipping carriers. The Commission's enabling act specified that it was to issue such an order only "after notice and hearing". Nevertheless, the court agreed with the FMC that it was not required to hold a trial-type hearing, complete with the procedures mandated by sections 556 and 557 of the APA, because "nothing in the terms of the statute or its legislative history indicates that a trial-type hearing . . . was intended. . . . "

Although no formal hearing was required, the court held that the ex parte contacts that had occurred should not have been allowed for

53. 564 F.2d 458 (D.C.Cir.1977). In *ACT,* the rule involved restrictions upon children's advertising, a manifestly non-valuable privilege context.

54. *See* Robinson, *The Federal Communications Commission: An Essay on*

Regulatory Watchdogs, 64 Va.L.Rev. 169, 227–30 (1978) (questioning whether even the pay cable rules in *HBO* involve a valuable privilege).

55. 584 F.2d 519 (D.C.Cir.1978) (Wright, J.).

two reasons. First, the court thought that such contacts were inconsistent with the FMC's statutory obligation to hold a hearing because "[t]he public right to participate in such a hearing ... is effectively nullified when the agency decision is based not on submissions and information known and available to all, but rather on the private conversations and secret points and arguments to which the public and participating parties have no access". Second, the court thought that such contacts "also foreclose effective judicial review of the agency's final decision according to the arbitrary and capricious test of the Administrative Procedure Act." The court quoted its concern in *HBO* that judicial review could not be effective if the reviewing court did not have all of the important arguments considered by an agency in making its decision.

In *Sierra Club v. Costle,* another panel of the District of Columbia Circuit attempted to summarize the effect of the previous decisions.[56] Reacting to claims that the Environmental Protection Agency had received ex parte contacts after the close of the comment period for a rulemaking proceeding, Judge Wald read the previous precedent to mean that "[w]here agency action resembles judicial action, where it involves formal rulemaking, adjudication, or quasi-adjudication among 'conflicting private claims to a valuable privilege,' the insulation of the decisionmaker from ex parte contacts is justified by basic notions of due process to the parties involved." Judge Wald noted, however, that "where agency action involves informal rulemaking of a policymaking sort, the concept of ex parte contacts is of more questionable utility." As a result, the court declined to extend the decision in *HBO* to cover all meetings during the post-comment period. Judge Wald explained that "[l]ater decisions of this court ... have declined to apply *Home Box Office* to informal rulemaking of the policymaking sort involved here, and there is no precedent for applying it to the procedures found in the Clean Air Act Amendments of 1977."

Despite the previous holding, the court did not think that EPA was entirely free to engage in ex parte contacts. The panel required EPA to place in the rulemaking record an adequate summary of all post-comment conversations and meetings that were of "central relevance" to the disposition of its proceeding. EPA was required to take this step because the Clean Air Act provided that the rulemaking docket was to be the sole repository of material upon which EPA relied to issue a rule. Judge Wald explained that unless "oral communications of central relevance to the rulemaking are also docketed in

56.   657 F.2d 298 (D.C.Cir.1981).

some fashion or other, information central to the justification of the rule could be obtained without ever appearing on the docket, simply by communicating it by voice rather than by pen, thereby frustrating the command of [the statute] that the final rule not be 'based (in whole or in part) on any information or data which has not been placed in the docket. . . . ' "

Although the indeterminate status of ex parte contacts in informal rulemaking initially created considerable confusion at agencies, some agencies reacted to *HBO* by promulgating regulations restricting ex parte contacts in the informal rulemaking setting.[57] Judging from this reaction, it might be concluded that agencies find the insulation offered by such restrictions to be a good thing. While such contacts will undoubtedly still occur during the pre-rulemaking period, commissioners and their staffs are at least freed from time-consuming, and often unproductive, meetings, during and after the comment period. In this way, *HBO* has had a positive effect on the informal administrative process. But the total elimination of ex parte contracts in the informal setting is not necessarily a good idea even if it could be achieved. Informed observers have persuasively argued that private meetings with the interested public can be as important to bureaucrats, as they are to members of Congress, or the executive branch.[58]

The disposition in *Sierra Club* offers a useful policy compromise between these two positions. An agency could be required to place a summary of all ex parte contacts of central relevance to the disposition of an informal proceeding in a record of that proceeding. This solution would have two advantages. First, it would allow such contacts to occur and an agency therefore could obtain whatever advantages would result from them. Second, it would ensure that a reviewing court had a complete record from which the court could determine whether the agency's actions were arbitrary and capricious. Finally, as the D.C. Circuit noted in *Air Transport Ass'n v. FAA*,[59] the important point is whether "*ex parte* material were to lead to an unanticipatable change in the final rule."

---

57. *See, e.g.,* 16 C.F.R. § 4.7 (FTC rules); 47 C.F.R. §§ 1.1201–13 (FCC rules); *see also* ACUS Rec. 77–3 (1977), 1 C.F.R. § 305.77–3 (rejecting a general prohibition against ex parte contacts in informal rulemaking, but suggesting agency experimentation with disclosure of significant oral or written information received outside the comment process).

58. *See* Robinson, *supra* note 54, at 228–30. It is virtually impossible to insulate commissioners from pre-rulemaking contacts unless one is prepared to isolate them from all members of the industry they regulate, which would of course reduce their effectiveness in other ways.

59. 161 F. 3d 1, 18 n.5 (D.C. Cir. 1999). The Court also queried whether HBO was "undermined" by *Vermont*

§ 9.3.3   Ex parte contacts by the White House

A distinction should be drawn between contacts between decisionmakers and private parties outside government and contacts between decisionmakers and officials from other branches of government. The issue arises because the last three Presidents have sought to oversee the rulemaking practices of federal agencies to control the burden of regulations upon the public. The technique for policy control has been to give the Office of Management and Budget (OMB) and other members of the White House staff unprecedented powers under executive orders to mediate, modify and approve major agency rules.[60] In exercising this power, OMB and other officials have engaged in post-comment contacts with agency officials who are assigned to draft rules.

OMB contacts and communications have led some to raise objections based upon the ex parte contact precepts of *HBO*.[61] The concern with off-the-record consultation by White House officials is based upon the potential such contacts have to introduce political factors into the rulemaking process which are not reflected in the rulemaking record. One presidential response to these concerns has been to exempt independent agencies from such controls.[62] Another has been to accept the fact that rulemaking is itself a political process and to adopt procedures that regulate contacts between the White House, agency staffs and outside parties without expressly forbidding them.[63]

In *Sierra Club v. Costle*[64] the D.C. Circuit considered the question of White House involvement in an EPA rulemaking proceeding to set national standards for coal dust emissions from power plants. The court accepted the fact that contacts between agency and White House staffs occurred throughout the rulemaking process, but it did not believe it was necessary to forbid all such contacts in order to

---

Yankee (*See* § 6.4.9) a result that should obtain only if *HBO* was interpreted as adding procedures to APA § 553 informal rulemaking by forbidding ex parte contacts at the outset of rulemaking.

60. For a description and discussion of these efforts, *see infra* § 9.5.2.

61. *See* ABA Comm. on Law and the Economy, Federal Regulation: Roads to Reform 157 (1979) (statement of William T. Coleman, Jr.); Morrison, *Presidential Intervention in Informal Rulemaking: Striking the Proper Balance,* 56 Tul. L.Rev. 879 (1983). *See also* Kagan, Presi-

dential Administration, 114 Harv. L. Rev. 2245, 2281–82 (2001).

62. *See infra* note 157 & accompanying text. For a consideration of the possible differences between presidential authority over independent and executive agencies, *see supra* § 4.4.

63. *See infra* notes 149–150 & accompanying text (describing OMB ex parte contact rules); *see generally*, Verkuil, *Jawboning Administrative Agencies: Ex Parte Contacts by the White House,* 80 Colum. L. Rev. 943 (1980).

64. 657 F.2d 298 (D.C.Cir.1981).

preserve its role in judicial review, that was earlier emphasized in *HBO*. Judge Wald's opinion accommodates both the legal and political nature of the informal rulemaking process while preserving the framework of judicial review:

> The purposes of full-record review which underlie the need for disclosing ex parte conversations in some settings do not require that courts know the details of every White House contact, including a Presidential one, in this informal rulemaking setting. After all, any rule issued here with or without White House assistance must have the requisite factual support in the rulemaking record, and under this particular statute the Administrator may not base the rule in whole or in part on any "information or data" which is not in the record, no matter what the source. The courts will monitor all this, but they need not be omniscient to perform their role effectively. Of course, it is always possible that undisclosed Presidential prodding may direct an outcome that is factually based on the record, but different from the outcome that would have obtained in the absence of Presidential involvement. In such a case, it would be true that the political process did affect the outcome in a way the courts could not police. But we do not believe that Congress intended that the courts convert informal rulemaking into a rarified technocratic process, unaffected by political considerations or the presence of presidential power.

The court, however, did not believe that the White House was free of all restrictions concerning ex parte contacts. Restrictions would be necessary to ensure due process where such conversations directly concern the outcome of adjudications or quasi-adjudications because "there is no inherent executive power to control the rights of individuals in such settings". Further, the court thought that summaries of such conversations may have to be docketed in the rulemaking record in situations "where a statute ... *specifically requires* that essential 'information or data' upon which the rule is based be docketed". Although such a statute existed in this case, the court found that because EPA did not rely on the White House ex parte contacts to establish the rule, they did not have to be docketed. The court felt uncomfortable in extending ex parte prohibitions any further because "[w]here the President himself is directly involved in oral communications with Executive Branch officials, Article II considerations—combined with the strictures of *Vermont Yankee*—require that the courts tread with extraordinary caution in mandating disclosure beyond that already required by statute".

§ 9.3.4   Ex parte contacts by Congress

Chapter Three explored the methods by which Congress assures some degree of control over the exercise of agency discretion. As part of that function, Congress makes private, as well as public, contacts with agency officials. This occurs most frequently for those institutions that have been given "independent agency" status by Congress.[65] So long as Congress and its staff limit private contacts to policy matters, it is difficult to distinguish congressional contacts from contacts by the President and the White House staff. The courts, however, draw the line at legislative pressure to force an agency to decide on the basis of factors not made relevant by Congress in the applicable statute.[66]

In *Sierra Club*, Judge Wald observed that due process required the restriction of ex parte contacts by the White House that directly concerned the outcome of adjudications or quasi-adjudications. The same limitation would apply to members of Congress. Nevertheless, there are situations in which members of Congress persist in intervening privately in adjudicative matters. To facilitate these contacts, Congress has specifically exempted itself from the ex parte contract prohibitions of section 557 by stating "[t]his subsection specifically does not constitute authority to withhold information from Congress".[67] One example is constituent inquiries in social security disability cases.[68] These inquiries are inappropriate because in effect they involve private pleading on behalf of some, but presumably not all, claimants for benefits. Nevertheless, the Social Security Administration responds to them in detail (and at considerable bureaucratic cost) in order to keep its political powder dry.[69] One has to question whether this is a valid form of political accountability, entrenched though it is. The most that can be said for the practice is that, because it is so routine, it is unlikely to have any significant effect on an individual disability decision by an ALJ. There probably are other adjudicatory-type programs with which members of Congress interfere on a less regular basis (awards of government contracts for example) that pose equal or greater threats to objective decisionmaking.[70]

---

65. *See supra* § 4.4.

66. *See supra* § 3.6.2 (discussing Congress and informal agency action).

67. 5 U.S.C. § 557(2).

68. *See* J. Mashaw, *supra* note 34, at 58–59 (Congress makes over 100,000 such inquiries per year).

69. SSA employs several hundred people whose sole job is to respond to Congressional inquiries. *Id.* at 78.

70. *See, e.g.,* D.C. Fed. of Civic Ass'ns v. Volpe, 459 F.2d 1231 (D.C.Cir.1971) (contacts by members of Congress with Secretary of Transportation concerning

Undoubtedly, political accountability is a banner under which Congress hides some private contacts that could easily be prejudicial. But such contacts are a recognized method of political oversight. This may be one reason that Congress is not anxious to forbid all ex parte contacts by the executive branch under the APA. Congress enjoys the freedom to intervene privately in the informal process and could not lightly deprive the President of a similar opportunity. To the extent that Congress were to place tight controls around executive branch contacts,[71] it might be forced, as a matter of separation of powers theory, to do the same to itself.[72] Such an outcome would serve neither branch interest nor, in most situations, the cause of political accountability.

§ 9.3.5   Ex parte contacts by agency staff: The role of separation of functions

The APA provides in section 554(d) that an ALJ may not be responsible to an agency employee engaged in the performance of investigative or prosecuting functions and that:

> [A]n employee or agent engaged in the performance of investigative or prosecutorial functions for an agency in a case may not, in that or a factually related case, participate or advise in the decision, recommended decision or agency review ... except as witness or counsel in public proceedings.

These separation of functions requirements, however, apply only to formal adjudication and do not pertain to formal rulemaking, initial licensing, informal adjudication, or rulemaking. As a result, separation of functions presently is a less important restraint on agency staff than are the ex parte communications restrictions. Because separation of functions serves the same interests within the agency as ex parte communications restrictions do outside the agency, the ABA and the Administrative Conference have recommended that they be extended to formal rulemaking and initial licensing.[73]

Hercules, Inc. v. EPA[74] warned that the separation of functions

---

funding for Three Sisters bridge); *see generally supra* § 3.6.

71. At some point the doctrine of executive privilege would place a constitutional limit upon Congress' ability to isolate the President from his staff, but Congress would certainly be able to formalize the methods of agency interaction to a greater degree than it has before

confronting that issue. *See* Verkuil, *supra* note 63, at 978–1006.

72. *See* Strauss, *The Place of Agencies in Government: Separation of Powers and the Fourth Branch*, 84 Colum.L.Rev. 573, 650–53 (1984) (arguing for branch parity in political oversight).

73. *See* ABA Comm. on Law and the Economy, *supra* note 61, at 95–96.

74. 598 F.2d 91 (D.C. Cir. 1978).

might be required in formal rulemaking even in the absence of APA limitations. The EPA judicial officer assigned to write the rule relied upon information provided by agency employees who had acted in an "adversary capacity" during the comment period. The D.C. Circuit was strongly influenced by its contemporaneous opinion in *HBO*, yet it was reluctant to apply that case's ex parte contact restrictions on a retroactive basis to the agency staff situation. Judge McGowan nevertheless counseled in *Hercules* that:

> [a]mendatory legislation may be justified if agencies do not themselves proscribe post-hearing contacts between staff advocates and decisionmaker in formal rulemaking proceedings, lest there be an erosion of public trust and confidence in the administrative process.

While the D.C. Circuit has not imposed separation of functions requirements in the cases that followed *Hercules*,[75] agencies themselves have adopted such requirements by regulation to contexts not required by the APA.

In the informal rulemaking setting, the proper role of separation of functions is even less certain. Agencies are at a considerable disadvantage if knowledgeable employees are restricted from conferring with their counterparts during the rule formulation process. William Pederson of EPA, a knowledgeable student of the administrative process, has raised important questions whether, in this type of non-accusatory situation, staff isolation from internal sources of vital technological information and experience, because of judicially or congressionally imposed separation of functions requirements, will "undermine seriously the quality of the agency's final product".[76] As a general matter, it seems advisable to limit separation of functions requirements in rulemaking to those few agency employees who act as staff advocates.[77] Differences in agency organization and staffing suggest that a uniform restriction is not advisable; rather, agency-by-agency experimentation with separation of functions seems the best

---

75. *See* United Steelworkers v. Marshall, 647 F.2d 1189, 1214–15 (D.C. Cir. 1980) (reserving the imposition of separation of functions requirements for "valuable privilege" situations).

76. *See* Pederson, *The Decline of Separation of Functions in Regulatory Agencies,* 64 Va. L. Rev. 991, 994 (1978) (advocating the inadvisability of separation of functions requirements in rulemaking

and questioning whether it even makes sense in formal adjudication when it prevents agency heads from conferring with ALJs about matters of record); *compare infra* § 9.3.6 (ALJ Corps plan).

77. *See* Asimow, *When the Curtain Falls: Separation of Functions in the Federal Administrative Agencies,* 81 Colum. L. Rev. 759 (1981).

way to work toward a definition of its proper role.[78]

§ 9.3.6 Ex parte contacts between commissioners and ALJs and the ALJ corps idea

Within agencies, there is also the potential of contacts between agency heads, or commissioners, and the ALJs who prepare initial decisions in formal adjudications. These contacts can involve matters of policy or even the merits of individual cases. Because section 554(d) forbids only those agency employees "engaged in the performance of investigative or prosecutorial functions" from making contact with ALJs in formal adjudication, agency heads, or commissioners, by the literal terms of the APA, are free to make contact with ALJs about matters before them.

Whether such contacts are a good idea, even if not forbidden, is a question whose answer turns on how one views the role of the ALJs in the administrative decision process. Agency heads, or commissioners, in whom is placed the statutory responsibility for decisionmaking, currently delegate that responsibility to the ALJs for a preliminary analysis. Therefore, the ALJ's initial decision is advisory, or only a recommendation, and it can be adopted, modified, or rejected at will by the agency authority responsible for making the final decision.

This view of the ALJ's role suggests that policy advice and direction from agency heads, or commissioners, might be a positive way to make the ALJ's decision better informed and, therefore, likely to carry more weight when it is reviewed by the agency itself.[79] In other words, since the ALJ's decision is entitled to no independent weight, its value would be enhanced if the agency communicated (presumably off the record) about priorities and goals before, or even during, the adjudicative process.

But in recent years there has been far greater emphasis placed on ALJ independence than upon policymaking coordination between agency and adjudicator. In a series of confrontations during the Reagan Administration, the Social Security Administrator sought to have ALJs follow agency policy in disability cases rather than that set out by the courts of appeals. This triggered a bitter legislative

---

78.   *See id.* at Appendix (documenting a variety of separation of functions solutions in six agencies).

79.   The ALJ is already bound to follow agency policy that is publicly de-

clared in rulemaking or adjudicatory proceedings. *See* Pacific Gas and Electric Co. v. FPC, 506 F.2d 33, 38 (D.C. Cir. 1974).

debate.[80]

The SSA had also sought to control the productivity of ALJs in disability cases by setting out case load levels and allowance rate goals. The ALJs challenged these practices directly as incursions upon their decisional independence, with inconclusive judicial results.[81] There has never been a clear understanding in the Congress or in the courts as to how "independent" ALJs are meant to be under the APA.[82] Not surprisingly, ALJs continue to push for independence approaching that of federal judges, while agencies continue to seek control of ALJs in order to maintain policy control of the adjudicative process.

The question whether ALJs should remain part of the agency or should be more independent was raised by proposals for an ALJ Corps. One proposal would have created an ALJ Corps under the direction of a chief ALJ separate from the agencies ALJs serve.[83] This proposal was opposed by the Department of Justice[84] and was not enacted into law, although the concept has been adopted in 26 states.[85] A critical aspect was whether the decisions of ALJs will be accorded conclusive effect. If they are not, and the agency makes the final decision, decisional control remains in the agency. If legislation were to grant decision finality on questions of fact or even law,[86] then

80. *See generally* Estreicher & Reverz, *Nonacquiescence by Federal Administrative Agencies,* 98 Yale L.J. 679, 699–705 (1989).

81. *See* Nash v. Bowen, 869 F.2d 675 (2d Cir.1989); Association of Administrative Law Judges, Inc. v. Heckler, 594 F.Supp. 1132 (D.D.C.1984). *See also* discussion at § 9.2.3.

82. *Compare* Ramspeck v. Fedral Trial Examiners Conference, 345 U.S. 128, 133 (1953) ("Agencies intended to make hearing examiners [as ALJs then were called] a special class of 'semi-independent, subordinate-hearing officers' "), *with* Butz v. Economou, 438 U.S. 478, 513 (1978) (granting ALJs, like judges, absolute immunity from tort damages because of their independent status).

83. S. 594, 101st Cong., 1st Sess., 135 Cong. Rec. 2711–13 (1989).

84. *See* Hearings on S. 594 before the Subcomm. on Courts and Admin. Practice of the Senate Comm. on the Judiciary, 101st Cong. 1st Sess. (1989). To some extent the growth of non-ALJ adjudica-tors in the Immigration and Naturalization Service (then under the Department of Justice) may have been a function of that agency's desire to achieve policy control over adjudication. Today, there are more non-ALJ adjudicators than ALJs in the federal system. *See* Frye, Study of Non–ALJ Hearing Programs, 44 Ad. L. Rev. 261 (1992) (listing some 2700 non-ALJ deciders). *See also* Office of ALJs, The Federal Administrative Judiciary 1992–2002 (Dec. 23, 2002) (listing 3,370 non-ALJ deciders, a 25% increase over the 1992 Frye study).

85. See Rossi, *Final, But Often Fallible: Recognizing Problems With ALJ Finality,* 56 Ad.L.Rev. 53, 57 (2004).

86. *See* M. Asimow, A. Bonfield, & R. Levin, 2003 Supplement to State and Federal Administrative Law 8 (2003) (a "notable trend in state administrative law is to make ALJ decisions final, either eliminating or greatly curtailing the ability of agency heads to alter an ALJ decision.").

the APA's assumption of agency control over ALJs in policy matters,[87] would be vitiated.

§ 9.4   Open–Government Legislation

During the 1970s Congress sought to expose the administrative process and potential conflicts of interest to greater public scrutiny. The Government-in-the-Sunshine Act,[88] the Federal Advisory Committee Act,[89] and the Ethics in Government Act[90] are the most prominent of those initiatives. These schemes manifest a sustained effort to satisfy the twin goals of fairness and political accountability and in many ways, they have transformed the agency deliberative process. Reconciliation of these goals, in these contexts, however, continues to be challenged by an inherent tension between the need for policy making privacy and public scrutiny of the government's business.

§ 9.4.1   The Sunshine Act: The statutory framework

The Sunshine Act requires that "every portion of every meeting of an agency" that is "headed by a collegial body" must be "open to public observation."[91] The Act requires an agency to follow a "detailed ritual" of procedures intended to give the public adequate notice of the meeting and its agenda.[92] Meetings, or a portion of them, can be closed only if one of ten exemptions applies. To close a meeting, the majority vote of an agency's governing board must determine that, and give adequate notice that, the meeting is "likely to disclose" some information covered by an exemption and that the public interest does not require nevertheless that the meeting be open. To give adequate notice, the agency must follow another "detailed ritual" of procedures required to close meetings.

The Sunshine Act includes seven of the nine FOIA exemptions and three original ones.[93] The only important FOIA exemption not

---

87. It has been difficult for agencies to achieve policy control in situations where the split enforcement model prevails. *See* Shapiro & McGarity, *Reorienting OSHA: Regulatory Alternatives and Legislative Reform,* 6 Yale J.Reg. 1, 59–62 (1989); Johnson, *The Split–Enforcement Model: Some Conclusions from the OSHA and MSHA Experiences,* 39 Ad. L. Rev. 315 (1987). *See generally* Verkuil, *The Purposes and Limits of Independent Agencies,* 1988 Duke L.J. 257, 268–71.

88. 5 U.S.C. § 552b; *see generally* J. O'Reilly, Federal Information Disclosure: Procedures, Forms and the Law §§ 32.01–.08 (1983); R. Berg & S. Klitzman, An Interpretative Guide to the Government in the Sunshine Act (1978).

89. 5 U.S.C. App.

90. 5 U.S.C. App.

91. 5 U.S.C. at § 552b(b).

92. 5 U.S.C. at § 552b(e)(1)–(3).

93. 5 U.S.C. at § 552b(c)(1)–(4), (6)–(8); *see supra* §§ 8.3.3a–g.

included is the one for intra-agency and inter-agency memoranda. It was dropped because it is inconsistent with the purpose of the Act. The Act was intended to open an agency's meetings so that the public could observe an agency's deliberations. As a result, no exemption is provided to protect those deliberations from public scrutiny. Protection is provided beyond the FOIA exemptions, however. Three original exemptions cover disclosure that is likely to involve accusations that a person has committed a crime, likely to disclose information the premature release of which would frustrate the agency's purpose in meeting, or is likely to concern matters of litigation strategy.[94] If sued concerning a decision to close a meeting, an agency bears the burden of establishing that any of the exemptions are applicable to justify the closing.

§ 9.4.2   The Sunshine Act definition of "Meeting"

An agency is not obligated to follow the previous requirements unless a "meeting" is held. A meeting is defined as "the deliberations of at least the number of individual agency members required to take action on behalf of the agency where such deliberations determine or result in the joint conduct of agency business."[95] Under that definition, an agency can make two arguments that the Act does not apply. It can argue that less than the number of members "required to take action" were present. It can also argue that the required number or more did not engage in "deliberations" that constituted the "official business of the agency".

Congress chose vague language to define "meeting" because it wanted a definition broad enough that agencies could not easily evade the open-meeting requirement. Rather than trying to find a universal definition of what type of informal agency communication was not included, Congress delegated that role to the federal courts.

In *ITT World Communications, Inc. v. FCC,*[96] the D.C. Circuit interpreted the act's vague language in an expansive fashion. FCC members had met with foreign telecommunication companies to discuss whether foreign operators would be willing to establish interconnections with American companies who wished to enter the international communications market. ITT World Communications, an established market participant, asked to attend those meetings and was denied access. ITT claimed that the FCC was obligated by the Sunshine Act to open the meetings to public participation.

94. 5 U.S.C. at § 552b(c)(5), (9)–(10).   **96.** 699 F.2d 1219 (D.C.Cir.1983).
95. 5 U.S.C. at § 552b(a)(2).

The FCC had argued that the Act did not apply because a majority of the seven members of the Commission was not present and because the Commission had not authorized the three Commissioners who were present to act on its behalf. In particular, the Commission argued that under the FCC Act certain procedures must be met to delegate any of the Commission's functions to a panel of Commissioners and that those procedures had not been invoked. The circuit court disagreed and invoked the Act's strictures on the basis that the discussions "play[ed] an integral role in the Commission's rulemaking processes".

On petition for certiorari, the Supreme Court unanimously reversed.[97] The Court held that the Sunshine Act requirements apply only when a subdivision of the Commission is "formally delegated authority to take official action for the agency." In rendering its decision, the Court was sensitive to the need for commissioners to meet informally in private for the exchange of views on important international matters, especially where the attendance was at a meeting abroad not organized by the agency itself. The Court appeared to accept criticism of the expansive definition of meeting proposed by the court of appeals and proffered a narrowing construction for future cases: "Congress in drafting the Act's definition of 'meeting' recognized that the administrative process cannot be conducted entirely in the public eye."[98] In *NRDC v. NRC*,[99] the D.C. Circuit approved NRC rules that defined "meeting" under the Sunshine Act in language identical to the Supreme Court's holding in *ITT Communications, Inc. v. FCC*, even though NRC had for the prior decade operated under definitional rules that were more expansive. The definitional language at issue involved when Commission discussions were "sufficiently focused on discrete proposals."

§ 9.4.3 The effect of openness on collegial decisionmaking

The Sunshine Act applies to over 50 collegial agencies of the federal government and many state agencies because of comparable legislation at the state level. The avowed purpose of the Act is to open closed meetings to public scrutiny, but it became a fair question

97. FCC v. ITT World Communications, Inc., 466 U.S. 463 (1984).

98. The American Bar Association submitted a memorandum amicus curiae that urged the court to grant certiorari and reverse on the grounds that the expansive definition of "meeting" would discourage agency commissioners from meeting or communicating with members of the public if they could only do so in an open format. ABA Memorandum No. 83–371, Oct. 3, 1983.

99. 216 F.3d 1180, 1183 (D.C. Cir. 2000).

whether it has achieved its goals at cost to the quality of collegiate decisionmaking.

The evidence is increasingly clear that, while the act has opened commission meetings to public scrutiny, it has done so at some injury to the process of decisionmaking, because collegial agencies meet less than they did prior to the act.[100] Survey research also discerned several disturbing trends in the nature of collegial decisionmaking: there has been an increase in notational (written) voting on matters before the agency, an increase in meetings by staff assistants of the commissioners (which are not covered by the Act), and a tendency for commissioners to make up their minds prior to their appearance at the open meetings.[101]

These findings left little doubt that the Sunshine Act had a deleterious impact upon the collegiality of multi-member agencies. Whether this translates into poorer quality decisions in some abstract sense is difficult to know. But in so far as the process of collegial decisionmaking is meant to produce better (or more acceptable) decisions,[102] these data invite a negative conclusion. Moreover, the increased use of commission staff to reach decisions outside the Act's requirements suggests a further difficulty. Agency control is shifting away from the politically appointed (and more accountable) commissioners to the permanent (and potentially less accountable) bureaucracy.

In light of these difficulties, a special committee of the Administrative Conference recommended a trial experiment of permitting some agencies to hold closed meetings subject to the requirement that such agencies publish a detailed summary of the meeting after it was held.[103] Congress, however, did not act on the proposal, which was vigorously opposed by the news media.

Open decisionmaking as a concept is attractive to those who seek to reform the administrative process. But it seems that even sunshine may not be an unqualified virtue. The perverse effect of the concept upon the process of collegial decisionmaking is indicates a more

---

100. The Chairman of the ICC, Reese Taylor, testified before the Senate Appropriations committee that his agency had not held regularly scheduled public meetings since the late 1970s. After stern warnings during the budgetary process, the chastened agency later reported that it held two public meetings. *Senate Panel Cuts Members, Budget of ICC*, Washington Post, June 30, 1984, at D11.

101. Welborn, Lynn & Thomas, *Implementation and Effects of the Federal Government in the Sunshine Act*, 1984 ACUS 197.

102. *Compare* discussion at *supra* § 4.4.1(b).

103. *See* May, *Taming The Sunshine Act*, Legal Times, Feb. 5, 1996 (describing committee proposals).

general problem institutional notions of fairness (implicit in the openness principle) have the potential to contradict equally important principles of political accountability. The larger lessons are contained in the nature of decision quality. Protections against backroom deals or inside arrangements are never easy to fashion; it may just be that there are sufficient other remedies, judicial or political, that can better control the problems. Having so acknowledged, however, it must be said that even in its less aggressive version, the Sunshine Act has served the valid public purpose of notion of ensuring that agencies act with the notion of public scrutiny in mind.

§ 9.4.4 The Federal Advisory Committee Act

In 1972, Congress enacted the Federal Advisory Committee Act because of concern about the influence of private advisory groups upon administrative activities. The purpose of the Act was to identify and reduce the number of such groups and to structure the remaining committees along established lines under the guidance of agency officials. In 1976, the Act was amended to conform it to the requirements of the Sunshine Act.[104] The Act is presently implemented by the General Services Administration (GSA).[105]

FACA requires advisory committees to provide advanced notice of their meetings and to open them to the public unless the President or the administrator to whom the committee reports determines the meeting may be closed in accordance with the Sunshine Act. FACA also stipulates that committees keep minutes and that the minutes and other committee records be open to the public unless the information falls within one of the FOIA exemptions and the government chooses to withhold it.

In *Public Citizen v. United States Department of Justice*,[106] the Court was required to decide the scope of the FACA. The FACA defines an "advisory committee" as "any committee, board, commission, council, conference, panel, task force, or other similar group ... which is (A) established by statute or reorganization plan, or (B) established or *utilized by* the President, or ... (C) ... by one or more agencies in the interest of obtaining advice or recommenda-

---

104. *See* 5 U.S.C. App.

105. The Act first placed control in the hands of the Director of OMB, but President Carter, by executive order, transferred that control to the Administrator of General Services. Exec. Order 12024, 42 Fed. Reg. 61445 (1977).

106. 491 U.S. 440 (1989); *see also* National Nutritional Foods Ass'n v. Califano, 603 F.2d 327 (2d Cir.1979); Aviation Consumer Action Project v. Washburn, 535 F.2d 101 (D.C. Cir. 1976).

tions. . . . "[107] A public interest group argued that the FACA applied to consultations between the Justice Department and the American Bar Association's Standing Committee on Federal Judiciary concerning the ABA's rating of Supreme Court nominees. The Supreme Court admitted it was a "close question whether FACA should be construed to apply to the ABA committee," but it rejected that interpretation for two reasons. First, an interpretation that excluded the ABA committee avoided the necessity of deciding whether inclusion unduly infringed on the President's Article II power to nominate federal judges and violated the doctrine of separation of powers. Second, Congress did not intend a literal reading of the words "utilized by" because it said FACA did not cover every situation where the government consulted a private group. The Court reasoned that the ABA committee was not the type of committee that Congress meant to include under the term "utilize" for three reasons: it was not formed at the federal government's prompting, the Department of Justice had no control over it, and it received no government funds.

The Court's decision is wary of the dangers of over-inclusion presented in the Sunshine Act, might affect FACA as well. By formalizing the relationship between agencies and the public, FACA threatens to discourage the ad hoc contacts between government and the private sector that often provide expert technical and scholarly advice to the government at little or no cost. For these reasons, the Administrative Conference recommended that ad hoc groups not be placed under the Act and has urged the GSA in its periodic review of existing committees to react accordingly.[108]

Nevertheless, *Public Citizen* may have created a loophole that will enable agencies to avoid the FACA altogether. *Public Citizen* invites lower courts to limit the FACA to situations where the government forms, controls, and funds a committee that it uses for advice. An agency can now avoid the act by the simple expedient of having a non-governmental outside group form the advisory committee. For example, in *Food Chemical News v. Young,*[109] the D.C. Circuit held that an advisory group formed by a governmental contractor was not "utilized" by an agency for advice. And in *Byrd v EPA,*[110] the court defined the terms "established" and "utilized"

---

107. 5 U.S.C. App. 3(2) (emphasis added).

108. ACUS Rec. 80–3, 1 C.F.R. § 305.80–3.

109. 900 F.2d 328 (D.C. Cir.), *cert. denied*, 498 U.S. 846 (1990).

110. 174 F.3d 239 (D.C. Cir. 1999), *cert. denied*, 529 U.S. 1018 (2000).

narrowly so as to exempt a peer review panel, created through a private consulting firm working for EPA, from scrutiny under FACA. *Public Citizen* thus could be viewed as a useful limitation on the scope of the FACA, but it might also invite agencies to escape the requirements of FACA by the expedient of relying on advisory groups formed by contractors and similar approaches.[111]

The National Academy of Sciences (NAS) failed in its attempt to take advantage of this loophole in *Animal Legal Defense Fund, Inc. v. Shalala*.[112] NAS had refused to permit members of the Fund to attend meetings of a committee responsible for updating the *Guide for the Care and Use of Laboratory Animals*, published by the Academy. The D.C. Circuit agreed with the Fund's argument that NAS, as a federal advisory committee, was legally obligated to hold open meetings and to make public any minutes, transcripts and records. The issue was whether the government had "utilized" the NAS as that term was defined in *Public Citizen*. The court interpreted *Public Citizen* as extending FACA to any private group that was used by the President or an agency *in the same manner* as advisory groups established by the government. The Academy met this definition because "NAS was created by Congress to answer the government's requests for investigations, examinations, experiments, and reports, and the government takes care of the expenses associated with performing these tasks." The opinion distinguished *Food Chemical News* because the committee in that case was formed by a wholly private organization.

After the decision, NAS asked Congress to exempt it from FACA, which it agreed to do.[113] Congress, however, required NAS to follow procedures similar to those in FACA, except it permitted the Academy to hold private meetings for purposes of deliberation, which FACA does not authorize.[114] Thus, Congress struck a different balance in the context of the NAS between the desirability of open meetings and the need to close meetings to aid candid debate.

Another FACA exemption is for committees composed "wholly of full-time, or permanent part-time, officers or employees of the Federal Government."[115] In *Association of American Physicians and Sur-*

111. *But see* Miccosukee Tribe v. Southern Everglades Restoration Alliance, 304 F.3d 1076 (11th Cir. 2002) (defining SERA as an advisory committee and reading *Public Citizen* as defining the statutory term "established" in a broad fashion).

112. 104 F.3d 424 (D.C. Cir.), *cert. denied,* 522 U.S. 949 (1997).

113. 5 U.S.C. App. § 3(2).

114. *Id.* § 15.

115. *Id.* § 3(2).

geons, Inc. v. Clinton,[116] a group of physicians argued that President Clinton's Task Force on National Health Care Reform could not qualify for this exemption because it was chaired by Hillary Rodham Clinton, who was not a government employee. The court disagreed for two reasons. First, it held that the President's spouse acted as the functional equivalent of an assistant to the President. This conclusion was based on the fact that Congress had authorized the payment of persons who assisted the spouse in White House duties. Second, the court decided that if the president's spouse were not considered a governmental employee, it might have to declare FACA to be unconstitutional. The judges reasoned that an interpretation of FACA that barred a President from obtaining confidential advice from private citizens, separate from or together with the President's closest governmental associates, could violate the "impermissible" burden test created in *Morrison v. Olsen*.[117] FACA could have this impact because it would hinder the President in obtaining the advice he needed to carry out his constitutional duties.

This case also illustrates the tension between open and effective government. It seems inconceivable that a president could effectively assemble a legislative proposal like the Clinton health care initiative if his advisors were required to hold public meetings. The FACA exemption for advisory committees composed of government officials recognizes this problem and, as the court indicated, an exemption may be constitutionally compelled for advisory committees containing private persons that directly report to the President.

Recently, various parties sought information about the National Energy Policy Development Group chaired by Vice President Dick Cheney. NRDC and Judicial Watch filed challenges under FACA. The government moved to dismiss arguing that the application of FACA to these actions of the Vice President would interfere with the President's constitutional authority.[118] At this stage, the Vice President is under a "carefully focused discovery order" to determine whether non-federal personnel participated in the NEPDG deliberations.[119]

116. 997 F.2d 898 (D.C. Cir. 1993).

117. 487 U.S. 654 (1988). This case is discussed in § 4.4.3.

118. Judicial Watch, Inc. v. National Energy Policy Development Group, 219 F.Supp.2d 20 (D.D.C. 2002) (ruling that no private right of action exists under FACA but that FACA could be enforceable through mandamus).

119. *In re Cheney*, 334 F.3d 1096 (D.C. Cir.) (2–1) (dismissing mandamus petitions by the Vice President seeking to vacate discovery orders), *cert. granted*, Cheney v. United States District Court, ___ U.S. ___, 124 S.Ct. 958 (2003).

§ 9.4.5   The Ethics in Government Act

In 1978, Congress enacted the Ethics in Government Act which broadly sought to reveal potential conflicts of interest by government officials.[120] The Act requires the filing of detailed financial reports by legislative, executive and judicial personnel, as well as administrative officials. The disclosure forms are monitored by the Office of Government Ethics which has the duty to determine whether conflicts exist and recommend corrective action.

The Act also imposes restrictions on what type of post-employment activities former government officials can accept.[121] These restrictions are intended to solve the so-called "revolving door" problem.[122] It is common for persons to move to government service from private employment and then to return later to private employment from their government service. When a person returns to private employment and is engaged in contacts with the agency he or she has just left, there is the potential for unfairness. By virtue of their government employment, those persons may have access to administrative decisionmakers (often in private) that is unavailable to others. In fact, a major activity of many Washington lawyers is trading on prior contacts and relationships developed while in government service.[123]

Besides the Act, former government lawyers are also regulated by state disciplinary codes concerning the type of post-government employment they can accept. These codes govern possible conflicts of interest that are created if a lawyer, or the lawyer's firm, seeks to represent a private party concerning a dispute in which the lawyer participated as a government employee.[124] By comparison, non-lawyers have no comparable set of disciplinary rules to back up the principles stated in the Ethics in Government Act.

While these types of restrictions promote fairness, they may also create negative side-effects that could ultimately decrease the political accountability of the bureaucracy. If the conflict rules are too

---

120. P.L. 95–521, 92 Stat. 1824, 5 U.S.C. App.

121. *See* 18 U.S.C. § 207 (an official is permanently forbidden to represent private parties in matters he or she directly participated on during government service; and is subjected to a one year cooling-off period on personal advocacy before his or her former agency).

122. *See generally,* Morgan, *Appropriate Limits on Participation By a For-*

mer Agency Official in Matters Before an Agency, 1980 Duke L.J. 1.

123. *See generally,* J. Goulden, The Superlawyers (1972) for a highly charged description of the problem.

124. *See* Morgan, *supra* note 122. The basic problem under the disciplinary rules has been the necessity of disqualification of law firms when some of their members are former government employees. *See* ABA Code DR 5–105(D).

strict, they can discourage individuals from entering government service because those persons will not be willing to jeopardize post-government employment opportunities. Ultimately, the rules could dry up sources of talented government employees, or make those currently in government service less effective, or both. Some have even suggested that overly stringent ethics rules could result in the creation of "permanent" civil servants who do not have the independence necessary to challenge erroneous official positions or practices because they may be unable to find post-government employment. At the other extreme is the danger of too short stays in government by political appointees who revolve the door at high speed, going back to the private sector after about two years of government service. Professor Ackerman has emphasized that this kind of "churning" of political officials leads to poor management.[125]

In light of the possible disadvantages of conflict of interest rules, there have been several suggestions that the scope of the rules should be narrowed.[126] Some of these reforms may be necessary to balance the costs and benefits posed by legislation like the Ethics in Government Act. Calibrations of the proper scope of such legislation takes place only over time and through the process of trial and error. What is necessary is sensitivity to the existence of conflicts between fairness and political accountability and the exercise of careful judgment concerning the public values at stake.

Of course even stringent ethics rules are no assurance of ethical conduct in government. Since the Ethics in Government Act was enacted, there have been several scandals of major proportions, notably among them are those involving the S & L industry and HUD. The HUD scandal involved agency officials who, acting under the direction of former Secretary Samuel Pierce, awarded HUD grants on the basis of politics rather than statutory criteria. These activities are also subject to criminal investigation. And, while the Ethics in Government Act does not have direct application to elected officials, the "Keating five" were all Senators who were deeply involved in the receipt of campaign funds from the head of now defunct Lincoln Savings and Loan of California, and some of them were disciplined by the Senate. These incidents certainly do not say much for the state of ethical conduct in government.

---

125. *See* Ackerman, *The New Separation of Powers*, 113 Harv. L. Rev. 633, 706–09 (2000) ("short-term appointments yields a remorselessly short-term policy focus").

126. *See* ACUS Rec. 79–7, 1 C.F.R. § 305.97–7; Morgan, *supra* note 122, at 54–58.

When President George W. Bush took office, he emphasized the need to confront the problem of ethics in government. Building on the work of his father (No. 41) who had established a Commission of Ethics Law Reform,[127] he made lobbyists sign a code of ethics. But it remains an open question whether lobbying has been more well-controlled in the current Administration, especially given the Iraqi contracts awarded to American companies with ties to Vice President Cheney and others in the Administration.

Almost twenty years ago, Paul Volcker, former head of the Federal Reserve Board, chaired a bipartisan committee that issued a report on the performance, morale and quality of government officials. This report spent less time on purely ethical issues and focused on equally critical issues like salary levels and recruiting strategies.[128] The quality and compensation of government employees is a crucial aspect of ethical conduct by the bureaucracy. The Volcker Commission's recommendations sought to reduce the number of political appointees (from about 3,000 to 2,000) in order to improve the morale and performance of the permanent bureaucracy. This solution could improve the ethics of bureaucrats by expanding career opportunities and countering the short-term perspective of political appointees noted above. It seems unlikely, however, that any President would want to reduce the number of political slots available for appointment.

Interest and concern with ethics in government issues have the potential to lead to further reforms, encompassing congressional as well as executive and judicial ethics. In the age of Enron, it may be that the ethical failures of the corporate sector will highlight the government's need for reform and produce further extensions in government ethical standards. [129]

§ 9.5   Regulatory Analysis and Political Accountability

Regulatory analysis is a management technique. It is employed by the White House and the Executive branch in order to make "better," more "responsible" and less "burdensome" agency decisions. These purposes suggest a desire to enhance political accountability. A President takes office with various mandates to achieve public goals. Efforts to incorporate those goals into regulatory policy

---

127. Exec. Order No. 12,668. The Commission's purpose is to review existing laws, orders and policies and make recommendations for reforms "needed to ensure full public confidence in the integrity of all public officials and employees."

128. Report of the National Commission on Ethics Law Reform (1989).

129. *Compare* J. Rohr, Ethics for Bureaucrats (2d Ed.1989) *with* Thompson, *The Possibility of Administrative Ethics* 45 Pub. Admin. Rev. 595 (1985).

can be viewed as an attempt to make agencies more accountable to the electorate. In this way, regulatory analysis becomes an accountability mechanism.

At the same time, regulatory analysis presents an accountability problem. First, regulatory analysis depends primarily on cost-benefit analysis to analyze and develop sound regulatory policy. Congress, however, has almost always rejected the use of cost-benefit analysis to establish the degree of regulatory protection that EPA, OSHA, and other similar agencies are to provide to the public and the environment.[130] Instead, Congress has employed several pragmatic methods of taking costs into account, but none of these methods requires that agencies equate costs and benefits in order to determine how stringent a regulation should be.[131] The accountability problem is how to ensure that agency decisions about the scope of regulation are consistent with the agency's statutory mandate when it requires a different outcome than would be indicated by cost-benefit analysis.

§ 9.5.1 Techniques of regulatory analysis

Shrouded as it is in scientific and economic jargon, regulatory analysis has taken on an aura of the occult. But it began life as a means for the President to control the bureaucracy through the use of common tools of analysis and evaluation. [132] It is nothing more (or less) than an examination of the advantages and disadvantages of a regulation, of alternative regulations, and of no regulation at all. It is the kind of analytical process that should be undertaken before any administrative agency attempts to regulate public behavior. During the 1970s, however, it became increasingly clear that many agencies were not engaging in this type of detailed analytical consideration. As a result, the executive branch, Congress and the courts began to impose policymaking standards upon them. This process began in the environmental field where first the courts and then Congress imposed upon government agencies the requirement that they attempt to measure the impact of a proposed regulatory decision upon the environment and try to minimize any costs created by the regula-

---

130. *See* Shapiro & Glicksman, Risk Regulation At Risk: Restoring a Pragmatic Approach 40 (2003) (finding that only two of 22 key health and safety and environment statutes use a cost-benefit test to establish the degree of regulatory protection).

131. *See id.* at 33–40 (explaining alternative methods).

132. Regulatory analysis actually began in the Nixon Administration when OMB instituted its "Quality of Life" review of EPA regulations. *See* J. Quarles, Cleaning up America: An Insider's View of the Environmental Protection Agency 117–42 (1976).

tion.[133] Thereafter, the focus was put upon deregulation as the preferred public policy option in industries formerly subjected to extensive economic controls.[134]

Today, agencies confront an array of regulatory analysis obligations that require them to jump through numerous analytical hoops before a regulation can be issued. The current focus upon centralized control of regulatory analysis has been accepted by the White House and Congress, and agency staffs have internalized the analytical techniques of regulatory analysis, making executive control less necessary to achieve political accountability. These shifts have caused some to lose sight of the fact that cost-benefit analysis is useful for identifying gross disproportions in regulatory outcomes, not for fine-tuning precise solutions.[135] The effort to measure costs and benefits confronts methodological problems[136] and the lack of relevant information[137] that often limit or distort the accuracy of cost and benefit estimates. There is, however, an on-gong debate whether these infirmities are as debilitating as the critics contend.[138]

§ 9.5.2 The Executive order requirements

President Ford began with "inflation impact statements"[139]; President Carter had "regulatory analysis";[140] Presidents Reagan and Bush had "regulatory impact analysis";[141] and President Clinton had

133. *See generally* 42 U.S.C. §§ 4331–4335; T. Schoenbaum, Environmental Policy Law (1982). The cost-benefit requirements contained in NEPA were initially imposed upon regulatory agencies by judicial review. *See* Scenic Hudson Preservation Conference v. FPC, 354 F.2d 608 (2d Cir.1965), *cert. denied,* 384 U.S. 941 (1966).

134. *See generally* S. Breyer, Regulation and its Reform (1983) (documenting weaknesses in classical regulation).

135. *See* Shapiro, *Political Oversight and the Deterioration of Regulatory Policy,* 46 Admin. L. Rev. 1 (1994); Pierce, *Encouraging Safety: The Limits of Tort Law and Government Regulation,* 33 Vand. L. Rev. 1281 (1980).

136. F. Ackerman & L. Heinzerling, Priceless: On Knowing the Price of Everything and the Value of Nothing (2004) (finding that the measurement of regulatory costs and benefits requires important and contested choices about values that greatly affect the outcome); Heinzer-

ling, *Regulatory Costs of Mythic Proportions,* 107 Yale L.J. 1981 (1998)(same).

137. *See* Parker, *Grading the Government,* 70 U. Chi. L. Rev. 1345 (2003) (finding after a close examination of widely cited studies of regulatory costs and benefits that the studies are so fundamentally flawed that they prove nothing at all about the rationality of regulation).

138. *Compare* Sunstein, *The Arithmetic of Arsenic,* 90 Geo. L.J. 2255 (2002) (finding cost-benefit analysis reliable enough to be useful) *with* McGarity, *Professor Sunstein's Fuzzy Math,* 90 Geo. L.J. 2341 (2002)(finding cost-benefit analysis too unreliable to be useful).

139. Exec. Order No. 11,821, 3 C.F.R. Pt. 926 (1975).

140. Exec. Order No. 12,044, 3 C.F.R. Pt. 152 (1979).

141. Exec. Order No. 12,291, 3 C.F.R. Pt. 127 (1982).

"Regulatory Planning and Review,";[142] and; President George W. Bush kept Clinton's Executive Order in place. These concepts amount essentially to the same thing: executive agencies are obligated to publish information about their rules and provide OMB with a cost-benefit analysis of those rules designated as "major" before they are promulgated.[143] Further, starting with the Reagan order, the White House has forbidden executive agencies, except where enabling statutes require otherwise, from issuing regulations unless the benefits outweigh the costs, and it requires the "regulatory impact analysis" to be submitted for approval to OMB and to be made public. As mentioned earlier, most safety and health and environmental protection statutes forbid using a cost-benefit test to set the level of regulation.

Because the last three presidents have required proposed rules to be submitted to OMB before being published as proposed or final rules, discussion between agency rulemaking officials and OMB occurs in private before the rule is proposed.[144] This process assumes the possibility that OMB review could make an agency alter or even abandon a rule before it is proposed for comment.[145] Critics of earlier administrations alleged that OMB served as a conduit for receiving evidence and comments that were not entered into the rulemaking record, significantly delayed promulgation of rules, and used its review process as a subterfuge to serve the goal of deregulation.[146] While OMB vigorously denied that it misused the process,[147] it reduced the time it took to complete its reviews[148] and adopted rules that limit *ex parte* contacts and require information transferred to OMB to be placed in the rulemaking record.[149] The Clinton order

---

142. Exec. Order No. 12866, 58 Fed. Reg. 51735 (1993).

143. *Id.* Major rules are defined as those rules likely to have an annual effect upon the economy of $100 million or more.

144. *See* Gray, *Presidential Involvement in Informal Rulemaking*, 56 Tul. L.Rev. 863, 864–65 (1982).

145. *See* De Muth, *Constraining Regulatory Costs: Part I, The White House Review Programs*, Regulation, Jan./Feb., 1980, at 21.

146. *See, e.g.,* Morrison, *OMB Interference with Agency Rulemaking: The Wrong Way To Write A Regulation*, 99 Harv. L. Rev. 1059 (1986); Comment,

OMB Interference In Agency Rulemaking: The Case of Broadened Review, 95 Yale L.J. 1789 (1986).

147. *See, e.g., Remarks of Jay Plager*, 4 Admin. L.J. 5 (1990).

148. For example, the average time for reviewing major rules of the Environmental Protection Agency (EPA) declined from 105 days in 1985 to 45 days in 1988 and the average time for reviewing major rules of the Occupational Safety and Health Administration (OSHA) declined from 173 days in 1985 to 39 days in 1988. 1988–89 Regulatory Program of the United States, app. IV, exhibit 11, at 555.

149. Additional Procedures Concerning OIRA Reviews Under Executive Orders 12291 & 12498 [Revised], June 13,

expanded on these reforms by establishing time periods for the completion of review, prohibiting ex parte contacts with OMB staff members, disclosing the existence of meetings between private parties and OMB administrators,[150] and requiring agencies to identify for the public changes made in response to OMB comments.[151] President George W. Bush had OMB transmit in September 2003, in its annual regulatory cost benefit report to Congress,[152] a detailed Circular A–4 describing the elements of a good regulatory analysis.[153]

While White House review is now a fixture of the regulatory landscape in Washington, it continues to be controversial. Its critics perceive that it is used to further a given administration's political aims in ways that are inconsistent with an agency's regulatory mission. An extensive empirical study by Professor Croley of White House regulatory review, however, finds that on balance the data indicate that "White House review can be substantive and evenhanded, albeit not perfectly so." Nevertheless, Croley concludes that "[i]n the absence of greater White House transparency, fears that the White House uses the rulemaking review process to deliver illicit regulatory favors to special interests will be impossible to dispel."[154] A recent GAO report finds that "[a]lthough both OIRA and some of the rulemaking agencies have improved the transparency of the regulatory review process, ... neither OIRA nor the agencies are required to disclose why rules are withdrawn from review, the descriptions that OIRA discloses about its contacts with outside parties is often not very helpful", and "neither [OIRA] nor the rulemaking agencies are required to disclose the changes made to rules while they are under informal review—the period in which OIRA said it can have its greatest effect."[155]

Despite the controversy concerning Executive oversight, the President's constitutional power to influence and control executive

---

1986, *reprinted in* 1988–89 Regulatory Program of the United States, app. III, 529–31.

150. Exec. Order No. 12866, § 6(b).

151. *Id.* § 6(a)(3)(E).

152. *See Informing Regulatory Decisions: 2003 Report to Congress on the Costs and Benefits of Federal Regulations and Unfunded Mandates on State, Local, and Tribal Entities* at *http://www.Whitehouse.gov/omp/inforeg/regpol-reports-congress.html*

153. The Circular describes thee key elements of Regulatory analysis: (1) need

for action; (2) examination of alternatives, and; an evaluation of quantitative and qualitative benefits and costs. *See* note 152 *supra.*

154. Croley, *White House Review of Agency Rulemaking: An Empirical Investigation,* 70 U. Chi. L. Rev. 821 (2003). Croley also notes that greater transparency would make it possible for studies like his to verify or contradict the critic's claims.

155. GAO, Rulemaking: OMB's Role in Review of Agencies' Draft Rules and the Transparency of Those Rules (2003)(GAO–03–029).

officials provides adequate justification for OMB review.[156] The Executive orders, however, have specifically made participation by independent agencies in the OMB regulatory analysis program voluntary.[157] Whether the President has the constitutional power to assert such authority is debatable.[158] but there is no doubt that as a political matter it would be a bold step for any president to take. President Clinton's order required independent agencies to participate in a government-wide planning process,[159] and this requirement continues under President Bush. There is little doubt that such actions are permissible under cases like *Sierra Club v. Costle.*[160] The case approved private contacts between the members of the White House staff, OMB and the rulemaking officials of EPA, and it can be read to have accepted the concept of presidential oversight by use of the regulatory analysis process.[161] The independent agencies remain "voluntary" participants in this process.

In *Chevron U.S.A., Inc. v. NRDC,*[162] the Court endorsed the practice of executive review. The Court emphasized the role of executive control of the agencies in words that continue to resonate:

> While agencies are not directly accountable to the people, the Chief Executive is, and it is entirely appropriate for this political branch of the government to make such policy choices—resolving the competing interests which Congress itself either inadvertently did not resolve, or intentionally left to be resolved by the agency charged with the administration of the statute in light of everyday realities.

§ 9.5.3 The statutory adjuncts to regulatory review

Congress has enacted three provisions that supplement, and often duplicate, the regulatory review provisions established by exec-

156. *See* Cutler, *Regulatory Mismatch and Its Cure,* 96 Harv. L. Rev. 545, 553 (1982); Shane, *Presidential Regulatory Oversight and the Separation of Powers: The Constitutionality of Executive Order No. 12,291,* 23 Ariz.L.Rev. 1235 (1981).

157. *E.g.* Exec. Order No. 12866, §§ 3(b), 5 (President Clinton's order exempting independent agencies from mandatory OMB oversight).

158. *See supra* § 4.4.2.

159. Exec. Order No. 12866, § 4. The planning process is intended to provide

for coordination of regulations, to maximize consultation between agencies, and to resolve potential conflicts between regulatory plans of agencies, to provide an opportunity for the White House and state, local and tribal officials to influence the regulatory agenda of agencies. *Id.*

160. 657 F.2d 298, 406 (D.C. Cir. 1981).

161. *See supra* § 9.3.3.

162. 467 U.S. 837 (1984).

utive order. The Regulatory Flexibility Act[163] Paperwork Reduction Act,[164] and Unfunded Mandates Act[165] have regulatory review requirements.

The Regulatory Flexibility Act, originally enacted in 1980 and significantly amended in 1996, requires agencies whose rules will have a "significant impact upon a substantial number of small entities"[166] to file initial and final regulatory flexibility analysis (RFAs). The purpose of an RFA is to assess the impact of a rule upon small entities, and explain why the final alternative was chosen. The original legislation prohibited judicial review of an agency's compliance with the Act. Instead, it assigned the responsibility to monitor compliance to the Chief Counsel for Advocacy of the Small Business Administration. Since the Act's requirements are potentially duplicative of regulatory analysis requirements under Executive Order 12,-866, Congress also gave OMB an active role in the administration of the Regulatory Flexibility Act. In 1996, acting on complaints about the ineffective nature of the Act from affected entities, Congress made two changes. First, it authorized a court to remand a rule back to an agency if it fails to comply with procedures required by the Act.[167] Further, the RFA is now part of the rulemaking record when there is judicial review of a rule. This means a court can consider the RFA in deciding whether a rule is arbitrary and capricious under section 706 of the APA, although it can not directly review the substance of an RFA. Second, Congress required EPA and OSHA to follow special procedures for rules that affect small entities. These require the agencies to establish special advisory committees composed of members of small entities to review proposed rules before they are published for public comment.

The Paperwork Reduction Act (PRA) is a form of regulatory relief that promotes some of the goals of the executive orders relating to regulatory analysis. Under the PRA, OMB is given authority to review and approve agency information requests to reduce the paperwork burdens on the public. Because reporting requirements are a method whereby agencies gather information for the purposes of rulemaking, and because the Act applies both to independent and

163. 5 U.S.C. §§ 601–12; *see generally* Verkuil, *A Critical Guide to the Regulatory Flexibility Act,* 1982 Duke L.J. 213.

164. 44 U.S.C. §§ 3501–3520.

165. Pub. L. No. 104–4, 109 Stat. 48.

166. An agency can opt out of the requirements of the RFA by certifying

that its rule does not have such an impact. 5 U.S.C. at § 605(b).

167. Small Business Regulatory Enforcement Fairness Act, Pub. L. No. 104–121, § 242, 110 Stat. 847 (1996) (codified at 5 U.S.C. § 611).

executive agencies,[168] Congress has given OMB considerable control over the regulatory process.

In *Dole v. United Steelworkers*,[169] however, the Supreme Court imposed an important limitation on OMB's authority under the Paperwork Act. OMB had rejected as unnecessary some aspects of a standard promulgated by the Occupational Safety and Health Administration (OSHA) that required employers to inform their employees about workplace hazards. The Court distinguished "information collection requirements," which involve the collection of information by the government, from "disclosure rules" such as the OSHA regulation, which involve the disclosure by one private party to another. After examining the language and purpose of the Act, the Court held the Act did not apply to disclosure rules. The Court noted that Congress' concern in passing the Act was to minimize the burden on individuals in providing information to the government and to minimize the government's cost of handling such information. Disclosure rules present neither of these problems. When Congress reauthorized the Paperwork Act in 1996, it overruled the Supreme Court's decision. The amendments make it clear that the Act also applies to rules which require regulated entities to disclose information directly to the public, such as workplace safety notices or product labeling requirements.

The Unfunded Mandates Act, passed in 1995, also contains provisions that require regulatory analysis. Title II of the legislation, which has the title "Regulatory Accountability and Reform," requires agencies to prepare a statement assessing the effect of any proposed or final regulation that includes a "mandate" resulting in costs of $100 annually on state, local, or tribal governments or on the private sector.[170] The analysis must "identify and consider a reasonable number of regulatory alternatives," and the agency must "select the least costly, most cost-effective, or least burdensome alternative that achieves the objectives of the rule." The "costs" that the agency must minimize are the costs and burdens to state, local, and tribal governments and the private sector. This limitation applies unless it is inconsistent with provisions of another law or the agency administrator explains why the agency did not meet the requirement.[171] Title IV of the legislation empowers the courts to order an agency to comply with certain procedures and related requirements, but a court

168. For a more detailed discussion of the Paperwork Act, *see supra* § 8.2.2.

169. 494 U.S. 26 (1990).

170. 2 U.S.C. § 1532(a).

171. *Id.* § 1535(b).

may not enjoin an agency rule because of noncompliance with these provisions.[172]

§ 9.5.4   Congressional review of rules

The previous analytical requirements are under the supervision of OMB. Finding this oversight insufficient, Congress established a mechanism in 1996 to permit it to do its own review.[173] Before a rule can become law, agencies must submit it to Congress, along with copies of any analyses done pursuant to executive orders, the Flexibility Act, and the Unfunded Mandates Act. The Comptroller General has the responsibility of ensuring that agencies comply with submission requirements. A major rule (generally one with an annual impact of $100 million or more on the economy) cannot take effect until 60 days after the prior information is submitted to Congress or after the rule is published in the Federal Register, whichever is later. This stay does not apply to rules that are not major or if any one of several exceptions applies, including that the President finds immediate implementation is necessary to prevent an imminent threat to health or safety.

Congress also established procedures for legislation that would bar an agency from adopting a rule. If a resolution of disapproval is introduced in both houses, the Senate and the House have a limited time period to employ fast-track procedures to obtain a vote on the resolution. In the Senate, for example, the resolution is subject to limited debate (which eliminates filibusters), it can not be amended or postponed, and it is not subject to certain procedural motions that normally apply to pending legislation. The joint resolution, however, may not amend the agency rule, it can only disapprove it. If the resolution is passed by both Houses and signed by the President,[174] a rule will not go into effect, or if it is already in effect, it will cease to

172. *Id.* § 1571.

173. Contract With America Advancement Act of 1996, Pub. L. No. 104–121, 251, 110 Stat. 847, 868–74 (1996) (codified at 5 U.S.C. §§ 801–808); *see generally* Cohen & Strauss, *Congressional Review of Agency Regulations*, 49 Ad. L. Rev. 95 (1997) (providing detailed review and assessment of congressional review provisions). Most states preceded Congress in creating legislative procedures to review rules before they become effective. The most typical pattern is a single, standing committee, composed of members of both houses. Rules become effective unless they are overridden by legislation signed by the governor. For more details, *see* A. Bonfield, State Administrative Rulemaking § 8.3.1(b) (1986).

174. The requirement of the President's signature is necessary after the *Chadha* decision which declared legislative vetoes to be unconstitutional. *See supra* § 3.5; *see also* Herz, *The Legislative Veto in Times of Political Reversal: Chadha and the 104th Congress*, 14 Const. Commentary 319 (1997) (discussing the interrelationship of *Chadha* and congressional review of new rules).

be in effect. In addition, a rule that has been disapproved "may not be reissued in substantially the same form, and a new rule that is substantially the same as such a rule may not be issued, unless the reissued rule is specifically authorized by a law enacted after the date of the joint resolution disapproving the original rule."

These procedures are unlikely to have a significant impact for several reasons.[175] First, Congress has been overwhelmed by the number of rules submitted. It chose not to limit the submission requirements to major rules, although the 60 day stay provisions are limited to such rules.[176] Second, because of the press of other business, Congress will usually find it difficult to act on more than a few of the 75 to 100 major new rules that agencies promulgate each year. Third, Congress already has the power to cancel a rule if it can get the President's concurrence (or to override a presidential veto).[177] The Congressional Review Act had been dormant until the waning months of the Clinton Administration when OSHA issued its Ergonomics regulation imposing estimated costs on industry of $60–90 billion. Congress passed its joint resolution of disapproval in March 2001 and President Bush promptly signed it.[178] Since 1995, 409 rules have been laid before Congress; 17 joint resolutions of disapproval have been introduced and only one (the Ergonomics rule) has been passed.[179]

The House of Representatives established another fast-track oversight device in 1995, known as "Corrections Day."[180] After a

---

175. *See* Troy, *Congressional Review Procedures of Agency Rules*, 21 Admin. & Reg. Law News 4, 19 (Summer, 1996).

176. In fact, because of its zeal to oversee the regulatory process, Congress required the submission of all "rules" which includes, under the APA's definition of rule, the thousands of policy statements and interpretive rules issued by agencies. *See* Pfohl, *Congressional Review of Agency Rulemaking: The 104th Congress and the Salvage Timber Directive*, 14 J.L. & Politics 1 (1998) (advocating that Congress narrow the review requirements). For an explanation of policy statements and interpretive rules, *see* § 6.4.4a–b.

177. Congress is unlikely to get that approval very often since the President will defend agency rules (and thereby protect the Executive branch from legis-

lative encroachment). However, with regard to some rules that are of particular interest to oversight committees or key legislators, agencies may respond to legislative threats to invoke the review procedures by pulling or modifying the rule.

178. Recently, another regulation was challenged under the Congressional Review Act when the Senate voted on September 13, 2003 to nullify the FCC rules permitting media cross ownership of television stations and newspaper in the same market. The House has not acted.

179. *See* Cong. Res. Serv., Congressional Review of Agency Rulemaking (Sept. 16, 2002).

180. 114 Cong. Rec. H6104 (daily ed. June 20, 1995); *see* Nagle, *Corrections Day*, 43 U.C.L.A. L. Rev. 1267 (1996) (describing debate over Corrections Day).

House committee passes legislation to reverse or amend an agency rule, the Speaker can schedule the bill for the one or two days a month that the House sets aside to rectify agency "mistakes." The House rules expedite consideration of the legislation by limiting amendments and procedural motions that would impede a vote on the bill, but the bill must pass by a 60 percent majority. Any bill that fails to pass can be considered at a later date under regular House procedures. Of course, any legislation passed in this manner must be approved by the Senate (which does not have a corrections day) and signed by the President before it becomes law.

§ 9.5.5   Regulatory Review Legislation

Congress has twice come close to enacting a regulatory analysis requirement for all administrative agencies. In 1982, the Senate passed a comprehensive regulatory reform bill (S. 1080),[181] but the bill failed to clear the House. In 1995, the House passed legislation requiring detailed analytical and substantive requirements for agency rulemaking,[182] as part of the "Contract with America" proposed by House Republicans elected in 1994. The Senate's version of the legislation, the "Comprehensive Regulatory Reform Act of 1995", was also known as the "Dole bill." Senator Dole's effort was blocked by a filibuster which the Republicans failed to end by two votes. Senators Levin and Thompson sponsored a similar bill in the next Congress,[183] that, as amended,[184] attracted broad, bipartisan support. Nevertheless, Congress did not pass comprehensive legislation on agency risk assessment.

In enacting a comprehensive requirement of regulatory analysis, Congress faces three issues. First, what events should trigger an agency's obligation to engage in rulemaking analysis before proposing and finalizing a rule? Second, what is the type of analysis in which the agency should engage? Third, should the agency's compliance

181. S. 1080, 97th Cong., 1st Sess. (1981). In return for explicit extension of regulatory analysis to independent agencies, the bill required officials in charge of the regulatory analysis program to be either the Vice President, or an officer within the executive branch whose appointment was subject to Senate confirmation. This requirement would have moved responsibility from the Director of OMB, who is not subject to Senate confirmation. *Compare* Cohen, *Regulatory Reform: Assessing the California Plan,* 1983 Duke L.J. 231 (describing the California Office of Administrative Law whose chief administrator is subject to Senate confirmation). *See supra* § 4.7.2.

182. H.R. 9, 104th Cong., 1st Sess. (1995).

183. S. 981, 105th Cong., 1st Sess. (1997).

184. S. Amdt. No. 1644 (Feb. 4, 1998).

with analytical requirements be subject to judicial review and what should be the consequences of noncompliance?

The issue of the regulatory trigger is important because regulatory analysis can impose substantial costs and delays. The Comptroller General estimated that analyses of new regulations in the Reagan Administration cost an average of $212,000 each,[185] and there is no reason to believe the cost has declined. Obviously, a regulatory analysis that costs this much (or more) can be justified only if it results in millions of dollars in savings to the public by revised regulations. Moreover, critics assert that requirements to analyze regulations add to the "ossification" of the rulemaking process caused by judicial demands for detailed analysis of regulatory issues.[186] According to this criticism, agencies spend too much time studying the impact of rules and not enough time actually issuing them. Supporters reply that analytical requirements lead to more rational rules. Because both sides have a legitimate point, this debate suggests that regulatory analysis is itself a technique that ought to be controlled by principles of cost-benefit analysis. Executive Order 12,866 accomplishes this need to some extent because it applies only to "major rules" with a $100 million annual effect upon the economy.[187] Legislative proposals would likewise limit regulatory analysis to major rules, usually defined as having a $100 million annual impact on the economy, although some legislators have favored a lower threshold, such as $50 million. An alternative is a sampling procedure for significant rules, which may be a better way of achieving quality control of the regulatory analysis process with less strain upon the political system.[188]

Another trigger issue is whether to subject the independent agencies to the analysis requirements. Presidents have traditionally exempted the independent agencies from the executive order analytical requirements out of deference to Congress' decision to make such agencies more independent from White House oversight than the executive branch agencies.[189] In the legislative proposals, Congress

---

185. General Accounting Office, Improved Quality, Adequate Resources, and Consistent Oversight Needed If Regulatory Analysis is to Help Control Costs of Regulation 3 (1982).

186. For a discussion relating to ossification, *see* § 7.6.

187. Exec. Order No. 12866, §§ 3(f), 6(a).

188. Much time is presently spent in debating whether or not a given rule is or is not "major." A sampling technique that looked at rules of all sizes on a limited, but objective basis, might be to everyone's advantage.

189. *See supra* notes 157–161 & accompanying text (discussing exemption for regulatory agencies from executive orders); § 4.4.1 (discussing distinction

would end this distinction and subject all agencies to the regulatory review requirements. Since there seems to be no defensible reason to exempt independent agencies, except Congress' desire to protect them from presidential oversight, it is appropriate for Congress to end the differential treatment of such agencies.

The proposed legislation would require agencies to prepare an analysis of a rule's potential benefits and costs, and, if the benefits of a rule included the reduction of a health or safety risk, a separate analysis of the risks that the agency proposed to reduce. Earlier versions of the legislation contained more detailed requirements concerning the scope of the analysis, while later versions have been less prescriptive. Not surprisingly, representatives of regulated entities have generally favored more detailed requirements, while representatives of regulatory beneficiaries, such as environmental groups, opposed them. The latter argued that reformers were seeking "paralysis by analysis."

The same groups battled over reform for another reason. Opponents claimed that some provisions that appeared to be procedural on their face would actually operate as substantive changes. For example, some reformers favored a requirement that agencies use "best estimates" or "average values" in estimating the risk of cancer or other diseases, which would dramatically change the method by which EPA and other agencies estimate risks. Uncertainty and lack of sufficient data are common occurrences in risk assessment. One reason is that disease mechanisms, especially for cancer, are poorly understood. In addition, because the routes of exposure from the environment to a target organ are so numerous and complex, the relationship between the exposure level (dose) and the onset of disease (response) are poorly defined. In light of the uncertainty, EPA makes worst-case estimates of how dangerous a toxic substance might be in the absence of convincing contrary evidence. EPA defends its approach as consistent with the preventative nature of the environmental legislation which it administers. The reader might agree or disagree with EPA's decision to err on the side of safety, but there should be no dispute that this is a substantive policy judgment rather than a matter of procedure.[190]

between executive and independent agencies).

190. *See* Campbell–Mohn & Applegate, *Using Risk Responsibly: Learning from NEPA*, 23 Harv. Envtl. L. Rev. 93 (1999) (describing and explaining the debate about risk assessment policy); Applegate, *A Beginning and Not an End in Itself: The Proper Role of Risk in Environmental Decisionmaking*, 63 U. Cin. L. Rev. 1643 (1995) (same).

Congress has debated three approaches to judicial review. The most restrictive approach, which follows the Regulatory Flexibility Act and the executive orders, prohibits judicial enforcement of the analysis requirements themselves, but any analyses would become part of the rulemaking record. A second approach follows the Unfunded Mandates Act and permits judicial review of compliance with analytical requirements. If there is noncompliance, however, a court could only order the agency to comply after-the-fact, and it could not enjoin the rule because of procedural violations. The final and most intrusive approach would make compliance with analytical requirements fully subject to judicial review. This approach would authorize a court to prohibit an agency from enforcing any rule if the agency violates any analytical requirements.

The difficulty with this last proposal is that it could lead to judicial invalidation of important rules because of relatively minor defects in agency compliance, particularly if agencies must comply with detailed and complex analytical requirements, as some legislators and interest groups favor. The better approach is to consider the results of regulatory analysis as part of the rulemaking record. In typically astute fashion, the late Judge McGowan predicted that an agency might benefit when a court considers its regulatory analysis as part of the rulemaking record: "It may well be that, if such analyses are well done, the agencies will be less vulnerable to judicial scrutiny."[191] Presumably, the opposite result would also occur: If an agency produces an analysis of poor quality, it will encourage the court to reject the rule. If these effects were to occur, the regulatory analysis process would indeed have an effect upon substantive review.

§ 9.5.6   The future of regulatory analysis

Regulatory analysis became a byword for executive policy-making in the 1980's when many felt that agencies should regulate with a light touch, if at all. In this sense, it served at least two purposes: regulatory relief and bureaucratic accountability. Those who favored these purposes found a sympathetic ear at the White House from Republican presidents and a less sympathetic reception in Congress which was then controlled by the Democrats. In the 1990s, the tables were turned. The Republican majority in Congress saw in regulatory analysis the opportunity for less regulation and more control over the

---

191. McGowan, *Regulatory Analysis*   627, 634 (1981).
and Judicial Review, 42 Ohio St. L.J.

bureaucracy, while the White House was far from convinced. There was less of a partisan split, however, concerning regulatory analysis as a tool of more rational decisionmaking.[192]

Regulatory analysis still offers the promise of "smarter" regulation, but it is not a magic bullet. One must consider the confusion and demoralization that befalls an agency whose policy-makers are consistently overruled or second-guessed by powerful agents of the White House. In some cases, such oversight will eliminate inefficient and wasteful regulation but, in other cases, it can discourage needed regulatory initiatives or delay their completion and implementation. The notion of deference to agency "expertise" may no longer be fashionable or even justified, but there is some merit still to reliance upon experienced officials with proximity to the regulatory problems. As agencies have become more experienced with the use of regulatory analysis, there is less need to impose it upon them. The Clinton administration seemed to have heeded this lesson, but the Bush administration has returned to a more interventionist regulatory approach.[193]

One should always be leery of accomplishing substantive purposes through procedural means, such as regulatory. Those who oppose regulation may find it politically easier to enact procedures that inhibit regulation than to amend legislation to adopt the substantive changes which they favor. Procedural efforts are less visible and comprehensible to the public and thus may attract less opposition. Still, the adoption of any procedure has the potential to slow down the regulatory process. Good faith advocates of procedural reform inevitably must resolve conflicts between the promotion of accountability and accurate decisions and the efficient realization of an agency's mandate.

§ 9.6 Concluding Note

Administration is meant to be a political process. Attempts to make it more fair or more accountable must accept that fact. Politics cannot be legislated away and political influences can be regulated, or moderated, only in modest ways. These conclusions are not alarming so long as the political system is itself open and accountable, as

---

192. *See* T. McGarity, Reinventing Rationality: Regulatory Analysis in the Federal Government (1991). *See also* Blumstein, Regulatory Review by the Executive Office of the President: An Overview and Policy Analysis of Current Issues, 51 Duke L.J. 851 (2001).

193. *See* GAO Report, *supra* note 155, at 5(describing the shift in a shift OMB's role from the Clinton administration to the Bush administration as "from counselor to gatekeeper").

Professor Ely has long ago noted. Thus, administrative law and process can never be superior to the system that produces it.

Reform efforts like those presented in this chapter arise from unease with the political process. Openness, neutrality, independence, and political accountability are enduring themes that have been given statutory content in the administrative setting. But they can be successful only to the extent that they accept the relationship between process and political reality. In our system, it is exceedingly difficult to legislate behavior in public law matters when those efforts incorporate values not fully shared in the private sector.

The judiciary has a limited, but important, role in implementing these reforms. As the least politically-accountable branch,[194] the judiciary's first responsibility is to ensure that the political process works. This obligation is of constitutional dimensions, but it also has an analogue in the implementation of the reforms discussed here. An important aspect of the political process is agency government. If one views the bureaucracy historically,[195] agencies are as much involved in the conflicts between majority rule and individual rights as the judiciary has been. In this situation, the courts have a responsibility to ensure the success of agency government as part of the political process.[196]

The judicial responsibility to police agencies has a due process core. It is implemented through the enforcement of statutes concerned with such doctrines as separation of powers, decider-neutrality, and ex parte contacts. The judiciary also draws its responsibility to police agencies from statutory requirements that administration be open to public scrutiny. The courts must ultimately decide whether a statutory requirement puts limits on the administrative process.

In making these statutory determinations, the courts engage in a process of balancing politics and law. The primary responsibility for good government remains with the voters, not the judges. Thus, courts should think twice about whether a better or fairer process can be produced by expanded procedural rules. While such rules can be beneficial, in many cases they will make the political process more

---

194. The Court has reminded us that "Judges are not experts in the field, and are not part of either political branch of the Government." Chevron U.S.A., Inc. v. NRDC, 467 U.S. 837, 865 (1984).

195. *See* W. Nelson, The Roots of American Bureaucracy (1830–1900) (1982).

196. *See* J. L. Mashaw, Greed, Chaos & Governance (1997) (describing the inevitable interrelation between the bureaucracy, politics and law).

difficult to implement for those in Congress, in the Executive, and in the agencies who have the immediate responsibility for shaping public policy in our system.[197]

197. These considerations are also addressed in the earlier sections on judi- cial review. *See supra* § 7.6.

*

Appendix

FEDERAL ADMINISTRATIVE
PROCEDURE ACT

United States Code. Title 5

CHAPTER 5—Administrative Procedure

SUBCHAPTER II—ADMINISTRATIVE PROCEDURE

---

§ 551. Definitions.

For the purpose of this subchapter—

(1) "agency" means each authority of the Government of the United States, whether or not it is within or subject to review by another agency, but does not include—

    (A) the Congress;

    (B) the courts of the United States;

    (C) the governments of the territories or possessions of the United States;

(D) the government of the District of Columbia; or except as to the requirements of section 552 of this title

(E) agencies composed of representatives of the parties or of representatives of organizations of the parties to the disputes determined by them;

(F) courts martial and military commissions;

(G) military authority exercised in the field in time of war or in occupied territory; or

(H) functions conferred by sections 1738, 1739, 1743, and 1744 of title 12; chapter 2 of title 41; subchapter II of chapter 471 of title 49; or sections 1884, 1891–1902, and former section 1641(b)(2), of title 50, appendix;

(2) "person" includes an individual, partnership, corporation, association, or public or private organization other than an agency;

(3) "party" includes a person or agency named or admitted as a party, or properly seeking and entitled as of right to be admitted as a party, in an agency proceeding, and a person or agency admitted by an agency as a party for limited purposes;

(4) "rule" means the whole or a part of an agency statement of general or particular applicability and future effect designed to implement, interpret, or prescribe law or policy or describing the organization, procedure, or practice requirements of an agency and includes the approval or prescription for the future of rates, wages, corporate or financial structures or reorganizations thereof, prices, facilities, appliances, services or allowances therefor or of valuations, costs, or accounting, or practices bearing on any of the foregoing;

(5) "rule making" means agency process for formulating, amending, or repealing a rule;

(6) "order" means the whole or a part of a final disposition, whether affirmative, negative, injunctive, or declaratory in form, of an agency in a matter other than rule making but including licensing;

(7) "adjudication" means agency process for the formulation of an order;

(8) "license" includes the whole or a part of an agency permit, certificate, approval, registration, charter, membership, statutory exemption or other form of permission;

(9) "licensing" includes agency process respecting the grant, renewal, denial, revocation, suspension, annulment, withdrawal, limitation, amendment, modification, or conditioning of a license;

(10) "sanction" includes the whole or a part of an agency—

(A) prohibition, requirement, limitation, or other condition affecting the freedom of a person;

(B) withholding of relief;

(C) imposition of penalty or fine;

(D) destruction, taking, seizure, or withholding of property;

(E) assessment of damages, reimbursement, restitution, compensation, costs, charges, or fees;

(F) requirement, revocation, or suspension of a license; or

(G) taking other compulsory or restrictive action;

(11) "relief" includes the whole or a part of an agency—

(A) grant of money, assistance, license, authority, exemption, exception, privilege, or remedy;

(B) recognition of a claim, right, immunity, privilege, exemption, or exception; or

(C) taking of other action on the application or petition of, and beneficial to, a person;

(12) "agency proceeding" means an agency process as defined by paragraphs (5), (7), and (9) of this section;

(13) "agency action" includes the whole or a part of an agency rule, order, license, sanction, relief, or the equivalent or denial thereof, or failure to act; and

(14) "ex parte communication" means an oral or written communication not on the public record with respect to which reasonable prior notice to all parties is not given, but it shall not include requests for status reports on any matter or proceeding covered by this subchapter.

§ 552. Public information; agency rules, opinions, orders, records, and proceedings.

(a) Each agency shall make available to the public information as follows:

(1) Each agency shall separately state and currently publish in the Federal Register for the guidance of the public—

(A) descriptions of its central and field organization and the established places at which, the employees (and in the case of a uniformed service, the members) from whom, and the methods whereby, the public may obtain information, make submittals or requests, or obtain decisions;

(B) statements of the general course and method by which its functions are channeled and determined, including the nature and requirements of all formal and informal procedures available;

(C) rules of procedure, descriptions of forms available or the places at which forms may be obtained, and instructions as to the scope and contents of all papers, reports, or examinations;

(D) substantive rules of general applicability adopted as authorized by law, and statements of general policy or interpretations of general applicability formulated and adopted by the agency; and

(E) each amendment, revision, or repeal of the foregoing. Except to the extent that a person has actual and timely notice of the terms thereof, a person may not in any manner be required to resort to, or be adversely affected by, a matter required to be published in the Federal Register and not so published. For the purpose of this paragraph, matter reasonably available to the class of persons affected thereby is deemed published in the Federal Register when incorporated by reference therein with the approval of the Director of the Federal Register.

(2) Each agency, in accordance with published rules, shall make available for public inspection and copying—

(A) final opinions, including concurring and dissenting opinions, as well as orders, made in the adjudication of cases;

(B) those statements of policy and interpretations which have been adopted by the agency and are not published in the Federal Register; and

(C) administrative staff manuals and instructions to staff that affect a member of the public;

unless the materials are promptly published and copies offered for sale. To the extent required to prevent a clearly unwarranted invasion of personal privacy, an agency may delete identifying details when it makes available or publishes an opinion, statement of policy, interpretation, or staff manual or instruction. However, in each case the justification for the deletion shall be explained fully in writing. Each agency shall also maintain and make available for public inspection and copying current indexes providing identifying information for the public as to any matter issued, adopted, or promulgated after July 4, 1967, and required by this paragraph to be made available or published. Each agency shall promptly publish, quarterly or more frequently, and distribute (by sale or otherwise) copies of each index or supplements thereto unless it determines by order published in the Federal Register that the publication would be unnecessary and impracticable, in which case the agency shall nonetheless provide copies of such index on request at a cost not to exceed the direct cost of duplication. A final order, opinion, statement of policy, interpretation, or staff manual or instruction that affects a member of the public may be relied on, used, or cited as precedent by an agency against a party other than an agency only if—

 (i) it has been indexed and either made available or published as provided by this paragraph; or

 (ii) the party has actual and timely notice of the terms thereof.

(3)(A) Except with respect to the records made available under paragraphs (1) and (2) of this subsection, and except as provided in subparagraph (E), each agency, upon any request for records which (i) reasonably describes such records and (ii) is made in accordance with published rules stating the time, place, fees (if any), and procedures to be followed, shall make the records promptly available to any person.

 (B) In making any record available to a person under this paragraph, an agency shall provide the record in any form or format requested by the person if the record is readily reproducible by the agency in that form or format. Each agency shall make reasonable efforts to maintain its records in forms or formats that are reproducible for purposes of this section.

 (C) In responding under this paragraph to a request for records, an agency shall make reasonable efforts to search for the records in electronic form or format, except when such efforts would significantly interfere with the operation of the agency's automated information system.

 (D) For purposes of this paragraph, the term "search" means to review, manually or by automated means, agency records for the purpose of locating those records which are responsive to a request.

(E) An agency, or part of an agency, that is an element of the intelligence community (as that term is defined in section 3(4) of the National Security Act of 1947 (50 U.S.C. 401a(4)) shall not make any record available under this paragraph to—

(i) any government entity, other than a State, territory, commonwealth, or district of the United States, or any subdivision thereof; or

(ii) a representative of a government entity described in clause (i).

(4)(A)(i) In order to carry out the provisions of this section, each agency shall promulgate regulations, pursuant to notice and receipt of public comment, specifying the schedule of fees applicable to the processing of requests under this section and establishing procedures and guidelines for determining when such fees should be waived or reduced. Such schedule shall conform to the guidelines which shall be promulgated, pursuant to notice and receipt of public comment, by the Director of the Office of Management and Budget and which shall provide for a uniform schedule of fees for all agencies.

(ii) Such agency regulations shall provide that—

(I) fees shall be limited to reasonable standard charges for document search, duplication, and review, when records are requested for commercial use;

(II) fees shall be limited to reasonable standard charges for document duplication when records are not sought for commercial use and the request is made by an educational or noncommercial scientific institution, whose purpose is scholarly or scientific research; or a representative of the news media; and

(III) for any request not described in (I) or (II), fees shall be limited to reasonable standard charges for document search and duplication.

(iii) Documents shall be furnished without any charge or at a charge reduced below the fees established under clause (ii) if disclosure of the information is in the public interest because it is likely to contribute significantly to public understanding of the operations or activities of the government and is not primarily in the commercial interest of the requester.

(iv) Fee schedules shall provide for the recovery of only the direct costs of search, duplication, or review. Review costs shall include only the direct costs incurred during the initial examination of a document for the purposes of determining whether the documents must be disclosed under this section and for the purposes of withholding any portions exempt from disclosure under this section. Review costs may not include any costs incurred in resolving issues of law or policy that may be raised in the course of processing a request under this section. No fee may be charged by any agency under this section—

(I) if the costs of routine collection and processing of the fee are likely to equal or exceed the amount of the fee; or

(II) for any request described in clause (ii) (II) or (III) of this subparagraph for the first two hours of search time or for the first one hundred pages of duplication.

(v) No agency may require advance payment of any fee unless the requester has previously failed to pay fees in a timely fashion, or the agency has determined that the fee will exceed $250.

(vi) Nothing in this subparagraph shall supersede fees chargeable under a statute specifically providing for setting the level of fees for particular types of records.

(vii) In any action by a requester regarding the waiver of fees under this section, the court shall determine the matter de novo: Provided, That the court's review of the matter shall be limited to the record before the agency.

(B) On complaint, the district court of the United States in the district in which the complainant resides, or has his principal place of business, or in which the agency records are situated, or in the District of Columbia, has jurisdiction to enjoin the agency from withholding agency records and to order the production of any agency records improperly withheld from the complainant. In such a case the court shall determine the matter de novo, and may examine the contents of such agency records in camera to determine whether such records or any part thereof shall be withheld under any of the exemptions set forth in subsection (b) of this section, and the burden is on the agency to sustain its action.

(C) Notwithstanding any other provision of law, the defendant shall serve an answer or otherwise plead to any complaint made under this subsection within thirty days after service upon the defendant of the pleading in which such complaint is made, unless the court otherwise directs for good cause shown.

(D) Repealed. Pub. L. 98–620, title IV, Sec. 402(2), Nov. 8, 1984, 98 Stat. 3357.)

(E) The court may assess against the United States reasonable attorney fees and other litigation costs reasonably incurred in any case under this section in which the complainant has substantially prevailed.

(F) Whenever the court orders the production of any agency records improperly withheld from the complainant and assesses against the United States reasonable attorney fees and other litigation costs, and the court additionally issues a written finding that the circumstances surrounding the withholding raise questions whether agency personnel acted arbitrarily or capriciously with respect to the withholding, the Special Counsel shall promptly initiate a proceeding to determine whether disciplinary action is warranted against the officer or employee who was primarily responsible for the withholding. The Special Counsel, after investigation and consideration of the evidence submitted, shall submit his findings and recommendations to the administrative authority of the agency concerned and shall send copies of the findings and recommendations to the officer or employee or his representative. The administrative authority shall take the corrective action that the Special Counsel recommends.

(G) In the event of noncompliance with the order of the court, the district court may punish for contempt the responsible employee, and in the case of a uniformed service, the responsible member.

(5) Each agency having more than one member shall maintain and make available for public inspection a record of the final votes of each member in every agency proceeding.

(6)(A) Each agency, upon any request for records made under paragraph (1), (2), or (3) of this subsection, shall—

(i) determine within ten days (excepting Saturdays, Sundays, and legal public holidays) after the receipt of any such request whether to comply with such request and shall immediately notify the person making such request of such determination and the reasons therefor, and of the right of such person to appeal to the head of the agency any adverse determination; and

(ii) make a determination with respect to any appeal within twenty days (excepting Saturdays, Sundays, and legal public holidays) after the receipt of such appeal. If on appeal the denial of the request for records is in whole or in part upheld, the agency shall notify the person making such request of the provisions for judicial review of that determination under paragraph (4) of this subsection.

(B) In unusual circumstances as specified in this subparagraph, the time limits prescribed in either clause (i) or clause (ii) of subparagraph (A) may be extended by written notice to the person making such request setting forth the reasons for such extension and the date on which a determination is expected to be dispatched. No such notice shall specify a date that would result in an extension for more than ten working days. As used in this subparagraph, "unusual circumstances" means, but only to the extent reasonably necessary to the proper processing of the particular request—

(i) the need to search for and collect the requested records from field facilities or other establishments that are separate from the office processing the request;

(ii) the need to search for, collect, and appropriately examine a voluminous amount of separate and distinct records which are demanded in a single request; or

(iii) the need for consultation, which shall be conducted with all practicable speed, with another agency having a substantial interest in the determination of the request or among two or more components of the agency having substantial subject-matter interest therein.

(C) Any person making a request to any agency for records under paragraph (1), (2), or (3) of this subsection shall be deemed to have exhausted his administrative remedies with respect to such request if the agency fails to comply with the applicable time limit provisions of this paragraph. If the Government can show exceptional circumstances exist and that the agency is exercising due diligence in responding to the request, the court may retain jurisdiction and allow the agency additional time to complete its review of the records. Upon any determination by an agency to comply with a request for records, the records shall be made promptly available to such person making such request. Any notification of denial of any request for records under this subsection shall set forth the names and titles or positions of each person responsible for the denial of such request.

(b) This section does not apply to matters that are—

(1)(A) specifically authorized under criteria established by an Executive order to be kept secret in the interest of national defense or foreign policy and (B) are in fact properly classified pursuant to such Executive order;

(2) related solely to the internal personnel rules and practices of an agency;

(3) specifically exempted from disclosure by statute (other than section 552b of this title), provided that such statute (A) requires that the matters be withheld from the public in such a manner as to leave no discretion on the issue, or (B) establishes particular criteria for withholding or refers to particular types of matters to be withheld;

(4) trade secrets and commercial or financial information obtained from a person and privileged or confidential;

(5) inter-agency or intra-agency memorandums or letters which would not be available by law to a party other than an agency in litigation with the agency;

(6) personnel and medical files and similar files the disclosure of which would constitute a clearly unwarranted invasion of personal privacy;

(7) records or information compiled for law enforcement purposes, but only to the extent that the production of such law enforcement records or information (A) could reasonably be expected to interfere with enforcement proceedings, (B) would deprive a person of a right to a fair trial or an impartial adjudication, (C) could reasonably be expected to constitute an unwarranted invasion of personal privacy, (D) could reasonably be expected to disclose the identity of a confidential source, including a State, local, or foreign agency or authority or any private institution which furnished information on a confidential basis, and, in the case of a record or information compiled by criminal law enforcement authority in the course of a criminal investigation or by an agency conducting a lawful national security intelligence investigation, information furnished by a confidential source, (E) would disclose techniques and procedures for law enforcement investigations or prosecutions, or would disclose guidelines for law enforcement investigations or prosecutions if such disclosure could reasonably be expected to risk circumvention of the law, or (F) could reasonably be expected to endanger the life or physical safety of any individual;

(8) contained in or related to examination, operating, or condition reports prepared by, on behalf of, or for the use of an agency responsible for the regulation or supervision of financial institutions; or

(9) geological and geophysical information and data, including maps, concerning wells. Any reasonably segregable portion of a

record shall be provided to any person requesting such record after deletion of the portions which are exempt under this subsection.

(c)(1) Whenever a request is made which involves access to records described in subsection (b)(7)(A) and—

(A) the investigation or proceeding involves a possible violation of criminal law; and

(B) there is reason to believe that

(i) the subject of the investigation or proceeding is not aware of its pendency, and

(ii) disclosure of the existence of the records could reasonably be expected to interfere with enforcement proceedings, the agency may, during only such time as that circumstance continues, treat the records as not subject to the requirements of this section.

(2) Whenever informant records maintained by a criminal law enforcement agency under an informant's name or personal identifier are requested by a third party according to the informant's name or personal identifier, the agency may treat the records as not subject to the requirements of this section unless the informant's status as an informant has been officially confirmed.

(3) Whenever a request is made which involves access to records maintained by the Federal Bureau of Investigation pertaining to foreign intelligence or counterintelligence, or international terrorism, and the existence of the records is classified information as provided in subsection (b)(1), the Bureau may, as long as the existence of the records remains classified information, treat the records as not subject to the requirements of this section.

(d) This section does not authorize withholding of information or limit the availability of records to the public, except as specifically stated in this section. This section is not authority to withhold information from Congress.

(e) On or before March 1 of each calendar year, each agency shall submit a report covering the preceding calendar year to the Speaker of the House of Representatives and President of the Senate for referral to the appropriate committees of the Congress. The report shall include—

(1) the number of determinations made by such agency not to comply with requests for records made to such agency under subsection (a) and the reasons for each such determination;

(2) the number of appeals made by persons under subsection (a)(6), the result of such appeals, and the reason for the action upon each appeal that results in a denial of information;

(3) the names and titles or positions of each person responsible for the denial of records requested under this section, and the number of instances of participation for each;

(4) the results of each proceeding conducted pursuant to subsection (a)(4)(F), including a report of the disciplinary action taken against the officer or employee who was primarily responsible for improperly withholding records or an explanation of why disciplinary action was not taken;

(5) a copy of every rule made by such agency regarding this section;

(6) a copy of the fee schedule and the total amount of fees collected by the agency for making records available under this section; and

(7) such other information as indicates efforts to administer fully this section.

The Attorney General shall submit an annual report on or before March 1 of each calendar year which shall include for the prior calendar year a listing of the number of cases arising under this section, the exemption involved in each case, the disposition of such case, and the cost, fees, and penalties assessed under subsections (a)(4)(E), (F), and (G). Such report shall also include a description of the efforts undertaken by the Department of Justice to encourage agency compliance with this section.

(f) For purposes of this section, the term "agency" as defined in section 551(1) of this title includes any executive department, military department, Government corporation, Government controlled corporation, or other establishment in the executive branch of the Government (including the Executive Office of the President), or any independent regulatory agency.

§ 552a. Records about individuals.

(a) Definitions.

For purposes of this section

(1) the term "agency" means agency as defined in section 552(e) of this title;

(2) the term "individual" means a citizen of the United States or an alien lawfully admitted for permanent residence;

(3) the term "maintain" includes maintain, collect, use, or disseminate;

(4) the term "record" means any item, collection, or grouping of information about an individual that is maintained by an agency, including, but not limited to, his education, financial transactions, medical history, and criminal or employment history and that contains his name, or the identifying number, symbol, or other identifying particular assigned to the individual, such as a finger or voice print or a photograph;

(5) the term "system of records" means a group of any records under the control of any agency from which information is retrieved by the name of the individual or by some identifying number, symbol, or other identifying particular assigned to the individual;

(6) the term "statistical record" means a record in a system of records maintained for statistical research or reporting purposes only and not used in whole or in part in making any determination about an identifiable individual, except as provided by section 8 of title 13;

(7) the term "routine use" means, with respect to the disclosure of a record, the use of such record for a purpose which is compatible with the purpose for which it was collected;

(8) the term "matching program"—

(A) means any computerized comparison of—

(i) two or more automated systems of records or a system of records with non-Federal records for the purpose of—

(I) establishing or verifying the eligibility of, or continuing compliance with statutory and regulatory requirements by, applicants for, recipients or beneficiaries of, participants in, or providers of services with respect to, cash or in-kind assistance or payments under Federal benefit programs, or

(II) recouping payments or delinquent debts under such Federal benefit programs, or

(ii) two or more automated Federal personnel or payroll systems of records or a system of Federal personnel or payroll records with non-Federal records,

(B) but does not include—

(i) matches performed to produce aggregate statistical data without any personal identifiers;

(ii) matches performed to support any research or statistical project, the specific data of which may not be used to make decisions concerning the rights, benefits, or privileges of specific individuals;

(iii) matches performed, by an agency (or component thereof) which performs as its principal function any activity pertaining to the enforcement of criminal laws, subsequent to the initiation of a specific criminal or civil law enforcement investigation of a named person or persons for the purpose of gathering evidence against such person or persons;

(iv) matches of tax information (I) pursuant to section 6103(d) of the Internal Revenue Code of 1986, (II) for purposes of tax administration as defined in section 6103(b)(4) of such Code, (III) for the purpose of intercepting a tax refund due an individual under authority granted by section 464 or 1137 of the Social Security Act; or (IV) for the purpose of intercepting a tax refund due an individual under any other tax refund intercept program authorized by statute which has been determined by the Director of the Office of Management and Budget to contain verification, notice, and hearing requirements that are substantially similar to the procedures in section 1137 of the Social Security Act;

(v) matches—

(I) using records predominantly relating to Federal personnel, that are performed for routine administrative purposes (subject to guidance provided by the Director of the Office of Management and Budget pursuant to subsection (v)); or

(II) conducted by an agency using only records from systems of records maintained by that agency; if the purpose of the match is not to take any adverse financial, personnel, disciplinary, or other adverse action against Federal personnel;

(vi) matches performed for foreign counterintelligence purposes or to produce background checks for security clearances of Federal personnel or Federal contractor personnel; or

(vii) matches performed pursuant to section 6103(l)(12) of the Internal Revenue Code of 1986 and section 1144 of the Social Security Act;

(viii) matches performed pursuant to section 202(x)(3) or 1611(e)(1) of the Social Security Act (42 U.S.C. 402(x)(3), 1382(e)(1));

(9) the term "recipient agency" means any agency, or contractor thereof, receiving records contained in a system of records from a source agency for use in a matching program;

(10) the term "non-Federal agency" means any State or local government, or agency thereof, which receives records contained in a system of records from a source agency for use in a matching program;

(11) the term "source agency" means any agency which discloses records contained in a system of records to be used in a matching program, or any State or local government, or agency thereof, which discloses records to be used in a matching program;

(12) the term "Federal benefit program" means any program administered or funded by the Federal Government, or by any agent or State on behalf of the Federal Government, providing cash or in-kind assistance in the form of payments, grants, loans, or loan guarantees to individuals; and

(13) the term "Federal personnel" means officers and employees of the Government of the United States, members of the uniformed services (including members of the Reserve Components), individuals entitled to receive immediate or deferred retirement benefits under any retirement program of the Government of the United States (including survivor benefits).

(b) Conditions of Disclosure.

No agency shall disclose any record which is contained in a system of records by any means of communication to any person, or to another agency, except pursuant to a written request by, or with the prior written consent of, the individual to whom the record pertains, unless disclosure of the record would be—

(1) to those officers and employees of the agency which maintains the record who have a need for the record in the performance of their duties;

(2) required under section 552 of this title;

(3) for a routine use as defined in subsection (a)(7) of this section and described under subsection (e)(4)(D) of this section;

(4) to the Bureau of the Census for purposes of planning or carrying out a census or survey or related activity pursuant to the provisions of title 13;

(5) to a recipient who has provided the agency with advance adequate written assurance that the record will be used solely as a statistical research or reporting record, and the record is to be transferred in a form that is not individually identifiable;

(6) to the National Archives and Records Administration as a record which has sufficient historical or other value to warrant its continued preservation by the United States Government, or for evaluation by the Archivist of the United States or the designee of the Archivist to determine whether the record has such value;

(7) to another agency or to an instrumentality of any governmental jurisdiction within or under the control of the United States for a civil or criminal law enforcement activity if the activity is authorized by law, and if the head of the agency or instrumentality has made a written request to the agency which maintains the record specifying the particular portion desired and the law enforcement activity for which the record is sought;

(8) to a person pursuant to a showing of compelling circumstances affecting the health or safety of an individual if upon such disclosure notification is transmitted to the last known address of such individual;

(9) to either House of Congress, or, to the extent of matter within its jurisdiction, any committee or subcommittee thereof, any joint committee of Congress or subcommittee of any such joint committee;

(10) to the Comptroller General, or any of his authorized representatives, in the course of the performance of the duties of the General Accounting Office;

(11) pursuant to the order of a court of competent jurisdiction; or

(12) to a consumer reporting agency in accordance with section 3711(f) of title 31.

(c) Accounting of Certain Disclosures.

Each agency, with respect to each system of records under its control, shall—

(1) except for disclosures made under subsections (b)(1) or (b)(2) of this section, keep an accurate accounting of—

(A) the date, nature, and purpose of each disclosure of a record to any person or to another agency made under subsection (b) of this section; and

(B) the name and address of the person or agency to whom the disclosure is made;

(2) retain the accounting made under paragraph (1) of this subsection for at least five years or the life of the record, whichever is longer, after the disclosure for which the accounting is made;

(3) except for disclosures made under subsection (b)(7) of this section, make the accounting made under paragraph (1) of this subsection available to the individual named in the record at his request; and

(4) inform any person or other agency about any correction or notation of dispute made by the agency in accordance with subsection (d) of this section of any record that has been disclosed to the person or agency if an accounting of the disclosure was made.

(d) Access to Records.

Each agency that maintains a system of records shall—

(1) upon request by any individual to gain access to his record or to any information pertaining to him which is contained in the system, permit him and upon his request, a person of his own choosing to accompany him, to review the record and have a copy made of all or any portion thereof in a form comprehensible to him, except that the agency may require the individual to furnish a written statement authorizing discussion of that individual's record in the accompanying person's presence;

(2) permit the individual to request amendment of a record pertaining to him and—

(A) not later than 10 days (excluding Saturdays, Sundays, and legal public holidays) after the date of receipt of such request, acknowledge in writing such receipt; and

(B) promptly, either—

(i) make any correction of any portion thereof which the individual believes is not accurate, relevant, timely, or complete; or

(ii) inform the individual of its refusal to amend the record in accordance with his request, the reason for the refusal, the procedures established by the agency for the individual to request a review of that refusal by the head of the agency or an officer designated by the head of the agency, and the name and business address of that official;

(3) permit the individual who disagrees with the refusal of the agency to amend his record to request a review of such refusal, and not later than 30 days (excluding Saturdays, Sundays, and legal public holidays) from the date on which the individual requests such review, complete such review and make a final determination unless, for good cause shown, the head of the agency extends such 30–day period; and if, after his review, the reviewing official also refuses to amend the record in accordance with the request, permit the individual to file with the agency a concise statement setting forth the reasons for his disagreement with the refusal of the agency, and notify the individual of the provisions for judicial review of the reviewing official's determination under subsection (g)(1)(A) of this section;

(4) in any disclosure, containing information about which the individual has filed a statement of disagreement, occurring after the filing of the statement under paragraph (3) of this subsection, clearly note any portion of the record which is disputed and provide copies of the statement and, if the agency deems it appropriate, copies of a concise statement of the reasons of the agency for not making the amendments requested, to persons or other agencies to whom the disputed record has been disclosed; and

(5) nothing in this section shall allow an individual access to any information compiled in reasonable anticipation of a civil action or proceeding.

(e) Agency Requirements.

Each agency that maintains a system of records shall—

(1) maintain in its records only such information about an individual as is relevant and necessary to accomplish a purpose of the agency required to be accomplished by statute or by executive order of the President;

(2) collect information to the greatest extent practicable directly from the subject individual when the information may result in adverse determinations about an individual's rights, benefits, and privileges under Federal programs;

(3) inform each individual whom it asks to supply information, on the form which it uses to collect the information or on a separate form that can be retained by the individual—

(A) the authority (whether granted by statute, or by executive order of the President) which authorizes the solicitation of the information and whether disclosure of such information is mandatory or voluntary;

(B) the principal purpose or purposes for which the information is intended to be used;

(C) the routine uses which may be made of the information, as published pursuant to paragraph (4)(D) of this subsection; and

(D) the effects on him, if any, of not providing all or any part of the requested information;

(4) subject to the provisions of paragraph (11) of this subsection, publish in the Federal Register upon establishment or revision a notice of the existence and character of the system of records, which notice shall include—

(A) the name and location of the system;

(B) the categories of individuals on whom records are maintained in the system;

(C) the categories of records maintained in the system;

(D) each routine use of the records contained in the system, including the categories of users and the purpose of such use;

(E) the policies and practices of the agency regarding storage, retrievability, access controls, retention, and disposal of the records;

(F) the title and business address of the agency official who is responsible for the system of records;

(G) the agency procedures whereby an individual can be notified at his request if the system of records contains a record pertaining to him;

(H) the agency procedures whereby an individual can be notified at his request how he can gain access to any record pertaining to him contained in the system of records, and how he can contest its content; and

(I) the categories of sources of records in the system;

(5) maintain all records which are used by the agency in making any determination about any individual with such accuracy, relevance, timeliness, and completeness as is reasonably necessary to assure fairness to the individual in the determination;

(6) prior to disseminating any record about an individual to any person other than an agency, unless the dissemination is made pursuant to subsection (b)(2) of this section, make reasonable efforts to assure that such records are accurate, complete, timely, and relevant for agency purposes;

(7) maintain no record describing how any individual exercises rights guaranteed by the First Amendment unless expressly authorized by statute or by the individual about whom the record is maintained or unless pertinent to and within the scope of an authorized law enforcement activity;

(8) make reasonable efforts to serve notice on an individual when any record on such individual is made available to any person under compulsory legal process when such process becomes a matter of public record;

(9) establish rules of conduct for persons involved in the design, development, operation, or maintenance of any system of records, or in maintaining any record, and instruct each such person with respect to such rules and the requirements of this section, including any other rules and procedures adopted pursuant to this section and the penalties for noncompliance;

(10) establish appropriate administrative, technical, and physical safeguards to insure the security and confidentiality of records and to protect against any anticipated threats or hazards to their security or integrity which could result in substantial harm, embarrassment, inconvenience, or unfairness to any individual on whom information is maintained;

(11) at least 30 days prior to publication of information under paragraph (4)(D) of this subsection, publish in the Federal Register notice of any new use or intended use of the information in the system, and provide an opportunity for interested persons to submit written data, views, or arguments to the agency; and

(12) if such agency is a recipient agency or a source agency in a matching program with a non-Federal agency, with respect to any establishment or revision of a matching program, at least 30 days prior to conducting such program, publish in the Federal Register notice of such establishment or revision.

(f) Agency Rules.

In order to carry out the provisions of this section, each agency that maintains a system of records shall promulgate rules, in accordance with the requirements (including general notice) of section 553 of this title, which shall—

(1) establish procedures whereby an individual can be notified in response to his request if any system of records named by the individual contains a record pertaining to him;

(2) define reasonable times, places, and requirements for identifying an individual who requests his record or information pertaining to him before the agency shall make the record or information available to the individual;

(3) establish procedures for the disclosure to an individual upon his request of his record or information pertaining to him, including special procedure, if deemed necessary, for the disclosure to an individual of medical records, including psychological records, pertaining to him;

(4) establish procedures for reviewing a request from an individual concerning the amendment of any record or information pertaining to the individual, for making a determination on the request, for an appeal within the agency of an initial adverse agency determination, and for whatever additional means may be necessary for each individual to be able to exercise fully his rights under this section; and

(5) establish fees to be charged, if any, to any individual for making copies of his record, excluding the cost of any search for and review of the record. The Office of the Federal Register shall biennially compile and publish the rules promulgated under this subsection and agency notices published under subsection (e)(4) of this section in a form available to the public at low cost.

(g) Civil Remedies.

Whenever any agency—

(1) (A) makes a determination under subsection (d)(3) of this section not to amend an individual's record in accordance with his request, or fails to make such review in conformity with that subsection;

(B) refuses to comply with an individual request under subsection (d)(1) of this section;

(C) fails to maintain any record concerning any individual with such accuracy, relevance, timeliness, and completeness as is necessary to assure fairness in any determination relating to the qualifications, character, rights, or opportunities of, or benefits to the individual that may be made on the basis of such record, and consequently a determination is made which is adverse to the individual; or

(D) fails to comply with any other provision of this section, or any rule promulgated thereunder, in such a way as to have an adverse effect on an individual, the individual may bring a civil action against the agency, and the district courts of the United States shall have jurisdiction in the matters under the provisions of this subsection.

(2)(A) In any suit brought under the provisions of subsection (g)(1)(A) of this section, the court may order the agency to amend the individual's record in accordance with his request or in such other way as the court may direct. In such a case the court shall determine the matter de novo.

(B) The court may assess against the United States reasonable attorney fees and other litigation costs reasonably incurred in any case under this paragraph in which the complainant has substantially prevailed.

(3) (A) In any suit brought under the provisions of subsection (g)(1)(B) of this section, the court may enjoin the agency from withholding the records and order the production to the complainant of any agency records improperly withheld from him. In such a case the court shall determine the matter de novo, and may examine the contents of any agency records in camera to determine whether the records or any portion thereof may be withheld under any of the exemptions set forth in subsection (k) of this section, and the burden is on the agency to sustain its action.

(B) The court may assess against the United States reasonable attorney fees and other litigation costs reasonably incurred in any case under this paragraph in which the complainant has substantially prevailed.

(4) In any suit brought under the provisions of subsection (g)(1)(C) or (D) of this section in which the court determines that the agency acted in a manner which was intentional or willful, the United States shall be liable to the individual in an amount equal to the sum of—

(A) actual damages sustained by the individual as a result of the refusal or failure, but in no case shall a person entitled to recovery receive less than the sum of $1,000; and

(B) the costs of the action together with reasonable attorney fees as determined by the court.

(5) An action to enforce any liability created under this section may be brought in the district court of the United States in the district in which the complainant resides, or has his principal place of business, or in which the agency records are situated, or in the District of Columbia, without regard to the amount in controversy, within two years from the date on which the cause of action arises, except that where an agency has materially and willfully misrepresented any information required under this section to be disclosed to an individual and the information so misrepresented is material to establishment of the liability of the agency to the individual under this section, the action may be brought at any time within two years after discovery by the individual of the misrepresentation. Nothing in this section shall be construed to authorize any civil action by reason of any injury sustained as the result of a disclosure of a record prior to September 27, 1975.

(h) Rights of Legal Guardians.

For the purposes of this section, the parent of any minor, or the legal guardian of any individual who has been declared to be incompetent due to physical or mental incapacity or age by a court of competent jurisdiction, may act on behalf of the individual.

(i) Criminal Penalties.

(1) Any officer or employee of an agency, who by virtue of his employment or official position, has possession of, or access to, agency records which contain individually identifiable information the disclosure of which is prohibited by this section or by rules or regulations established thereunder, and who knowing that disclosure of the specific material is so prohibited, willfully discloses the material in any manner to any person or agency not entitled to receive it, shall be guilty of a misdemeanor and fined not more than $5,000.

(2) Any officer or employee of any agency who willfully maintains a system of records without meeting the notice requirements of subsection (e)(4) of this section shall be guilty of a misdemeanor and fined not more than $5,000.

(3) Any person who knowingly and willfully requests or obtains any record concerning an individual from an agency under false pretenses shall be guilty of a misdemeanor and fined not more than $5,000.

(j) General Exemptions.

The head of any agency may promulgate rules, in accordance with the requirements (including general notice) of sections 553(b)(1), (2), and (3), (c), and (e) of this title, to exempt any system of records within the agency from any part of this section except subsections (b), (c)(1) and (2), (e)(4)(A) through (F), (e)(6), (7), (9), (10), and (11), and (i) if the system of records is—

(1) maintained by the Central Intelligence Agency; or

(2) maintained by an agency or component thereof which performs as its principal function any activity pertaining to the enforcement of criminal laws, including police efforts to prevent, control, or reduce crime or to apprehend criminals, and the activities of prosecutors, courts, correctional, probation, pardon, or parole authorities, and which consists of (A) information compiled for the purpose of identifying individual criminal offenders and alleged offenders and consisting only of identifying data and notations of arrests, the nature and disposition of criminal charges, sentencing, confinement, release, and parole and probation status; (B) information compiled for the purpose of a criminal investigation, including reports of informants and investigators, and associated with an identifiable individual; or (C) reports identifiable to an individual compiled at any stage of the process of enforcement of the criminal laws from arrest or indictment through release from supervision. At the time rules are adopted under this subsection, the agency shall include in the statement required under section 553(c) of this title, the reasons why the system of records is to be exempted from a provision of this section.

(k) Specific Exemptions.

The head of any agency may promulgate rules, in accordance with the requirements (including general notice) of sections 553(b)(1), (2), and (3), (c), and (e) of this title, to exempt any system of records within the agency from subsections (c)(3), (d), (e)(1), (e)(4)(G), (H), and (I) and (f) of this section if the system of records is—

(1) subject to the provisions of section 552(b)(1) of this title;

(2) investigatory material compiled for law enforcement purposes, other than material within the scope of subsection (j)(2) of this section: Provided, however, That if any individual is denied any right, privilege, or benefit that he would otherwise be entitled by Federal law, or for which he would otherwise be eligible, as a result of the maintenance of such material, such material shall be provided to such individual, except to the extent that the disclosure of such material would reveal the identity of a source who furnished information to the Government under an express promise that the identity of the source would be held in confidence, or, prior to the effective date

of this section, under an implied promise that the identity of the source would be held in confidence;

(3) maintained in connection with providing protective services to the President of the United States or other individuals pursuant to section 3056 of title 18;

(4) required by statute to be maintained and used solely as statistical records;

(5) investigatory material compiled solely for the purpose of determining suitability, eligibility, or qualifications for Federal civilian employment, military service, Federal contracts, or access to classified information, but only to the extent that the disclosure of such material would reveal the identity of a source who furnished information to the Government under an express promise that the identity of the source would be held in confidence, or, prior to the effective date of this section, under an implied promise that the identity of the source would be held in confidence;

(6) testing or examination material used solely to determine individual qualifications for appointment or promotion in the Federal service the disclosure of which would compromise the objectivity or fairness of the testing or examination process; or

(7) evaluation material used to determine potential for promotion in the armed services, but only to the extent that the disclosure of such material would reveal the identity of a source who furnished information to the Government under an express promise that the identity of the source would be held in confidence, or, prior to the effective date of this section, under an implied promise that the identity of the source would be held in confidence. At the time rules are adopted under this subsection, the agency shall include in the statement required under section 553(c) of this title, the reasons why the system of records is to be exempted from a provision of this section.

(l) Archival Records.

(1) Each agency record which is accepted by the Archivist of the United States for storage, processing, and servicing in accordance with section 3103 of title 44 shall, for the purposes of this section, be considered to be maintained by the agency which deposited the record and shall be subject to the provisions of this section. The Archivist of the United States shall not disclose the record except to the agency which maintains the record, or under rules established by that agency which are not inconsistent with the provisions of this section.

(2) Each agency record pertaining to an identifiable individual which was transferred to the National Archives of the United States as a record which has sufficient historical or other value to warrant its continued preservation by the United States Government, prior to the effective date of this section, shall, for the purposes of this section, be considered to be maintained by the National Archives and shall not be subject to the provisions of this section, except that a statement generally describing such records (modeled after the requirements relating to records subject to subsections (e)(4)(A) through (G) of this section) shall be published in the Federal Register.

(3) Each agency record pertaining to an identifiable individual which is transferred to the National Archives of the United States as a record which has sufficient historical or other value to warrant its continued preservation by the United States Government, on or after the effective date of this section, shall, for the purposes of this section, be considered to be maintained by the National Archives and shall be exempt from the requirements of this section except subsections (e)(4)(A) through (G) and (e)(9) of this section.

(m) Government Contractors.

(1) When an agency provides by a contract for the operation by or on behalf of the agency of a system of records to accomplish an agency function, the agency shall, consistent with its authority, cause the requirements of this section to be applied to such system. For purposes of subsection (i) of this section any such contractor and any employee of such contractor, if such contract is agreed to on or after the effective date of this section, shall be considered to be an employee of an agency.

(2) A consumer reporting agency to which a record is disclosed under section 3711(f) of title 31 shall not be considered a contractor for the purposes of this section.

(n) Mailing Lists.

An individual's name and address may not be sold or rented by an agency unless such action is specifically authorized by law. This provision shall not be construed to require the withholding of names and addresses otherwise permitted to be made public.

(o) Matching Agreements.

(1) No record which is contained in a system of records may be disclosed to a recipient agency or non-Federal agency for use in a computer matching program except pursuant to a written agreement

between the source agency and the recipient agency or non-Federal agency specifying—

(A) the purpose and legal authority for conducting the program;

(B) the justification for the program and the anticipated results, including a specific estimate of any savings;

(C) a description of the records that will be matched, including each data element that will be used, the approximate number of records that will be matched, and the projected starting and completion dates of the matching program;

(D) procedures for providing individualized notice at the time of application, and notice periodically thereafter as directed by the Data Integrity Board of such agency (subject to guidance provided by the Director of the Office of Management and Budget pursuant to subsection (v)), to—

(i) applicants for and recipients of financial assistance or payments under Federal benefit programs, and

(ii) applicants for and holders of positions as Federal personnel, that any information provided by such applicants, recipients, holders, and individuals may be subject to verification through matching programs;

(E) procedures for verifying information produced in such matching program as required by subsection (p);

(F) procedures for the retention and timely destruction of identifiable records created by a recipient agency or non-Federal agency in such matching program;

(G) procedures for ensuring the administrative, technical, and physical security of the records matched and the results of such programs;

(H) prohibitions on duplication and redisclosure of records provided by the source agency within or outside the recipient agency or the non-Federal agency, except where required by law or essential to the conduct of the matching program;

(I) procedures governing the use by a recipient agency or non-Federal agency of records provided in a matching program by a source agency, including procedures governing return of the records to the source agency or destruction of records used in such program;

(J) information on assessments that have been made on the accuracy of the records that will be used in such matching program; and

(K) that the Comptroller General may have access to all records of a recipient agency or a non-Federal agency that the Comptroller General deems necessary in order to monitor or verify compliance with the agreement.

(2)(A) A copy of each agreement entered into pursuant to paragraph (1) shall—

(i) be transmitted to the Committee on Governmental Affairs of the Senate and the Committee on Government Operations of the House of Representatives; and

(ii) be available upon request to the public.

(B) No such agreement shall be effective until 30 days after the date on which such a copy is transmitted pursuant to subparagraph (A)(i).

(C) Such an agreement shall remain in effect only for such period, not to exceed 18 months, as the Data Integrity Board of the agency determines is appropriate in light of the purposes, and length of time necessary for the conduct, of the matching program.

(D) Within 3 months prior to the expiration of such an agreement pursuant to subparagraph (C), the Data Integrity Board of the agency may, without additional review, renew the matching agreement for a current, ongoing matching program for not more than one additional year if—

(i) such program will be conducted without any change; and

(ii) each party to the agreement certifies to the Board in writing that the program has been conducted in compliance with the agreement.

(p) Verification and Opportunity to Contest Findings.

(1) In order to protect any individual whose records are used in a matching program, no recipient agency, non-Federal agency, or source agency may suspend, terminate, reduce, or make a final denial of any financial assistance or payment under a Federal benefit program to such individual, or take other adverse action against such individual, as a result of information produced by such matching program, until—

(A)(i) the agency has independently verified the information; or

(ii) the Data Integrity Board of the agency, or in the case of a non-Federal agency the Data Integrity Board of the source agency, determines in accordance with guidance issued by the Director of the Office of Management and Budget that—

(I) the information is limited to identification and amount of benefits paid by the source agency under a Federal benefit program; and

(II) there is a high degree of confidence that the information provided to the recipient agency is accurate;

(B) the individual receives a notice from the agency containing a statement of its findings and informing the individual of the opportunity to contest such findings; and

(C)(i) the expiration of any time period established for the program by statute or regulation for the individual to respond to that notice; or

(ii) in the case of a program for which no such period is established, the end of the 30–day period beginning on the date on which notice under subparagraph (B) is mailed or otherwise provided to the individual.

(2) Independent verification referred to in paragraph (1) requires investigation and confirmation of specific information relating to an individual that is used as a basis for an adverse action against the individual, including where applicable investigation and confirmation of—

(A) the amount of any asset or income involved;

(B) whether such individual actually has or had access to such asset or income for such individual's own use; and

(C) the period or periods when the individual actually had such asset or income. (3) Notwithstanding paragraph (1), an agency may take any appropriate action otherwise prohibited by such paragraph if the agency determines that the public health or public safety may be adversely affected or significantly threatened during any notice period required by such paragraph.

(q) Sanctions.

(1) Notwithstanding any other provision of law, no source agency may disclose any record which is contained in a system of records

to a recipient agency or non-Federal agency for a matching program if such source agency has reason to believe that the requirements of subsection (p), or any matching agreement entered into pursuant to subsection (o), or both, are not being met by such recipient agency.

(2) No source agency may renew a matching agreement unless—

(A) the recipient agency or non-Federal agency has certified that it has complied with the provisions of that agreement; and

(B) the source agency has no reason to believe that the certification is inaccurate.

(r) Report on New Systems and Matching Programs.

Each agency that proposes to establish or make a significant change in a system of records or a matching program shall provide adequate advance notice of any such proposal (in duplicate) to the Committee on Government Operations of the House of Representatives, the Committee on Governmental Affairs of the Senate, and the Office of Management and Budget in order to permit an evaluation of the probable or potential effect of such proposal on the privacy or other rights of individuals.

(s) Biennial Report.

The President shall biennially submit to the Speaker of the House of Representatives and the President pro tempore of the Senate a report—

(1) describing the actions of the Director of the Office of Management and Budget pursuant to section 6 of the Privacy Act of 1974 during the preceding 2 years;

(2) describing the exercise of individual rights of access and amendment under this section during such years;

(3) identifying changes in or additions to systems of records;

(4) containing such other information concerning administration of this section as may be necessary or useful to the Congress in reviewing the effectiveness of this section in carrying out the purposes of the Privacy Act of 1974.

(t) Effect of Other Laws.

(1) No agency shall rely on any exemption contained in section 552 of this title to withhold from an individual any record which is otherwise accessible to such individual under the provisions of this section.

(2) No agency shall rely on any exemption in this section to withhold from an individual any record which is otherwise accessible to such individual under the provisions of section 552 of this title.

(u) Data Integrity Boards.

(1) Every agency conducting or participating in a matching program shall establish a Data Integrity Board to oversee and coordinate among the various components of such agency the agency's implementation of this section.

(2) Each Data Integrity Board shall consist of senior officials designated by the head of the agency, and shall include any senior official designated by the head of the agency as responsible for implementation of this section, and the inspector general of the agency, if any. The inspector general shall not serve as chairman of the Data Integrity Board.

(3) Each Data Integrity Board—

(A) shall review, approve, and maintain all written agreements for receipt or disclosure of agency records for matching programs to ensure compliance with subsection (o), and all relevant statutes, regulations, and guidelines;

(B) shall review all matching programs in which the agency has participated during the year, either as a source agency or recipient agency, determine compliance with applicable laws, regulations, guidelines, and agency agreements, and assess the costs and benefits of such programs;

(C) shall review all recurring matching programs in which the agency has participated during the year, either as a source agency or recipient agency, for continued justification for such disclosures;

(D) shall compile an annual report, which shall be submitted to the head of the agency and the Office of Management and Budget and made available to the public on request, describing the matching activities of the agency, including—

(i) matching programs in which the agency has participated as a source agency or recipient agency;

(ii) matching agreements proposed under subsection (o) that were disapproved by the Board;

(iii) any changes in membership or structure of the Board in the preceding year;

(iv) the reasons for any waiver of the requirement in paragraph (4) of this section for completion and submission of a cost-benefit analysis prior to the approval of a matching program;

(v) any violations of matching agreements that have been alleged or identified and any corrective action taken; and

(vi) any other information required by the Director of the Office of Management and Budget to be included in such report;

(E) shall serve as a clearinghouse for receiving and providing information on the accuracy, completeness, and reliability of records used in matching programs;

(F) shall provide interpretation and guidance to agency components and personnel on the requirements of this section for matching programs;

(G) shall review agency recordkeeping and disposal policies and practices for matching programs to assure compliance with this section; and

(H) may review and report on any agency matching activities that are not matching programs.

(4)(A) Except as provided in subparagraphs (B) and (C), a Data Integrity Board shall not approve any written agreement for a matching program unless the agency has completed and submitted to such Board a cost-benefit analysis of the proposed program and such analysis demonstrates that the program is likely to be cost effective.

(B) The Board may waive the requirements of subparagraph (A) of this paragraph if it determines in writing, in accordance with guidelines prescribed by the Director of the Office of Management and Budget, that a cost-benefit analysis is not required.

(C) A cost-benefit analysis shall not be required under subparagraph (A) prior to the initial approval of a written agreement for a matching program that is specifically required by statute. Any subsequent written agreement for such a program shall not be approved by the Data Integrity Board unless the agency has submitted a cost-benefit analysis of the program as conducted under the preceding approval of such agreement.

(5)(A) If a matching agreement is disapproved by a Data Integrity Board, any party to such agreement may appeal the disapproval to the Director of the Office of Management and Budget. Timely notice of the filing of such an appeal shall be provided by the Director of the Office of Management and Budget to the Committee on Governmental Affairs of the Senate and the Committee on Government Operations of the House of Representatives.

(B) The Director of the Office of Management and Budget may approve a matching agreement notwithstanding the disapproval of a Data Integrity Board if the Director determines that—

(i) the matching program will be consistent with all applicable legal, regulatory, and policy requirements;

(ii) there is adequate evidence that the matching agreement will be cost-effective; and

(iii) the matching program is in the public interest.

(C) The decision of the Director to approve a matching agreement shall not take effect until 30 days after it is reported to committees described in subparagraph (A).

(D) If the Data Integrity Board and the Director of the Office of Management and Budget disapprove a matching program proposed by the inspector general of an agency, the inspector general may report the disapproval to the head of the agency and to the Congress.

(6) The Director of the Office of Management and Budget shall, annually during

the first 3 years after the date of enactment of this subsection and biennially thereafter, consolidate in a report to the Congress the information contained in the reports from the various Data Integrity Boards under paragraph (3)(D). Such report shall include detailed information about costs and benefits of matching programs that are conducted during the period covered by such consolidated report, and shall identify each waiver granted by a Data Integrity Board of the requirement for completion and submission of a cost-benefit analysis and the reasons for granting the waiver.

(7) In the reports required by paragraphs (3)(D) and (6), agency matching activities that are not matching programs may be reported on an aggregate basis, if and to the extent necessary to protect ongoing law enforcement or counterintelligence investigations.

(v) Office of Management and Budget Responsibilities.

The Director of the Office of Management and Budget shall—

(1) develop and, after notice and opportunity for public comment, prescribe guidelines and regulations for the use of agencies in implementing the provisions of this section; and

(2) provide continuing assistance to and oversight of the implementation of this section by agencies.

§ 552b. Open meetings.

(a) For purposes of this section—

(1) the term "agency" means any agency, as defined in section 552(e) of this title, headed by a collegial body composed of two or more individual members, a majority of whom are appointed to such position by the President with the advice and consent of the Senate, and any subdivision thereof authorized to act on behalf of the agency;

(2) the term "meeting" means the deliberations of at least the number of individual agency members required to take action on behalf of the agency where such deliberations determine or result in the joint conduct or disposition of official agency business, but does not include deliberations required or permitted by subsection (d) or (e); and ·

(3) the term "member" means an individual who belongs to a collegial body heading an agency.

(b) Members shall not jointly conduct or dispose of agency business other than in accordance with this section. Except as provided in subsection (c), every portion of every meeting of an agency shall be open to public observation.

(c) Except in a case where the agency finds that the public interest requires otherwise, the second sentence of subsection (b) shall not apply to any portion of an agency meeting, and the requirements of subsections (d) and (e) shall not apply to any information pertaining to such meeting otherwise required by this section to be disclosed to the public, where the agency properly determines that such portion or portions of its meeting or the disclosure of such information is likely to—

(1) disclose matters that are (A) specifically authorized under criteria established by an Executive order to be kept secret in the interests of national defense or foreign policy and (B) in fact properly classified pursuant to such Executive order;

(2) relate solely to the internal personnel rules and practices of an agency;

(3) disclose matters specifically exempted from disclosure by statute (other than section 552 of this title), provided that such

statute (A) requires that the matters be withheld from the public in such a manner as to leave no discretion on the issue, or (B) establishes particular criteria for withholding or refers to particular types of matters to be withheld;

(4) disclose trade secrets and commercial or financial information obtained from a person and privileged or confidential;

(5) involve accusing any person of a crime, or formally censuring any person;

(6) disclose information of a personal nature where disclosure would constitute a clearly unwarranted invasion of personal privacy;

(7) disclose investigatory records compiled for law enforcement purposes, or information which if written would be contained in such records, but only to the extent that the production of such records or information would (A) interfere with enforcement proceedings, (B) deprive a person of a right to a fair trial or an impartial adjudication, (C) constitute an unwarranted invasion of personal privacy, (D) disclose the identity of a confidential source and, in the case of a record compiled by a criminal law enforcement authority in the course of a criminal investigation, or by an agency conducting a lawful national security intelligence investigation, confidential information furnished only by the confidential source, (E) disclose investigative techniques and procedures, or (F) endanger the life or physical safety of law enforcement personnel;

(8) disclose information contained in or related to examination, operating, or condition reports prepared by, on behalf of, or for the use of an agency responsible for the regulation or supervision of financial institutions;

(9) disclose information the premature disclosure of which would—

(A) in the case of an agency which regulates currencies, securities, commodities, or financial institutions, be likely to (i) lead to significant financial speculation in currencies, securities, or commodities, or (ii) significantly endanger the stability of any financial institution; or

(B) in the case of any agency, be likely to significantly frustrate implementation of a proposed agency action, except that subparagraph (B) shall not apply in any instance where the agency has already disclosed to the public the content or nature of its proposed action, or where the agency is required by law to make such disclosure on its own initiative prior to taking final agency action on such proposal; or

(10) specifically concern the agency's issuance of a subpena, or the agency's participation in a civil action or proceeding, an action in a foreign court or international tribunal, or an arbitration, or the initiation, conduct, or disposition by the agency of a particular case of formal agency adjudication pursuant to the procedures in section 554 of this title or otherwise involving a determination on the record after opportunity for a hearing.

(d)(1) Action under subsection (c) shall be taken only when a majority of the entire membership of the agency (as defined in subsection (a)(1)) votes to take such action. A separate vote of the agency members shall be taken with respect to each agency meeting a portion or portions of which are proposed to be closed to the public pursuant to subsection (c), or with respect to any information which is proposed to be withheld under subsection (c). A single vote may be taken with respect to a series of meetings, a portion or portions of which are proposed to be closed to the public, or with respect to any information concerning such series of meetings, so long as each meeting in such series involves the same particular matters and is scheduled to be held no more than thirty days after the initial meeting in such series. The vote of each agency member participating in such vote shall be recorded and no proxies shall be allowed.

(2) Whenever any person whose interests may be directly affected by a portion of a meeting requests that the agency close such portion to the public for any of the reasons referred to in paragraph (5), (6), or (7) of subsection (c), the agency, upon request of any one of its members, shall vote by recorded vote whether to close such meeting.

(3) Within one day of any vote taken pursuant to paragraph (1) or (2), the agency shall make publicly available a written copy of such vote reflecting the vote of each member on the question. If a portion of a meeting is to be closed to the public, the agency shall, within one day of the vote taken pursuant to paragraph (1) or (2) of this subsection, make publicly available a full written explanation of its action closing the portion together with a list of all persons expected to attend the meeting and their affiliation.

(4) Any agency, a majority of whose meetings may properly be closed to the public pursuant to paragraph (4), (8), (9)(A), or (10) of subsection (c), or any combination thereof, may provide by regulation for the closing of such meetings or portions thereof in the event that

a majority of the members of the agency votes by recorded vote at the beginning of such meeting, or portion thereof, to close the exempt portion or portions of the meeting, and a copy of such vote, reflecting the vote of each member on the question, is made available to the public. The provisions of paragraphs (1), (2), and (3) of this subsection and subsection (e) shall not apply to any portion of a meeting to which such regulations apply: Provided, That the agency shall, except to the extent that such information is exempt from disclosure under the provisions of subsection (c), provide the public with public announcement of the time, place, and subject matter of the meeting and of each portion thereof at the earliest practicable time. **(e)**(1) In the case of each meeting, the agency shall make public announcement, at least one week before the meeting, of the time, place, and subject matter of the meeting, whether it is to be open or closed to the public, and the name and phone number of the official designated by the agency to respond to requests for information about the meeting. Such announcement shall be made unless a majority of the members of the agency determines by a recorded vote that agency business requires that such meeting be called at an earlier date, in which case the agency shall make public announcement of the time, place, and subject matter of such meeting, and whether open or closed to the public, at the earliest practicable time.

(2) The time or place of a meeting may be changed following the public announcement required by paragraph (1) only if the agency publicly announces such change at the earliest practicable time. The subject matter of a meeting, or the determination of the agency to open or close a meeting, or portion of a meeting, to the public, may be changed following the public announcement required by this subsection only if (A) a majority of the entire membership of the agency determines by a recorded vote that agency business so requires and that no earlier announcement of the change was possible, and (B) the agency publicly announces such change and the vote of each member upon such change at the earliest practicable time.

(3) Immediately following each public announcement required by this subsection, notice of the time, place, and subject matter of a meeting, whether the meeting is open or closed, any change in one of the preceding, and the name and phone number of the official designated by the agency to respond to requests for information about the meeting, shall also be submitted for publication in the Federal Register.

(f)(1) For every meeting closed pursuant to paragraphs (1) through (10) of subsection (c), the General Counsel or chief legal officer of the agency shall publicly certify that, in his or her opinion, the meeting may be closed to the public and shall state each relevant exemptive provision. A copy of such certification, together with a statement from the presiding officer of the meeting setting forth the time and place of the meeting, and the persons present, shall be retained by the agency. The agency shall maintain a complete transcript or electronic recording adequate to record fully the proceedings of each meeting, or portion of a meeting, closed to the public, except that in the case of a meeting, or portion of a meeting, closed to the public pursuant to paragraph (8), (9)(A), or (10) of subsection (c), the agency shall maintain either such a transcript or recording, or a set of minutes. Such minutes shall fully and clearly describe all matters discussed and shall provide a full and accurate summary of any actions taken, and the reasons therefor, including a description of each of the views expressed on any item and the record of any rollcall vote (reflecting the vote of each member on the question). All documents considered in connection with any action shall be identified in such minutes.

(2) The agency shall make promptly available to the public, in a place easily accessible to the public, the transcript, electronic recording, or minutes (as required by paragraph (1)) of the discussion of any item on the agenda, or of any item of the testimony of any witness received at the meeting, except for such item or items of such discussion or testimony as the agency determines to contain information which may be withheld under subsection (c). Copies of such transcript, or minutes, or a transcription of such recording disclosing the identity of each speaker, shall be furnished to any person at the actual cost of duplication or transcription. The agency shall maintain a complete verbatim copy of the transcript, a complete copy of the minutes, or a complete electronic recording of each meeting, or portion of a meeting, closed to the public, for a period of at least two years after such meeting, or until one year after the conclusion of any agency proceeding with respect to which the meeting or portion was held, whichever occurs later.

(g) Each agency subject to the requirements of this section shall, within 180 days after the date of enactment of this section, following consultation with the Office of the Chairman of the Administrative Conference of the United States and published notice in the Federal Register of at least thirty days and opportunity for written comment by any person, promulgate regulations to implement the requirements of subsections (b) through (f) of this section. Any person may bring a proceeding in the United States District Court for the District of Columbia to require an agency to promulgate such regulations if such agency has not promulgated such regulations within the time period specified herein. Subject to any limitations of time provided by law, any person may bring a proceeding in the United States Court of Appeals for the District of Columbia to set aside agency regulations issued pursuant to this subsection that are not in accord with the requirements of subsections (b) through (f) of this section and to require the promulgation of regulations that are in accord with such subsections.

(h)(1) The district courts of the United States shall have jurisdiction to enforce the requirements of subsections (b) through (f) of this section by declaratory judgment, injunctive relief, or other relief as may be appropriate. Such actions may be brought by any person against an agency prior to, or within sixty days after, the meeting out of which the violation of this section arises, except that if public announcement of such meeting is not initially provided by the agency in accordance with the requirements of this section, such action may be instituted pursuant to this section at any time prior to sixty days after any public announcement of such meeting. Such actions may be brought in the district court of the United States for the district in which the agency meeting is held or in which the agency in question has its headquarters, or in the District Court for the District of Columbia. In such actions a defendant shall serve his answer within thirty days after the service of the complaint. The burden is on the defendant to sustain his action. In deciding such cases the court may examine in camera any portion of the transcript, electronic recording, or minutes of a meeting closed to the public, and may take such additional evidence as it deems necessary. The court, having due regard for orderly administration and the public interest, as well as the interests of the parties, may grant such equitable relief as it deems appropriate, including granting an injunction against future violations of this section or ordering the agency to make available to the public such portion of the transcript, recording, or minutes of a meeting as is not authorized to be withheld under subsection (c) of this section.

(2) Any Federal court otherwise authorized by law to review agency action may, at the application of any person properly participating in the proceeding pursuant to other applicable law, inquire into violations by the agency of the requirements of this section and afford such relief as it deems appropriate. Nothing in this section authorizes any Federal court having jurisdiction solely on the basis of paragraph (1) to set aside, enjoin, or invalidate any agency action

(other than an action to close a meeting or to withhold information under this section) taken or discussed at any agency meeting out of which the violation of this section arose.

(i) The court may assess against any party reasonable attorney fees and other litigation costs reasonably incurred by any other party who substantially prevails in any action brought in accordance with the provisions of subsection (g) or (h) of this section, except that costs may be assessed against the plaintiff only where the court finds that the suit was initiated by the plaintiff primarily for frivolous or dilatory purposes. In the case of assessment of costs against an agency, the costs may be assessed by the court against the United States.

(j) Each agency subject to the requirements of this section shall annually report to the Congress regarding the following:

(1) The changes in the policies and procedures of the agency under this section that have occurred during the preceding 1–year period.

(2) A tabulation of the number of meetings held, the exemptions applied to close meetings, and the days of public notice provided to close meetings.

(3) A brief description of litigation or formal complaints concerning the implementation of this section by the agency.

(4) A brief explanation of any changes in law that have affected the responsibilities of the agency under this section.

(k) Nothing herein expands or limits the present rights of any person under section 552 of this title, except that the exemptions set forth in subsection (c) of this section shall govern in the case of any request made pursuant to section 552 to copy or inspect the transcripts, recordings, or minutes described in subsection (f) of this section. The requirements of chapter 33 of title 44, United States Code, shall not apply to the transcripts, recordings, and minutes described in subsection (f) of this section.

(l) This section does not constitute authority to withhold any information from Congress, and does not authorize the closing of any agency meeting or portion thereof required by any other provision of law to be open.

(m) Nothing in this section authorizes any agency to withhold from any individual any record, including transcripts, recordings, or minutes required by this section, which is otherwise accessible to such individual under section 552a of this title.

§ 553. Rule making.

(a) This section applies, according to the provisions thereof, except to the extent that there is involved—

(1) a military or foreign affairs function of the United States; or

(2) a matter relating to agency management or personnel or to public property, loans, grants, benefits, or contracts.

(b) General notice of proposed rule making shall be published in the Federal Register, unless persons subject thereto are named and either personally served or otherwise have actual notice thereof in accordance with law. The notice shall include—

(1) a statement of the time, place, and nature of public rule making proceedings;

(2) reference to the legal authority under which the rule is proposed; and

(3) either the terms or substance of the proposed rule or a description of the subjects and issues involved. Except when notice or hearing is required by statute, this subsection does not apply—

(A) to interpretative rules, general statements of policy, or rules of agency organization, procedure, or practice; or

(B) when the agency for good cause finds (and incorporates the finding and a brief statement of reasons therefor in the rules issued) that notice and public procedure thereon are impracticable, unnecessary, or contrary to the public interest.

(c) After notice required by this section, the agency shall give interested persons an opportunity to participate in the rule making through submission of written data, views, or arguments with or without opportunity for oral presentation. After consideration of the relevant matter presented, the agency shall incorporate in the rules adopted a concise general statement of their basis and purpose. When rules are required by statute to be made on the record after opportunity for an agency hearing, sections 556 and 557 of this title apply instead of this subsection.

(d) The required publication or service of a substantive rule shall be made not less than 30 days before its effective date, except—

(1) a substantive rule which grants or recognizes an exemption or relieves a restriction;

(2) interpretative rules and statements of policy; or

(3) as otherwise provided by the agency for good cause found and published with the rule.

(e) Each agency shall give an interested person the right to petition for the issuance, amendment, or repeal of a rule.

§ 554. Adjudications.

(a) This section applies, according to the provisions thereof, in every case of adjudication required by statute to be determined on the record after opportunity for an agency hearing, except to the extent that there is involved—

(1) a matter subject to a subsequent trial of the law and the facts de novo in a court;

(2) the selection or tenure of an employee, except an administrative law judge appointed under section 3105 of this title; So in original.

(3) proceedings in which decisions rest solely on inspections, tests, or elections;

(4) the conduct of military or foreign affairs functions;

(5) cases in which an agency is acting as an agent for a court; or

(6) the certification of worker representatives.

(b) Persons entitled to notice of an agency hearing shall be timely informed of—

(1) the time, place, and nature of the hearing;

(2) the legal authority and jurisdiction under which the hearing is to be held; and

(3) the matters of fact and law asserted. When private persons are the moving parties, other parties to the proceeding shall give prompt notice of issues controverted in fact or law; and in other instances agencies may by rule require responsive pleading. In fixing the time and place for hearings, due regard shall be had for the convenience and necessity of the parties or their representatives.

(c) The agency shall give all interested parties opportunity for—

(1) the submission and consideration of facts, arguments, offers of settlement, or proposals of adjustment when time, the nature of the proceeding, and the public interest permit; and

(2) to the extent that the parties are unable so to determine a controversy by consent, hearing and decision on notice and in accordance with sections 556 and 557 of this title.

(d) The employee who presides at the reception of evidence pursuant to section 556 of this title shall make the recommended decision or initial decision required by section 557 of this title, unless he becomes unavailable to the agency. Except to the extent required for the disposition of ex parte matters as authorized by law, such an employee may not—

(1) consult a person or party on a fact in issue, unless on notice and opportunity for all parties to participate; or

(2) be responsible to or subject to the supervision or direction of an employee or agent engaged in the performance of investigative or prosecuting functions for an agency. An employee or agent engaged in the performance of investigative or prosecuting functions for an agency in a case may not, in that or a factually related case, participate or advise in the decision, recommended decision, or agency review pursuant to section 557 of this title, except as witness or counsel in public proceedings. This subsection does not apply—

(A) in determining applications for initial licenses;

(B) to proceedings involving the validity or application of rates, facilities, or practices of public utilities or carriers; or

(C) to the agency or a member or members of the body comprising the agency.

(e) The agency, with like effect as in the case of other orders, and in its sound discretion, may issue a declaratory order to terminate a controversy or remove uncertainty.

§ 555. Ancillary matters.

(a) This section applies, according to the provisions thereof, except as otherwise provided by this subchapter.

(b) A person compelled to appear in person before an agency or representative thereof is entitled to be accompanied, represented, and advised by counsel or, if permitted by the agency, by other qualified representative. A party is entitled to appear in person or by or with counsel or other duly qualified representative in an agency proceeding. So far as the orderly conduct of public business permits, an interested person may appear before an agency or its responsible employees for the presentation, adjustment, or determination of an issue, request, or controversy in a proceeding, whether interlocutory, summary, or otherwise, or in connection with an agency function. With due regard for the convenience and necessity of the parties or their representatives and within a reasonable time, each agency shall proceed to conclude a matter presented to it. This subsection does not grant or deny a person who is not a lawyer the right to appear for or represent others before an agency or in an agency proceeding.

(c) Process, requirement of a report, inspection, or other investigative act or demand may not be issued, made, or enforced except as authorized by law. A person compelled to submit data or evidence is entitled to retain or, on payment of lawfully prescribed costs, procure a copy or transcript thereof, except that in a nonpublic investigatory proceeding the witness may for good cause be limited to inspection of the official transcript of his testimony.

(d) Agency subpenas authorized by law shall be issued to a party on request and, when required by rules of procedure, on a statement or showing of general relevance and reasonable scope of the evidence sought. On contest, the court shall sustain the subpena or similar process or demand to the extent that it is found to be in accordance with law. In a proceeding for enforcement, the court shall issue an order requiring the appearance of the witness or the production of the evidence or data within a reasonable time under penalty of punishment for contempt in case of contumacious failure to comply.

(e) Prompt notice shall be given of the denial in whole or in part of a written application, petition, or other request of an interested person made in connection with any agency proceeding. Except in affirming a prior denial or when the denial is self-explanatory, the notice shall be accompanied by a brief statement of the grounds for denial.

§ 556. Hearings; presiding employees; powers and duties; burden of proof; evidence; record as basis of decision.

(a) This section applies, according to the provisions thereof, to hearings required by section 553 or 554 of this title to be conducted in accordance with this section.

(b) There shall preside at the taking of evidence—

    (1) the agency;

    (2) one or more members of the body which comprises the agency; or

    (3) one or more administrative law judges appointed under section 3105 of this title.

This subchapter does not supersede the conduct of specified classes of proceedings, in whole or in part, by or before boards or other employees specially provided for by or designated under statute. The functions of presiding employees and of employees participating in decisions in accordance with section 557 of this title shall be conducted in an impartial manner. A presiding or participating employee may at any time disqualify himself. On the filing in good faith of a timely and sufficient affidavit of personal bias or other disqualification of a presiding or participating employee, the agency shall determine the matter as a part of the record and decision in the case.

(c) Subject to published rules of the agency and within its powers, employees presiding at hearings may—

(1) administer oaths and affirmations;

(2) issue subpenas authorized by law;

(3) rule on offers of proof and receive relevant evidence;

(4) take depositions or have depositions taken when the ends of justice would be served;

(5) regulate the course of the hearing;

(6) hold conferences for the settlement or simplification of the issues by consent of the parties or by the use of alternative means of dispute resolution as provided in subchapter IV of this chapter;

(7) inform the parties as to the availability of one or more alternative means of dispute resolution, and encourage use of such methods;

(8) require the attendance at any conference held pursuant to paragraph (6) of at least one representative of each party who has authority to negotiate concerning resolution of issues in controversy;

(9) dispose of procedural requests or similar matters;

(10) make or recommend decisions in accordance with section 557 of this title; and

(11) take other action authorized by agency rule consistent with this subchapter.

(d) Except as otherwise provided by statute, the proponent of a rule or order has the burden of proof. Any oral or documentary evidence may be received, but the agency as a matter of policy shall provide for the exclusion of irrelevant, immaterial, or unduly repetitious evidence. A sanction may not be imposed or rule or order issued except on consideration of the whole record or those parts thereof cited by a party and supported by and in accordance with the reliable, probative, and substantial evidence. The agency may, to the extent consistent with the interests of justice and the policy of the underlying statutes administered by the agency, consider a violation of section

557(d) of this title sufficient grounds for a decision adverse to a party who has knowingly committed such violation or knowingly caused such violation to occur. A party is entitled to present his case or defense by oral or documentary evidence, to submit rebuttal evidence, and to conduct such cross-examination as may be required for a full and true disclosure of the facts. In rule making or determining claims for money or benefits or applications for initial licenses an agency may, when a party will not be prejudiced thereby, adopt procedures for the submission of all or part of the evidence in written form.

(e) The transcript of testimony and exhibits, together with all papers and requests filed in the proceeding, constitutes the exclusive record for decision in accordance with section 557 of this title and, on payment of lawfully prescribed costs, shall be made available to the parties. When an agency decision rests on official notice of a material fact not appearing in the evidence in the record, a party is entitled, on timely request, to an opportunity to show the contrary.

§ 557. Initial decisions; conclusiveness; review by agency; submissions by parties; contents of decisions; record.

(a) This section applies, according to the provisions thereof, when a hearing is required to be conducted in accordance with section 556 of this title.

(b) When the agency did not preside at the reception of the evidence, the presiding employee or, in cases not subject to section 554(d) of this title, an employee qualified to preside at hearings pursuant to section 556 of this title, shall initially decide the case unless the agency requires, either in specific cases or by general rule, the entire record to be certified to it for decision. When the presiding employee makes an initial decision, that decision then becomes the decision of the agency without further proceedings unless there is an appeal to, or review on motion of, the agency within time provided by rule. On appeal from or review of the initial decision, the agency has all the powers which it would have in making the initial decision except as it may limit the issues on notice or by rule. When the agency makes the decision without having presided at the reception of the evidence, the presiding employee or an employee qualified to preside at hearings pursuant to section 556 of this title shall first recommend a decision, except that in rule making or determining applications for initial licenses—

(1) instead thereof the agency may issue a tentative decision or one of its responsible employees may recommend a decision; or

(2) this procedure may be omitted in a case in which the agency finds on the record that due and timely execution of its functions imperatively and unavoidably so requires.

(c) Before a recommended, initial, or tentative decision, or a decision on agency review of the decision of subordinate employees, the parties are entitled to a reasonable opportunity to submit for the consideration of the employees participating in the decisions—

(1) proposed findings and conclusions; or

(2) exceptions to the decisions or recommended decisions of subordinate employees or to tentative agency decisions; and

(3) supporting reasons for the exceptions or proposed findings or conclusions. The record shall show the ruling on each finding, conclusion, or exception presented. All decisions, including initial, recommended, and tentative decisions, are a part of the record and shall include a statement of—

(A) findings and conclusions, and the reasons or basis therefor, on all the material issues of fact, law, or discretion presented on the record; and

(B) the appropriate rule, order, sanction, relief, or denial thereof.

(d)(1) In any agency proceeding which is subject to subsection (a) of this section, except to the extent required for the disposition of ex parte matters as authorized by law—

(A) no interested person outside the agency shall make or knowingly cause to be made to any member of the body comprising the agency, administrative law judge, or other employee who is or may reasonably be expected to be involved in the decisional process of the proceeding, an ex parte communication relevant to the merits of the proceeding;

(B) no member of the body comprising the agency, administrative law judge, or other employee who is or may reasonably be expected to be involved in the decisional process of the proceeding, shall make or knowingly cause to be made to any interested person outside the agency an ex parte communication relevant to the merits of the proceeding;

(C) a member of the body comprising the agency, administrative law judge, or other employee who is or may reasonably be expected to be involved in the decisional process of such proceeding who receives, or who makes or knowingly causes to be made, a communication prohibited by this subsection shall place on the public record of the proceeding:

    (i) all such written communications;

    (ii) memoranda stating the substance of all such oral communications; and

    (iii) all written responses, and memoranda stating the substance of all oral responses, to the materials described in clauses (i) and (ii) of this subparagraph;

(D) upon receipt of a communication knowingly made or knowingly caused to be made by a party in violation of this subsection, the agency, administrative law judge, or other employee presiding at the hearing may, to the extent consistent with the interests of justice and the policy of the underlying statutes, require the party to show cause why his claim or interest in the proceeding should not be dismissed, denied, disregarded, or otherwise adversely affected on account of such violation; and

(E) the prohibitions of this subsection shall apply beginning at such time as the agency may designate, but in no case shall they begin to apply later than the time at which a proceeding is noticed for hearing unless the person responsible for the communication has knowledge that it will be noticed, in which case the prohibitions shall apply beginning at the time of his acquisition of such knowledge.

(2) This subsection does not constitute authority to withhold information from Congress.

§ 558. Imposition of sanctions; determination of applications for licenses; suspension, revocation, and expiration of licenses.

(a) This section applies, according to the provisions thereof, to the exercise of a power or authority.

(b) A sanction may not be imposed or a substantive rule or order issued except within jurisdiction delegated to the agency and as authorized by law.

(c) When application is made for a license required by law, the agency, with due regard for the rights and privileges of all the interested parties or adversely affected persons and within a reasonable time, shall set and complete proceedings required to be conducted in accordance with sections 556 and 557 of this title or other proceedings required by law and shall make its decision. Except in cases of willfulness or those in which public health, interest, or safety requires otherwise, the withdrawal, suspension, revocation, or annulment of a license is lawful only if, before the institution of agency proceedings therefor, the licensee has been given—

(1) notice by the agency in writing of the facts or conduct which may warrant the action; and

(2) opportunity to demonstrate or achieve compliance with all lawful requirements.

When the licensee has made timely and sufficient application for a renewal or a new license in accordance with agency rules, a license with reference to an activity of a continuing nature does not expire until the application has been finally determined by the agency.

§ 559. Effect on other laws; effect of subsequent statute.

This subchapter, chapter 7, and sections 1305, 3105, 3344, 4301(2)(E), 5372, and 7521 of this title, and the provisions of section 5335(a)(B) of this title that relate to administrative law judges, do not limit or repeal additional requirements imposed by statute or otherwise recognized by law. Except as otherwise required by law, requirements or privileges relating to evidence or procedure apply equally to agencies and persons. Each agency is granted the authority necessary to comply with the requirements of this subchapter through the issuance of rules or otherwise. Subsequent statute may not be held to supersede or modify this subchapter, chapter 7, sections 1305, 3105, 3344, 4301(2)(E), 5372, or 7521 of this title, or the provisions of section 5335(a)(B) of this title that relate to administrative law judges, except to the extent that it does so expressly.

Appendix

FEDERAL ADMINISTRATIVE PROCEDURE ACT

United States Code. Title 5

CHAPTER 7—Judicial Review

SUBCHAPTER II—ADMINISTRATIVE PROCEDURE

---

§ 701. Application; definitions.

(a) This chapter applies, according to the provisions thereof, except to the extent that—

(1) statutes preclude judicial review; or

(2) agency action is committed to agency discretion by law.

(b) For the purpose of this chapter—

(1) "agency" means each authority of the Government of the United States, whether or not it is within or subject to review by another agency, but does not include—

(A) the Congress;

(B) the courts of the United States;

(C) the governments of the territories or possessions of the United States;

(D) the government of the District of Columbia;

(E) agencies composed of representatives of the parties or of representatives of organizations of the parties to the disputes determined by them;

(F) courts martial and military commissions;

(G) military authority exercised in the field in time of war or in occupied territory; or

(H) functions conferred by sections 1738, 1739, 1743, and 1744 of title 12; chapter 2 of title 41; subchapter II of chapter 471 of title 49; or sections 1884, 1891–1902, and former section 1641(b)(2), of title 50, appendix; and

(2) "person", "rule", "order", "license", "sanction", "relief", and "agency action" have the meanings given them by section 551 of this title.

§ 702. Right of review.

A person suffering legal wrong because of agency action, or adversely affected or aggrieved by agency action within the meaning of a relevant statute, is entitled to judicial review thereof. An action in a court of the United States seeking relief other than money damages and stating a claim that an agency or an officer or employee thereof acted or failed to act in an official capacity or under color of legal authority shall not be dismissed nor relief therein be denied on the ground that it is against the United States or that the United States is an indispensable party. The United States may be named as a defendant in any such action, and a judgment or decree may be entered against the United States: Provided, That any mandatory or injunctive decree shall specify the Federal officer or officers (by name or by title), and their successors in office, personally responsible for compliance. Nothing herein (1) affects other limitations on judicial review or the power or duty of the court to dismiss any action or deny relief on any other appropriate legal or equitable ground; or (2) confers authority to grant relief if any other statute that grants consent to suit expressly or impliedly forbids the relief which is sought.

§ 703. Form and venue of proceeding.

The form of proceeding for judicial review is the special statutory review proceeding relevant to the subject matter in a court specified by statute or, in the absence or inadequacy thereof, any applicable form of legal action, including actions for declaratory judgments or writs of prohibitory or mandatory injunction or habeas corpus, in a court of competent jurisdiction. If no special statutory review proceeding is applicable, the action for judicial review may be brought against the United States, the agency by its official title, or the appropriate officer. Except to the extent that prior, adequate, and exclusive opportunity for judicial review is provided by law, agency action is subject to judicial review in civil or criminal proceedings for judicial enforcement.

§ 704.   Actions reviewable.

Agency action made reviewable by statute and final agency action for which there is no other adequate remedy in a court are subject to judicial review. A preliminary, procedural, or intermediate agency action or ruling not directly reviewable is subject to review on the review of the final agency action. Except as otherwise expressly required by statute, agency action otherwise final is final for the purposes of this section whether or not there has been presented or determined an application for a declaratory order, for any form of reconsideration, or, unless the agency otherwise requires by rule and provides that the action meanwhile is inoperative, for an appeal to superior agency authority.

§ 705.   Relief pending review.

When an agency finds that justice so requires, it may postpone the effective date of action taken by it, pending judicial review. On such conditions as may be required and to the extent necessary to prevent irreparable injury, the reviewing court, including the court to which a case may be taken on appeal from or on application for certiorari or other writ to a reviewing court, may issue all necessary and appropriate process to postpone the effective date of an agency action or to preserve status or rights pending conclusion of the review proceedings.

§ 706.   Scope of review.

To the extent necessary to decision and when presented, the reviewing court shall decide all relevant questions of law, interpret constitutional and statutory provisions, and determine the meaning or applicability of the terms of an agency action. The reviewing court shall—

(1) compel agency action unlawfully withheld or unreasonably delayed; and

(2) hold unlawful and set aside agency action, findings, and conclusions found to be—

(A) arbitrary, capricious, an abuse of discretion, or otherwise not in accordance with law;

(B) contrary to constitutional right, power, privilege, or immunity;

(C) in excess of statutory jurisdiction, authority, or limitations, or short of statutory right;

(D) without observance of procedure required by law;

(E) unsupported by substantial evidence in a case subject to sections 556 and 557 of this title or otherwise reviewed on the record of an agency hearing provided by statute; or

(F) unwarranted by the facts to the extent that the facts are subject to trial de novo by the reviewing court. In making the foregoing determinations, the court shall review the whole record or those parts of it cited by a party, and due account shall be taken of the rule of prejudicial error.

*

TABLE OF CASES

References are to Pages.

*

TABLE OF STATUTES, REGULATIONS, AND EXECUTIVE ORDERS

*

BIBLIOGRAPHY

BOOKS

———

ABA Commission on Law and the Economy, Federal Regulation: Roads to Reform (1979), 79, 90, 490, 493

Ackerman, Reconstructing American Law (1984), 6

Ackerman, The New Separation of Powers, 113 Harv. L. Rev. 633 (2000), 506

Administrative Conference of the United States, 1992 Recommendations and Reports (1992), 481

Arnold, R., Congress and the Bureaucracy: A Theory of Influence (1979), 48

Arrow, K., Social Choice & Individual Values (1951), 44

Asimow, M., Bonfield, A. & Levin, R., State and Federal Administrative Law (2d ed. 1998), 117

Asimow, M., Bonfield, A. & Levin, R., Supplement to State and Federal Administrative Law (2003), 496

Auerbach, J., Unequal Justice: Lawyers and Social Change in Modern America (1976), 32

Baldwin, R. & Cave, M., Understanding Regulation: Theory, Strategy, & Practice (1999), 6

Bardach, E. & Kagan, R., Going by the Book: The Problem of Regulatory Unreasonableness (1982), 14

Benefit–Cost Analysis of Social Regulation: Case Studies from the Council on Wage and Price Stability (J. Miller III & B. Yandle, eds. 1979), 14

Berg, R. & Klitzman, E., An Interpretive Guide to the Government in the Sunshine Act (1978), 497

Bernstein, M., Regulating Business by Independent Commission (1955), 18, 94

Beyond Self–Interest (J. Mansbridge ed. 1990), 19

Blumstein, Regulatory Review by the Executive Office of the President: An Overview and Policy Analysis of Current Issues, 51 Duke L.J. 851 (2002), 521

Bonfield, A., State Administrative Rulemaking (1986), 515

Breger, M., Halting Taxpayer Subsidy of Partisan Advocacy (Heritage Foundation Lecture 1983), 181

Breyer, S., Breaking the Vicious Cycle: Toward Effective Risk Regulation (1993), 14

Breyer, S., Regulation and its Reform (1982), 14, 15, 124, 509

Breyer, S., Stewart, R., Sunstein, C. & Spitzer, M., Administrative Law and Regulatory Policy (5th ed. 2002), 29

Brown, L. Neville & Bell, John S., French Administrative Law (4th ed. 1993), 3

Buchanen, J. & Tullock, G., The Calculus of Consent (1962), 17

Burns, J.M., The Power to Lead—The Crisis of the American Presidency (1984), 79

Caldwell, L., The Administrative Theories of Hamilton & Jefferson (1964), 24

Carrow, M., Background of Administrative Law (1948), 4

Cass, R., Diver, C., Beermann, R., Administrative Law: Cases & Materials (2d ed. 1994), 6

Chase, W., The American Law School and the Rise of Administrative Government (1982), 4

Choper, J., Judicial Review and the National Political Process (1980), 26

Chubb, J., Interest Groups and the Bureaucracy: The Politics of Energy (1983), 16

Commission on Federal Paperwork Final Summary Report (1977), 409

Congressional Research Service, Congressional Review of Agency Rulemaking (Sept. 16, 2002), 516

Cooper, F., State Administrative Law (1965), 61

Corwin, E., The President—Office and Powers (4th ed. 1957), 81, 110

Council for Public Interest Law, Balancing the Scales of Justice: Financing Public Interest Law in America (1976), 178, 179

Council of State Governments, The Book of States (1981–1982) (1980), 115, 116

Cound, J., Friedental, J., Miller, A., & Sexton, J., Civil Procedure: Cases and Materials (7th ed. 1997), 320

Cox, E., Fellmeth, R. & Schultz, J., "The Nader Report" On the Federal Trade Commission (1969), 45

Cross, H., The People's Right to Know: Legal Access to Public Records and Proceedings (1953), 432

Crunden, R., Ministers of Reform: The Progressive's Achievement in American Civilization (1889–1920) (1982), 29

Cushman, R., The Independent Regulatory Commissions (1941), 29, 94

Dahl, R., Pluralistic Democracy in the United States (1967), 26

Dahl, R., Preface to Democratic Theory (1956), 26

Dahl, R. & Lindblom, C., Politics, Economics & Welfare (1953), 26

Davis, K., Administrative Law Treatise (1978), 61

Davis, K., Administrative Law Treatise (2d ed. 1979), 234, 258, 271, 418, 421

Davis, K., Administrative Law Treatise (2d ed. 1980), 69, 70, 176, 178

Davis, K. & Pierce, R., Administrative Law Treatise (4th ed. 2002), 271, 301, 388, 428, 431, 432

Department of Justice, Office of Information and Privacy, Freedom of Information Act Guide & Privacy Act Overview (May 2002 edition), 435, 440, 441

Dicey, A., Introduction to the Study of the Law of the Constitution (10th ed. 1959), 25

Dodd, L. & Schott, R., Congress and the Administrative State (1979), 41, 48

Downs, A., Inside Bureaucracy (1967), 84

Ely, J., Democracy & Distrust (1980), 38, 57, 260, 474

Farber, D. & Frickey, P., Law & Public Choice: A Critical Introduction (1991), 19, 43

Fiorina, M., Congress, Keystone of the Washington Establishment (1977), 43

Fisher, L., Presidential Spending Power (1975), 87

Fisher, L., The Politics of Shared Power (1981), 113

Foreman Jr., C., Signals From the Hill: Congressional Oversight and the Challenge of Social Regulation (1988), 47

Freedman, J., Crisis and Legitimacy: The Administrative Process and American Government (1978), 23, 58

Freund, E., Administrative Powers Over Persons and Property: A Comparative Survey (1928), 5

Freund, E., Historical Survey In the Growth of American Administrative Law (1923), 5

Friedman, M., Capitalism & Freedom (1962), 24

Friendly, H., The Federal Administrative Agencies: The Need for Better Definition of Standards (1962), 31

Funk, W., Shapiro, S. & Weaver, R., Administrative Practice and Procedure (2d ed. 2001), 415

Galbraith, J., Economics and the Public Purpose (1973), 24

Goodnow, F., Comparative Administrative Law (reprint of 1893 edition 1970), 5

Goulden, J., The Superlawyers (1972), 505

Graham & Kramer, Appointments to the Regulatory Agencies; Federal Communications Commission and Federal Trade Commission (1949–1974) (1976), 96

Gwyn, W.B., The Meaning of Separation of Powers (1965), 25, 103

Hamilton, A., Federalist No. 81, (B. Wright ed. 1961), 24

Hamilton, A., Federalist No. 77, (B. Wright ed. 1961), 97

Harrison, J., Morgan, T. & Verkuil, P., Regulation and Deregulation (2nd ed. 2004), 12

Hart, J., An Introduction to Administrative Law with Selected Cases (2d ed. 1950), 5

Hartz, L., The Liberal Tradition in America (1955), 23

Hayek, F., Law, Legislation, and Liberty (1973), 24

Heclo, H., A Government of Strangers: Executive Politics in Washington (1977), 21, 114

Heinzerling, L. & Ackermann, F., Priceless: On Knowing the Price of Everything and the Value of Nothing (2004), 14, 509

Irons, P., The New Deal Lawyers (1982), 50

Josephson, M.M., The Politicos (1938), 17

Kahn, A., The Economics of Regulation: Principles and Institutions (1970), 12

Kariel, H., The Decline of American Pluralism (1961), 27

Katzmann, R., Regulatory Bureaucracy: The Federal Trade Commission and Antitrust Policy (1980), 45

Kaufman, A., Cardozo (1998), 52

Kaufman, H., The Administrative Behavior of Federal Bureau Chiefs (1981), 47

Kaufman, H., Redtape: Its Origins, Uses and Abuses (1977), 409

Kelman, S., Regulating America, Regulating Sweden: A Comparative Study of Occupational Safety and Health Policy (1981), 31

Kennedy, J., Profiles in Courage (1956), 20

Kingdon, J., Congressmen's Voting Decisions (2d ed. 1981), 20

Kirst, M., Government Without Passing Laws (1979), 41

Kolko, G., Railroads and Regulation (1965), 17

LaFave, Search and Seizure: A Treatise on the Fourth Amendment (2d ed. 1987), 415, 416

Landis, J., Report on the Regulatory Agencies to the President–Elect (1960), 83, 339

Landis, J., The Administrative Process (1938), 30

Lasswell, H., Politics: Who Gets What, When, How? (1936), 15

Leone, R., Who Profits?: Winners, Losers & Government Regulation (1986), 15

Levitan, S., The Great Society's Poor Law (1969), 32

Lindblom, C. & Cohen, D., Usable Knowledge (1979), 21

Linde, H. & Bunn, G., Legislative and Administrative Processes (1976), 61

Lipson, L., The Democratic Civilization (1964), 24

Litan, R. & Nordhous, W., Reforming Federal Regulation (1983), 67

Litigation Under the Federal Freedom of Information Act and Privacy Act (A. Adler ed. 1990), 432, 436, 437, 439, 440, 442, 444, 450, 457, 463

Lowi, T., The End of Liberalism: The Second Republic of the United States (2d ed. 1979), 27, 38, 58

McConnell, G., Private Power and American Democracy (1966), 27

McGarity, T., Reinventing Rationality: Regulatory Analysis in the Federal Government (1991), 521

McGraw, T., Prophets of Regulation (1984), 83

Madison, J., Federalist 47, 48 and 51, (B. Wright ed. 1961) 24

Maglebey, D., Direct Legislation (1984), 116

Mann, T., Unsafe at any Margin: Interpreting Congressional Elections (1978), 26

Margolis, M., Viable Democracy (1979), 26

Mashaw, J., Bureaucratic Justice: Managing Social Security Disability Claims (1983), 20, 40, 224, 480, 492

Mashaw, J., Greed, Chaos & Governance: Using Public Choice To Improve Public Law (1997), 23, 203, 522

Mashaw, J. & Harfst, D., The Struggle for Auto Safety (1990), 8, 336, 337

Mashaw, J., Merrill, R. & Shane, P., The American Public Law System (5th ed. 2003), 196

Mayhew, D., Party Loyalty Among Congressmen (1966), 20

McGreer, M., A Fierce Discontent: The Risk and Fall of the Progressive Movement 1870–1920 (2003), 29

Meier, K., Politics and the Bureaucracy: Policy–Making in the Fourth Branch of Government (1979), 113

Melnick, S., Regulation in the Courts (1983), 225

Mendeloff, J., The Dilemma of Toxic Substance Regulation (1988), 336

Merryman, J., The Civil Law Tradition (1969), 2, 3

Meyer, K., Pedersen, D., Thorsen, N. & Davidson, J., Agricultural Law: Cases and Materials (1985), 12

Miller, G., The Legislative Evolution of the Interstate Commerce Commission (1930), 94

Miller, F. & Clark, B., Cases and Materials on Consumer Protection (1980), 14

Mills, C., The Power Elite (1956), 27

Mosher, F., Democracy and Public Service (2d ed. 1982), 20

Mueller, D., Public Choice II 1 (1989), 16

Nelson, W., The Roots of American Bureaucracy (1830–1900) (1982), 522

Niskanen, W., Bureaucracy and Representative Government (1971), 17

Noll, R., The Political Economy of Deregulation: Interest Groups and the Political Process (1983), 16

Office of Administrative Law Judges, The Federal Administrative Judiciary 1992–2002 (December 23, 2002), 496

Ogus, A., Regulation': Legal Form & Economic Theory (1994), 11

Okun, A., Equality and Efficiency: The Big Trade–Off (1975), 14

Olsen, M., Jr., The Logic of Collective Action: Public Goods and a Theory of Groups (rev. ed. 1971), 171

O'Reilly, J., Federal Information Disclosure: Procedures, Forms, and the Law (2d ed. 1990), 431, 432, 440, 450, 457, 497

Parker, R., Administrative Law (1952), 5

Pennock, J., Liberal Democracy: Its Merits and Prospects (1950), 23

Pertschuk, M., Revolt Against Regulation: The Rise and Fall of the Consumer Movement (1982), 19, 32, 46

Pfohl, Congressional Review of Agency Rulemaking: The 104th Congress and the Salvage Timber Directive, 14 J. L. & Politics 1 (1998), 516

Price, D., America's Unwritten Constitution: Science, Religion and Political Responsibility (1983), 26

Purcell, E., The Crisis of Democratic Theory: Scientific Naturalism and the Problem of Value (1973), 26

Quarles, J., Cleaning Up America: An Insider's View of the Environmental Protection Agency (1976), 508

Quirk, P., Industry Influence in Federal Regulatory Agencies (1981), 17

Rawls, J., A Theory of Justice (1971), 24

Redford, E., The President and the Regulatory Commissions (1960), 80

Report of the National Commission on Ethics Law Reform (1989), 507

Robinson, G., Gellhorn, E. & Bruff, H., The Administrative Process (4th ed. 1993), 6

Robinson, G., Public Choice & Public Law (1991), 6, 80

Rohr, J., Ethics for Bureaucrats (2d ed. 1989), 507

Scherer, F., Industrial Market Structure and Economic Performance (2d ed. 1980), 12

Schlesinger, A., The Coming of the New Deal (1959), 31, 32

Schlesinger, A., The Imperial Presidency (1973), 81

Schlesinger, A., The Politics of Upheaval (1960), 52

Schoenbrod, D., Power Without Responsibility (1995), 57

Schoenbaum, T., Environmental Policy Law (1982), 509

Schuck, P., Suing Government (1983), 112

Schumpter, J., Capitalism, Socialism & Democracy (1950), 26

Schwartz, B., Administrative Law (2d ed. 1983), 61

Shapiro, S. & Glicksman, R., Risk Regulation At Risk: Restoring a Pragmatic Approach (2003), 14, 225, 508

Shapiro, S. & Tomain, J., Regulatory Law & Policy: Cases and Materials (3d ed. 2003), 10, 28

Shepsle, K. & Bonchek, M., Analyzing Politics: Rationality, Behavior, and Institutions (1997), 44

Social Regulation: Strategies for Reform (E. Bardach & R. Kagan, eds. 1982), 14

Social Security Administration, Office of Hearings and Appeals, Key Workload Indicators (Fiscal Year 2002), 480

Strauss, P., Rakoff, T., & Farina, C., Administrative Law (10th ed. 2003), 133, 424, 430

Sunstein, C., After the Rights Revolution: Reconceiving the Regulatory State (1990), 10, 27

Sunstein, C., Free Markets & Social Justice (1997), 6, 13, 474

Taft, W.H., The President and His Powers (1916), 82

The Power of Public Ideas (R. Reich, ed. 1988), 19

The Truman Wit (A. Goldman, ed. 1966), 111

Tolchin, S. & Tolchin, M., Dismantling America: The Rush to Deregulate (1983), 46

Tribe, L., American Constitutional Law (2d ed. 1988), 119, 154, 236, 474

Truman, D., The Governmental Process (1955), 26

Tullock, G., The Politics of Bureaucracy (1965), 17

Verkuil, Gifford, Koch, Pierce & Lubbers, The Administrative Judiciary (1992), 310

Viscusi, W., Fatal Tradeoffs: Public & Private Responsibilities For Risk (1992), 14

Weidenbaum, M., Business, Government and the Public (2d ed. 1981), 18, 32, 33

Welborn, D., Governance of Federal Regulatory Agencies (1977), 83

Whitebread, C. & Slobogin, C., Criminal Procedure: An Analysis of Constitutional Cases and Concepts (1980), 429

Wilson, The Politics of Regulation, in The Politics of Regulation (J.Q. Wilson ed. 1980), 18, 19

Wolff, R., The Poverty of Liberalism (1968), 27

Wood, G., The Creation of the American Republic 1776–1887 (1969), 27

Wright, C., Law of Federal Courts (1983), 196

Wyman, B., The Principles of Administrative Law Governing the Relations of Public Officers (1903), 4

Yates, D., Bureaucratic Democracy: The Search for Democracy and Efficiency in American Government (1982), 27

ARTICLES

A Blackletter Statement of Administrative Law, 54 Ad. L. Rev. 1 (Verkuil, Duffy, & Herz eds. 2002), 409

Abbott, Case Studies on the Costs and Benefits of Federal Statutory and Judicial Deadlines, 39 Admin.L.Rev. 467 (1987), 226

Abourezk, The Congressional Veto: A Contemporary Response to Executive Encroachment on Legislative Prerogatives, 52 Ind. L.Rev. 323 (1977), 44

Agency Diplomacy: Relations With Congress and the White Houuse, and Ethics in the Administrative Process, 4 Admin.L.Rev. 3 (1990)(Comments of David M. Klaus), 69

Aman, Administrative Equity: An Analysis of Exceptions to Administrative Rules, 1982 Duke L.J. 277 (1982), 345

Applegate, A Beginning and Not an End in Itself: The Proper Role of Risk in Environmental Decision Making, 63 U.Cin.L.Rev. 1643 (1995), 519

Aronson, Gellhorn & Robinson, A Theory of Legislative Delegation, 68 Cornell L.Rev. 1 (1982), 43, 58

Asimow, When the Curtain Falls: Separation of Functions in the Federal Administrative Agencies, 81 Colum.L.Rev. 759 (1981), 494

Baker, The Prices of Rights: Toward a Positive Theory of Unconstitutional Condition, 73 Cornell L.Rev. 1185 (1990), 236

Bazelon, Coping with Technology Through the Legal Process, 62 Cornell L.Rev. 817 (1977), 21

Benston, An Appraisal of the Costs and Benefits of Government Required Disclosure: SEC and FTC Requirements, Law & Contemp.Probs. 41 (Summer 1977), 412

Berger, Standing To Sue in Public Actions: Is It A Constitutional Requirement?, 78 Yale L.J. 816 (1969), 141

Bernstein, The NLRB's Adjudication Rule Making Dilemma Under the Administrative Procedure Act, 79 Yale L.J. 571 (1970), 286

Bloch, Lubbers, & Verkuil, Developing A Full and Fair Evidentiary Record in A Nonadversary Setting: Two Proposals For Improving Social Security Disability Adjudications, 25 Car. L. Rev. 1 (2003), 479, 480, 481

Bloch & Stein, The Public Counsel Concept in Practice: The Regional Organization Act of 1973, 16 Wm. & Mary L.Rev. 215 (1974), 180

Boyer, Report on the Trade Regulation Rulemaking Procedures of the Federal Trade Commission (Phase II), 1979 ACUS Ann.Rep. 41 (1979), 349

Brecher, Venue in Conservation Cases: A Potential Pitfall for Environmental Lawyers, 2 Ecology L.Q. 91 (1972), 184

Breyer, Analyzing Regulatory Failure: Mismatches, Less Restrictive Alternatives, and Reform, 92 Harv.L.Rev. 549 (1979), 15

Breyer, Judicial Review of Questions of Law and Policy, 38 Admin.L.Rev. 363 (1986), 338

Breyer, Vermont Yankee and the Court's Role in the Nuclear Energy Controversy, 91 Harv.L.Rev. 1804 (1978), 399

Bruff & Gellhorn, Congressional Control of Administrative Regulation: A Study of Legislative Vetoes, 90 Harv.L.Rev. 1369 (1977), 44, 66

Campbell–Mohn & Applegate, Using Risk Responsibly: Learning From NEPA, 23 Harv.Envt'l.L.Rev. 93 (1999), 519

Carbonneau, The French Legal Studies Curriculum: Its History and Relevance As A Model Of Reform, 25 McGill L.J. 445 (1980), 3

Chayes, The Role of the Judge In Public Law Litigation, 89 Harv. L.Rev. 1281 (1976), 2

Clark, Holding Government Accountable: The Amended Freedom of Information Act, 84 Yale L.J. 741 (1975), 433

Coase, The Problem of Social Cost, 3 J. Law & Econ. 1 (1960), 12

Coglianese, Assessing Consensus: The Promise and Performance of Negotiated Rulemaking, 68 Duke L.J. 1255 (1997), 343

Cohen, Regulatory Reform: Assessing the California Plan, 1983 Duke L.J. 231 (1983), 517

Cohen & Strauss, Congressional Review of Agency Regulations, 49 Admin.L.Rev. (1997), 515

Comment, Chevron Deference to Agency Interpretations That Delimit the Scope of the Agency's Jurisdiction, 61 U.Chi.L.Rev. 957 (1994), 387

Comment, Developments Under the Freedom of Information Act—1981, 1982 Duke L.J. 423 (1982), 440 , 443

Comment, Discovery in Federal Administrative Proceedings, 16 Stan. L.Rev. 1035 (1964),

Comment, OMB Interference in Agency Rulemaking: The Case of Broadened Review, 95 Yale L.J. 1789 (1986), 510

Cooper, Administrative Law: The Substantial Evidence Rule, 44 A.B.A.J. 945 (1958), 371

Cooper, Federal Agency Investigations: Requirements for the Production of Documents, 60 Mich.L.Rev. 187 (1961), 422

Costle, Brave New Chemical: The Future Regulatory History of Phlogiston, 33 Ad.L.Rev. 195 (1981), 329, 336

Craine & Miller, Budget Process and Spending Growth, 31 Wm. & Mary L.Rev. 1021 (1990), 88, 90

Cramton, A Comment on Trial–Type Hearings in a Nuclear Power Plan Siting, 58 Va.L.Rev. 585 (1972), 122

Cramton, The Why, Where and How of Broadened Participation in the Administrative Process, 60 Geo.L.J. 525 (1972), 179

Croley, Theories of Regulation: Incorporating the Administrative Process, 98 Colum. L. Rev. 1 (1998), 6

Croley, White House Review of Agency Rulemaking: An Empirical Investigation, 70 U. Chi. L. Rev. 821 (2003), 511

Cutler, Regulatory Mismatch and Its Cure, 96 Harv.L.Rev. 645 (1982), 512

Cutler & Johnson, Regulation and the Political Process, 84 Yale L.J. 1395 (1976),

Davis, A New Approach to Delegation, 36 U. Chi. L. Rev. 713 (1969), 43

Davis, An Approach to Legal Control of the Police, 52 Tex.L.Rev. 703 (1974), 353

Davis, An Approach to Problems of Evidence, 55 Harv.L.Rev. 364 (1942), 70

Davis, Congress and the Emergency of Public Health Policy, 10 Health Care Management 61 (1985), 59

Davis, The Liberalized Law of Standing, 37 U.Chi.L.Rev. 450 (1970), 164

Davis, The Information Act: A Preliminary Analysis, 34 U.Chi.L.Rev. 761 (1967) 432

Demsetz, Information and Efficiency: Another Viewpoint, 12 J.Law & Econ. 1 (1969), 410

DeMuth, Constraining Regulatory Costs: Part I, The White House Review Programs, Regulation (Jan./Feb. 1980), 510

Devins, Budget Reform and the Balance of Powers, 31 Wm. & Mary L.Rev. 993 (1990), 88

Dickinson, Crowell v. Benson: Judicial Review of Administrative Determinations or Questions of "Constitutional Fact," 80 U.Pa. L.Rev. 1055 (1932), 133

Diver, Policymaking Paradigms in Administrative Law, 95 Harv. L.Rev. 393 (1981), 39

Duffy, Administrative Common Law in Judicial Review, 77 Tex. L.Rev. 121 (1998), 199

Efficiency as a Legal Concern, 8 Hofstra L.Rev. 485 (1980) (Symposium), 15

Elliot, INS v. Chadha: The Administrative Constitution, the Constitution, and the Legislative Veto, 1983 Sup.Ct.Rev. 125, 64, 66

Estreicher & Revesz, Nonacquiescence by Federal Agencies, 98 Yale L.J. 679 (1989), 405, 496

Fallon, "The Rule of Law" As A Concept in Constitutional Discourse, 97 Colum.L.Rev. 1 (1997), 25

Farina & Rachlinski, Forward: Post–Public Choice?, 87 Corn. L. Rev. 267 (2002), 19

Farina, On Misusing "Revolution" and "Reform": Procedural Due Process and the New Welfare Act, 50 Admin.L.Rev. 591 (1998), 249

Farina, Statutory Interpretation and the Balance of Power in the Administrative State, 89 Colum.L.Rev. 452 (1989), 6

Fein, Fighting Off Congress: A Bill of Rights for the Independent Agency, 8 District Lawyer 37 (1983), 48

Force & Griffith, The Louisiana Administrative Procedure Act, 42 La.L.Rev. 1227 (1982), 115

Friendly, Some Kind of Hearing, 123 U.Pa.L.Rev. 1267 (1975), 90, 261, 263, 474

Freeman, Collaborative Governance n the Administrative State, 34 UCLA L. Rev. 1 (1997), 39

Freeman, Extending Public Law Norms Through Privatization, 116 Harv. L. Rev. 1285 (2003), 2

Freeman & Langbein, Regulatory Negotiation and the Legitimacy Benefit, 31 Env't L. Rep. 10811 (2001), 343

Frug, The Ideology of Bureacracy in American Law, 97 Harv.L.Rev. 1277 (1984), 19

Frye, Study of Non–ALJ Hearing Programs, 44 Ad. L. Rev. 261 (1992), 496

Funk, When Is a "Rule" a Regulation? Marking a Clear Line Between Nonlegislative Rules and Legislative Rules, 54 Admin. L. Rev. 659 (2002)

Gardner, The Procedures by Which Informal Action is Taken, 24 Ad.L.Rev. 155 (1972), 352

Gellhorn, Public Participation in Administrative Proceedings, 81 Yale L.J. 359 (1972), 179

Gellhorn, Rules of Evidence and Official Notice in Formal Administrative Hearings, 1971 Duke L.J. 1 (1971), 311

Gellhorn, The Wages of Zealotry: The FTC Under Siege, Regulation (Jan./Feb. 1980), 46

Gellhorn, & Verkuil, Controlling Chevron Based Delegations, 20 Cardoza L.Rev. 989 (1999), 388

Gifford, Rulemaking and Rulemaking Review: Struggling Toward a New Paradigm, 32 Ad.L.Rev. 577 (1980), 373

Gray, Presidential Involvement in Informal Rulemaking, 56 Tul. L.Rev. 863 (1982), 114, 510

Greenawalt & Noam, Confidentiality Claims of Business Organizations, in Business Disclosure: Government's Need to Know (H. Goldschmid ed. 1979), 410

Hamilton, Procedures for the Adoption of Rules of General Applicability: The Need for Procedural Innovation in Administrative Rulemaking, 60 Calif.L.Rev. 1276 (1972), 324

Hamilton, Rulemaking on a Record by the Food and Drug Administration, 50 Tex.L.Rev. 1132 (1972), 34, 230, 324

Harris & Navarro, Does Electing Public Utility Commissioners Bring Lower Electric Rates?, Pub.Util. Fortnightly (Sept. 1, 1983), 115

Hart, The Power of Congress to Limit the Jurisdiction of Federal Courts: An Exercise in Dialectic, 66 Harv.L.Rev. 1362 (1953), 127

Heinzerling, Regulatory Costs of Mythic Proportions, 107 Yale L.J. 181 (1998), 15, 509

Herman, The New Liberty: The Procedural Due Process Rights of Prisoners and Others Under the Burger Court, 59 N.Y.U.L.Rev. 482 (1984), 250

Herz, The Legislative Veto in the Times of Political Reversal: Chadha and the 104th Congress, 14 Const.Comm. 319 (1997), 515

Hochman, The Supreme Court and the Constitutionality of Retroactive Legislation, 73 Harv.L.Rev. 692 (1960), 292

Hovenkamp, Legislation, Well–Being and Public Choice, 57 U.Chi. L.Rev. 63 (1990), 19

Jaffe, Law Making by Private Groups, 51 Harv.L.Rev. 201 (1937), 52

Jaffee, Standing To Secure Judicial Review, 74 Harv.L.Rev. 1265 (1961), 141

Johnson, The Split–Enforcement Model: Some Conclusions from the OSHA and MSHA Experiences, 39 Ad.L.Rev. 315 (1987), 497

Jones, Multitude of Counselors: Appellate Adjudication as Group Decision Making, 54 Tul.L.Rev. 541 (1979), 96

Jordan, The Administrative Procedure Act's "Good Cause" Exemption, 36 Ad.L.Rev. 113 (1984), 322

Kagan, Presidential Administration, 114 Harv. L. Rev. 2245 (2001), 6, 79, 490

Kaiser, Congressional Action to Overturn Rules: Alternatives to the "Legislative Veto", 32 Ad.L.Rev. 667 (1980), 41, 44, 45

Karl, Executive Reorganization and Presidential Power, 1977 Sup.Ct. Rev. 1 (1977), 85

Kaufman, Emerging Conflicts in the Doctrines of Public Administration, in The Politics of the Federal Bureaucracy 75 (A. Altshuler ed. 1968), 21

Kerr, Shedding Light on Chevron: A Empirical Survey of the Chevron Doctrine in the U.S. Courts of Appeal, 15 Yale J. on Reg. 1 (1998), 387

Koch, Administrative Presiding Officials Today, 46 Admin.L.Rev. 271 (1994), 481

Koch, Discovery In Rulemaking, 1977 Duke L.J. 295 (1977), 466

Koch, Prejudgment: An Unavailable Challenge to Official Administrative Action, 33 Fed.Bar.J. 218 (1974), 478

Koch & Rubin, A Proposal for Comprehensive Restructuring of the Public Information System, 1979 Duke L.J. 1 (1979), 435

Kovacic, The Federal Trade Commission and Congressional Oversight of Antitrust Enforcement, 17 Tulsa L.J. 587 (1982),45

Krasnow & Shooshan, Congressional Oversight: The Ninety–Second Congress and the Federal Communications Commission, 10 Harv.L.J. on Legis. 297 (1973), 41

Lazarus & Onek, The Regulators and the People, 57 Va.L.Rev. 1069 (1971), 178, 179

Lemke, The Federal Trade Commission's Use of Investigational Subpoenas, 1 Loyola U.L.J. 15 (1970), 422

Levin, Understanding Unreviewability in Administrative Law, 74 Minn.L.Rev. 689 (1990), 139

Levin, "Vacation" at Sea: Judicial Remedies and Equitable Discretion in Administrative Law, 53 Duke L.J. __ (2003), 125

Levinson, Legislative and Executive Veto of Rules of Administrative Agencies: Models and Alternatives, 24 Wm. & Mary L.Rev. 79 (1982), 67

Linde, Due Process of Lawmaking, 55 Neb.L.Rev. 197 (1976), 483

Luneberg, Petitioning Federal Agencies for Rulemaking, 1988 Wis. L.Rev. 1, 172

Lyndon, Information Economics and Chemical Toxicity: Defining Laws To Produce and Use Data, 87 Mich.L.Rev. 1795 (1989), 11

MacCarthy, A Review of Some Normative and Conceptual Issues in Occupational Safety and Health, 9 B.C.Env.Affairs L.Rev. 773 (1981), 15

McCubbins, Noll Weingast, Administrative Procedures as Instruments of Political Control, 3 J.L.Econ. & Org. 243 (1987), 286

McGarity, Media Quality, Technology, and the Utilitarian Ideal: Alternative Strategies for Health and Environmental Regulation of the Chemical Industry, 46 Law & Contemp.Probs. 159 (1984), 15

McGarity, Multi–Party Forum Shopping for Appellate Review of Administrative Action, 129 U.Pa.L.Rev. 302 (1980), 185, 186

McGarity, Professor Sunstein's Fuxy Math, 90 Geo. L. J. 2341 (2002), 509

McGarity, Regulatory Analysis and Reform, 65 Tex.L.Rev. 1243 (1987), 340

McGarity, Some Thoughts on "Deossifying" the Rulemaking Process, 41 Duke L.J. 1385 (1992), 401

McGarity, Substantive and Procedural Discretion in Administrative Resolution of Science Policy Questions: Regulating Carcinogens in EPA and OSHA, 67 Geo.L.J. 729 (1979), 21, 377, 398

McGarity, The Courts and the Ossification of Rulemaking: A Response To Professor Seidenfeld, 85 Tex.L.Rev. 525 (1997), 39, 401

McGarity & Shapiro, OSHA's Critics & Regulatory Reform, 31 Wake Forrest L.Rev. 587 (1996), 15, 95

McGarity & Shapiro, The Trade Secret Status of Health and Safety Testing Information: Reforming Agency Disclosure Policies, 93 Harv.L.Rev. 837 (1980), 410, 445

McGowan, Regulatory Analysis and Judicial Review, 42 Ohio St.L.J. 627 (1981), 520

McKay, Self Incrimination and New Privacy, 1967 Sup.Ct.Rev. 193 (1967), 429

Mansfield, The Albertson Case: Conflict Between the Privilege Against Self–Incrimination and the Government's Need for Information, 1966 Sup.Ct.Rev. 103 (1966), 429

Mashaw, Explaining Administrative Process: Normative, Positive, and Critical Stories of Legal Development, 6 J.Law, Econ. & Org. 267 (1990), 6

Mashaw, Prodelegation: Why Administrators Should Make Political Decisions, 1 J.L.Econ. & Org. 1 (1985), 58

Mashaw, The Legal Structure of Frustration: Alternative Strategies For Public Choice Concerning Federally Aided Highway Construction, 122 U.Pa.L.Rev. 1 (1973), 73

Mashaw, The Management Side of Due Process: Accuracy, Fairness and Timeliness in Adjudication of Social Welfare Claims, 59 Cornell L.Rev. 772 (1974), 263

Mashaw, "Rights" in the Federal Administrative State, 92 Yale L.J. 1129 (1984), 6

May, Taming the Sunshine Act, Legal Times, Feb. 5, 1996, 500

Meier, FTC Re–Emerges As a Watchdog on Prices, N.Y. Times, Jan. 28, 1991, at A1 (nat'l ed.),

Merrill, Textualism and the Future of the Chevron Doctrine, 72 Wash.U.L.Q. 351 (1994), 387

Merryman, The Public Law–Private Law Distinction in European and American Law, 17 J.Pub.L. 3 (1968), 2

Monaghan, Marbury and the Administrative State, 83 Colum.L.Rev. 1 (1983), 110

Moore, The Purpose of Licensing, 4 J.Law & Econ. 93 (1961), 15

Morgan, Appropriate Limits on Participation by a Former Agency Official in Matters Before an Agency, 1980 Duke L.J. 1 (1980), 505, 506

Morrison, OMB Interference with Agency Rulemaking: The Wrong Way to Write a Regulation, 99 Harv.L.Rev. 1059 (1986), 510

Morrison, Presidential Intervention in Informal Rulemaking: Striking the Proper Balance, 56 Tul.L.Rev. 879 (1983), 490

Murphy & Hoffman, Current Models for Improving Public Representation in the Administrative Process, 28 Ad.L.Rev. 391 (1976), 180

Nader, Freedom from Information: The Act and the Agencies, 5 Harv.C.R.–C.L.Rev. 1 (1970), 433

Nagle, Corrections Day, 43 UCLA L.Rev. 1267 (1996), 516

Nichol, Re–Thinking Standing, 72 Cal.L.Rev. 68 (1984), 140, 155, 159

Nichols & Zeckhauser, Government Comes to the Workplace: An Assessment of OSHA, 49 The Public Interest 39 (1977), 36

Nonet, The Legitimation of Purposive Decision, 68 Cal.L.Rev. 263 (1980), 19, 20

Note, Discovery of Government Documents and the Official Information Privilege, 76 Colum.L.Rev. 142 (1976), 466

Note, Disqualification of Federal Judges for Bias or Prejudice, 46 Chi.L.Rev. 236 (1978), 477

Note, Regulatory Values and the Exceptions Process, 93 Yale L.J. 938 (1984), 345

Note, The Office of Public Counsel: Institutionalizing Public Interest Representation in State Government, 64 Geo.L.J. 895 (1976), 180

Note, Venue for Judicial Review of Administrative Actions: A New Approach, 93 Harv.L.Rev. 1735 (1980), 185

Parker, Grading the Government, 70 U. Chi. L. Rev. 1345 (2003), 509

Parnell, Congressional Interference in Agency Enforcement: The IRS Experience, 89 Yale L.J. 1360 (1980), 48

Pederson, The Decline of Separation of Functions in Regulatory Agencies, 64 Va.L.Rev. 991 (1978), 494

Peltzman, Toward A General Theory of Regulation, 19 J.Law & Econ. 211 (1976), 16, 18

Penn, Advocate From Within, Trial (Feb. 1976), 180

Peterson, Attorney–Client Privilege in Internal Revenue Service Investigations, 54 Minn.L.Rev. 67 (1969), 430

Pfohl, Congressional Review of Agency Rulemaking, the 104th Congress and the Salvage Timber Rule, 14 J.L. & Politics 1 (1998), 516

Pierce, Distinguishing Legislative Rules from Interpretative Rules, 52 Admin. L. Rev. 547 (2000), 317

Pierce, Encouraging Safety: The Limits of Tort Law and Government Regulation, 33 Vand.L.Rev. 1281 (1980), 13, 509

Pierce, Is Standing Law or Politics?, 77 N.C.L.Rev. 1741 (1999), 161

Pierce, Judicial Review of Agency Actions in a Period of Diminished Resources, 49 Ad.L.Rev. 61 (1997), 87, 226

Pierce, Obtaining Agency Consideration of a Competing Proposal: Alternatives to Ashbacker, 26 Kan.L.Rev. 185 (1978), 171

Pierce, Political Accountability and Delegated Power: A Response to Professor Lowi, 36 Am.U.L.Rev. 391 (1987), 58

Pierce, Political Control Versus Impermissible Bias in Agency Decisionmaking: Lessons from Chevron and Mistretta, 57 U.Chi. L.Rev. 481 (1990), 69, 309

Pierce, Reconsidering the Roles of Regulation and Competition in the Natural Gas Industry, 97 Harv.L.Rev. 345 (1983), 221

Pierce, The APA and Regulatory Reform, 10 Ad.L.J. 81 (1996), 40

Pierce, The Choice Between Adjudicating and Rulemaking for Formulating and Implementing Energy Policy, 31 Hastings L.J. 1 (1979), 187, 259, 272, 274, 287, 324

Pierce, The Due Process Counterrevolution of the 1990s?, 96 Colum.L.Rev. 1973 (1996), 249

Pierce, The Supreme Court's New Hypertextualism: An Invitation to Cacaphony and Incoherence, 95 Colum.L.Rev. 749 (1995), 387

Pierce, The Role of Constitutional and Political Theory in Administrative Law, 64 Tex.L.Rev. 469 (1985), 5

Pierce, The Role of the Judiciary in Implementing an Agency Theory of Government, 64 NYU L.Rev. 1239 (1989), 168, 171

Pierce, The Unintended Effects of Judicial Review of Agency Rules: How Federal Courts Have Contributed to the Electricity Crisis of the 1990s, 43 Admin.L.Rev. 7 (1991), 336

Pierce, Two Problems in Administrative Law: Political Polarity on the D.C. Circuit and Judicial Deterrence of Agency Rulemaking, 1988 Duke L.J. 300, 336

Pierce, Use of The Federal Rules of Evidence in Federal Agency Adjudications, 39 Admin.L.Rev. 1 (1987), 311

Pierce & Shapiro, Political and Judicial Review of Agency Action, 59 Tex.L.Rev. 1175 (1981), 6

Pitofsky, Beyond Nader: Consumer Protection and the Regulation of Advertising, 90 Harv.L.Rev. 661 (1977), 11

Posner, The Federal Trade Commission, 37 U.Chi.L.Rev. 47 (1973), 11

Posner, Theories of Economic Regulation, 5 Bell J.Econ. & Management & Sci. 335 (1974), 16, 18

Purcell, Ideas and Interests: Business and the Interstate Commerce Act, 54 J.Am. History 561 (1967), 17

Rabin, Administrative Law in Transition: A Discipline In Search of An Organizing Principle, 72 N.W.L.Rev. 120 (1977), 6, 34

Rabin, Federal Regulation in Historical Perspective, 38 Stan.L.Rev. 29 (1985), 29

Redford, Regulation Revisited, 28 Ad.L.Rev. 543 (1976), 43

Reich, Individual Rights and Social Welfare: The Emerging Legal Issues, 74 Yale L.J. 1245 (1965), 237

Reich, The Liberty Impact of the New Property, 21 W. & M. L. Rev. 295 (1990), 238

Reich, The New Property, 73 Yale L.J. 733 (1964), 237

Reich, Toward A New Consumer Protection, 128 U.Pa.L.Rev. 1 (1979), 11

Reiter & Hughes, A Preface on Modeling the Regulated United States Economy, 9 Hofstra L.Rev. 1381 (1981), 16

Remarks of Jay Plager, 4 Admin.L.J. 5 (1990), 510

Revesz, Environmental Regulation, Ideology, and the D.C. Circuit, 83 Va.L.Rev. (1997), 387, 401

Robinson, The Federal Communications Commission: An Essay in Regulatory Watchdogs, 64 Va.L.Rev. 169 (1978), 114, 487

Robinson, The Making of Administrative Policy: Another Look at Rulemaking and Adjudication and Administrative Procedure Reform, 118 U.Pa.L.Rev. 485 (1970), 34, 286

Rodgers, A Hard Look at Vermont Yankee: Environmental Law Under Close Scrutiny, 67 Geo.L.J. 699 (1979), 399

Rose, Occupational Licensing: A Framework For Analysis, 1979 Ariz. St.L.J. 189 (1979), 15, 17

Rossi, Final, But Often Fallible: Recognizing Problems With ALJ Finality, 56 Ad.L.Rev. 53 (2004), 496

Rubin, It's Time to Make the Administrative Procedures Act Administrative, 89 Corn. L. Rev. 101 (2002), 38

Rubin, Public Choice Phenomenology and the Meaning of the Modern State: Keep the Bathwater But Throw Out the Baby, 87 Corn. L. Rev. 309 (2002), 19

Sable & Simon, Destablizing Rights: How Public Law Litigation Succeeds, 1117 Harv. L. Rev. 1015 (2004), 2

Scalia, Back to Basics: Making Law Without Rules, Regulation 25 (July/Aug. 1981), 286

Scalia, Rulemaking As Politics, 34 Ad.L.Rev. v (1982) (Chairman's message, summer 1982), 22

Scalia, The Doctrine of Standing as an Essential Element of the Separation of Powers, 17 Suffolk L.Rev. 881 (1983), 143

Scalia, The Legislative Veto: A False Remedy for System Overload, Regulation, (Nov./Dec. 1979), 66

Scalia, Vermont Yankee: The APA, The D.C. Circuit, and the Supreme Court, 1978 Sup.Ct.Rev. 345 (1978), 346, 347, 349

Schroeder & Shapiro, Responses to Occupational Disease: The Role of Markets, Regulation, and Information, 72 Geo.L.J. 1231 (1984), 17, 21, 36, 450

Schuck, Organization Theory and the Teaching of Administrative Law, 33 J.Legal Ed. 13 (1983), 6, 112

Schuck, The Transformation of Immigration Law, 84 Colum.L.Rev. 1 (1984), 284

Schuck & Elliott, Studying Administrative Law: A Methodology For, and Report on, New Empirical Research, 42 Admin.L.Rev. 519 (1990), 336, 341

Scott, Standing in the Supreme Court—A Functional Analysis, 86 Harv.L.Rev. 645 (1973), 154

Seidenfeld, A Civil Republican Justification for the Bureaucratic State, 105 Harv.L.Rev. 1520 (1992), 28, 38

Seidenfeld, Hard Look in a World of Techno–Bureaucratic Rationality: A Reply to Professor McGarity, 75 Tex.L.Rev. 559 (1997), 39

Shane, Political Accountability in a System of Checks and Balances: The Case of Presidential Review of Rulemaking, 48 Ark.L.Rev. (1995), 340

Shane, Presidential Regulatory Oversight and the Separation of Powers: The Constitutionality of Executive Order 12,291, 23 Ariz.L.Rev. 1236 (1981), 512

Shapiro, A Delegation Theory of the APA, 10 Ad.L.J. 89 (1996), 40

Shapiro, Abstention and Primary Jurisdiction: Two Chips Off the Same Block?—A Comparative Analysis, 60 Cornell L.Rev. 75 (1974), 215

Shapiro, APA: Past, Present, Future, 72 Va.L.Rev. 447, 453–54 (1986), 338

Shapiro, Political Oversight and the Deterioration of Regulatory Policy, 46 Ad.L.Rev. 1 (1994), 67, 68, 80, 92, 509

Shapiro, Limiting Physician Freedom to Prescribe a Drug for Any Purpose: The Need for FDA Regulation, 72 N.W.U.L.Rev. 801 (1978), 410

Shapiro, OMB's Dubious Peer Review Procedures, 34 Env. L. Rev. 10064 (2004), 471, 472

Shapiro, Some Thoughts on Intervention Before Courts, Agencies and Arbitrators, 81 Harv.L.Rev. 721 (1968), 176

Shapiro, Substantive Reform, Judicial Review and Agency Resources, 49 Ad.L.Rev. 645 (1997), 87

Shapiro, The Choice of Rulemaking and Adjudication in the Development of Administrative Policy, 78 Harv.L.Rev. 921 (1965), 286

Shapiro, The Information Quality Act and Environmental Protection: The Perils of Regulatory Reform by Appropriations Rider, ___ W. & M. Env. L. & Pol. Rev. ___ (2004), 469, 472

Shapiro & Glicksman, Congress, The Supreme Court, and the Quiet Revolution in Administrative Law, 1988 Duke L.J. 879, 45

Shapiro & McGarity, Not So Paradoxical: The Rationale for Technology–Based Regulation, 1991 Duke L.Rev. 729, 15, 21

Shapiro & McGarity, Reorienting OSHA: Regulatory Alternatives and Legislative Reforms, 6 Yale J.Reg. 1 (1989), 224, 497

Simeone, The Function, Flexibility and Future of United States Judges of the Executive Department, 44 Admin.L.Rev. 159 (1992), 481

Steinzor, Democracies Die Behind Closed Doors: The Homeland Security Act and Corporate Accountability, 12 Kan. J. L. & Pub. Pol. 641 (2003), 463

Stevens, Reform in Haste & Repent in Leisure: Lolanthe, The Lord High Executioner and Brave New World, 24 J. Legal Studies 1 (2004), 25

Stewart, The Reformation of American Administrative Law, 88 Harv. L.Rev. 1669 (1975), 6, 34, 40, 59, 474

Stewart & Sunstein, Public Programs and Private Rights, 95 Harv. L.Rev. 1193 (1982), 6, 32, 359

Stichman, The Veterans Judicial Review Act of 1988: Congress Introduces Courts and Attorneys to Veterans' Benefits Proceedings, 41 Admin.L.Rev. 365 (1989), 126

Stigler, The Theory of Economic Regulation, 2 Bell J.Econ. & Management Sci. 3 (1981), 16

Strauss, Disqualifications of Decisional Officials in Rulemaking, 80 Colum.L.Rev. 990 (1980), 482

Strauss, One Hundred Fifty Cases Per Year: Some Implications of the Supreme Court's Limited Resources for Judicial Review of Agency Action, 87 Colum.L.Rev. 1093 (1987), 387

Strauss, Teaching Administrative Law: The Wonder of the Unknown, 33 J.Legal Ed. 1 (1983), 5

Strauss, The Place of Agencies in Government: Separation of Powers and the Fourth Branch, 84 Colum.Rev. 573 (1984), 102, 103, 493

Strauss, Was There a Baby in the Bathwater? A Comment on the Supreme Court's Legislative Veto Decision, 1983 Duke L.J. 789, 64, 67, 86

Strauss & Sunstein, The Role of the President and OMB in Informal Rulemaking, 38 Admin.L.Rev. 181 (1985),

Sunset Review—Effective Oversight Tool or New Political Football, 32 Ad.L.Rev. 209 (1980) (panel discussion), 68

Sunstein, Beyond the Republican Revival, 89 Yale L.J. 1539 (1988), 28

Sunstein, Interest Groups in American Public Law, 38 Stan.L.Rev. 29 (1985), 39

Sunstein, Participation, Public Law and Venue Reform, 49 U.Chi. L.Rev. 976 (1982), 185

Sunstein, The Arithmetic of Arsenic, 90 Geo. L. J. 2255 (2002), 809

Sunstein, What's Standing After Lujan?: Of Citizens Suits, "Injuries," and Article III, 91 Mich.L.Rev. 163 (1992), 141

Symposium on Administrative Law: The Uneasy Constitutional Status of Administrative Agencies, 36 Am.U.L.Rev. 277 (1987), 48

Symposium on the Theory of Public Choice, 74 Va.L.Rev. 167 (1988), 16

Symposium on Science in the Regulatory Process, 66 Law & Contemp. Prob. 1 (2003), 473

Szladits, The Civil Law System, in II International Encyclopedia of Comparative Law 2–26 (1974), 2

Thayer, Public Wrong and Private Action, 27 Harv.L.Rev. 317 (1914), 360

Thompson, The Possibility of Administrative Ethics, 45 Pub.Admin.Rev. 595 (1985), 507

Tobias, Of Public Funds and Public Participation: Resolving the Issue of Agency Authority to Reimburse Public Participants in Administrative Proceedings, 82 Col.L.Rev. 906 (1982), 179, 180, 181

Tomlinson, Discovery In Agency Adjudication, 1971 Duke L.J. 89 (1971), 466

Tomlinson, Use of the Freedom of Information Act for Discovery Purposes, 43 Md.L.Rev. 119 (1984), 411, 467

Tribe, The Legislative Veto Process: A Law By Any Other Name, 21 Harv.J. on Legis. 1 (1984), 67

Troy, Congressional Review Procedures of Agency Rules, 21 Admin. & Reg. Law News (Summer, 1996), 516

Trubek & Trubek, Civil Justice Through Civil Justice: A New Approach to Public Interest Advocacy in the United States, in Access to Justice in the Welfare State (M. Cappelletti ed. 1981), 178

Van Alstyne, Cracks in "The New Property," Adjudicative Due Process in the Administrative State, 62 Cornell L.Rev. 445 (1977), 234, 474

Van Alstyne, The Recrudescence of Property Rights as the Foremost Principle of Civil Liberties: The First of the Burger Court, 43 Law & Contemp.Prob. 66 (1980), 254

Verkuil, A Critical Guide to the Regulatory Flexibility Act, 1982 Duke L.J. 213, 513

Verkuil, A Study of Immigration Procedures, 31 U.C.L.A.Rev. 1141 (1984), 352

Verkuil, A Study of Informal Adjudication Procedures, 43 U.Chi. L.Rev. 739 (1976), 352

Verkuil, An Outcomes Analysis of Scope of Review Standards, 44 W. & M. L. Rev. 679 (2002), 376, 462

Verkuil, Congressional Limitations on Judicial Review of Rules, 57 Tul.L.Rev. 733 (1983), 129, 132, 133

Verkuil, Jawboning Administrative Agencies: Ex Parte Contacts by the White House, 80 Colum.L.Rev. 943 (1980), 103, 490, 493

Verkuil, Reflections Upon the Federal Administrative Judiciary, 39 UCLA L.Rev. 1341 (1992), 481

Verkuil, Revisiting the New Property After Twenty–Five Years, 31 W. & M. L. Rev. 365 (1990), 238

Verkuil, Separation of Powers, the Rule of Law and the Ideal of Independence, 30 Wm. & M.L.Rev. 301 (1989), 25

Verkuil, The Emerging Concept of Administrative Procedure, 78 Colum.L.Rev. 258 (1978), 32,

Verkuil, The Purposes and Limits of Independent Agencies, 1988 Duke L.J. 257, 95, 497

Verkuil, Understanding the "Public Interest" Justifications for Government Actions, 39 Acta Juridica Hungarica 141 (1998), 10

Verkuil, Waiting for Vermont Yankee II, 55 Tul.L.Rev. 418 (1981), 401

Wald, Making Informed Decisions on the District of Columbia Circuit, 50 G.W.L.Rev. 135 (1982), 391, 401

Wald, Remarks to the Administrative Conference of the United States (July 7, 1983),

Weaver, Regulation, Social Policy and Class Conflict, 50 Public Interest 45 (1978), 19

Weingast, Regulation, Reregulation, and Deregulation: The Political Foundations of Agency–Clientele Relationships, 44 Law & Contemp.Probs. 147 (Winter 1981), 17

Weingast & Moran, The Myth of the Runaway Bureaucracy: The Case of the FTC, Regulation (May/June 1982), 45

Welborn, Lynn & Thomas, Implementation and Effects of the Federal Government in the Sunshine Act, 1984 Administrative Conference of the United States 197 (June 1984), 500

Williams, Liberty and Property: The Problem of Government Benefits, 12 J.Leg. Studies 3 (1983), 237

Wilson, The Study of Administration, 2 Political Sci.Q. 197 (1887), 20

Winter, The Metaphor of Standing and the Problem of Self–Government, 40 Stan.L.Rev. 1371 (1988), 141

Wood, Federal Venue: Locating the Place Where the Claim Arose, 54 Tex.L.Rev. 392 (1976), 184

Wood, Laws & Breen, Restraining the Regulators: Legal Perspectives on a Regulatory Budget for Federal Agencies, 18 Harv.J. On Legis. 1 (1981), 67

Wright, Book Review, 81 Yale L.J. 575 (1972) (reviewing K. Davis, Discretionary Justice: A Preliminary Inquiry (1971)), 58

DOCUMENTS

ABA Memorandum No. 83–371, Oct. 3, 1983, 499

ABA, Administrative Law Section, Resolution and Report (1983), 301

General Accounting Office, Freedom of Information Act: Agency Views on Changes Resulting From New Policy (2003), 434

General Accounting Office, Improved Quality, Adequate Resources, and Consistent Oversight Needed if Regulatory Analysis is to Help Control Costs of Regulation (1982), 518

General Accounting Office, Rulemaking: OMB's Role in Review of Agencies' Draft Rules and the Transparency of Those Rules (2003), 511, 521

Oversight of Federal Trade Commission Law Enforcement: Fiscal Years 1982 and 1983 Before the Commerce, Consumer, and Monetary Affairs Subcomm. of the House Comm. on Government Operations, 88th Cong., 1st Sess. 298 (1983), 47

President's Advisory Comm'n on Executive Organization, Report on Selected Independent Regulatory Agencies, 94

Report of the ABA Committee to Study the Federal Trade Commission (1969), 45

Report Of The Committee With Studies Of Administrative Management In The Federal Government (1937), 31, 79

S.Rep. No. 364, 100th Cong., 2d Sess. (1988), 107

S.Rep. No. 752, 79th Cong., 1st Sess., 26 (1945), 134

Senate Comm. on Gov't Affairs, Vol. I.—The Regulatory Appointments Process, S.Doc. No. 95–25, 95th Cong., 1st Sess. 1 (1977), 83, 84, 86

Senate Commission on Government Affairs, Vol. II.—Congressional Oversight of Regulatory Agencies, S.Doc. No. 95–26, 95th Cong. 1st Sess. (1977), 41

Senate Comm. on Gov't Affairs, Vol. V.—Regulatory Organization, S.Doc. No. 95–91, 95th Cong., 2d Sess. 26–27 (1977), 94, 95, 96

Senate Comm. on Governmental Affairs, The Role of the Administrative Law Judge in the Title II Social Security Disability Program, 98th Cong., 1st Sess. (1983), 481

Senate Committee on Governmental Affairs, Study on Federal Regulation, Vol. IV, Delay in the Regulatory Process, S.Doc. No. 95–72, 95th Cong., 1st Sess. (1977), 223

Staff of Senate Comm. on Government Operations, Vol. III.—Public Participation in Regulatory Agency Proceedings, 95th Cong., 1st Sess. 65–71 (Comm.Print 1977), 180

INDEX

References are to pages.

ACTION COMMITTED TO AGENCY DIS-CRETION

See Jurisdiction, Action committed to agency discretion.

ADEQUATE CONSIDERATION TEST

See Scope of Review, Adequate consideration test.

ADJUDICATION

Administrative law judges. See ALJ function, this topic.

Administrator independence. See Independent Agencies, Executive authority to remove agency officials.

Agency power to choose. See Procedural Requirement, Choice of procedures.

ALJ function, 308–310.

Effects of rulemaking. See Rulemaking, Effects on adjudication.

Elements of, 308–313.

Ex parte contacts. See Ex Parte Contacts, And ALJs; Ex Parte Contacts, APA restrictions.

Findings and conclusions, 311–313.

Formal, 304–313.

Humphrey's Executor and administrator independence, 97–104.

Hybrid procedures. See Hybrid Procedures.

Informal, 304–308, 350–353.

Notice, 310.

Presentation of evidence, 310–311.

Required by due process. See Due Process, Procedures required by.

Required by statute. See Procedural Requirements, Required by statute.

Separation of Functions. See Separation of Functions, In adjudication.

ADMINISTRATIVE LAW

And democracy, 23–24.

And public law model, 1–11.

Future of, 37–40.

ADMINISTRATIVE LAW JUDGE

Ex parte contacts. See Ex Parte Contacts, And ALJs.

ADMINISTRATIVE LAW JUDGE—Cont'd

Function in adjudication. See Adjudication, ALJ function.

Independence of. See Separation of Functions, And ALJs.

ADMINISTRATIVE PROCESS

And democratic theory, 23, 34–35.

And public choice, 15–21.

And the modern state, 32–34.

And the new deal, 31–32.

Beginning of, 29–31.

Connection to public law, 10–11.

Example of, 7–10.

Future of, 37–40.

Nature of, 7.

ADMINISTRATIVE REORGANIZATION

See Executive Control of Discretion, Reorganization process.

AGENCY CAPTURE

See Regulation, Theories of capture.

AGENCY DELAY

See Timing of Judicial Review, Problem of agency delay.

AGENCY PROCEDURES

Choice of form of rulemaking. See Rulemaking, Choice between formal and informal procedures.

Choice of procedures. See Procedural Requirements, Choice of procedures.

Ethics in Government Act. See Ethics in Government Act.

Ex parte contacts. See Ex Parte Contacts.

Federal Advisory Committee Act. See Federal Advisory Committee Act.

Financing of intervention. See Standing to Intervene in Agency Proceedings, Public financing for intervention.

Formal adjudication. See Adjudication, Formal.

Hybrid procedures. See Hybrid Procedures.

Informal adjudication. See Adjudication, Informal.

†